JOSS WHEDON

Zack **Whedon** • Brett **Matthews** • Patton **Oswalt** • Will **Conrad** • Chris **Samnee**

firefly™

LEGACY EDITION BOOK ONE

Collection Designer
Scott Newman

Original Series Editors
Scott Allie, **Sierra Hahn**,
Freddye Miller, **Jim Gibbons**

Legacy Edition Assistant Editor
Gavin Gronenthal

Legacy Edition Editors
Jeanine Schaefer and **Sierra Hahn**

Special Thanks to **Nicole Speigel** and
Carol Roeder at **Twentieth Century Fox**,
Becca J. Sadowsky, **Chris Harbert**.

Originally published by
Dark Horse Comics

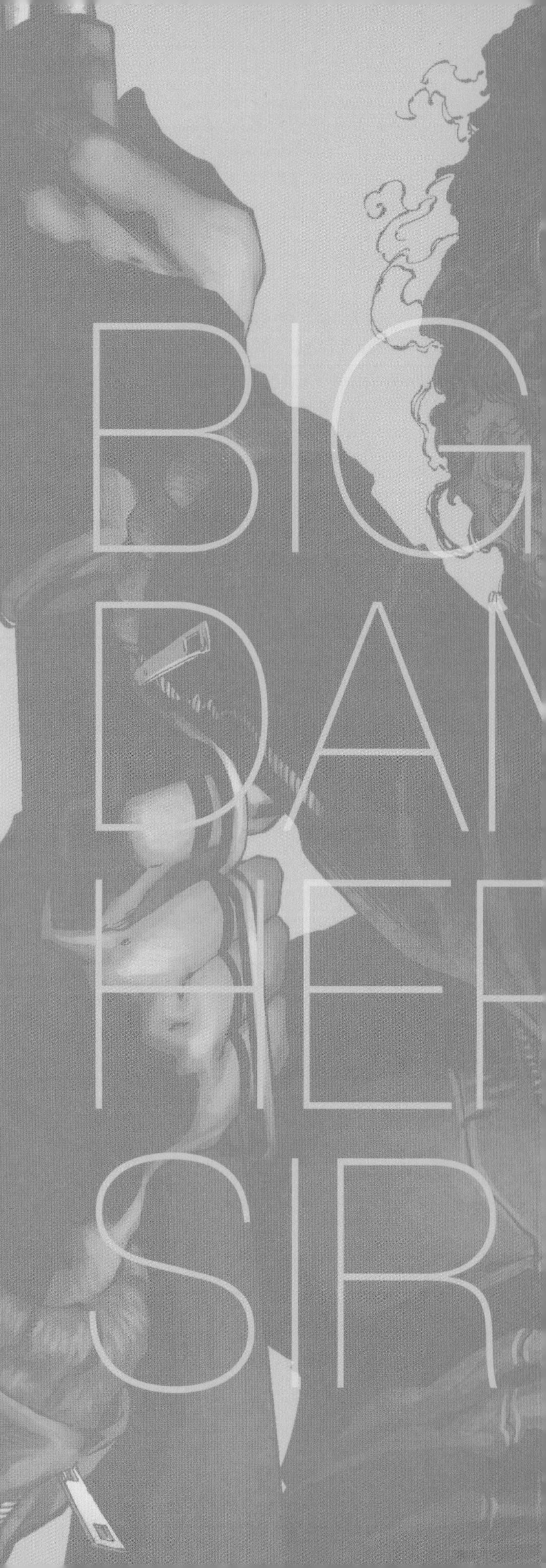
BIG
SIR

FIREFLY LEGACY EDITION Book One, November 2018. Published by BOOM! Studios, a division of Boom Entertainment, Inc.

For information regarding the CPSIA on this printed material, call: (203) 595-3636 and provide reference #RICH – 816390.

BOOM! Studios, 5670 Wilshire Boulevard, Suite 400,
Los Angeles, CA 90036-5679. Printed in USA. First Printing.

ISBN: 978-1-68415-320-6, eISBN: 978-1-64144-277-0

Big Damn Heroes Edition
ISBN: 978-1-68415-403-6

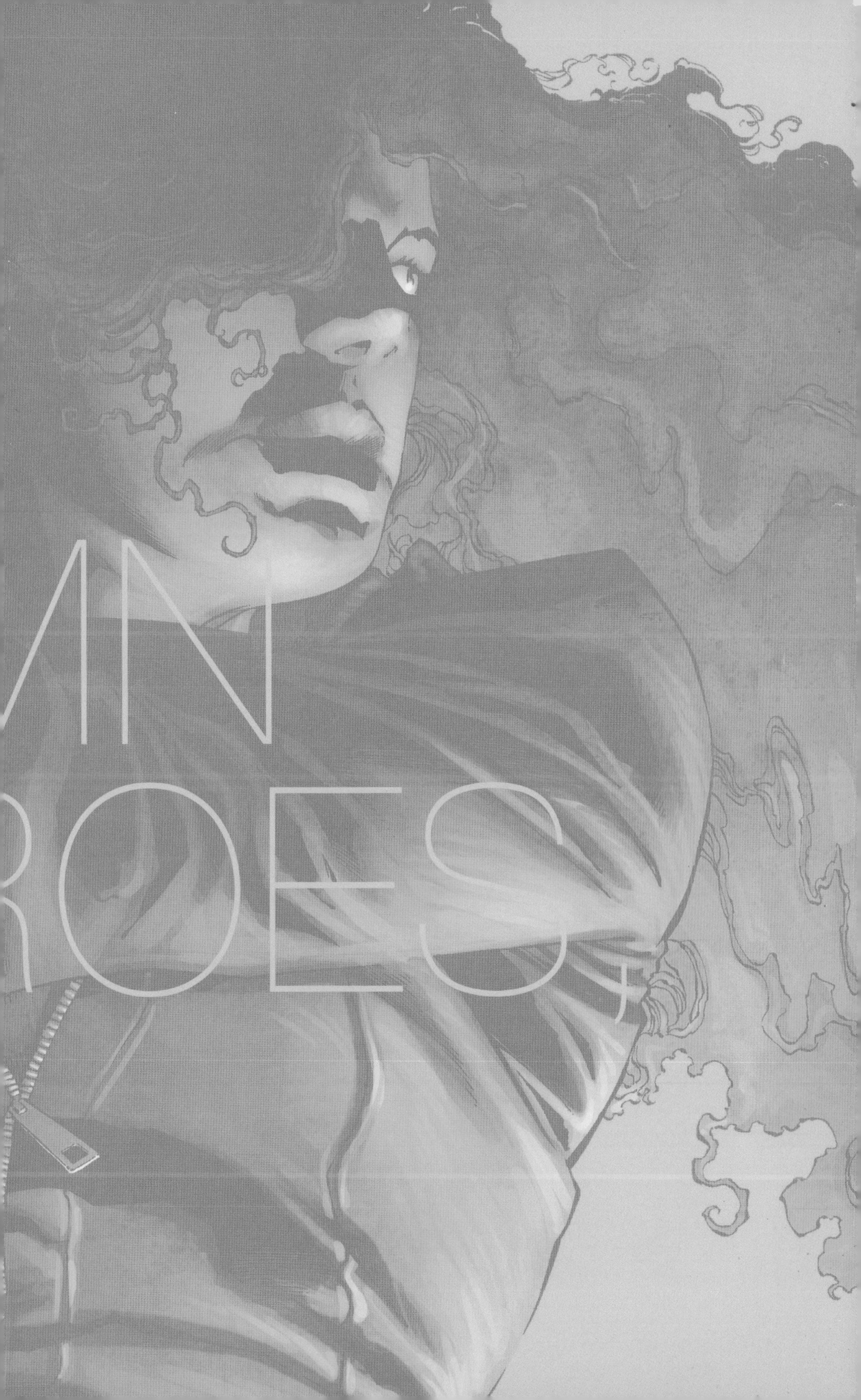

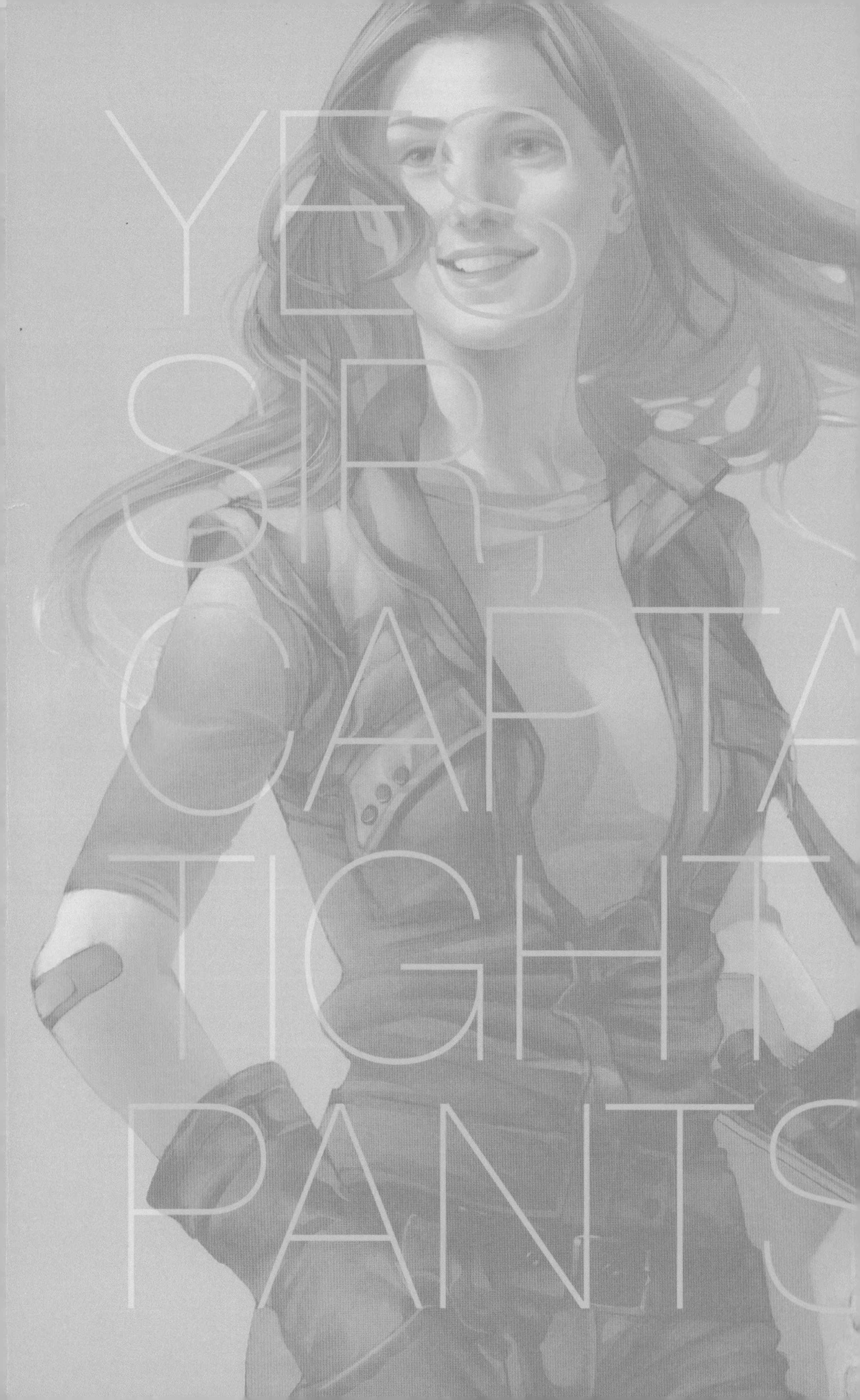
YES
SIR,
CAPTA
TIGHT
PANTS

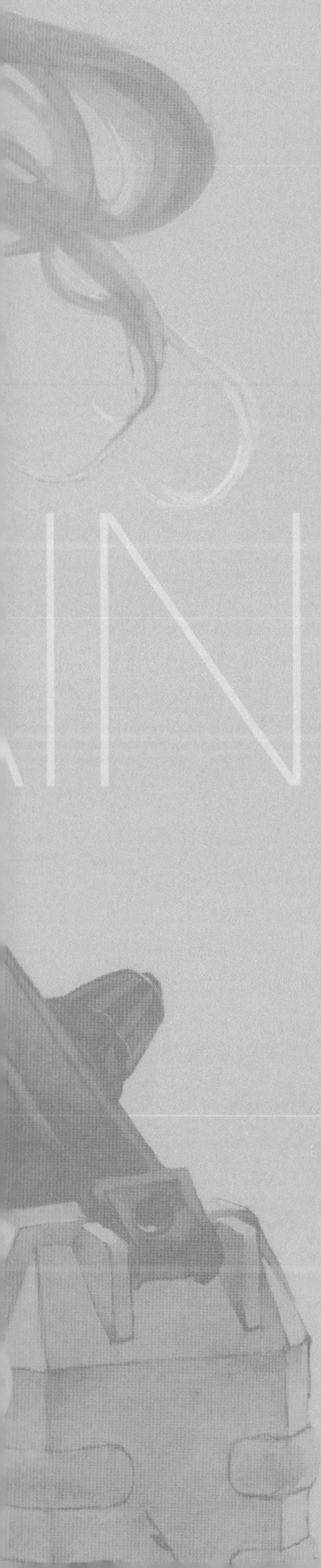

Created By
Joss Whedon

THOSE LEFT BEHIND
Story by
**Joss Whedon
& Brett Matthews**
Written by
Brett Matthews
Illustrated by
Will Conrad
Colored by
Laura Martin
Lettered by
Michael Heisler

BETTER DAYS
Story by
**Joss Whedon
& Brett Matthews**
Written by
Brett Matthews
Illustrated by
Will Conrad
Colored by
Michelle Madsen
Lettered by
Michael Heisler

THE OTHER HALF
Written by
Jim Krueger
Illustrated by
Will Conrad
Colored by
Julius Ohta
Lettered by
Michael Heisler

DOWNTIME
Script by
Zack Whedon
Illustrated by
Chris Samnee
Colored by
Dave Stewart
Lettered by
Michael Heisler

THE SHEPHERD'S TALE
Story by
Joss & Zack Whedon
Written by
Zack Whedon
Illustrated by
Chris Samnee
Colored by
Dave Stewart
Lettered by
Michael Heisler

FLOAT OUT
Written by
Patton Oswalt
Illustrated by
Patric Reynolds
Colored by
Dave Stewart
Lettered by
Michael Heisler

IT'S NEVER EASY
Written by
Zack Whedon
Illustrated by
Fábio Moon
Colored by
Cris Peter
Lettered by
Michael Heisler

Cover by
Nimit Malavia

Big Damn Heroes
Exclusive Variant Cover by
Rahzzah

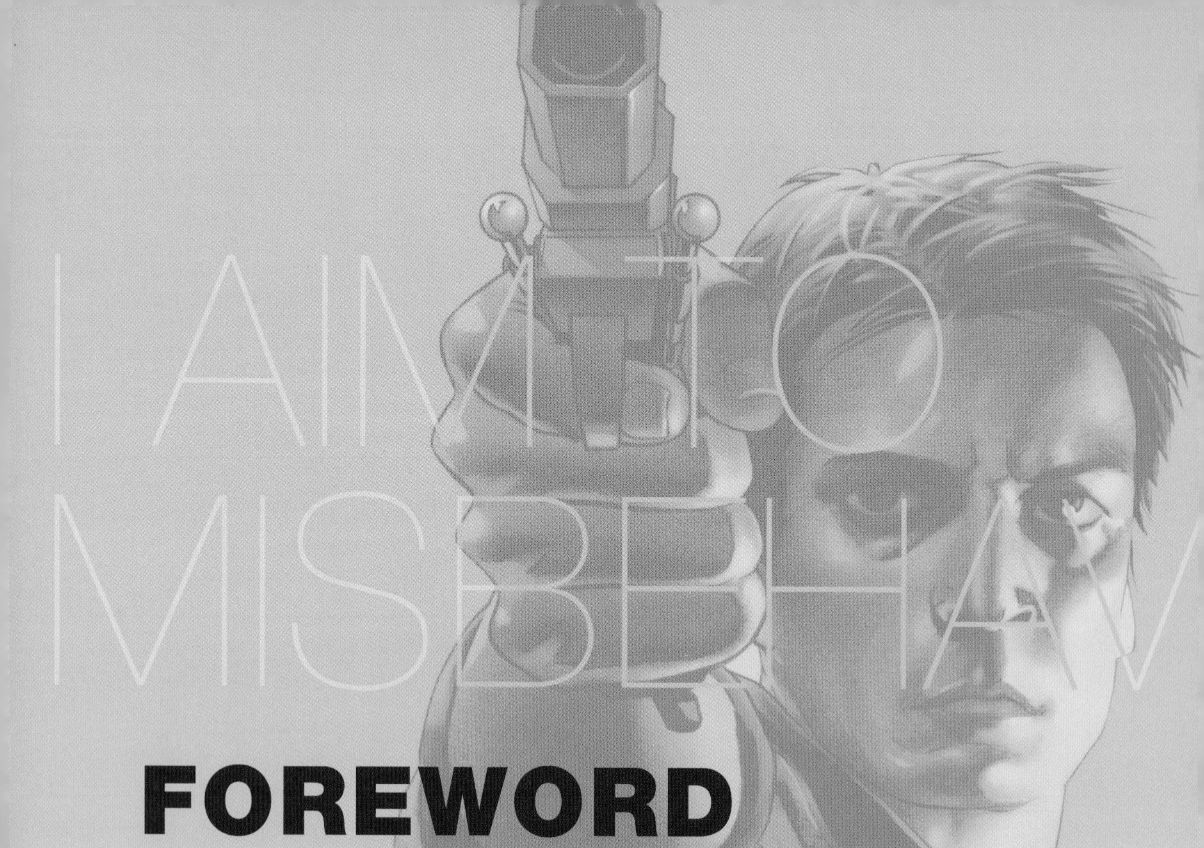
I AIM TO
MISBEHAV

FOREWORD

When I was very young, before I could read, I remember being interested in comic books. Our bedtime was not negotiable, but we could delay "lights out" for another half hour if we read anything. I mostly looked at the pictures; I could make out "a" and "the," and then simply tried to piece together a story. I could tell that Jughead liked to eat, Archie was broke, Betty was nice, and Veronica was mean. There are only so many times you can read the same ones, though, so my dad would take my brother and me to Whyte Avenue. Not too far down from Uncle Albert's Pancake House (burned down since then) was the Wee Book Inn, a store that had an odor a bit like someone's grandmother's house. Not mine, but someone's. I remember the dirty orange carpet, frayed and ragged. The wooden shelves were tall and packed with worn covers of books read many times over. Pages were yellowed and paperbacks had arched spines like old swaybacked horses. It was an old-folks' home for secondhand books, with that smell of old newsprint and slightly musty wood. There were stacks of magazines with fat, contented cats sleeping on them that you could pet without fear of being scratched. If ever there was a mystical "Ye Olde Magic Shoppe" in my life, this was it. It was a trading post for old books, and more importantly, comics. My dad would have us bring all the comics we could bear to part with, and we would watch as the clerk would shuffle through them, calculating their value. I felt as though I was in the days of the Klondike, come down from my claim in the hills and waiting for the assayer to separate the fool's gold from the real thing. His appraisal would determine how many secondhand comics we could walk away with. Always fewer than what we came in with, but my pops would pull out his wallet, careful to make sure we never left with a smaller stack. Comics were our treasure, our booty, and we would rush up to our rooms and file them away carefully on our very own spinning comic rack.

Soon, Archie, Dot, and Richie Rich gave way to Spider-Man, Captain America, X-Men, and Alpha Flight (Canada's very own superteam). Now, around this time, my memories blur a bit, but what I remember is this—I wanted to be a superhero. My brain was constantly calculating my supermoves, my supercostume, what powers I would have, how I would use them, and with whom I would share my incredible secret. My brother was in, my parents were out—lest they force me to use my newfound abilities on chores. There were, however, no radioactive spiders available to me, no toxic-waste sites, and I found out very quickly, despite my brother's urging, that jumping off the garage roof with two kites to sweep over the neighborhood didn't work. When the price of comics increased, so did my interest in girls and cars, and my treasure was relegated to the darkness of the crawlspace of our house, carefully packed in plastic bags and taped twice, not once. My desire to be a superhero, however, never abated. I couldn't help but think about how being able to fly and being bulletproof would help me in any endeavor I chose.

And then there was Joss. I met him in a small, dimly lit office, where he regaled me with tales of adventure, swashbuckling, shooting, spaceships, and narrow escapes. Um, where do I sign? He gave me a new identity, a costume, a gun, and a long brown duster for a cape. I remember that meeting so well; it was like a superhero "origin" issue. I remember Joss looking at Polaroid photos of my first costume fitting, holding up the one with the duster and gun, saying, "Action figure, anyone?"

Never in my wildest. Like some sort of superteam benefactor, Joss made superheroes out of all of us, complete with a superhideout spaceship. During filming, we'd all retreat to our dressing-room trailers and emerge like supermen with our alter egos. The boots, the suspenders, gun holstered low on my hip...with a flick and a spin of that wicked-awesome coat over my shoulders, I became someone else.

So, I guess the message I want to leave you with is this: What you hold in your hand is not just a comic. It is much more. It is a handbook. It is a guide. It is reference material for when you become a superhero. I have found the secret, you see. To become a superhero, all you have to do is want it badly enough, and comics are the fuel to that fire.

Incidentally, you hold in your hand my favorite (favourite for Canadians)...comic...ever.

Dark Horse and our cover artists have given us a great introduction to Joss's world of comic action heroes. They amazed us from the first issue, packed with shooting, crashing, punching, and splatting. Thank you, everyone. I'll be placing this series in my comic-book rack, just as soon as I get this home. It will be wrapped and double taped.

Nathan Fillion

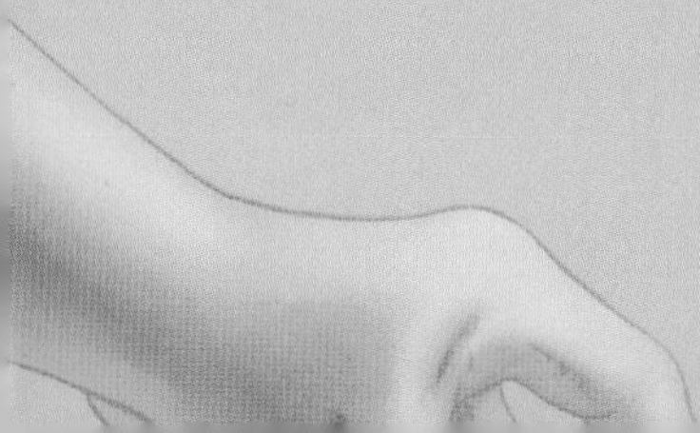

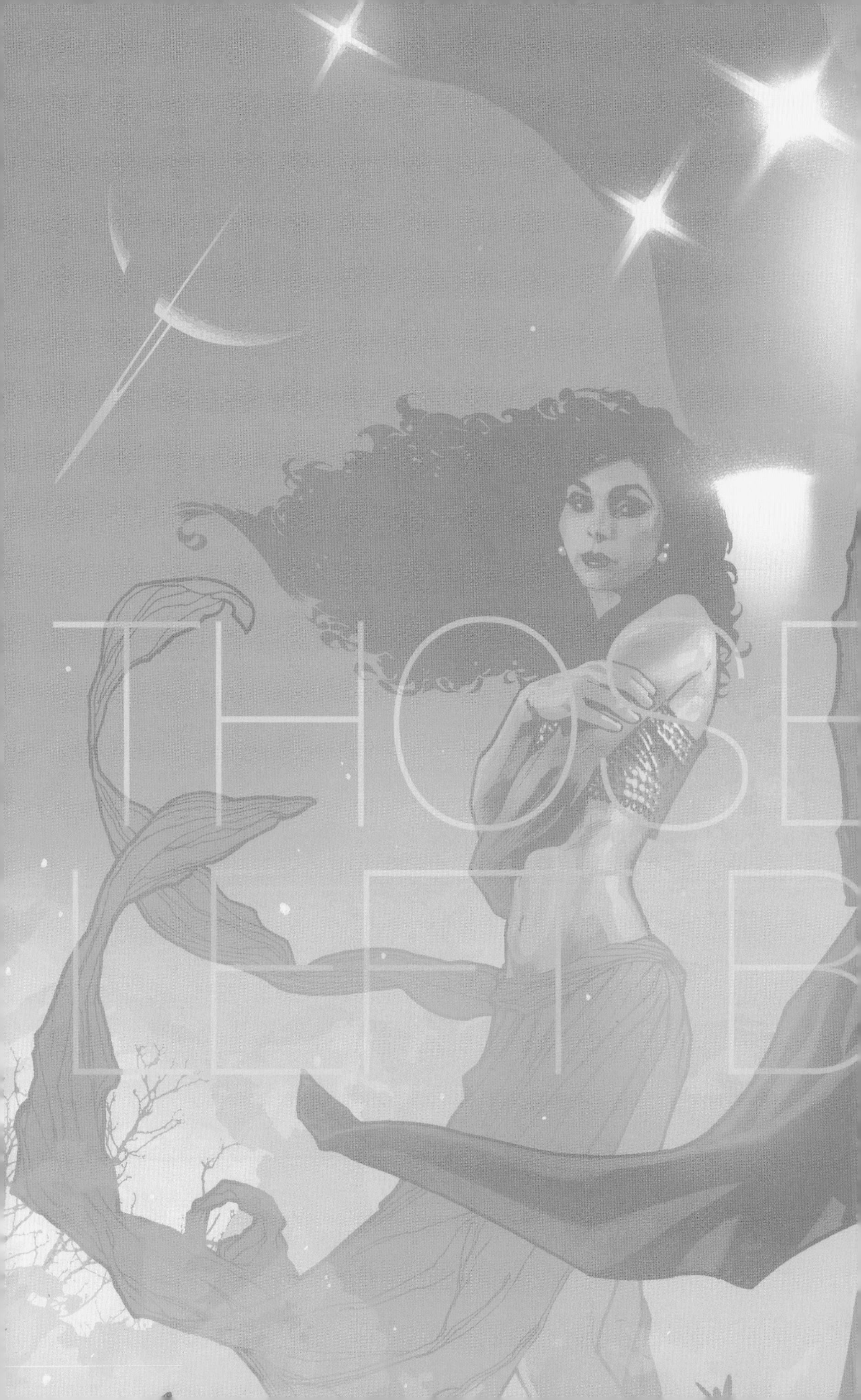

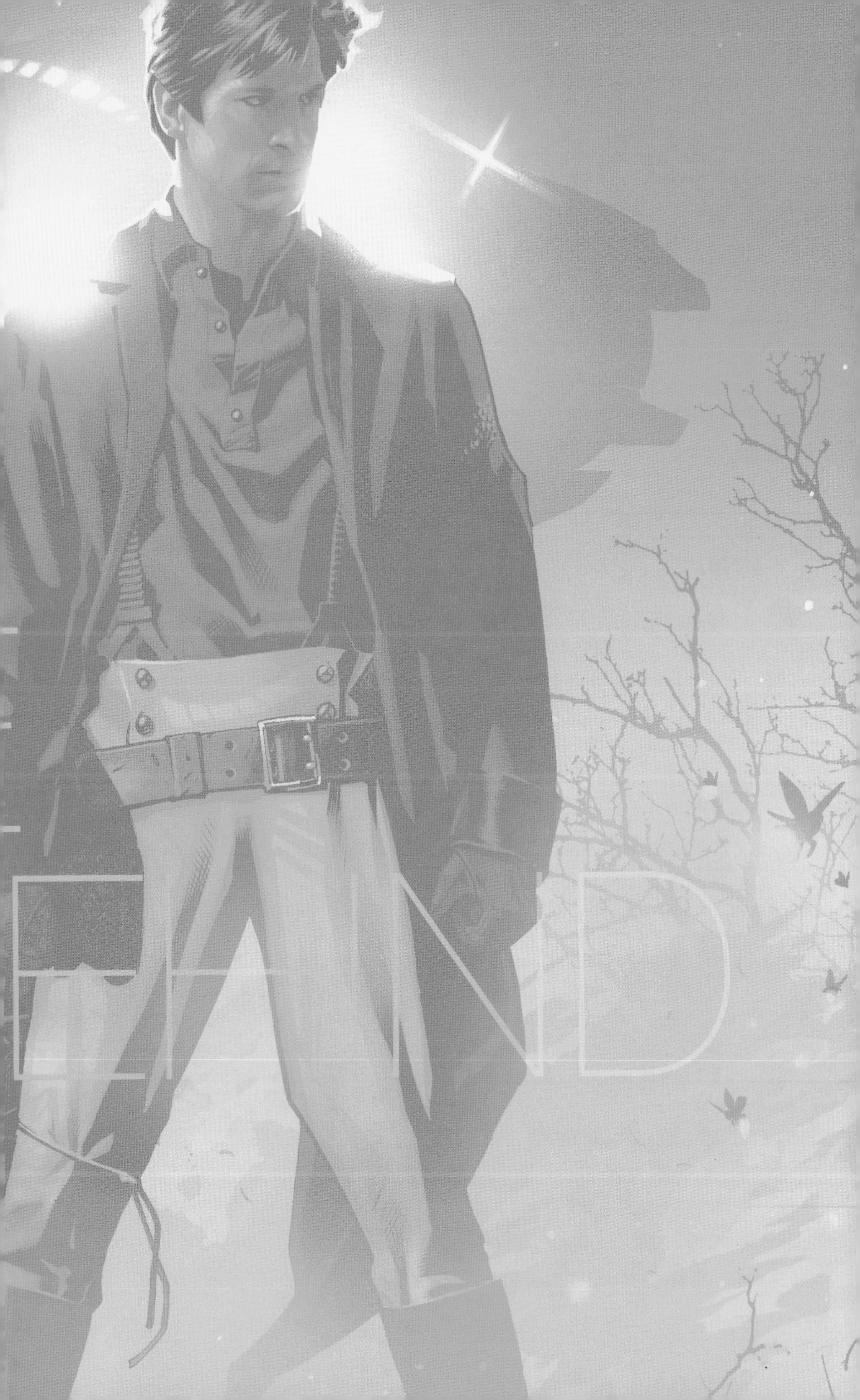

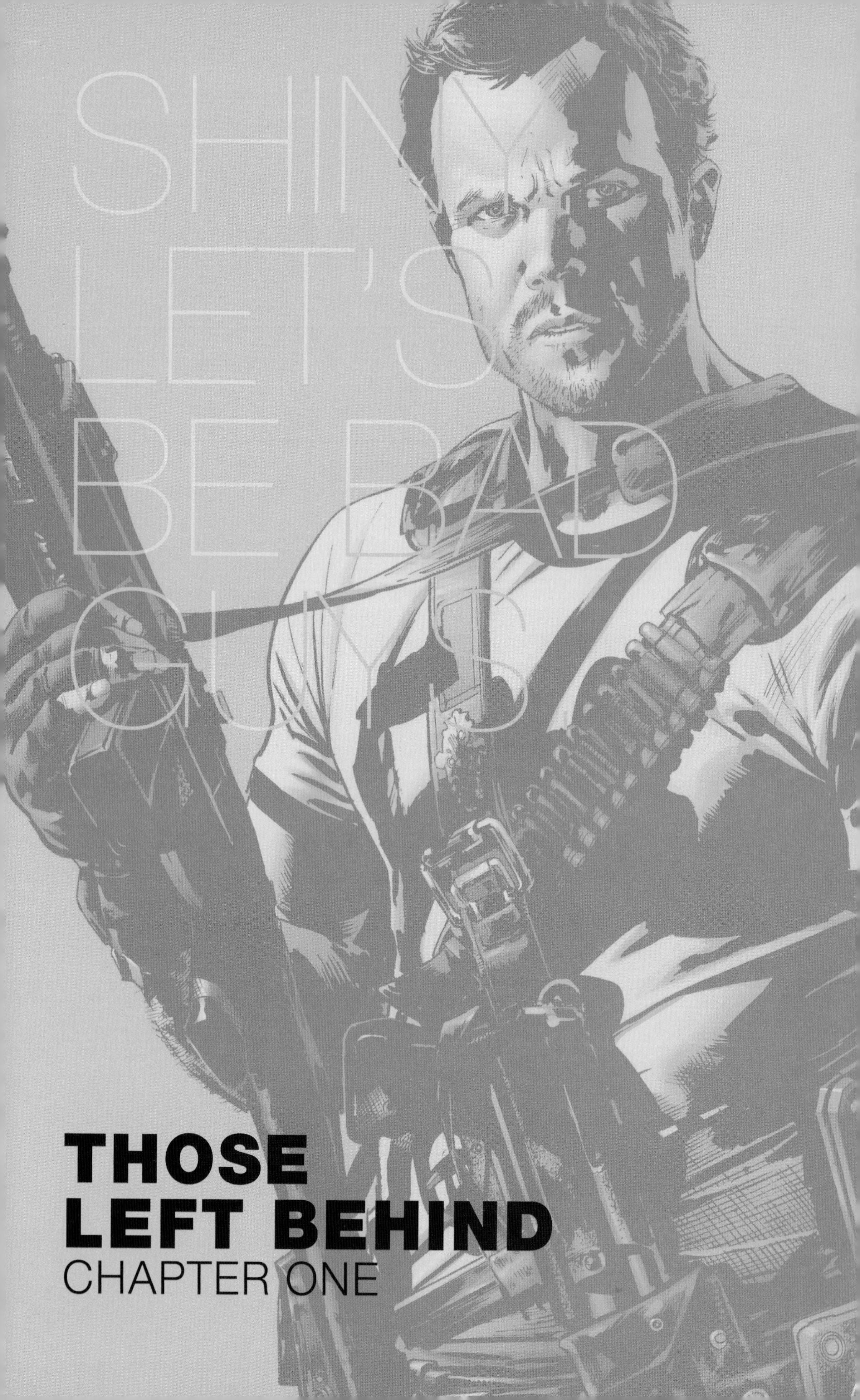
SHINY
LET'S
BE BAD
GUYS

THOSE LEFT BEHIND
CHAPTER ONE

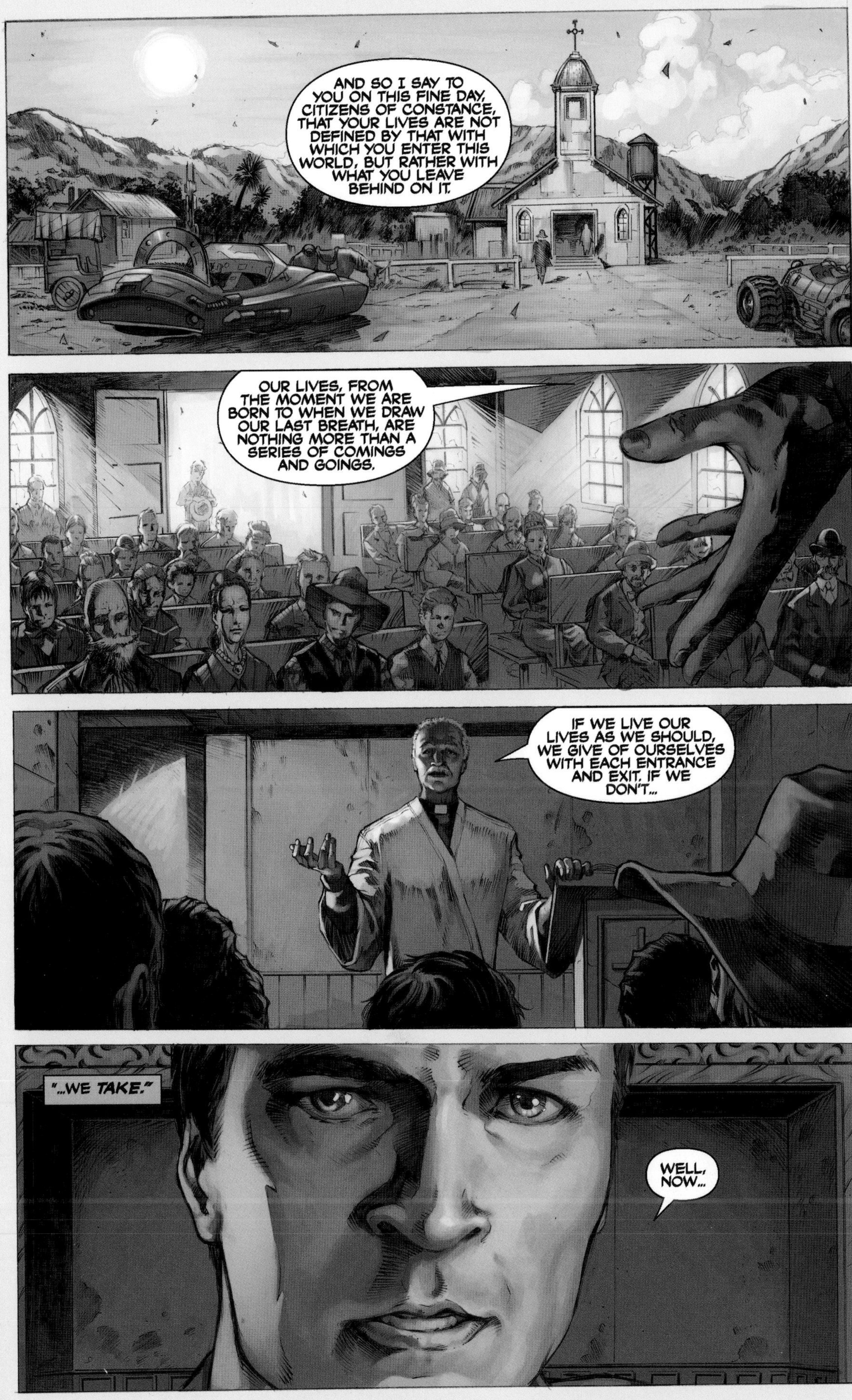
AND SO I SAY TO YOU ON THIS FINE DAY, CITIZENS OF CONSTANCE, THAT YOUR LIVES ARE NOT DEFINED BY THAT WITH WHICH YOU ENTER THIS WORLD, BUT RATHER WITH WHAT YOU LEAVE BEHIND ON IT.
OUR LIVES, FROM THE MOMENT WE ARE BORN TO WHEN WE DRAW OUR LAST BREATH, ARE NOTHING MORE THAN A SERIES OF COMINGS AND GOINGS.
IF WE LIVE OUR LIVES AS WE SHOULD, WE GIVE OF OURSELVES WITH EACH ENTRANCE AND EXIT. IF WE DON'T...
"...WE TAKE."
WELL, NOW...

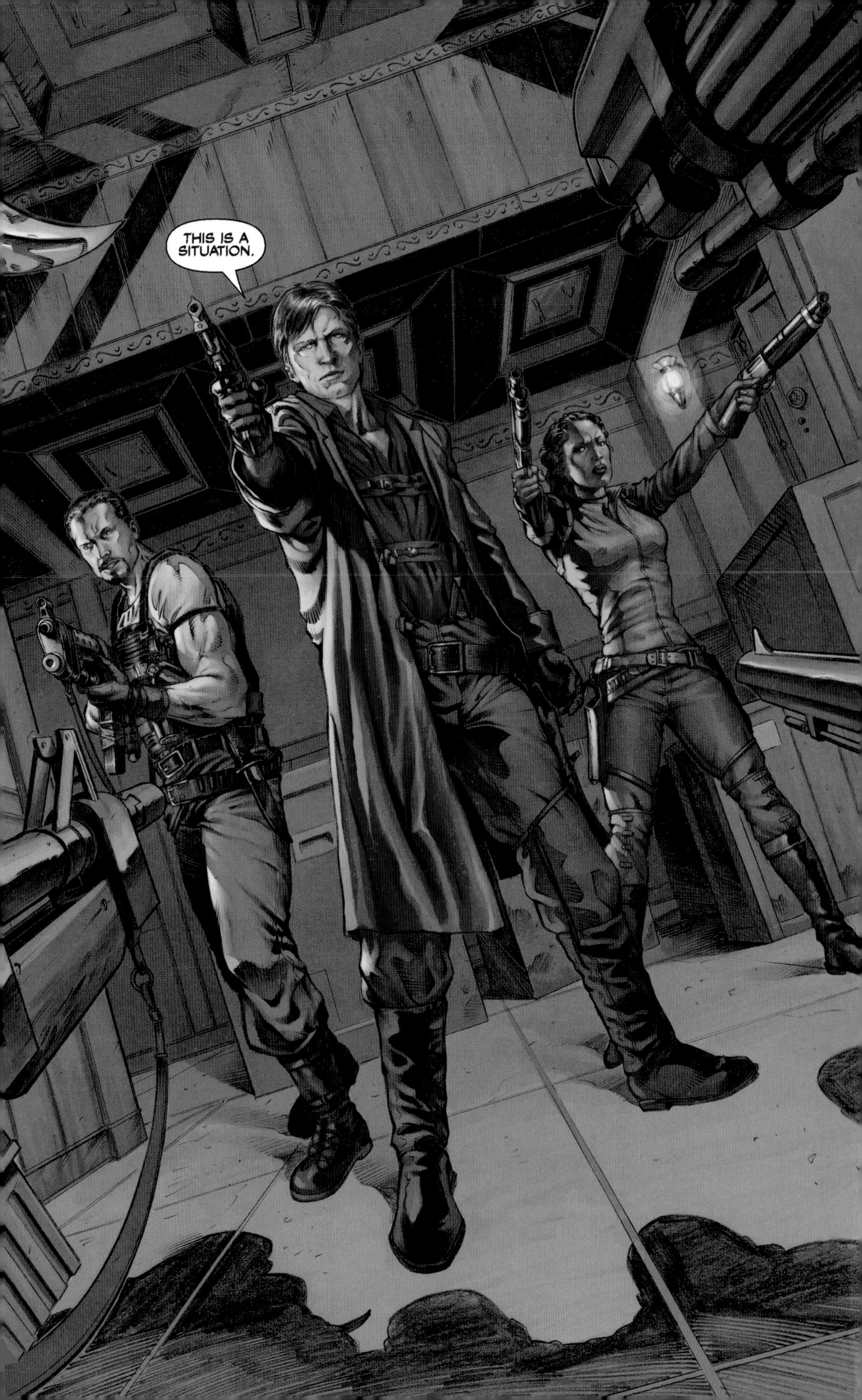
THIS IS A SITUATION.

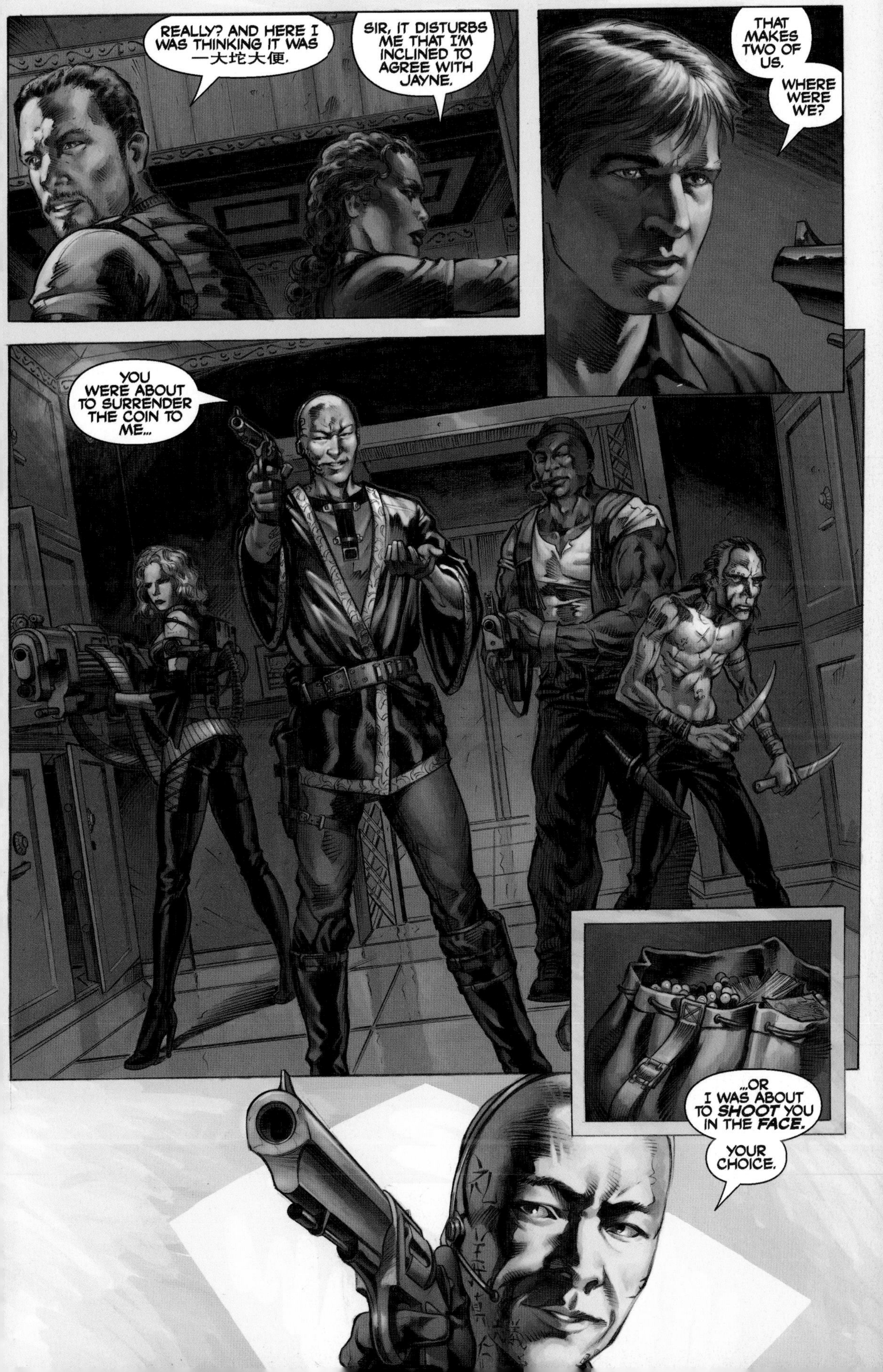
REALLY? AND HERE I WAS THINKING IT WAS 一大坨大便.
SIR, IT DISTURBS ME THAT I'M INCLINED TO AGREE WITH JAYNE.
THAT MAKES TWO OF US.
WHERE WERE WE?
YOU WERE ABOUT TO SURRENDER THE COIN TO ME...
...OR I WAS ABOUT TO *SHOOT* YOU IN THE *FACE*.
YOUR CHOICE.

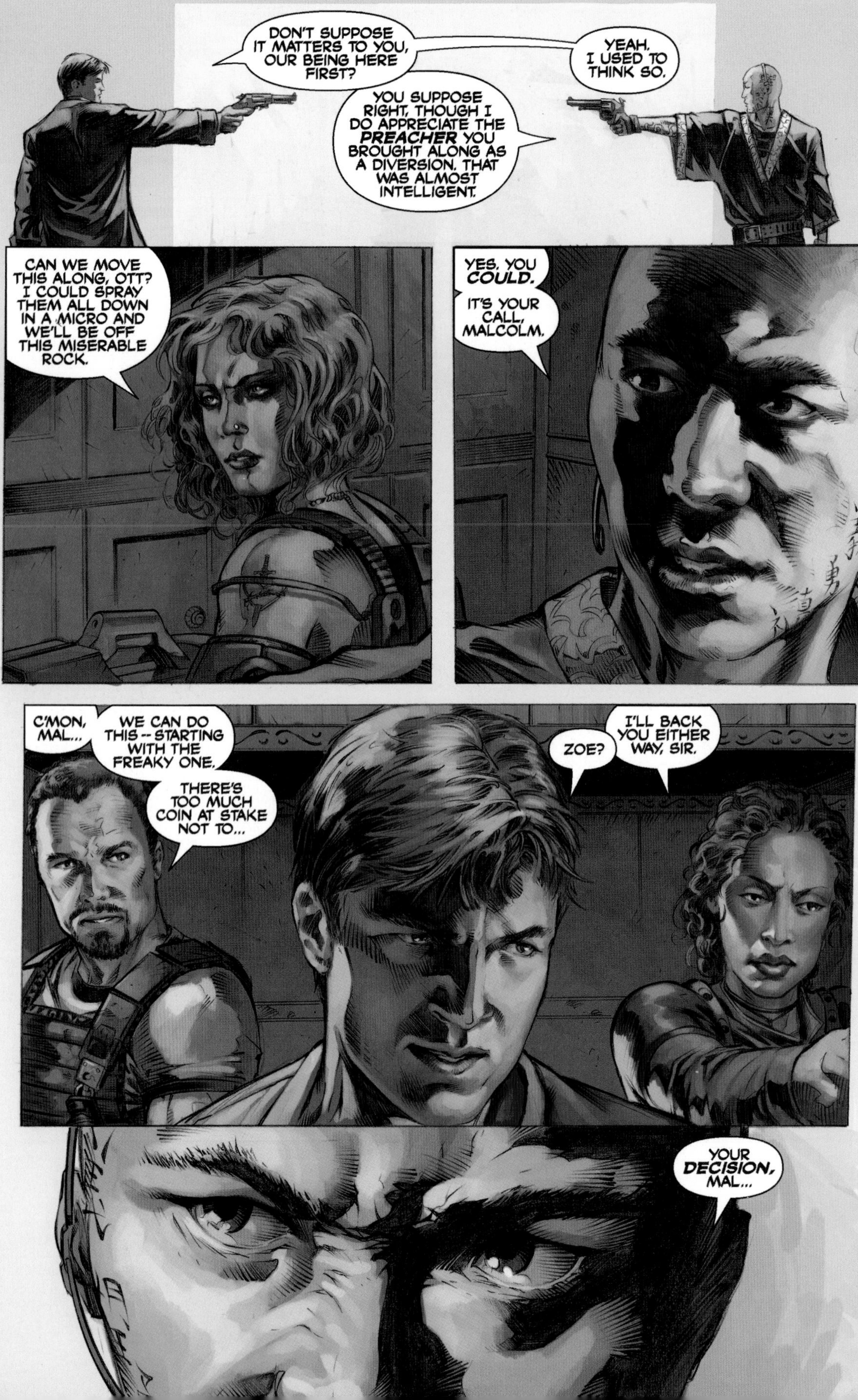

DON'T SUPPOSE IT MATTERS TO YOU, OUR BEING HERE FIRST?
YEAH, I USED TO THINK SO.
YOU SUPPOSE RIGHT, THOUGH I DO APPRECIATE THE **PREACHER** YOU BROUGHT ALONG AS A DIVERSION. THAT WAS ALMOST INTELLIGENT.
CAN WE MOVE THIS ALONG, OTT? I COULD SPRAY THEM ALL DOWN IN A MICRO AND WE'LL BE OFF THIS MISERABLE ROCK.
YES, YOU ***COULD.***
IT'S YOUR CALL, MALCOLM.
C'MON, MAL...
WE CAN DO THIS -- STARTING WITH THE FREAKY ONE.
THERE'S TOO MUCH COIN AT STAKE NOT TO...
ZOE?
I'LL BACK YOU EITHER WAY, SIR.
YOUR ***DECISION,*** MAL...

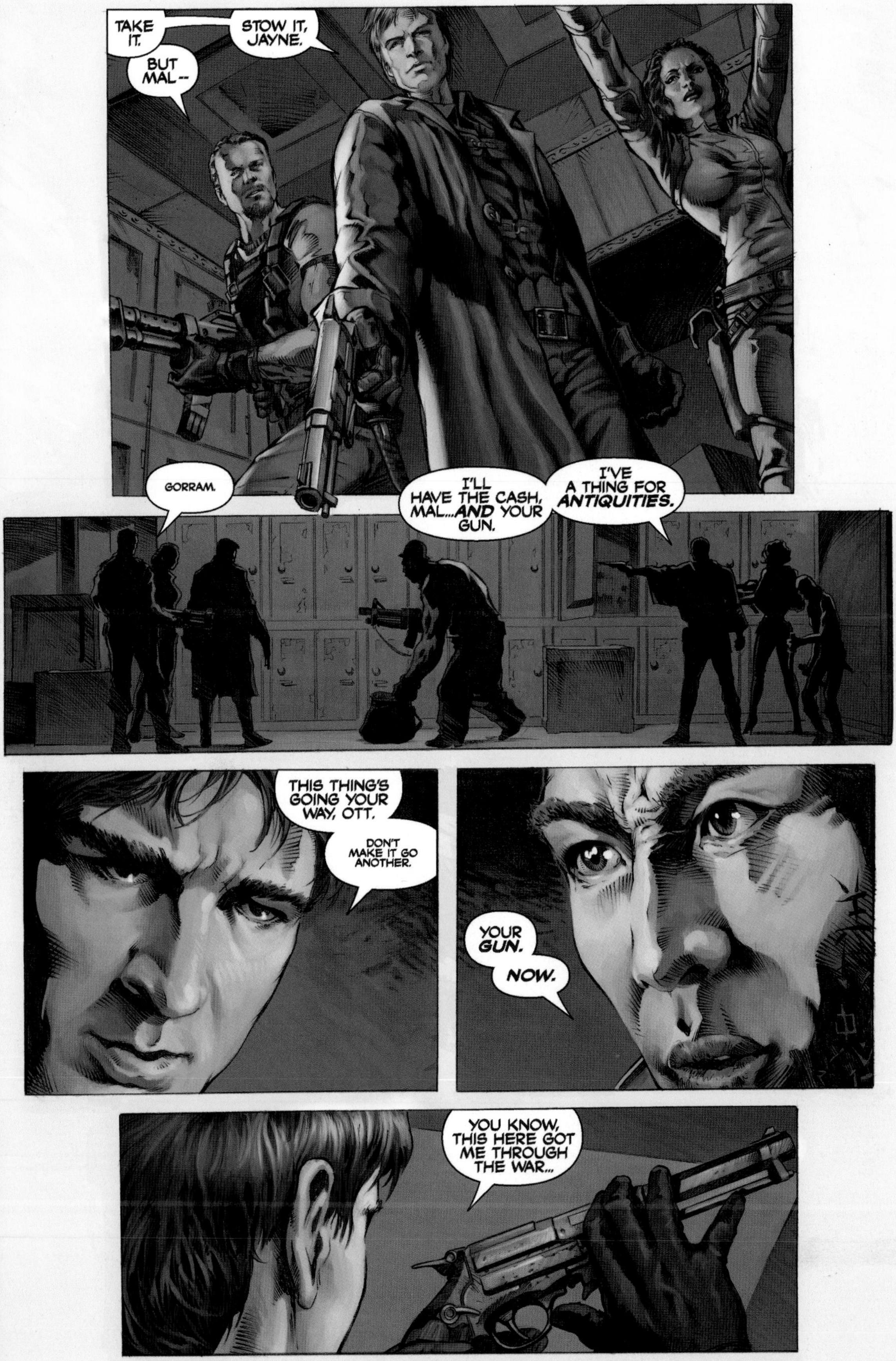
TAKE IT.
BUT MAL--
STOW IT, JAYNE.
GORRAM.
I'LL HAVE THE CASH, MAL...AND YOUR GUN.
I'VE A THING FOR ANTIQUITIES.
THIS THING'S GOING YOUR WAY, OTT.
DON'T MAKE IT GO ANOTHER.
YOUR GUN.
NOW.
YOU KNOW, THIS HERE GOT ME THROUGH THE WAR...

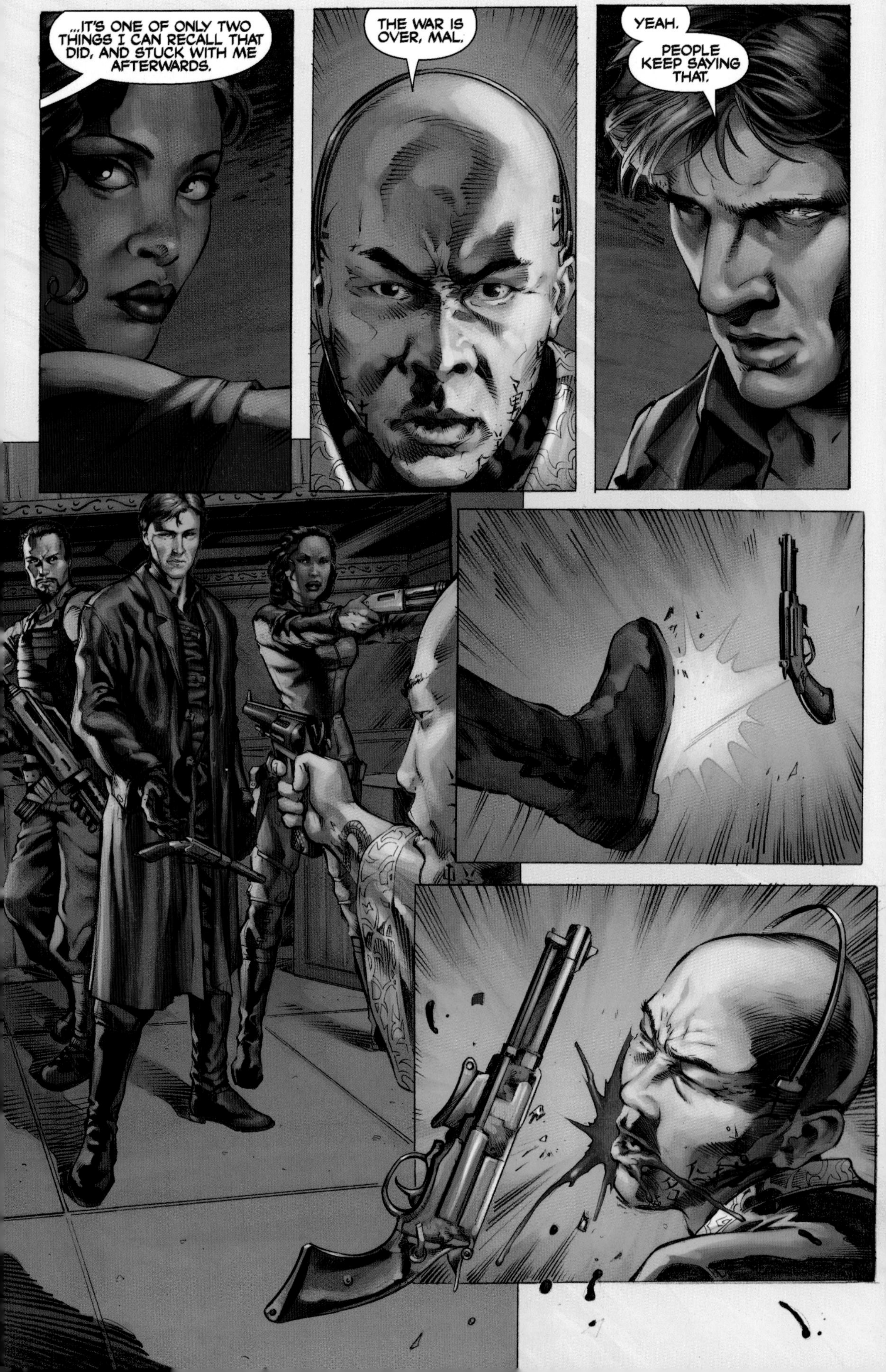
...IT'S ONE OF ONLY TWO THINGS I CAN RECALL THAT DID, AND STUCK WITH ME AFTERWARDS.
THE WAR IS OVER, MAL.
YEAH.
PEOPLE KEEP SAYING THAT.

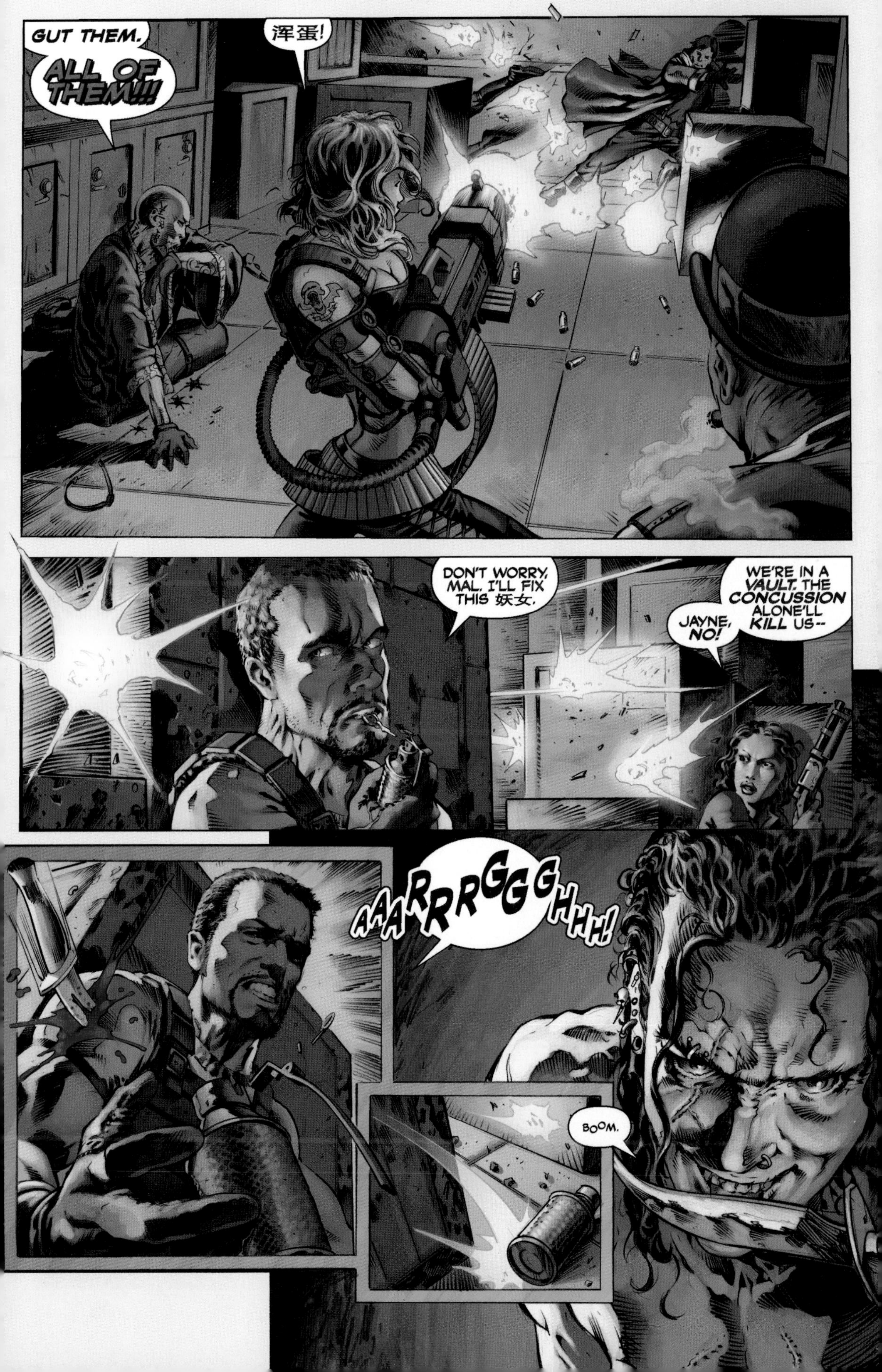
GUT THEM. ALL OF THEM!!!
浑蛋!
DON'T WORRY, MAL. I'LL FIX THIS 妖女.
JAYNE, NO!
WE'RE IN A VAULT. THE CONCUSSION ALONE'LL KILL US--
AAARRRGGGHHH!
BOOM.

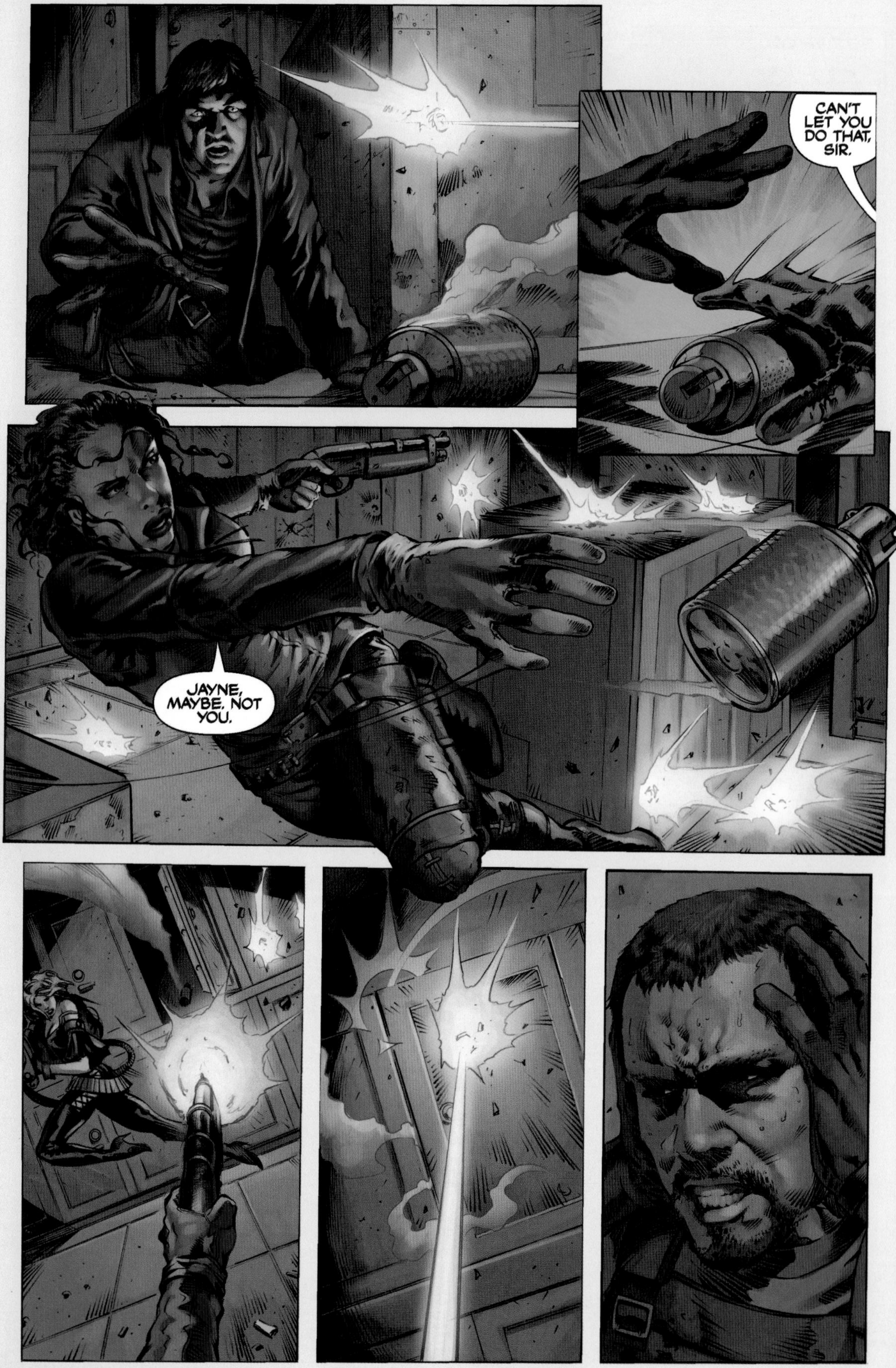
CAN'T LET YOU DO THAT, SIR.
JAYNE, MAYBE. NOT YOU.

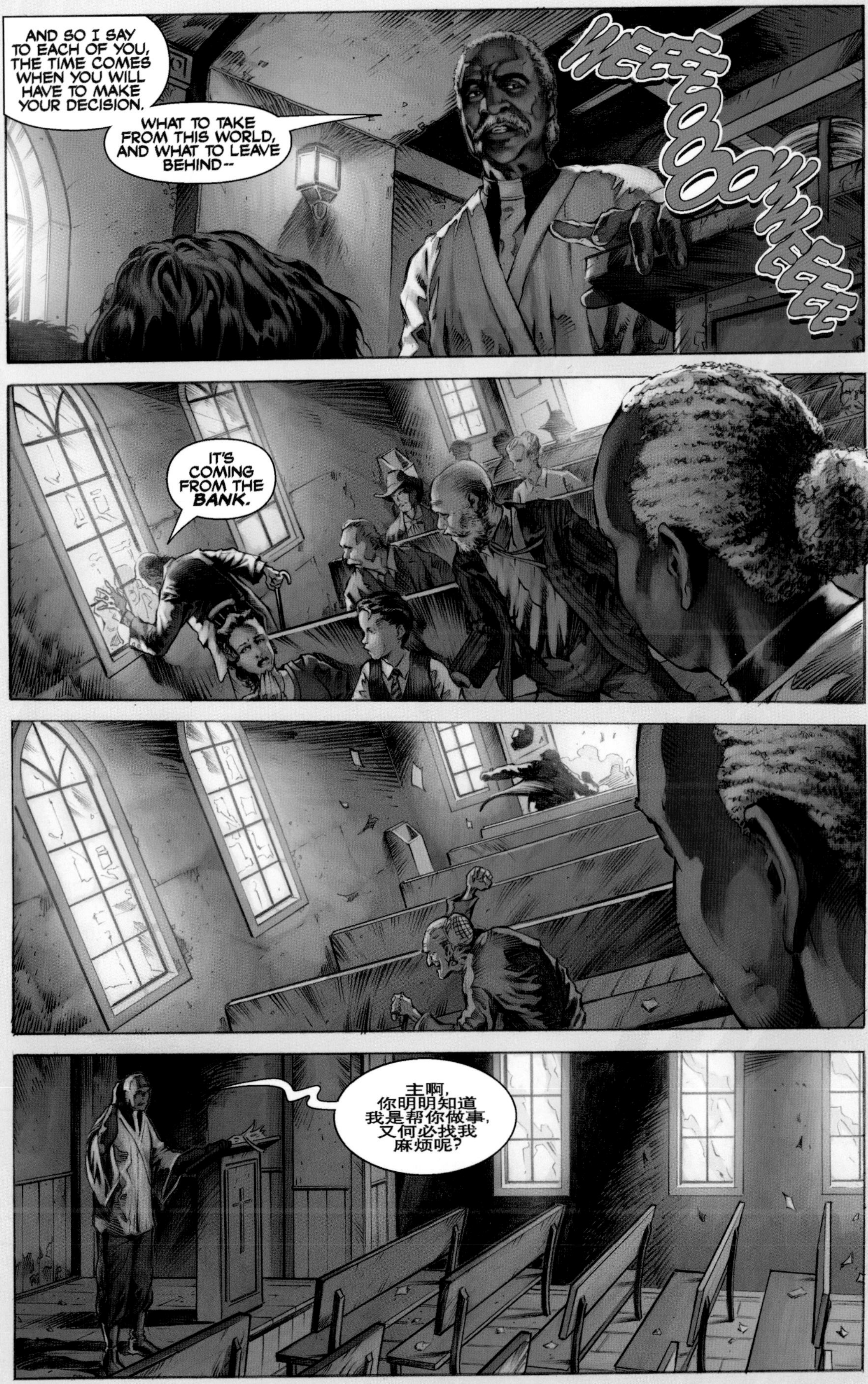
AND SO I SAY TO EACH OF YOU, THE TIME COMES WHEN YOU WILL HAVE TO MAKE YOUR DECISION.
WHAT TO TAKE FROM THIS WORLD, AND WHAT TO LEAVE BEHIND--
WEEEOOOWEEEE
IT'S COMING FROM THE BANK.
主啊,你明明知道我是帮你做事,又何必找我麻烦呢?

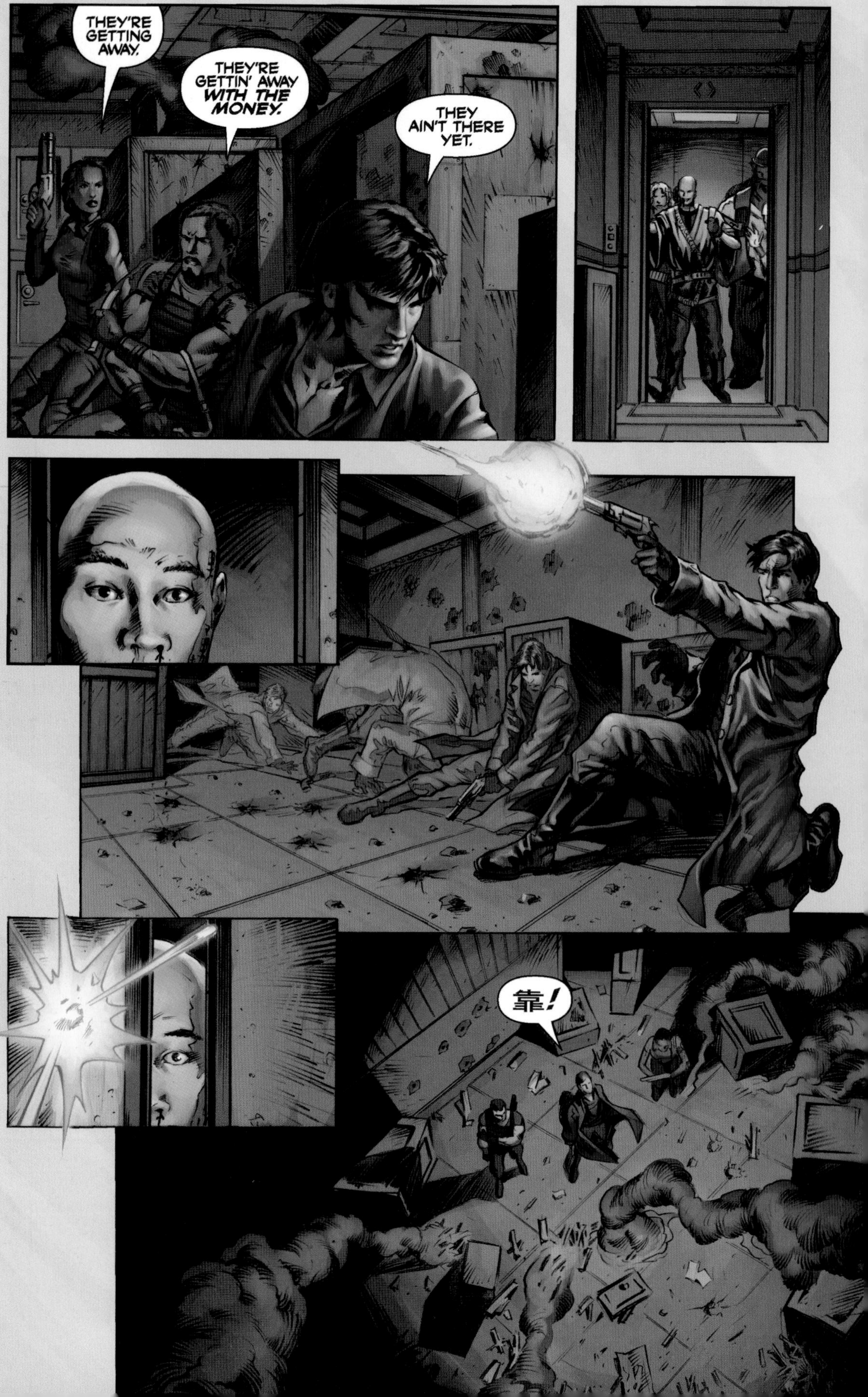
THEY'RE GETTING AWAY.
THEY'RE GETTIN' AWAY WITH THE MONEY.
THEY AIN'T THERE YET.
靠!

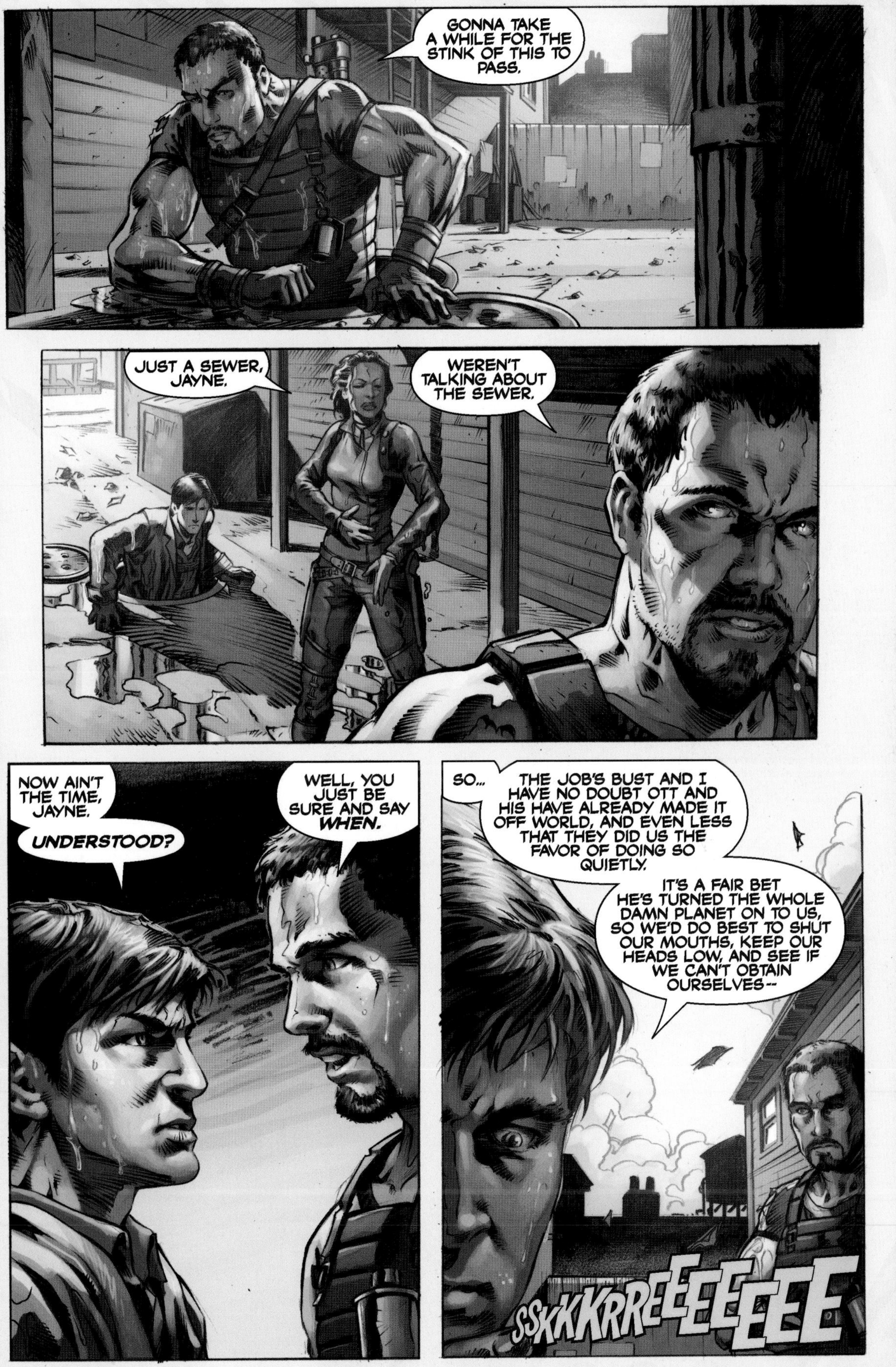
GONNA TAKE A WHILE FOR THE STINK OF THIS TO PASS.
JUST A SEWER, JAYNE.
WEREN'T TALKING ABOUT THE SEWER.
NOW AIN'T THE TIME, JAYNE.
UNDERSTOOD?
WELL, YOU JUST BE SURE AND SAY WHEN.
SO...
THE JOB'S BUST AND I HAVE NO DOUBT OTT AND HIS HAVE ALREADY MADE IT OFF WORLD, AND EVEN LESS THAT THEY DID US THE FAVOR OF DOING SO QUIETLY.
IT'S A FAIR BET HE'S TURNED THE WHOLE DAMN PLANET ON TO US, SO WE'D DO BEST TO SHUT OUR MOUTHS, KEEP OUR HEADS LOW, AND SEE IF WE CAN'T OBTAIN OURSELVES--
SSKKKRREEEEEEEE

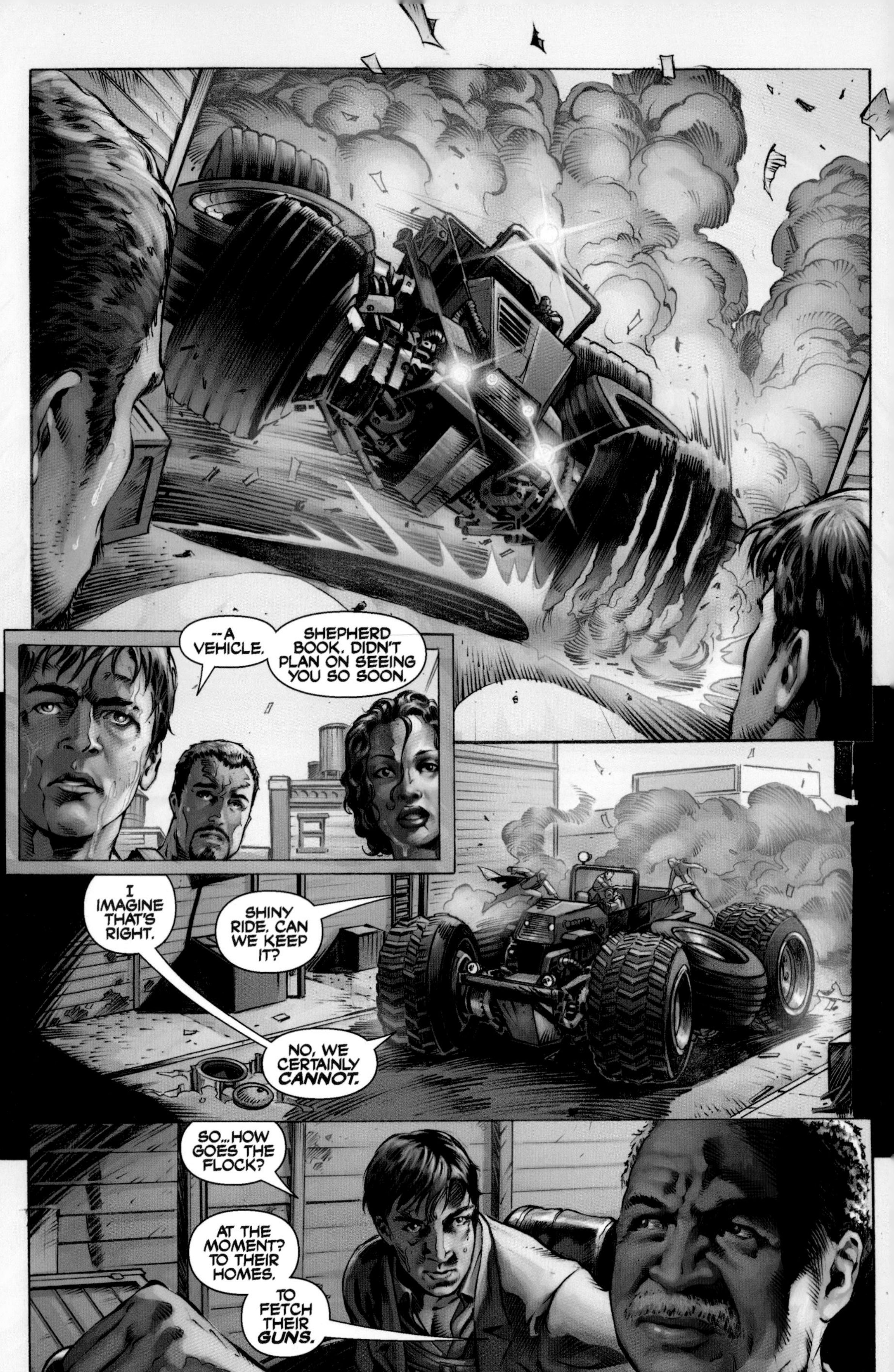
--A VEHICLE.
SHEPHERD BOOK. DIDN'T PLAN ON SEEING YOU SO SOON.
I IMAGINE THAT'S RIGHT.
SHINY RIDE. CAN WE KEEP IT?
NO, WE CERTAINLY CANNOT.
SO...HOW GOES THE FLOCK?
AT THE MOMENT? TO THEIR HOMES.
TO FETCH THEIR GUNS.

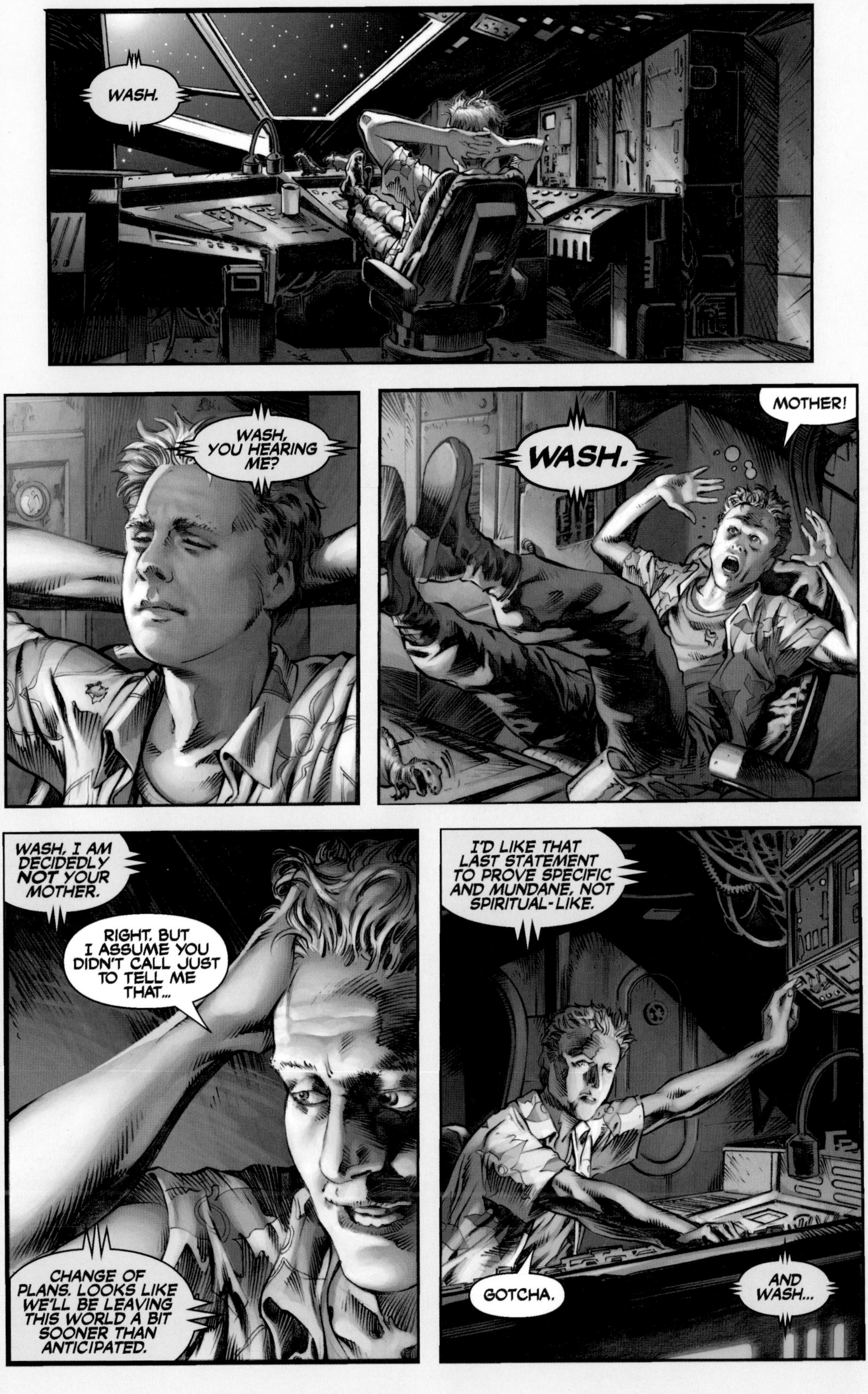

WASH.
WASH, YOU HEARING ME?
WASH.
MOTHER!
WASH, I AM DECIDEDLY NOT YOUR MOTHER.
RIGHT. BUT I ASSUME YOU DIDN'T CALL JUST TO TELL ME THAT...
CHANGE OF PLANS. LOOKS LIKE WE'LL BE LEAVING THIS WORLD A BIT SOONER THAN ANTICIPATED.
I'D LIKE THAT LAST STATEMENT TO PROVE SPECIFIC AND MUNDANE, NOT SPIRITUAL-LIKE.
GOTCHA.
AND WASH...

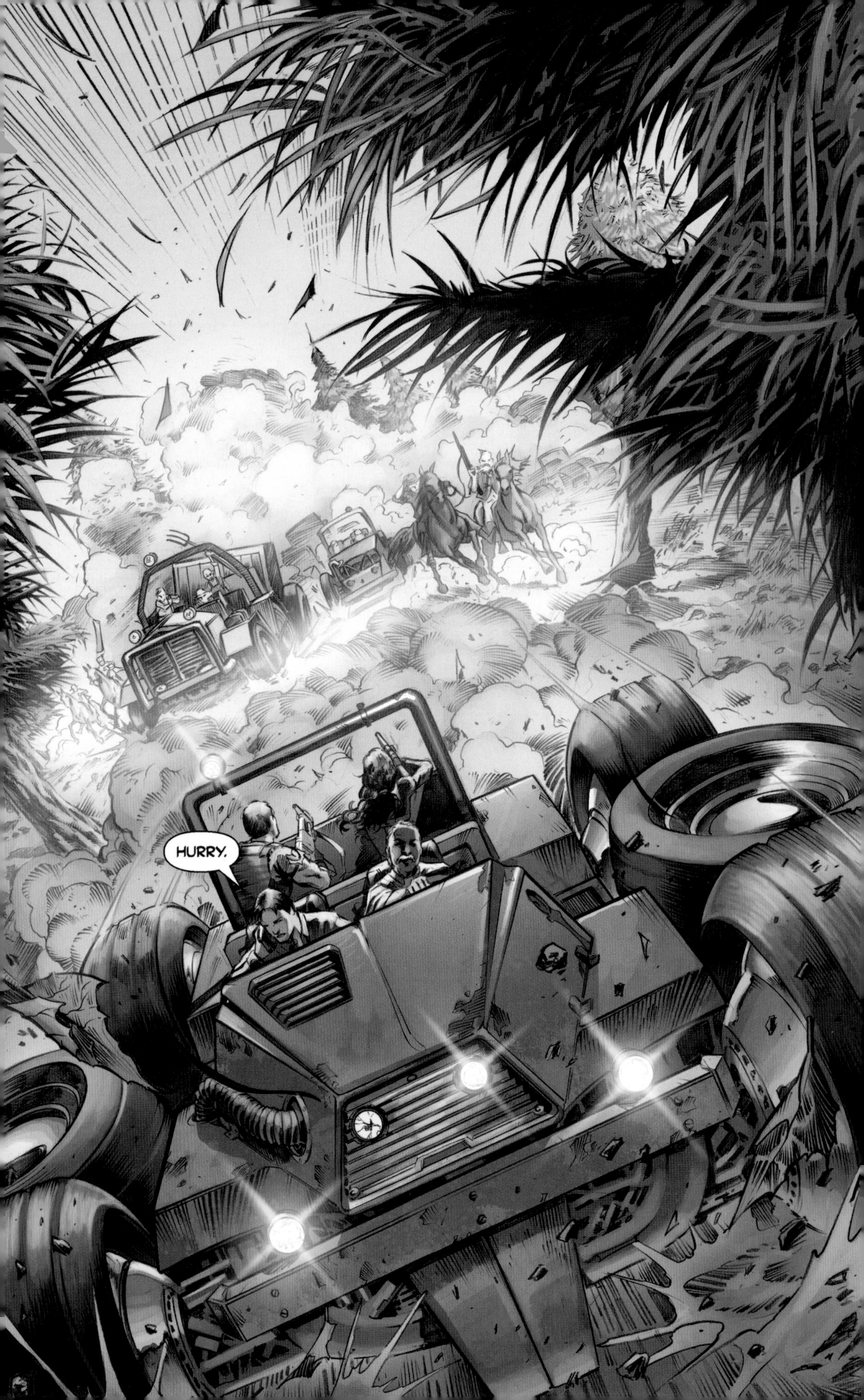
HURRY.

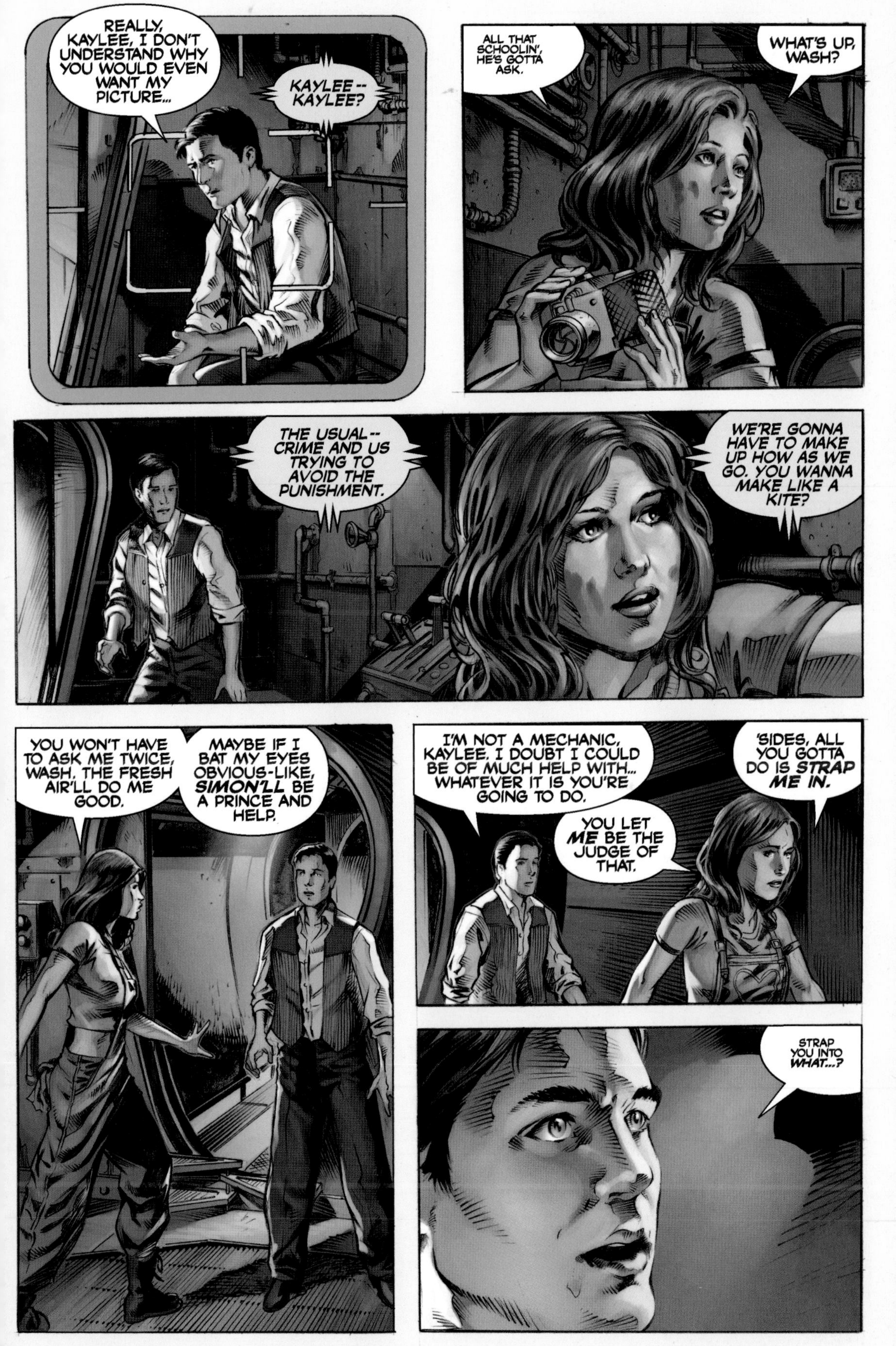
REALLY, KAYLEE, I DON'T UNDERSTAND WHY YOU WOULD EVEN WANT MY PICTURE...
KAYLEE -- KAYLEE?
ALL THAT SCHOOLIN', HE'S GOTTA ASK.
WHAT'S UP, WASH?
THE USUAL-- CRIME AND US TRYING TO AVOID THE PUNISHMENT.
WE'RE GONNA HAVE TO MAKE UP HOW AS WE GO. YOU WANNA MAKE LIKE A KITE?
YOU WON'T HAVE TO ASK ME TWICE, WASH. THE FRESH AIR'LL DO ME GOOD.
MAYBE IF I BAT MY EYES OBVIOUS-LIKE, SIMON'LL BE A PRINCE AND HELP.
I'M NOT A MECHANIC, KAYLEE. I DOUBT I COULD BE OF MUCH HELP WITH... WHATEVER IT IS YOU'RE GOING TO DO.
'SIDES, ALL YOU GOTTA DO IS STRAP ME IN.
YOU LET ME BE THE JUDGE OF THAT.
STRAP YOU INTO WHAT...?

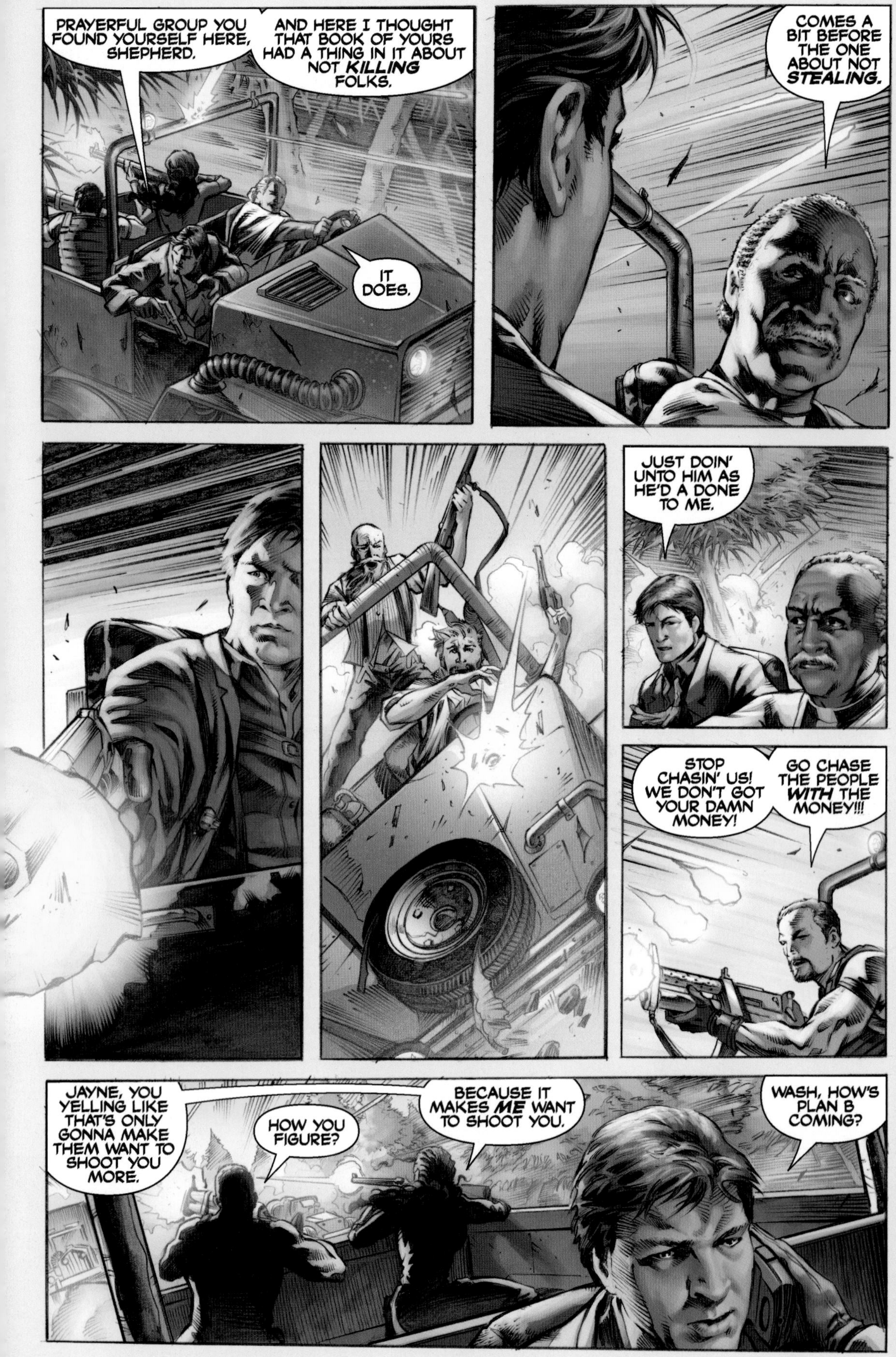
PRAYERFUL GROUP YOU FOUND YOURSELF HERE, SHEPHERD.
AND HERE I THOUGHT THAT BOOK OF YOURS HAD A THING IN IT ABOUT NOT KILLING FOLKS.
IT DOES.
COMES A BIT BEFORE THE ONE ABOUT NOT STEALING.
JUST DOIN' UNTO HIM AS HE'D A DONE TO ME.
STOP CHASIN' US! WE DON'T GOT YOUR DAMN MONEY!
GO CHASE THE PEOPLE WITH THE MONEY!!!
JAYNE, YOU YELLING LIKE THAT'S ONLY GONNA MAKE THEM WANT TO SHOOT YOU MORE.
HOW YOU FIGURE?
BECAUSE IT MAKES ME WANT TO SHOOT YOU.
WASH, HOW'S PLAN B COMING?

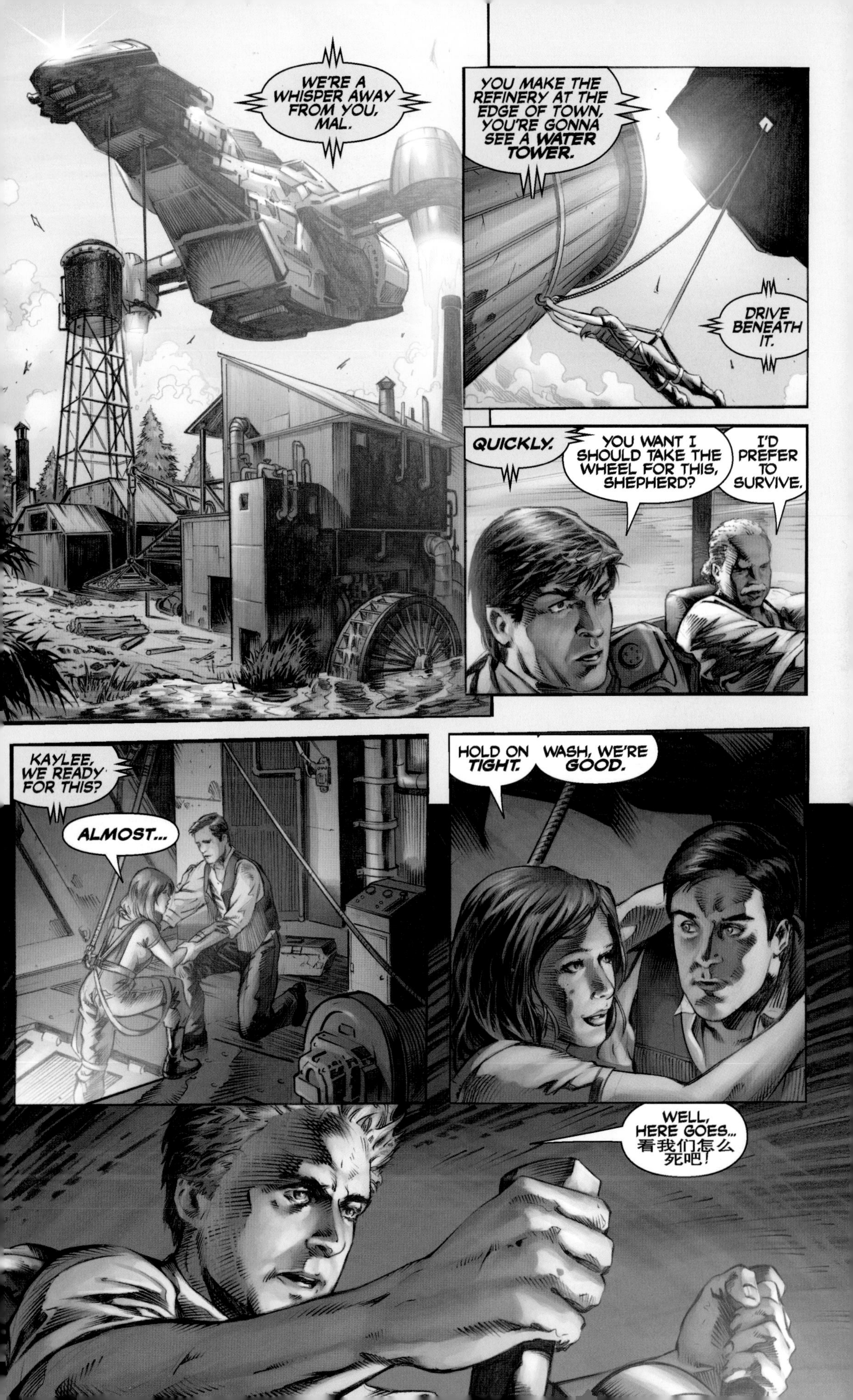
WE'RE A WHISPER AWAY FROM YOU, MAL.
YOU MAKE THE REFINERY AT THE EDGE OF TOWN, YOU'RE GONNA SEE A WATER TOWER.
DRIVE BENEATH IT.
QUICKLY.
YOU WANT I SHOULD TAKE THE WHEEL FOR THIS, SHEPHERD?
I'D PREFER TO SURVIVE.
KAYLEE, WE READY FOR THIS?
ALMOST...
HOLD ON TIGHT.
WASH, WE'RE GOOD.
WELL, HERE GOES... 看我们怎么死吧!

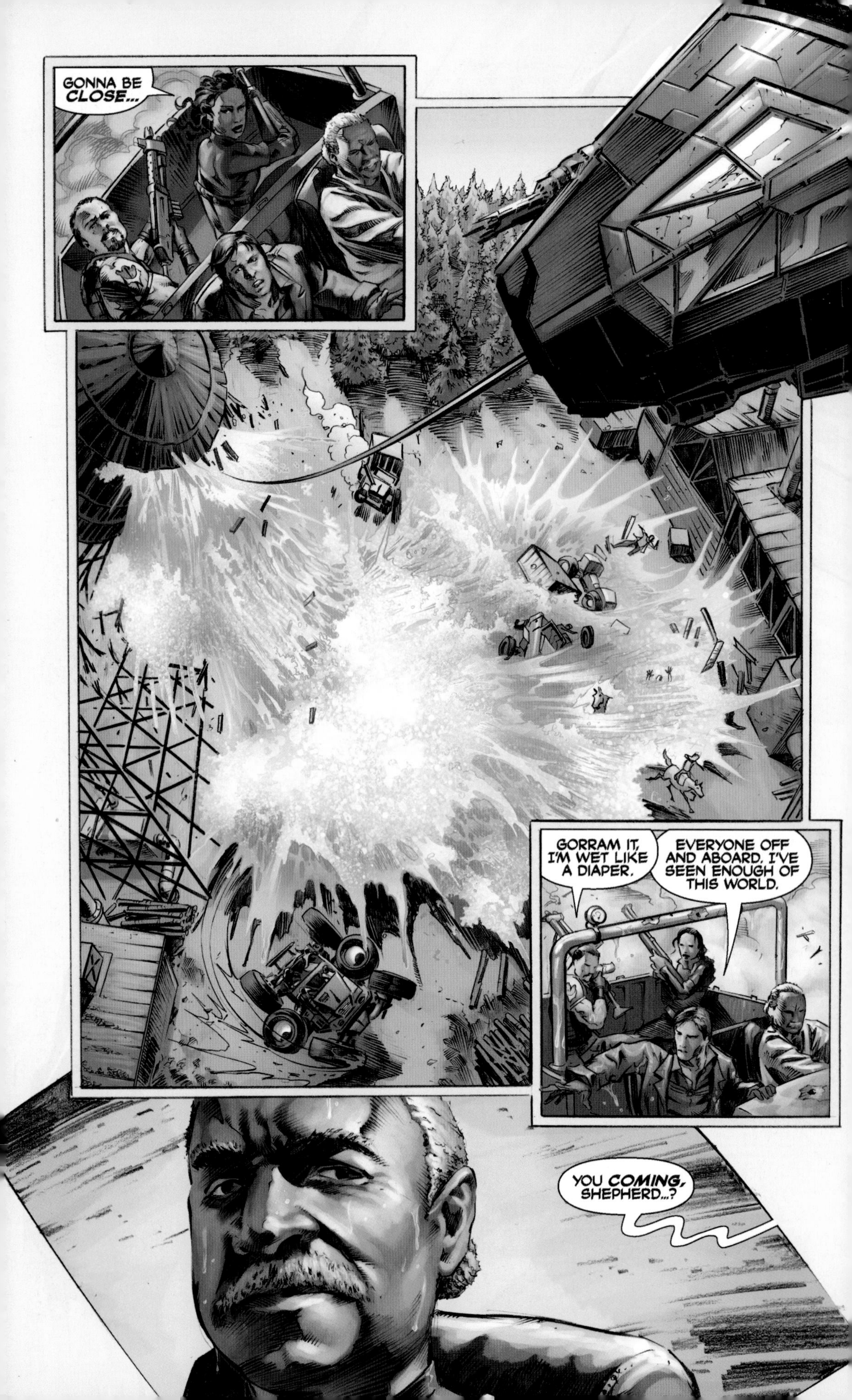
GONNA BE CLOSE...
GORRAM IT, I'M WET LIKE A DIAPER.
EVERYONE OFF AND ABOARD. I'VE SEEN ENOUGH OF THIS WORLD.
YOU COMING, SHEPHERD...?

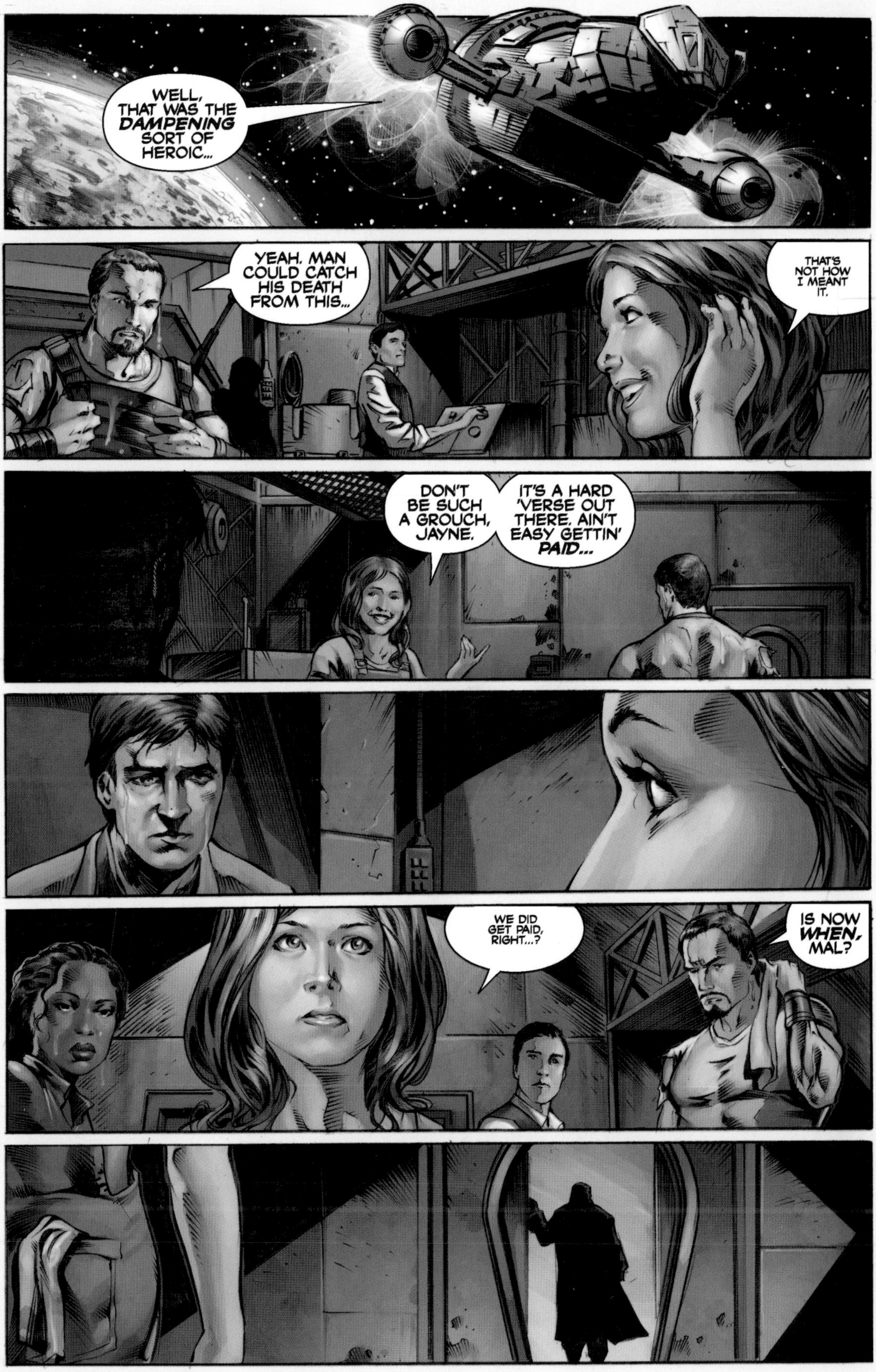

WELL, THAT WAS THE DAMPENING SORT OF HEROIC...
YEAH, MAN COULD CATCH HIS DEATH FROM THIS...
THAT'S NOT HOW I MEANT IT.
DON'T BE SUCH A GROUCH, JAYNE.
IT'S A HARD 'VERSE OUT THERE. AIN'T EASY GETTIN' PAID...
WE DID GET PAID, RIGHT...?
IS NOW WHEN, MAL?

RIVER? WHAT IN THE HELL ARE YOU--

BALL OF YARN...

ALL KNOTTED AND TANGLED WITH DIFFERENT WEIGHTS AND COLORS.

BUT PULL ONE STRING, YOU PULL THEM ALL...

THERE YOU ARE...

I'VE BEEN LOOKING ALL OVER THE SHIP FOR HER.

YOU CHEATED.

INARA.

SIMON ASKED THAT I LOOK AFTER HER, AND RIVER WAS BEING SO KIND AS TO HELP ME PACK--

IF IT'S ALL THE SAME TO YOU, INARA, NOW'S NOT THE TIME TO HAVE THIS CONVERSATION. AGAIN.

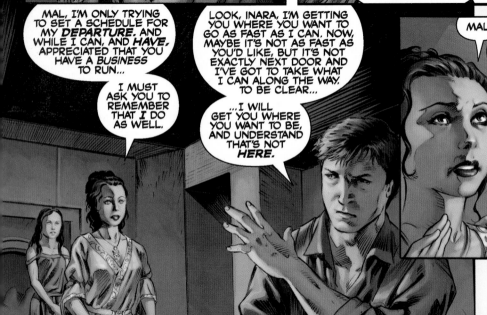

MAL, I'M ONLY TRYING TO SET A SCHEDULE FOR MY DEPARTURE. AND WHILE I CAN, AND HAVE, APPRECIATED THAT YOU HAVE A BUSINESS TO RUN...

I MUST ASK YOU TO REMEMBER THAT I DO AS WELL.

LOOK, INARA, I'M GETTING YOU WHERE YOU WANT TO GO AS FAST AS I CAN. NOW, MAYBE IT'S NOT AS FAST AS YOU'D LIKE, BUT IT'S NOT EXACTLY NEXT DOOR AND I'VE GOT TO TAKE WHAT I CAN ALONG THE WAY. TO BE CLEAR...

...I WILL GET YOU WHERE YOU WANT TO BE, AND UNDERSTAND THAT'S NOT HERE.

MAL...

LET THE BALL OF YARN GO.

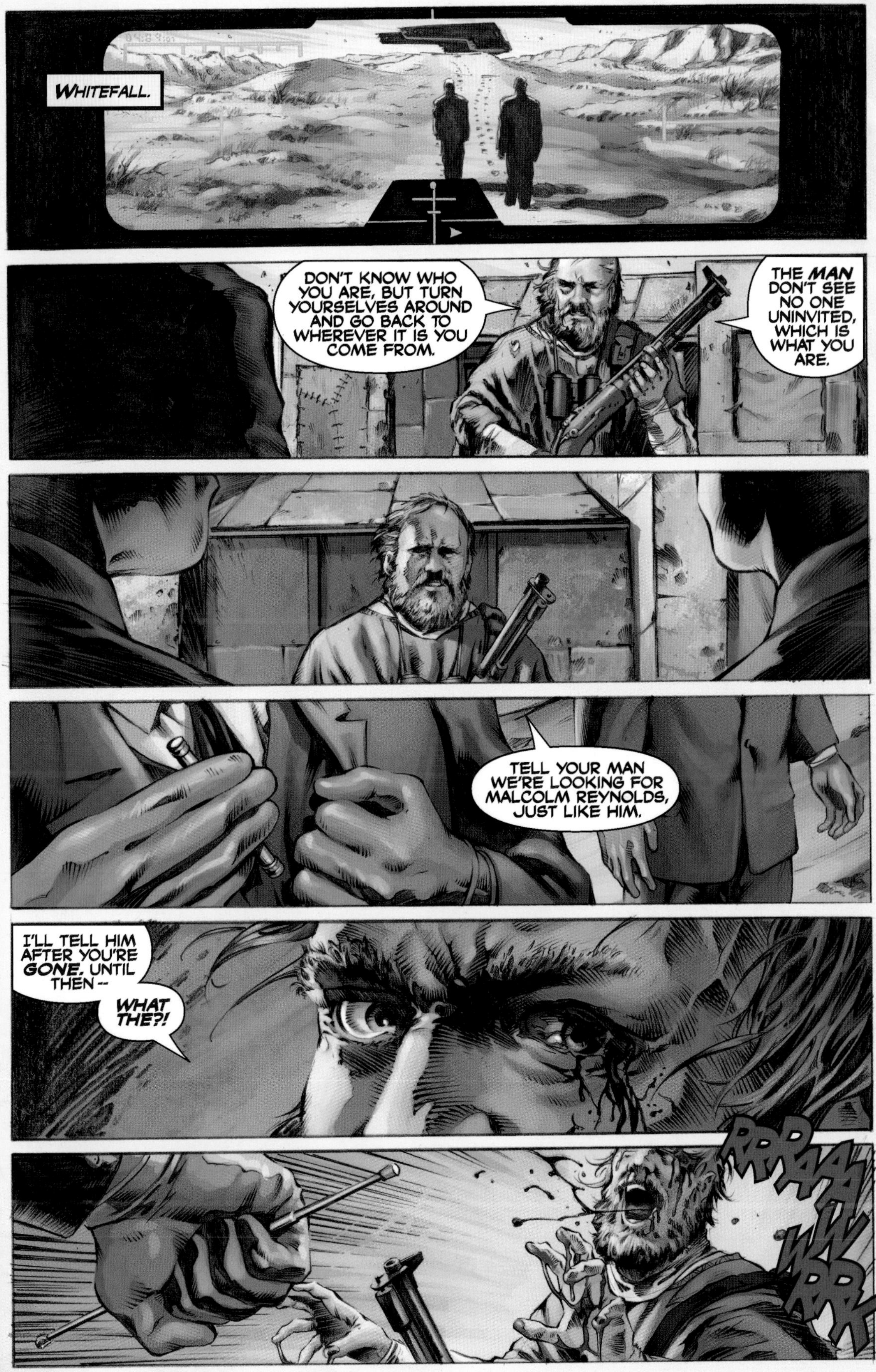
WHITEFALL.
DON'T KNOW WHO YOU ARE, BUT TURN YOURSELVES AROUND AND GO BACK TO WHEREVER IT IS YOU COME FROM.
THE MAN DON'T SEE NO ONE UNINVITED, WHICH IS WHAT YOU ARE.
TELL YOUR MAN WE'RE LOOKING FOR MALCOLM REYNOLDS, JUST LIKE HIM.
I'LL TELL HIM AFTER YOU'RE GONE. UNTIL THEN --
WHAT THE?!
RRRAAAWWRRK

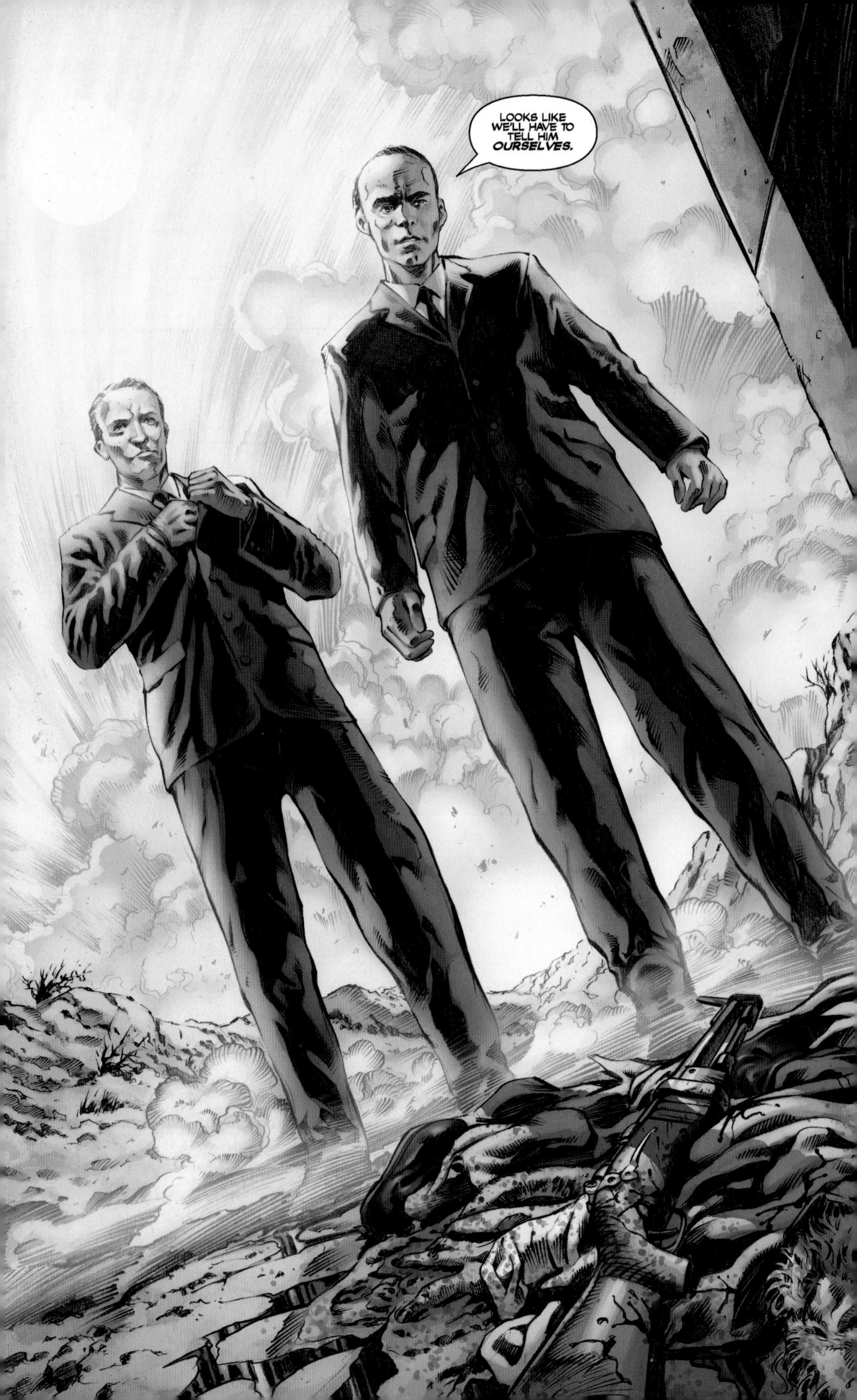
LOOKS LIKE WE'LL HAVE TO TELL HIM *OURSELVES.*

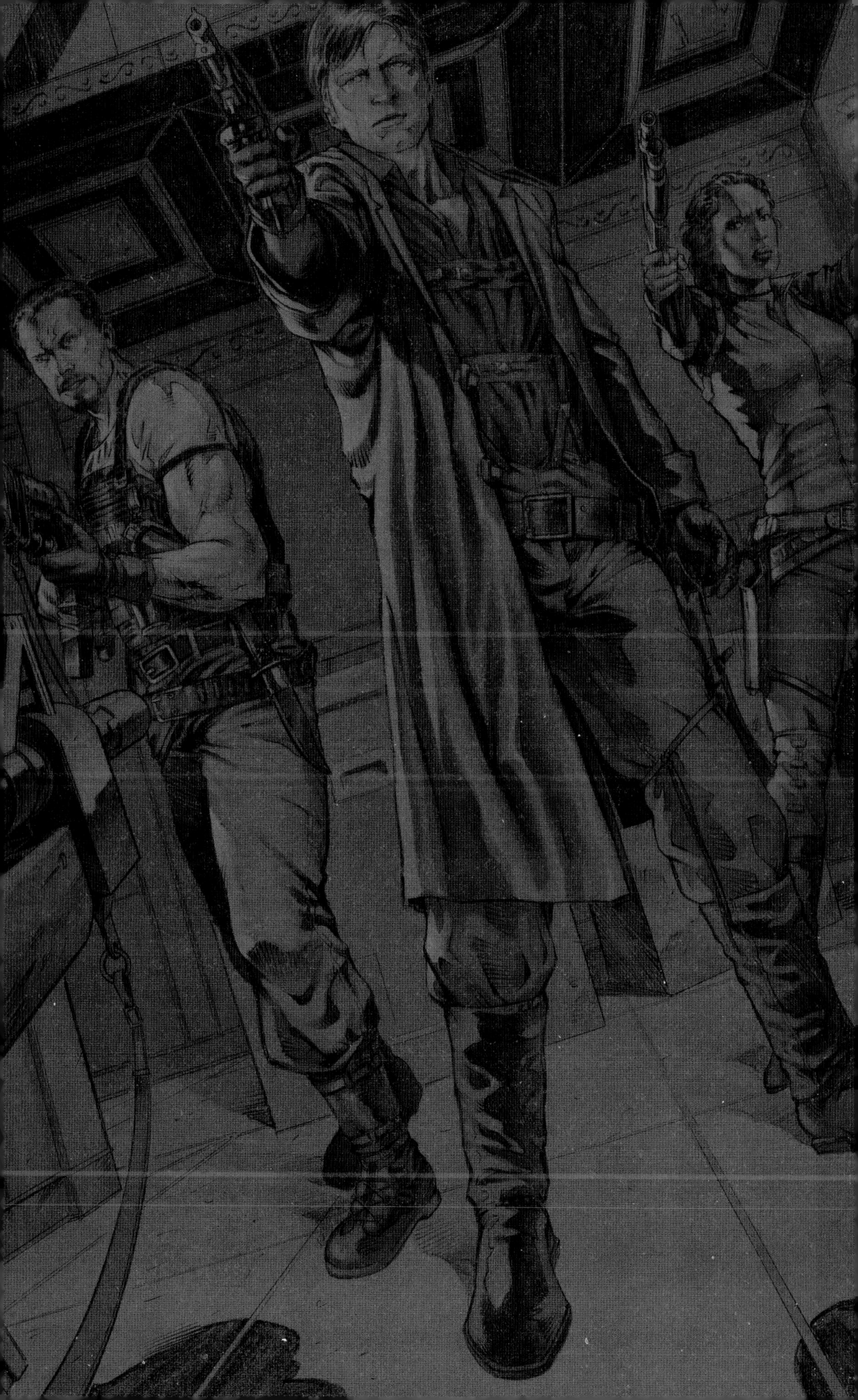

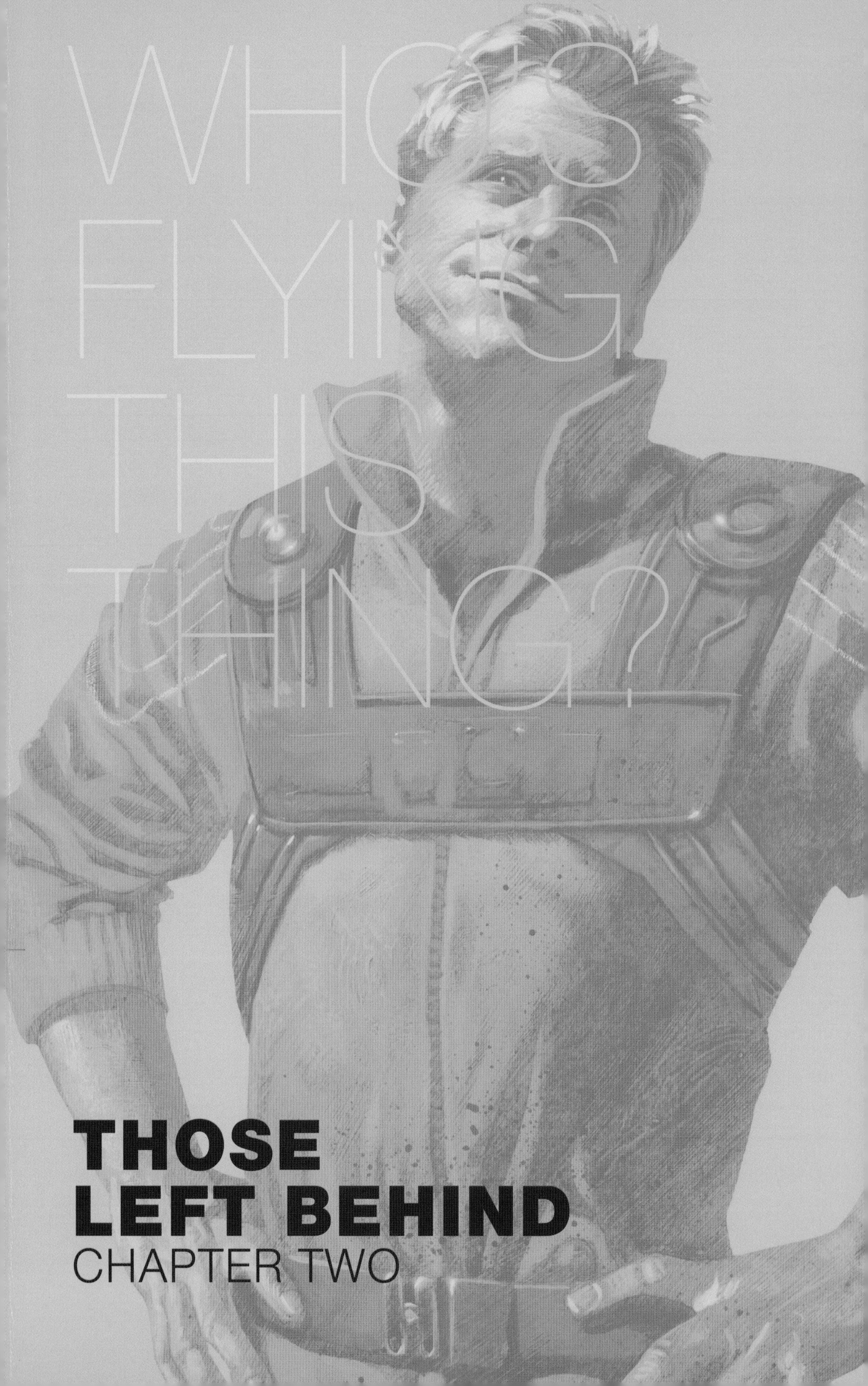
WHO'S
FLYING
THIS
THING?

THOSE LEFT BEHIND

CHAPTER TWO

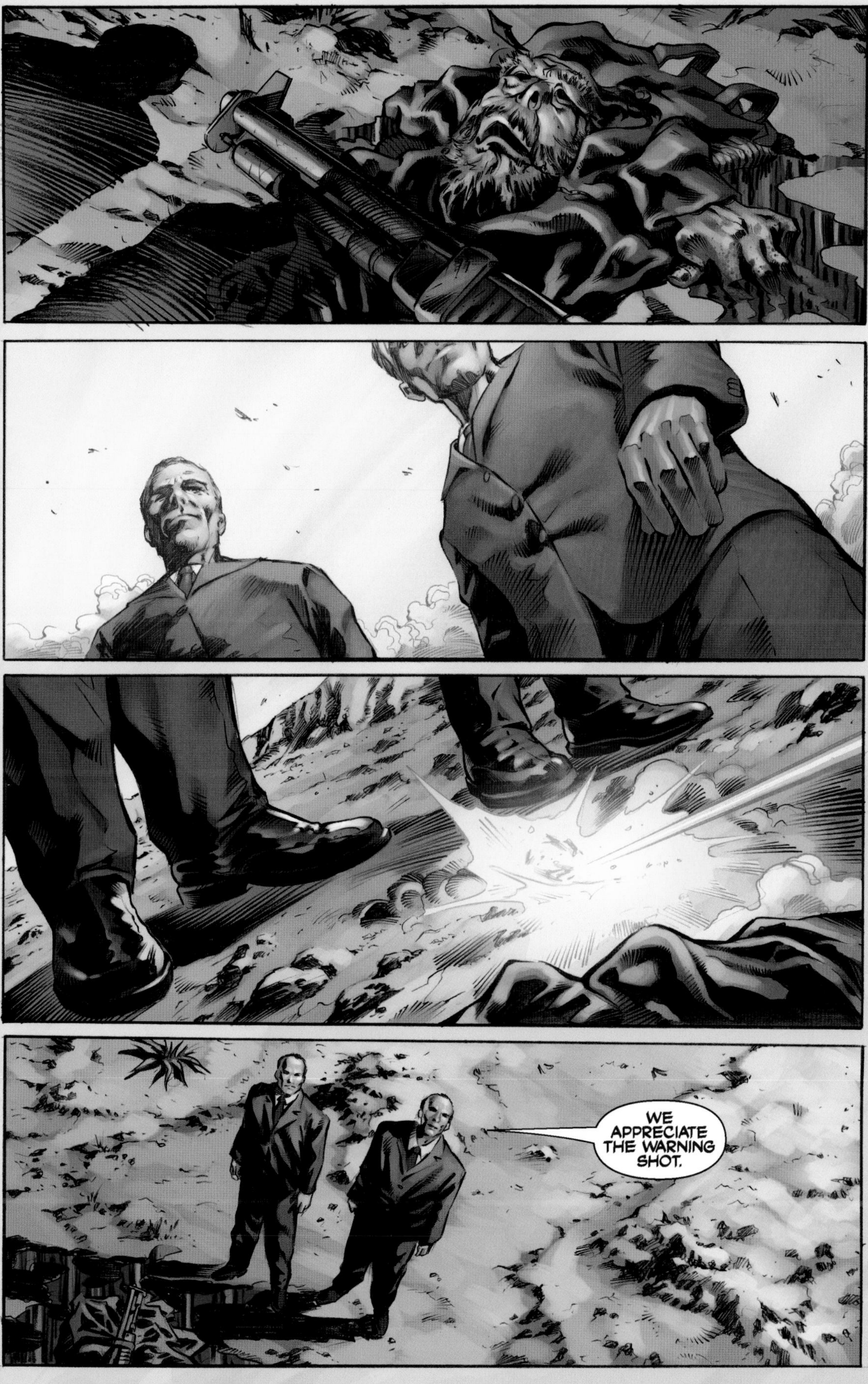
WE APPRECIATE THE WARNING SHOT.

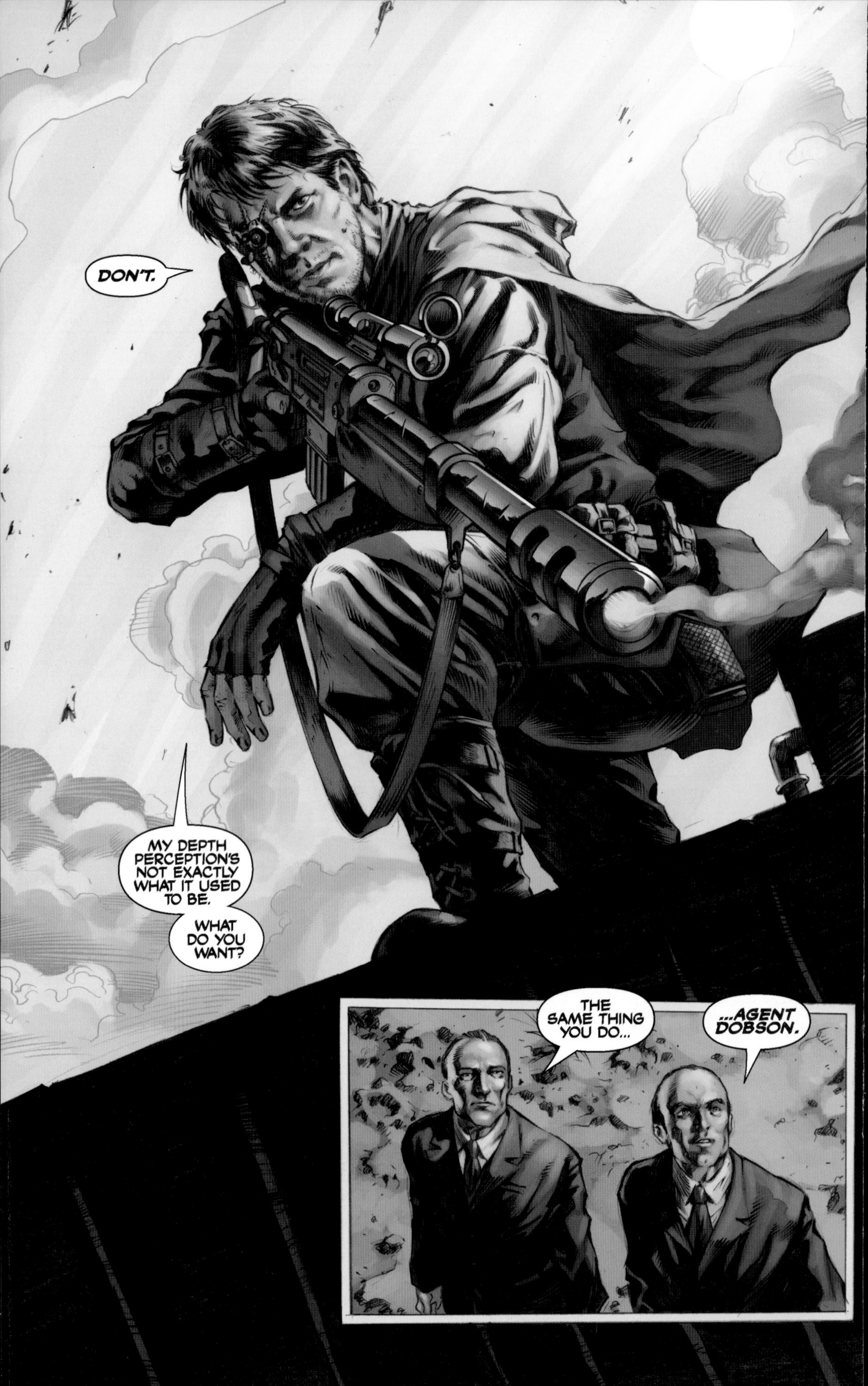
DON'T.
MY DEPTH PERCEPTION'S NOT EXACTLY WHAT IT USED TO BE.
WHAT DO YOU WANT?
THE SAME THING YOU DO...
...AGENT DOBSON.

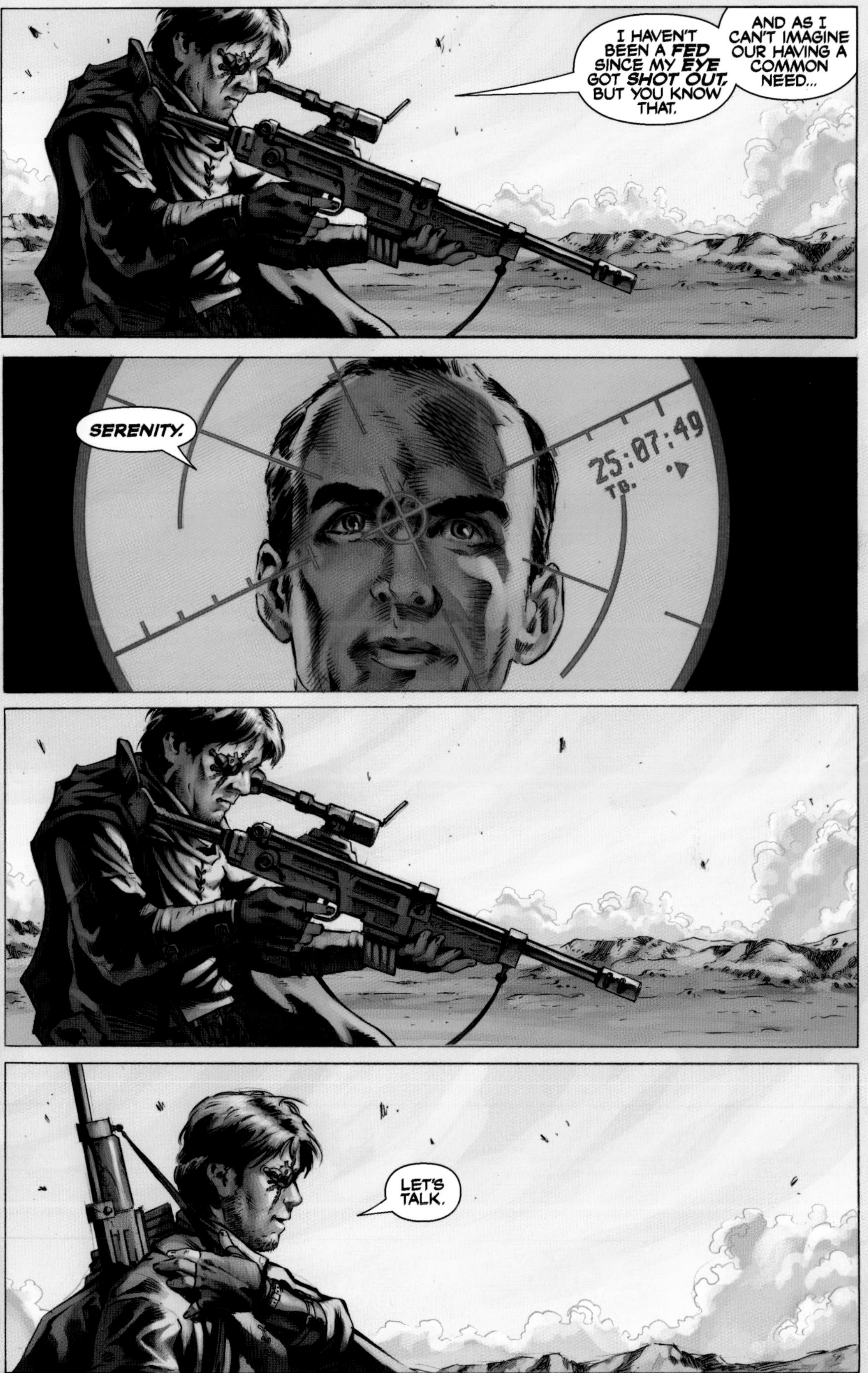
I HAVEN'T BEEN A FED SINCE MY EYE GOT SHOT OUT, BUT YOU KNOW THAT.
AND AS I CAN'T IMAGINE OUR HAVING A COMMON NEED...
SERENITY.
25:07:49
TB.
LET'S TALK.

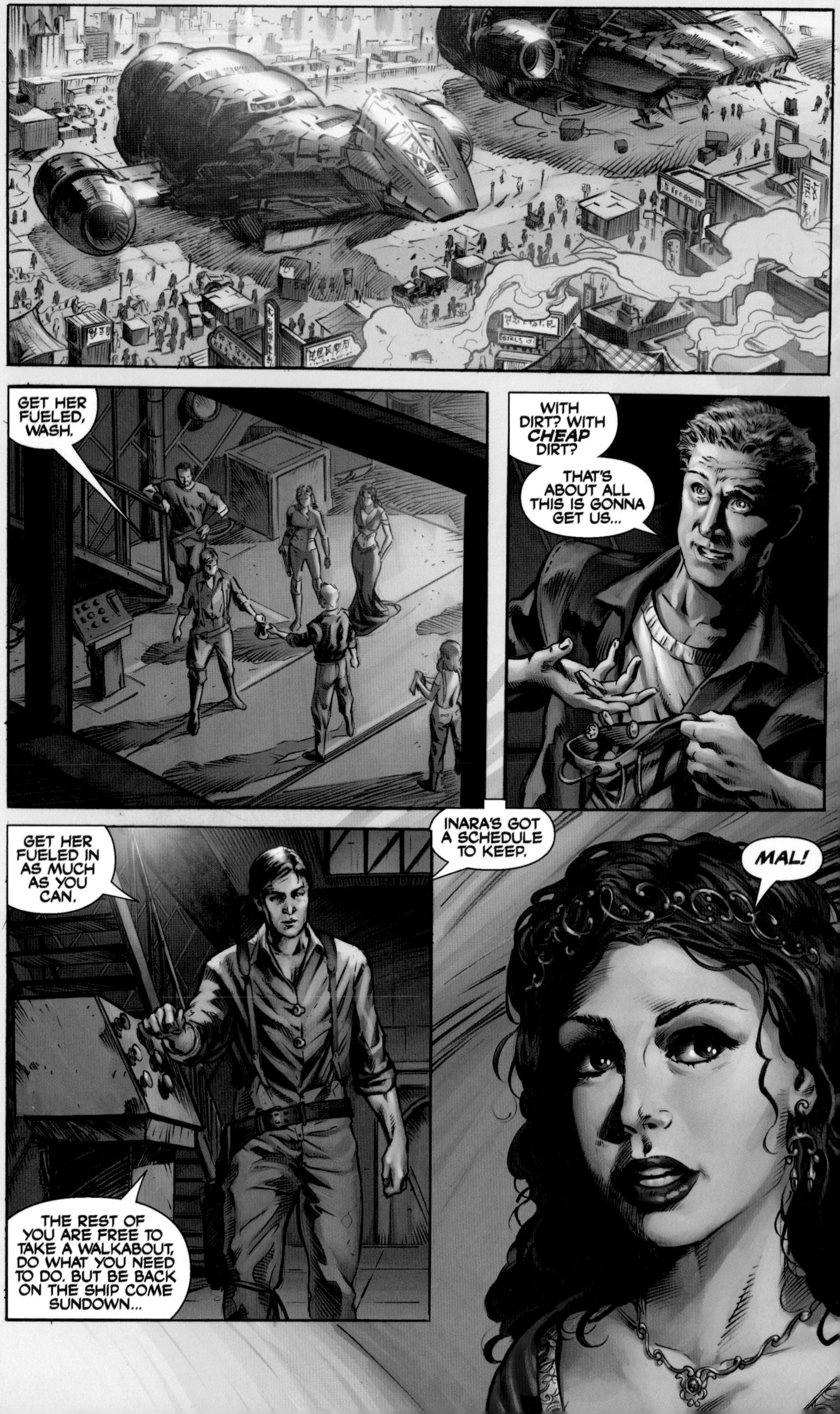
GET HER FUELED, WASH.
WITH DIRT? WITH *CHEAP* DIRT?
THAT'S ABOUT ALL THIS IS GONNA GET US...
GET HER FUELED IN AS MUCH AS YOU CAN.
INARA'S GOT A SCHEDULE TO KEEP.
THE REST OF YOU ARE FREE TO TAKE A WALKABOUT, DO WHAT YOU NEED TO DO. BUT BE BACK ON THE SHIP COME SUNDOWN...
MAL!

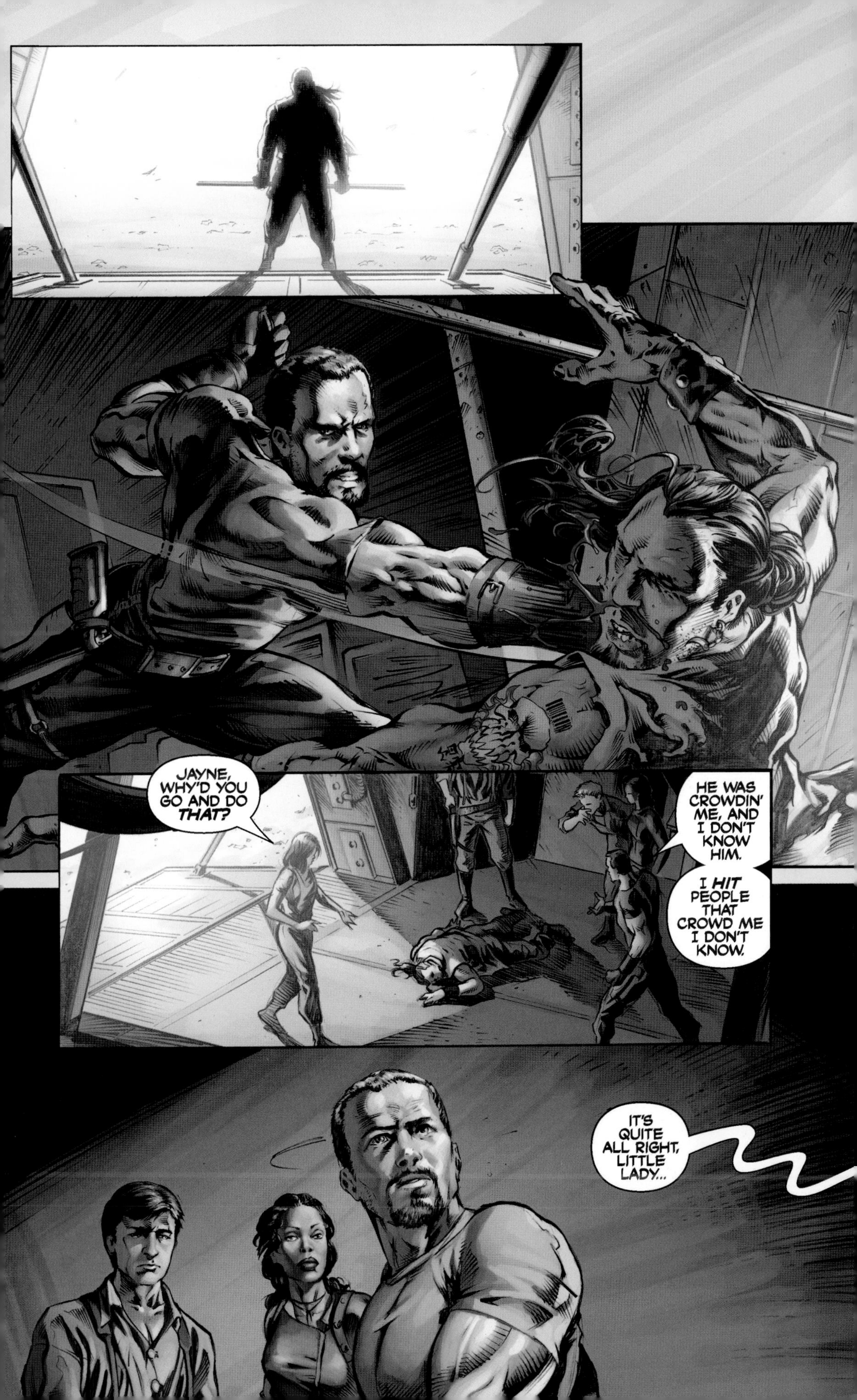
JAYNE, WHY'D YOU GO AND DO *THAT?*
HE WAS CROWDIN' ME, AND I DON'T KNOW HIM.
I *HIT* PEOPLE THAT CROWD ME I DON'T KNOW.
IT'S QUITE ALL RIGHT, LITTLE LADY...

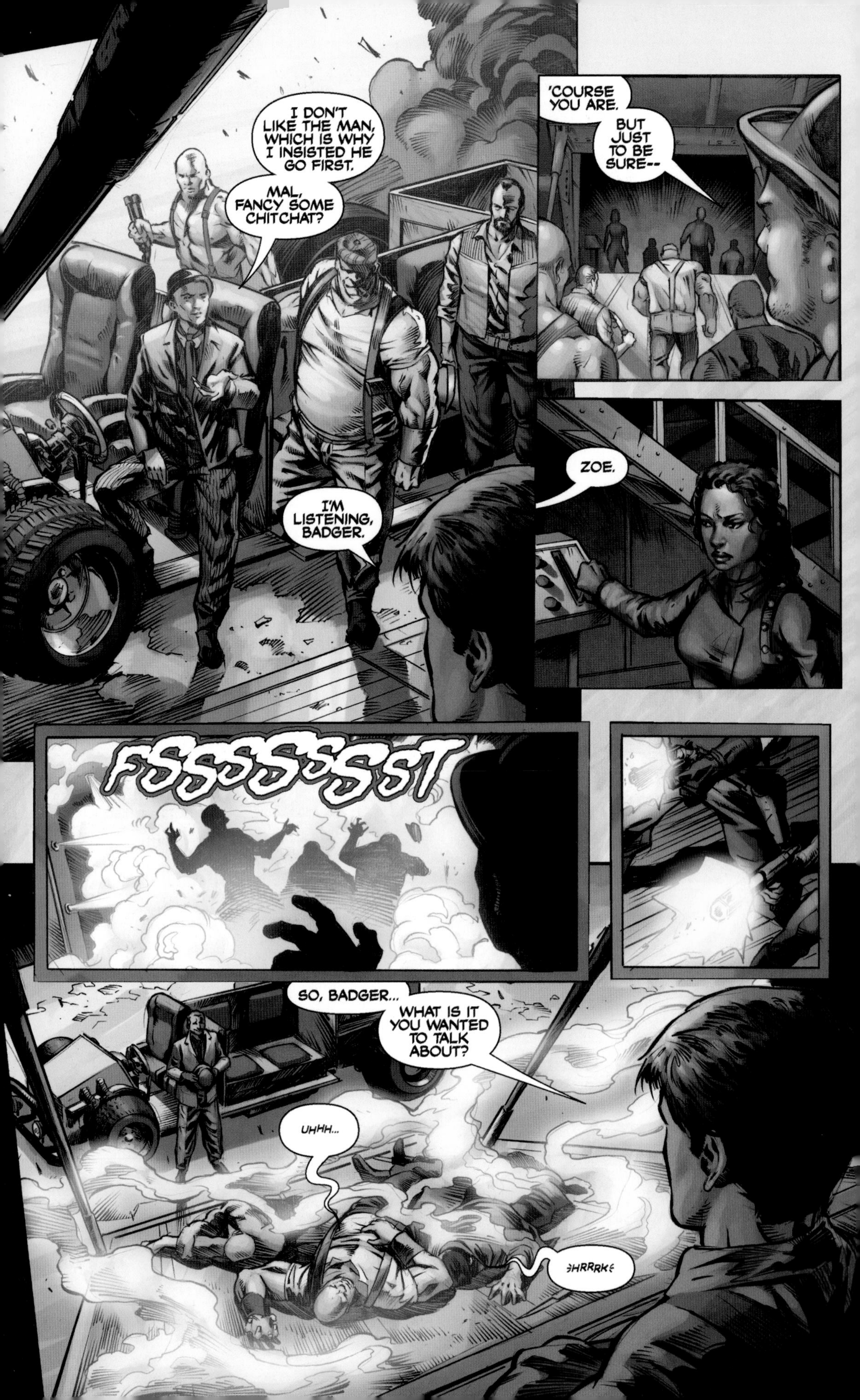
I DON'T LIKE THE MAN, WHICH IS WHY I INSISTED HE GO FIRST.
MAL, FANCY SOME CHITCHAT?
I'M LISTENING, BADGER.
'COURSE YOU ARE.
BUT JUST TO BE SURE--
ZOE.
FSSSSSSST
SO, BADGER...
WHAT IS IT YOU WANTED TO TALK ABOUT?
UHHH...
HRRRK

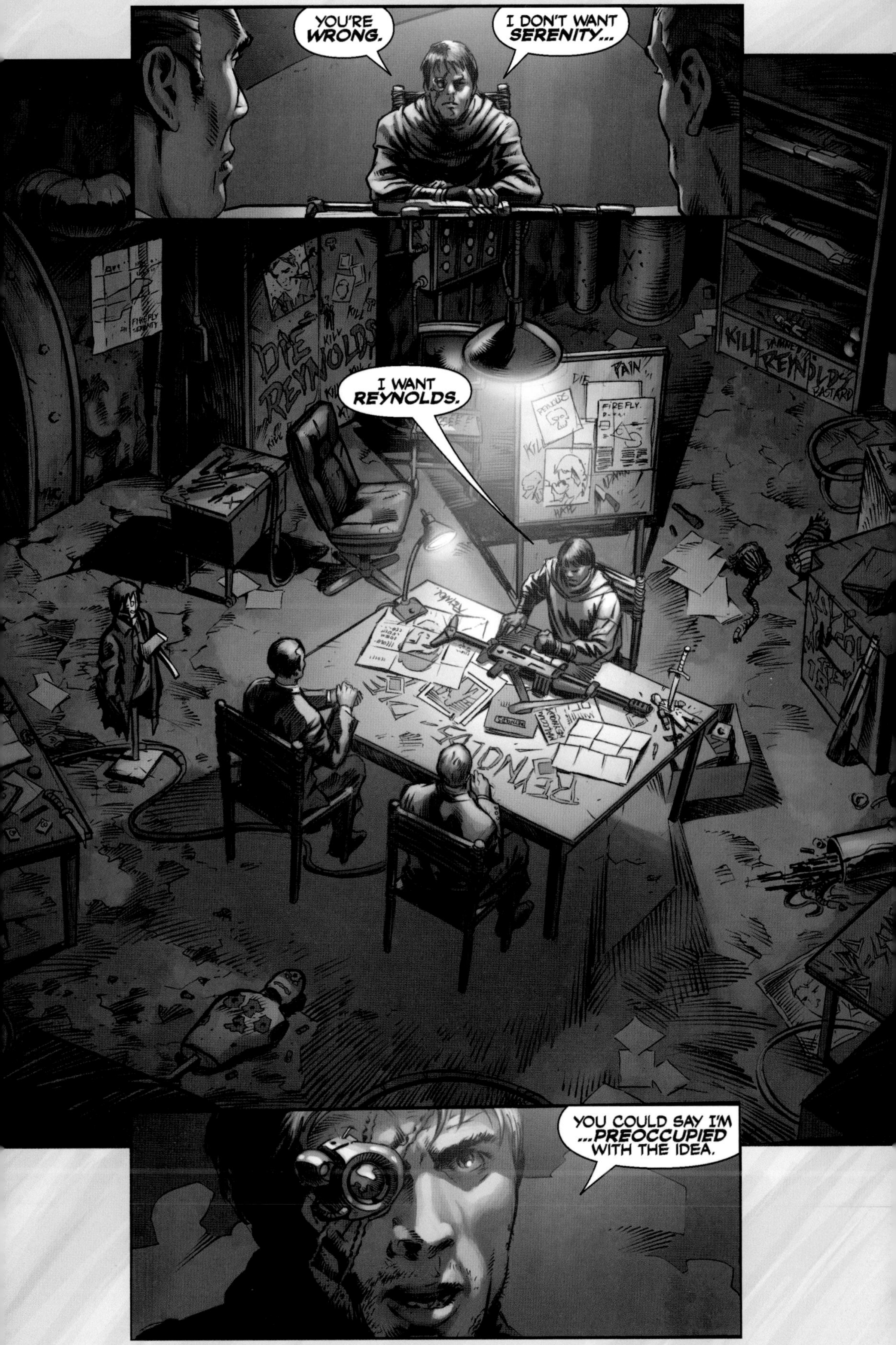
YOU'RE WRONG.
I DON'T WANT SERENITY...
I WANT REYNOLDS.
YOU COULD SAY I'M ...PREOCCUPIED WITH THE IDEA.

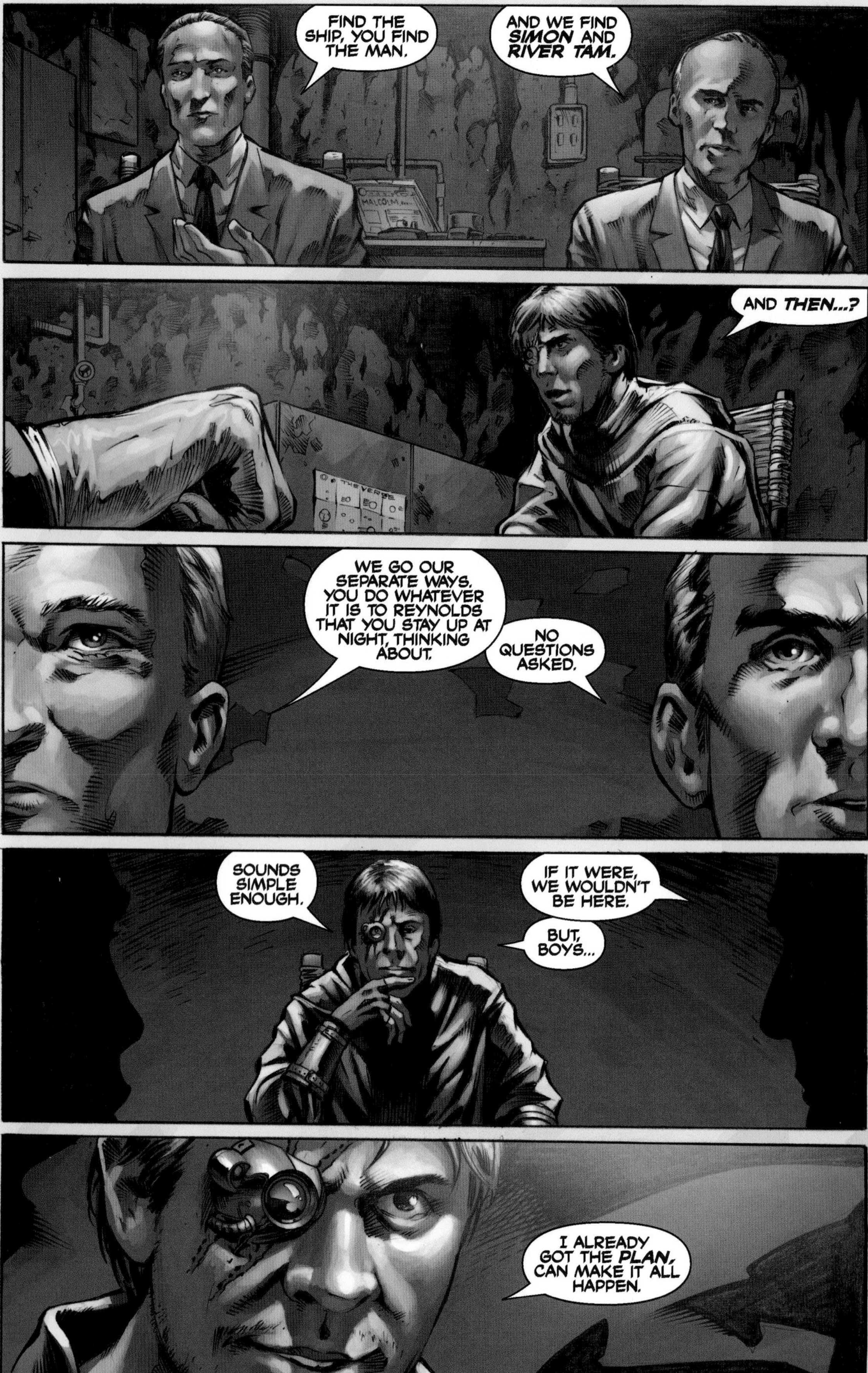

FIND THE SHIP, YOU FIND THE MAN.
AND WE FIND *SIMON* AND *RIVER TAM.*
AND *THEN*...?
WE GO OUR SEPARATE WAYS. YOU DO WHATEVER IT IS TO REYNOLDS THAT YOU STAY UP AT NIGHT, THINKING ABOUT.
NO QUESTIONS ASKED.
SOUNDS SIMPLE ENOUGH.
IF IT WERE, WE WOULDN'T BE HERE.
BUT, BOYS...
I ALREADY GOT THE *PLAN,* CAN MAKE IT ALL HAPPEN.

FOR SOMEONE WHO CAME HERE TO TALK, BADGER...

YOU SURE AIN'T.

WHERE ARE YOU TAKING ME?

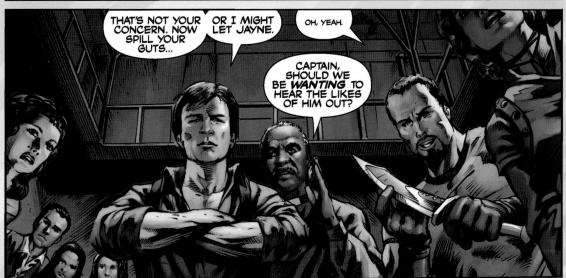

THAT'S NOT YOUR CONCERN. NOW SPILL YOUR GUTS...

OR I MIGHT LET JAYNE.

OH, YEAH.

CAPTAIN, SHOULD WE BE *WANTING* TO HEAR THE LIKES OF HIM OUT?

DON'T WORRY, SHEPHERD. HE'S GOT SOMETHING FOR US. I'LL SEE YOU GET YOUR CUT.

MAL, I HAD NOTHING TO DO WITH OTT AND HIS CREW SKANKING YOUR JOB.

COULD BE IT WAS THOSE TWO BACKBIRTHS, *FANTY AND MINGO,* TURNED THEM ONTO IT--

THEN MAYBE I SHOULD BE TALKING TO THEM, THEY MAKE A HABIT OF GETTING THEIR CREWS THE DROP.

NOW, UNLESS YOU'VE GOT SOMETHING *PROFITABLE* TO ADD...

THE BATTLE OF STURGES.

HEARD OF IT?

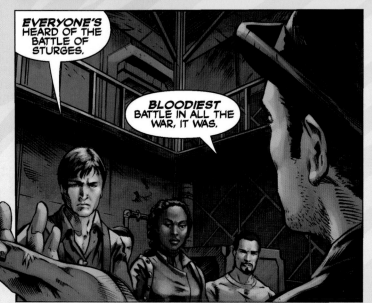

EVERYONE'S HEARD OF THE BATTLE OF STURGES.

BLOODIEST BATTLE IN ALL THE WAR, IT WAS.

I'D HOLD IT WAS A DISTANT SECOND.

BUT GO ON.

SHORTEST, TOO. ALL THOSE LIVES...

WANNA HEAR 'BOUT COIN, NOT SOME RUTTIN' HISTORY LESSON.

...SNUFFED IN A BLINK.

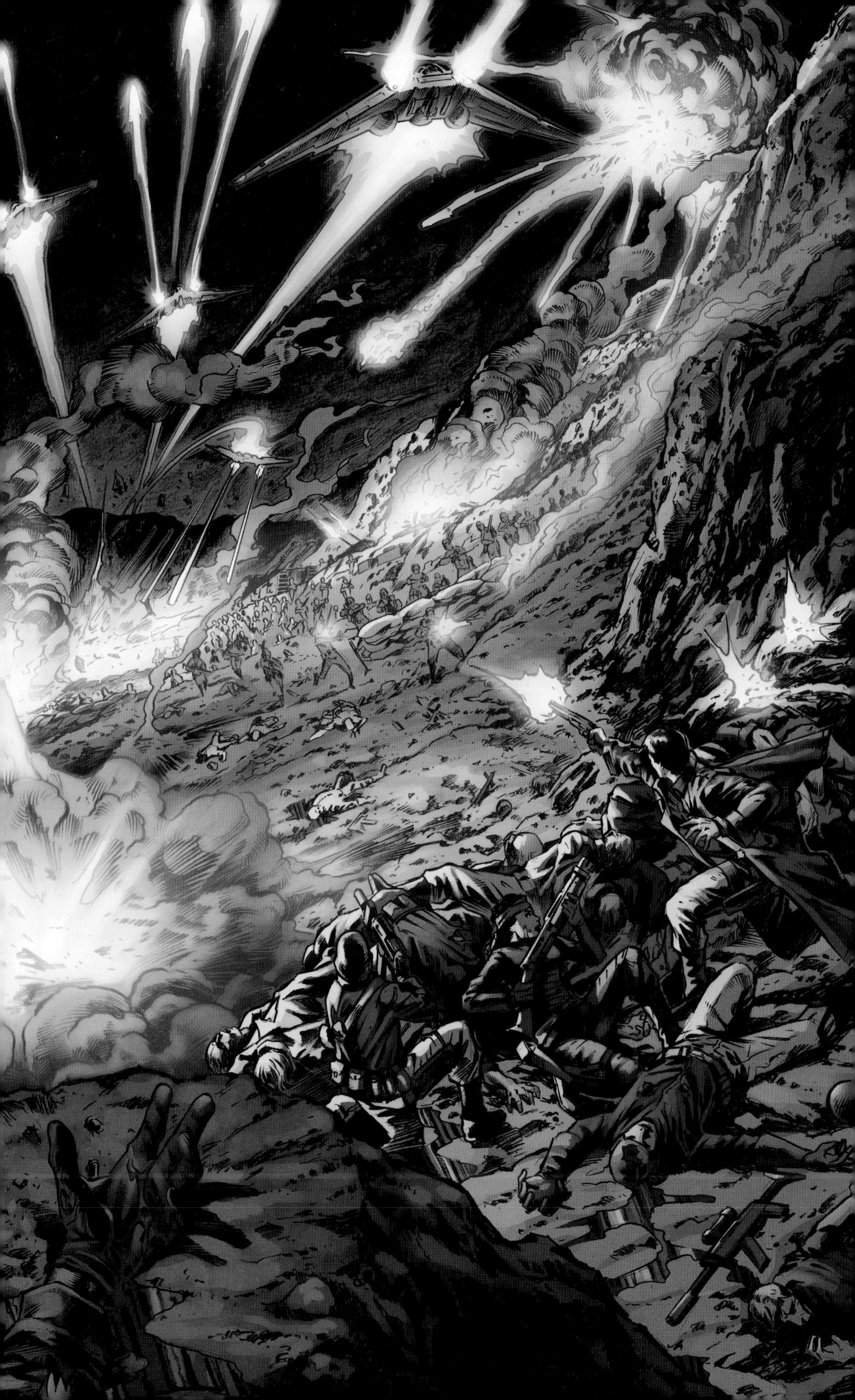

A BLINK'S AN AWFUL LONG TIME WHEN YOU'RE ON THE GROUND.

WE'RE NOT REQUIRIN' A LECTURE ON THE SUBJECT. OR HAD YOU NOT NOTICED THE *COLOR* THE CAPTAIN AND I ARE PARTIAL TO WEARING?

HERE'S WHAT YOU AND THE HISTORY BOOKS *DON'T* KNOW.

WHAT THE BATTLE OF STURGES WAS FOUGHT FOR -- WHAT ALL THEM BOYS AND GIRLS *DIED* FOR -- WAS A BOATLOAD OF *CASH.*

A BOATLOAD OF CASH THAT'S STILL THERE.

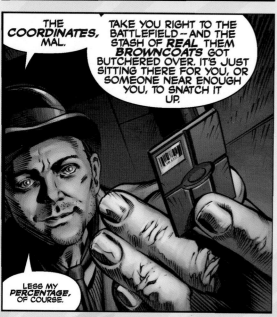

THE *COORDINATES,* MAL.

TAKE YOU RIGHT TO THE BATTLEFIELD -- AND THE STASH OF *REAL* THEM *BROWNCOATS* GOT BUTCHERED OVER. IT'S JUST SITTING THERE FOR YOU, OR SOMEONE NEAR ENOUGH YOU, TO SNATCH IT UP.

LESS MY *PERCENTAGE,* OF COURSE.

WHAT DO YOU SAY?

I SAY I'LL THINK ABOUT IT.

NOW GET OFF MY SHIP BEFORE THE STAIN SETS...

"YOU'VE GOT A LONG WALK AHEAD OF YOU."

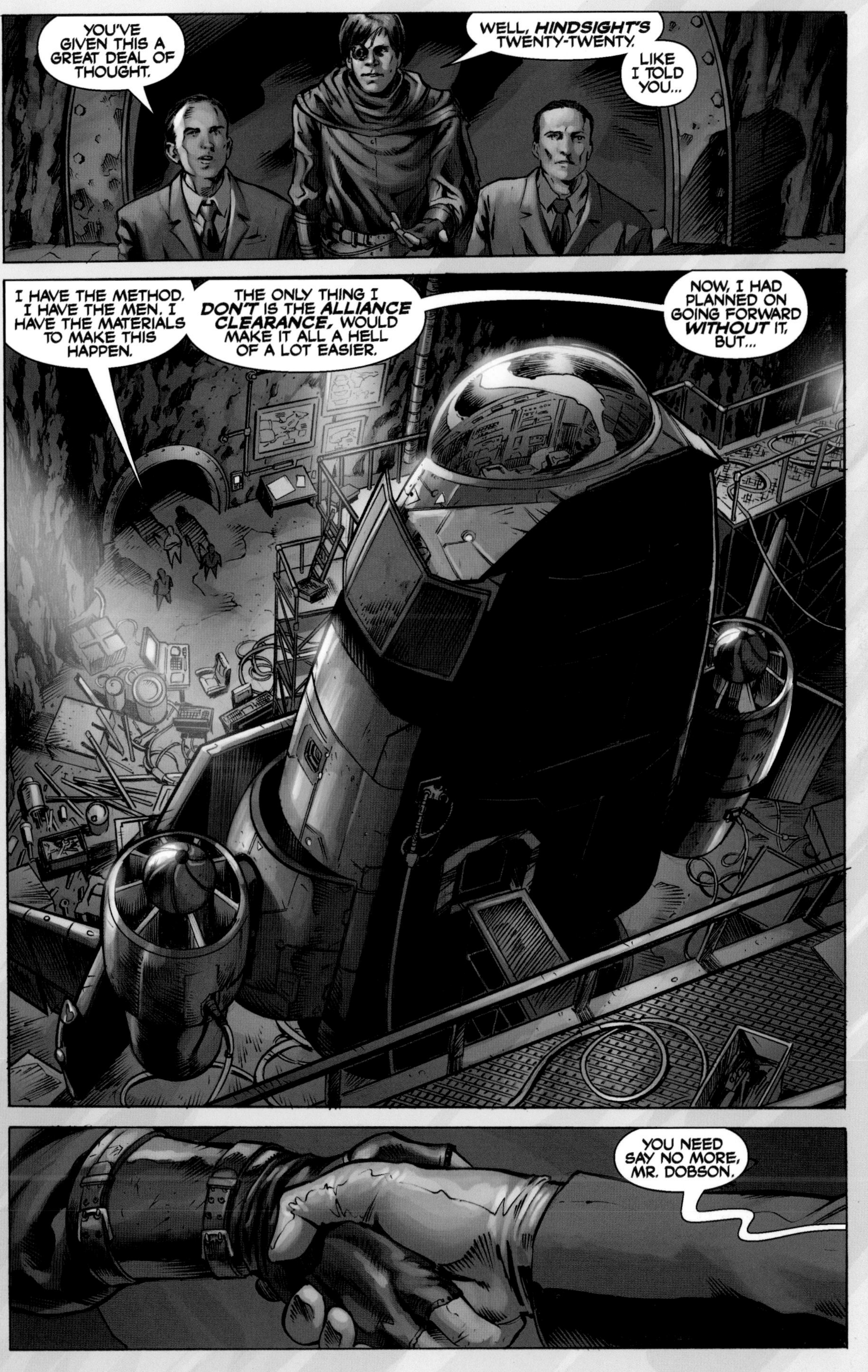
YOU'VE GIVEN THIS A GREAT DEAL OF THOUGHT.
WELL, HINDSIGHT'S TWENTY-TWENTY.
LIKE I TOLD YOU...
I HAVE THE METHOD. I HAVE THE MEN. I HAVE THE MATERIALS TO MAKE THIS HAPPEN.
THE ONLY THING I DON'T IS THE ALLIANCE CLEARANCE, WOULD MAKE IT ALL A HELL OF A LOT EASIER.
NOW, I HAD PLANNED ON GOING FORWARD WITHOUT IT, BUT...
YOU NEED SAY NO MORE, MR. DOBSON.

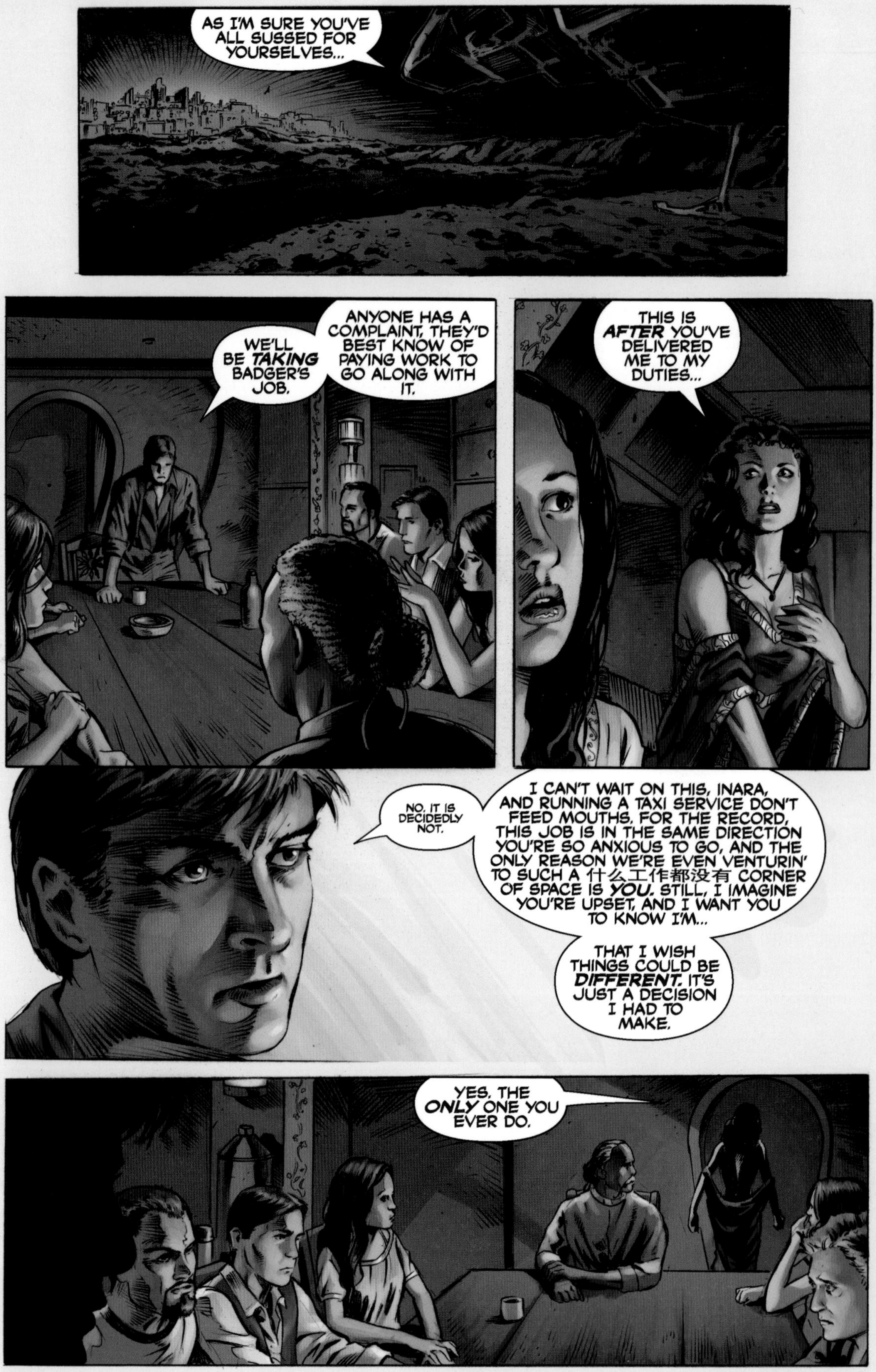
AS I'M SURE YOU'VE ALL SUSSED FOR YOURSELVES...
WE'LL BE TAKING BADGER'S JOB.
ANYONE HAS A COMPLAINT, THEY'D BEST KNOW OF PAYING WORK TO GO ALONG WITH IT.
THIS IS AFTER YOU'VE DELIVERED ME TO MY DUTIES...
NO, IT IS DECIDEDLY NOT.
I CAN'T WAIT ON THIS, INARA, AND RUNNING A TAXI SERVICE DON'T FEED MOUTHS. FOR THE RECORD, THIS JOB IS IN THE SAME DIRECTION YOU'RE SO ANXIOUS TO GO, AND THE ONLY REASON WE'RE EVEN VENTURIN' TO SUCH A 什么工作都没有 CORNER OF SPACE IS YOU. STILL, I IMAGINE YOU'RE UPSET, AND I WANT YOU TO KNOW I'M...
THAT I WISH THINGS COULD BE DIFFERENT. IT'S JUST A DECISION I HAD TO MAKE.
YES. THE ONLY ONE YOU EVER DO.

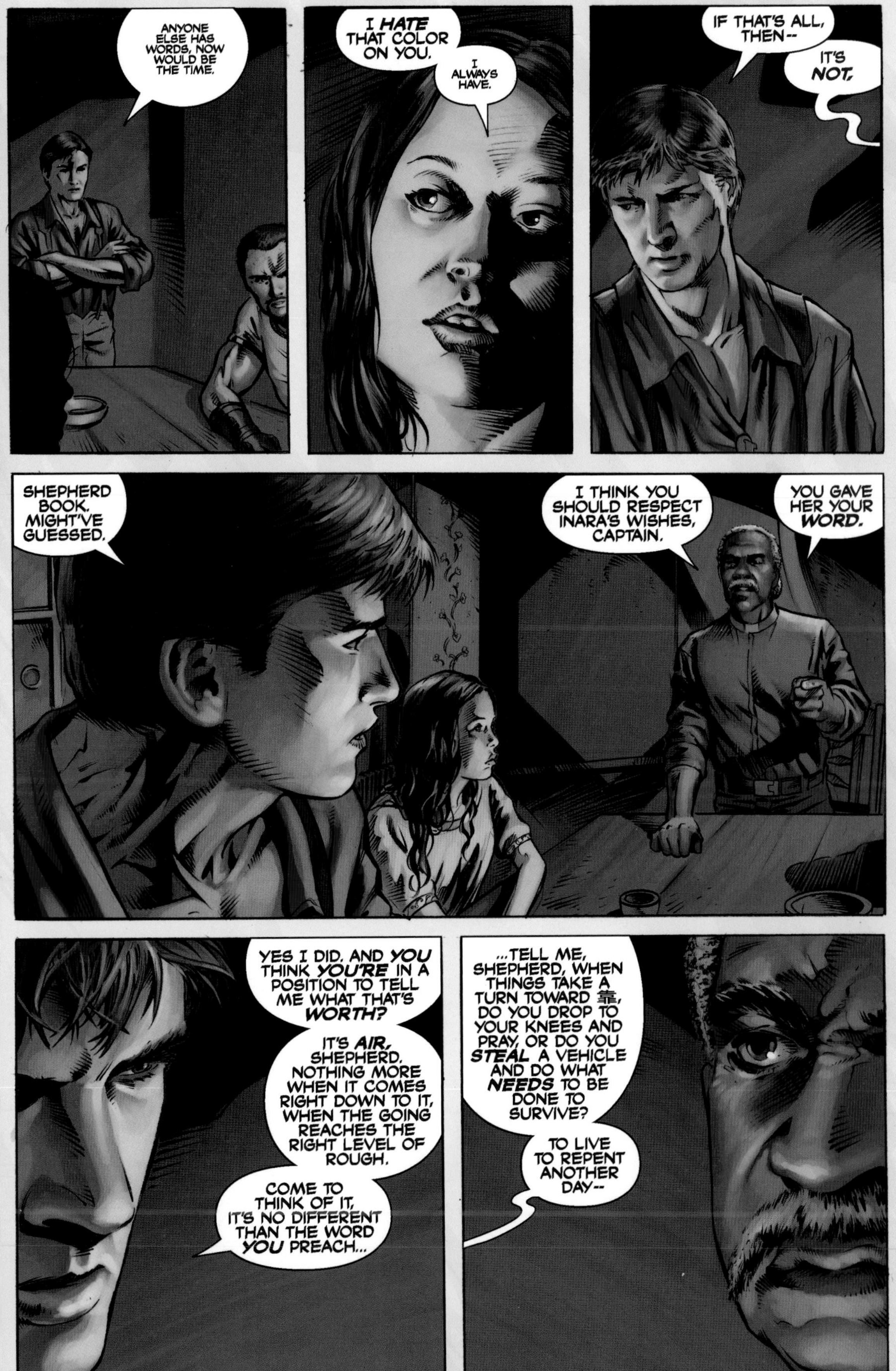
ANYONE ELSE HAS WORDS, NOW WOULD BE THE TIME.
I HATE THAT COLOR ON YOU.
I ALWAYS HAVE.
IF THAT'S ALL, THEN--
IT'S NOT.
SHEPHERD BOOK. MIGHT'VE GUESSED.
I THINK YOU SHOULD RESPECT INARA'S WISHES, CAPTAIN.
YOU GAVE HER YOUR WORD.
YES I DID. AND YOU THINK YOU'RE IN A POSITION TO TELL ME WHAT THAT'S WORTH?
IT'S AIR, SHEPHERD. NOTHING MORE WHEN IT COMES RIGHT DOWN TO IT, WHEN THE GOING REACHES THE RIGHT LEVEL OF ROUGH.
COME TO THINK OF IT, IT'S NO DIFFERENT THAN THE WORD YOU PREACH...
...TELL ME, SHEPHERD, WHEN THINGS TAKE A TURN TOWARD 靠, DO YOU DROP TO YOUR KNEES AND PRAY, OR DO YOU STEAL A VEHICLE AND DO WHAT NEEDS TO BE DONE TO SURVIVE?
TO LIVE TO REPENT ANOTHER DAY--

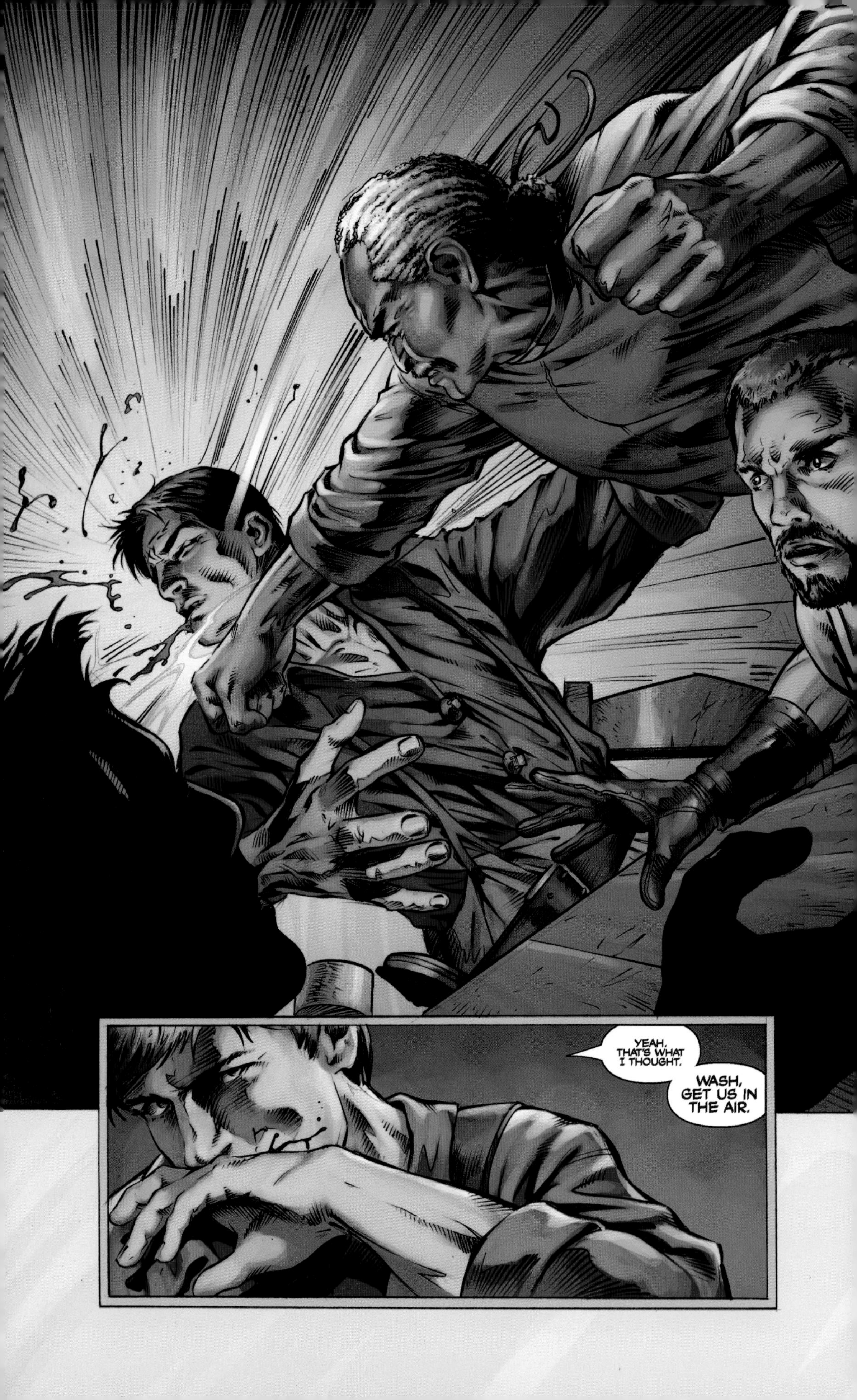
YEAH, THAT'S WHAT I THOUGHT.
WASH, GET US IN THE AIR.

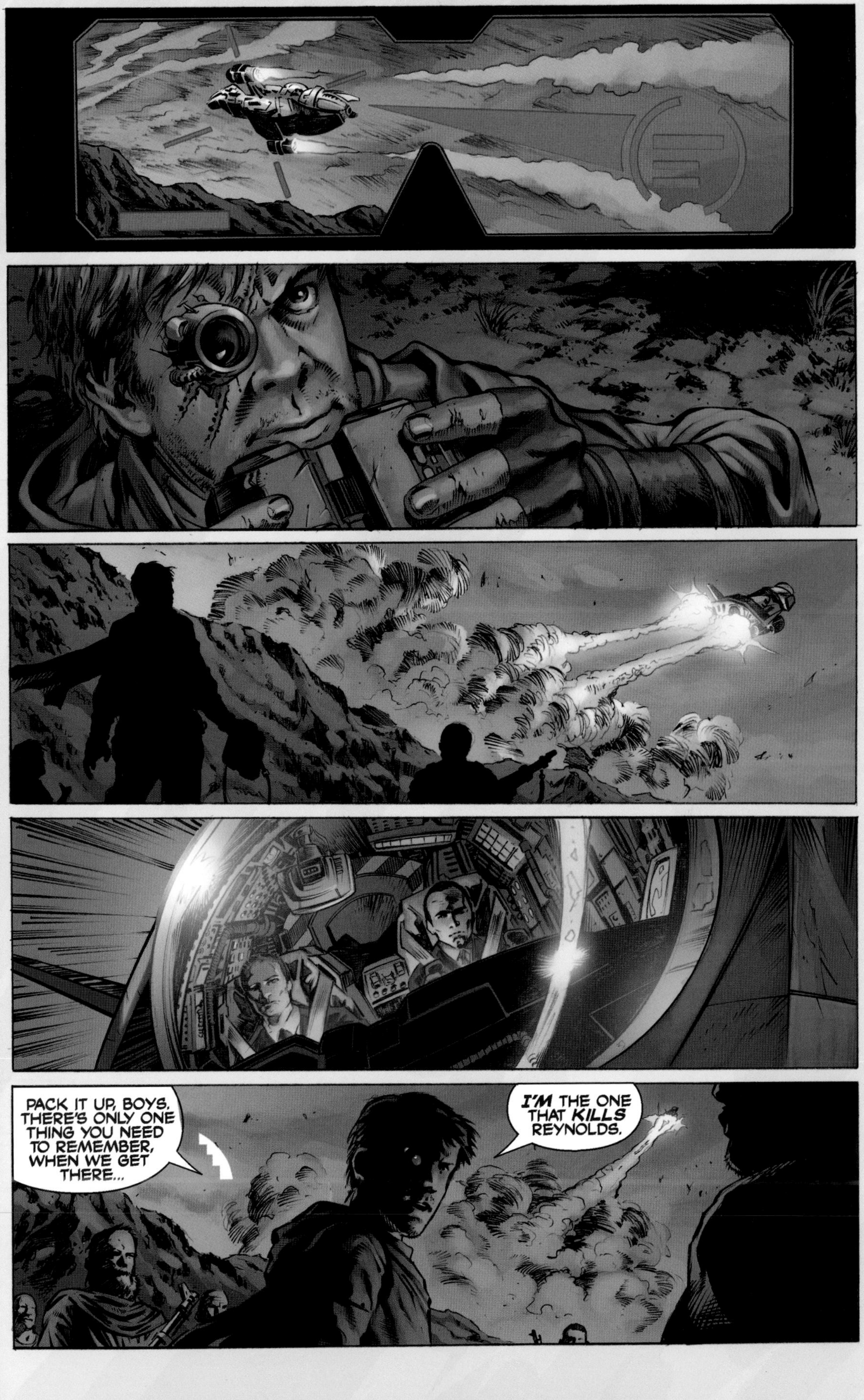
PACK IT UP, BOYS. THERE'S ONLY ONE THING YOU NEED TO REMEMBER, WHEN WE GET THERE...
I'M THE ONE THAT KILLS REYNOLDS.

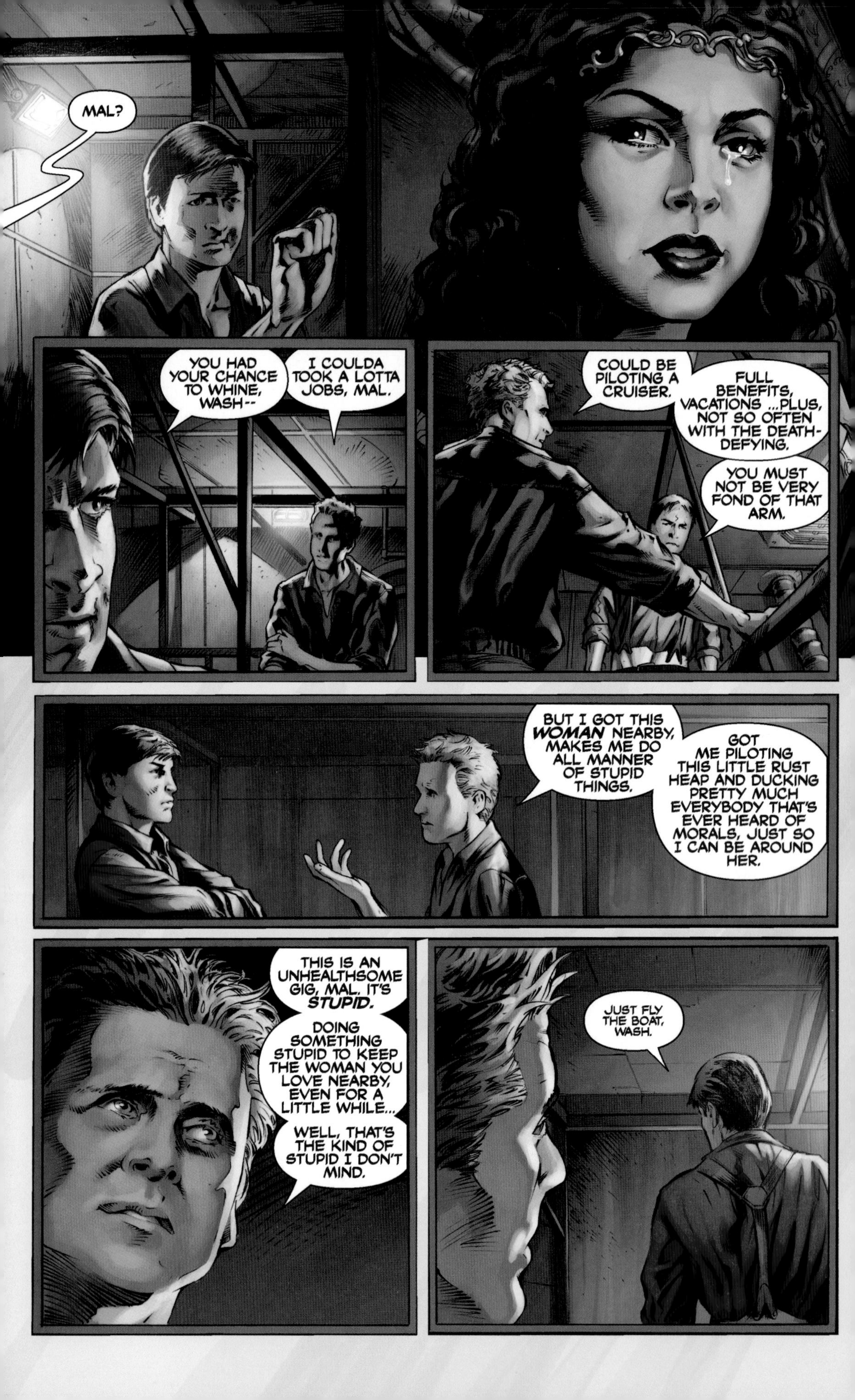
MAL?
YOU HAD YOUR CHANCE TO WHINE, WASH--
I COULDA TOOK A LOTTA JOBS, MAL.
COULD BE PILOTING A CRUISER.
FULL BENEFITS, VACATIONS ...PLUS, NOT SO OFTEN WITH THE DEATH-DEFYING.
YOU MUST NOT BE VERY FOND OF THAT ARM.
BUT I GOT THIS WOMAN NEARBY, MAKES ME DO ALL MANNER OF STUPID THINGS.
GOT ME PILOTING THIS LITTLE RUST HEAP AND DUCKING PRETTY MUCH EVERYBODY THAT'S EVER HEARD OF MORALS, JUST SO I CAN BE AROUND HER.
THIS IS AN UNHEALTHSOME GIG, MAL. IT'S STUPID.
DOING SOMETHING STUPID TO KEEP THE WOMAN YOU LOVE NEARBY, EVEN FOR A LITTLE WHILE...
WELL, THAT'S THE KIND OF STUPID I DON'T MIND.
JUST FLY THE BOAT, WASH.

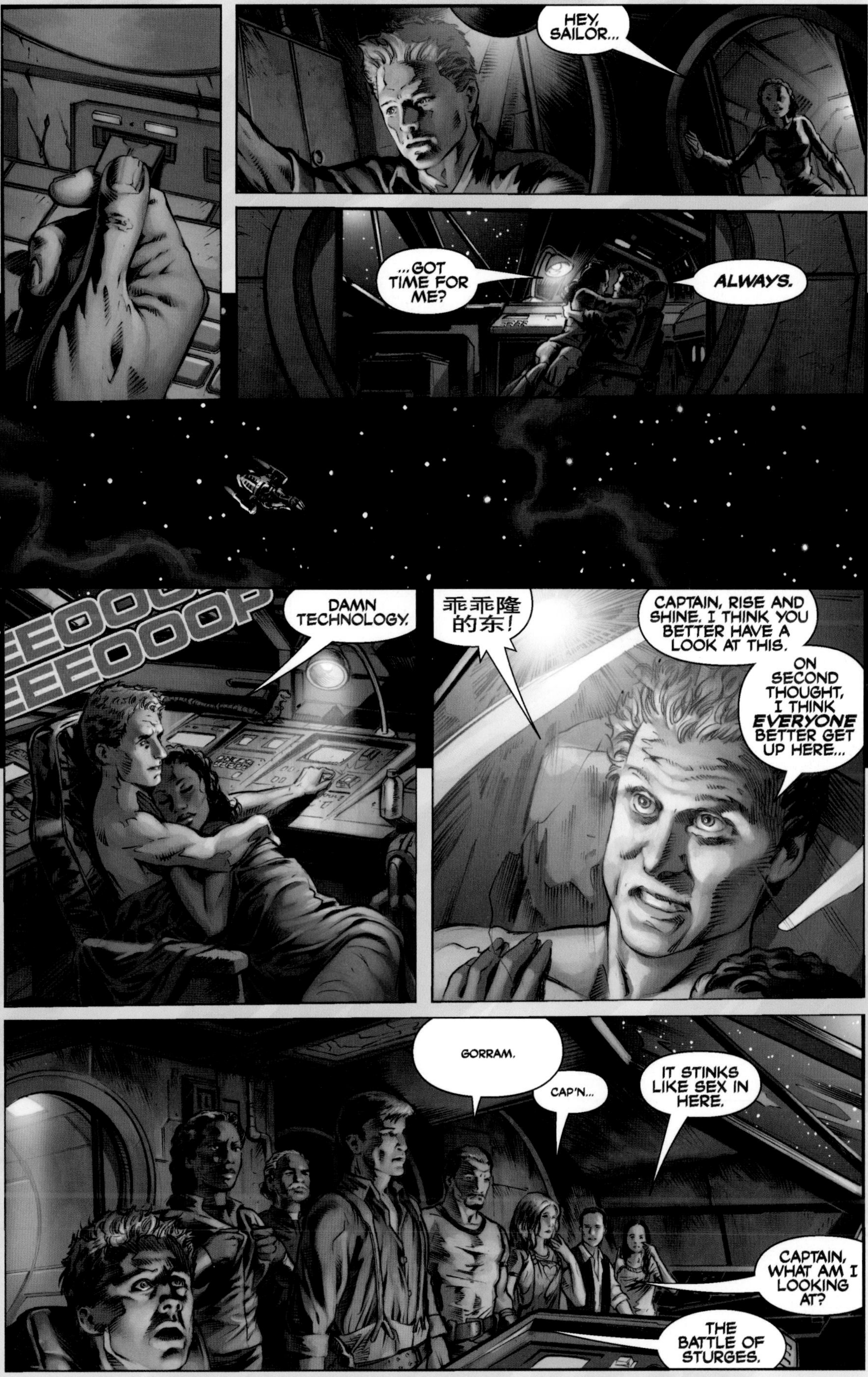
HEY, SAILOR...
...GOT TIME FOR ME?
ALWAYS.
DAMN TECHNOLOGY.
乖乖隆的东!
CAPTAIN, RISE AND SHINE. I THINK YOU BETTER HAVE A LOOK AT THIS.
ON SECOND THOUGHT, I THINK EVERYONE BETTER GET UP HERE...
GORRAM.
CAP'N...
IT STINKS LIKE SEX IN HERE.
CAPTAIN, WHAT AM I LOOKING AT?
THE BATTLE OF STURGES.

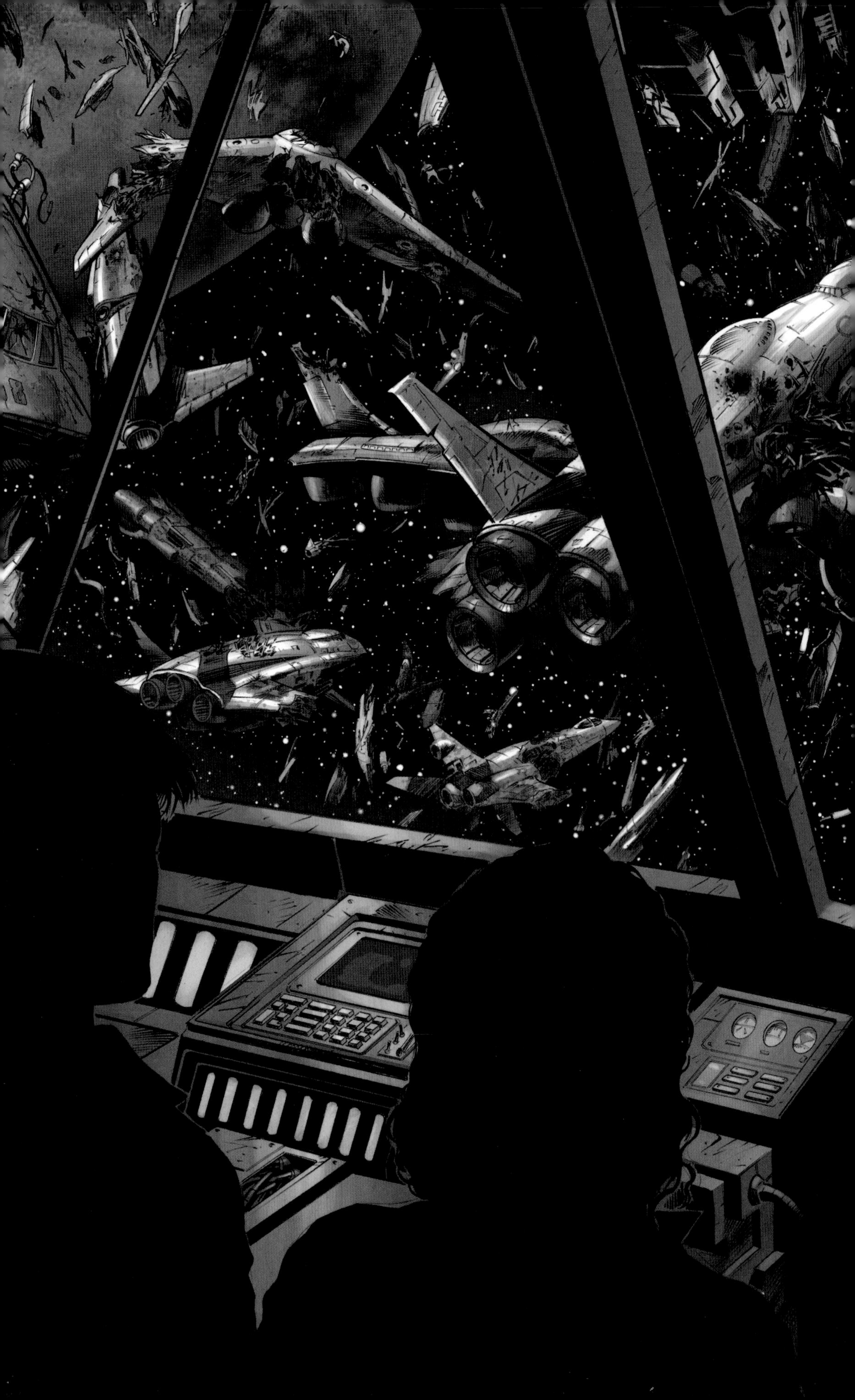

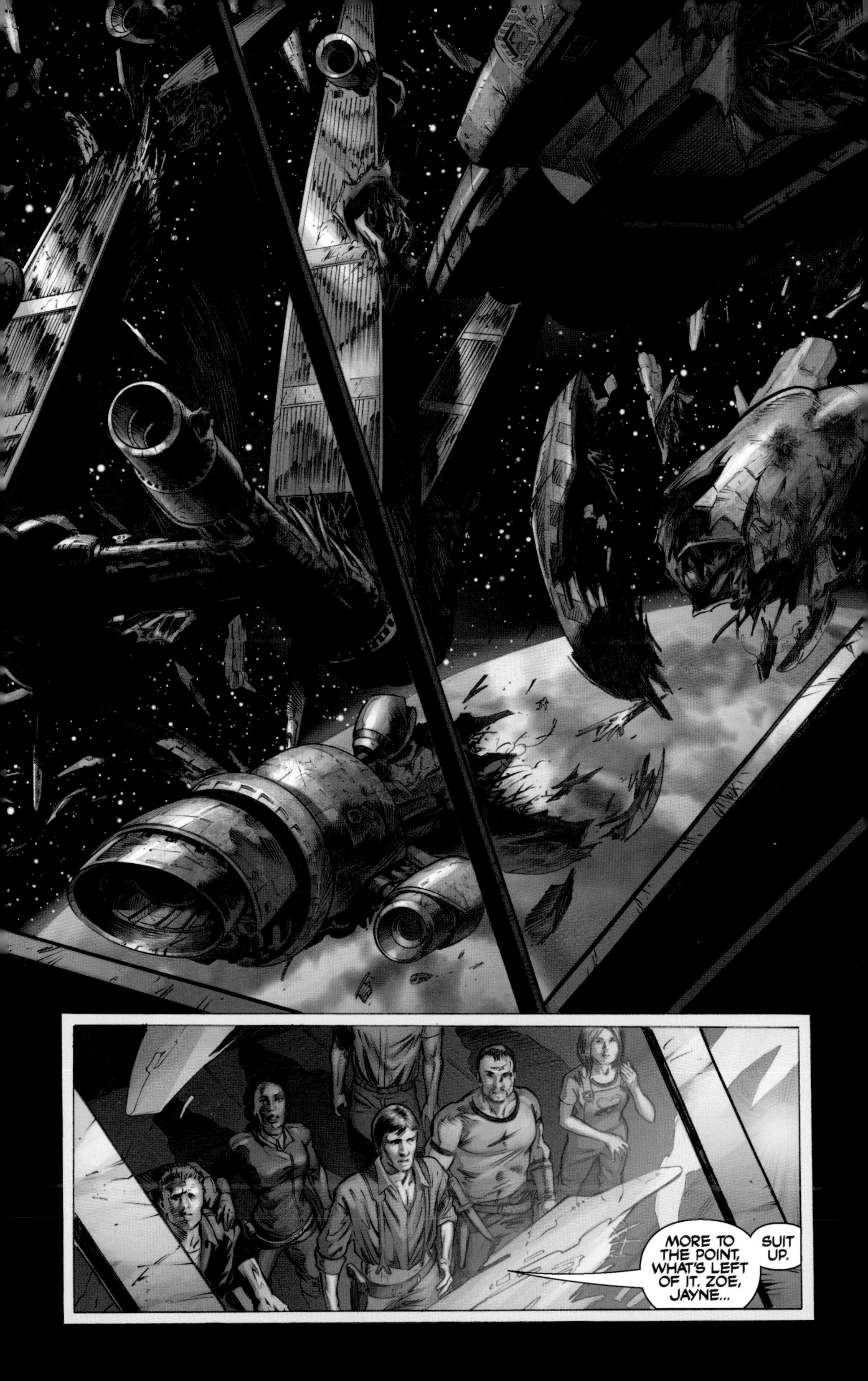
MORE TO THE POINT, WHAT'S LEFT OF IT. ZOE, JAYNE...
SUIT UP.

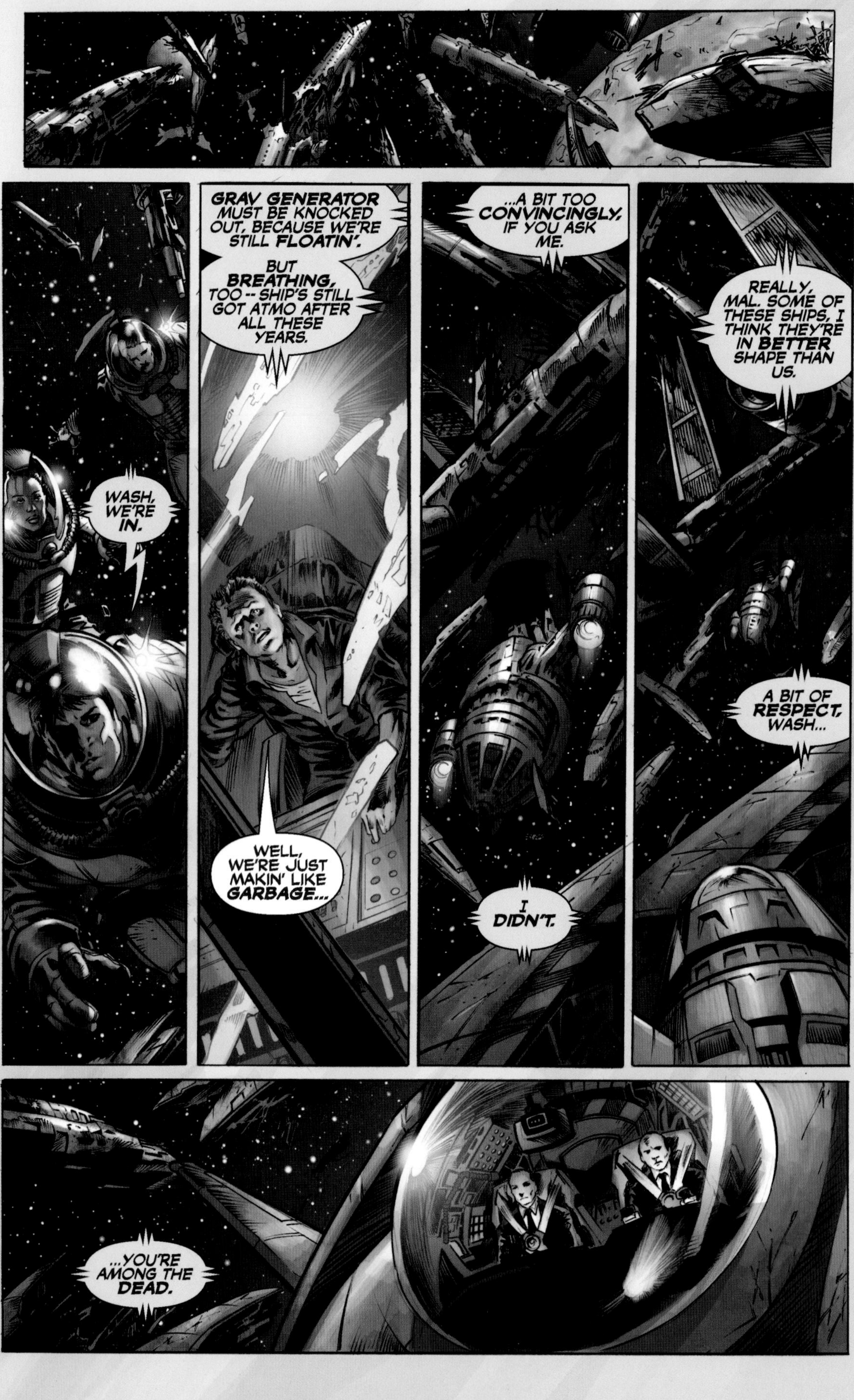
WASH, WE'RE IN.
GRAV GENERATOR MUST BE KNOCKED OUT, BECAUSE WE'RE STILL FLOATIN'.
BUT BREATHING, TOO -- SHIP'S STILL GOT ATMO AFTER ALL THESE YEARS.
WELL, WE'RE JUST MAKIN' LIKE GARBAGE...
...A BIT TOO CONVINCINGLY, IF YOU ASK ME.
I DIDN'T.
REALLY, MAL. SOME OF THESE SHIPS, I THINK THEY'RE IN BETTER SHAPE THAN US.
A BIT OF RESPECT, WASH...
...YOU'RE AMONG THE DEAD.

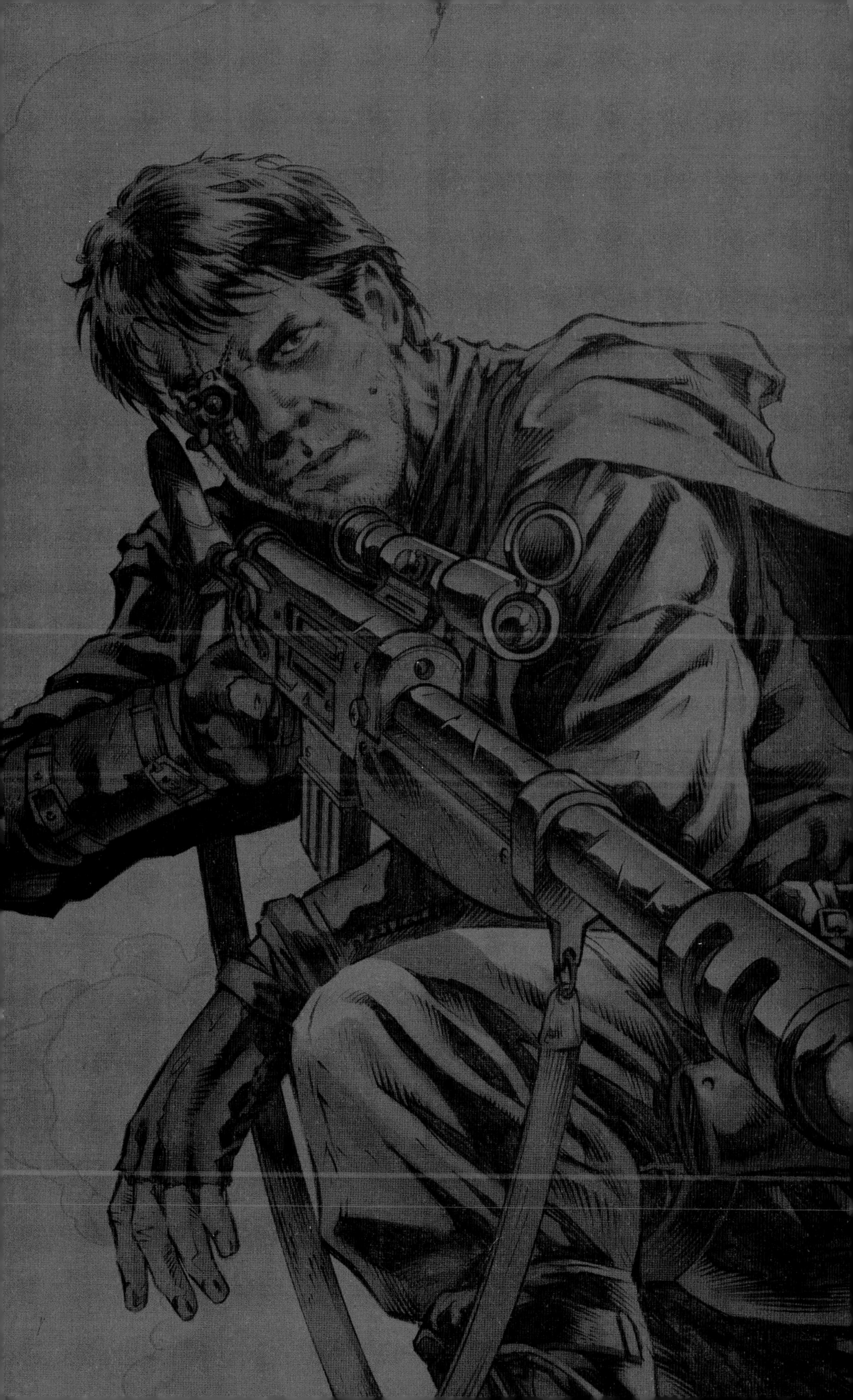

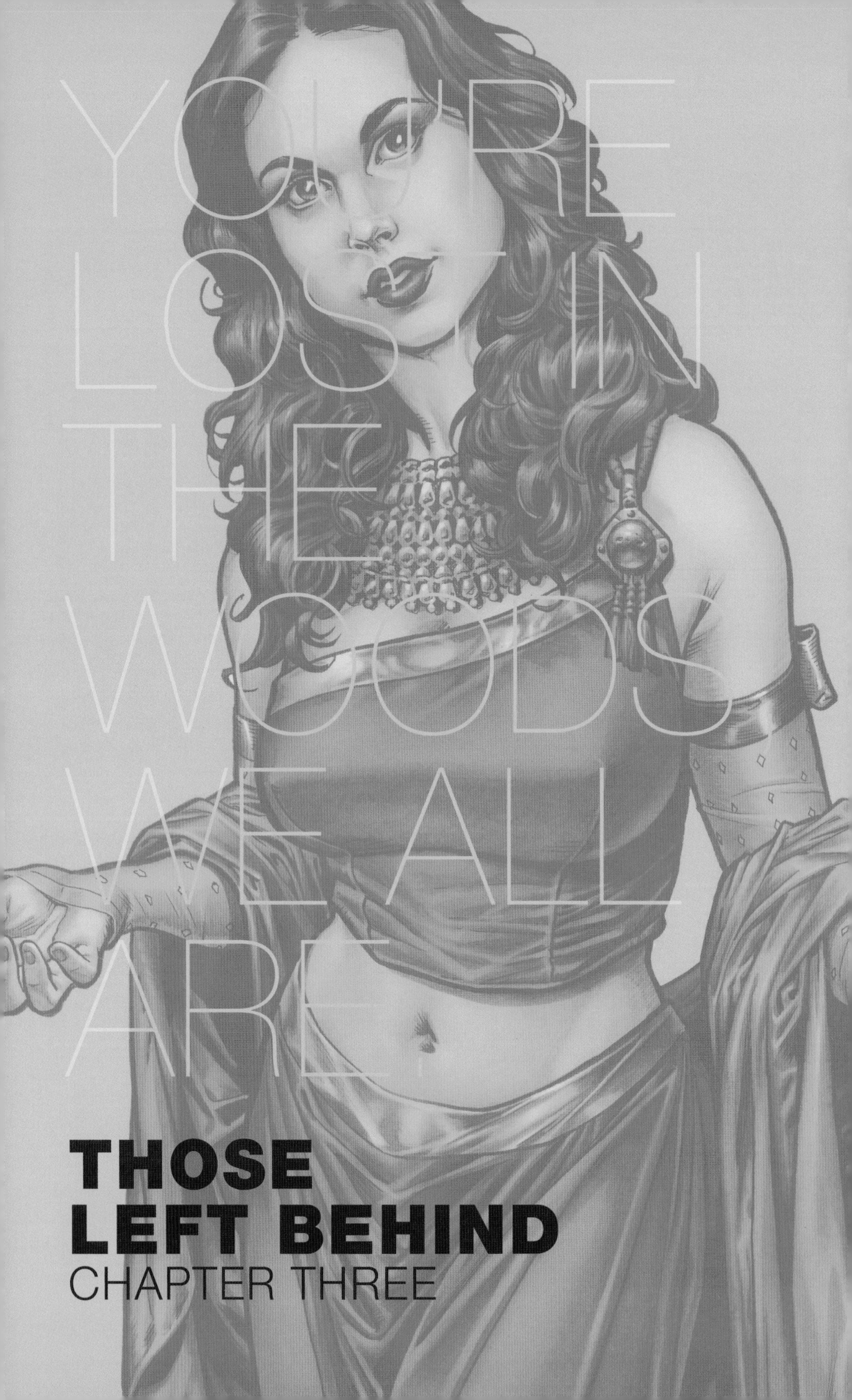
YOU'RE
LOST IN
THE
WOODS
WE ALL
ARE.

THOSE LEFT BEHIND
CHAPTER THREE

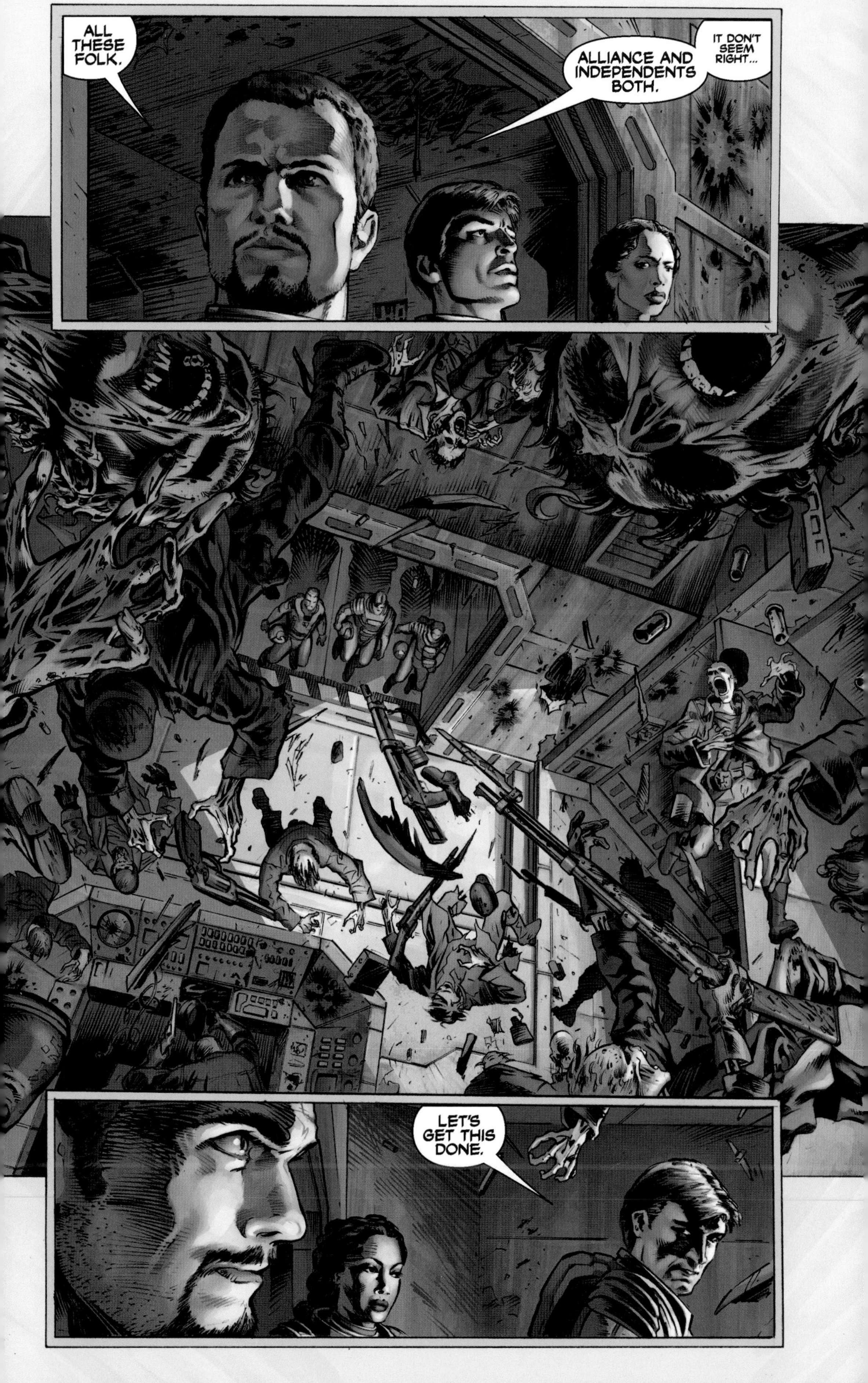
ALL THESE FOLK.
ALLIANCE AND INDEPENDENTS BOTH.
IT DON'T SEEM RIGHT...
LET'S GET THIS DONE.

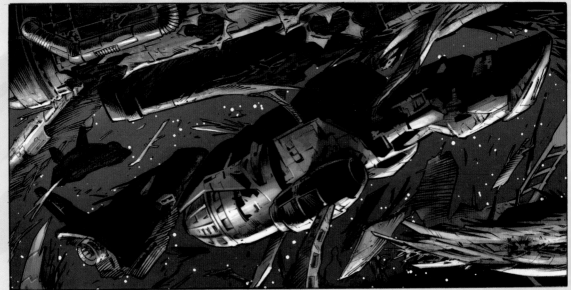

AIRLOCK ESTABLISHED.

PREPARE TO *BREACH.*

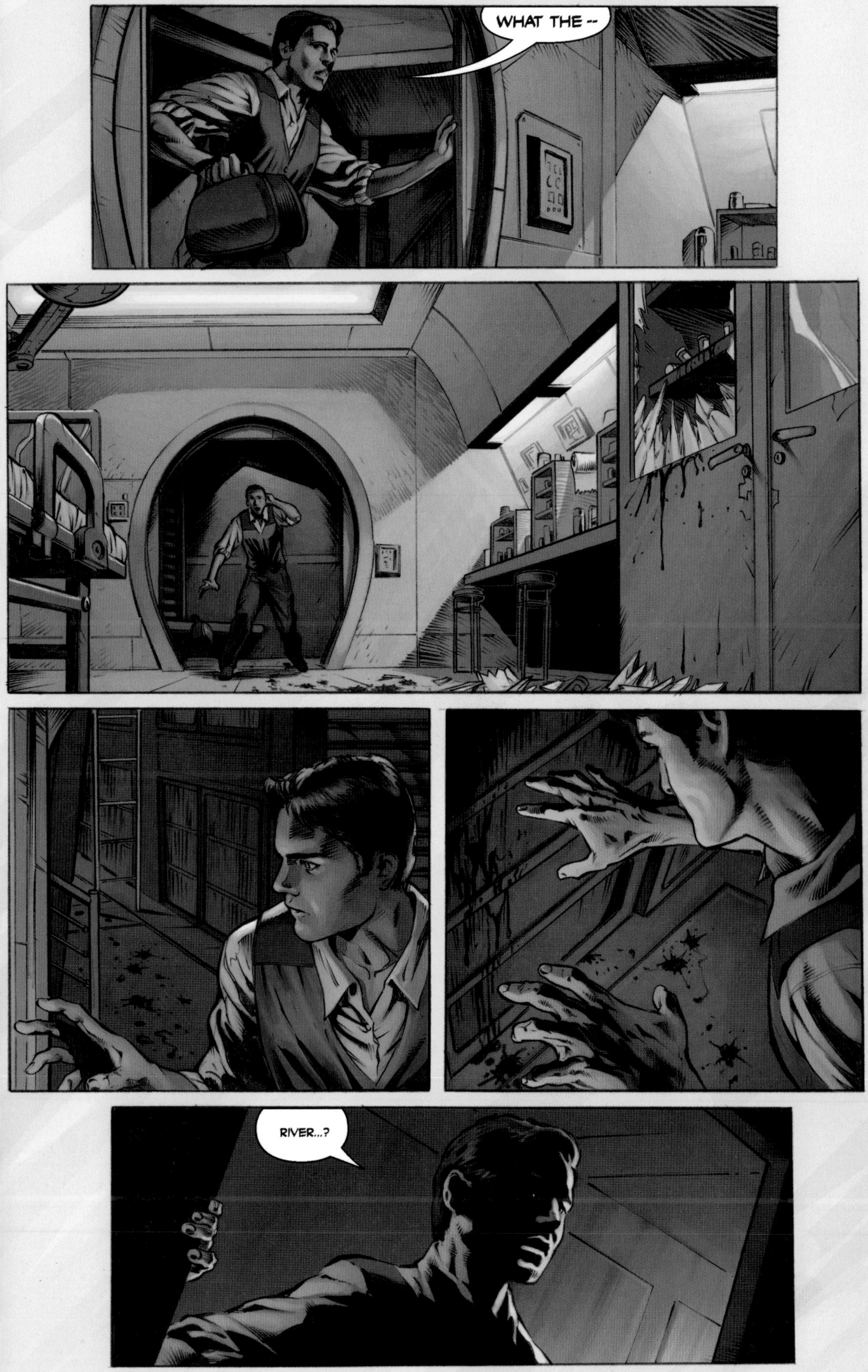
WHAT THE --
RIVER...?

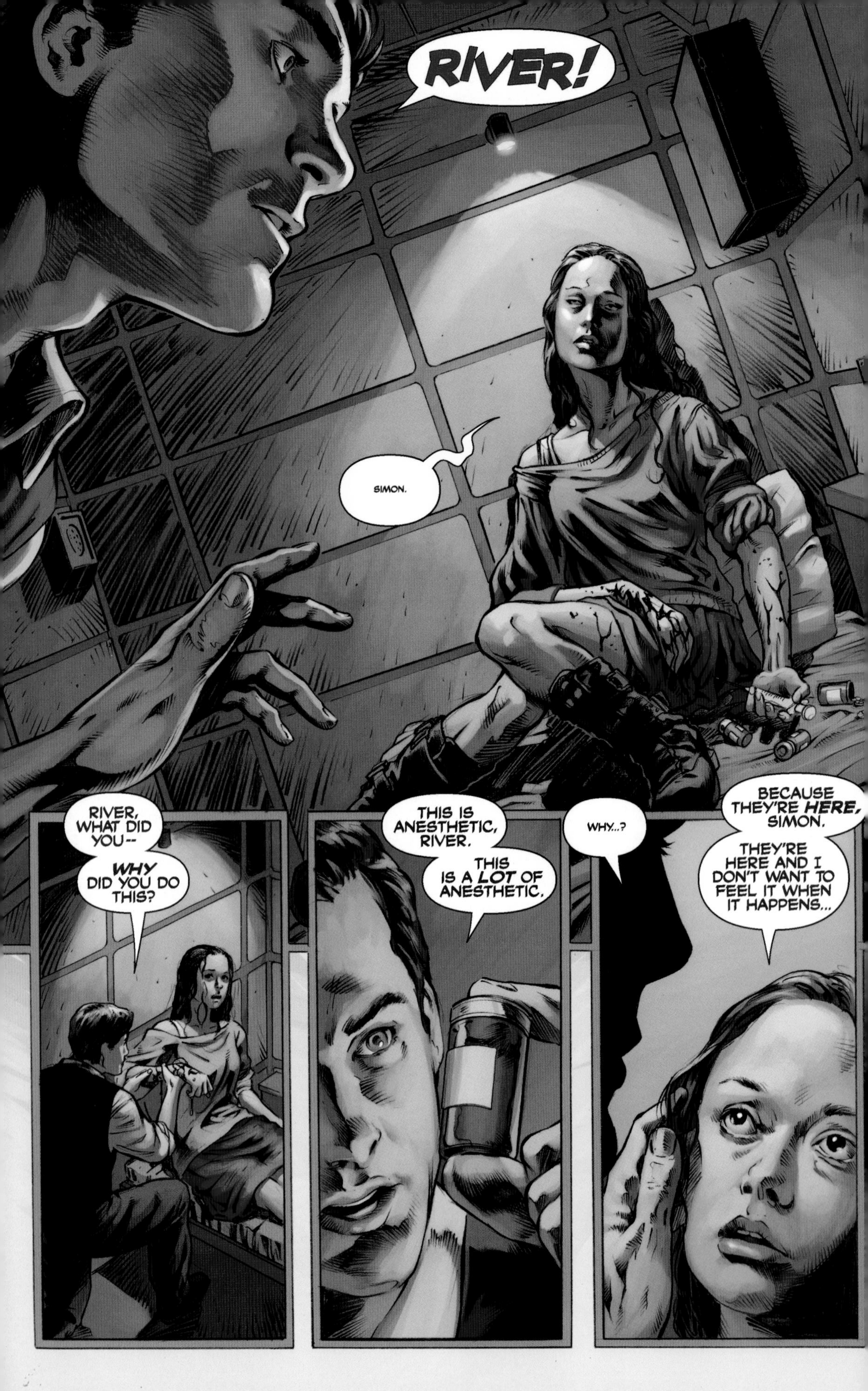
RIVER!
SIMON.
RIVER, WHAT DID YOU--
WHY DID YOU DO THIS?
THIS IS ANESTHETIC, RIVER.
THIS IS A LOT OF ANESTHETIC.
WHY...?
BECAUSE THEY'RE HERE, SIMON.
THEY'RE HERE AND I DON'T WANT TO FEEL IT WHEN IT HAPPENS...

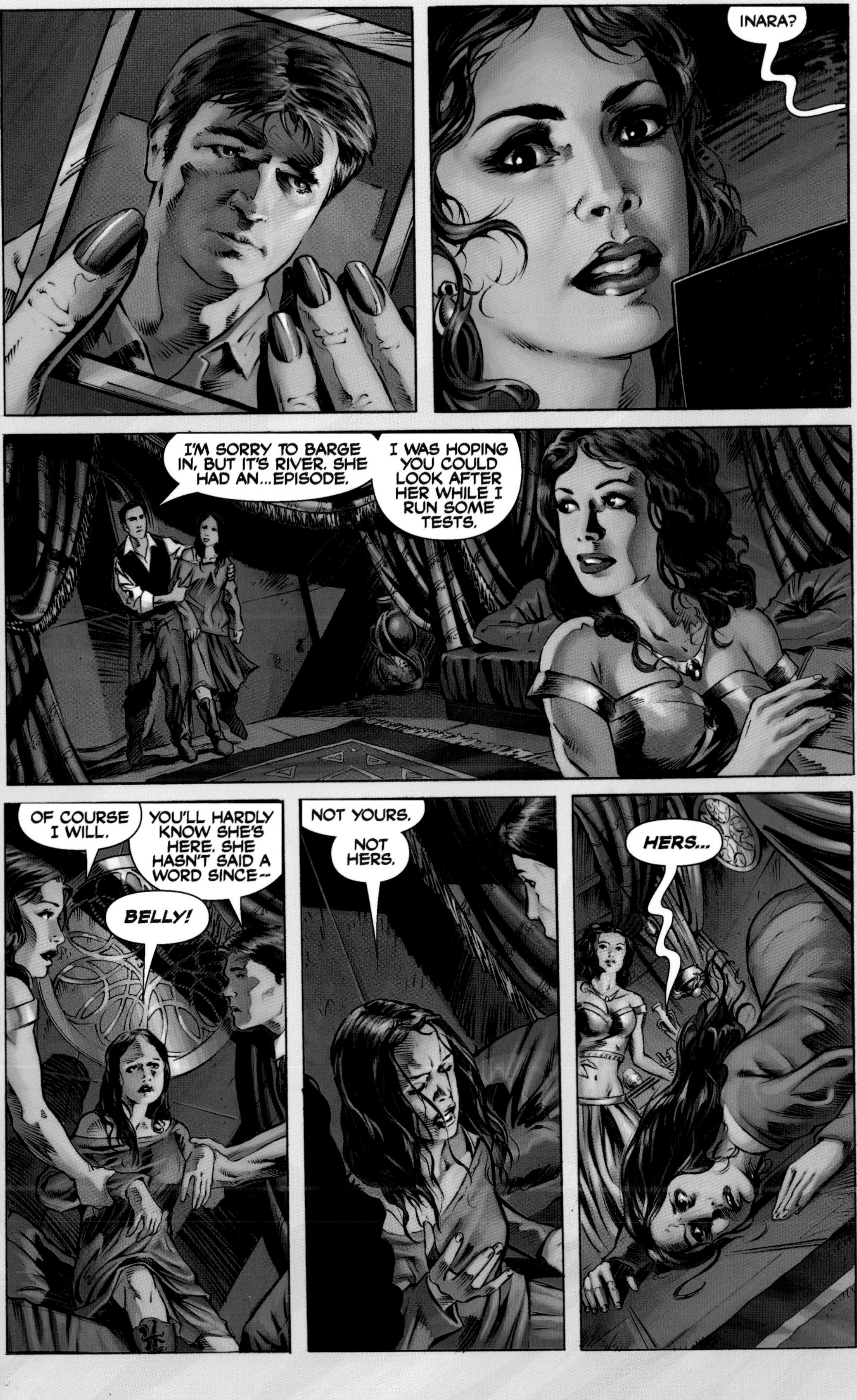
INARA?
I'M SORRY TO BARGE IN, BUT IT'S RIVER. SHE HAD AN...EPISODE.
I WAS HOPING YOU COULD LOOK AFTER HER WHILE I RUN SOME TESTS.
OF COURSE I WILL.
YOU'LL HARDLY KNOW SHE'S HERE. SHE HASN'T SAID A WORD SINCE--
BELLY!
NOT YOURS.
NOT HERS.
HERS...

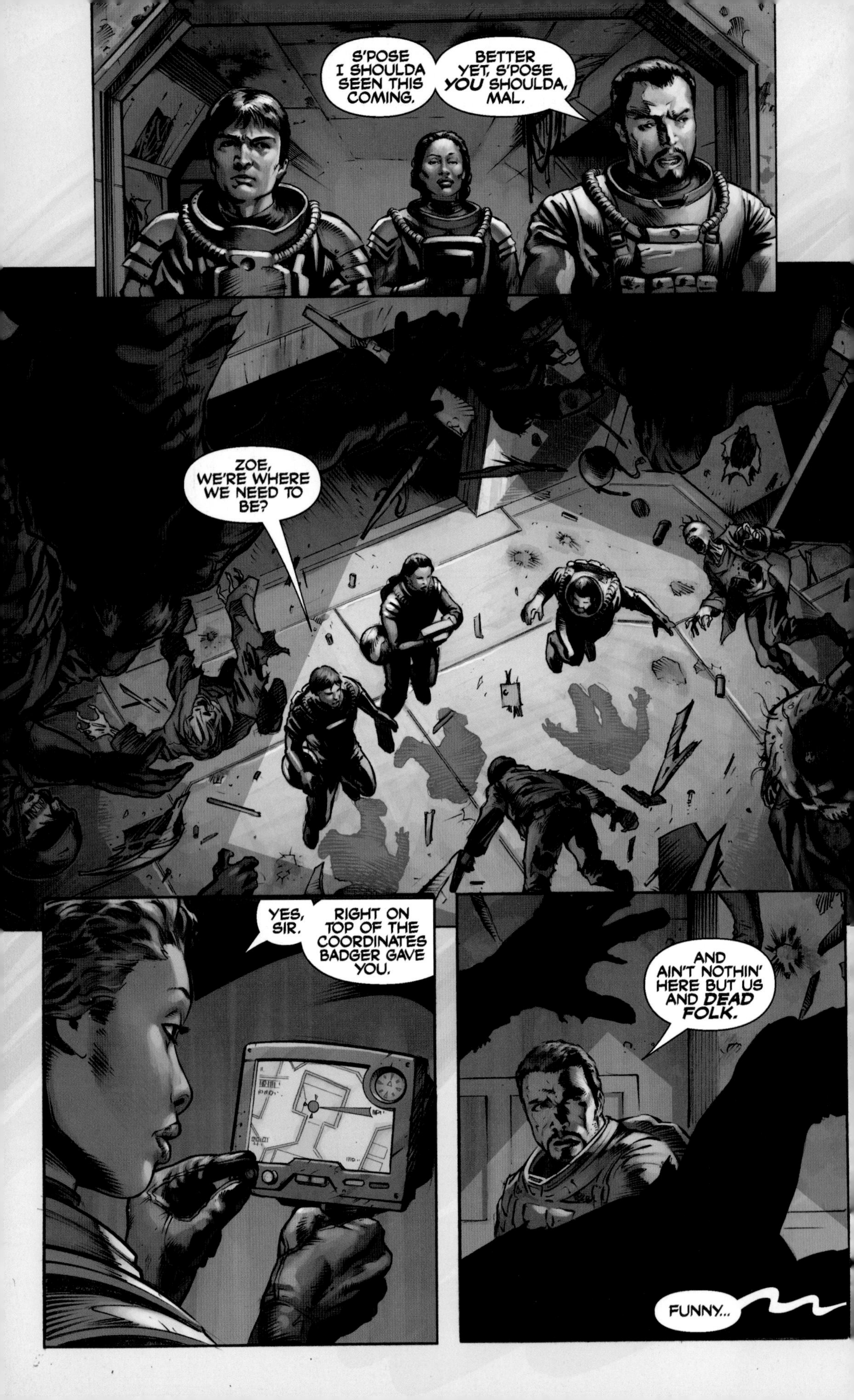
S'POSE I SHOULDA SEEN THIS COMING.
BETTER YET, S'POSE YOU SHOULDA, MAL.
ZOE, WE'RE WHERE WE NEED TO BE?
YES, SIR.
RIGHT ON TOP OF THE COORDINATES BADGER GAVE YOU.
AND AIN'T NOTHIN' HERE BUT US AND DEAD FOLK.
FUNNY...

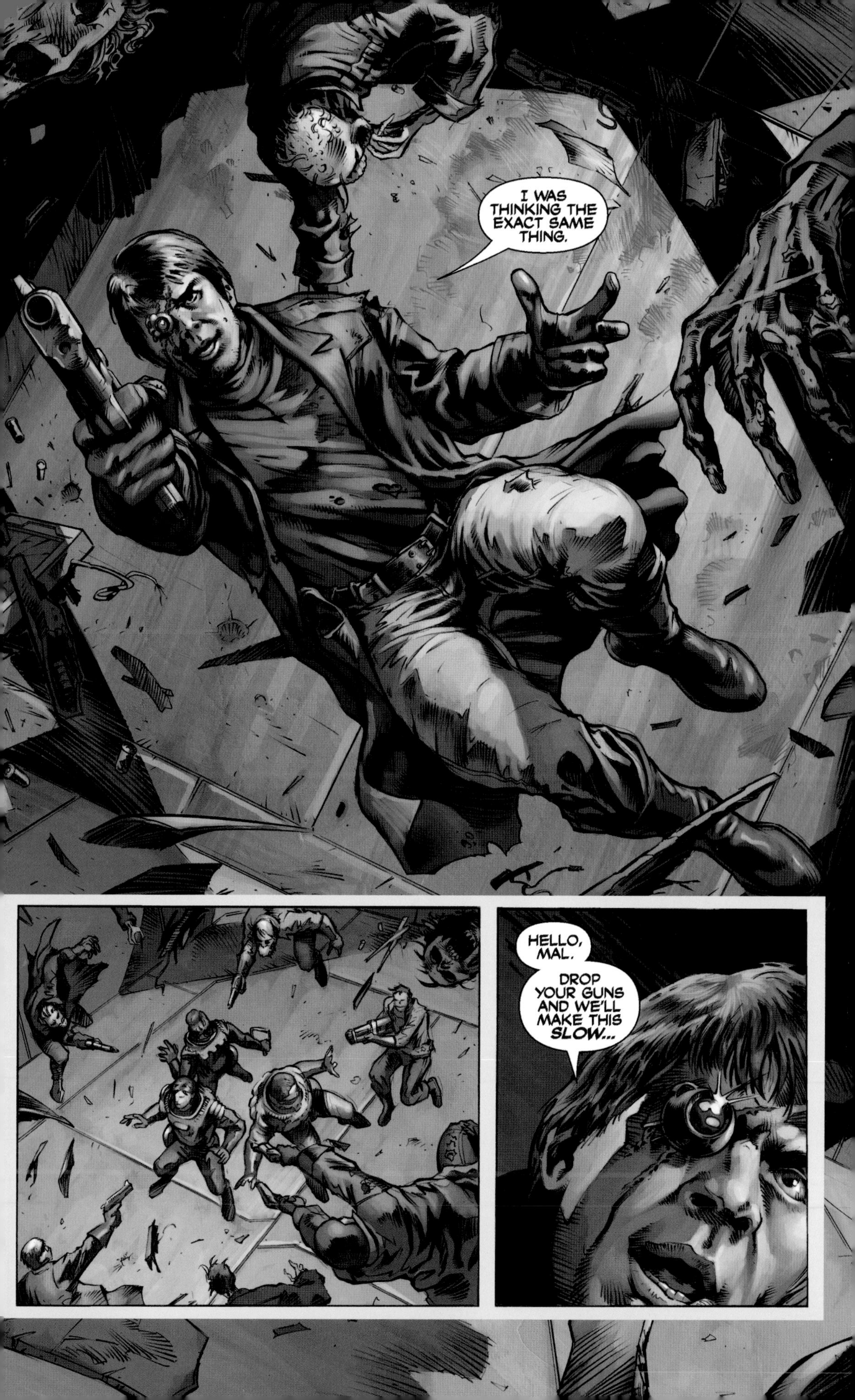
I WAS THINKING THE EXACT SAME THING.
HELLO, MAL.
DROP YOUR GUNS AND WE'LL MAKE THIS SLOW...

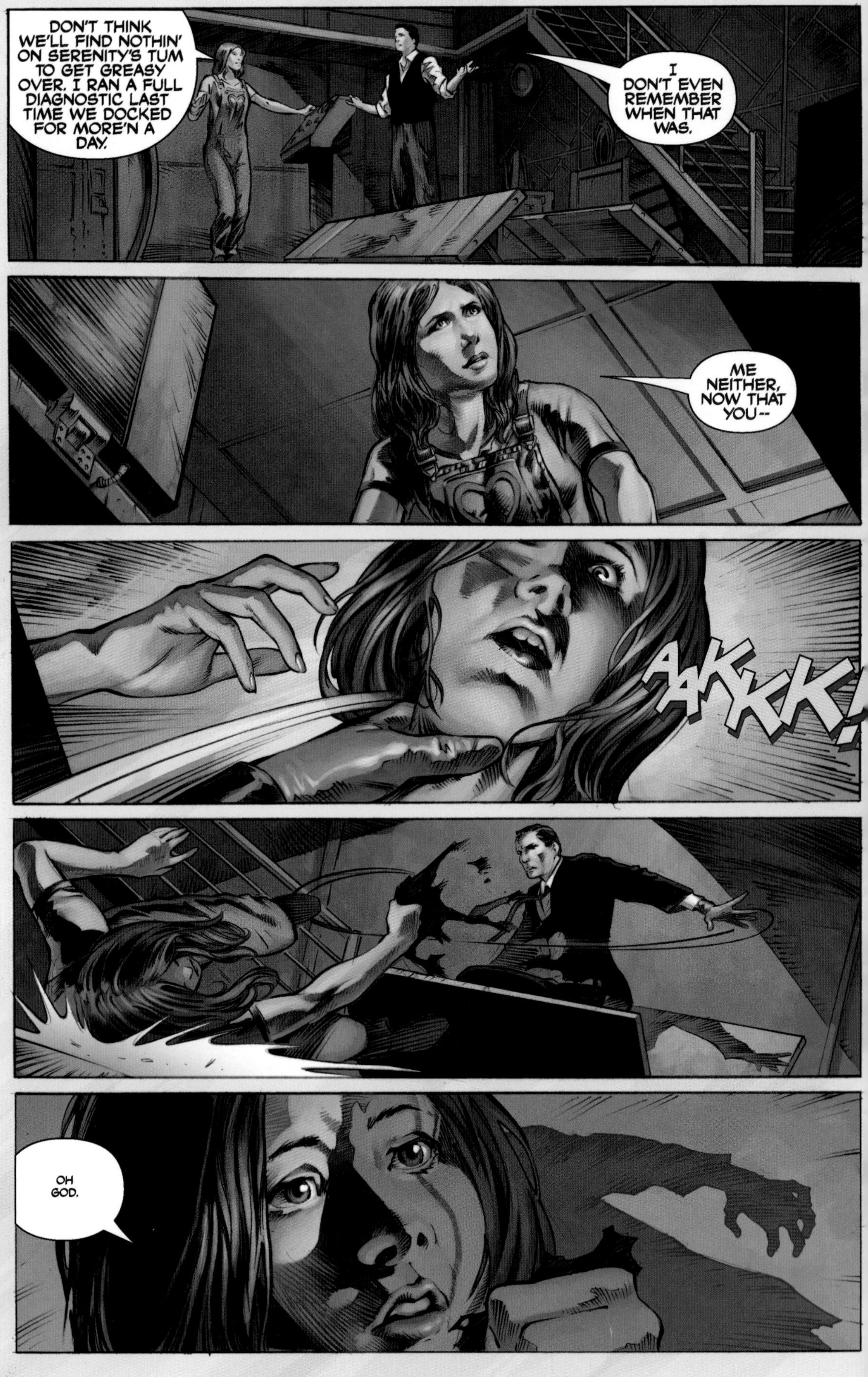
DON'T THINK WE'LL FIND NOTHIN' ON SERENITY'S TUM TO GET GREASY OVER. I RAN A FULL DIAGNOSTIC LAST TIME WE DOCKED FOR MORE'N A DAY.
I DON'T EVEN REMEMBER WHEN THAT WAS.
ME NEITHER, NOW THAT YOU--
AAKKK!
OH GOD.

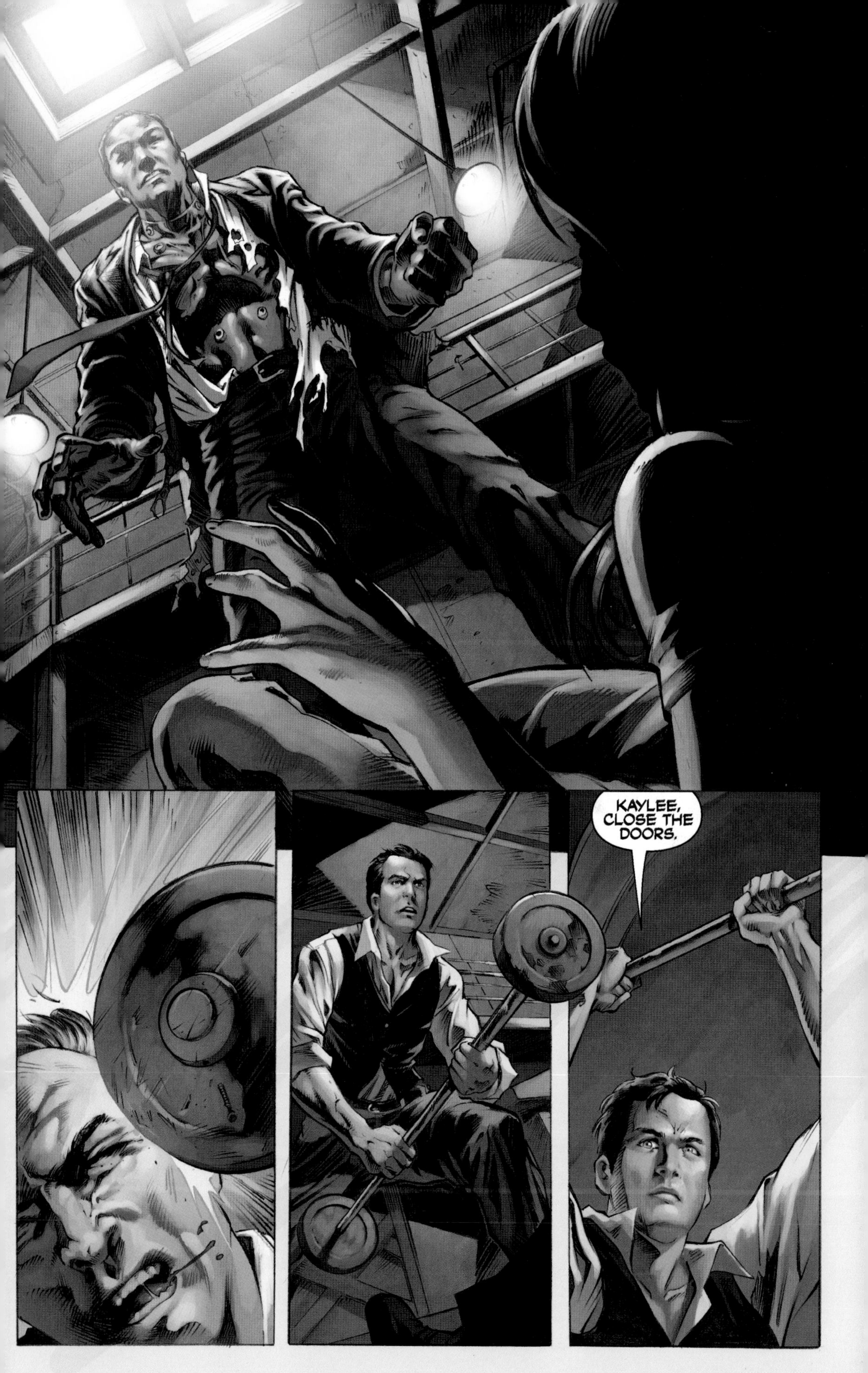
KAYLEE, CLOSE THE DOORS,

UH, MAL... DIDN'T YOU SHOOT THIS GUY IN THE HEAD --

NO, YOU MORON. THE POUND OF METAL GRAFTED TO MY FACE, IT'S PURELY COSMETIC.

WHAT IS IT YOU WANT, DOBSON?

YOU. *DEAD*.

ALL THIS TIME, YOU BEEN TRACKIN' US, THE TROUBLE AND RESOURCES THAT MUST HAVE TOOK.

GOT TO BE MORE TO IT THAN THAT...

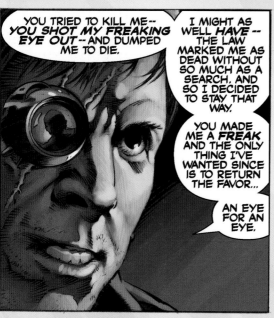

YOU TRIED TO KILL ME -- *YOU SHOT MY FREAKING EYE OUT* -- AND DUMPED ME TO DIE.

I MIGHT AS WELL *HAVE* -- THE LAW MARKED ME AS DEAD WITHOUT SO MUCH AS A SEARCH, AND SO I DECIDED TO STAY THAT WAY.

YOU MADE ME A *FREAK* AND THE ONLY THING I'VE WANTED SINCE IS TO RETURN THE FAVOR...

AN EYE FOR AN EYE.

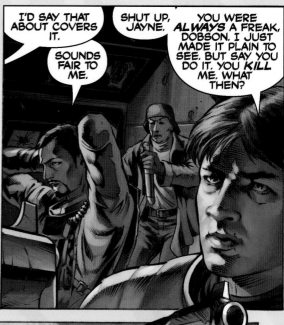

I'D SAY THAT ABOUT COVERS IT.

SOUNDS FAIR TO ME.

SHUT UP, JAYNE.

YOU WERE *ALWAYS* A FREAK, DOBSON. I JUST MADE IT PLAIN TO SEE. BUT SAY YOU DO IT. YOU *KILL* ME. WHAT THEN?

I DUNNO.

I IMAGINE I'LL GET A HOBBY OR SOMETHING...

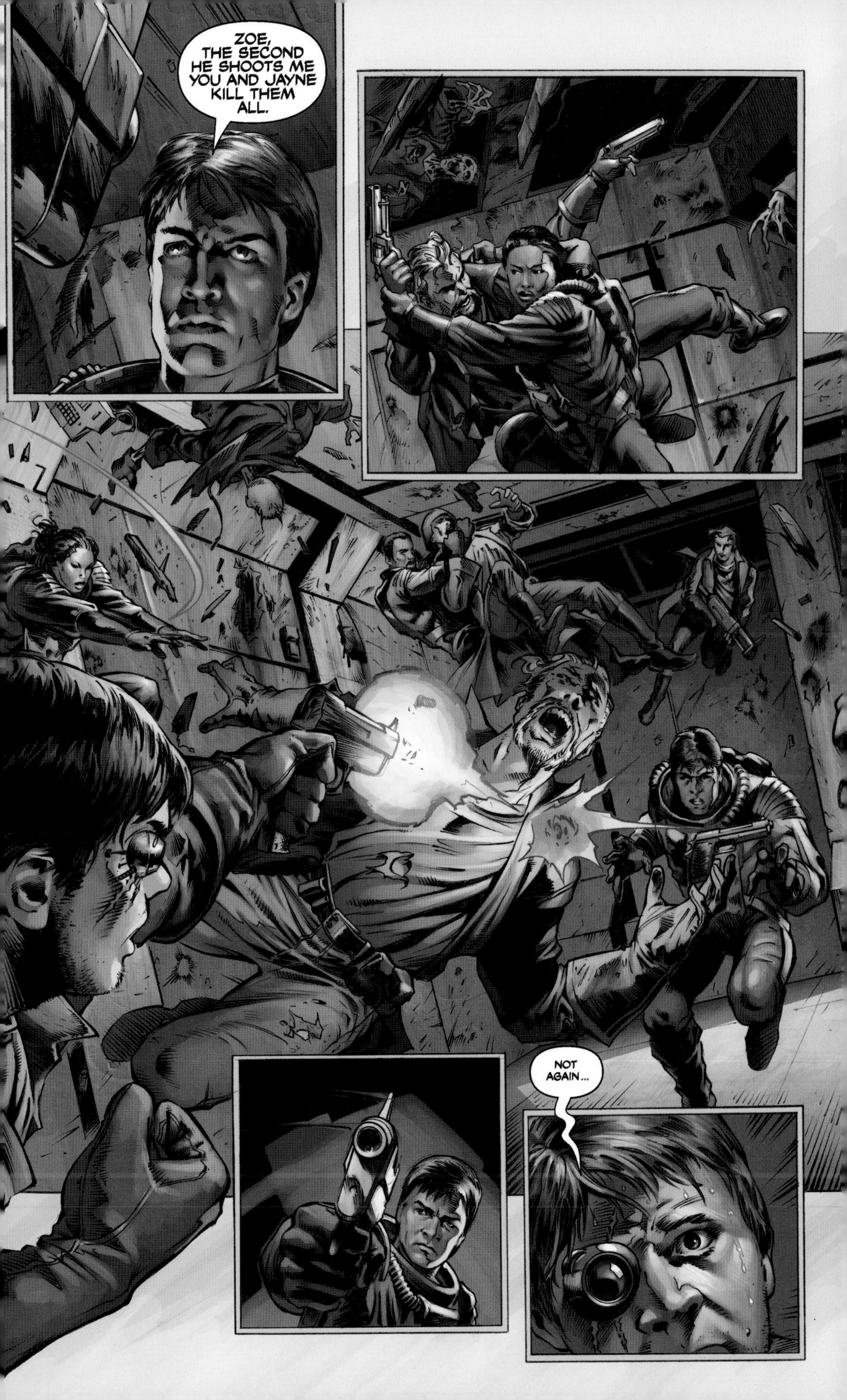
ZOE, THE SECOND HE SHOOTS ME YOU AND JAYNE KILL THEM ALL.
NOT AGAIN...

YOU MISSED
THIS ONE.

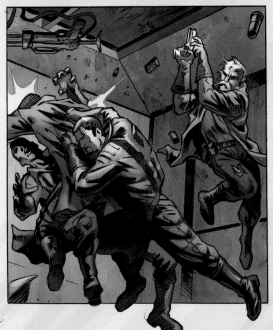

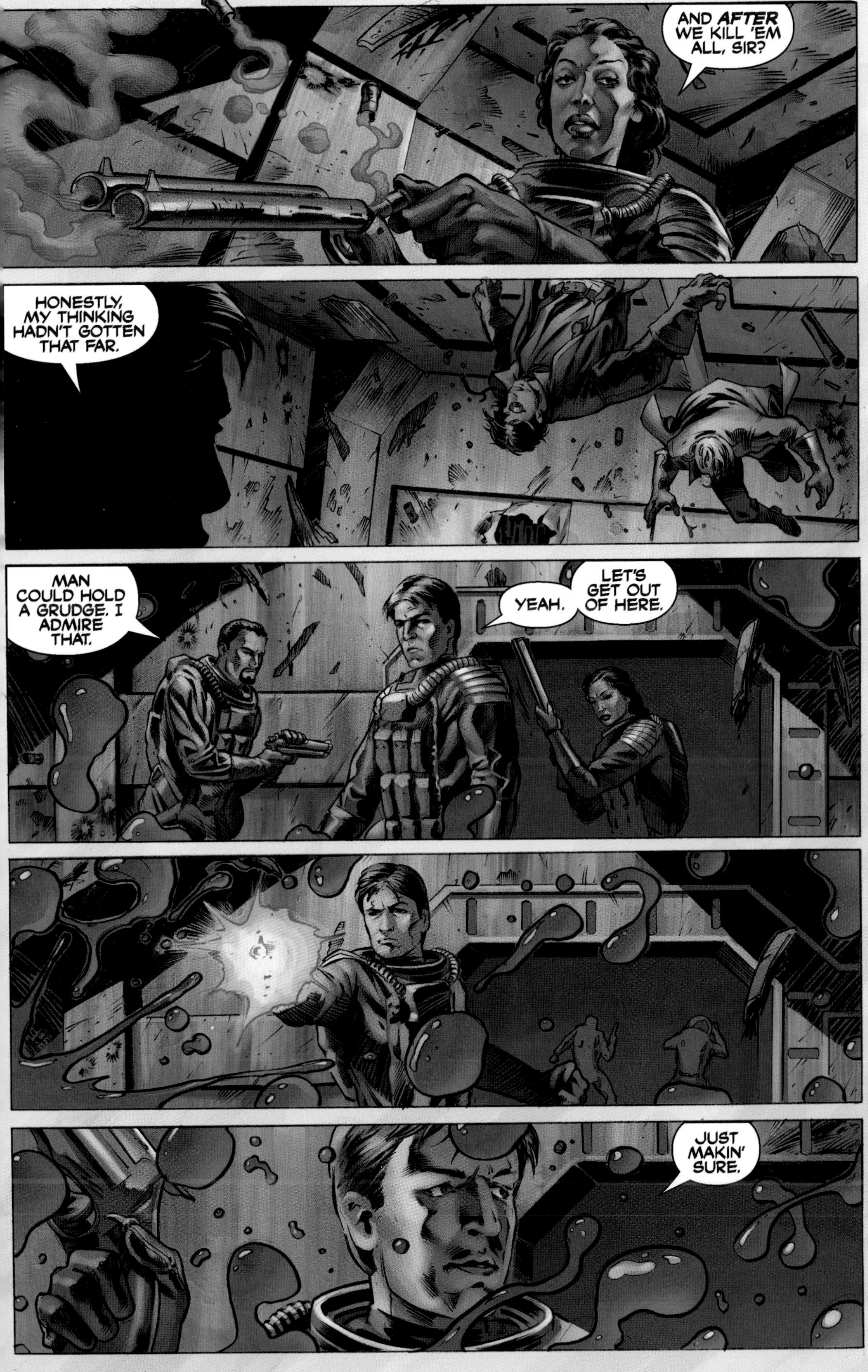
AND AFTER WE KILL 'EM ALL, SIR?
HONESTLY, MY THINKING HADN'T GOTTEN THAT FAR.
MAN COULD HOLD A GRUDGE, I ADMIRE THAT.
YEAH.
LET'S GET OUT OF HERE.
JUST MAKIN' SURE.

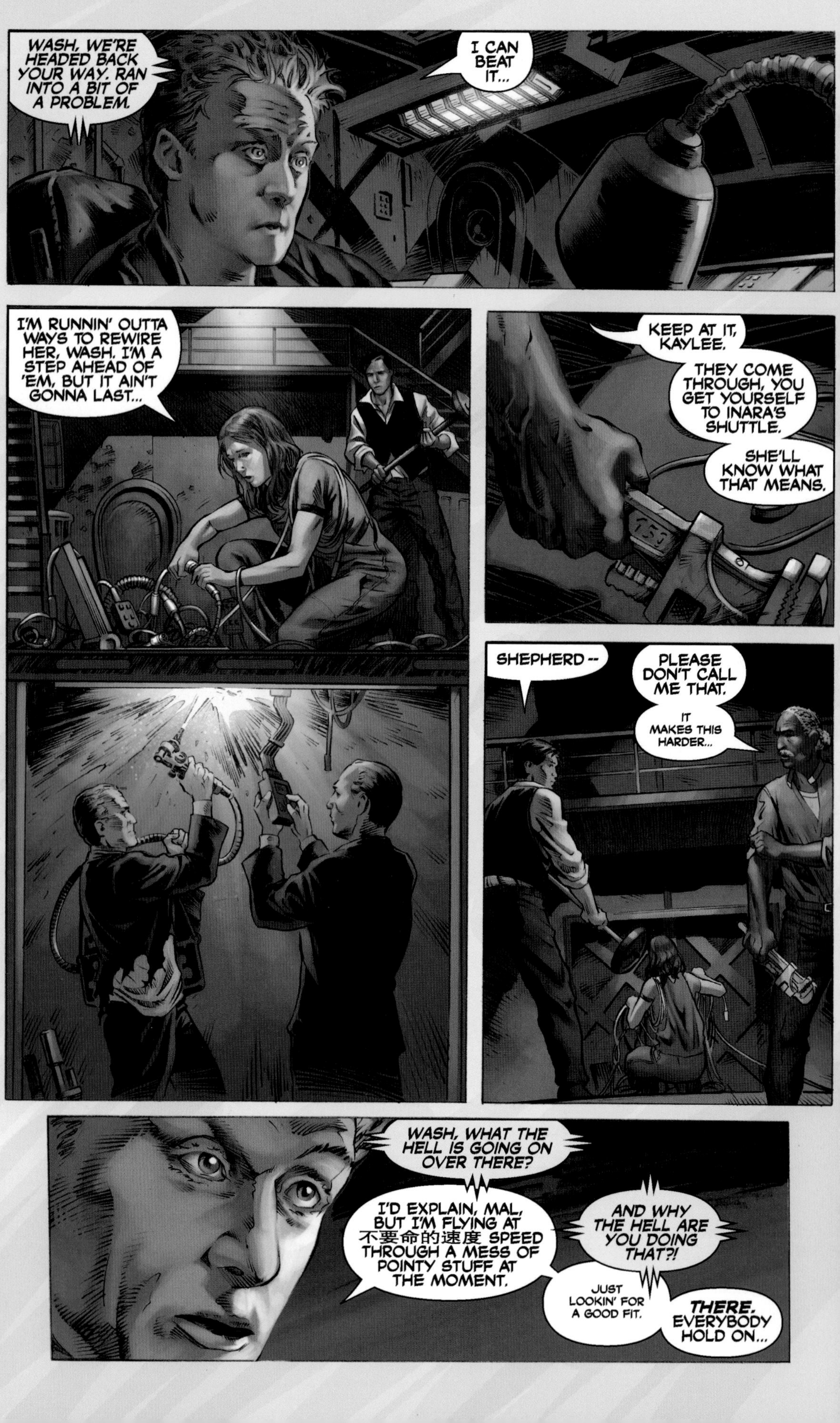
WASH, WE'RE HEADED BACK YOUR WAY. RAN INTO A BIT OF A PROBLEM.
I CAN BEAT IT...
I'M RUNNIN' OUTTA WAYS TO REWIRE HER, WASH. I'M A STEP AHEAD OF 'EM, BUT IT AIN'T GONNA LAST...
KEEP AT IT, KAYLEE.
THEY COME THROUGH, YOU GET YOURSELF TO INARA'S SHUTTLE.
SHE'LL KNOW WHAT THAT MEANS.
SHEPHERD --
PLEASE DON'T CALL ME THAT.
IT MAKES THIS HARDER...
WASH, WHAT THE HELL IS GOING ON OVER THERE?
I'D EXPLAIN, MAL, BUT I'M FLYING AT 不要命的速度 SPEED THROUGH A MESS OF POINTY STUFF AT THE MOMENT.
AND WHY THE HELL ARE YOU DOING THAT?!
JUST LOOKIN' FOR A GOOD FIT.
THERE. EVERYBODY HOLD ON...

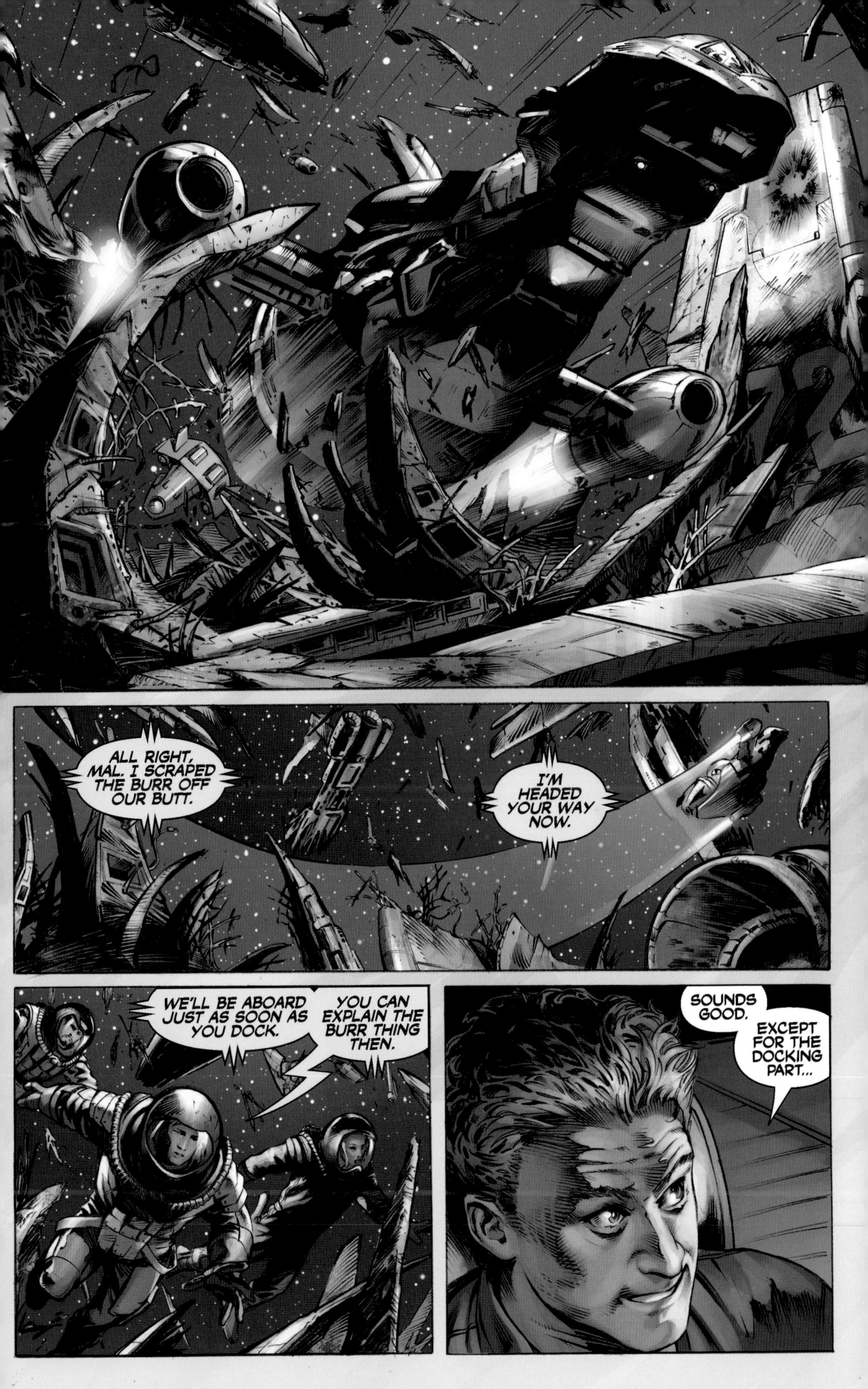
ALL RIGHT, MAL. I SCRAPED THE BURR OFF OUR BUTT.
I'M HEADED YOUR WAY NOW.
WE'LL BE ABOARD JUST AS SOON AS YOU DOCK.
YOU CAN EXPLAIN THE BURR THING THEN.
SOUNDS GOOD.
EXCEPT FOR THE DOCKING PART...

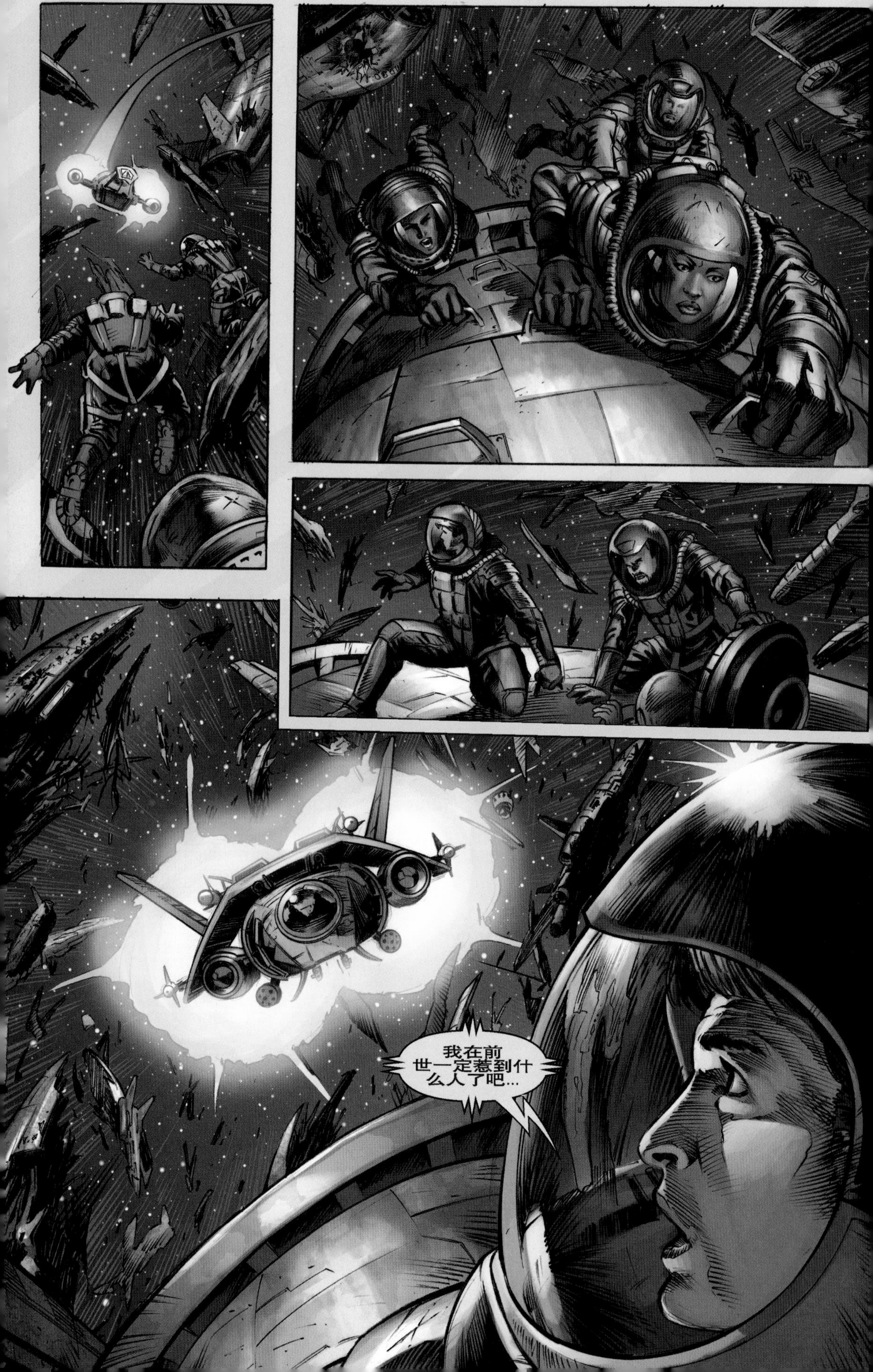
我在前
世一定惹到什
么人了吧...

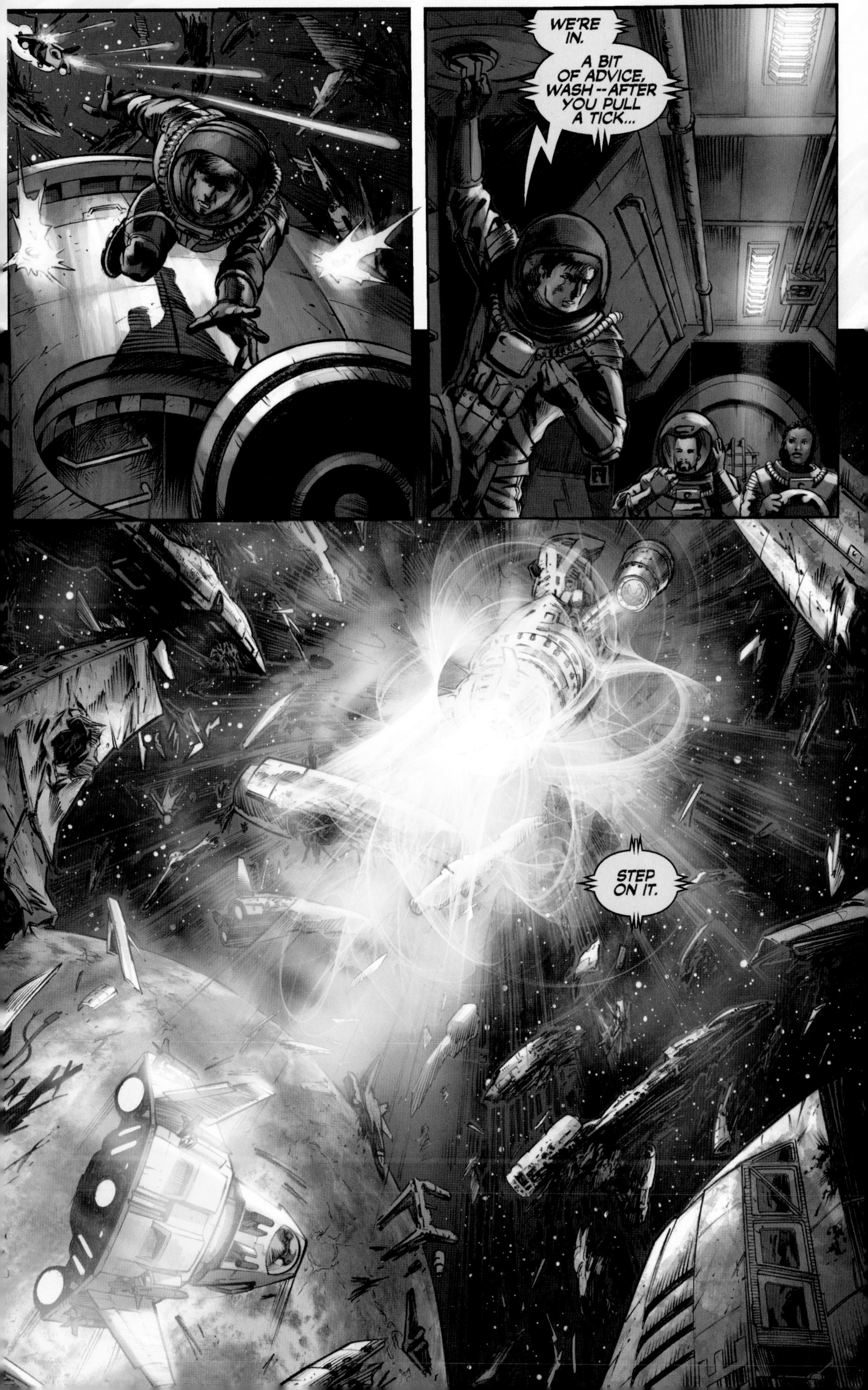
WE'RE IN.
A BIT OF ADVICE, WASH -- AFTER YOU PULL A TICK...
STEP ON IT.

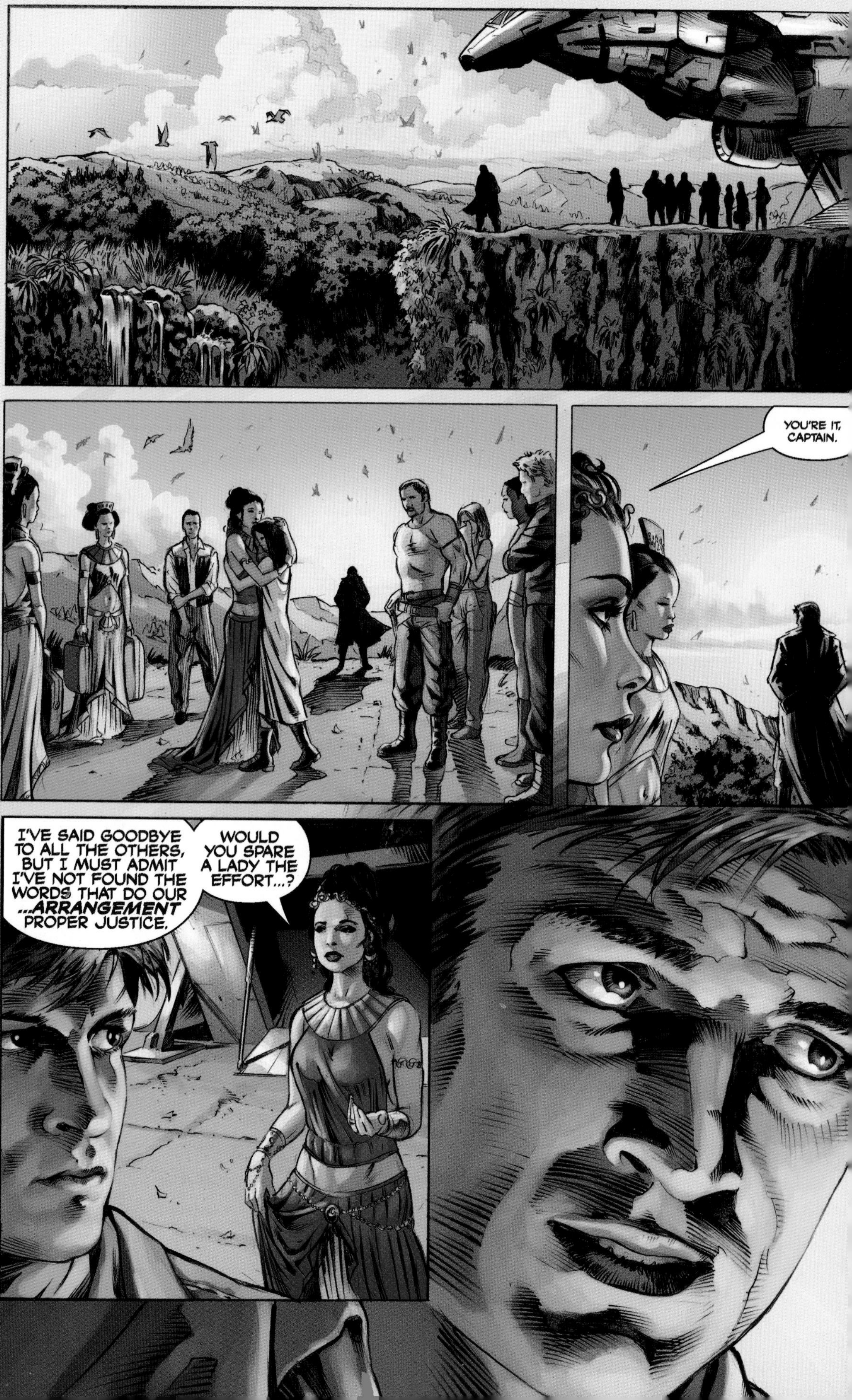
YOU'RE IT, CAPTAIN.
I'VE SAID GOODBYE TO ALL THE OTHERS, BUT I MUST ADMIT I'VE NOT FOUND THE WORDS THAT DO OUR ...ARRANGEMENT PROPER JUSTICE.
WOULD YOU SPARE A LADY THE EFFORT...?

I'LL MISS YOU, INARA.

I KEEP COMING UP WITH ALL MANNER OF THINGS TO SAY BUT THAT'S WHAT THEY ALL MEAN, IT COMES RIGHT DOWN TO IT.

I DON'T WANT YOU TO --

AM I INTERRUPTING SOMETHING, CAPTAIN?

NOT THAT I KNOW WHAT THAT WOULD BE, YOU STANDING HERE ALONE IN THE MIDDLE OF THE NIGHT.

WE'RE IN SPACE, SHEPHERD. IT'S ALWAYS THE MIDDLE OF THE NIGHT.

WHAT'S ON YOUR MIND?

I'M LEAVING THE SHIP.

DON'T KNOW WHERE FOR JUST YET, BUT IT'S TIME FOR ME TO MOVE ON, I THOUGHT YOU SHOULD BE THE FIRST TO KNOW.

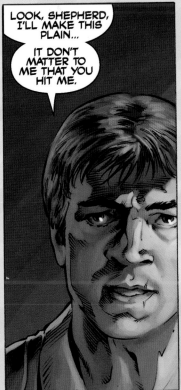

LOOK, SHEPHERD, I'LL MAKE THIS PLAIN...

IT DON'T MATTER TO ME THAT YOU HIT ME.

WHICH IS EXACTLY WHY I NEED TO BE AWAY FROM YOU.

BECAUSE SOONER OR LATER, IT WON'T MATTER TO ME, EITHER.

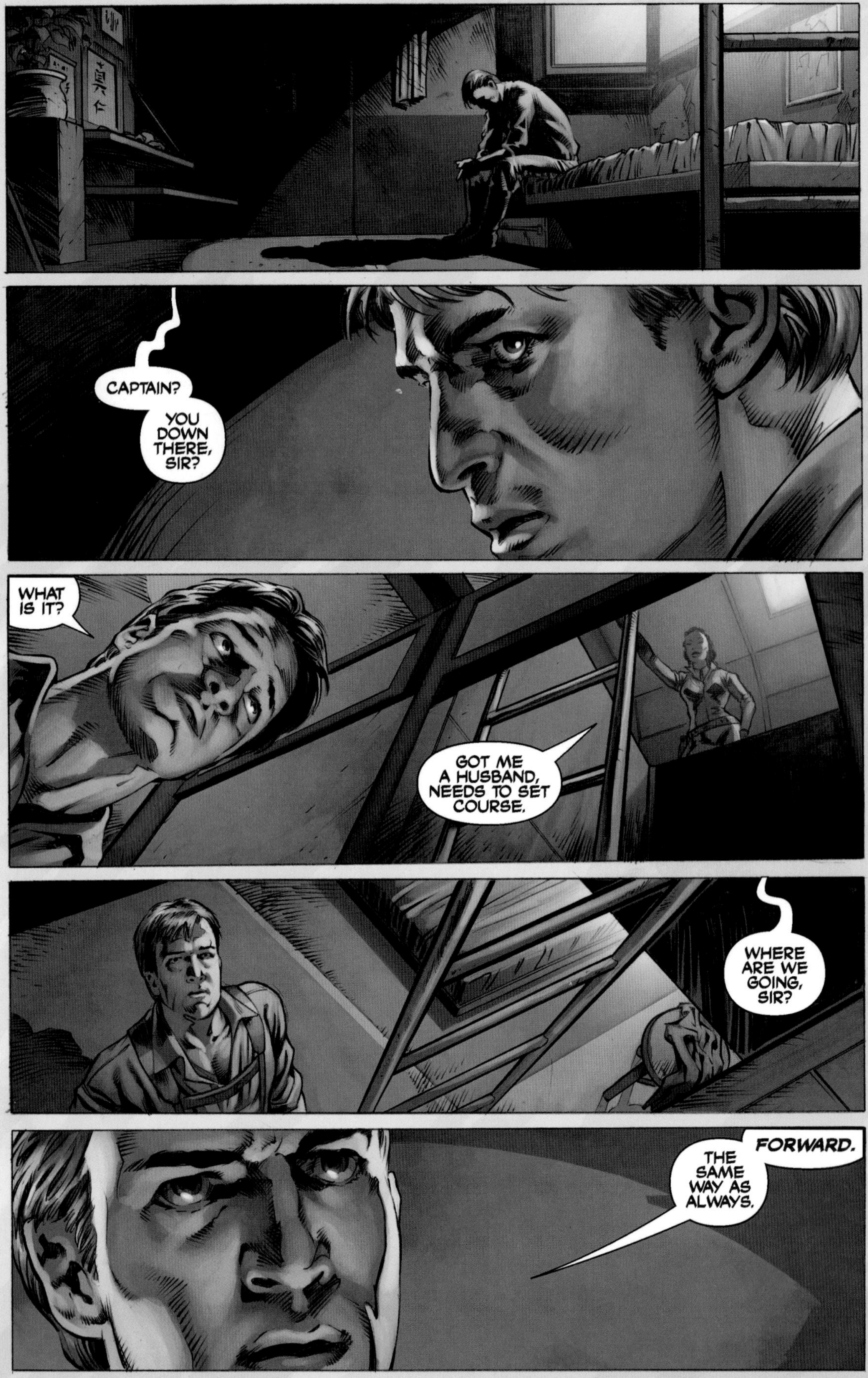
CAPTAIN?
YOU DOWN THERE, SIR?
WHAT IS IT?
GOT ME A HUSBAND, NEEDS TO SET COURSE.
WHERE ARE WE GOING, SIR?
FORWARD.
THE SAME WAY AS ALWAYS.

OUR INDEPENDENT CONTRACTORS HAVE... DISAPPEARED.

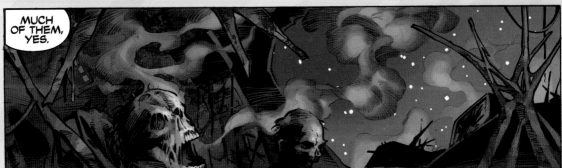

MUCH OF THEM, YES.

THEIR WORK FALLS TO YOU.

I ACCEPT IT.

I AM TRANSMITTING THE ASSIGNMENT NOW...

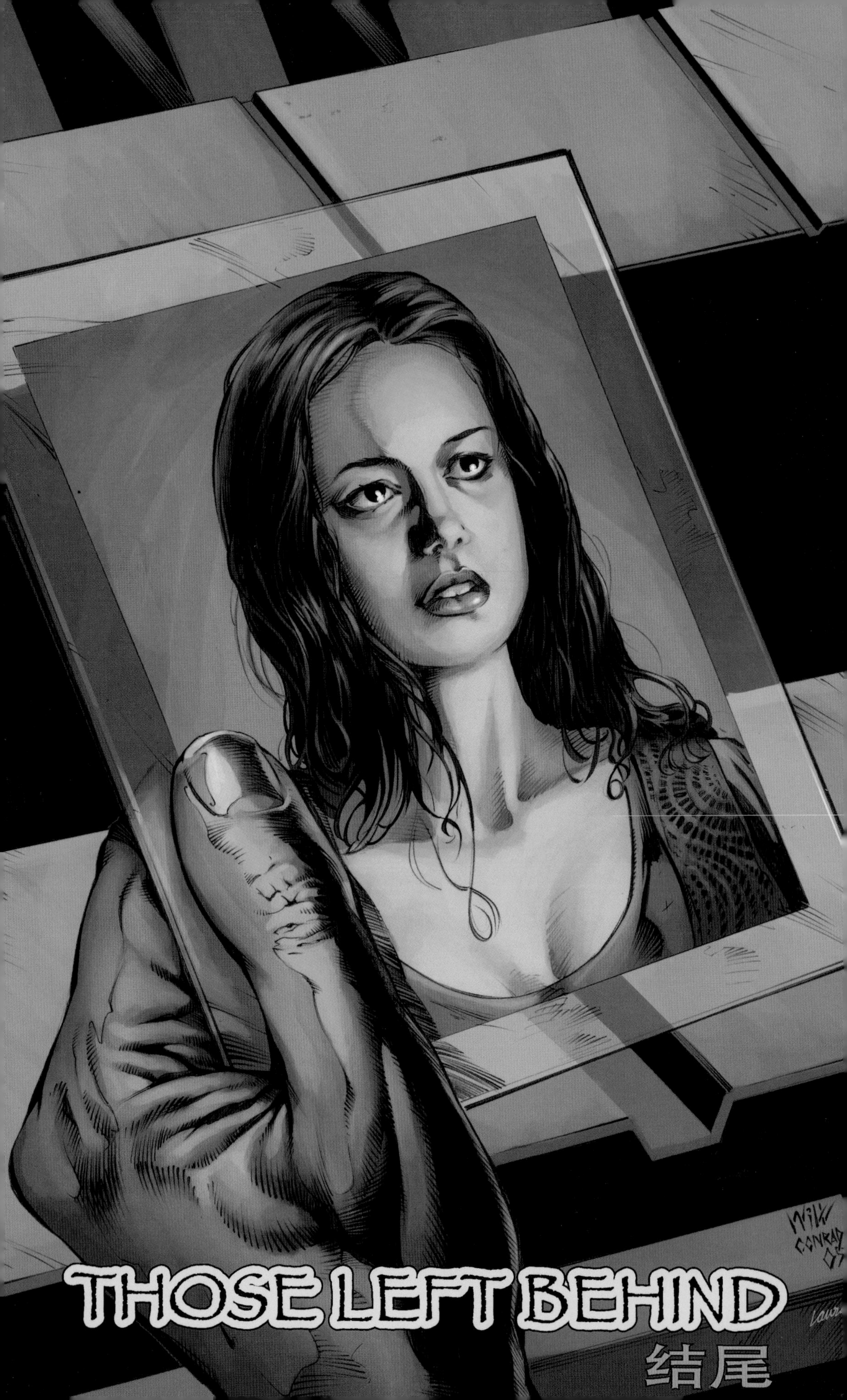
THOSE LEFT BEHIND
结尾

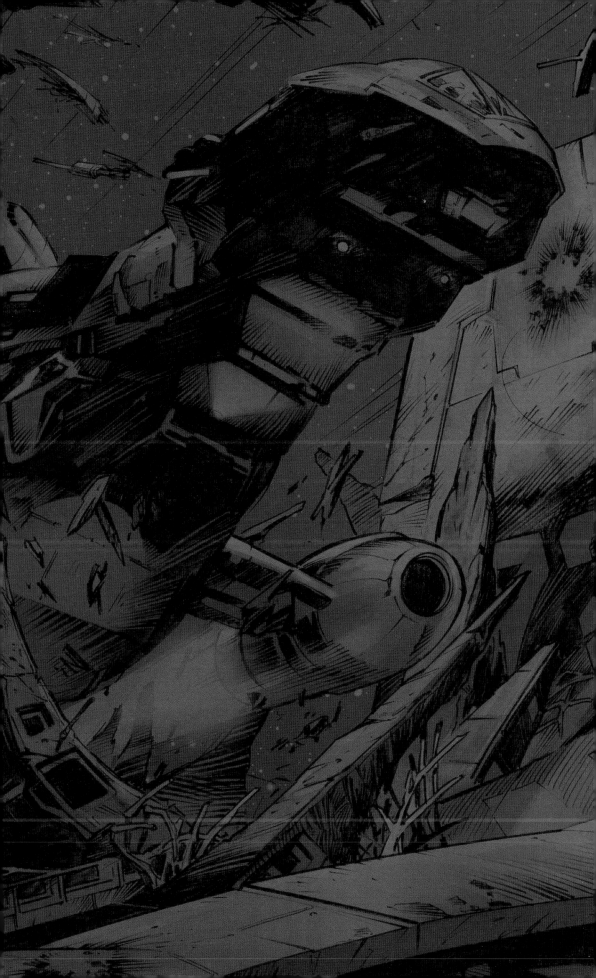

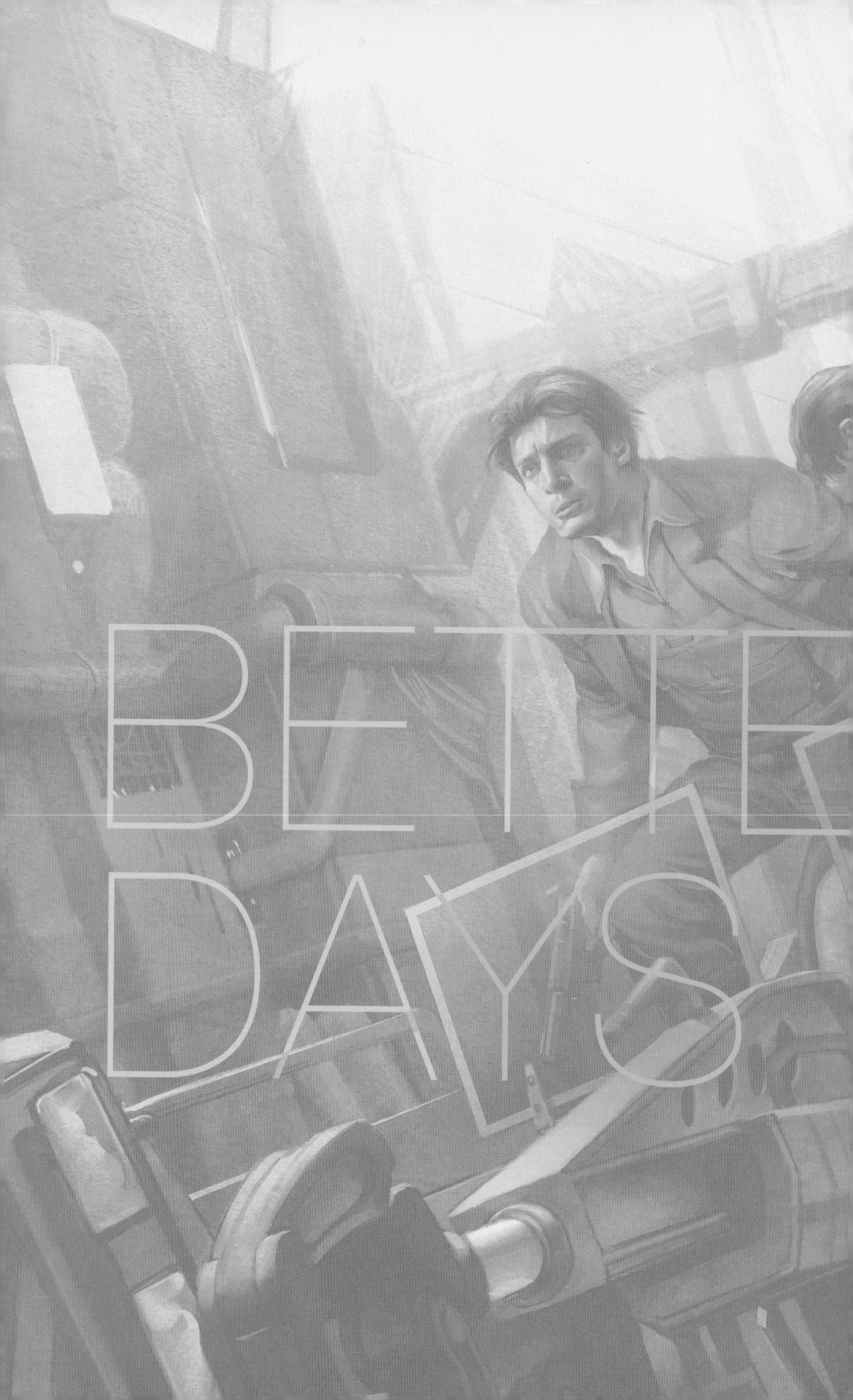
BETTE
DAYS

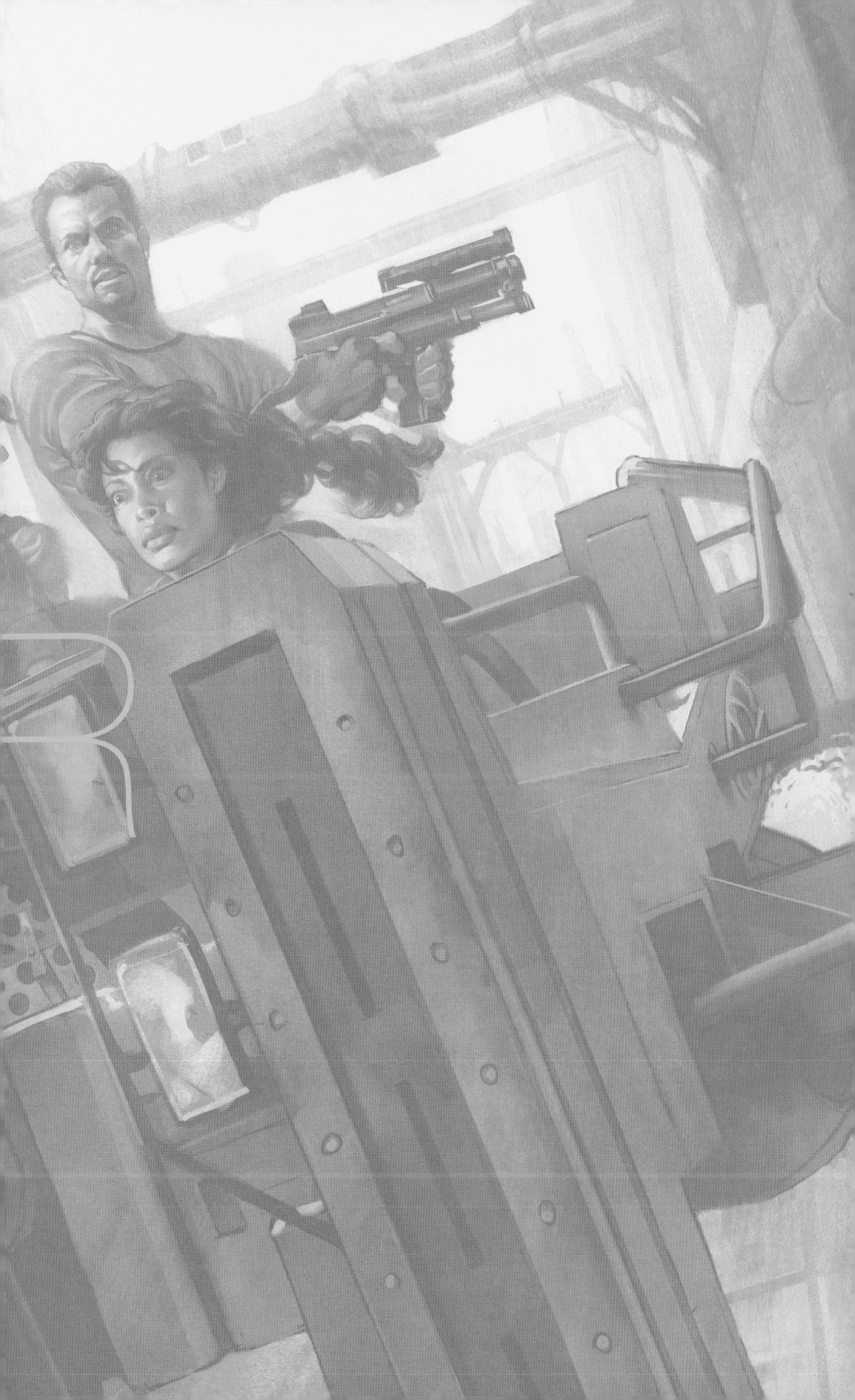

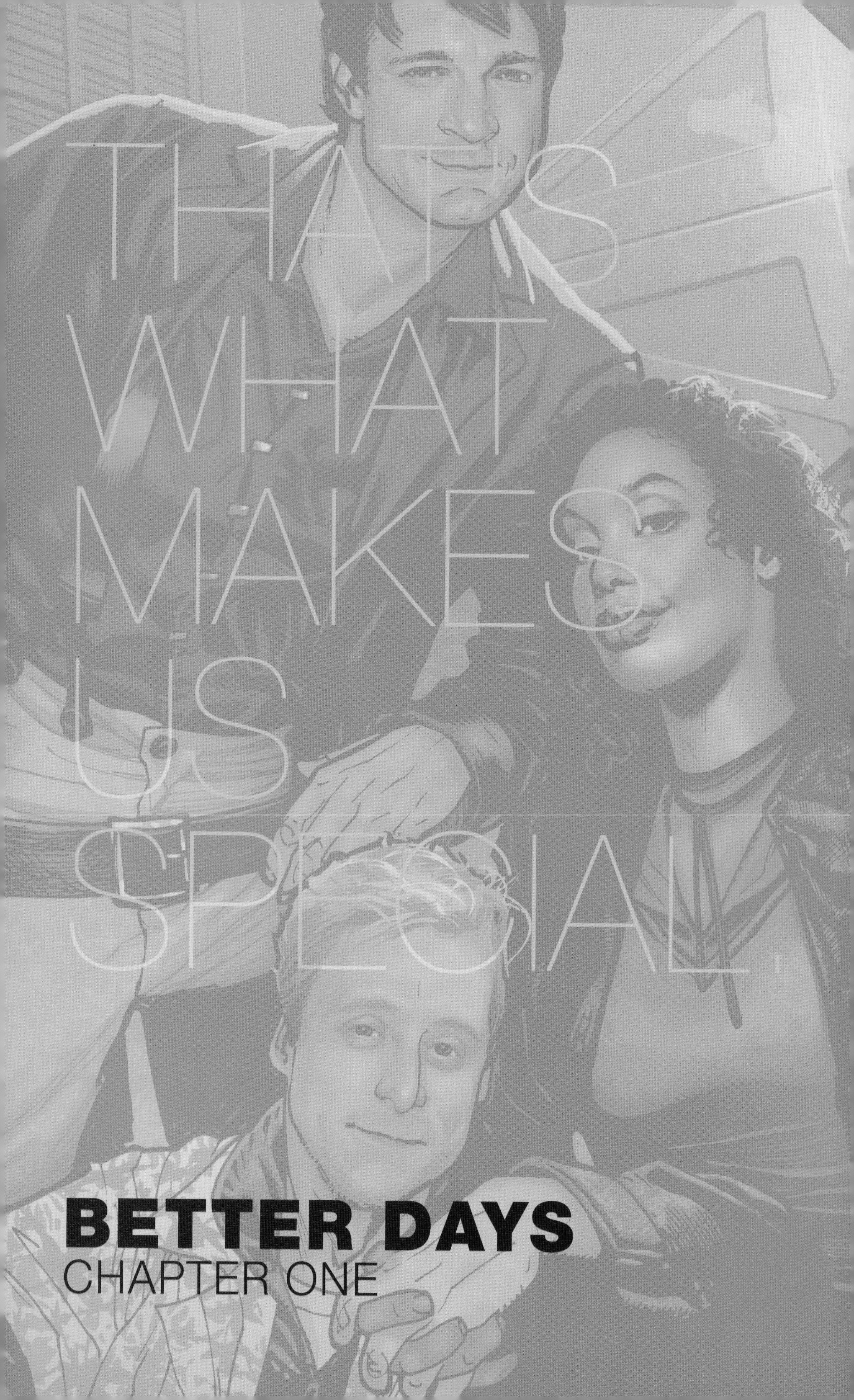
THAT'S
WHAT
MAKES
US
SPECIAL

BETTER DAYS
CHAPTER ONE

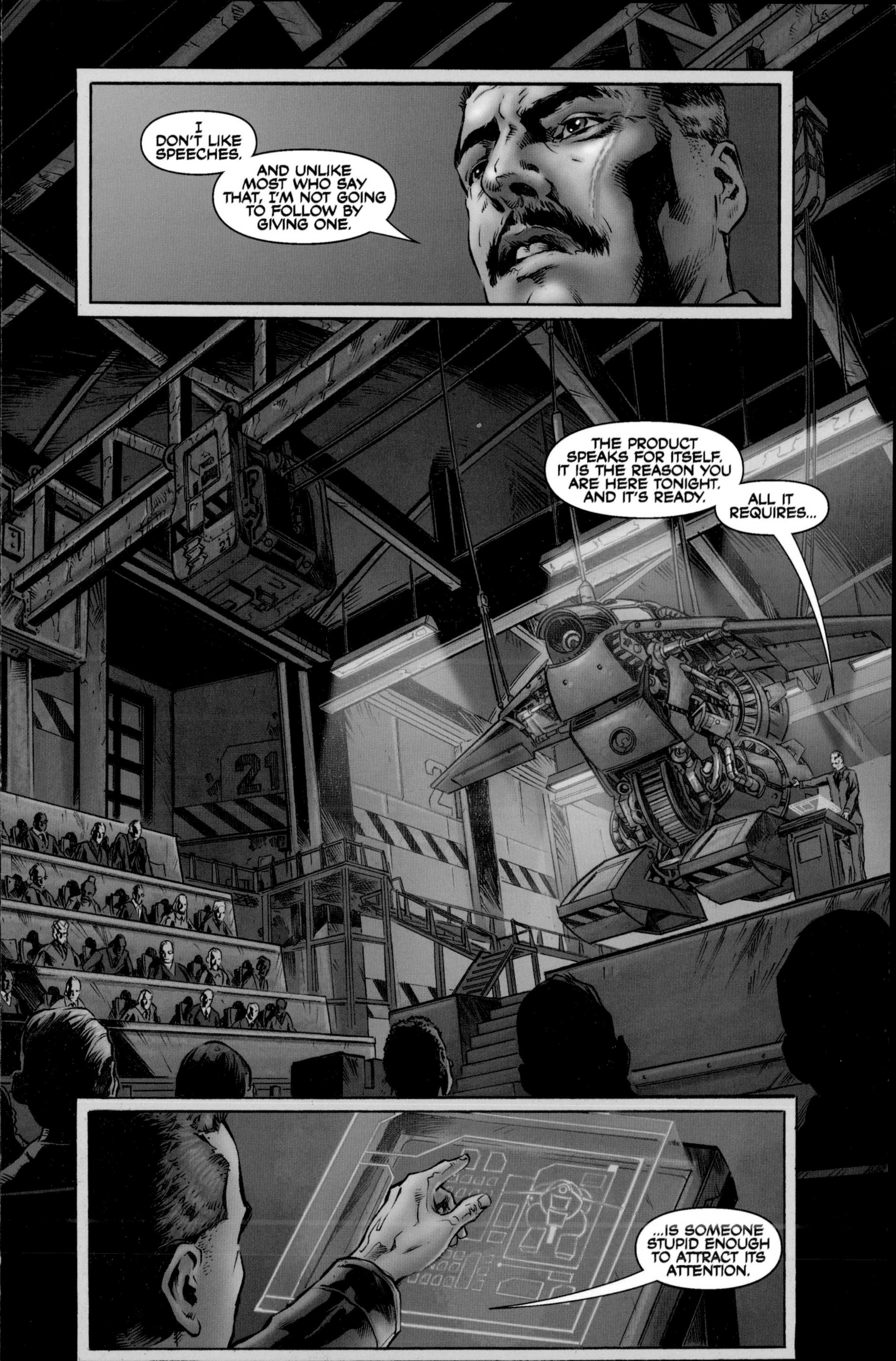
I DON'T LIKE SPEECHES.
AND UNLIKE MOST WHO SAY THAT, I'M NOT GOING TO FOLLOW BY GIVING ONE.
THE PRODUCT SPEAKS FOR ITSELF. IT IS THE REASON YOU ARE HERE TONIGHT. AND IT'S READY.
ALL IT REQUIRES...
...IS SOMEONE STUPID ENOUGH TO ATTRACT ITS ATTENTION.

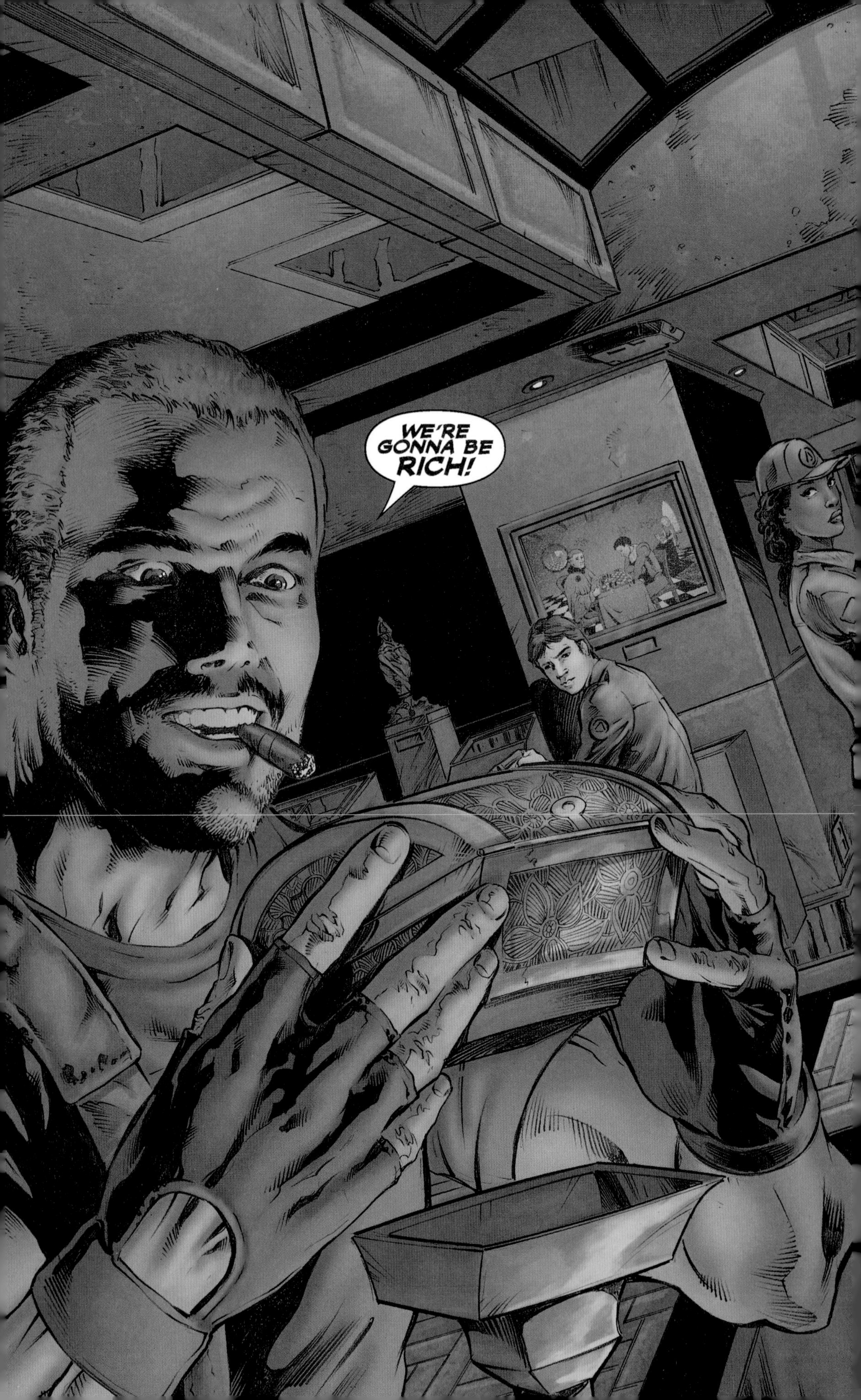
WE'RE GONNA BE RICH!

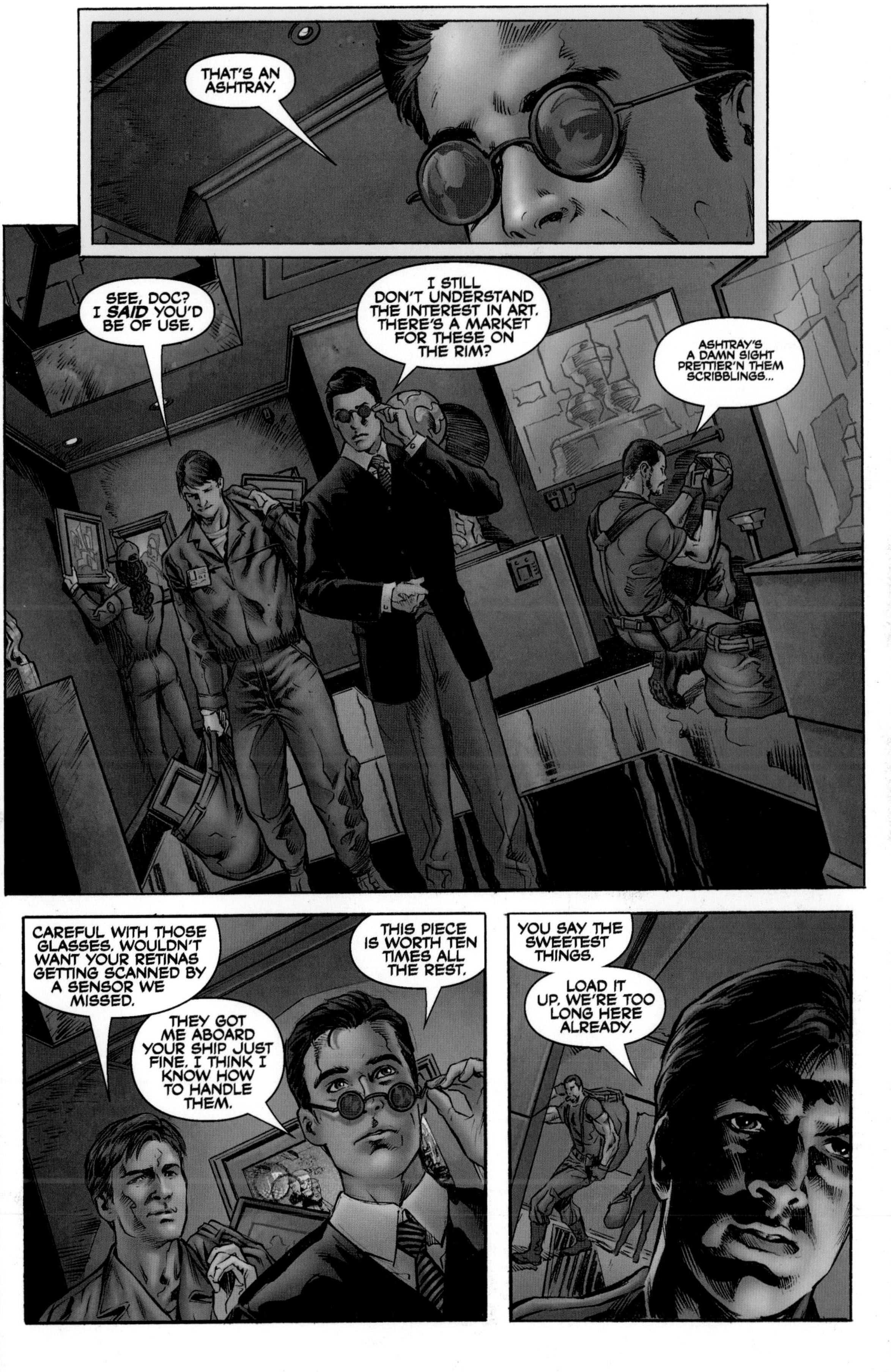
THAT'S AN ASHTRAY.
SEE, DOC? I *SAID* YOU'D BE OF USE.
I STILL DON'T UNDERSTAND THE INTEREST IN ART. THERE'S A MARKET FOR THESE ON THE RIM?
ASHTRAY'S A DAMN SIGHT PRETTIER'N THEM SCRIBBLINGS...
CAREFUL WITH THOSE GLASSES. WOULDN'T WANT YOUR RETINAS GETTING SCANNED BY A SENSOR WE MISSED.
THEY GOT ME ABOARD YOUR SHIP JUST FINE. I THINK I KNOW HOW TO HANDLE THEM.
THIS PIECE IS WORTH TEN TIMES ALL THE REST.
YOU SAY THE SWEETEST THINGS.
LOAD IT UP. WE'RE TOO LONG HERE ALREADY.

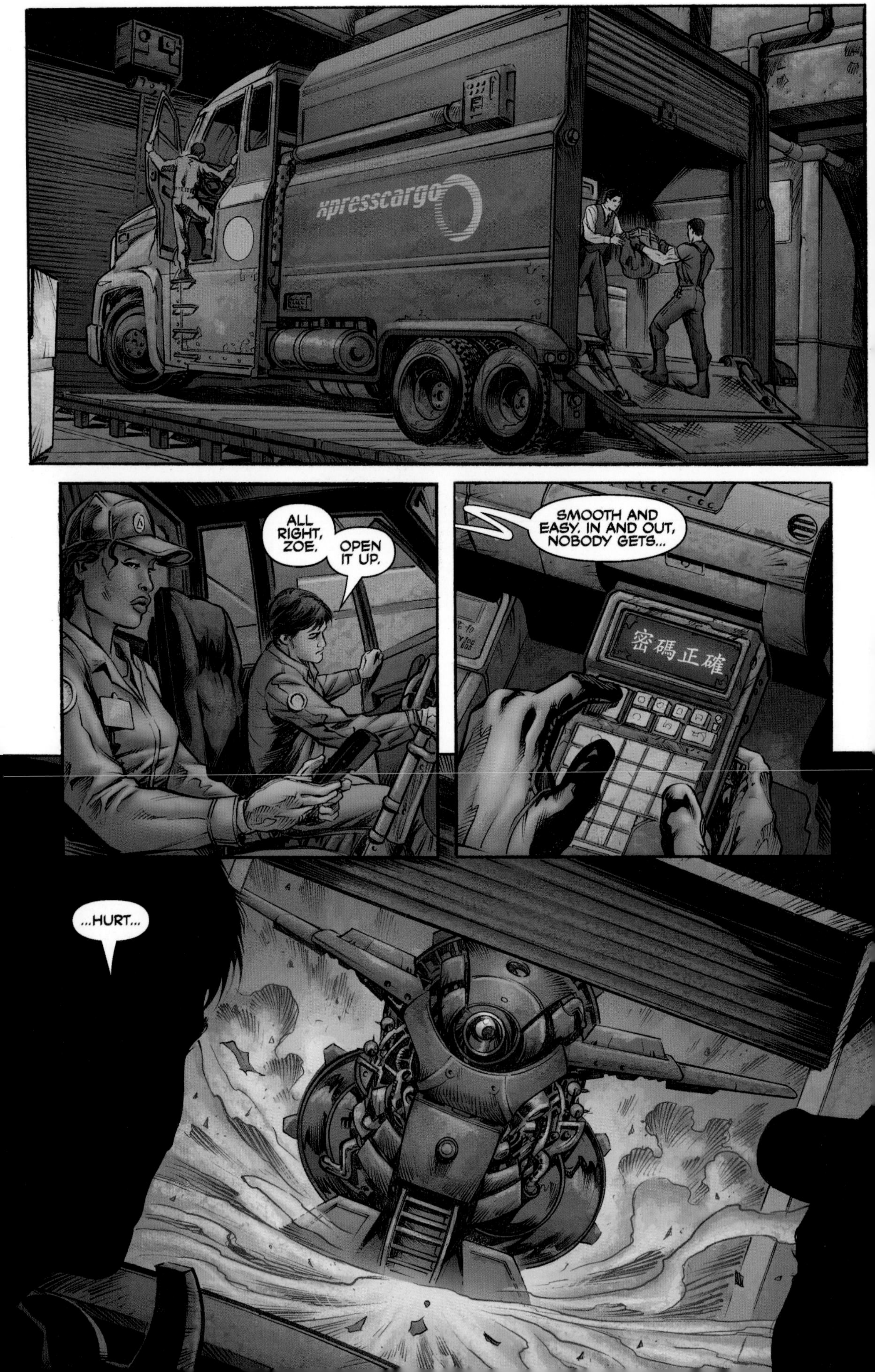
xpresscargo
ALL RIGHT, ZOE,
OPEN IT UP.
SMOOTH AND EASY. IN AND OUT, NOBODY GETS...
密碼正確
...HURT...

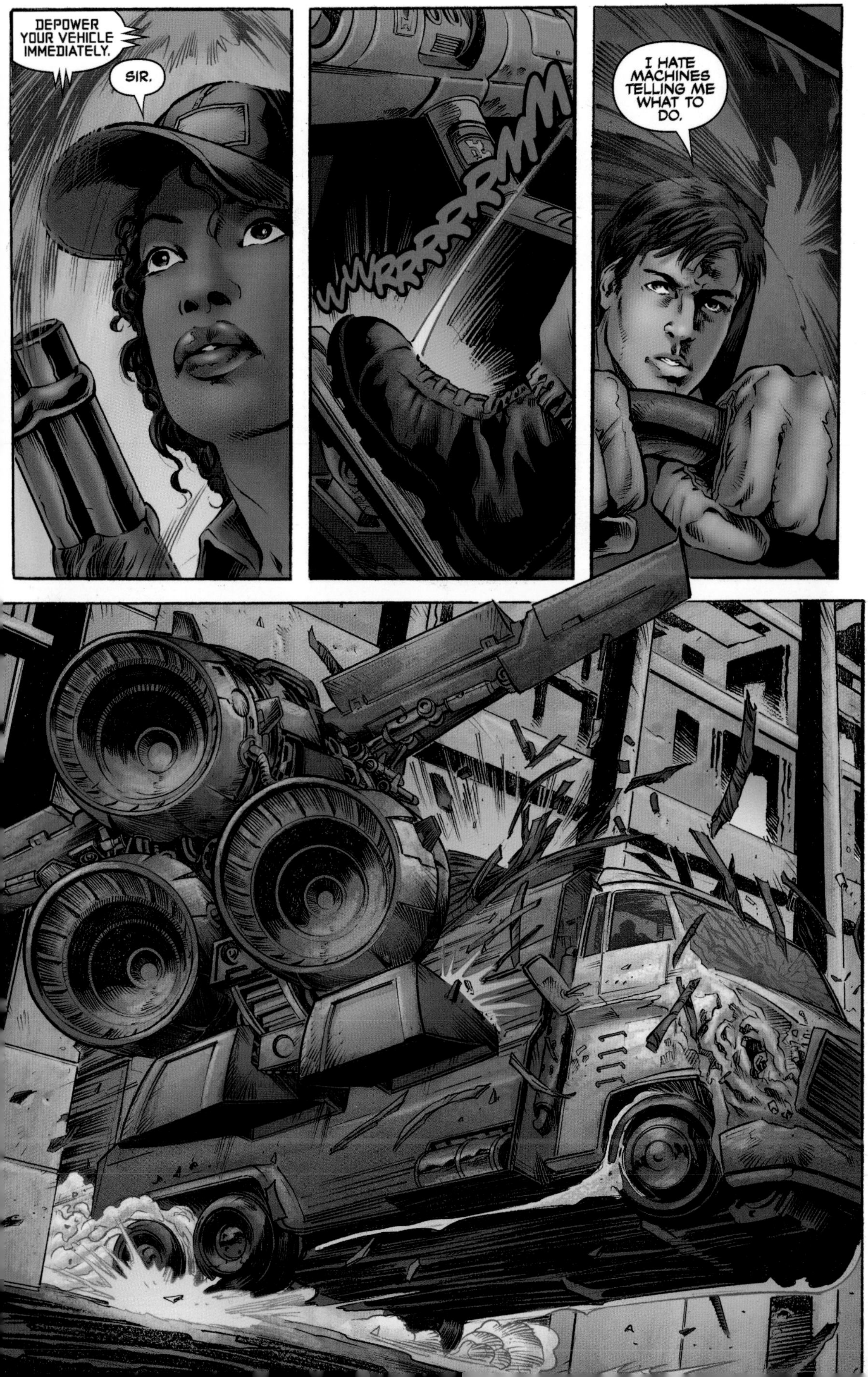
DEPOWER YOUR VEHICLE IMMEDIATELY.
SIR.
WWRRRRRRMM
I HATE MACHINES TELLING ME WHAT TO DO.

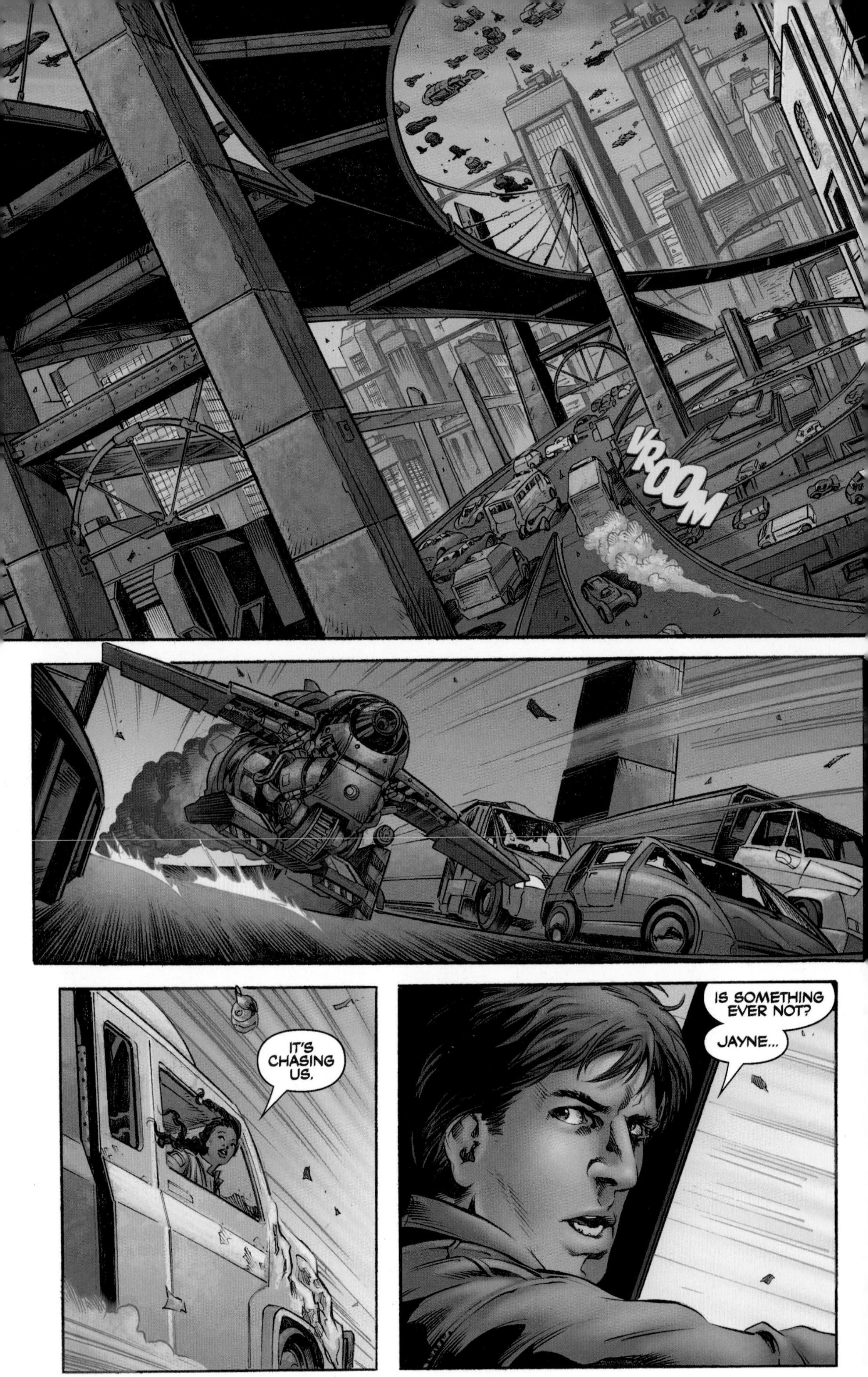
VROOM
IT'S CHASING US.
IS SOMETHING EVER NOT?
JAYNE...

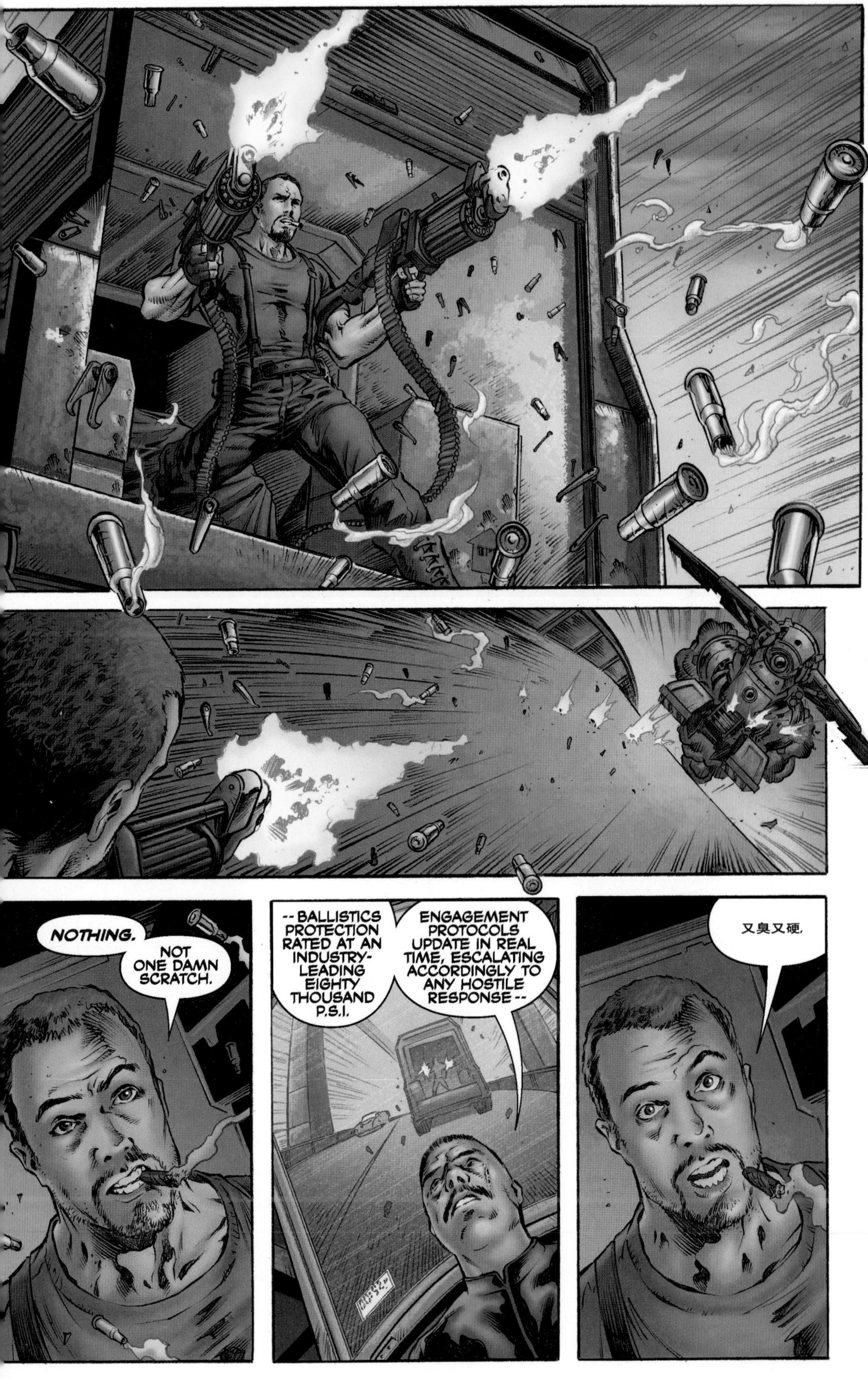
NOTHING.
NOT ONE DAMN SCRATCH.
-- BALLISTICS PROTECTION RATED AT AN INDUSTRY-LEADING EIGHTY THOUSAND P.S.I.
ENGAGEMENT PROTOCOLS UPDATE IN REAL TIME, ESCALATING ACCORDINGLY TO ANY HOSTILE RESPONSE --
又臭又硬,

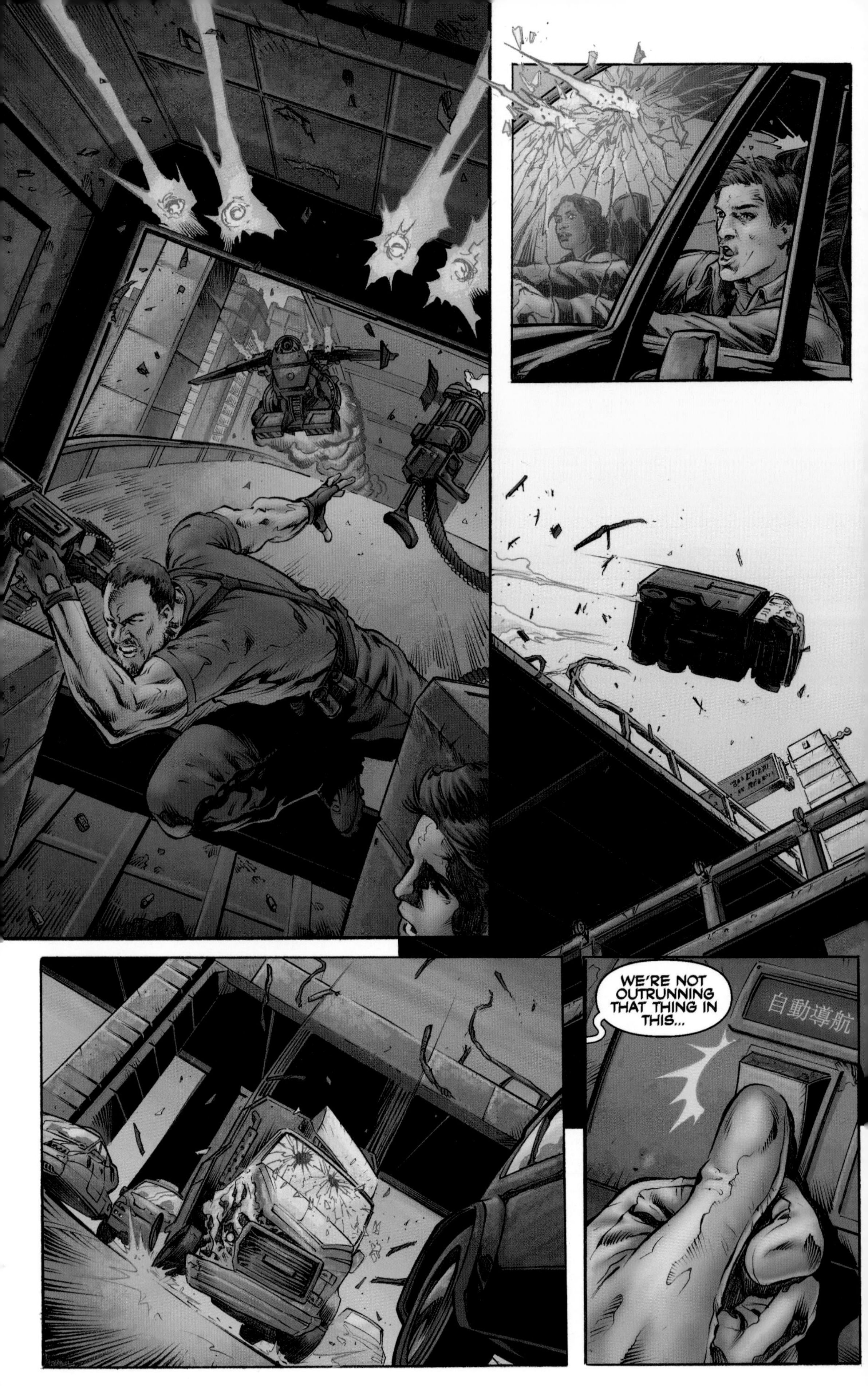
WE'RE NOT OUTRUNNING THAT THING IN THIS...
自動導航

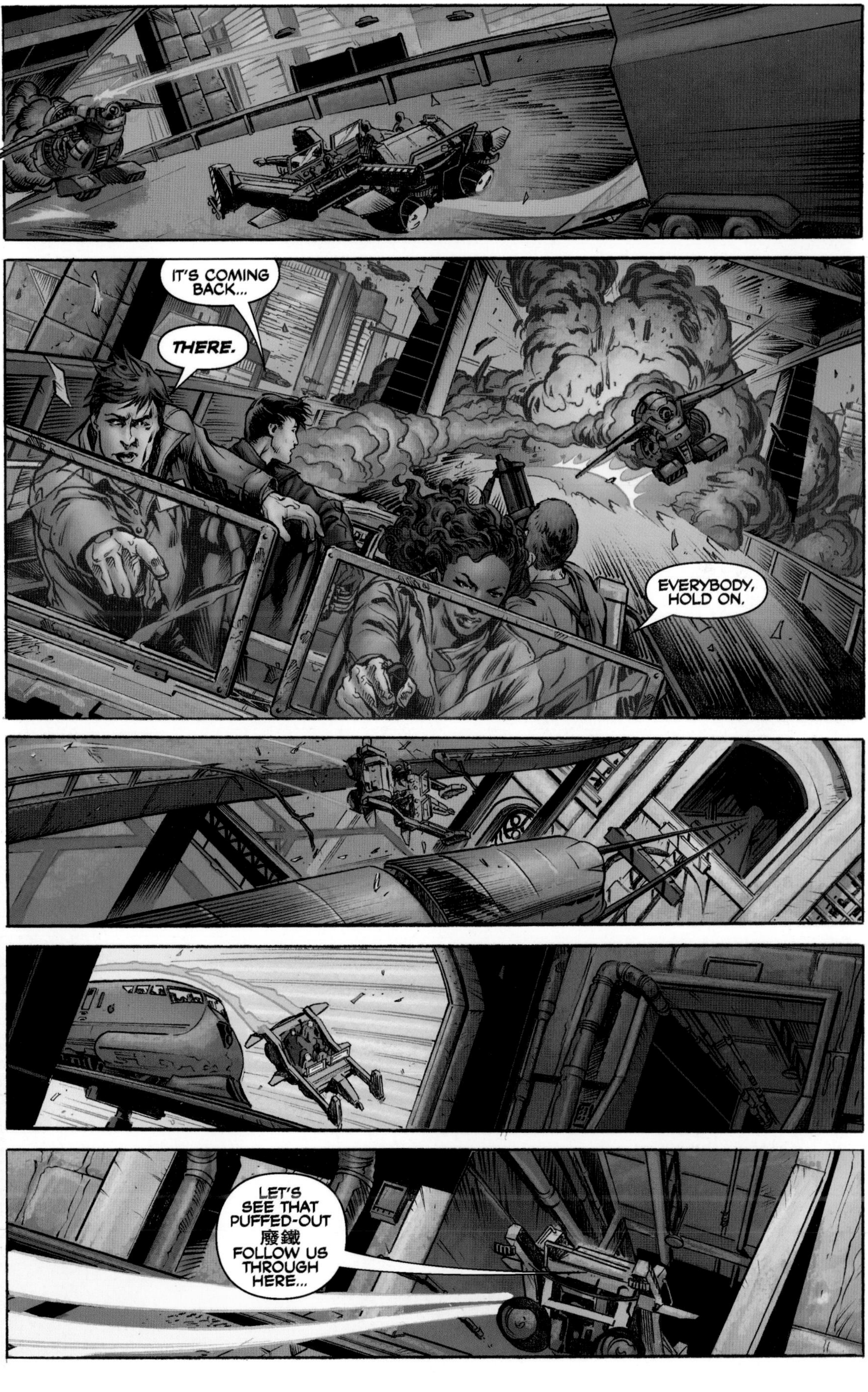
IT'S COMING BACK...
THERE.
EVERYBODY, HOLD ON.
LET'S SEE THAT PUFFED-OUT 廢鐵 FOLLOW US THROUGH HERE...

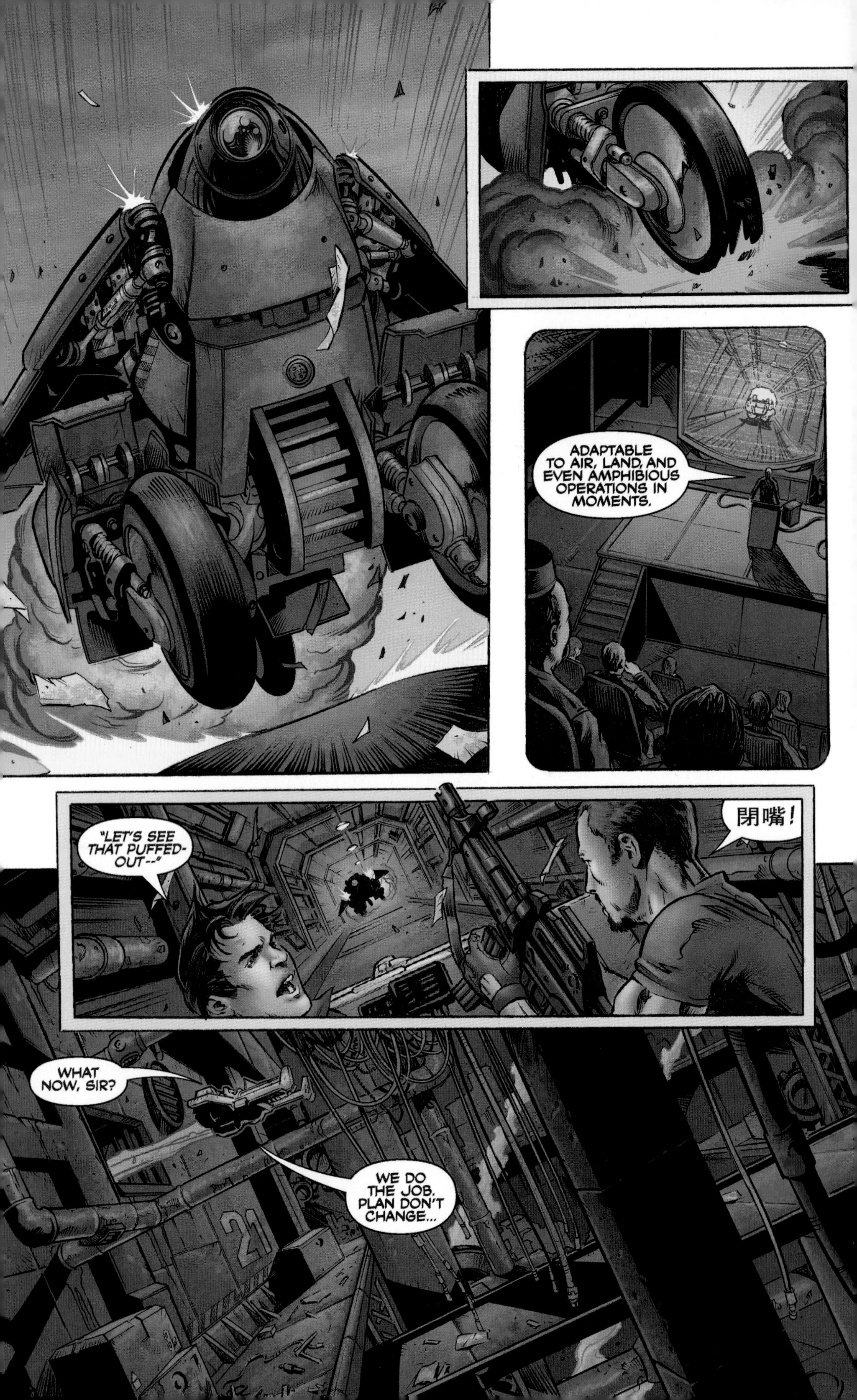
ADAPTABLE TO AIR, LAND, AND EVEN AMPHIBIOUS OPERATIONS IN MOMENTS.
"LET'S SEE THAT PUFFED-OUT--"
閉嘴!
WHAT NOW, SIR?
WE DO THE JOB. PLAN DON'T CHANGE...

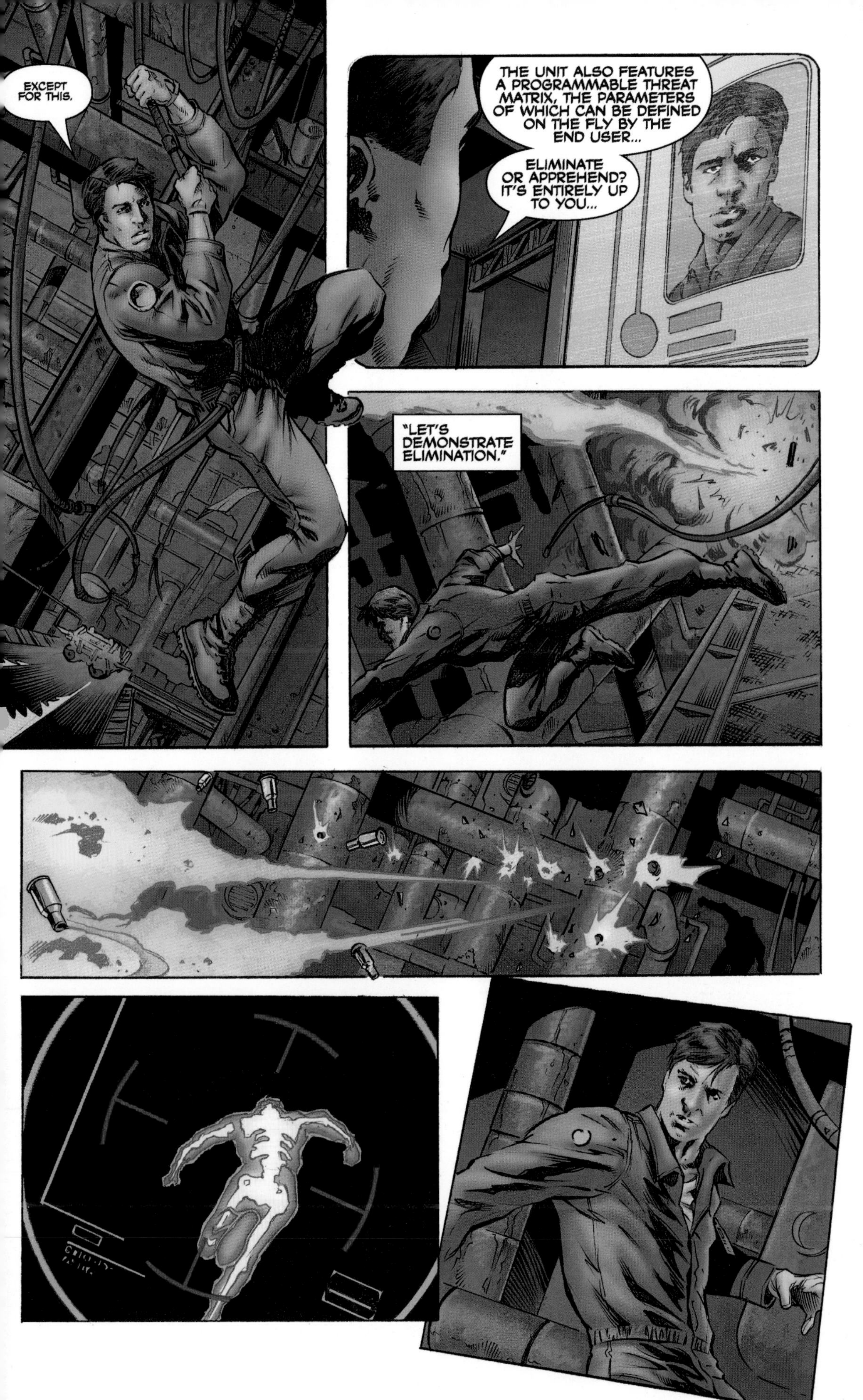
EXCEPT FOR THIS.
THE UNIT ALSO FEATURES A PROGRAMMABLE THREAT MATRIX, THE PARAMETERS OF WHICH CAN BE DEFINED ON THE FLY BY THE END USER...
ELIMINATE OR APPREHEND? IT'S ENTIRELY UP TO YOU...
"LET'S DEMONSTRATE ELIMINATION."

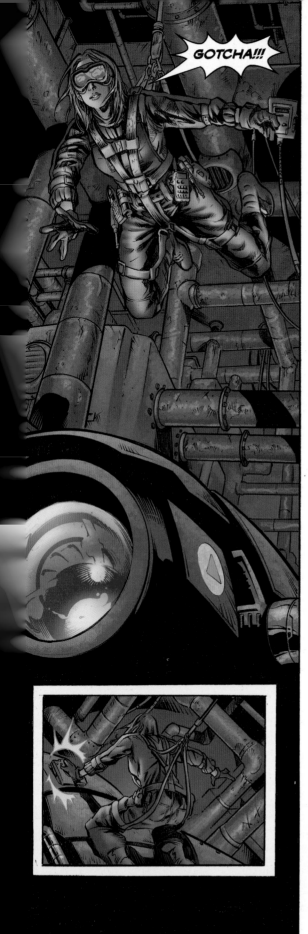

GOTCHA!!!

JEEPERS, CAP'N, DID YOU REALLY HAFTA--

I REALLY DID.

YOU MADE IT.

DON'T SOUND SO DISAPPOINTED, JAYNE.

GIVE KAYLEE A HAND GETTING IT TIED DOWN, AND BE CAREFUL. THING'S WORTH MORE THAN ALL OF US PUT TOGETHER.

WE GOT A DELIVERY TO MAKE.

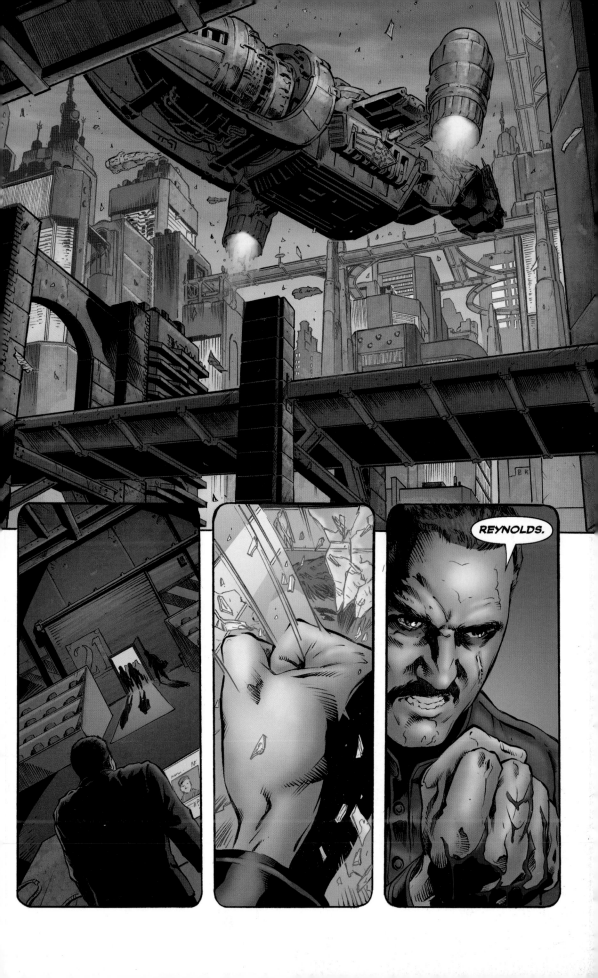

REYNOLDS.

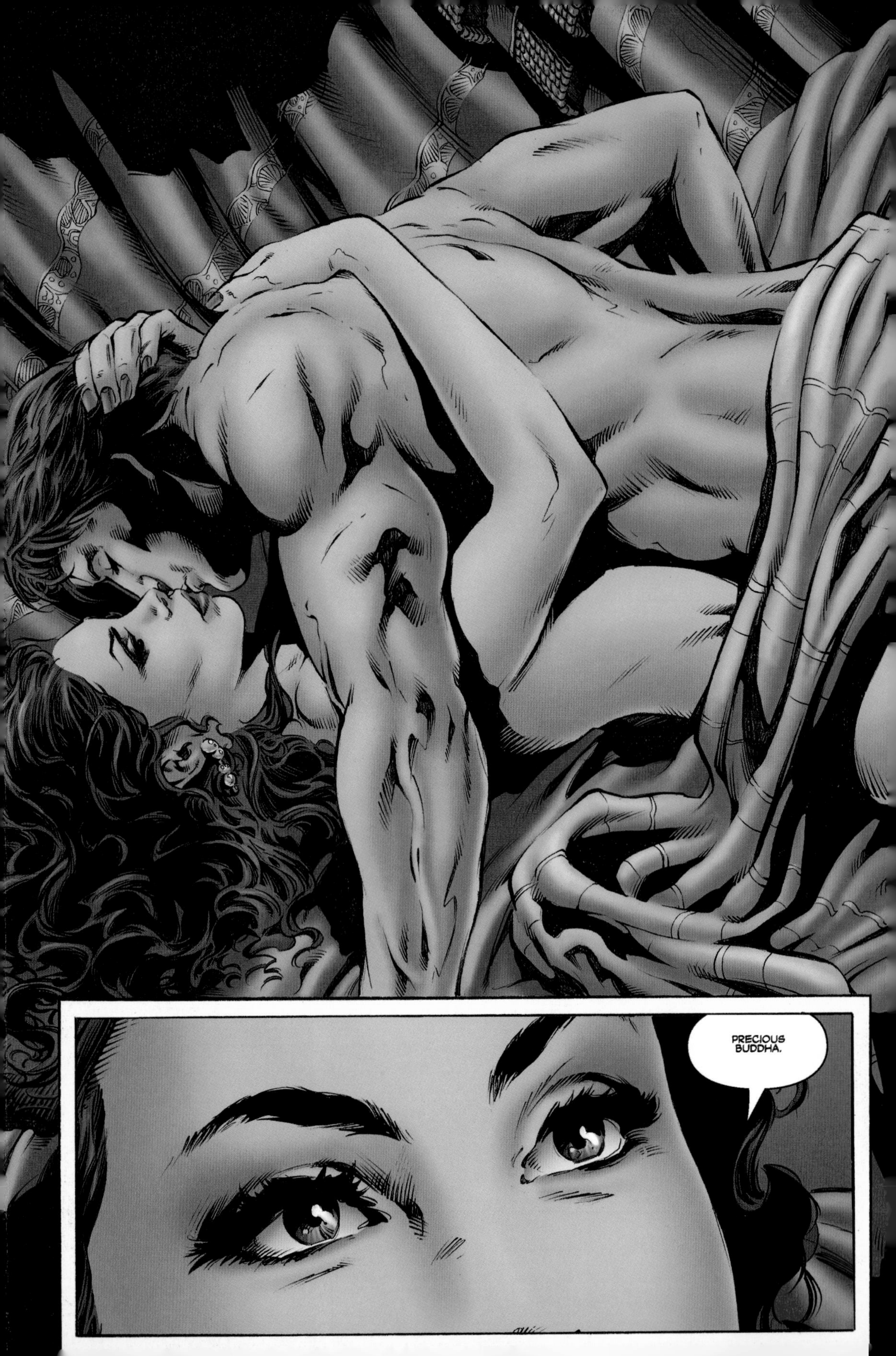
PRECIOUS BUDDHA.

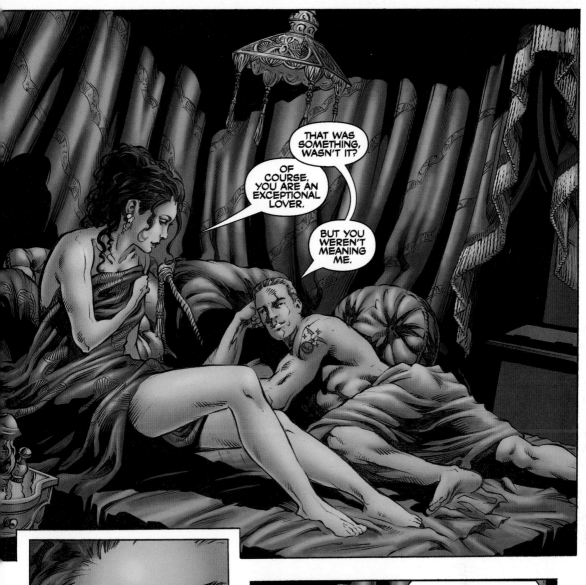

THAT WAS SOMETHING, WASN'T IT?

OF COURSE, YOU ARE AN EXCEPTIONAL LOVER.

BUT YOU WEREN'T MEANING ME.

AND IF YOU WISH TO REMAIN AN EXCEPTIONAL LOVER, WE'RE GOING TO HAVE TO DO SOMETHING ABOUT THAT NERVE CLUSTER I COULD FEEL MISFIRING.

TURN OVER.

I DON'T HOLD IT AGAINST YOU.

BEST NOT TO DWELL ON AN OLD SOLDIER LIKE ME. OR HIS WOUNDS.

THERE'S MUCH MORE TO YOU THAN THAT, EPHRAIM.

AND AS I EXPECTED, YOU'RE COMPLETELY OUT OF ALIGNMENT.

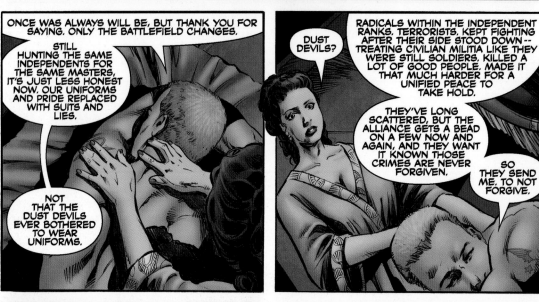

ONCE WAS ALWAYS WILL BE, BUT THANK YOU FOR SAYING. ONLY THE BATTLEFIELD CHANGES.

STILL HUNTING THE SAME INDEPENDENTS FOR THE SAME MASTERS, IT'S JUST LESS HONEST NOW. OUR UNIFORMS AND PRIDE REPLACED WITH SUITS AND LIES.

NOT THAT THE DUST DEVILS EVER BOTHERED TO WEAR UNIFORMS.

DUST DEVILS?

RADICALS WITHIN THE INDEPENDENT RANKS. TERRORISTS, KEPT FIGHTING AFTER THEIR SIDE STOOD DOWN -- TREATING CIVILIAN MILITIA LIKE THEY WERE STILL SOLDIERS, KILLED A LOT OF GOOD PEOPLE, MADE IT THAT MUCH HARDER FOR A UNIFIED PEACE TO TAKE HOLD.

THEY'VE LONG SCATTERED, BUT THE ALLIANCE GETS A BEAD ON A FEW NOW AND AGAIN, AND THEY WANT IT KNOWN THOSE CRIMES ARE NEVER FORGIVEN.

SO THEY SEND ME. TO NOT FORGIVE.

I'M SURPRISED YOU DON'T KNOW THE TERM, *"DUST DEVILS"* IS SPOKEN WITH PRIDE OUT HERE ON THE RIM. LOCAL HEROES TO SOME FOOLS. YOU KNOW THE TYPE:

HEADSTRONG, SUSPICIOUS, USUALLY SOME KIND OF PETTY THIEF --

KARAKK

THANKS FOR THE ADJUSTMENT. I FEEL A WORLD BETTER ALREADY.

ANYTIME.

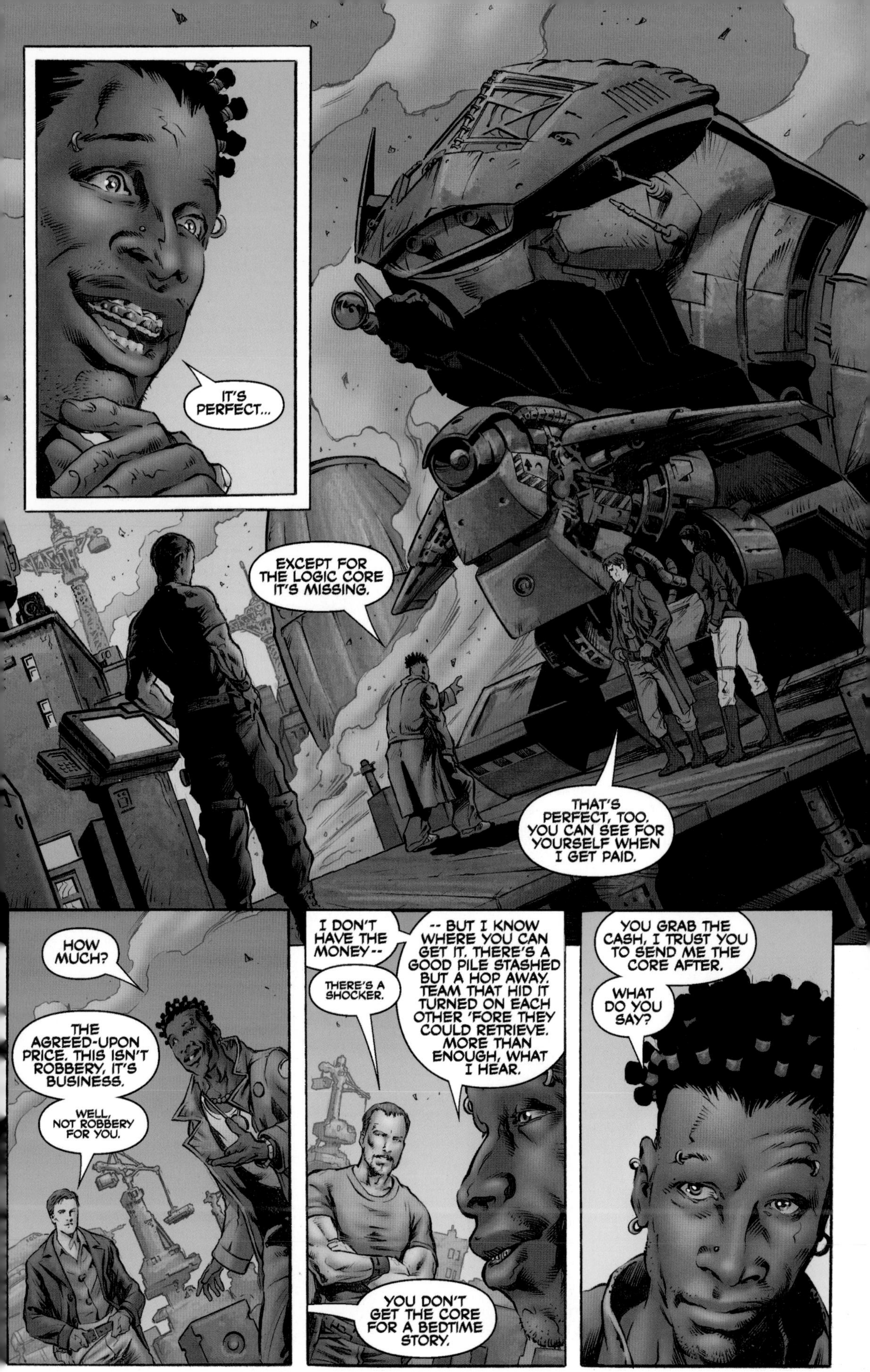
IT'S PERFECT...
EXCEPT FOR THE LOGIC CORE IT'S MISSING.
THAT'S PERFECT, TOO. YOU CAN SEE FOR YOURSELF WHEN I GET PAID.
HOW MUCH?
THE AGREED-UPON PRICE. THIS ISN'T ROBBERY, IT'S BUSINESS.
WELL, NOT ROBBERY FOR YOU.
I DON'T HAVE THE MONEY--
THERE'S A SHOCKER.
-- BUT I KNOW WHERE YOU CAN GET IT. THERE'S A GOOD PILE STASHED BUT A HOP AWAY. TEAM THAT HID IT TURNED ON EACH OTHER 'FORE THEY COULD RETRIEVE. MORE THAN ENOUGH, WHAT I HEAR.
YOU DON'T GET THE CORE FOR A BEDTIME STORY.
YOU GRAB THE CASH, I TRUST YOU TO SEND ME THE CORE AFTER.
WHAT DO YOU SAY?

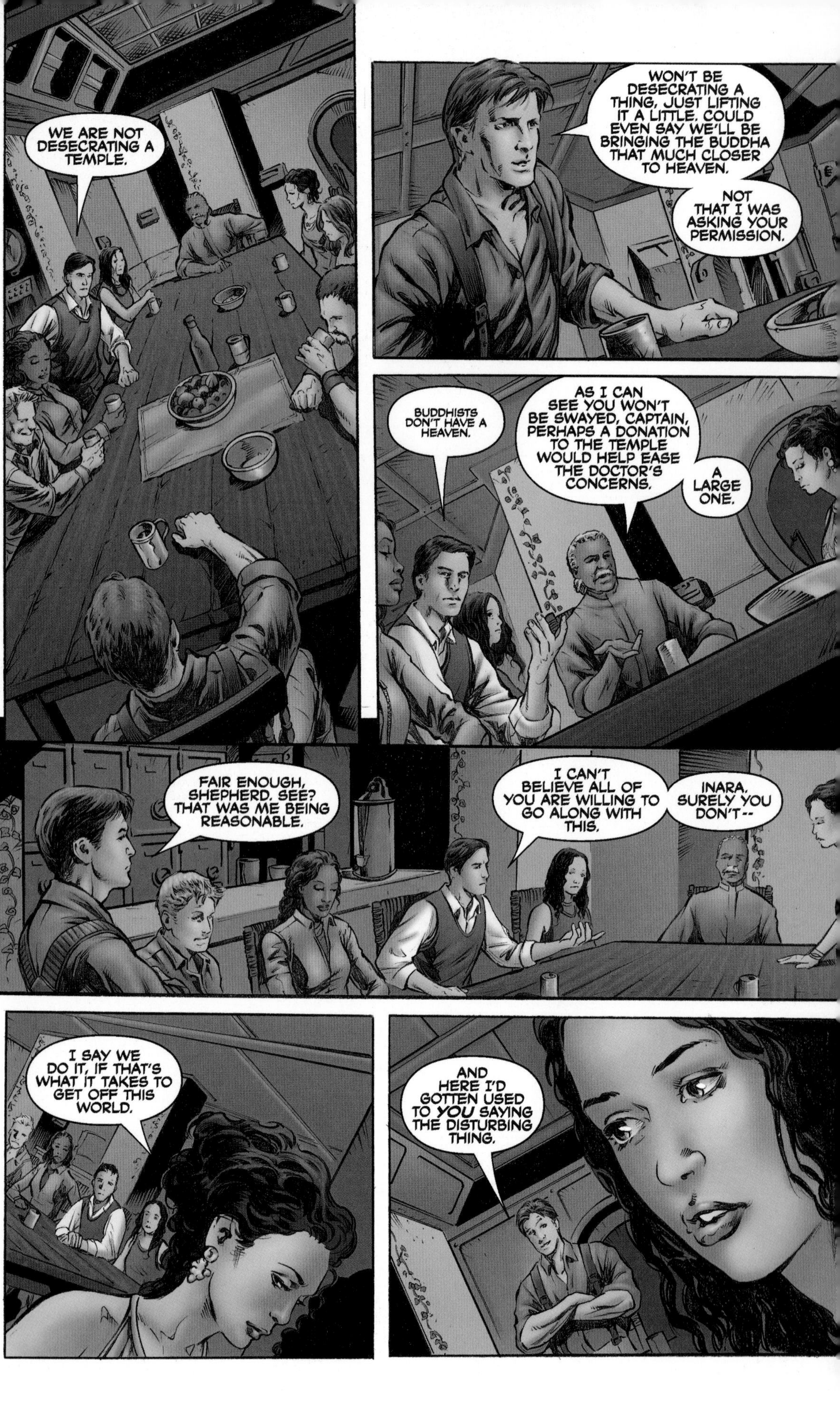
WE ARE NOT DESECRATING A TEMPLE.
WON'T BE DESECRATING A THING, JUST LIFTING IT A LITTLE. COULD EVEN SAY WE'LL BE BRINGING THE BUDDHA THAT MUCH CLOSER TO HEAVEN.
NOT THAT I WAS ASKING YOUR PERMISSION.
BUDDHISTS DON'T HAVE A HEAVEN.
AS I CAN SEE YOU WON'T BE SWAYED, CAPTAIN, PERHAPS A DONATION TO THE TEMPLE WOULD HELP EASE THE DOCTOR'S CONCERNS.
A LARGE ONE.
FAIR ENOUGH, SHEPHERD. SEE? THAT WAS ME BEING REASONABLE.
I CAN'T BELIEVE ALL OF YOU ARE WILLING TO GO ALONG WITH THIS.
INARA, SURELY YOU DON'T--
I SAY WE DO IT, IF THAT'S WHAT IT TAKES TO GET OFF THIS WORLD.
AND HERE I'D GOTTEN USED TO *YOU* SAYING THE DISTURBING THING.

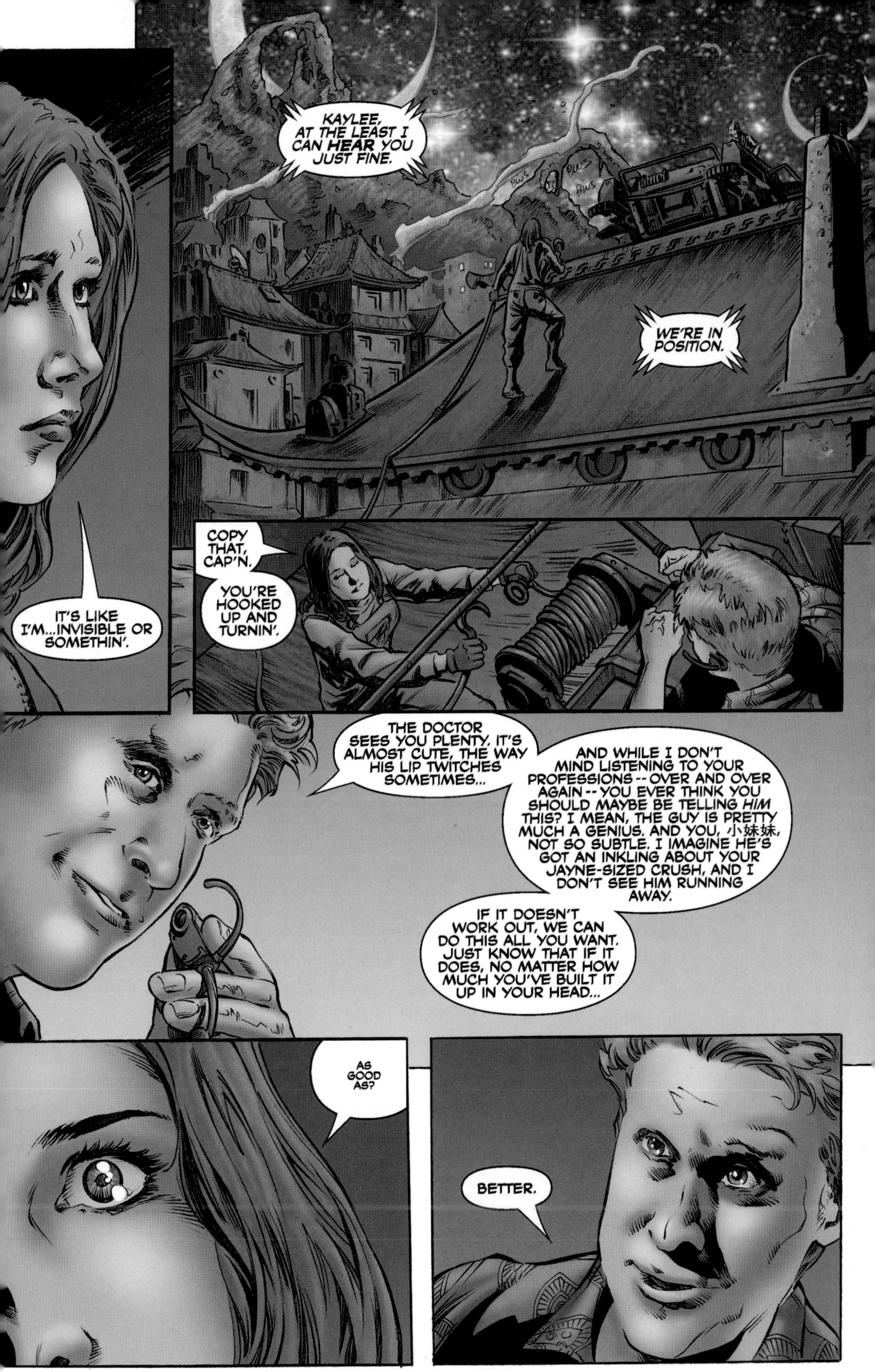

KAYLEE, AT THE LEAST I CAN HEAR YOU JUST FINE.
WE'RE IN POSITION.
IT'S LIKE I'M...INVISIBLE OR SOMETHIN'.
COPY THAT, CAP'N.
YOU'RE HOOKED UP AND TURNIN'.
THE DOCTOR SEES YOU PLENTY. IT'S ALMOST CUTE, THE WAY HIS LIP TWITCHES SOMETIMES...
AND WHILE I DON'T MIND LISTENING TO YOUR PROFESSIONS -- OVER AND OVER AGAIN -- YOU EVER THINK YOU SHOULD MAYBE BE TELLING *HIM* THIS? I MEAN, THE GUY IS PRETTY MUCH A GENIUS. AND YOU, 小妹妹, NOT SO SUBTLE. I IMAGINE HE'S GOT AN INKLING ABOUT YOUR JAYNE-SIZED CRUSH, AND I DON'T SEE HIM RUNNING AWAY.
IF IT DOESN'T WORK OUT, WE CAN DO THIS ALL YOU WANT. JUST KNOW THAT IF IT DOES, NO MATTER HOW MUCH YOU'VE BUILT IT UP IN YOUR HEAD...
AS GOOD AS?
BETTER.

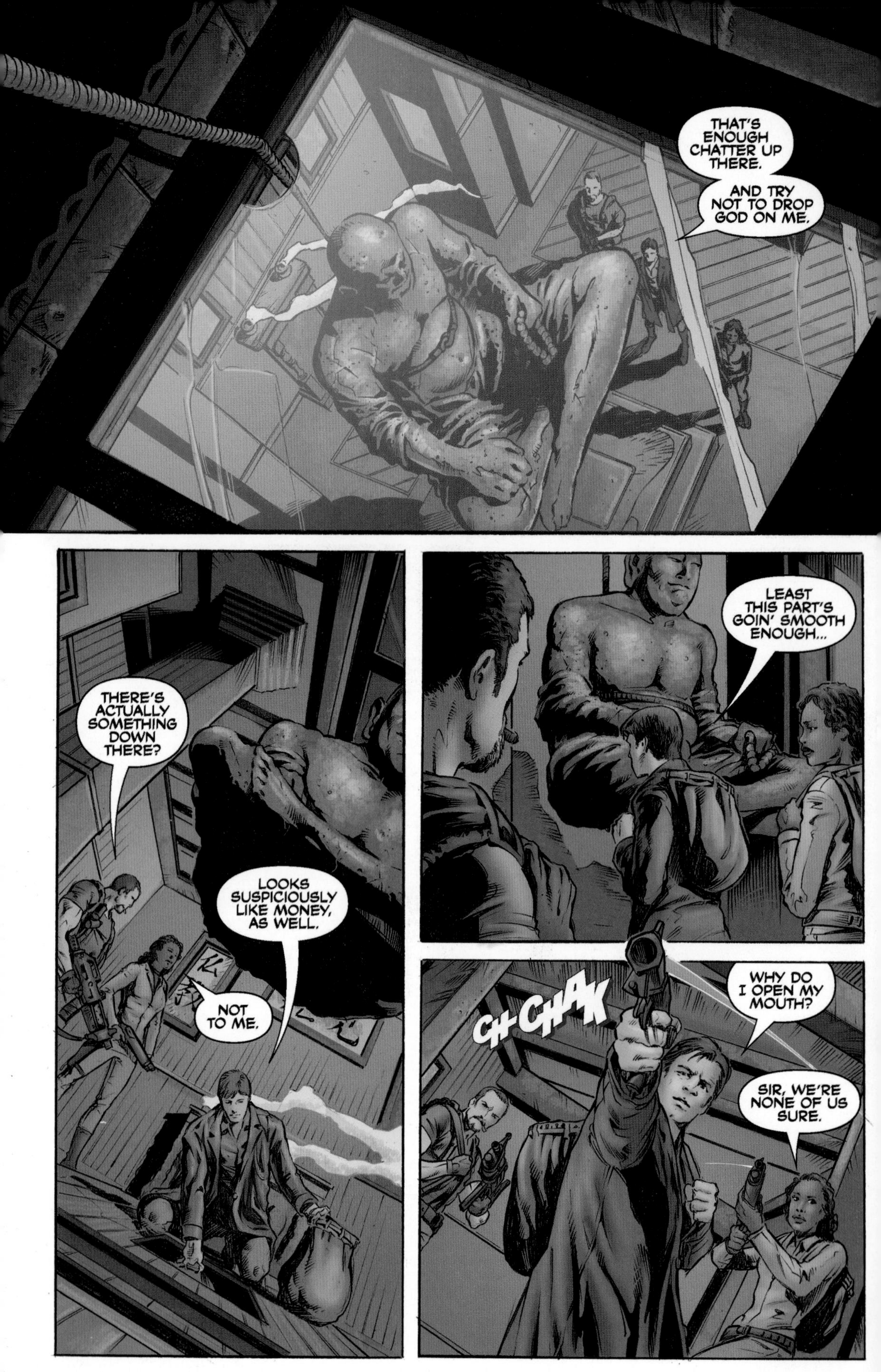

THAT'S ENOUGH CHATTER UP THERE.
AND TRY NOT TO DROP GOD ON ME.
THERE'S ACTUALLY SOMETHING DOWN THERE?
LOOKS SUSPICIOUSLY LIKE MONEY, AS WELL.
NOT TO ME.
LEAST THIS PART'S GOIN' SMOOTH ENOUGH...
CH-CHAK
WHY DO I OPEN MY MOUTH?
SIR, WE'RE NONE OF US SURE.

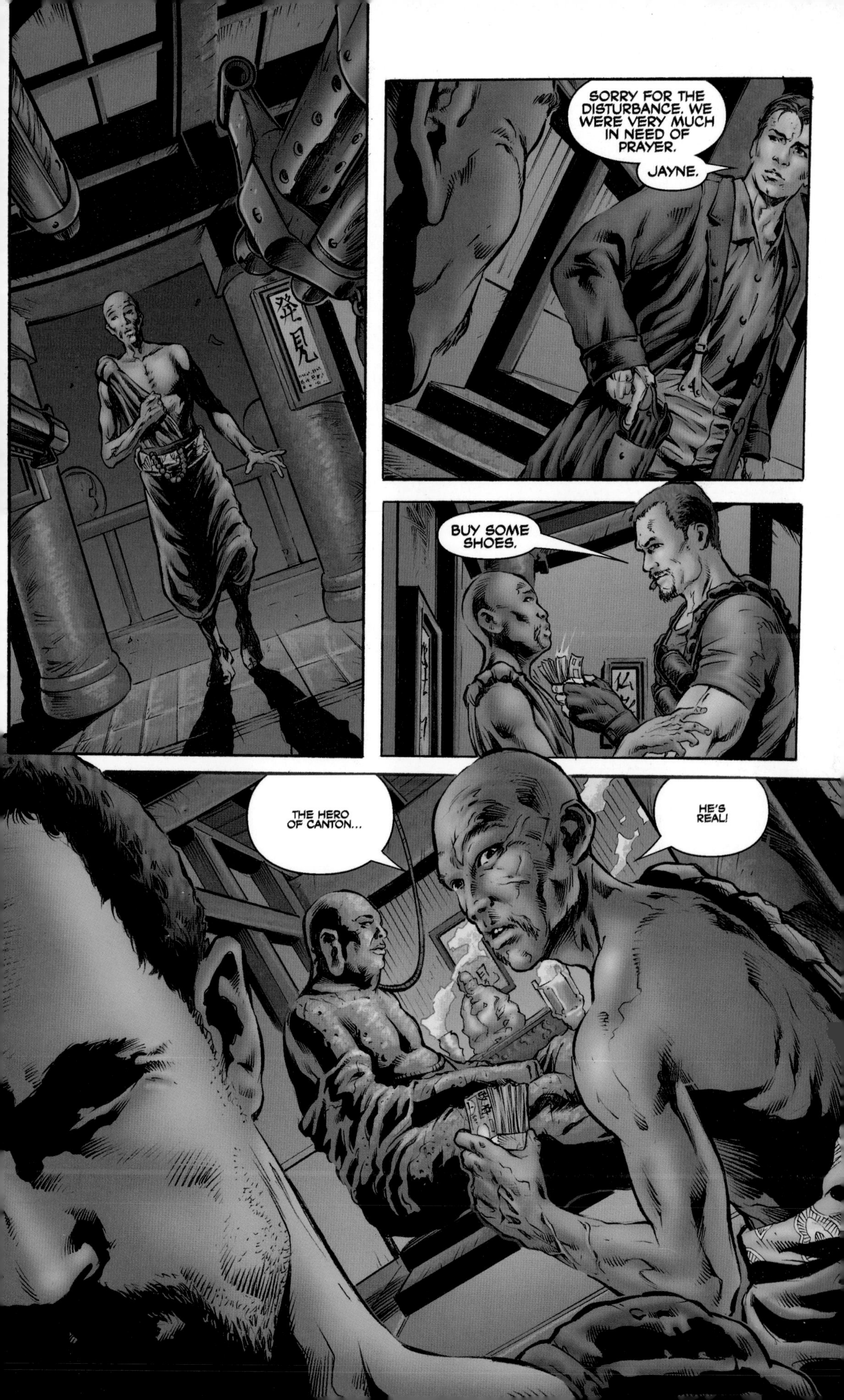
発見
SORRY FOR THE DISTURBANCE. WE WERE VERY MUCH IN NEED OF PRAYER.
JAYNE.
BUY SOME SHOES.
THE HERO OF CANTON...
HE'S REAL!

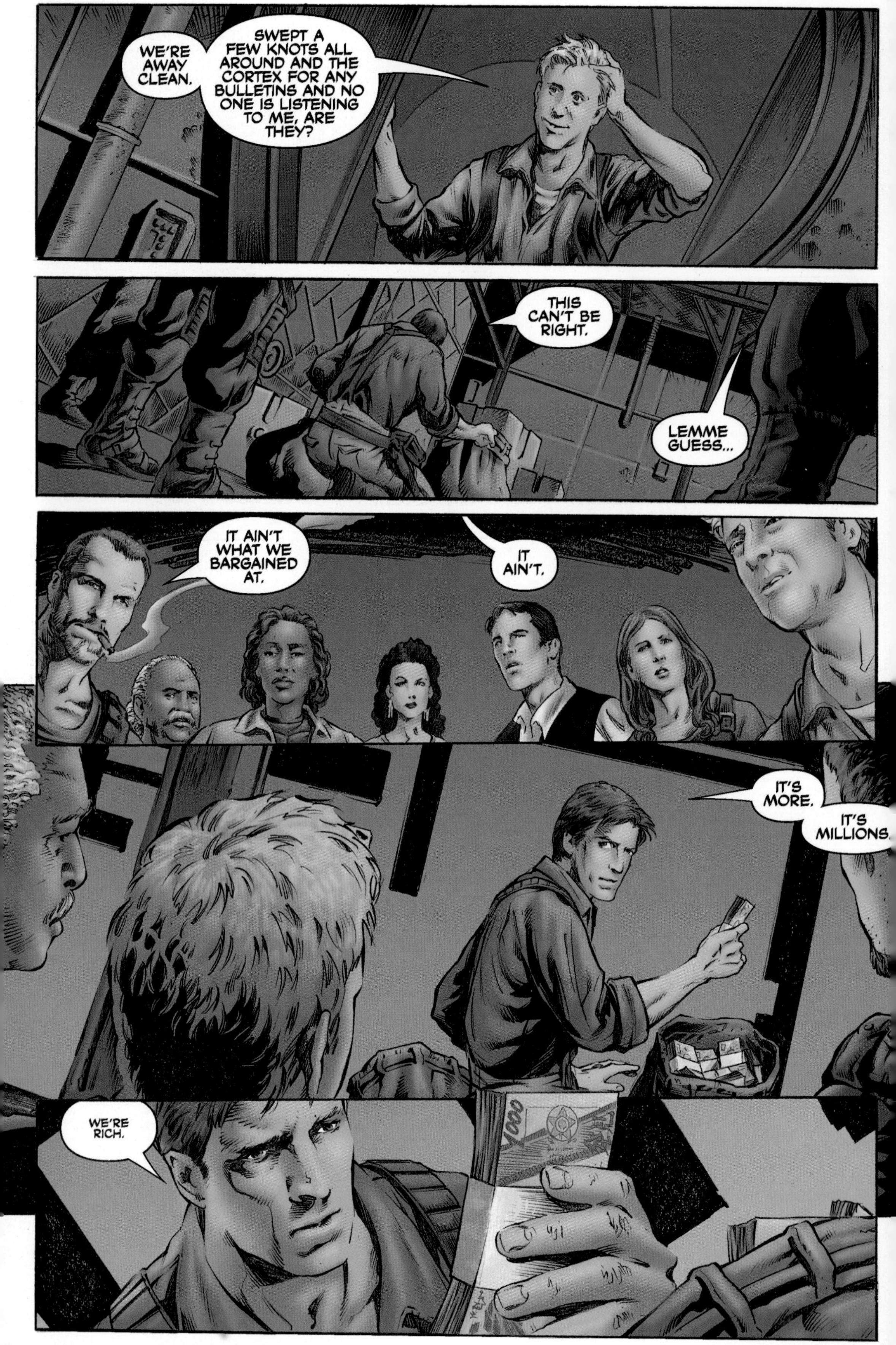
WE'RE AWAY CLEAN.
SWEPT A FEW KNOTS ALL AROUND AND THE CORTEX FOR ANY BULLETINS AND NO ONE IS LISTENING TO ME, ARE THEY?
THIS CAN'T BE RIGHT.
LEMME GUESS...
IT AIN'T WHAT WE BARGAINED AT.
IT AIN'T.
IT'S MORE.
IT'S MILLIONS.
WE'RE RICH.

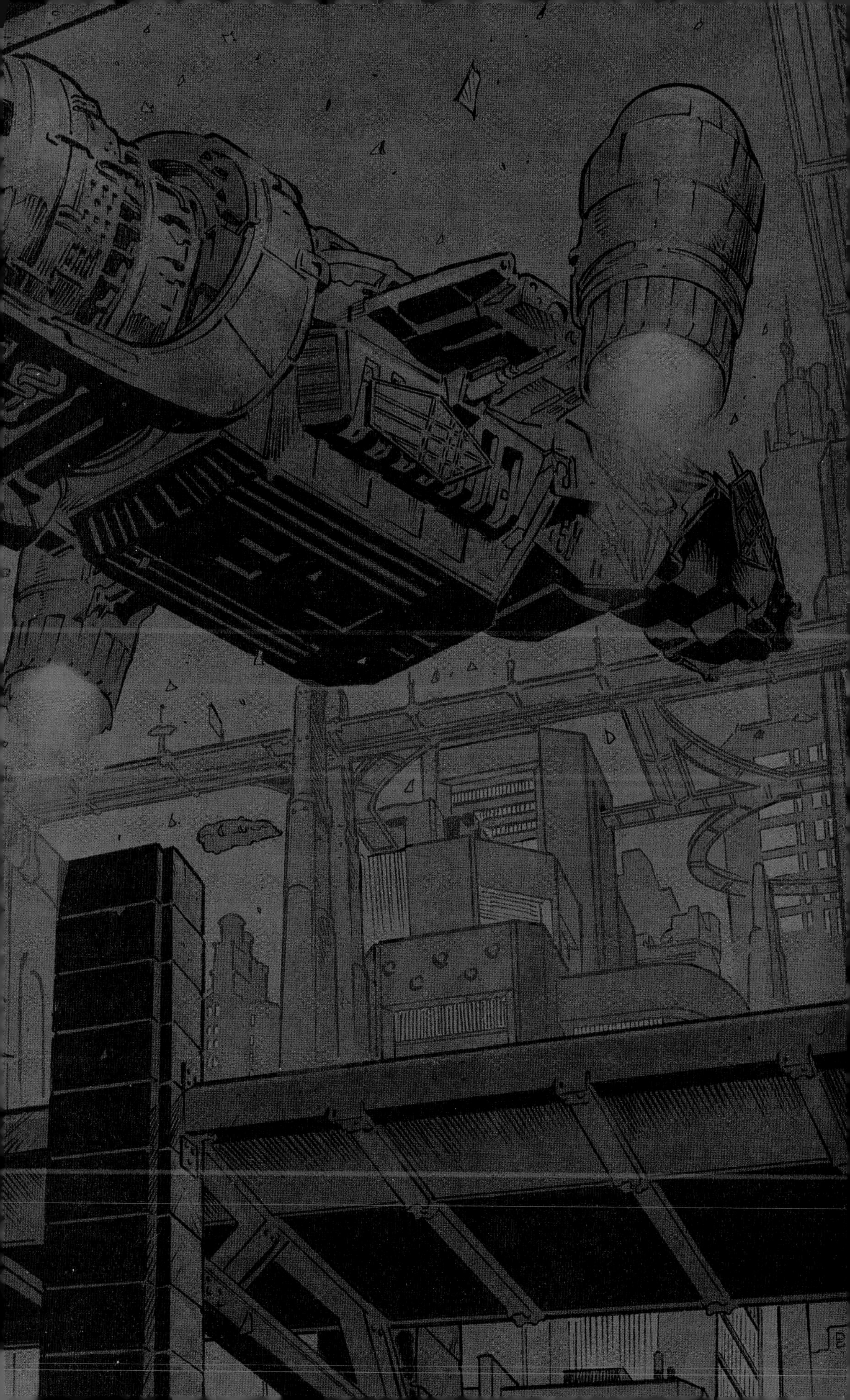

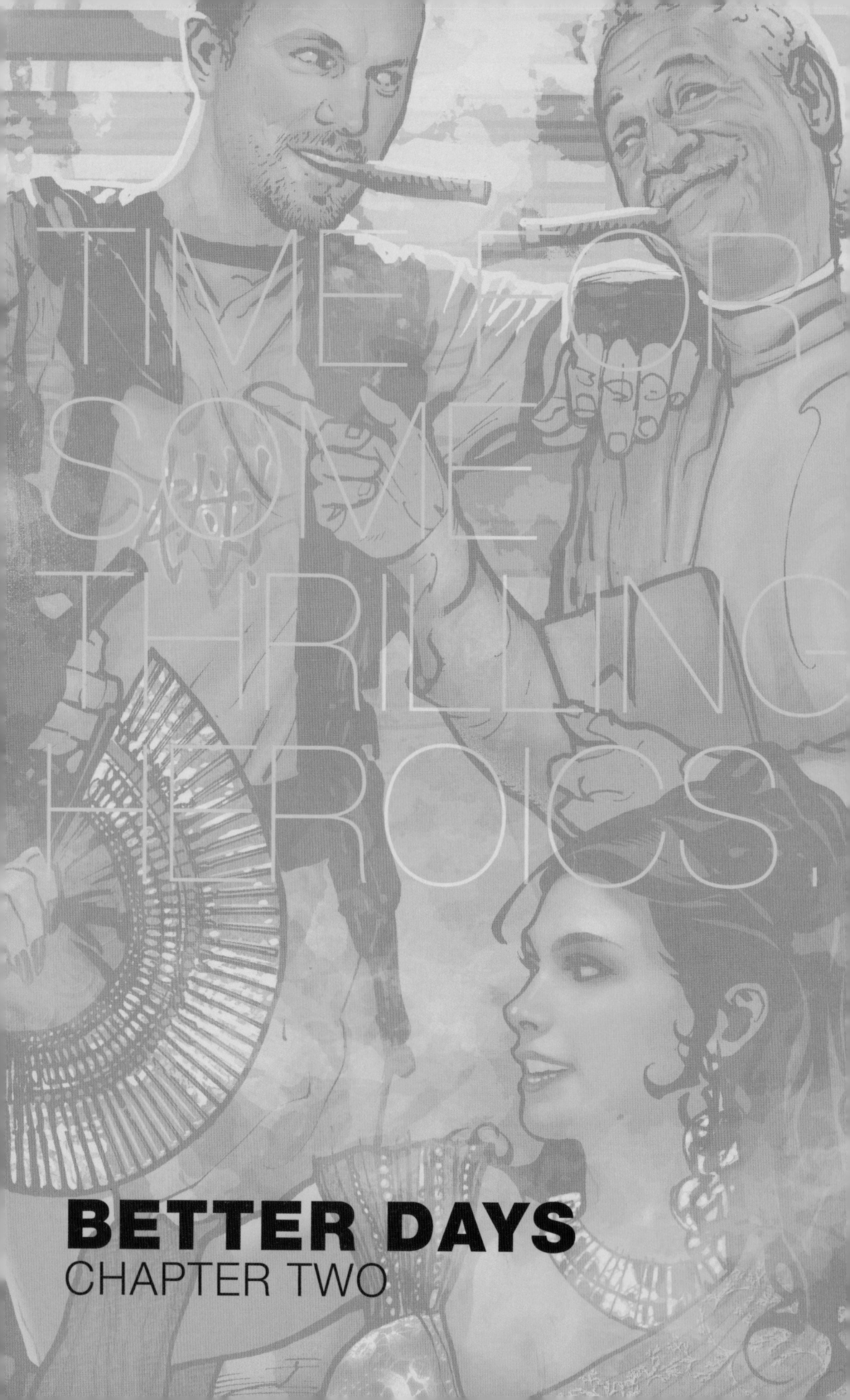
TIME FOR SOME THRILLING HEROICS.

BETTER DAYS
CHAPTER TWO

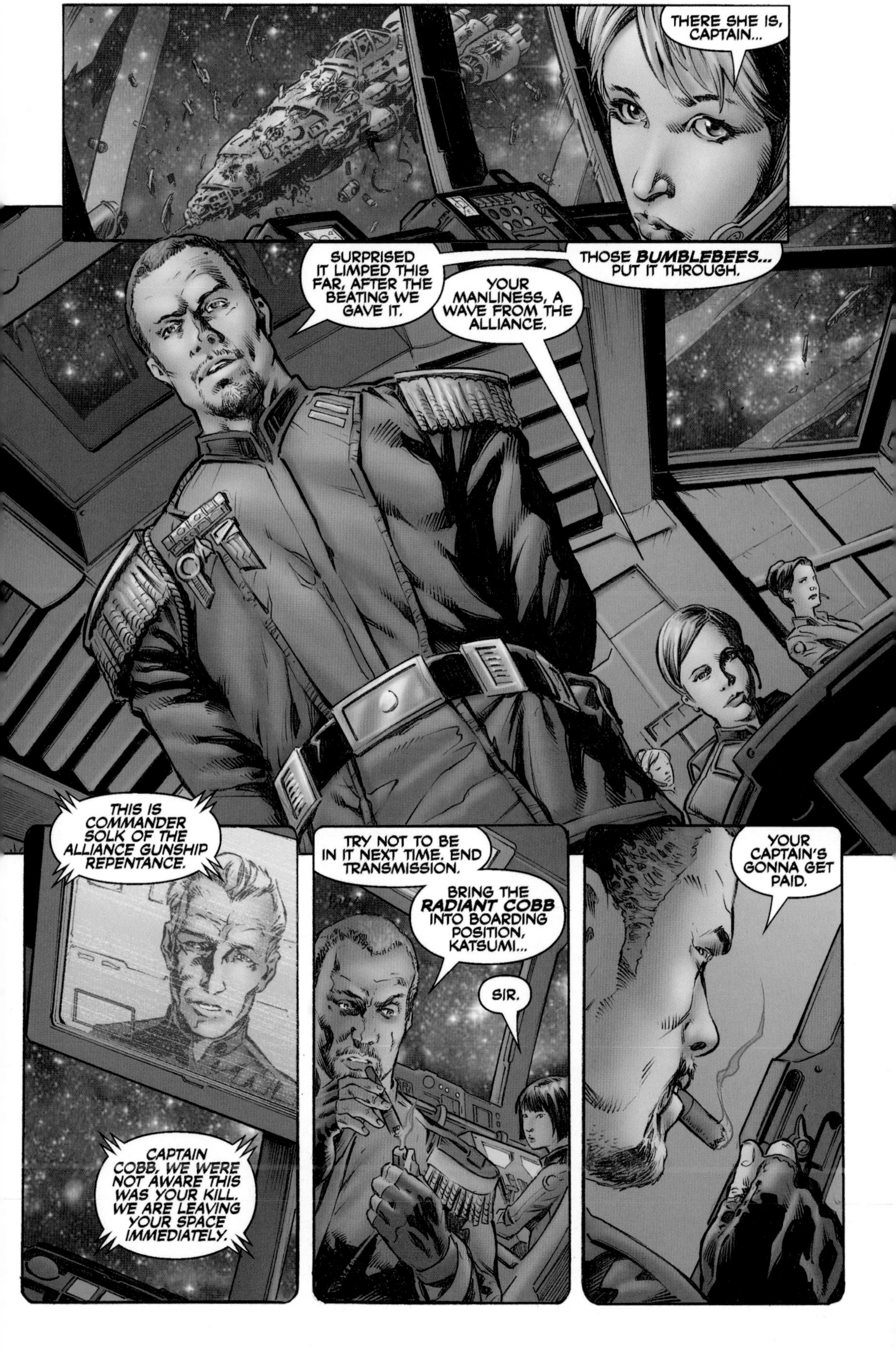
THERE SHE IS, CAPTAIN...
SURPRISED IT LIMPED THIS FAR, AFTER THE BEATING WE GAVE IT.
THOSE BUMBLEBEES... PUT IT THROUGH.
YOUR MANLINESS, A WAVE FROM THE ALLIANCE.
THIS IS COMMANDER SOLK OF THE ALLIANCE GUNSHIP REPENTANCE.
CAPTAIN COBB, WE WERE NOT AWARE THIS WAS YOUR KILL. WE ARE LEAVING YOUR SPACE IMMEDIATELY.
TRY NOT TO BE IN IT NEXT TIME. END TRANSMISSION.
BRING THE RADIANT COBB INTO BOARDING POSITION, KATSUMI...
SIR.
YOUR CAPTAIN'S GONNA GET PAID.

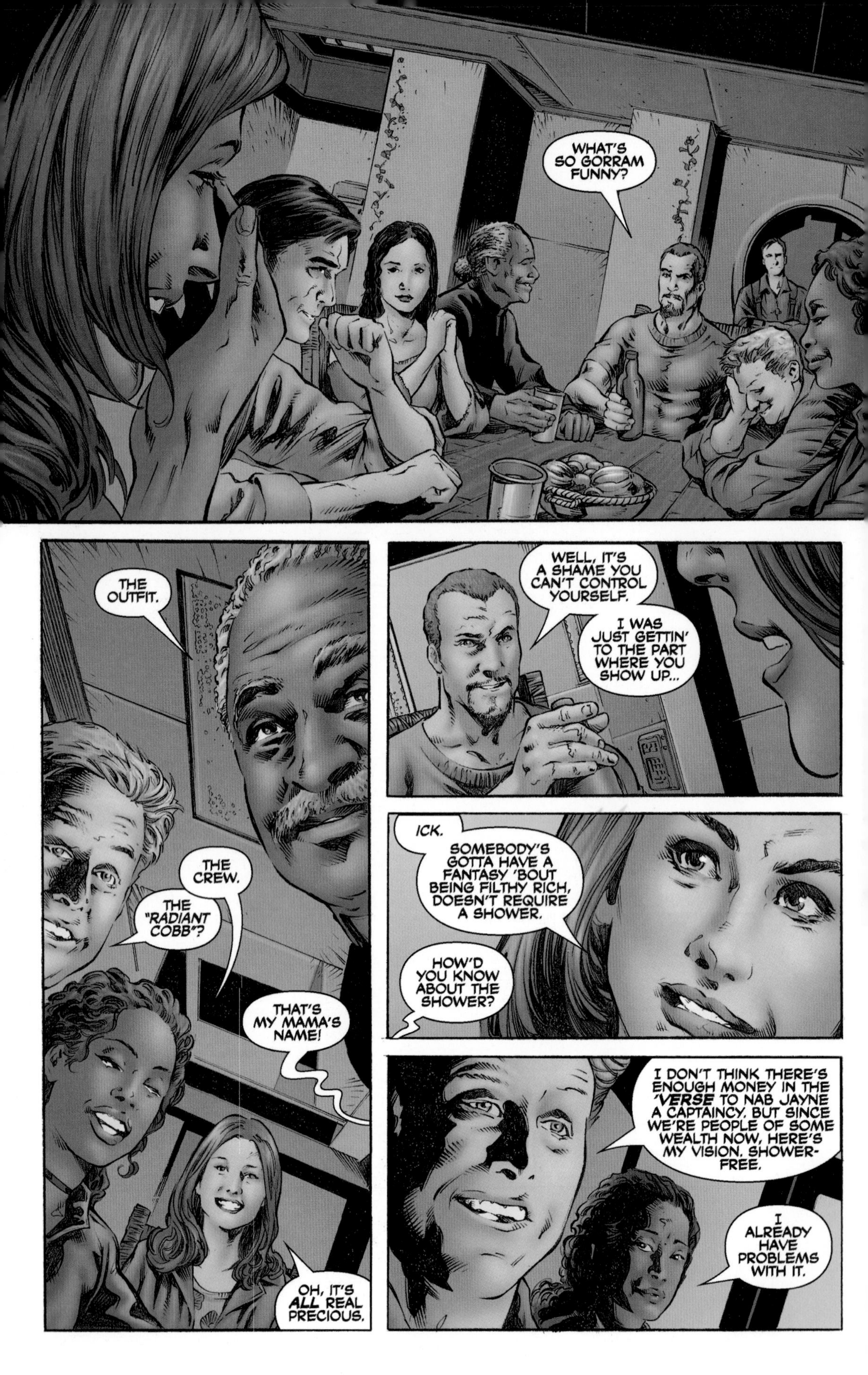
WHAT'S SO GORRAM FUNNY?
THE OUTFIT.
THE CREW.
THE "RADIANT COBB"?
THAT'S MY MAMA'S NAME!
OH, IT'S ALL REAL PRECIOUS.
WELL, IT'S A SHAME YOU CAN'T CONTROL YOURSELF.
I WAS JUST GETTIN' TO THE PART WHERE YOU SHOW UP...
ICK.
SOMEBODY'S GOTTA HAVE A FANTASY 'BOUT BEING FILTHY RICH, DOESN'T REQUIRE A SHOWER.
HOW'D YOU KNOW ABOUT THE SHOWER?
I DON'T THINK THERE'S ENOUGH MONEY IN THE 'VERSE TO NAB JAYNE A CAPTAINCY. BUT SINCE WE'RE PEOPLE OF SOME WEALTH NOW, HERE'S MY VISION. SHOWER-FREE.
I ALREADY HAVE PROBLEMS WITH IT.

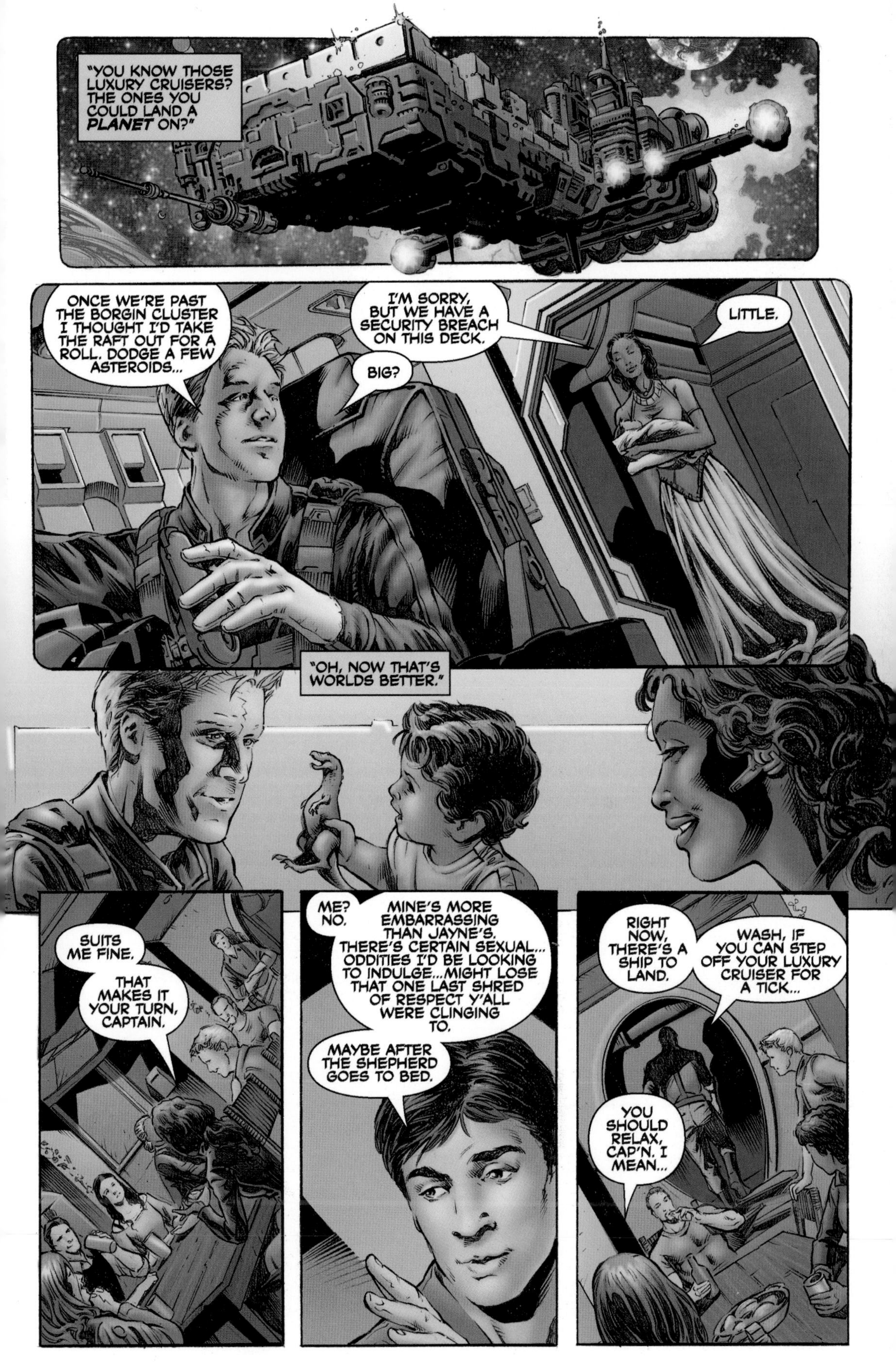
"YOU KNOW THOSE LUXURY CRUISERS? THE ONES YOU COULD LAND A PLANET ON?"
ONCE WE'RE PAST THE BORGIN CLUSTER I THOUGHT I'D TAKE THE RAFT OUT FOR A ROLL. DODGE A FEW ASTEROIDS...
I'M SORRY, BUT WE HAVE A SECURITY BREACH ON THIS DECK.
BIG?
LITTLE.
"OH, NOW THAT'S WORLDS BETTER."
SUITS ME FINE.
THAT MAKES IT YOUR TURN, CAPTAIN.
ME? NO.
MINE'S MORE EMBARRASSING THAN JAYNE'S. THERE'S CERTAIN SEXUAL... ODDITIES I'D BE LOOKING TO INDULGE...MIGHT LOSE THAT ONE LAST SHRED OF RESPECT Y'ALL WERE CLINGING TO.
MAYBE AFTER THE SHEPHERD GOES TO BED.
RIGHT NOW, THERE'S A SHIP TO LAND.
WASH, IF YOU CAN STEP OFF YOUR LUXURY CRUISER FOR A TICK...
YOU SHOULD RELAX, CAP'N. I MEAN...

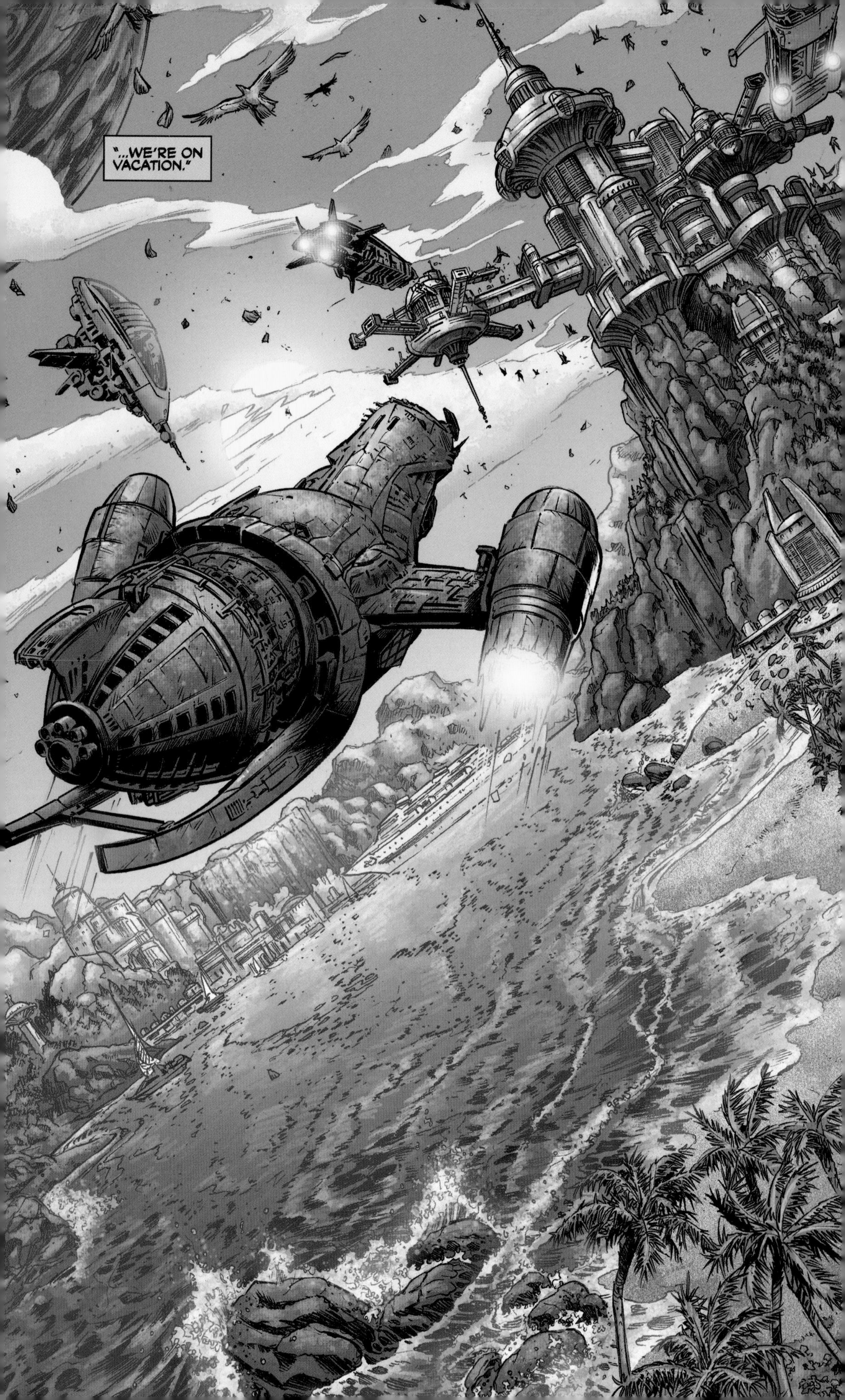
"...WE'RE ON VACATION."

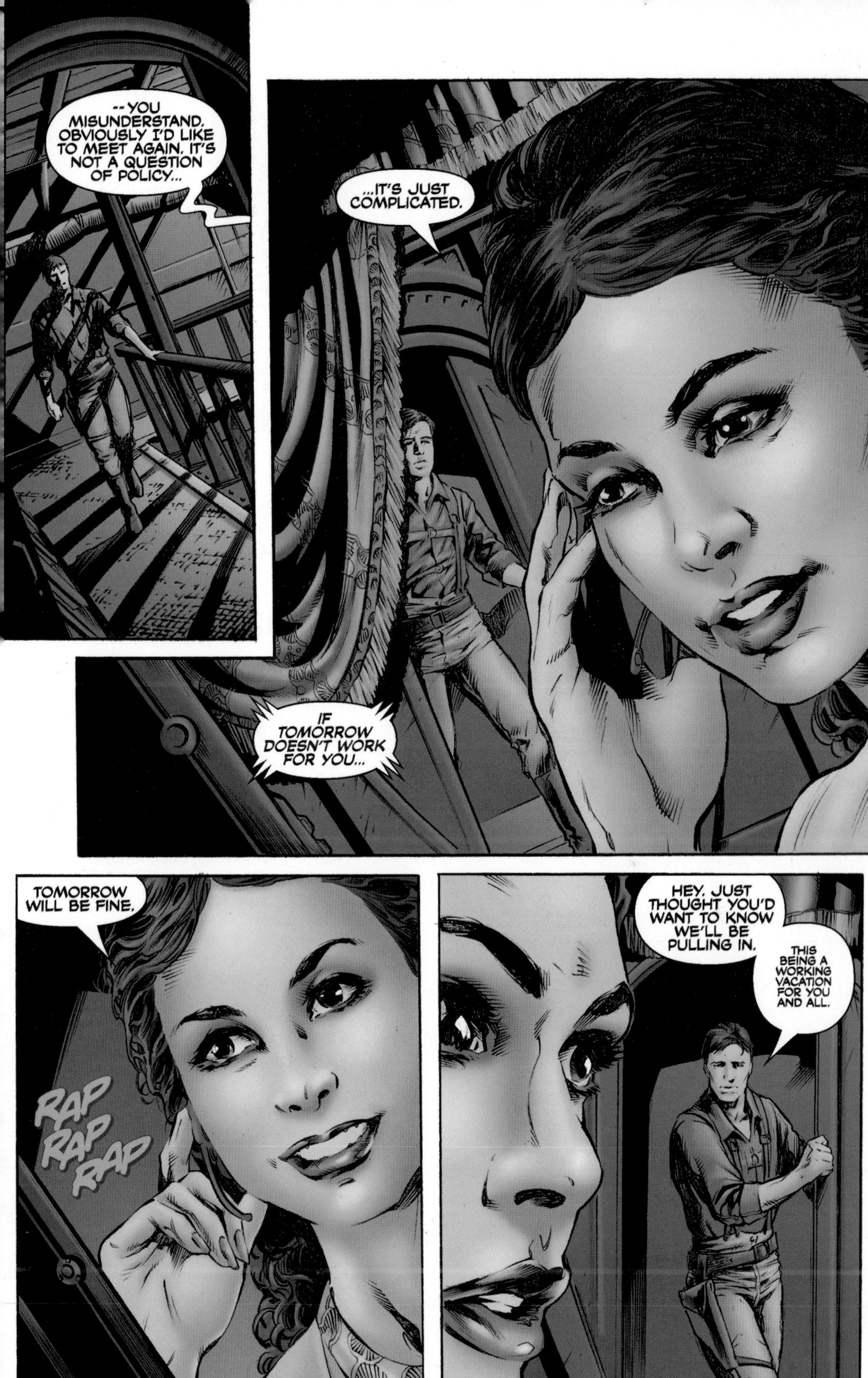
--YOU MISUNDERSTAND. OBVIOUSLY I'D LIKE TO MEET AGAIN. IT'S NOT A QUESTION OF POLICY...
...IT'S JUST COMPLICATED.
IF TOMORROW DOESN'T WORK FOR YOU...
TOMORROW WILL BE FINE.
RAP RAP RAP
HEY, JUST THOUGHT YOU'D WANT TO KNOW WE'LL BE PULLING IN.
THIS BEING A WORKING VACATION FOR YOU AND ALL.

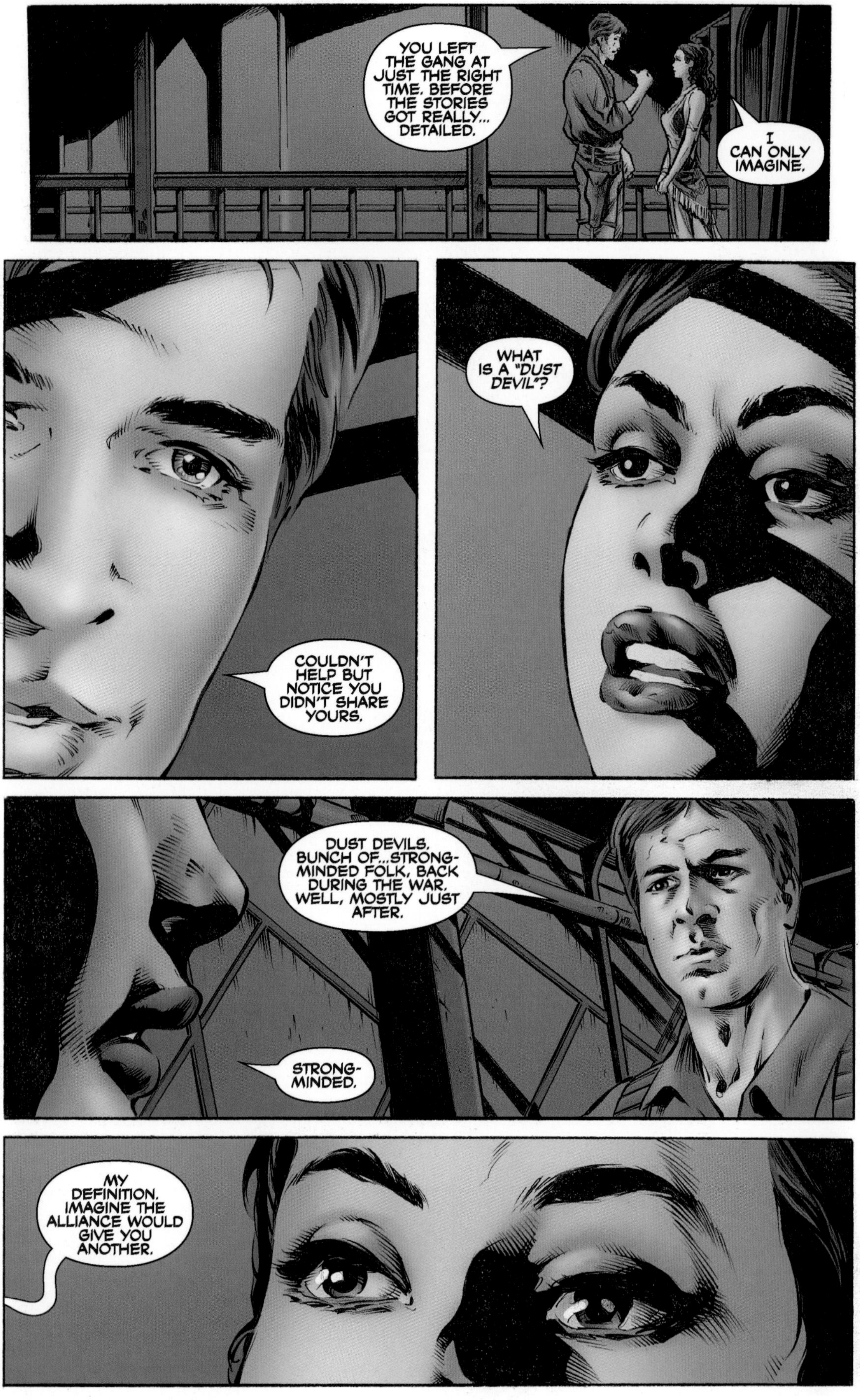
YOU LEFT THE GANG AT JUST THE RIGHT TIME. BEFORE THE STORIES GOT REALLY... DETAILED.
I CAN ONLY IMAGINE.
COULDN'T HELP BUT NOTICE YOU DIDN'T SHARE YOURS.
WHAT IS A "DUST DEVIL"?
DUST DEVILS. BUNCH OF...STRONG-MINDED FOLK, BACK DURING THE WAR. WELL, MOSTLY JUST AFTER.
STRONG-MINDED.
MY DEFINITION. IMAGINE THE ALLIANCE WOULD GIVE YOU ANOTHER.

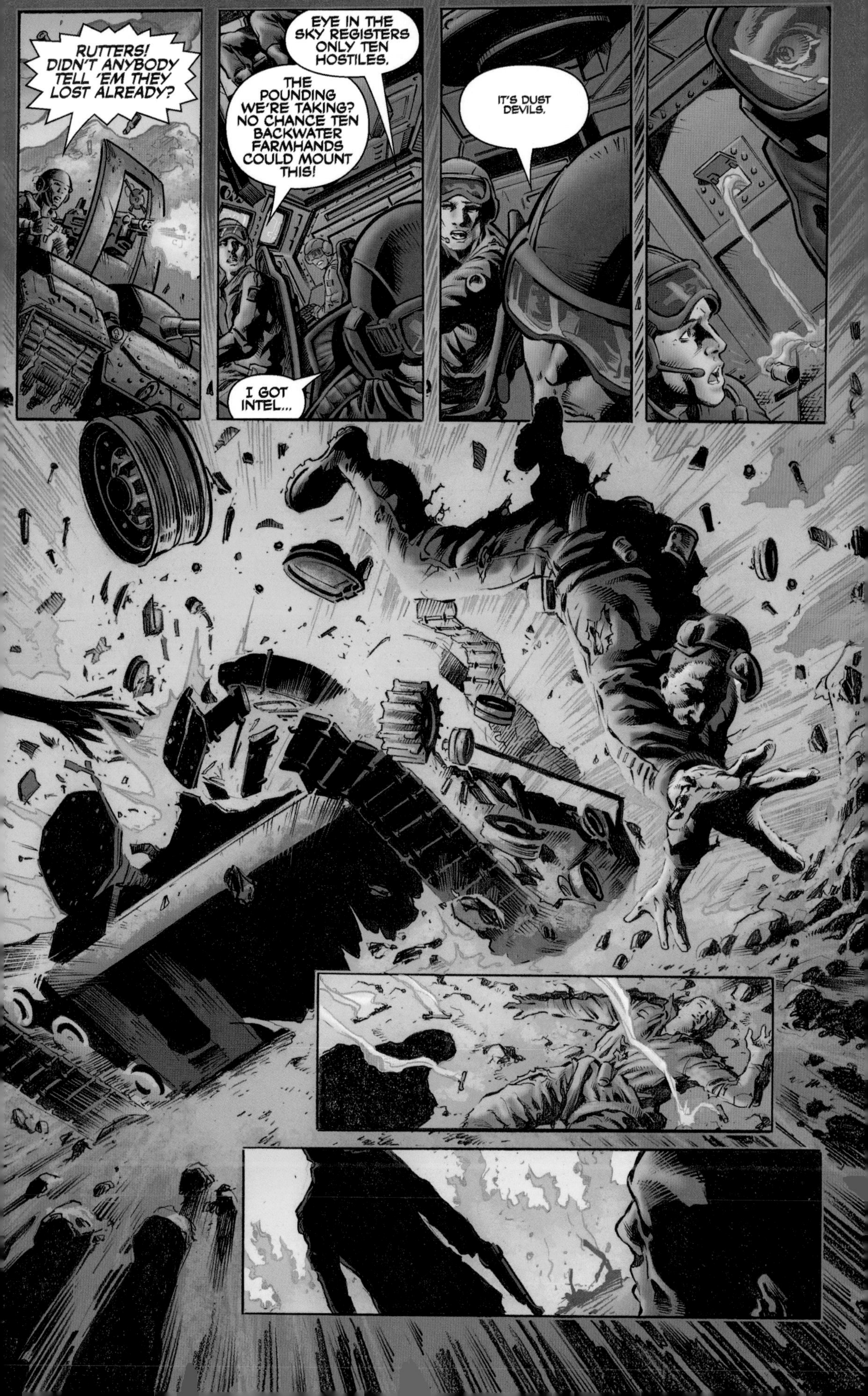
RUTTERS! DIDN'T ANYBODY TELL 'EM THEY LOST ALREADY?
EYE IN THE SKY REGISTERS ONLY TEN HOSTILES.
THE POUNDING WE'RE TAKING? NO CHANCE TEN BACKWATER FARMHANDS COULD MOUNT THIS!
I GOT INTEL...
IT'S DUST DEVILS.

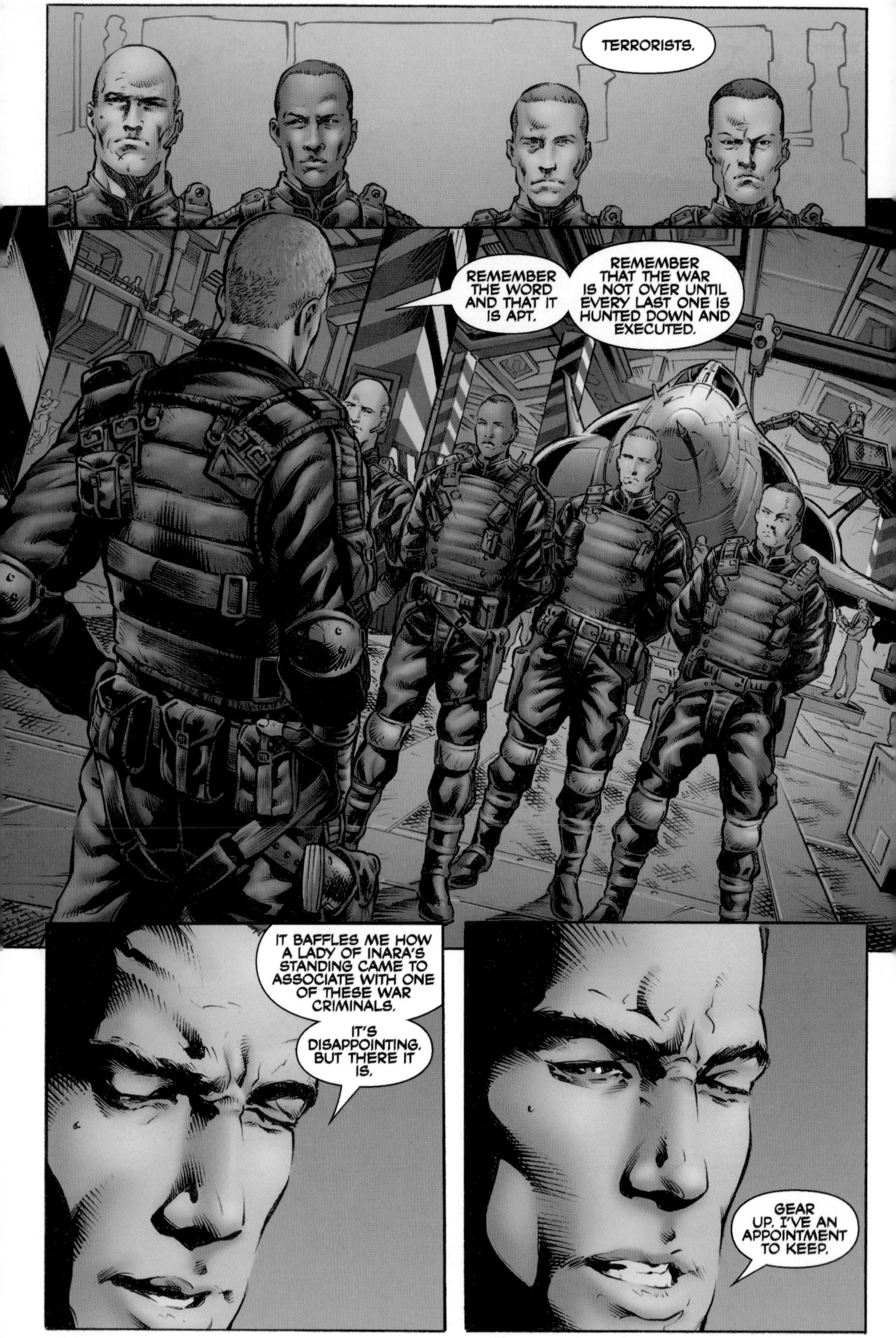
TERRORISTS.
REMEMBER THE WORD AND THAT IT IS APT.
REMEMBER THAT THE WAR IS NOT OVER UNTIL EVERY LAST ONE IS HUNTED DOWN AND EXECUTED.
IT BAFFLES ME HOW A LADY OF INARA'S STANDING CAME TO ASSOCIATE WITH ONE OF THESE WAR CRIMINALS.
IT'S DISAPPOINTING, BUT THERE IT IS.
GEAR UP. I'VE AN APPOINTMENT TO KEEP.

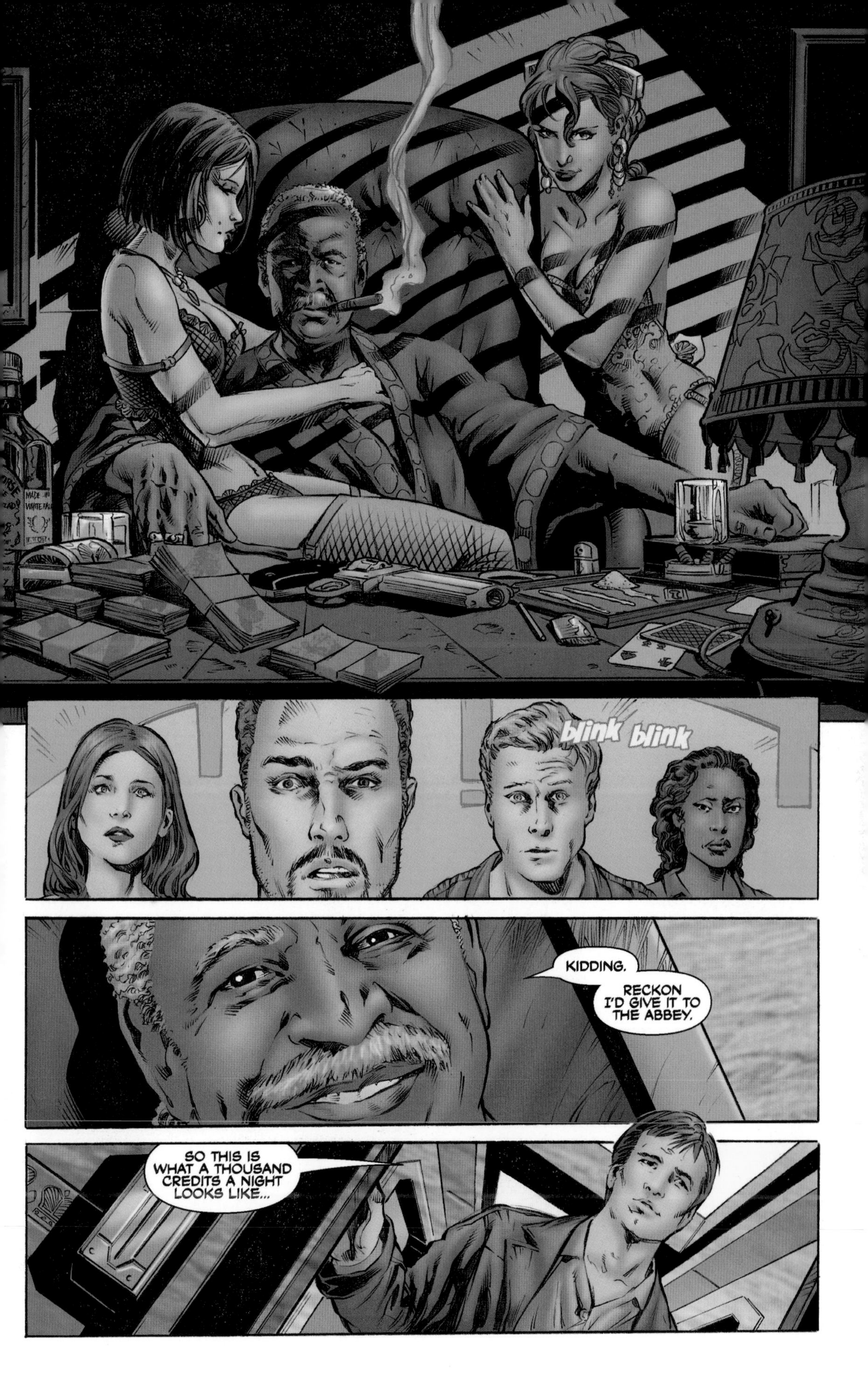
blink blink
KIDDING.
RECKON I'D GIVE IT TO THE ABBEY.
SO THIS IS WHAT A THOUSAND CREDITS A NIGHT LOOKS LIKE...

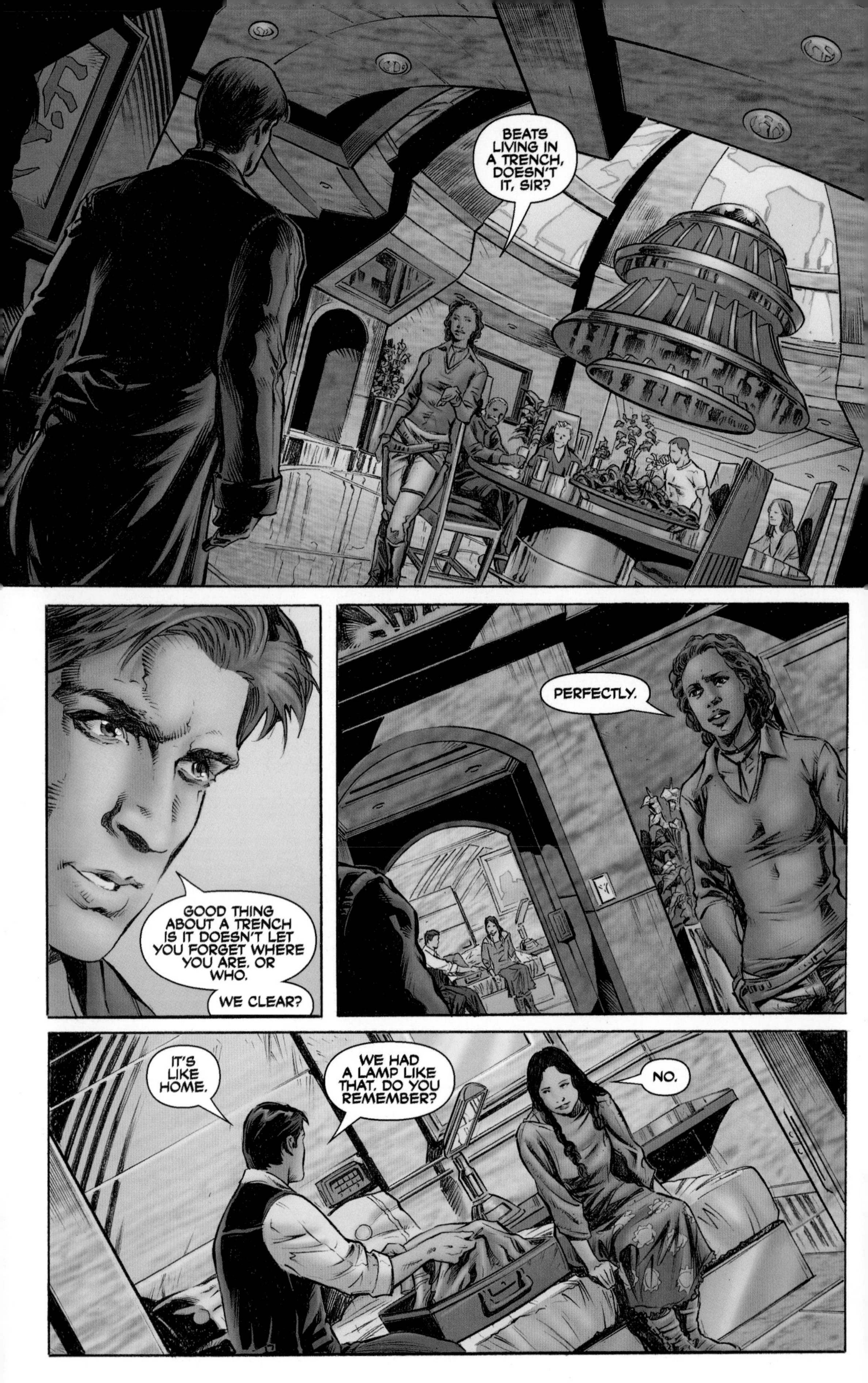
BEATS LIVING IN A TRENCH, DOESN'T IT, SIR?
GOOD THING ABOUT A TRENCH IS IT DOESN'T LET YOU FORGET WHERE YOU ARE. OR WHO.
WE CLEAR?
PERFECTLY.
IT'S LIKE HOME.
WE HAD A LAMP LIKE THAT. DO YOU REMEMBER?
NO.

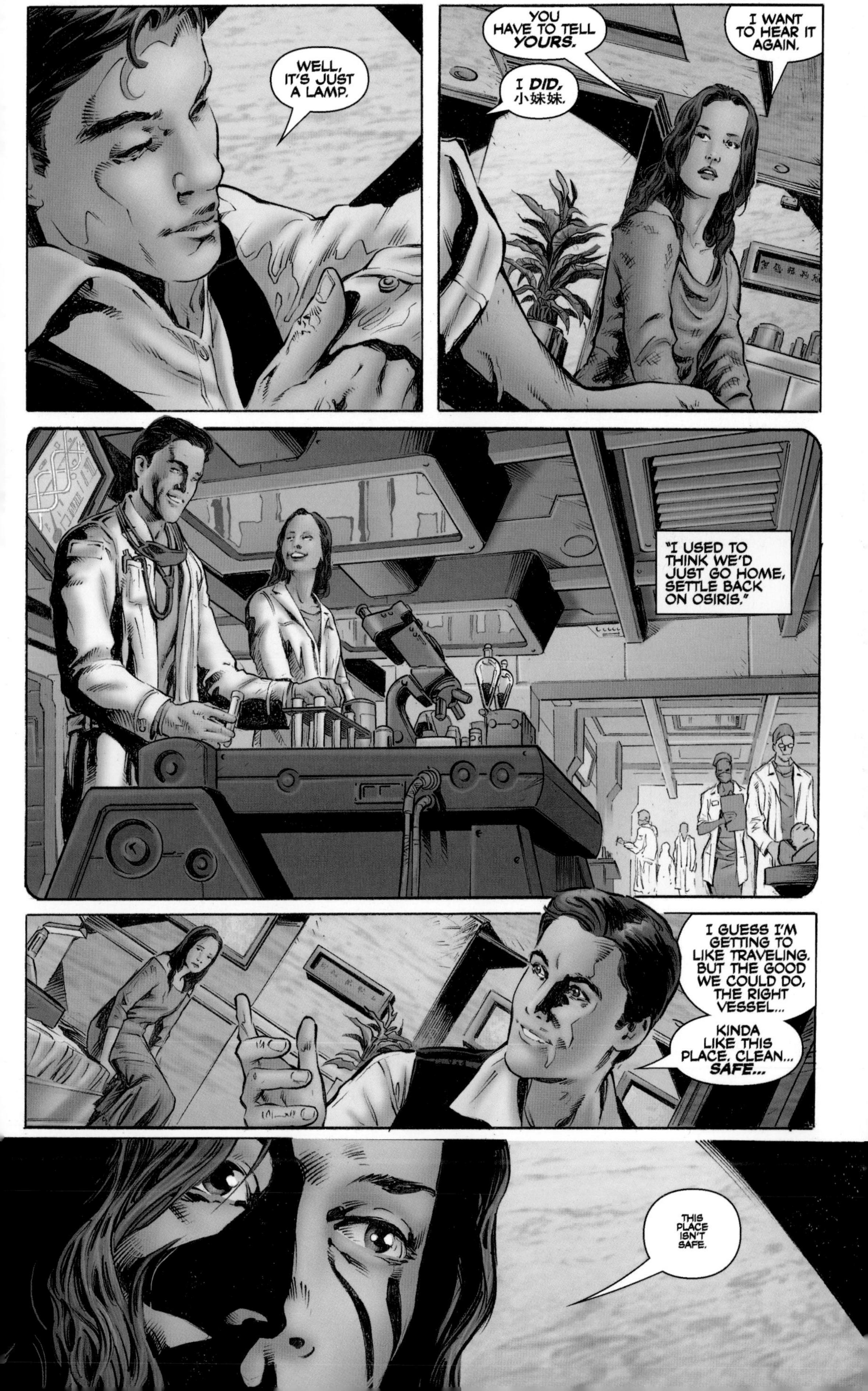
WELL, IT'S JUST A LAMP.
YOU HAVE TO TELL YOURS.
I WANT TO HEAR IT AGAIN.
I DID, 小妹妹.
"I USED TO THINK WE'D JUST GO HOME, SETTLE BACK ON OSIRIS."
I GUESS I'M GETTING TO LIKE TRAVELING. BUT THE GOOD WE COULD DO, THE RIGHT VESSEL...
KINDA LIKE THIS PLACE. CLEAN... SAFE...
THIS PLACE ISN'T SAFE.

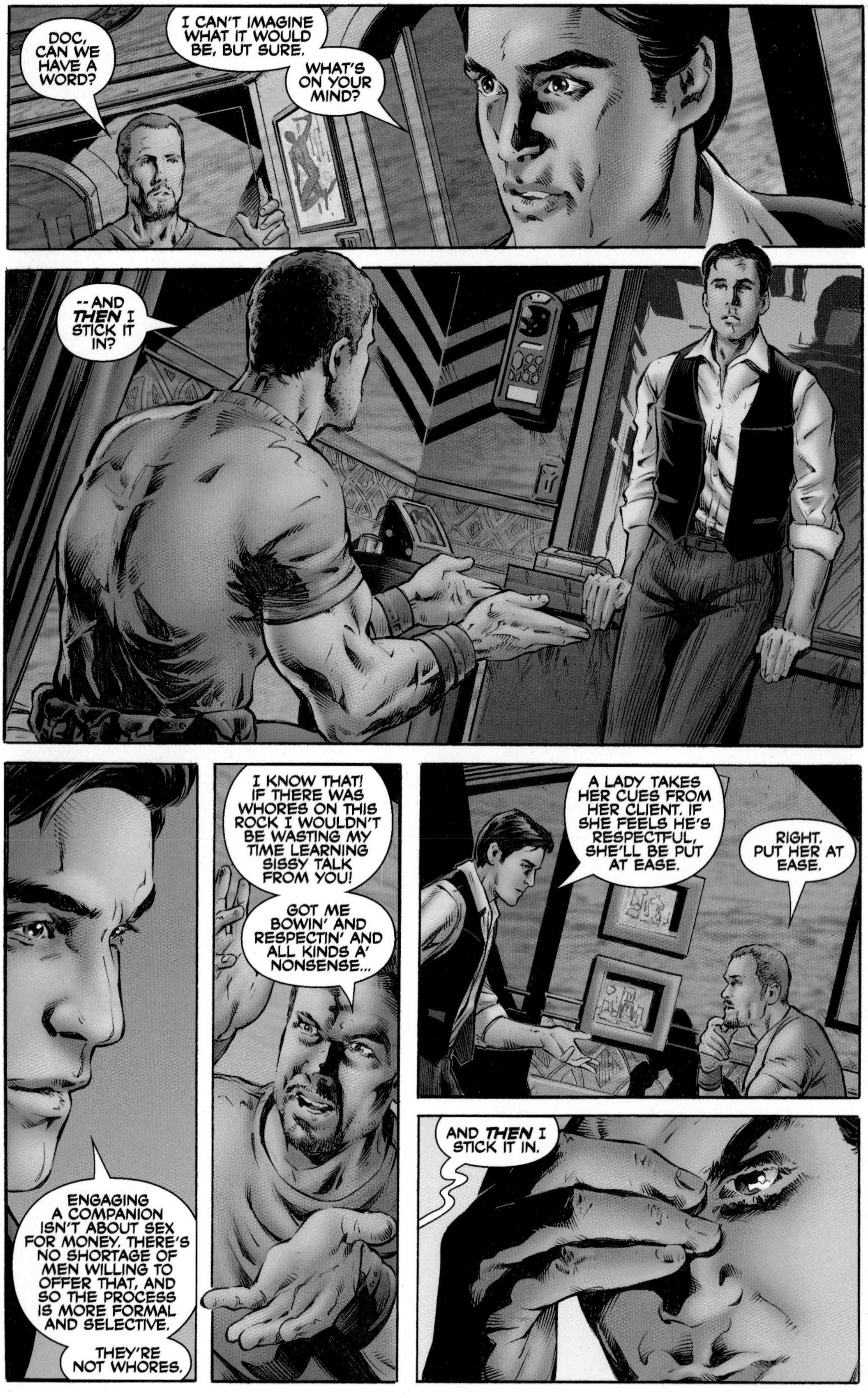
DOC, CAN WE HAVE A WORD?
I CAN'T IMAGINE WHAT IT WOULD BE, BUT SURE.
WHAT'S ON YOUR MIND?
--AND *THEN* I STICK IT IN?
ENGAGING A COMPANION ISN'T ABOUT SEX FOR MONEY. THERE'S NO SHORTAGE OF MEN WILLING TO OFFER THAT, AND SO THE PROCESS IS MORE FORMAL AND SELECTIVE.
THEY'RE NOT WHORES.
I KNOW THAT! IF THERE WAS WHORES ON THIS ROCK I WOULDN'T BE WASTING MY TIME LEARNING SISSY TALK FROM YOU!
GOT ME BOWIN' AND RESPECTIN' AND ALL KINDS A' NONSENSE...
A LADY TAKES HER CUES FROM HER CLIENT. IF SHE FEELS HE'S RESPECTFUL, SHE'LL BE PUT AT EASE.
RIGHT. PUT HER AT EASE.
AND *THEN* I STICK IT IN.

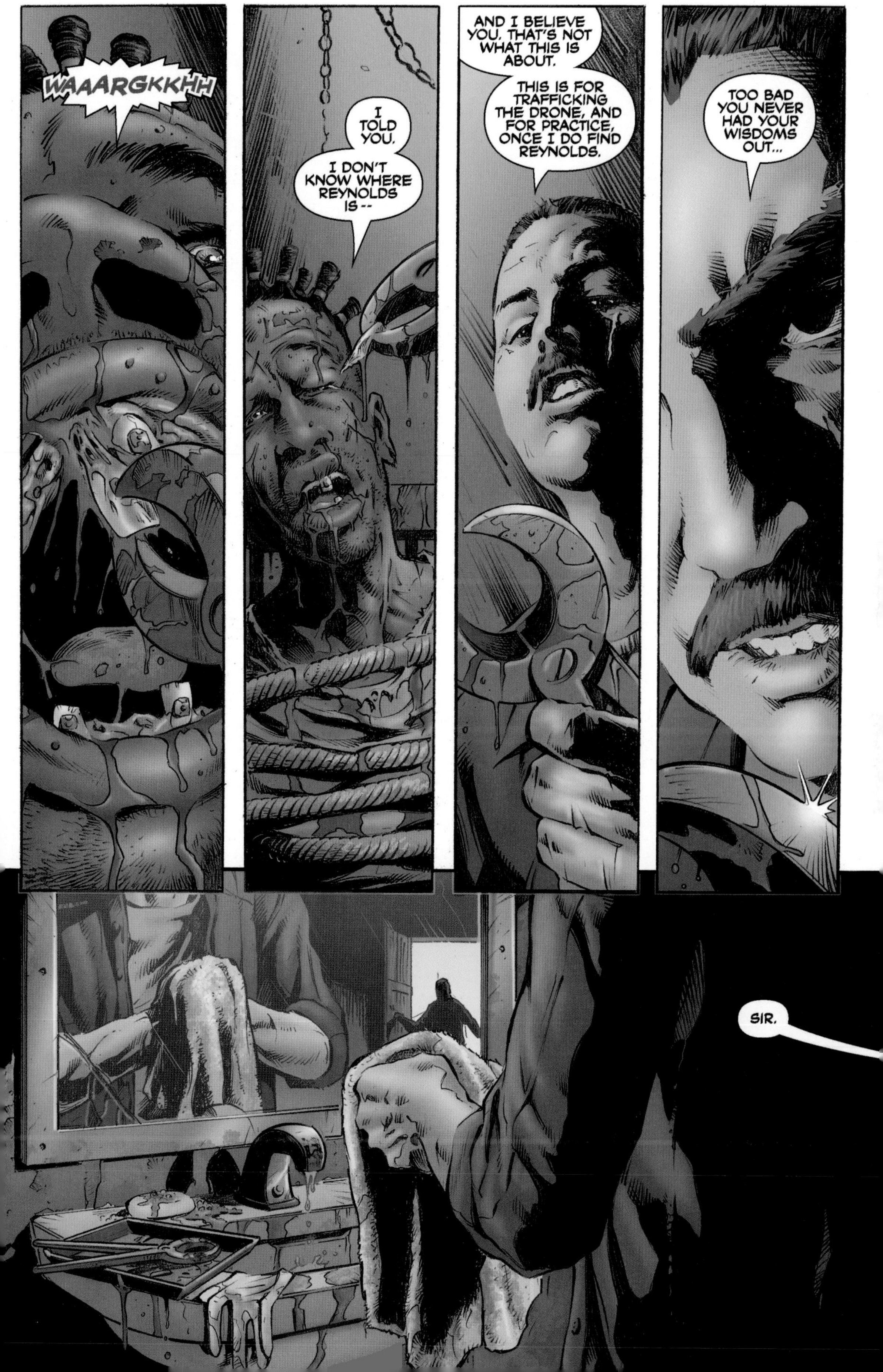
WAAARGKKHH
I TOLD YOU.
I DON'T KNOW WHERE REYNOLDS IS --
AND I BELIEVE YOU. THAT'S NOT WHAT THIS IS ABOUT.
THIS IS FOR TRAFFICKING THE DRONE, AND FOR PRACTICE, ONCE I DO FIND REYNOLDS.
TOO BAD YOU NEVER HAD YOUR WISDOMS OUT...
SIR.

ARE YOU AWARE THE DRONE WAS DESIGNED TO EXPEL MICROSCOPIC TRACKING BEACONS UPON UNEXPECTED SHUTDOWN OR SYSTEM FAILURE?

SIR...

YOU'VE GOT A HIT.

YES. A COUPLE HUNDRED BEACONS MOVING IN UNISON. A SHIP.

MOVEMENT CEASED AT PELORUM, A RESORT WORLD. CARBON SCORING AT THE POINT OF DEPARTURE SUGGESTS --

FIREFLY CLASS?

IT CHECKS.

PELORUM.

YOU'D BETTER BRING YOUR SUNBLOCK, THEN.

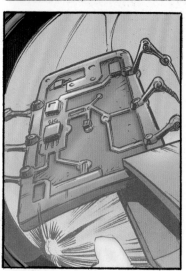

IT'S NOTHING FANCY OR ANYTHING...

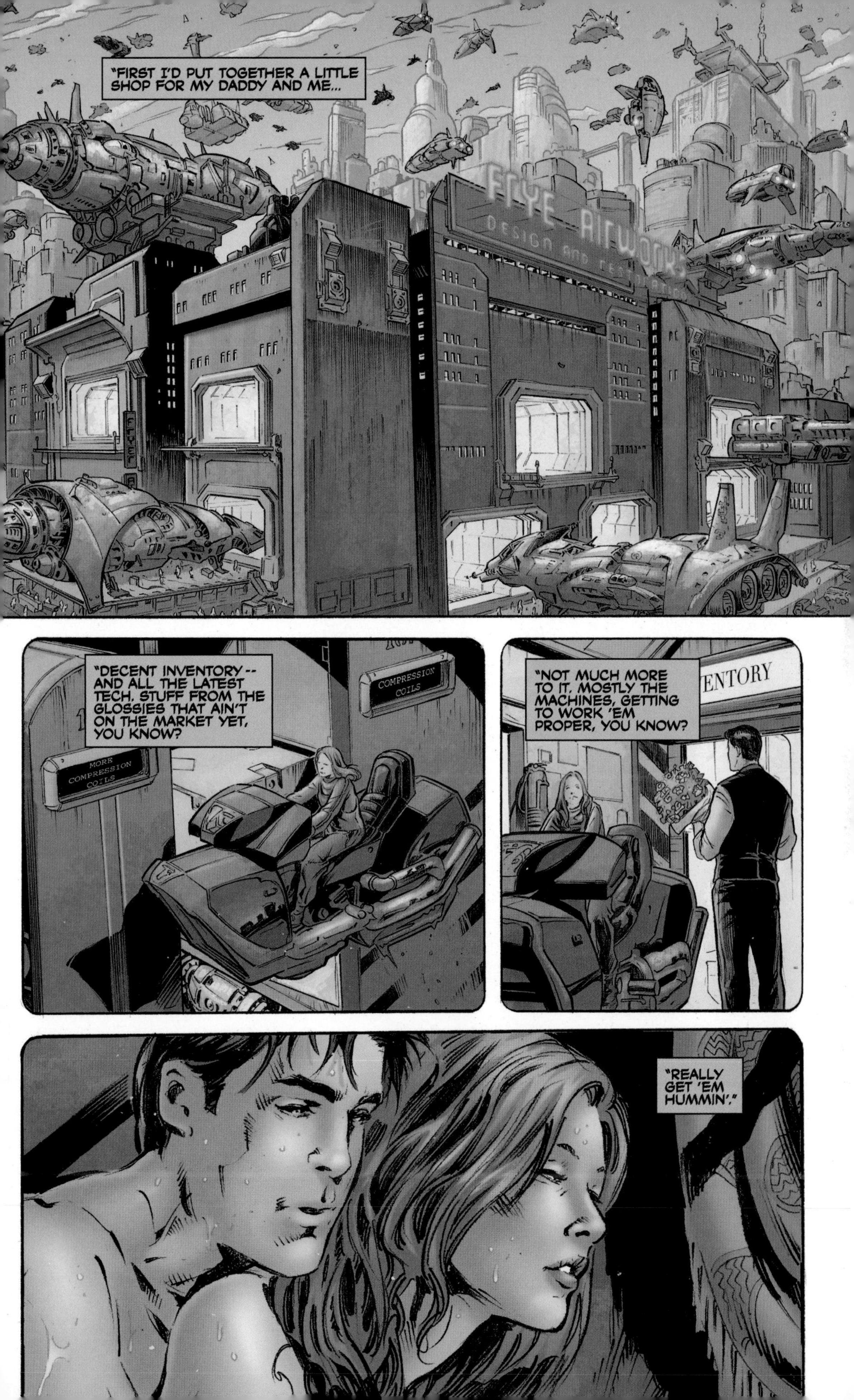
"FIRST I'D PUT TOGETHER A LITTLE SHOP FOR MY DADDY AND ME...
FRYE AIRWORKS
"DECENT INVENTORY-- AND ALL THE LATEST TECH. STUFF FROM THE GLOSSIES THAT AIN'T ON THE MARKET YET, YOU KNOW?
COMPRESSION COILS
MORE COMPRESSION COILS
"NOT MUCH MORE TO IT. MOSTLY THE MACHINES, GETTING TO WORK 'EM PROPER, YOU KNOW?
"REALLY GET 'EM HUMMIN'."

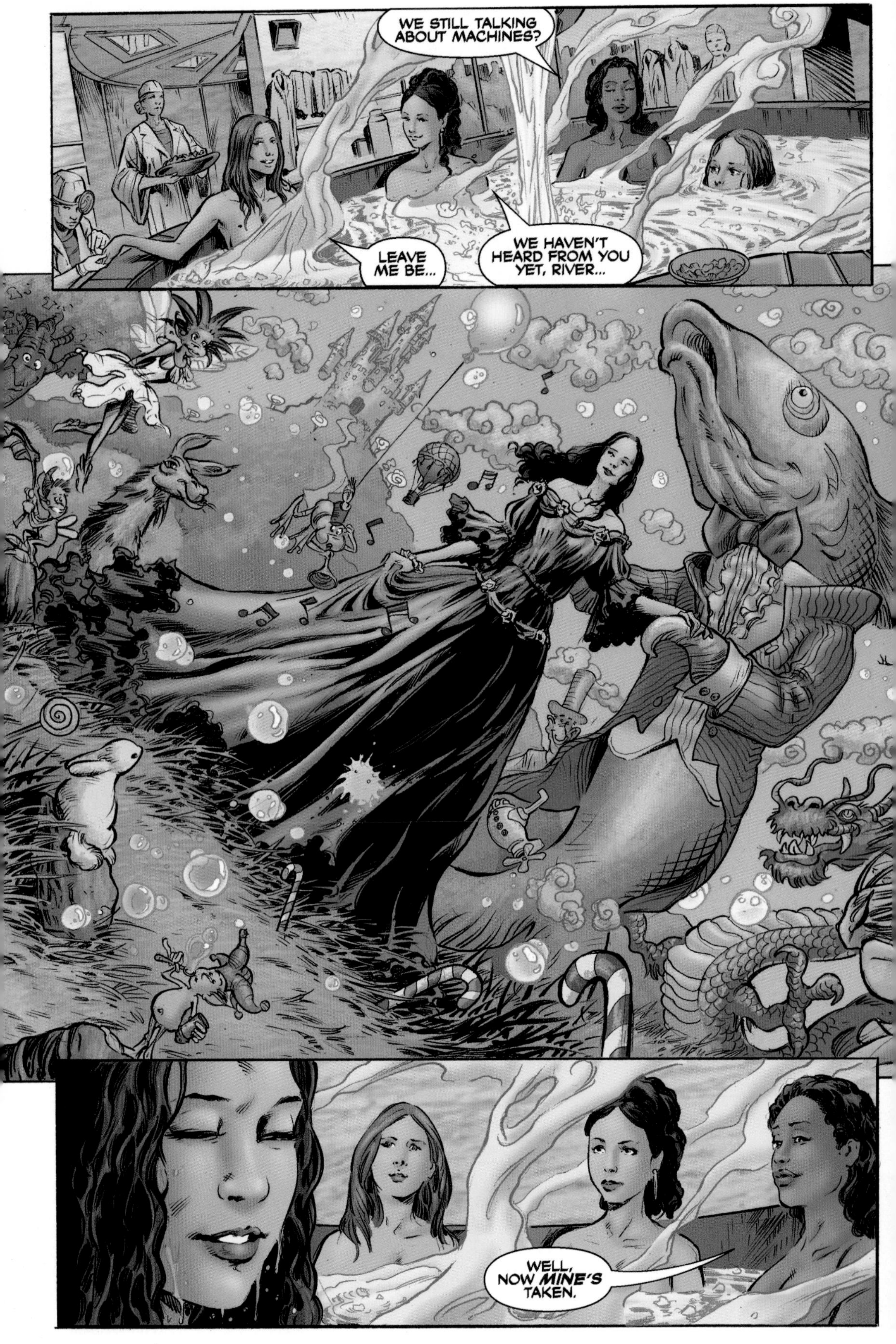
WE STILL TALKING ABOUT MACHINES?
WE HAVEN'T HEARD FROM YOU YET, RIVER...
LEAVE ME BE...
WELL, NOW *MINE'S* TAKEN.

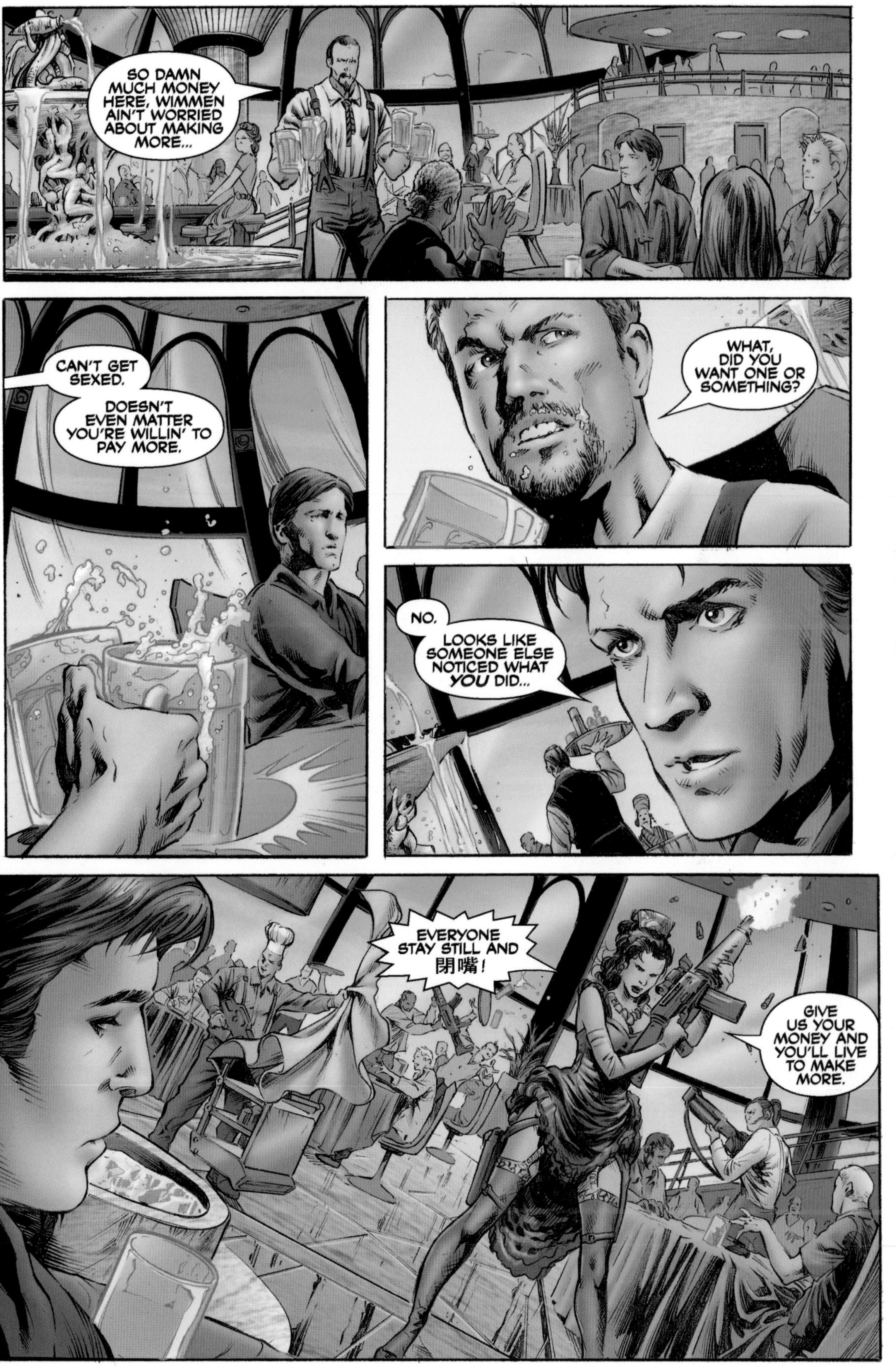
SO DAMN MUCH MONEY HERE, WIMMEN AIN'T WORRIED ABOUT MAKING MORE...
CAN'T GET SEXED.
DOESN'T EVEN MATTER YOU'RE WILLIN' TO PAY MORE.
WHAT, DID YOU WANT ONE OR SOMETHING?
NO.
LOOKS LIKE SOMEONE ELSE NOTICED WHAT *YOU* DID...
EVERYONE STAY STILL AND 閉嘴!
GIVE US YOUR MONEY AND YOU'LL LIVE TO MAKE MORE.

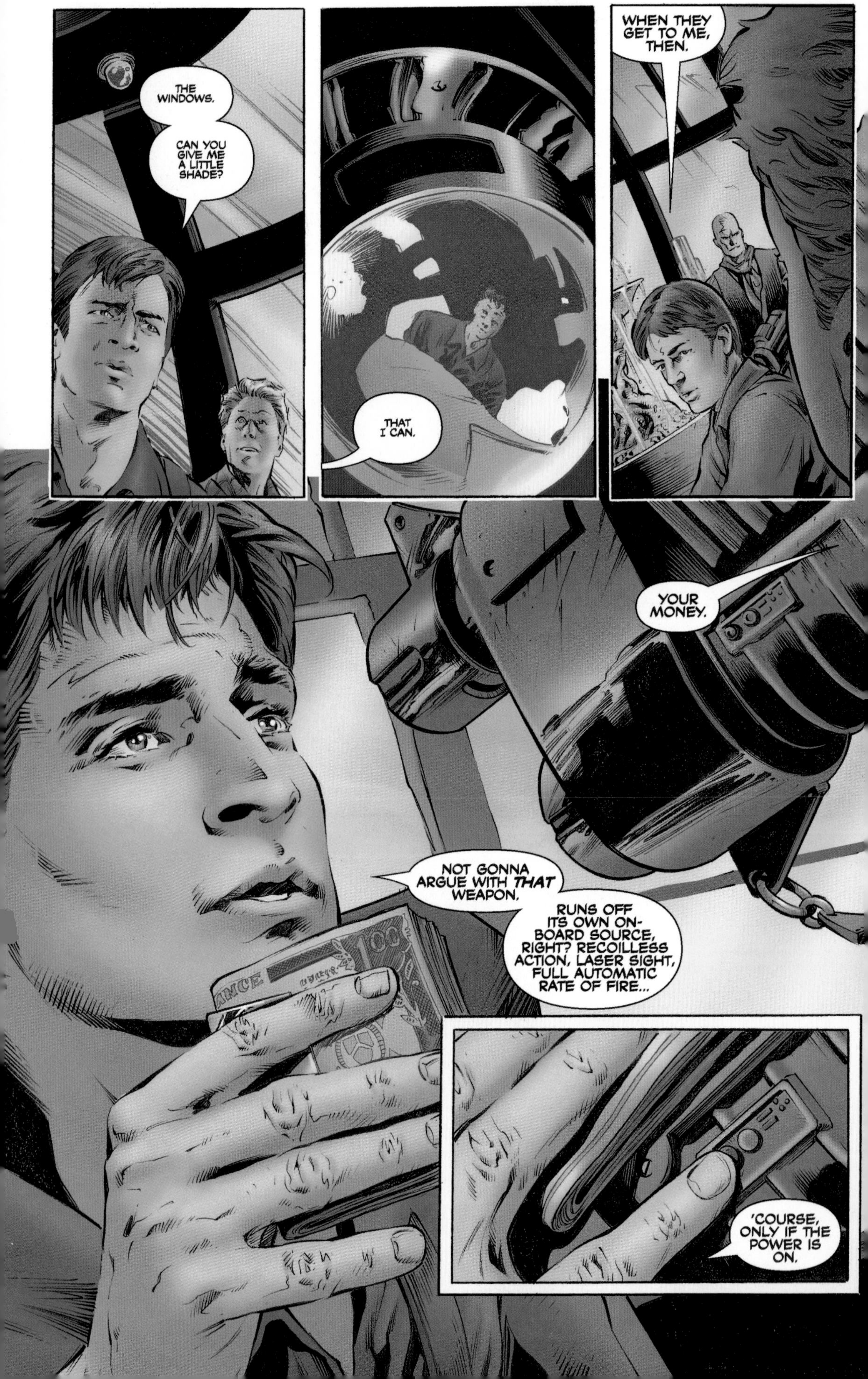
THE WINDOWS.
CAN YOU GIVE ME A LITTLE SHADE?
THAT I CAN.
WHEN THEY GET TO ME, THEN.
YOUR MONEY.
NOT GONNA ARGUE WITH *THAT* WEAPON.
RUNS OFF ITS OWN ON-BOARD SOURCE, RIGHT? RECOILLESS ACTION, LASER SIGHT, FULL AUTOMATIC RATE OF FIRE...
'COURSE, ONLY IF THE POWER IS ON.

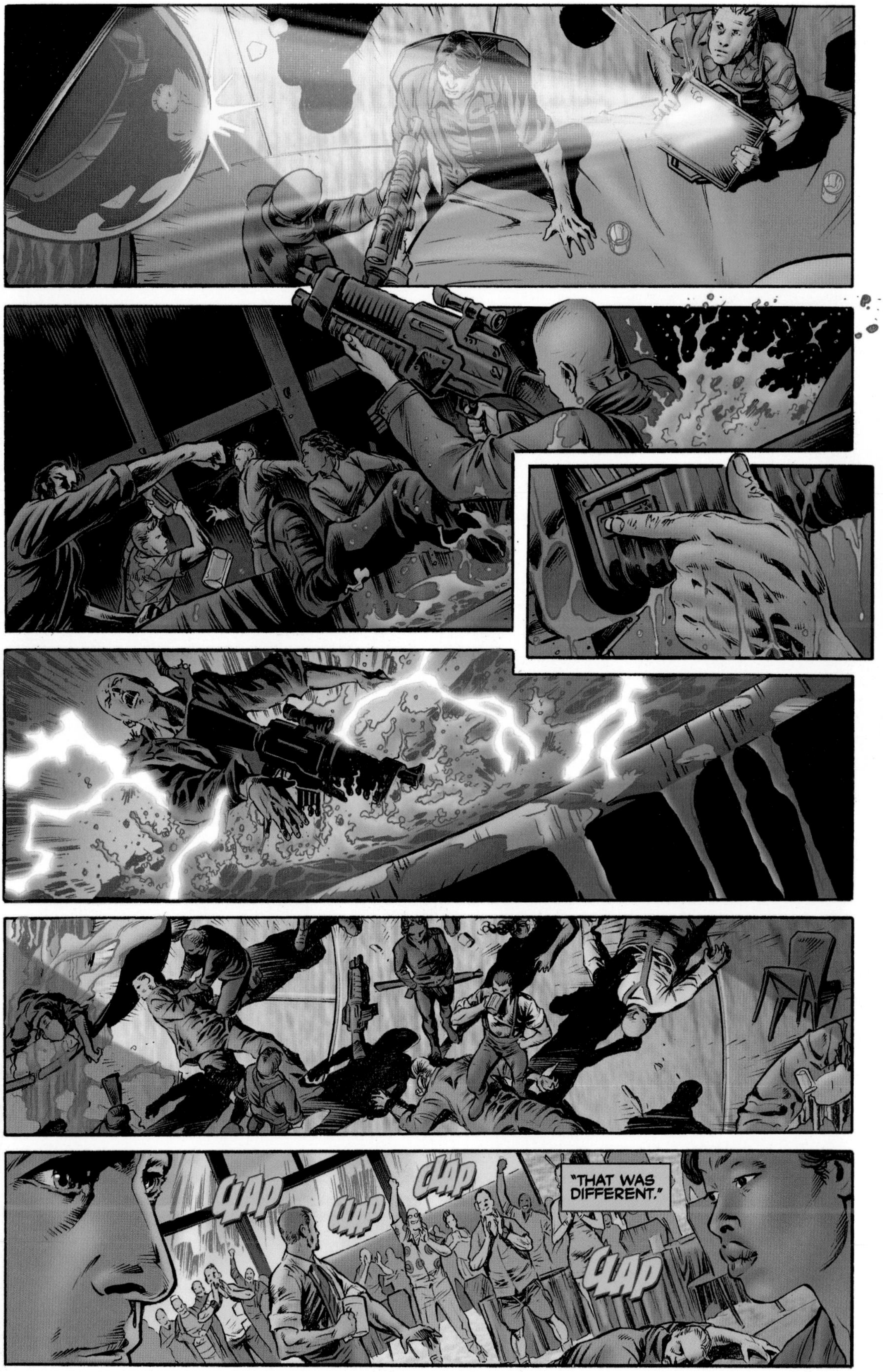
CLAP
CLAP
CLAP
"THAT WAS DIFFERENT."
CLAP

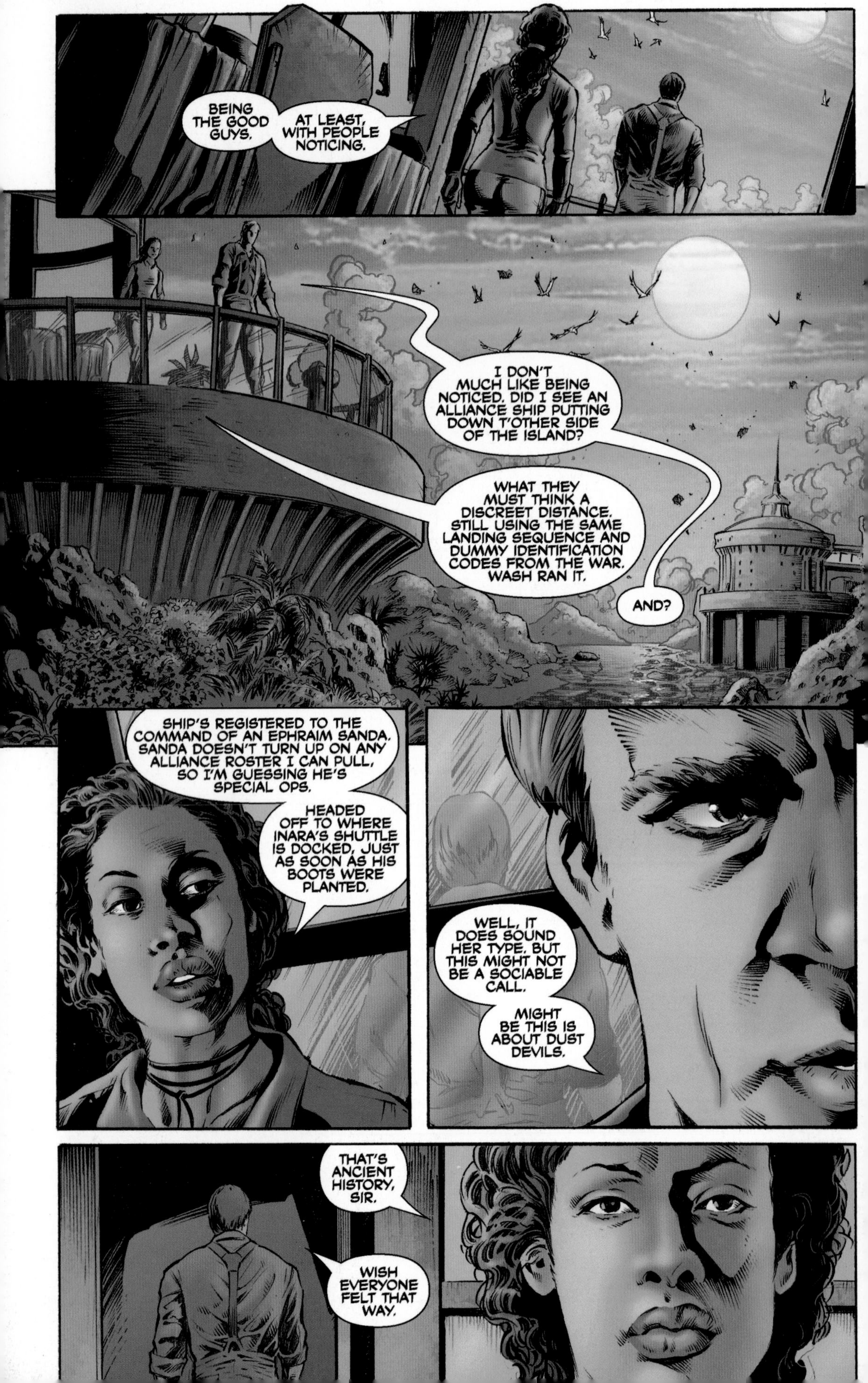

BEING THE GOOD GUYS.
AT LEAST, WITH PEOPLE NOTICING.
I DON'T MUCH LIKE BEING NOTICED. DID I SEE AN ALLIANCE SHIP PUTTING DOWN T'OTHER SIDE OF THE ISLAND?
WHAT THEY MUST THINK A DISCREET DISTANCE. STILL USING THE SAME LANDING SEQUENCE AND DUMMY IDENTIFICATION CODES FROM THE WAR. WASH RAN IT.
AND?
SHIP'S REGISTERED TO THE COMMAND OF AN EPHRAIM SANDA. SANDA DOESN'T TURN UP ON ANY ALLIANCE ROSTER I CAN PULL, SO I'M GUESSING HE'S SPECIAL OPS.
HEADED OFF TO WHERE INARA'S SHUTTLE IS DOCKED, JUST AS SOON AS HIS BOOTS WERE PLANTED.
WELL, IT DOES SOUND HER TYPE, BUT THIS MIGHT NOT BE A SOCIABLE CALL.
MIGHT BE THIS IS ABOUT DUST DEVILS.
THAT'S ANCIENT HISTORY, SIR.
WISH EVERYONE FELT THAT WAY.

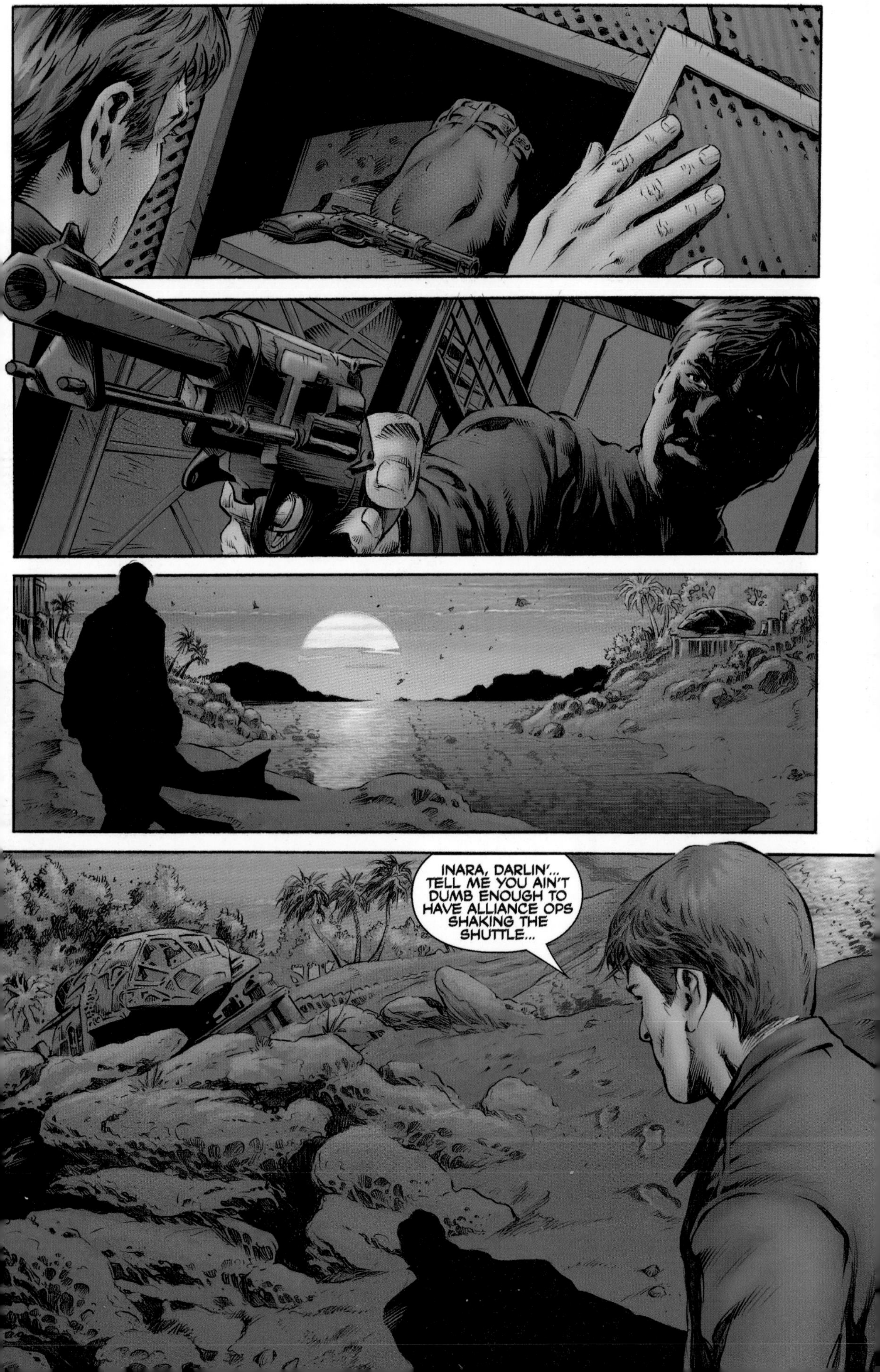
INARA, DARLIN'... TELL ME YOU AIN'T DUMB ENOUGH TO HAVE ALLIANCE OPS SHAKING THE SHUTTLE...

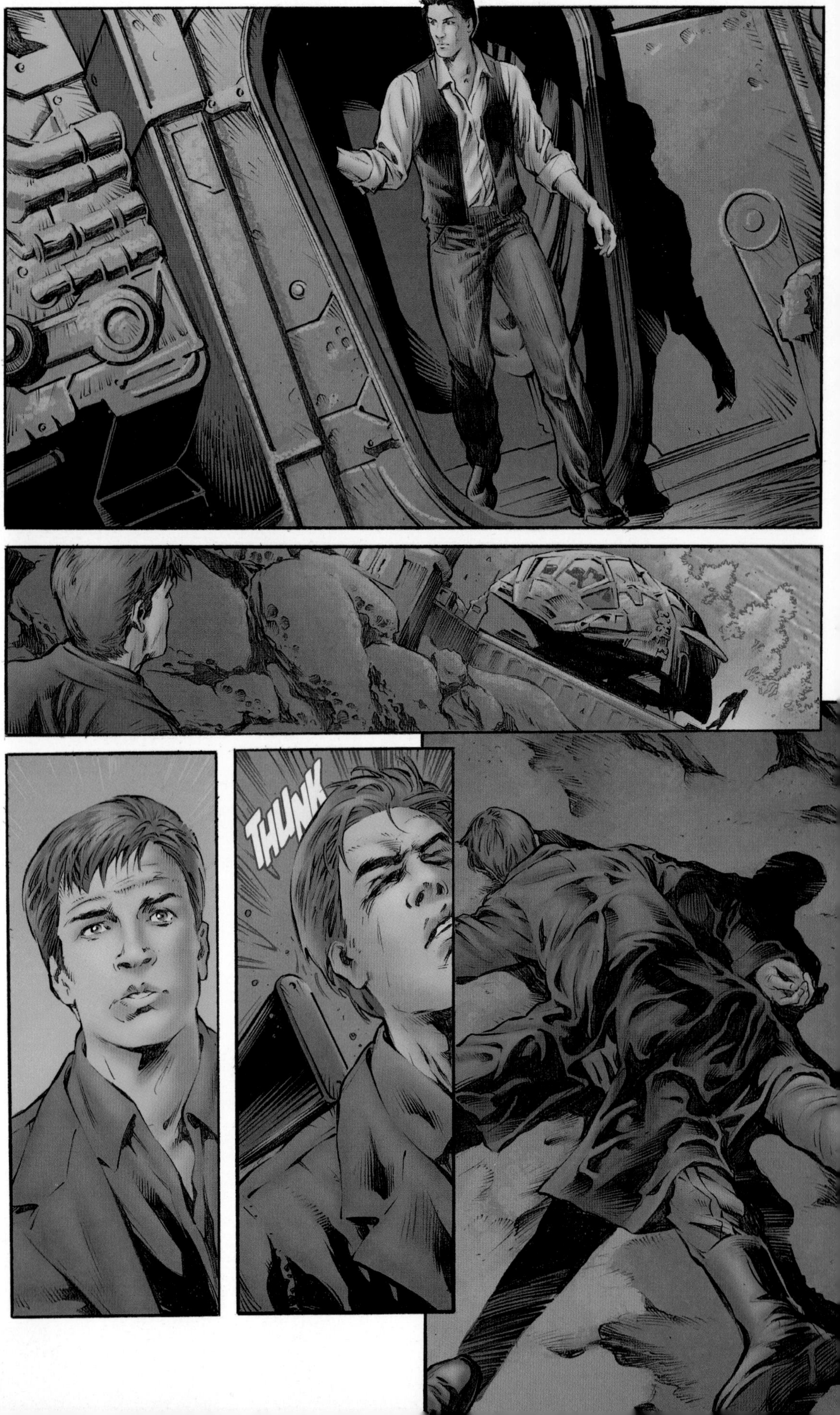
THUNK

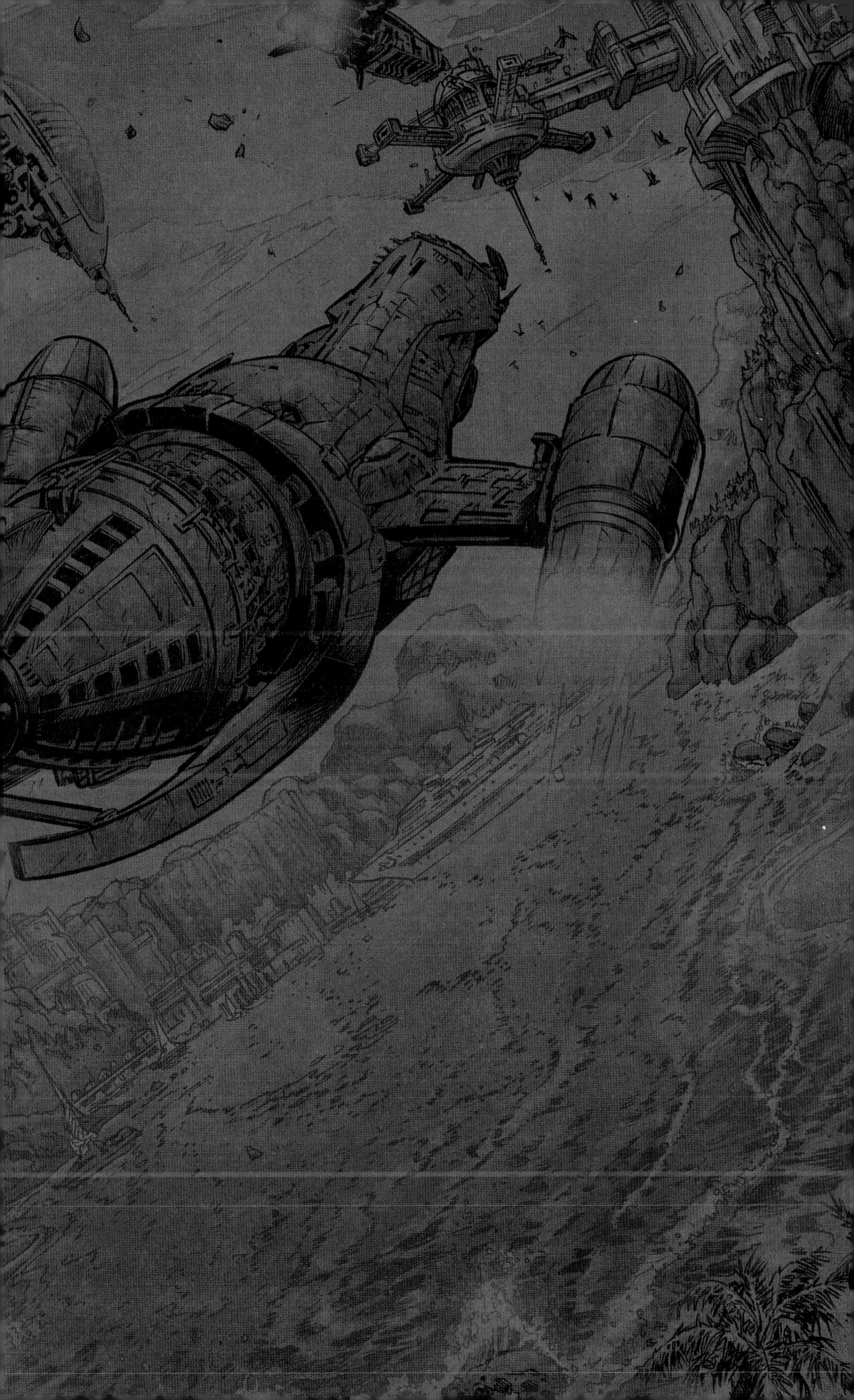

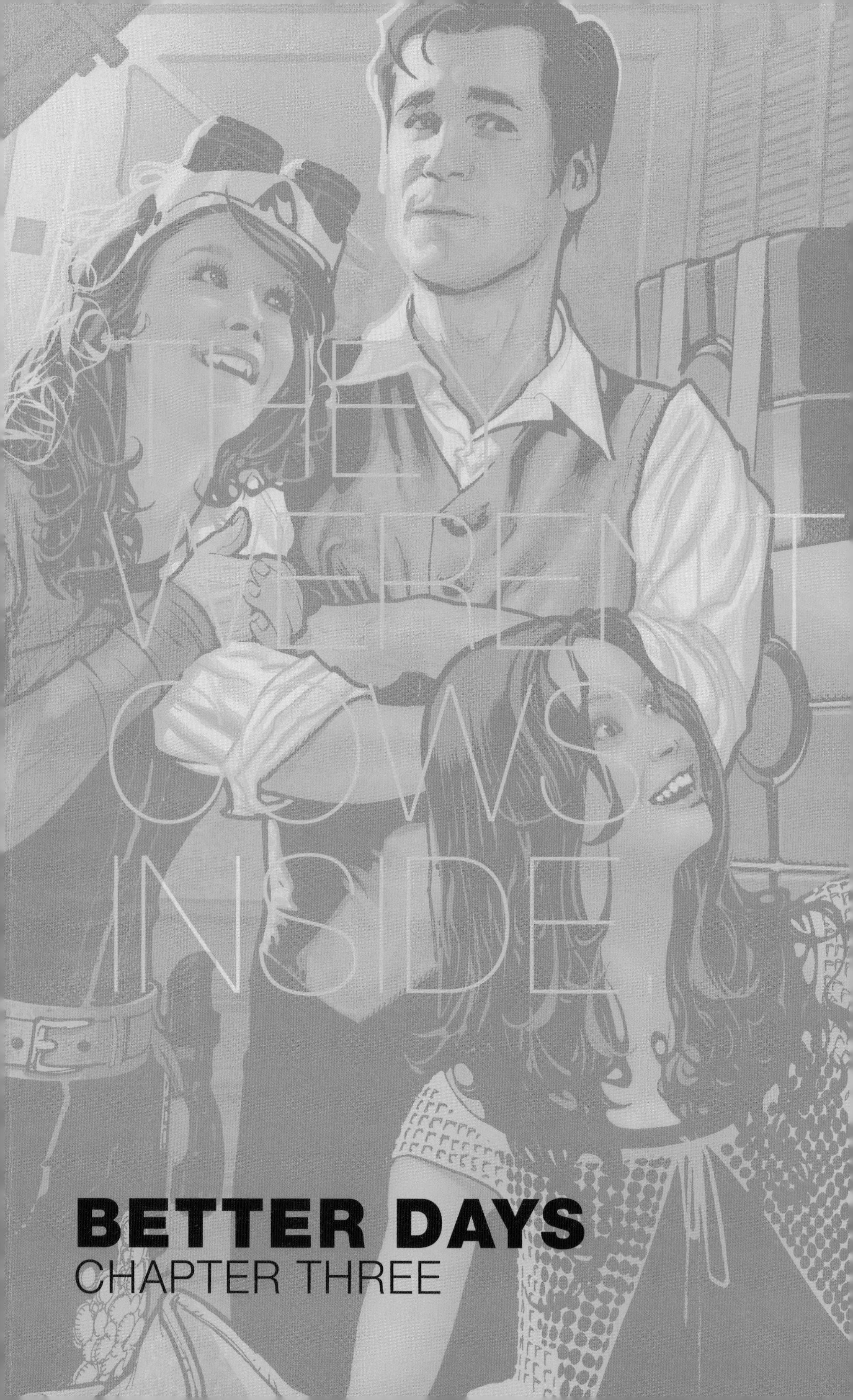
THEY
WERENT
COWS
INSIDE

BETTER DAYS
CHAPTER THREE

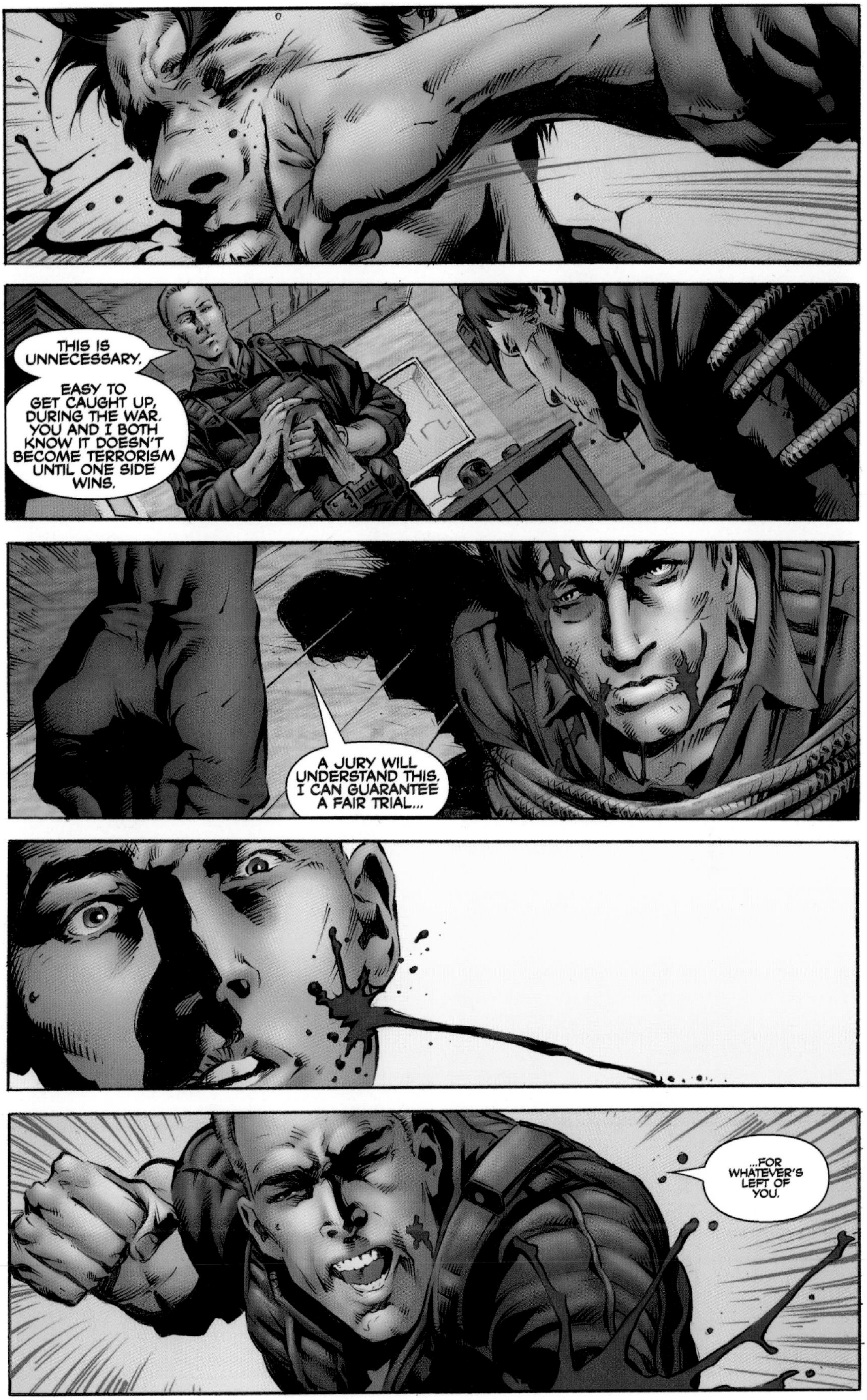
THIS IS UNNECESSARY.
EASY TO GET CAUGHT UP, DURING THE WAR. YOU AND I BOTH KNOW IT DOESN'T BECOME TERRORISM UNTIL ONE SIDE WINS.
A JURY WILL UNDERSTAND THIS. I CAN GUARANTEE A FAIR TRIAL...
...FOR WHATEVER'S LEFT OF YOU.

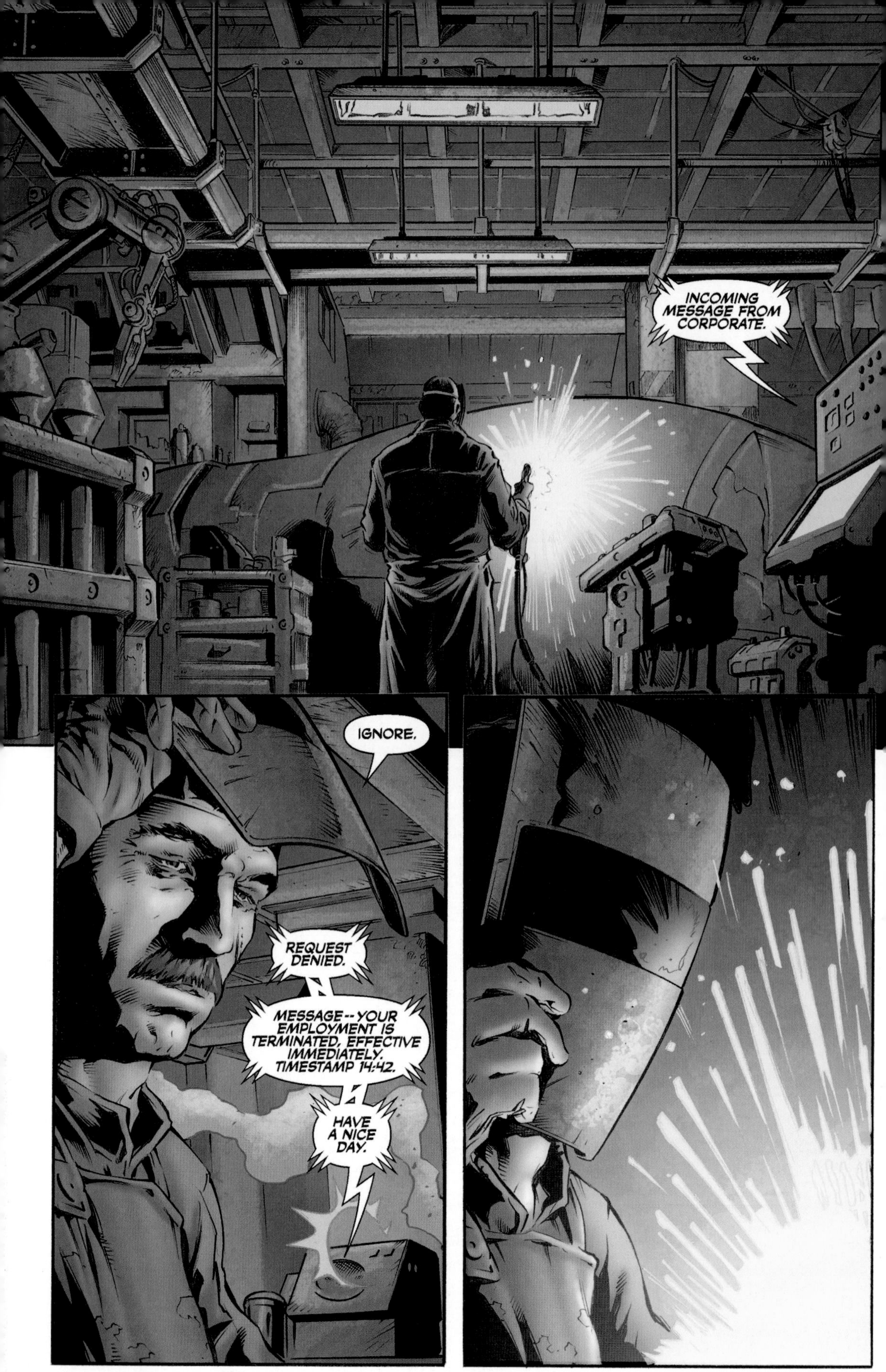
INCOMING MESSAGE FROM CORPORATE.
IGNORE.
REQUEST DENIED.
MESSAGE-- YOUR EMPLOYMENT IS TERMINATED, EFFECTIVE IMMEDIATELY. TIMESTAMP 14:42.
HAVE A NICE DAY.

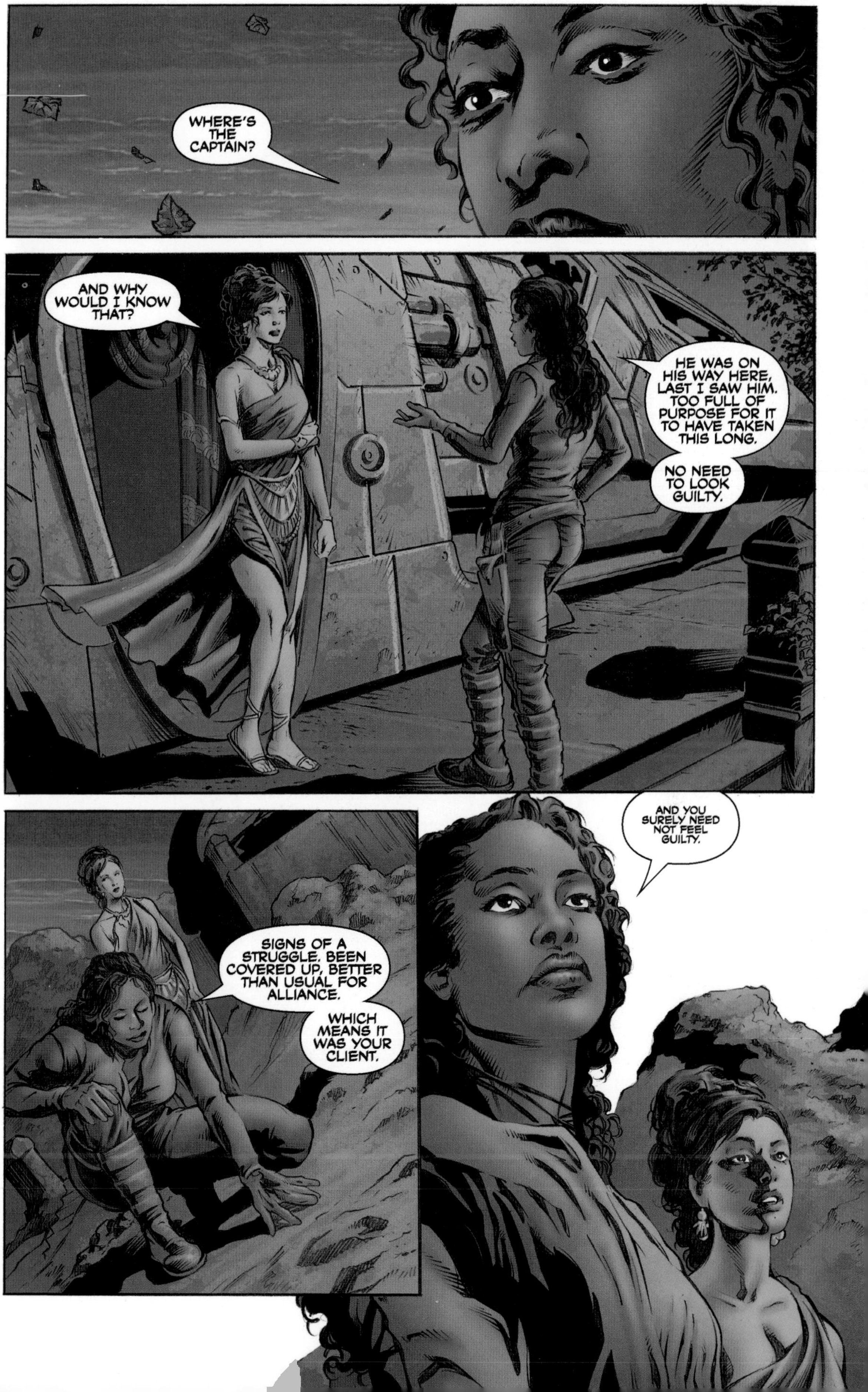
WHERE'S THE CAPTAIN?
AND WHY WOULD I KNOW THAT?
HE WAS ON HIS WAY HERE, LAST I SAW HIM. TOO FULL OF PURPOSE FOR IT TO HAVE TAKEN THIS LONG.
NO NEED TO LOOK GUILTY.
SIGNS OF A STRUGGLE. BEEN COVERED UP, BETTER THAN USUAL FOR ALLIANCE.
WHICH MEANS IT WAS YOUR CLIENT.
AND YOU SURELY NEED NOT FEEL GUILTY.

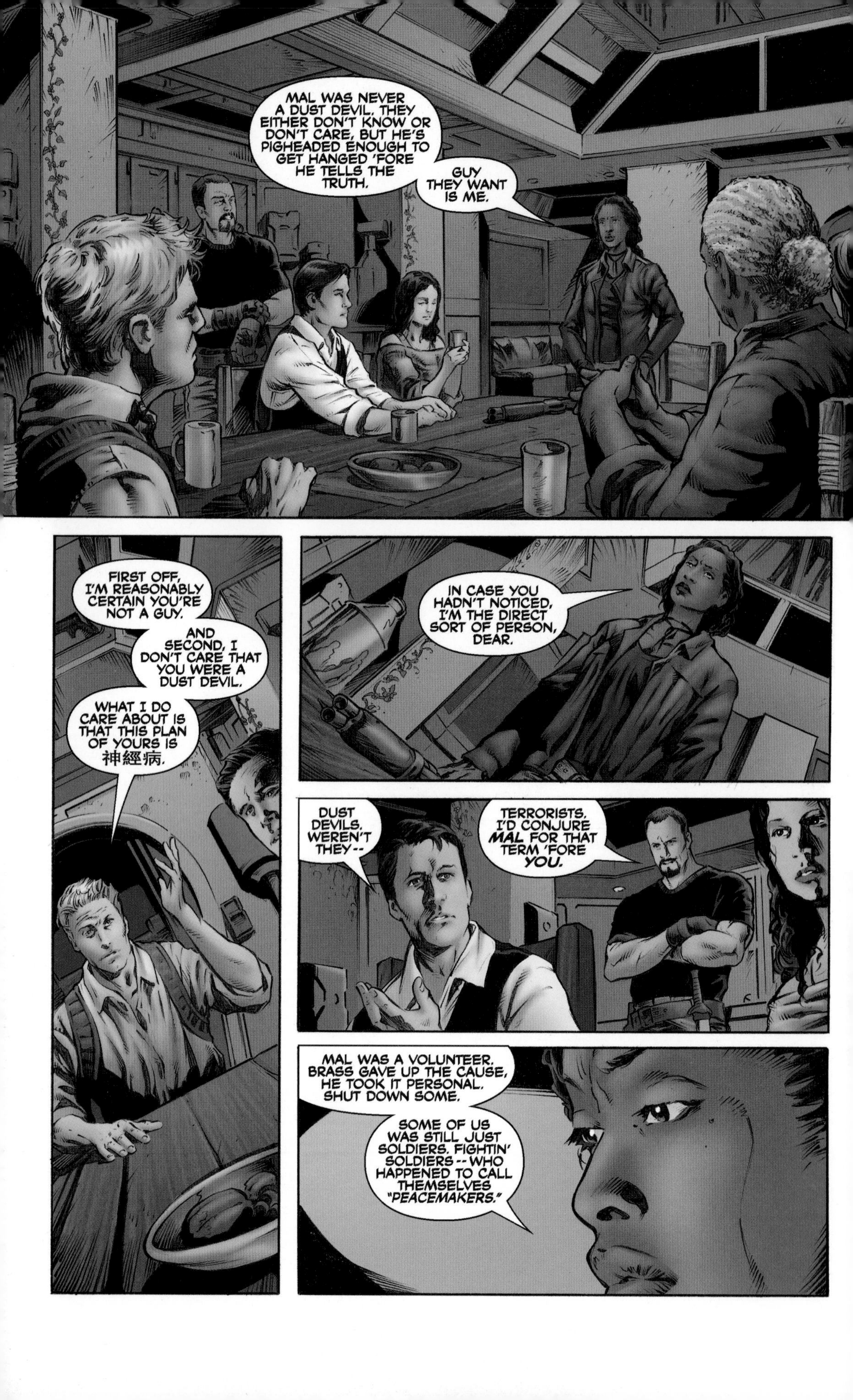
MAL WAS NEVER A DUST DEVIL. THEY EITHER DON'T KNOW OR DON'T CARE, BUT HE'S PIGHEADED ENOUGH TO GET HANGED 'FORE HE TELLS THE TRUTH.
GUY THEY WANT IS ME.
FIRST OFF, I'M REASONABLY CERTAIN YOU'RE NOT A GUY.
AND SECOND, I DON'T CARE THAT YOU WERE A DUST DEVIL.
WHAT I DO CARE ABOUT IS THAT THIS PLAN OF YOURS IS 神經病.
IN CASE YOU HADN'T NOTICED, I'M THE DIRECT SORT OF PERSON, DEAR.
DUST DEVILS. WEREN'T THEY--
TERRORISTS. I'D CONJURE *MAL* FOR THAT TERM 'FORE *YOU.*
MAL WAS A VOLUNTEER. BRASS GAVE UP THE CAUSE, HE TOOK IT PERSONAL. SHUT DOWN SOME.
SOME OF US WAS STILL JUST SOLDIERS. FIGHTIN' SOLDIERS -- WHO HAPPENED TO CALL THEMSELVES *"PEACEMAKERS."*

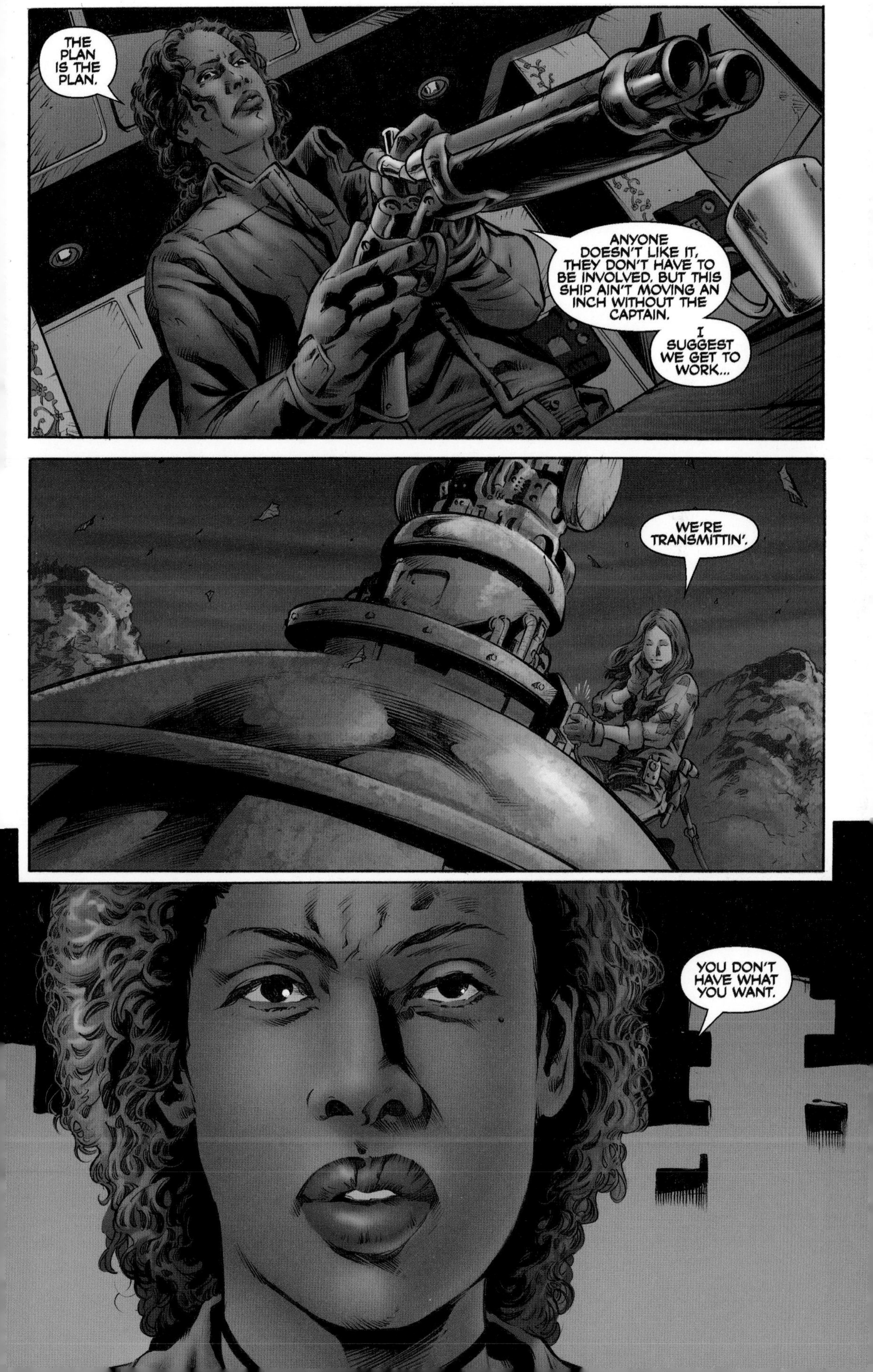
THE PLAN IS THE PLAN.
ANYONE DOESN'T LIKE IT, THEY DON'T HAVE TO BE INVOLVED. BUT THIS SHIP AIN'T MOVING AN INCH WITHOUT THE CAPTAIN.
I SUGGEST WE GET TO WORK...
WE'RE TRANSMITTIN'.
YOU DON'T HAVE WHAT YOU WANT.

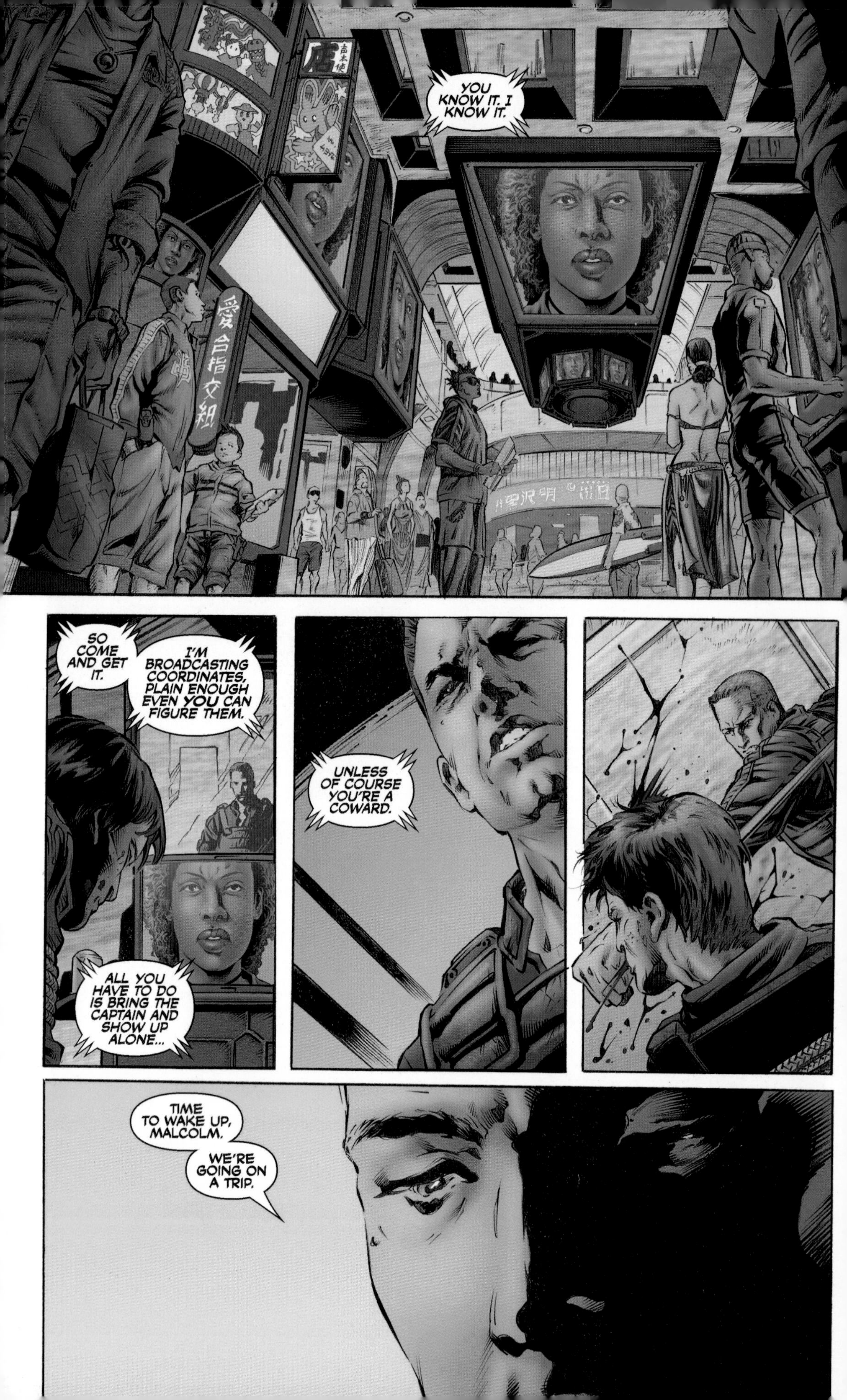
YOU KNOW IT. I KNOW IT.
SO COME AND GET IT.
I'M BROADCASTING COORDINATES, PLAIN ENOUGH EVEN YOU CAN FIGURE THEM.
ALL YOU HAVE TO DO IS BRING THE CAPTAIN AND SHOW UP ALONE...
UNLESS OF COURSE YOU'RE A COWARD.
TIME TO WAKE UP, MALCOLM.
WE'RE GOING ON A TRIP.

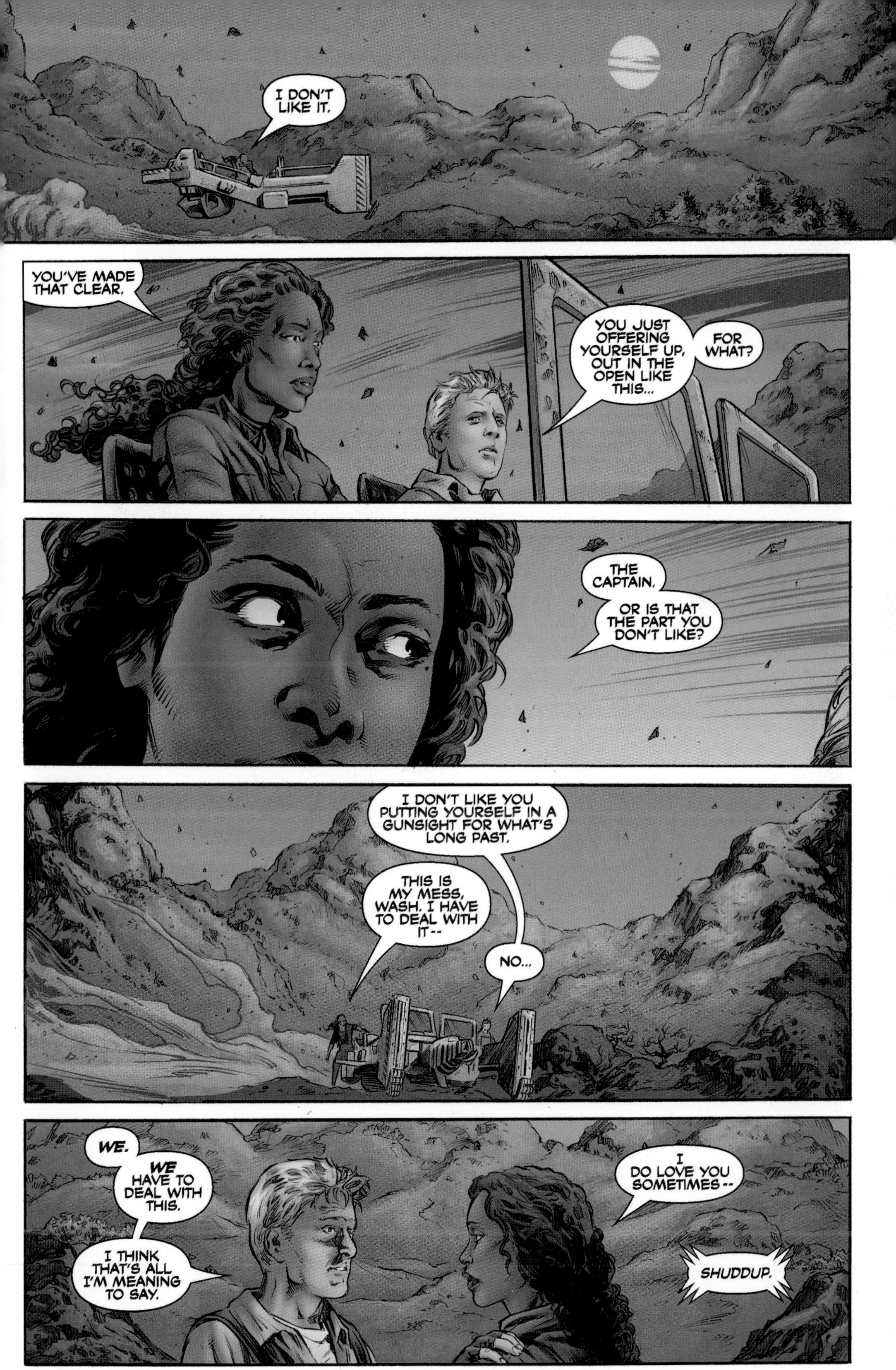
I DON'T LIKE IT.
YOU'VE MADE THAT CLEAR.
YOU JUST OFFERING YOURSELF UP, OUT IN THE OPEN LIKE THIS...
FOR WHAT?
THE CAPTAIN.
OR IS THAT THE PART YOU DON'T LIKE?
I DON'T LIKE YOU PUTTING YOURSELF IN A GUNSIGHT FOR WHAT'S LONG PAST.
THIS IS MY MESS, WASH. I HAVE TO DEAL WITH IT--
NO...
WE.
WE HAVE TO DEAL WITH THIS.
I THINK THAT'S ALL I'M MEANING TO SAY.
I DO LOVE YOU SOMETIMES--
SHUDDUP.

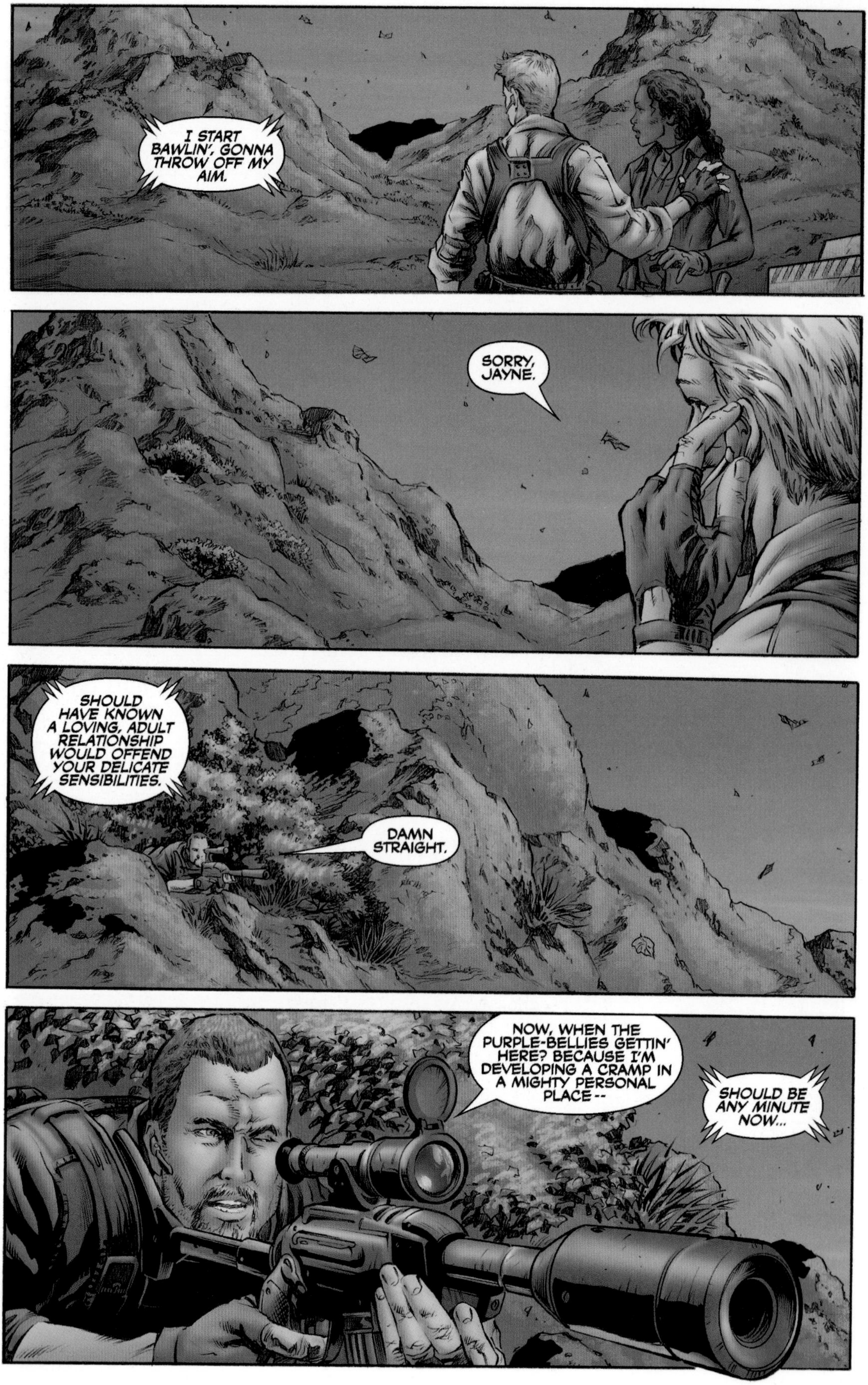
I START BAWLIN', GONNA THROW OFF MY AIM.
SORRY, JAYNE.
SHOULD HAVE KNOWN A LOVING, ADULT RELATIONSHIP WOULD OFFEND YOUR DELICATE SENSIBILITIES.
DAMN STRAIGHT.
NOW, WHEN THE PURPLE-BELLIES GETTIN' HERE? BECAUSE I'M DEVELOPING A CRAMP IN A MIGHTY PERSONAL PLACE --
SHOULD BE ANY MINUTE NOW...

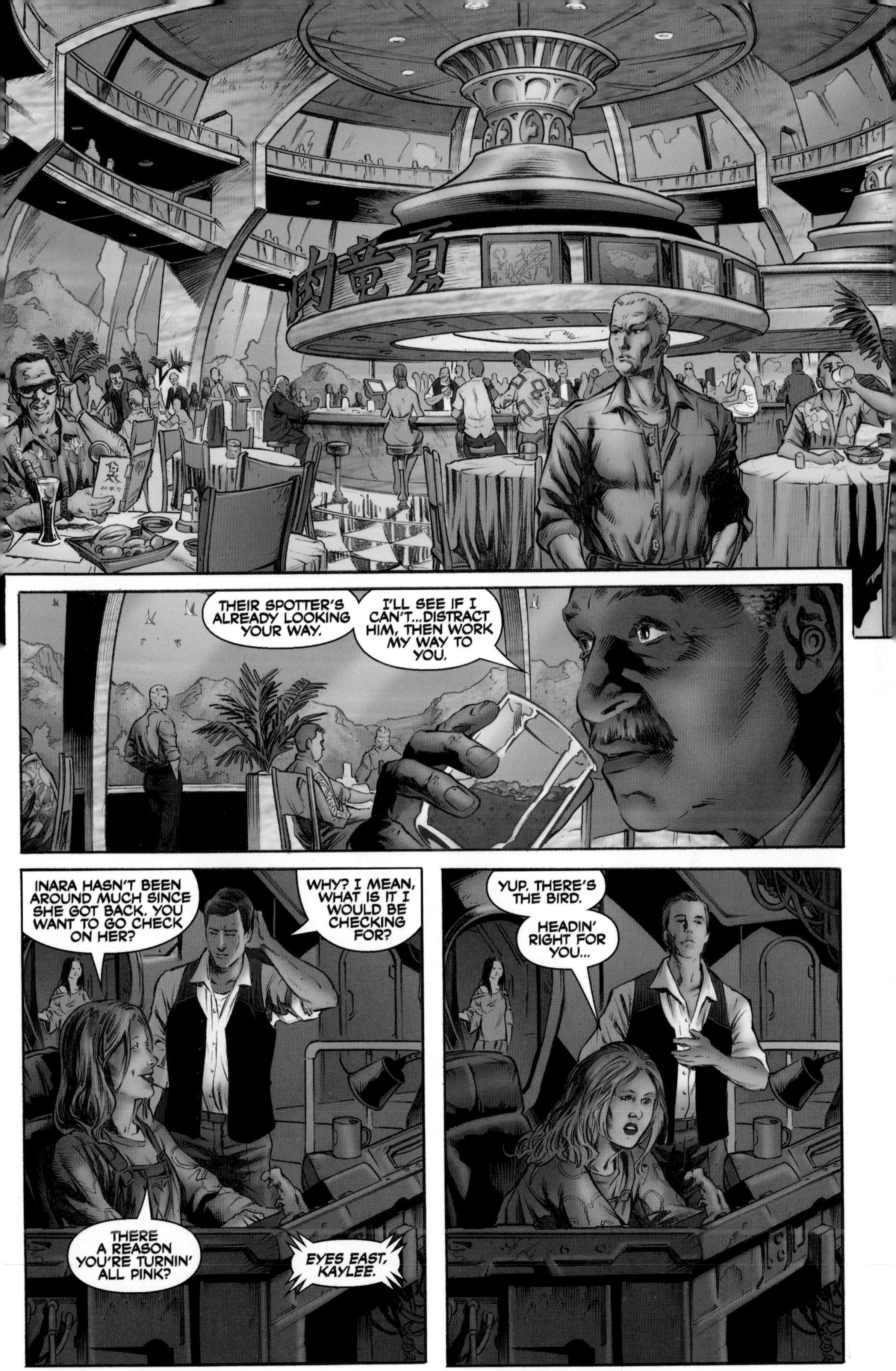
THEIR SPOTTER'S ALREADY LOOKING YOUR WAY.
I'LL SEE IF I CAN'T...DISTRACT HIM, THEN WORK MY WAY TO YOU.
INARA HASN'T BEEN AROUND MUCH SINCE SHE GOT BACK. YOU WANT TO GO CHECK ON HER?
WHY? I MEAN, WHAT IS IT I WOULD BE CHECKING FOR?
THERE A REASON YOU'RE TURNIN' ALL PINK?
EYES EAST, KAYLEE.
YUP. THERE'S THE BIRD.
HEADIN' RIGHT FOR YOU...

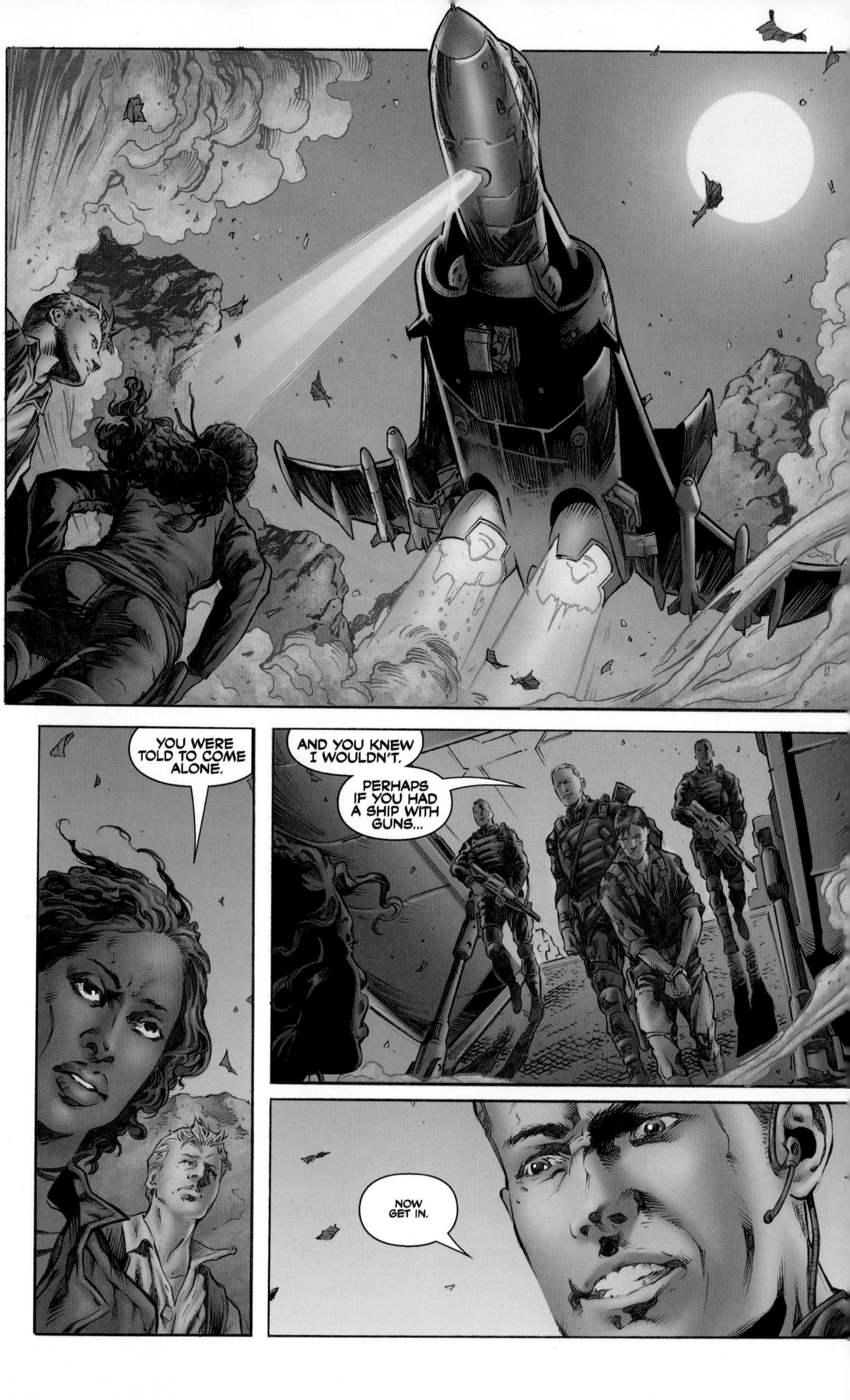

YOU WERE TOLD TO COME ALONE.
AND YOU KNEW I WOULDN'T.
PERHAPS IF YOU HAD A SHIP WITH GUNS...
NOW GET IN.

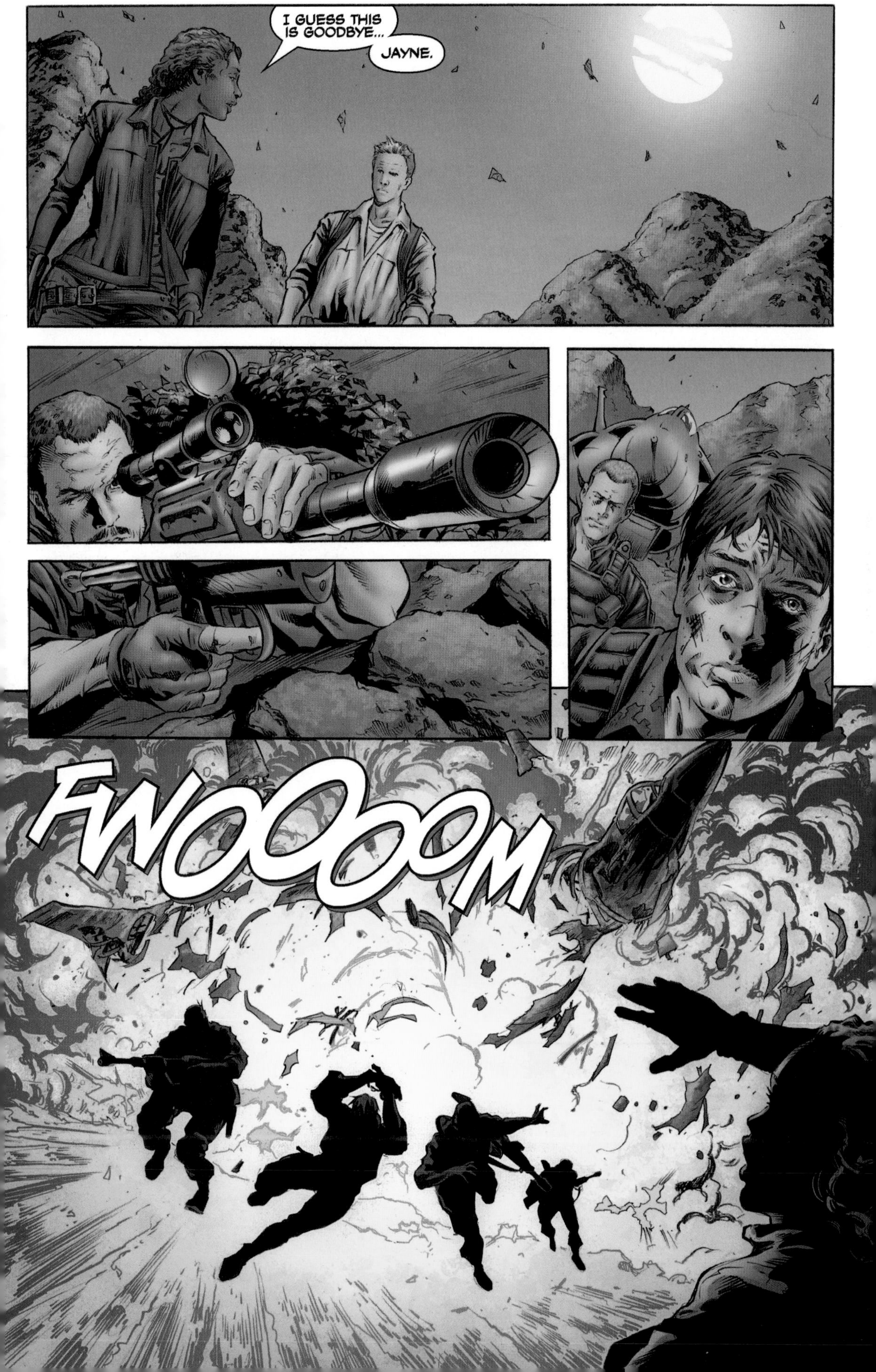
I GUESS THIS IS GOODBYE...
JAYNE.
FWOOOOM

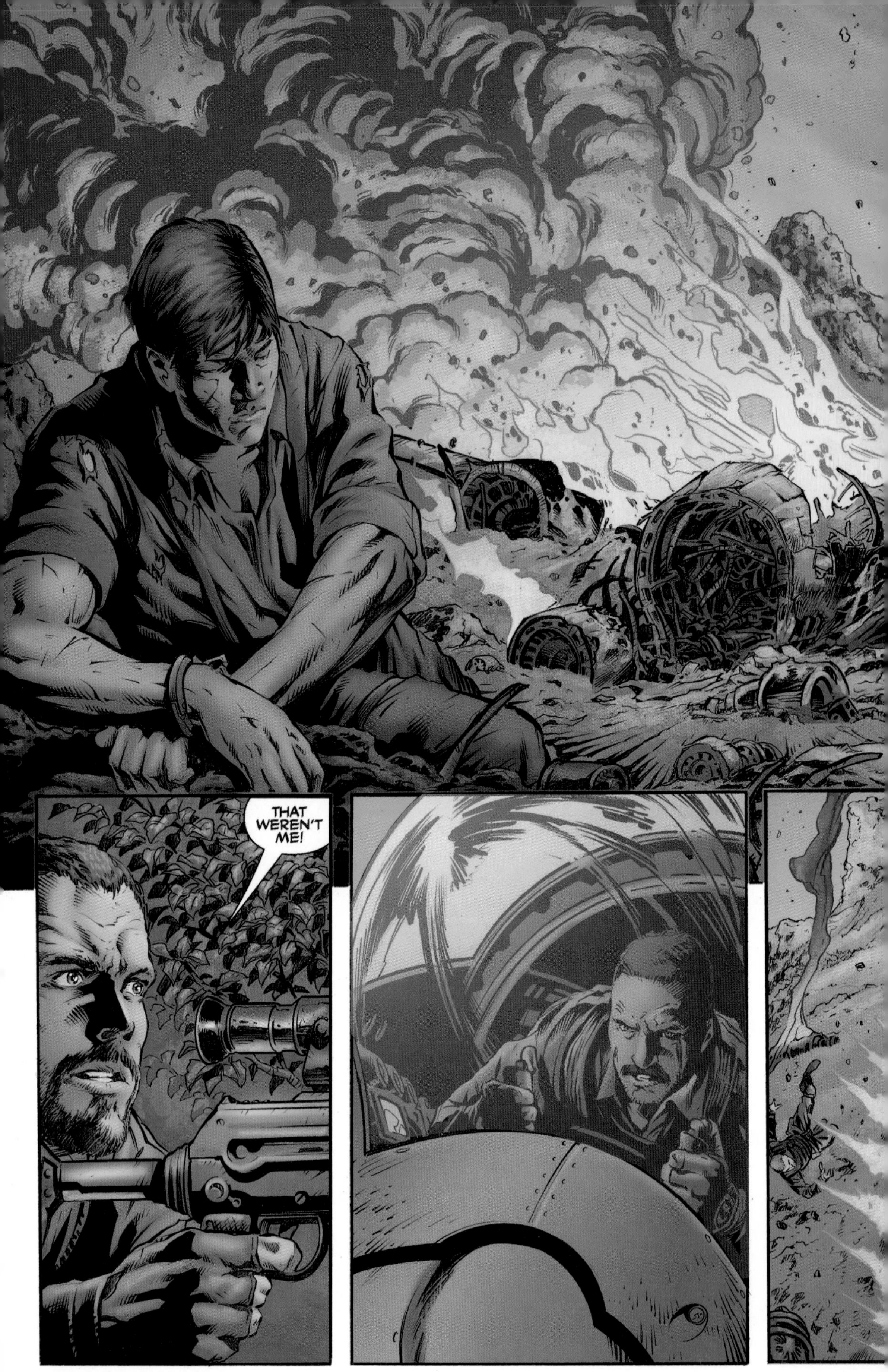
THAT WEREN'T ME!

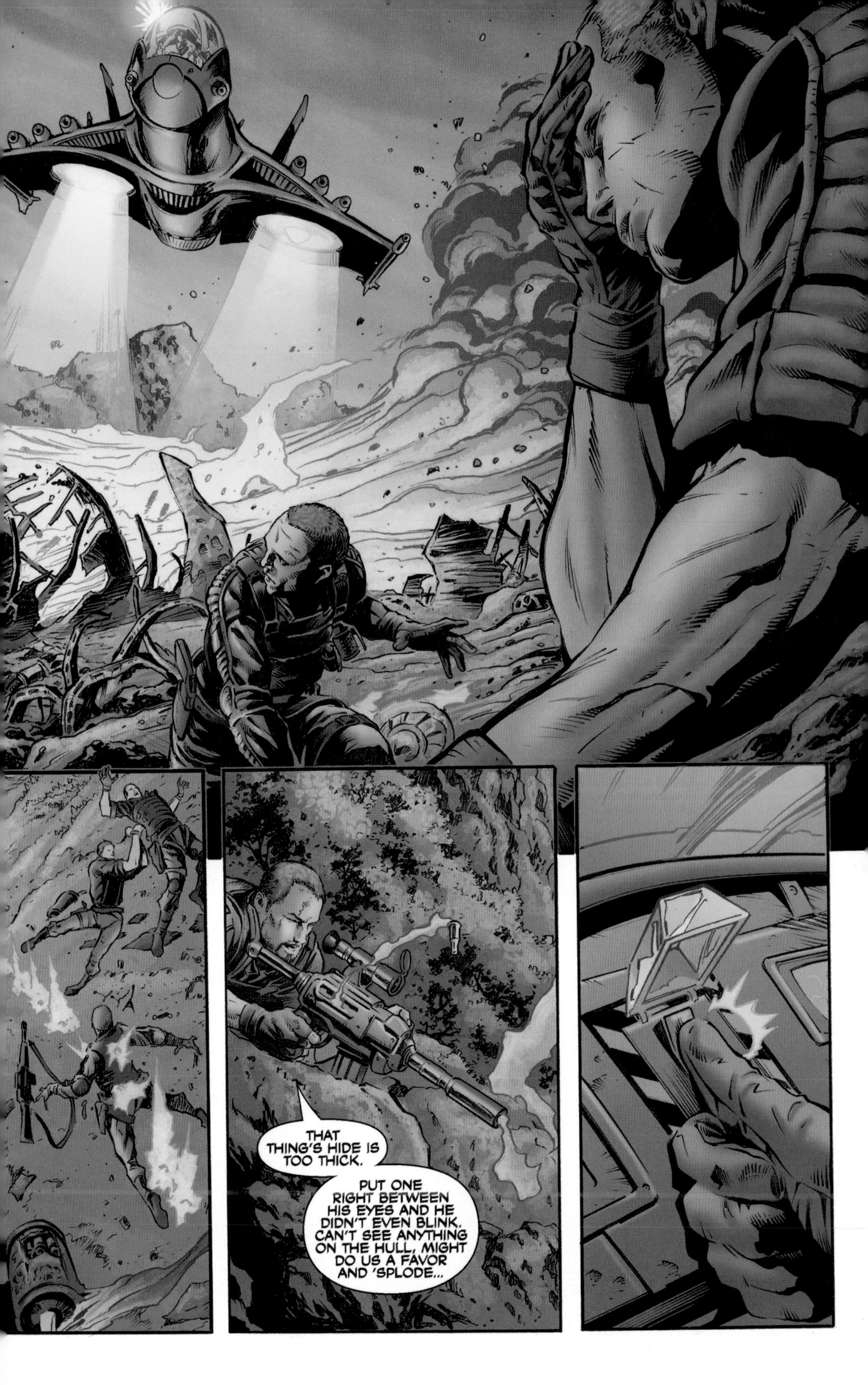
THAT THING'S HIDE IS TOO THICK.
PUT ONE RIGHT BETWEEN HIS EYES AND HE DIDN'T EVEN BLINK. CAN'T SEE ANYTHING ON THE HULL, MIGHT DO US A FAVOR AND 'SPLODE...

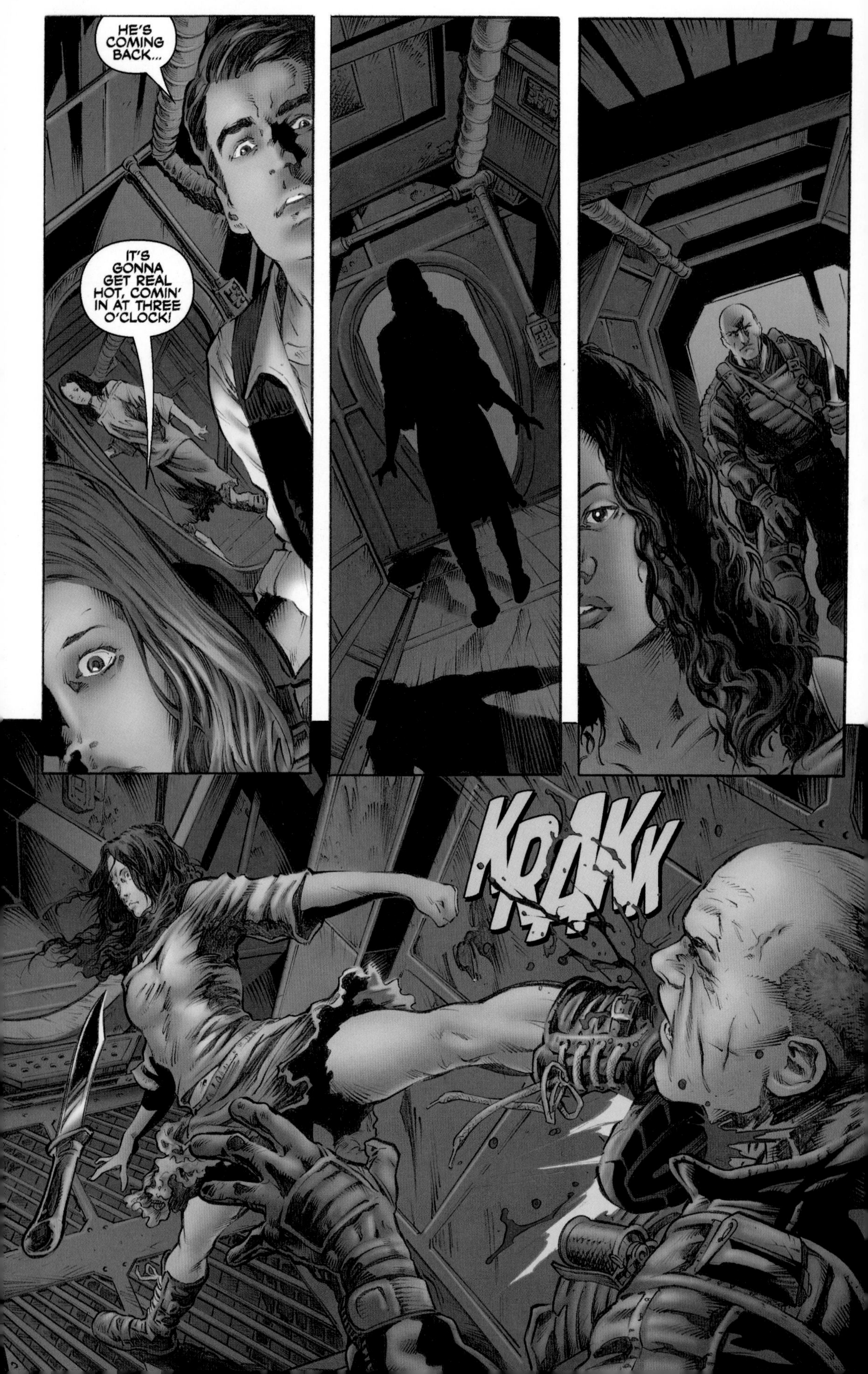
HE'S COMING BACK...
IT'S GONNA GET REAL HOT, COMIN' IN AT THREE O'CLOCK!
KRAKK

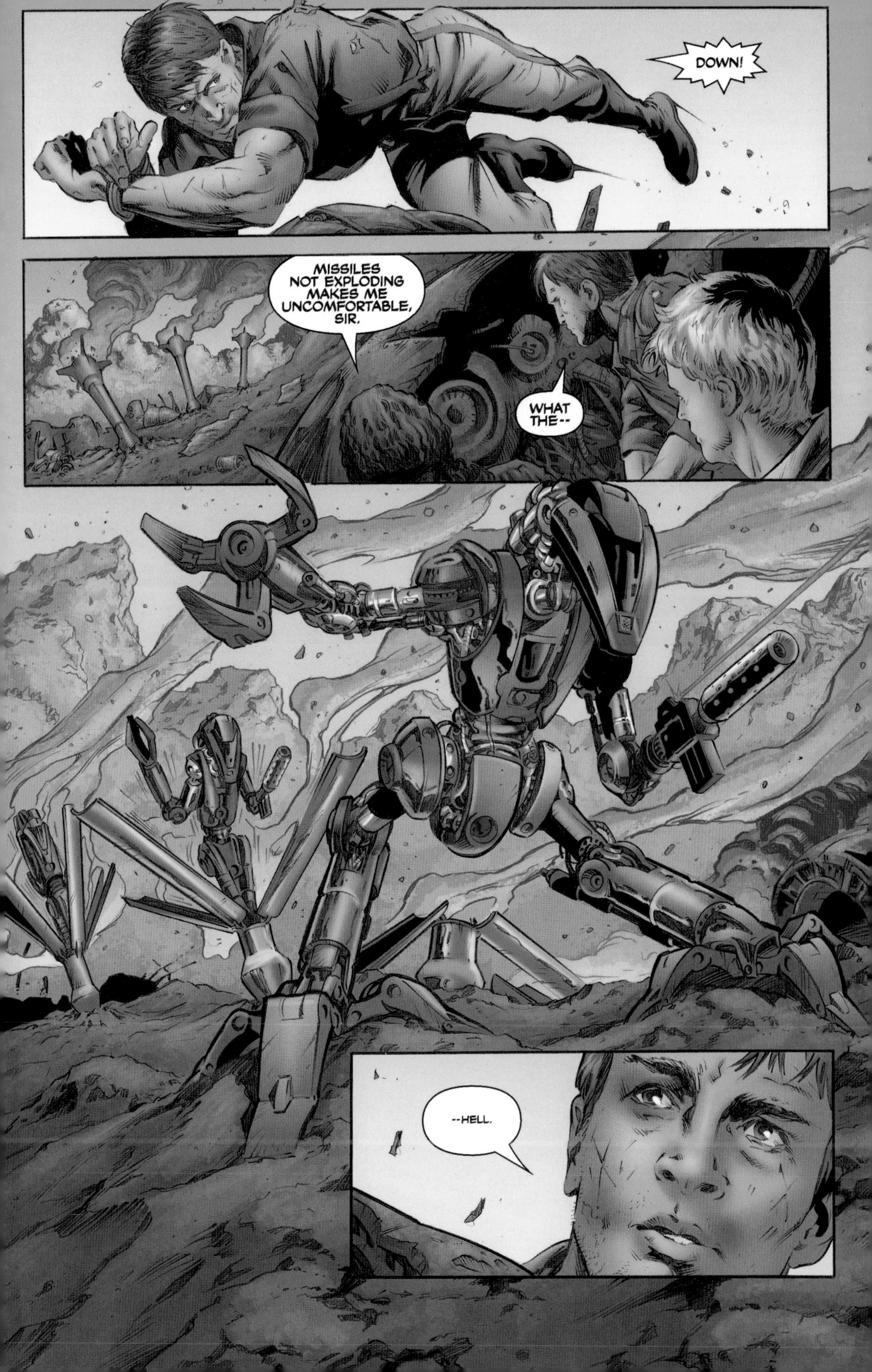
DOWN!
MISSILES NOT EXPLODING MAKES ME UNCOMFORTABLE, SIR.
WHAT THE--
--HELL.

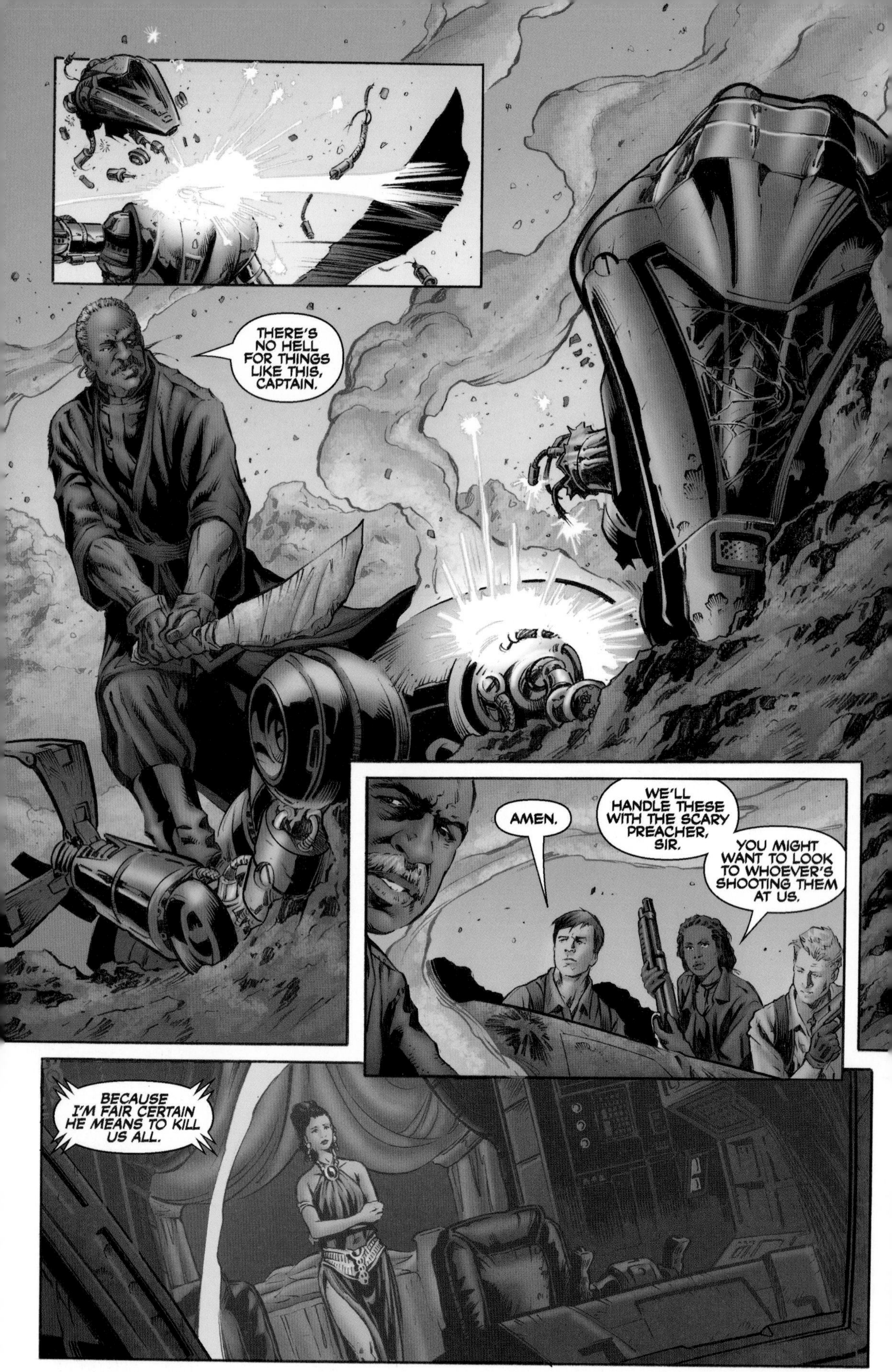
THERE'S NO HELL FOR THINGS LIKE THIS, CAPTAIN.
AMEN.
WE'LL HANDLE THESE WITH THE SCARY PREACHER, SIR.
YOU MIGHT WANT TO LOOK TO WHOEVER'S SHOOTING THEM AT US.
BECAUSE I'M FAIR CERTAIN HE MEANS TO KILL US ALL.

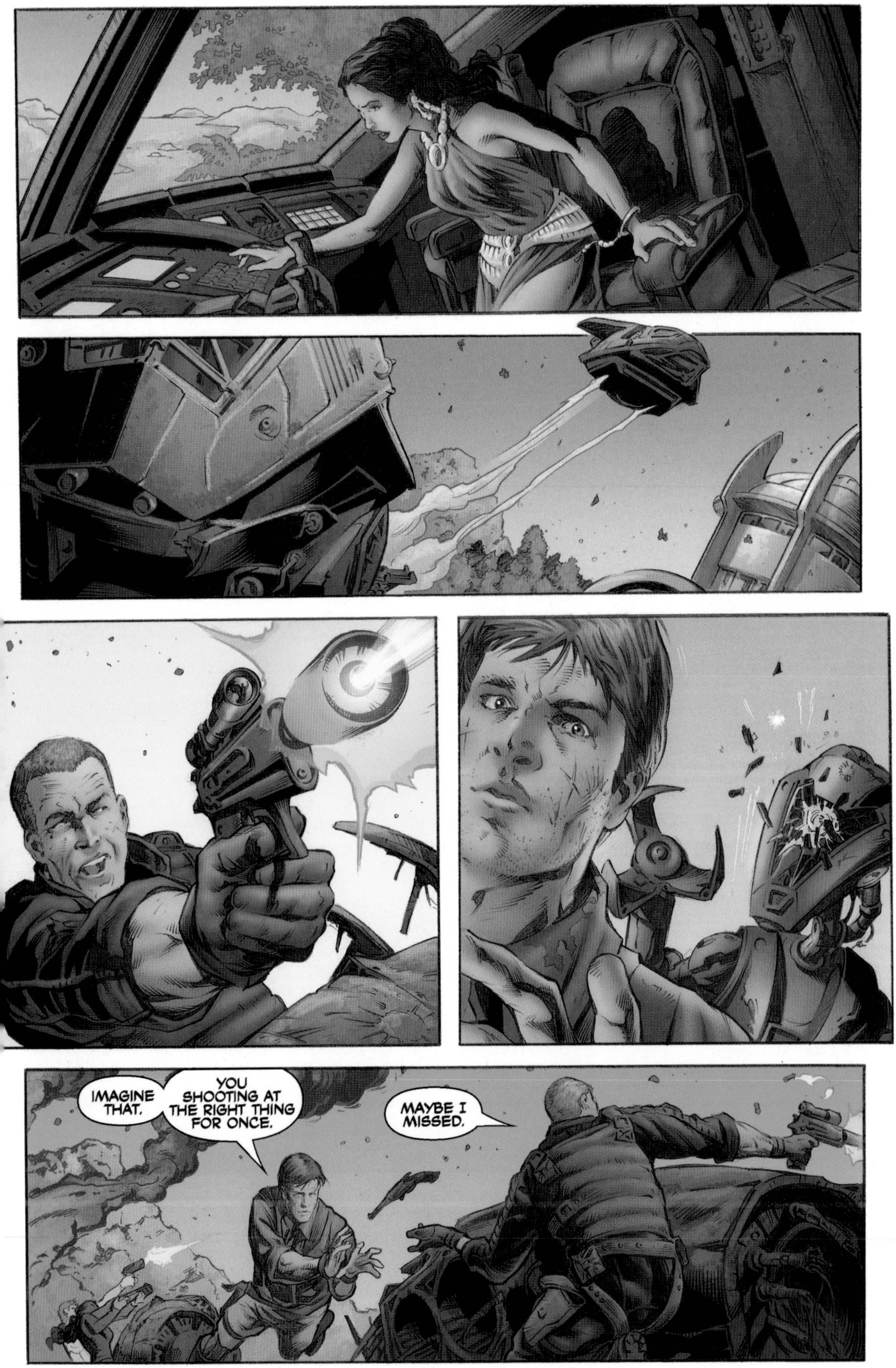
IMAGINE THAT.
YOU SHOOTING AT THE RIGHT THING FOR ONCE.
MAYBE I MISSED.

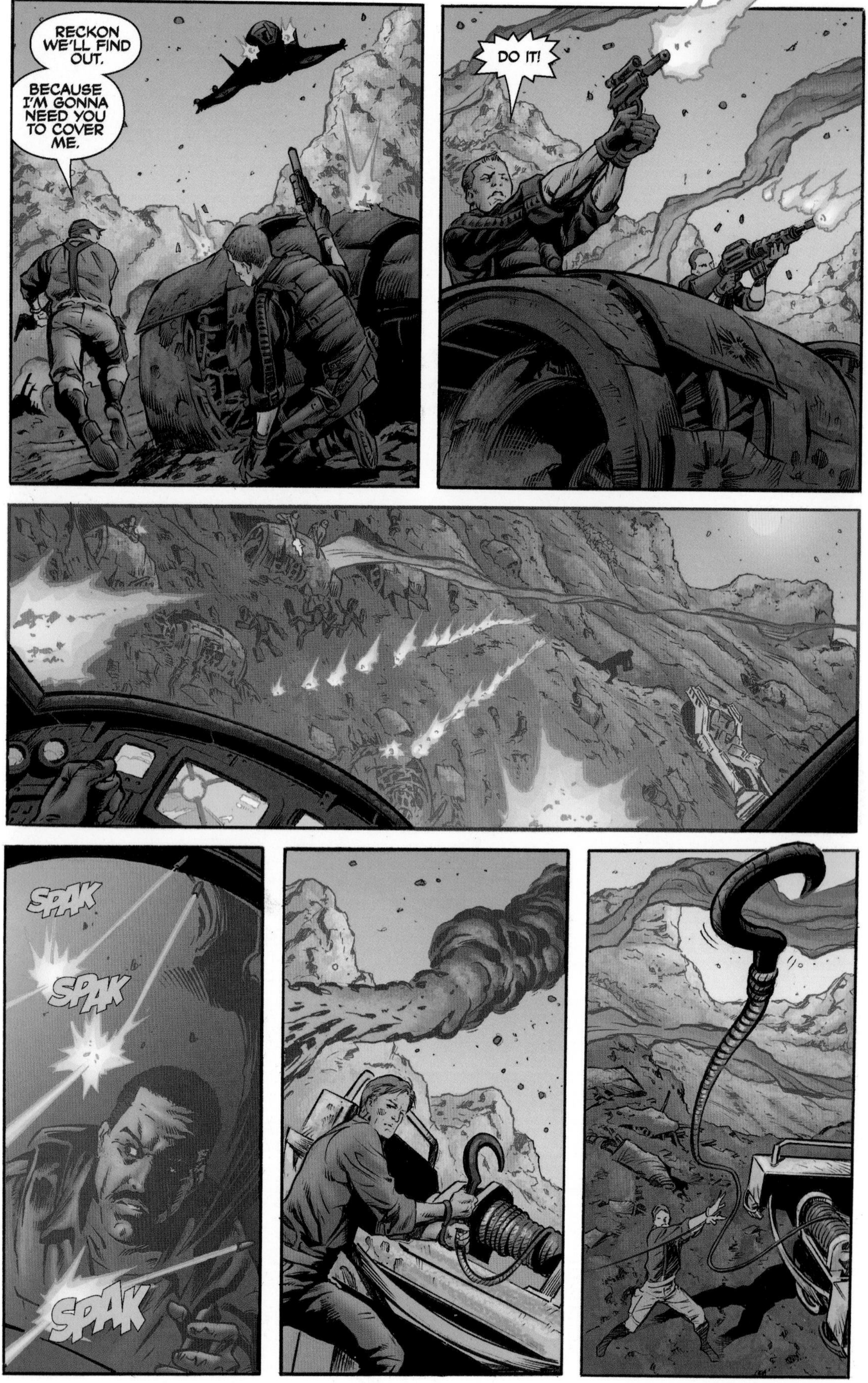
RECKON WE'LL FIND OUT.
BECAUSE I'M GONNA NEED YOU TO COVER ME.
DO IT!
SPAK
SPAK
SPAK

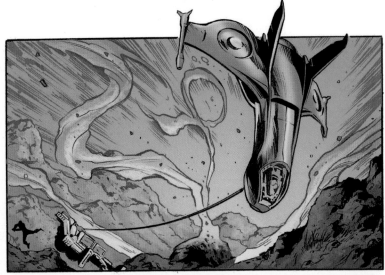

GUESS WE'LL NEVER KNOW WHAT HIS PROBLEM WAS...

WE GOOD HERE?

GOOD ENOUGH.

ACTUALLY, THERE'S THIS ONE THING...

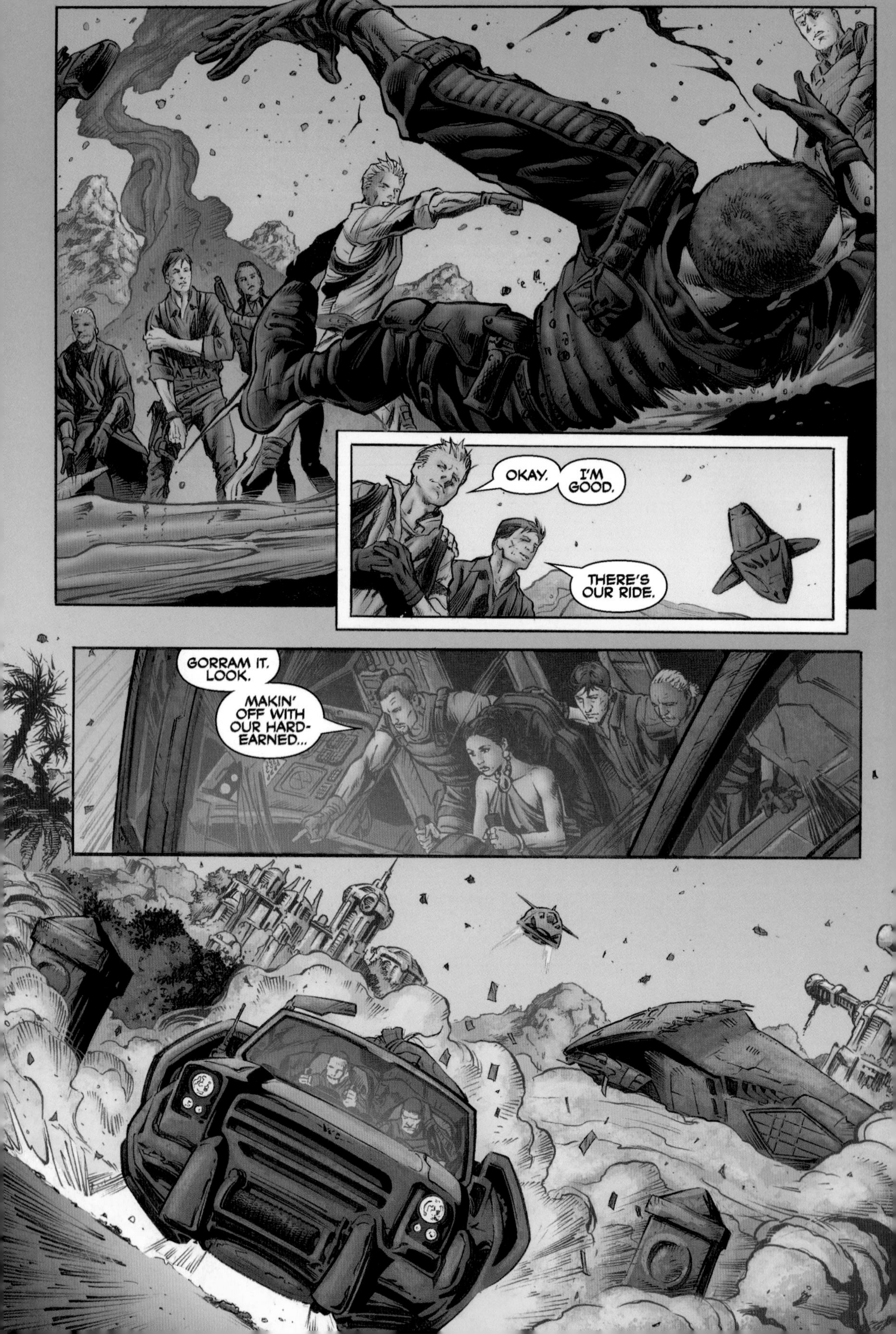
OKAY.
I'M GOOD.
THERE'S OUR RIDE.
GORRAM IT. LOOK.
MAKIN' OFF WITH OUR HARD-EARNED...

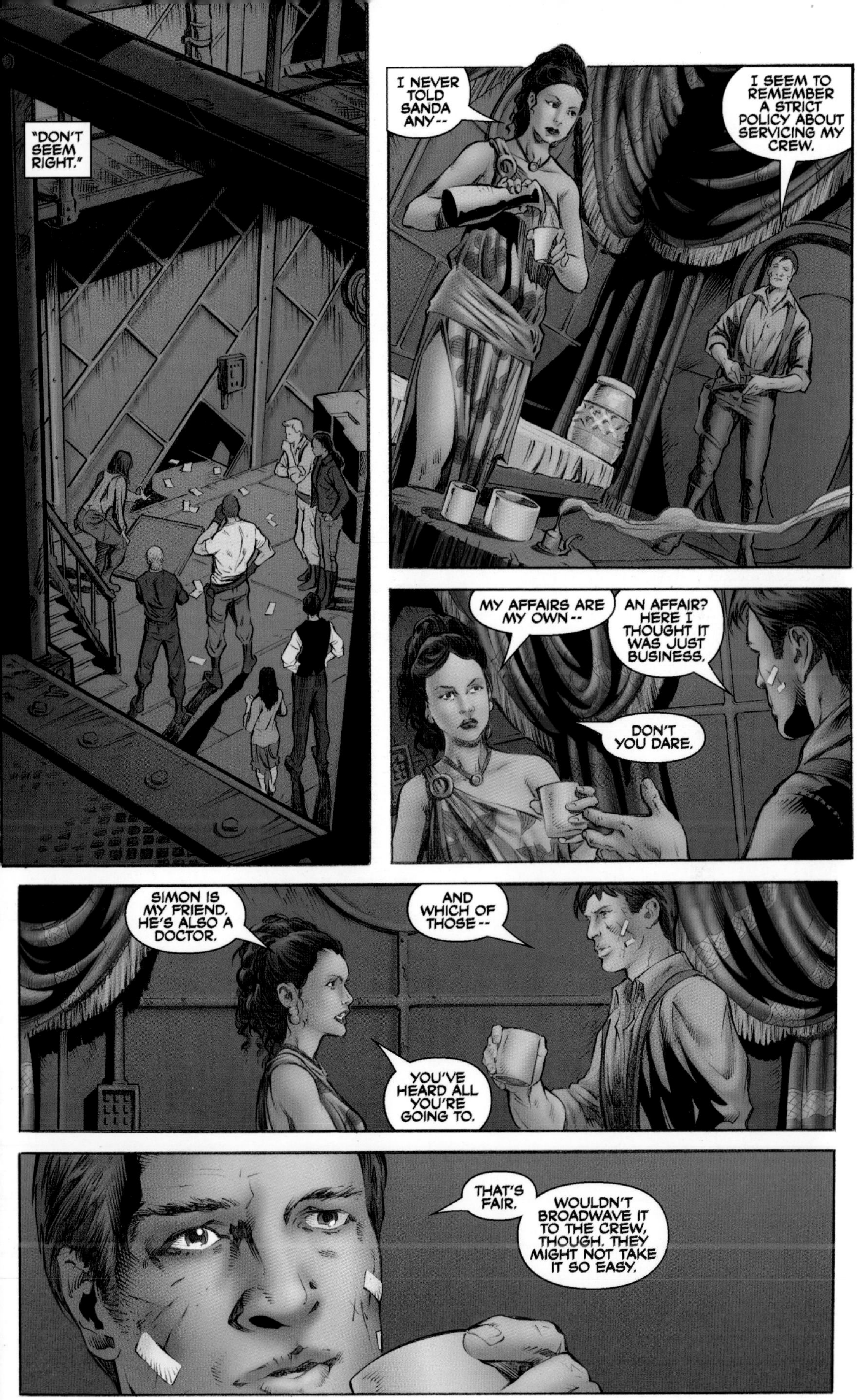
"DON'T SEEM RIGHT."
I NEVER TOLD SANDA ANY--
I SEEM TO REMEMBER A STRICT POLICY ABOUT SERVICING MY CREW.
MY AFFAIRS ARE MY OWN--
AN AFFAIR? HERE I THOUGHT IT WAS JUST BUSINESS.
DON'T YOU DARE.
SIMON IS MY FRIEND. HE'S ALSO A DOCTOR.
AND WHICH OF THOSE--
YOU'VE HEARD ALL YOU'RE GOING TO.
THAT'S FAIR.
WOULDN'T BROADWAVE IT TO THE CREW, THOUGH. THEY MIGHT NOT TAKE IT SO EASY.

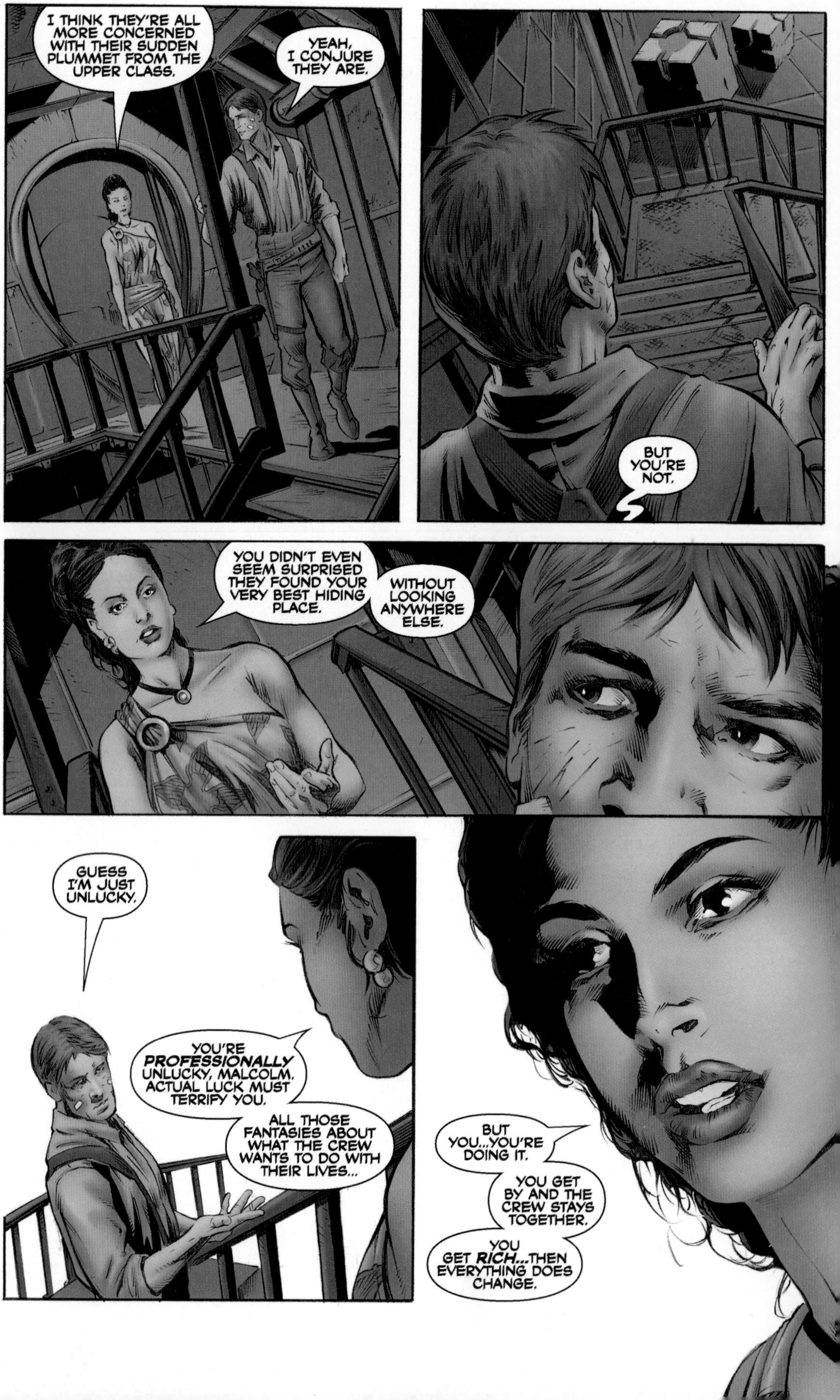
I THINK THEY'RE ALL MORE CONCERNED WITH THEIR SUDDEN PLUMMET FROM THE UPPER CLASS.
YEAH, I CONJURE THEY ARE.
BUT YOU'RE NOT.
YOU DIDN'T EVEN SEEM SURPRISED THEY FOUND YOUR VERY BEST HIDING PLACE.
WITHOUT LOOKING ANYWHERE ELSE.
GUESS I'M JUST UNLUCKY.
YOU'RE *PROFESSIONALLY* UNLUCKY, MALCOLM. ACTUAL LUCK MUST TERRIFY YOU.
ALL THOSE FANTASIES ABOUT WHAT THE CREW WANTS TO DO WITH THEIR LIVES...
BUT YOU...YOU'RE DOING IT.
YOU GET BY AND THE CREW STAYS TOGETHER.
YOU GET *RICH*...THEN EVERYTHING DOES CHANGE.

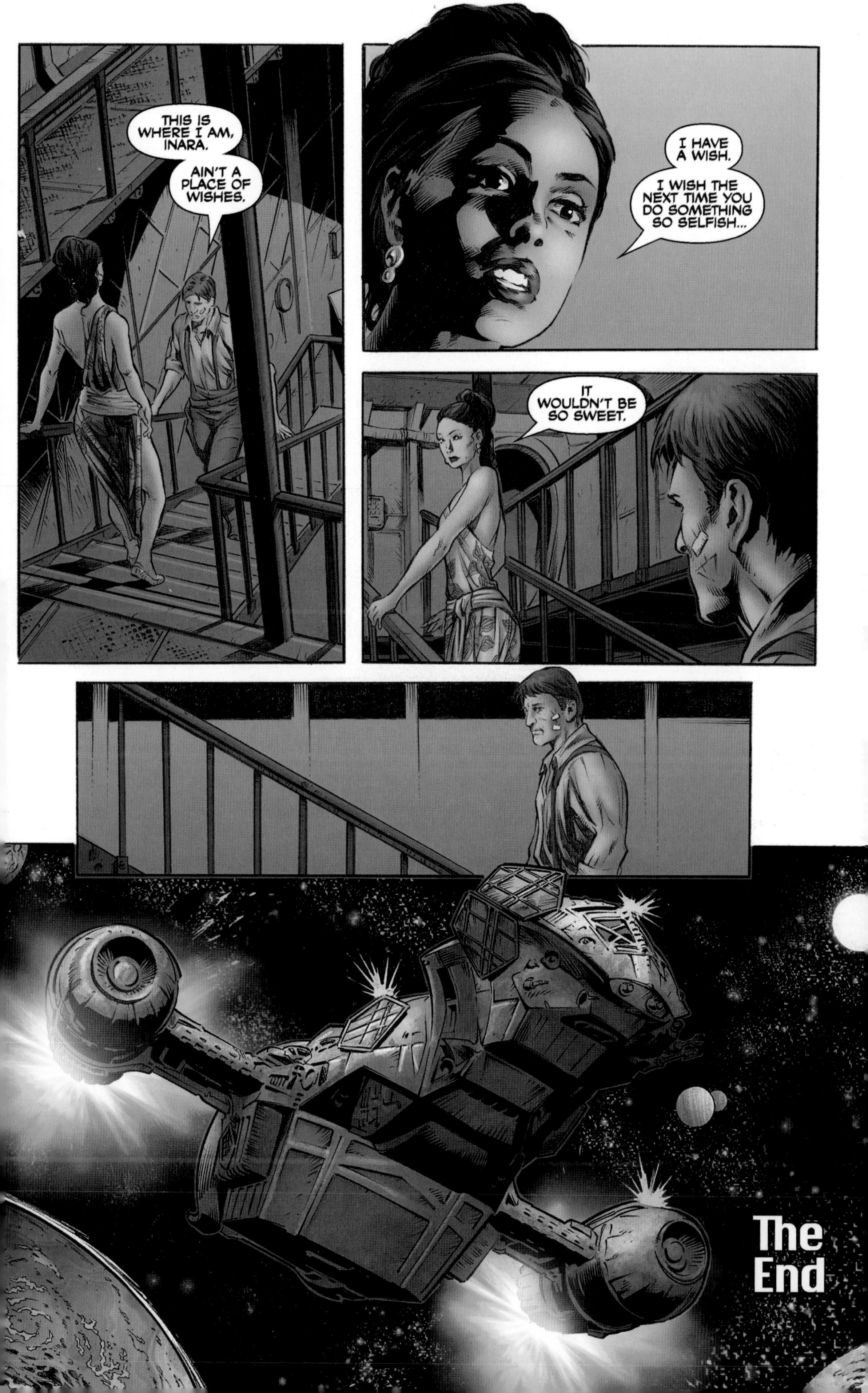
THIS IS WHERE I AM, INARA.
AIN'T A PLACE OF WISHES.
I HAVE A WISH.
I WISH THE NEXT TIME YOU DO SOMETHING SO SELFISH...
IT WOULDN'T BE SO SWEET.
The End

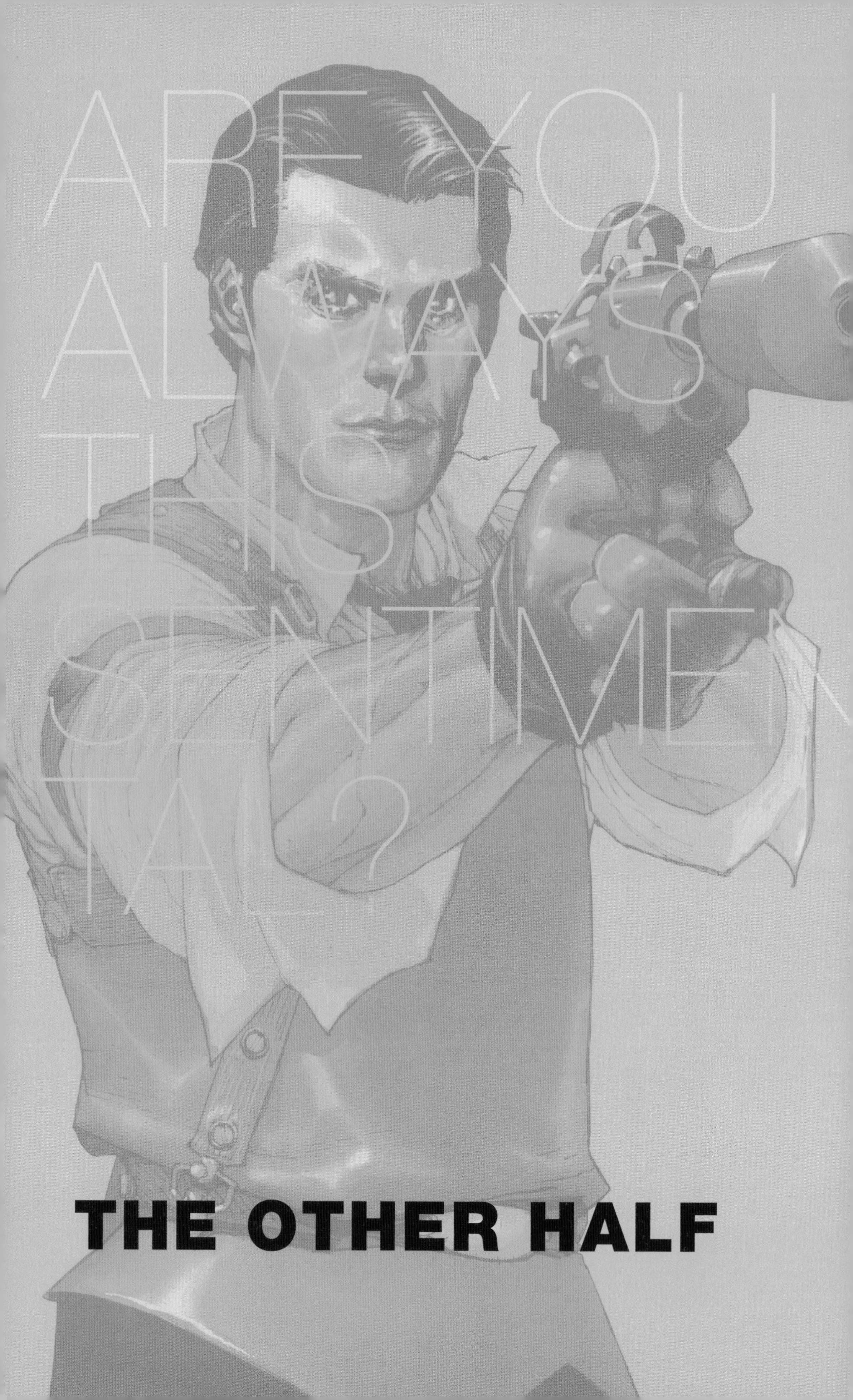
ARE YOU ALWAYS THIS SENTIMENTAL?

THE OTHER HALF

我這個身子不是用來餵 **REAVERS** 的!

YOU *KNOW*, ZOE -- IT JUST AIN'T *RIGHT* THAT EVERY ONCE IN A WHILE WE ACTUALLY GET A CHANCE TO *EARN* OUR GOLD!

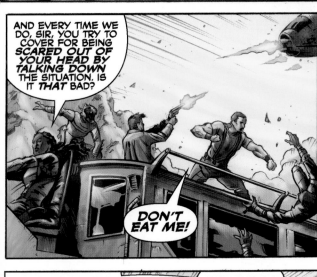

AND EVERY TIME WE DO, SIR, YOU TRY TO COVER FOR BEING *SCARED OUT OF YOUR HEAD* BY *TALKING DOWN* THE SITUATION, IS IT *THAT* BAD?

DON'T EAT ME!

WHAT DO *YOU* THINK?

HOW'S THE SHIP?

WASH'S ON HIS WAY. I'M MORE WORRIED ABOUT OUR CARGO. THAT LAST REAVER SHOT COULD HAVE MADE THIS TRIP A BIG WASTE.

WHY DO YOU THINK I INSIST ON HALF UP FRONT?

HALF UP FRONT *THIS* TIME.

WELL, JUST 'CAUSE I INSIST DOESN'T MEAN THEY AGREE.

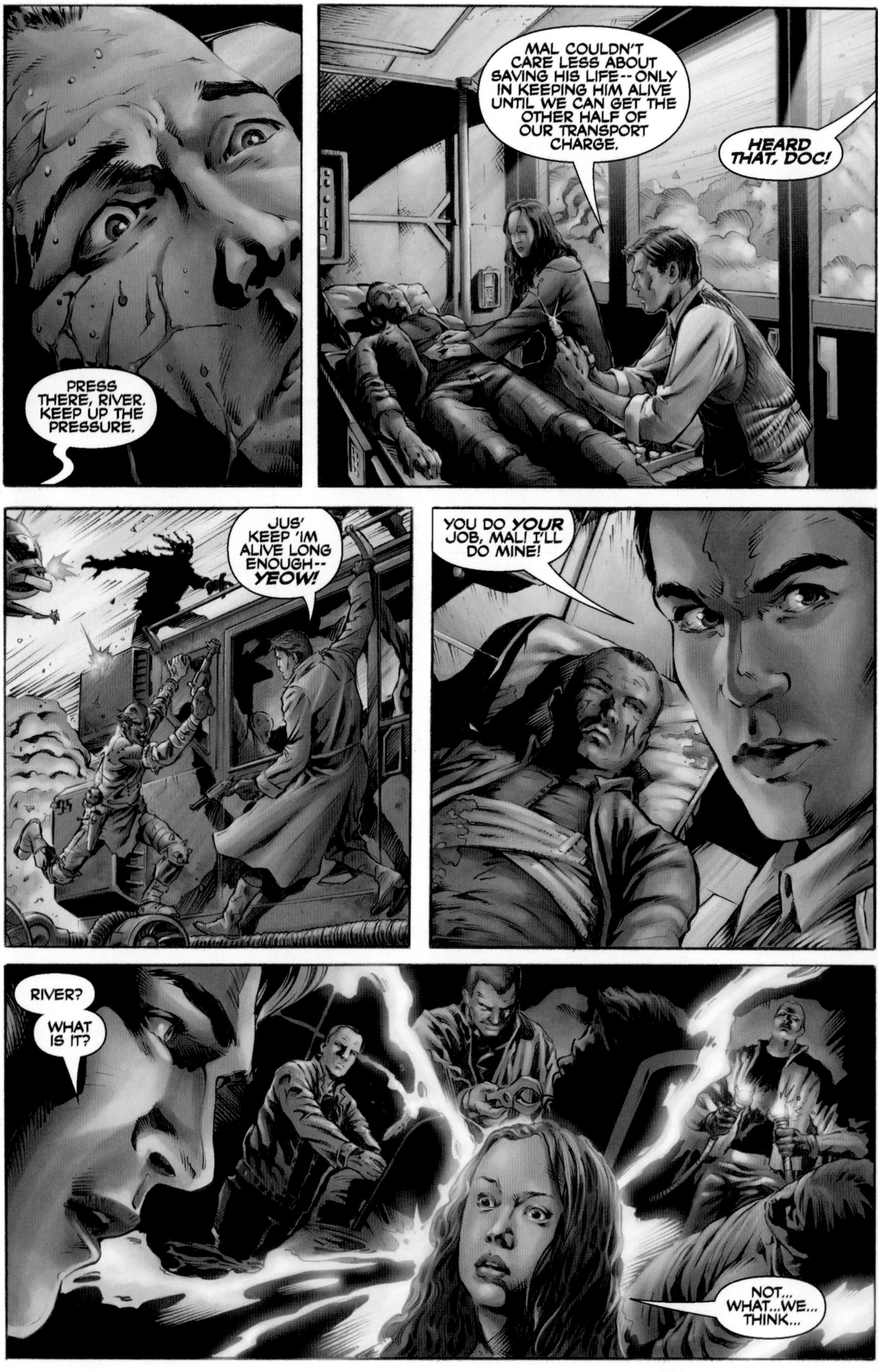
PRESS THERE, RIVER. KEEP UP THE PRESSURE.
MAL COULDN'T CARE LESS ABOUT SAVING HIS LIFE--ONLY IN KEEPING HIM ALIVE UNTIL WE CAN GET THE OTHER HALF OF OUR TRANSPORT CHARGE.
HEARD THAT, DOC!
JUS' KEEP 'IM ALIVE LONG ENOUGH--YEOW!
YOU DO YOUR JOB, MAL! I'LL DO MINE!
RIVER?
WHAT IS IT?
NOT... WHAT...WE... THINK...

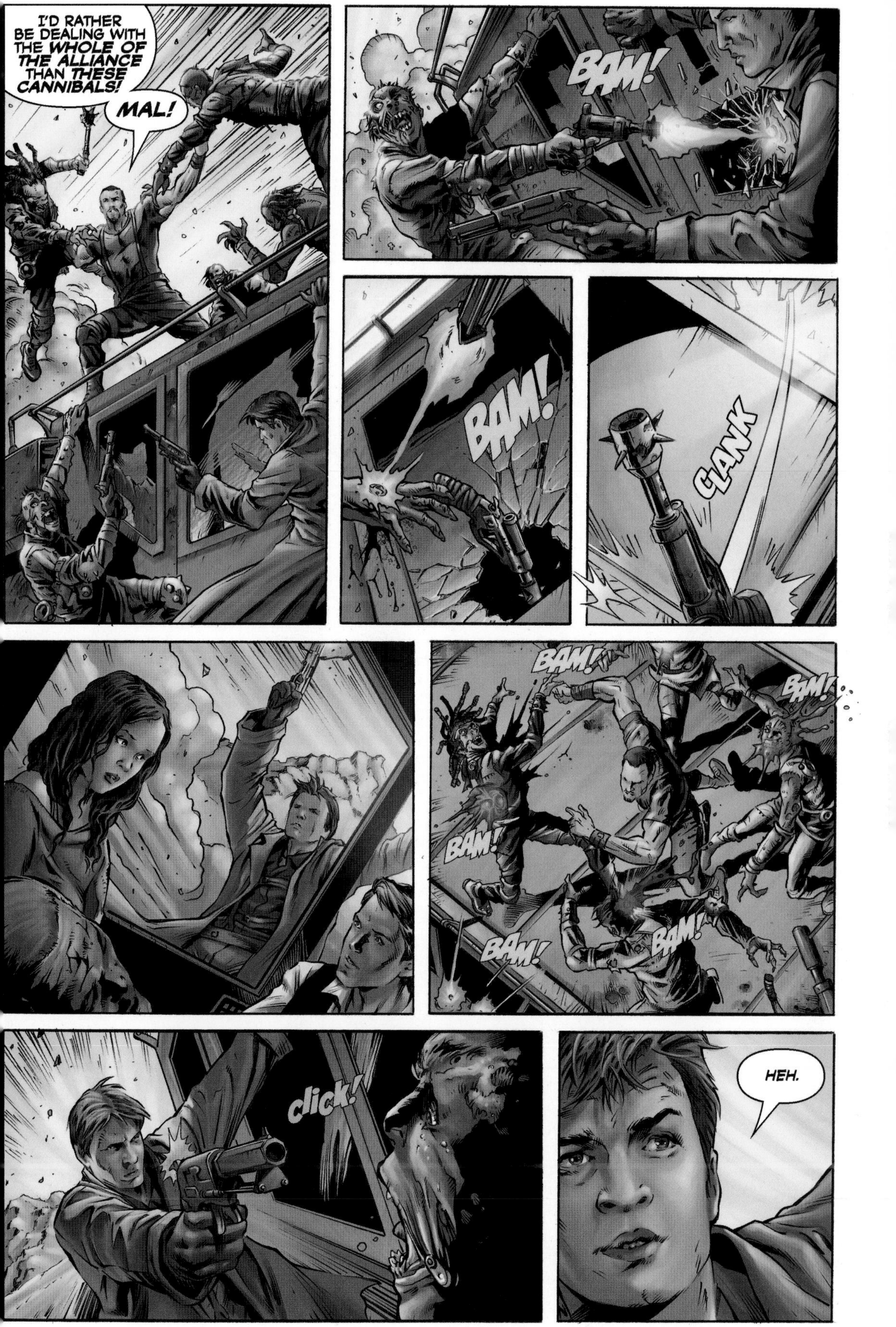
I'D RATHER BE DEALING WITH THE WHOLE OF THE ALLIANCE THAN THESE CANNIBALS!
MAL!
BAM!
BAM!
CLANK
BAM!
BAM!
BAM!
BAM!
BAM!
click!
HEH.

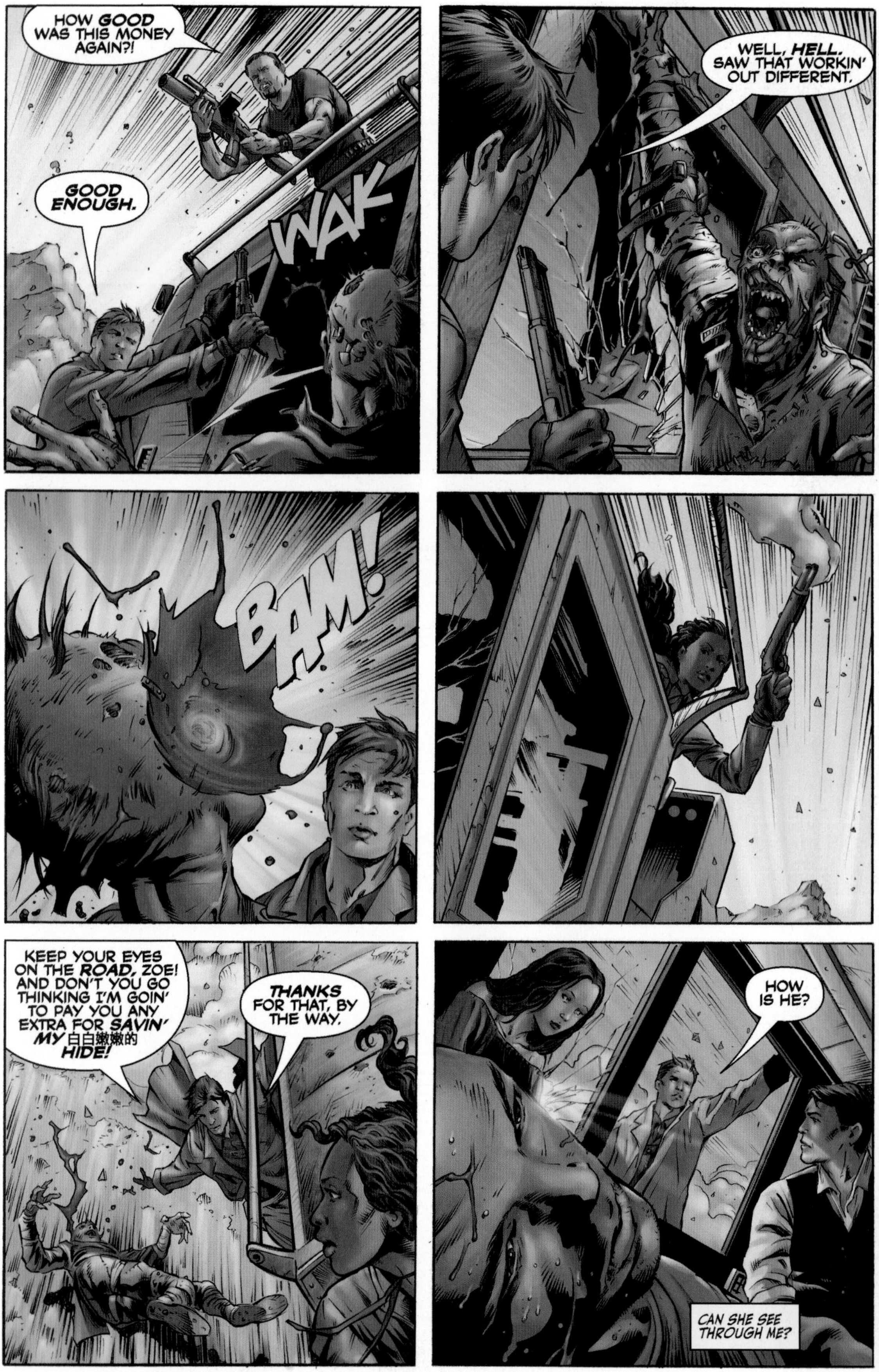
HOW GOOD WAS THIS MONEY AGAIN?!
GOOD ENOUGH.
WAK
WELL, HELL. SAW THAT WORKIN' OUT DIFFERENT.
BAM!
KEEP YOUR EYES ON THE ROAD, ZOE! AND DON'T YOU GO THINKING I'M GOIN' TO PAY YOU ANY EXTRA FOR SAVIN' MY 白白嫩嫩的 HIDE!
THANKS FOR THAT, BY THE WAY.
HOW IS HE?
CAN SHE SEE THROUGH ME?

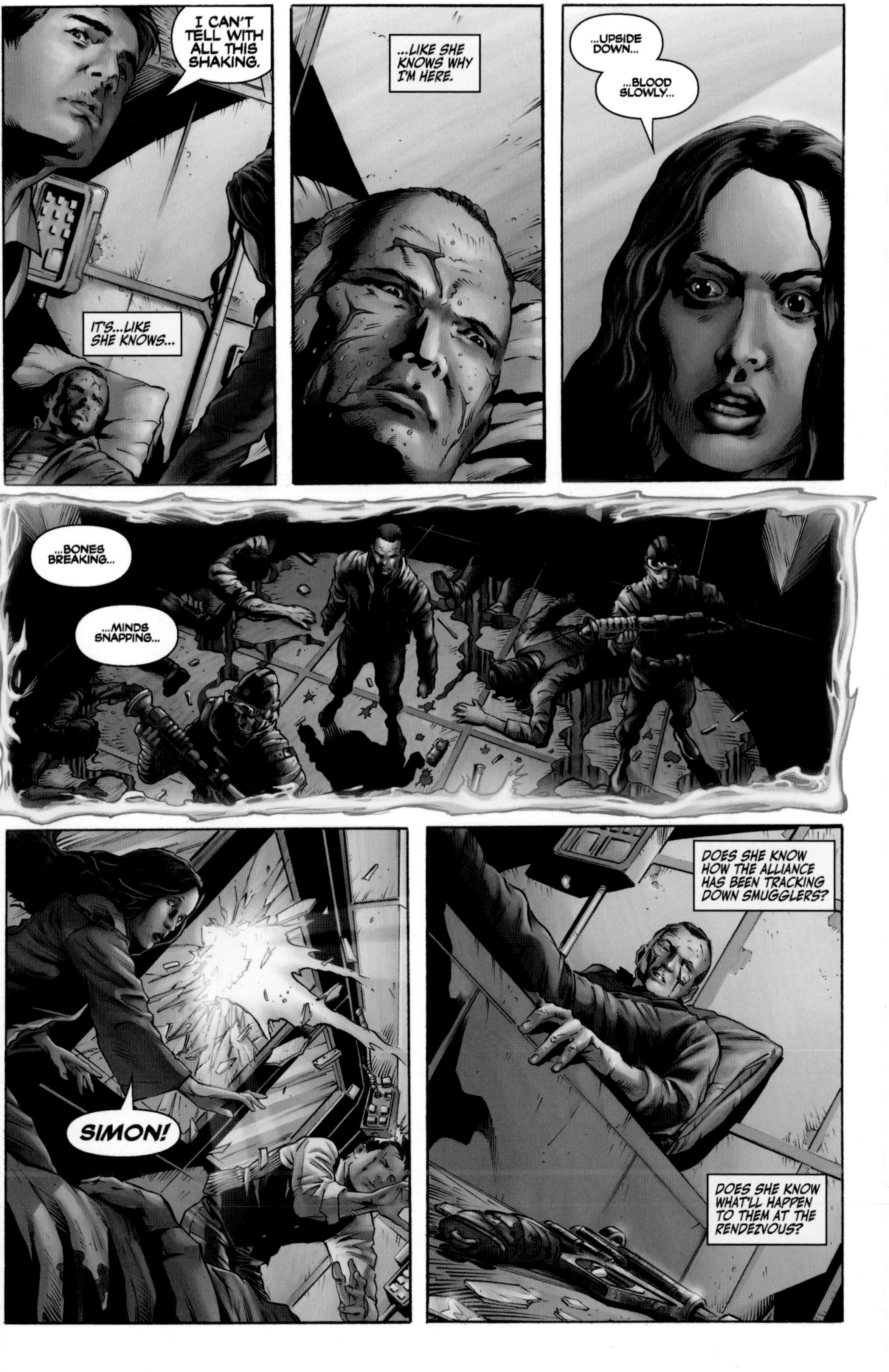
I CAN'T TELL WITH ALL THIS SHAKING.
IT'S...LIKE SHE KNOWS...
...LIKE SHE KNOWS WHY I'M HERE.
...UPSIDE DOWN...
...BLOOD SLOWLY...
...BONES BREAKING...
...MINDS SNAPPING...
SIMON!
DOES SHE KNOW HOW THE ALLIANCE HAS BEEN TRACKING DOWN SMUGGLERS?
DOES SHE KNOW WHAT'LL HAPPEN TO THEM AT THE RENDEZVOUS?

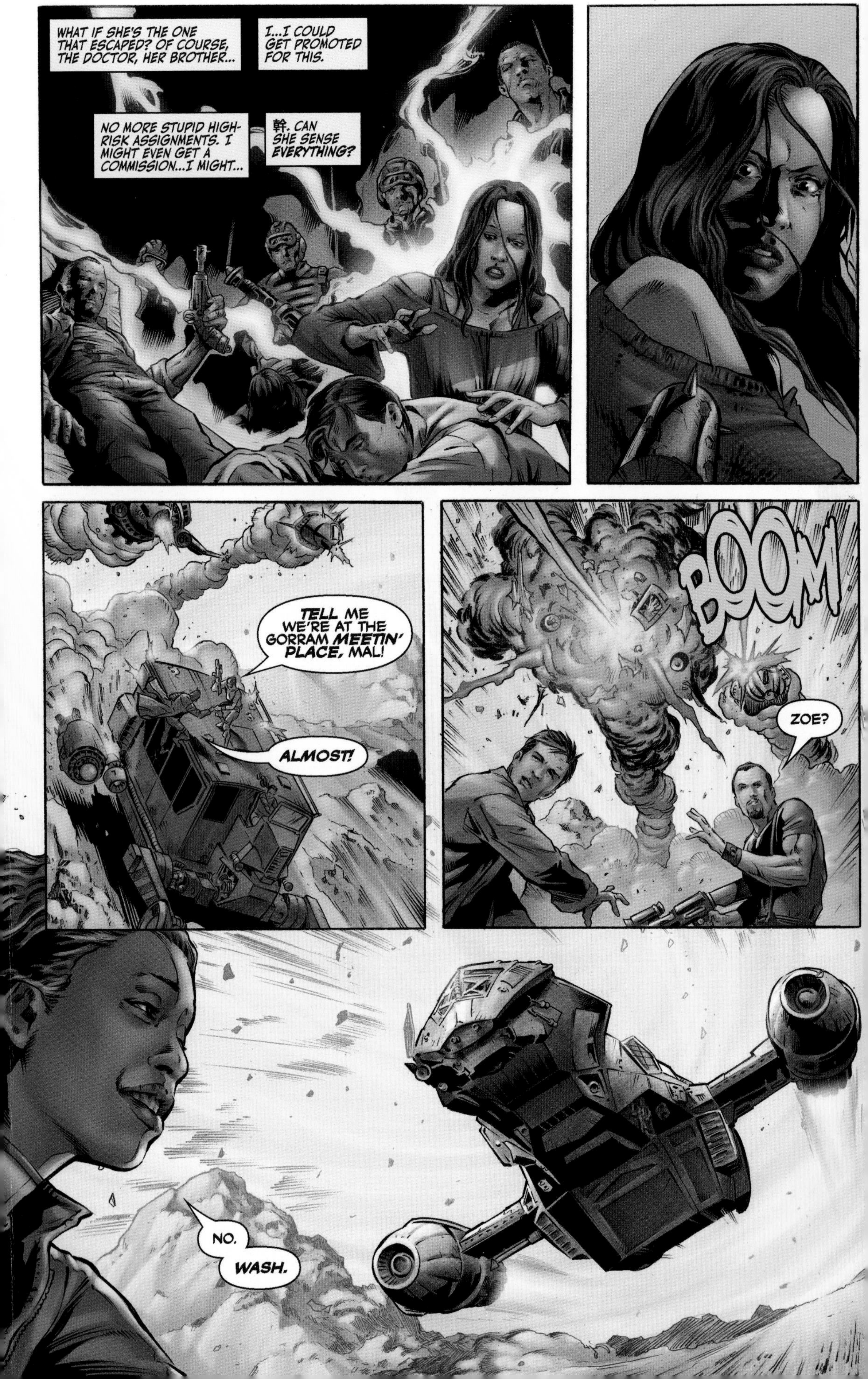
WHAT IF SHE'S THE ONE THAT ESCAPED? OF COURSE, THE DOCTOR, HER BROTHER...
I...I COULD GET PROMOTED FOR THIS.
NO MORE STUPID HIGH-RISK ASSIGNMENTS. I MIGHT EVEN GET A COMMISSION...I MIGHT...
幹. CAN SHE SENSE EVERYTHING?
TELL ME WE'RE AT THE GORRAM MEETIN' PLACE, MAL!
ALMOST!
BOOM
ZOE?
NO.
WASH.

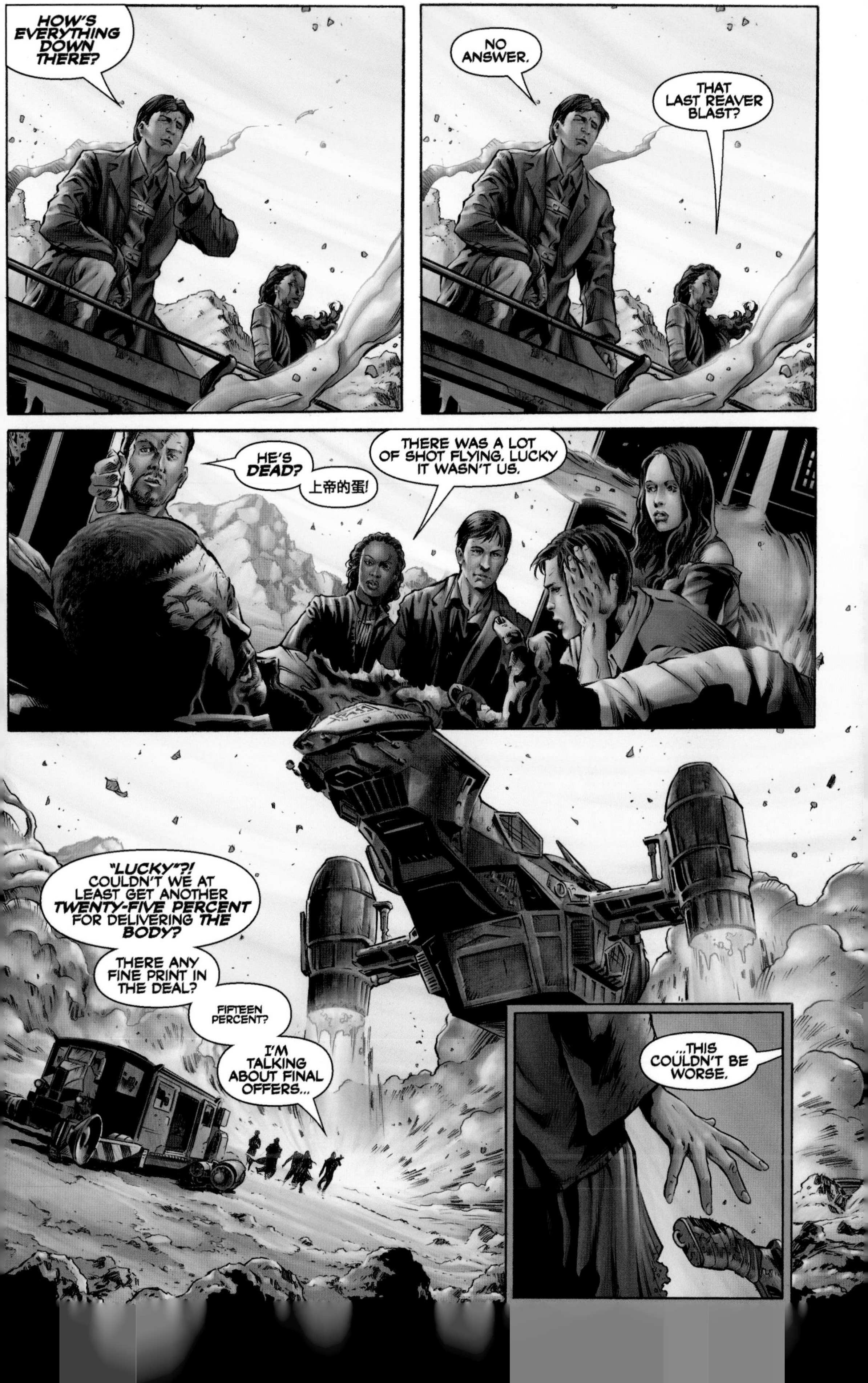
HOW'S EVERYTHING DOWN THERE?
NO ANSWER.
THAT LAST REAVER BLAST?
HE'S DEAD?
上帝的蛋!
THERE WAS A LOT OF SHOT FLYING. LUCKY IT WASN'T US.
"LUCKY"?! COULDN'T WE AT LEAST GET ANOTHER TWENTY-FIVE PERCENT FOR DELIVERING THE BODY?
THERE ANY FINE PRINT IN THE DEAL?
FIFTEEN PERCENT?
I'M TALKING ABOUT FINAL OFFERS...
...THIS COULDN'T BE WORSE.

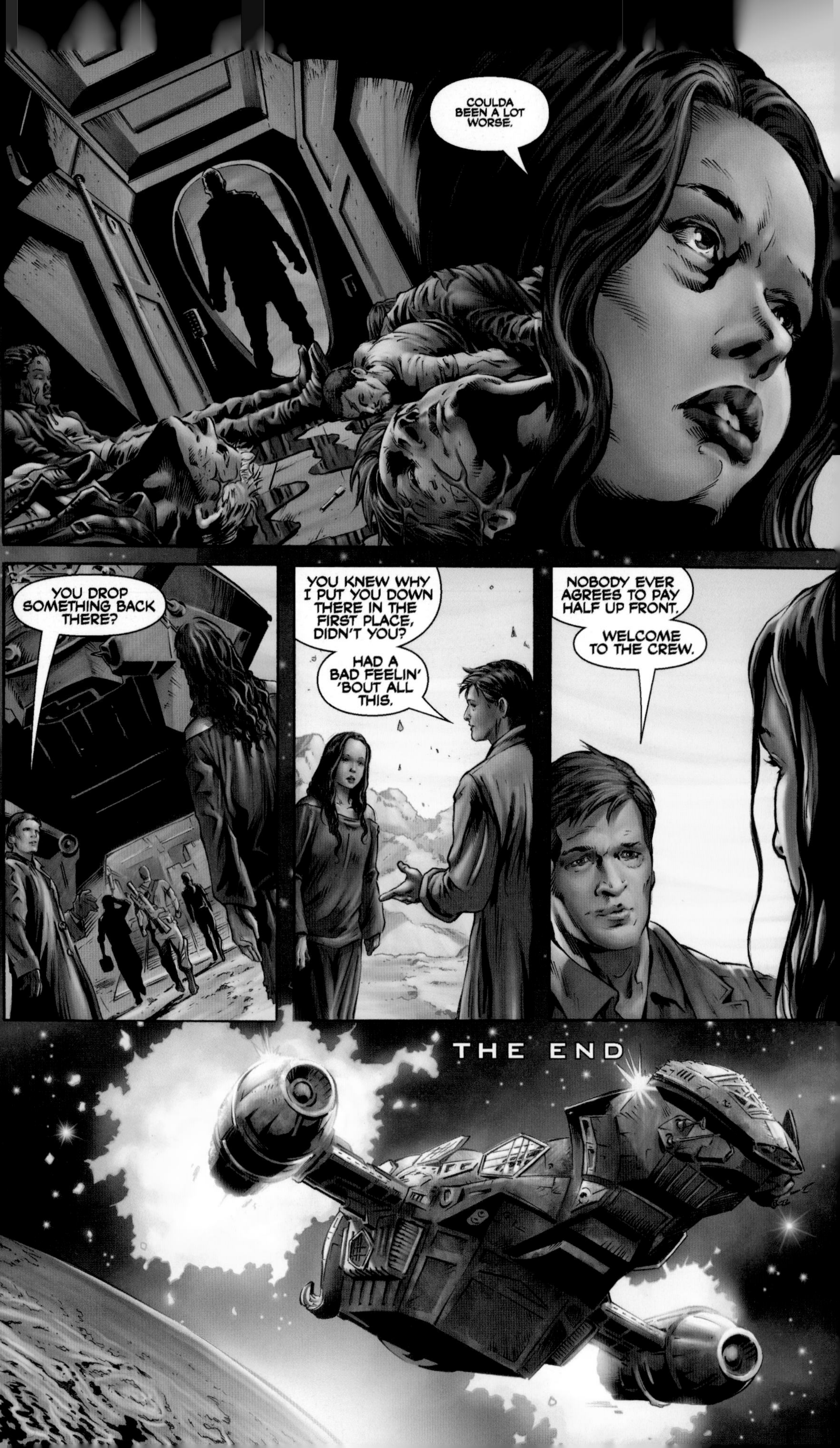
COULDA BEEN A LOT WORSE.
YOU DROP SOMETHING BACK THERE?
YOU KNEW WHY I PUT YOU DOWN THERE IN THE FIRST PLACE, DIDN'T YOU?
HAD A BAD FEELIN' 'BOUT ALL THIS.
NOBODY EVER AGREES TO PAY HALF UP FRONT.
WELCOME TO THE CREW.
THE END

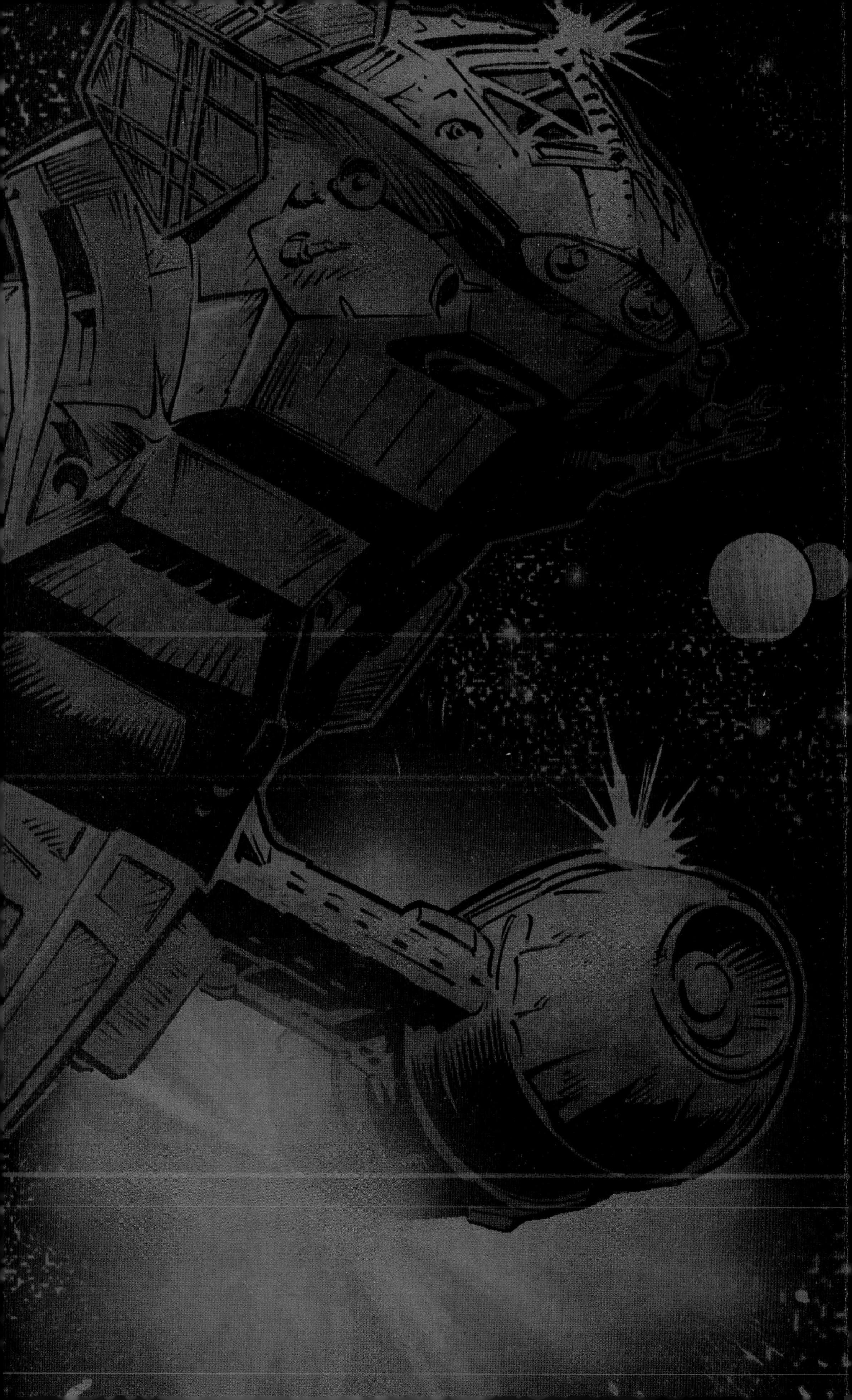

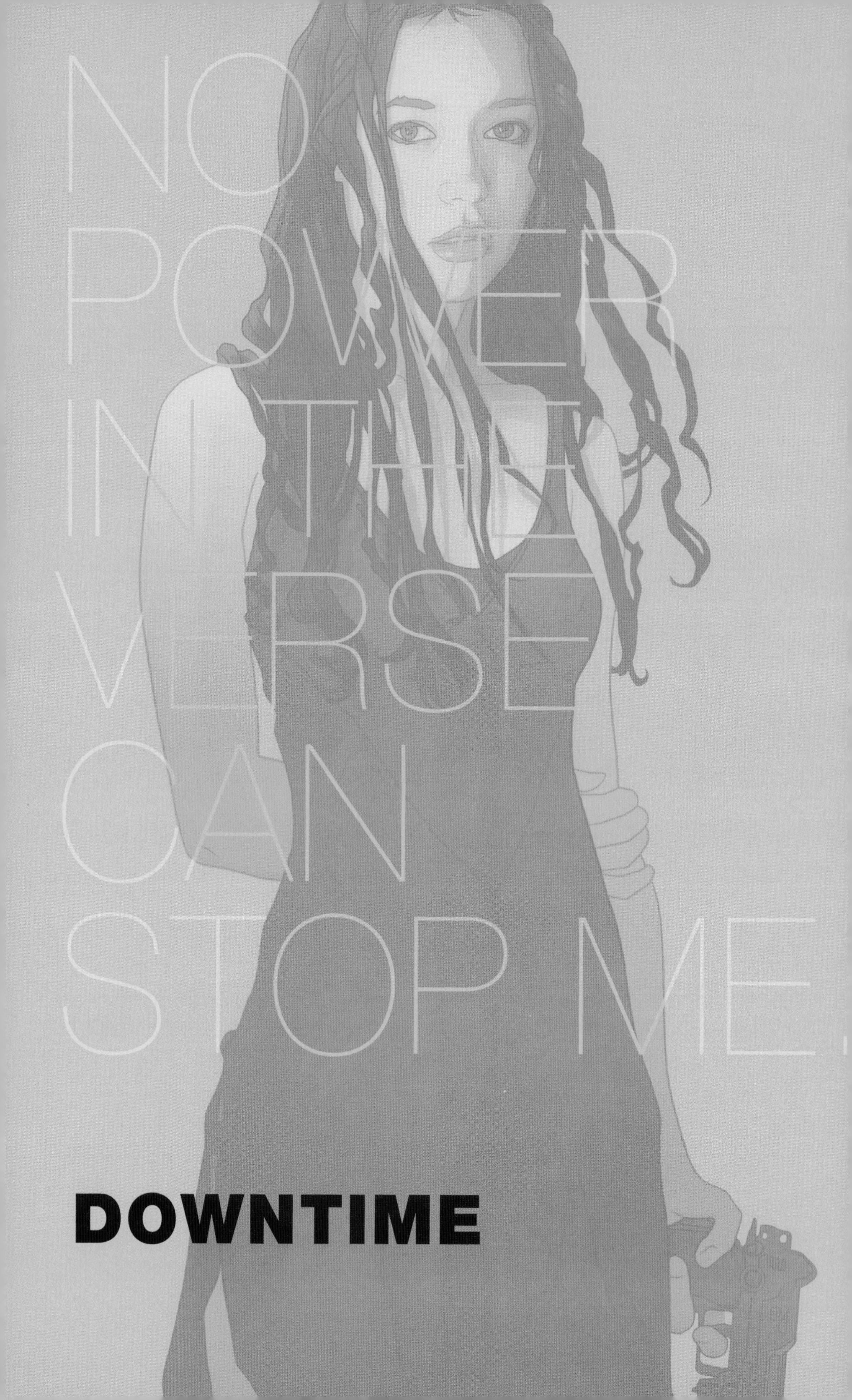
NO
POWER
IN THE
VERSE
CAN
STOP ME.

DOWNTIME

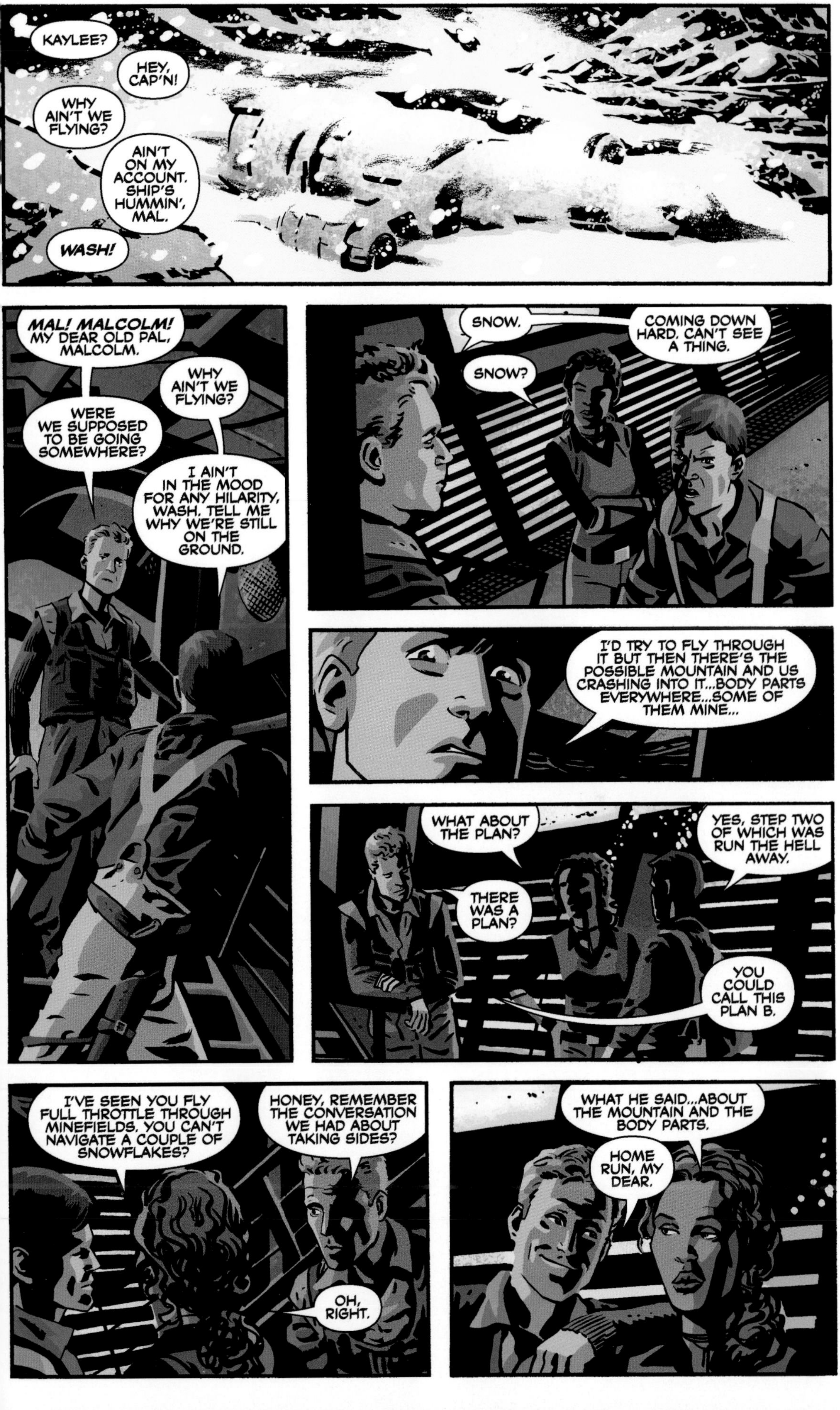
KAYLEE?
HEY, CAP'N!
WHY AIN'T WE FLYING?
AIN'T ON MY ACCOUNT. SHIP'S HUMMIN', MAL.
WASH!
MAL! MALCOLM! MY DEAR OLD PAL, MALCOLM.
WERE WE SUPPOSED TO BE GOING SOMEWHERE?
WHY AIN'T WE FLYING?
I AIN'T IN THE MOOD FOR ANY HILARITY, WASH. TELL ME WHY WE'RE STILL ON THE GROUND.
SNOW.
COMING DOWN HARD. CAN'T SEE A THING.
SNOW?
I'D TRY TO FLY THROUGH IT BUT THEN THERE'S THE POSSIBLE MOUNTAIN AND US CRASHING INTO IT...BODY PARTS EVERYWHERE...SOME OF THEM MINE...
WHAT ABOUT THE PLAN?
YES, STEP TWO OF WHICH WAS RUN THE HELL AWAY.
THERE WAS A PLAN?
YOU COULD CALL THIS PLAN B.
I'VE SEEN YOU FLY FULL THROTTLE THROUGH MINEFIELDS. YOU CAN'T NAVIGATE A COUPLE OF SNOWFLAKES?
HONEY, REMEMBER THE CONVERSATION WE HAD ABOUT TAKING SIDES?
OH, RIGHT.
WHAT HE SAID...ABOUT THE MOUNTAIN AND THE BODY PARTS.
HOME RUN, MY DEAR.

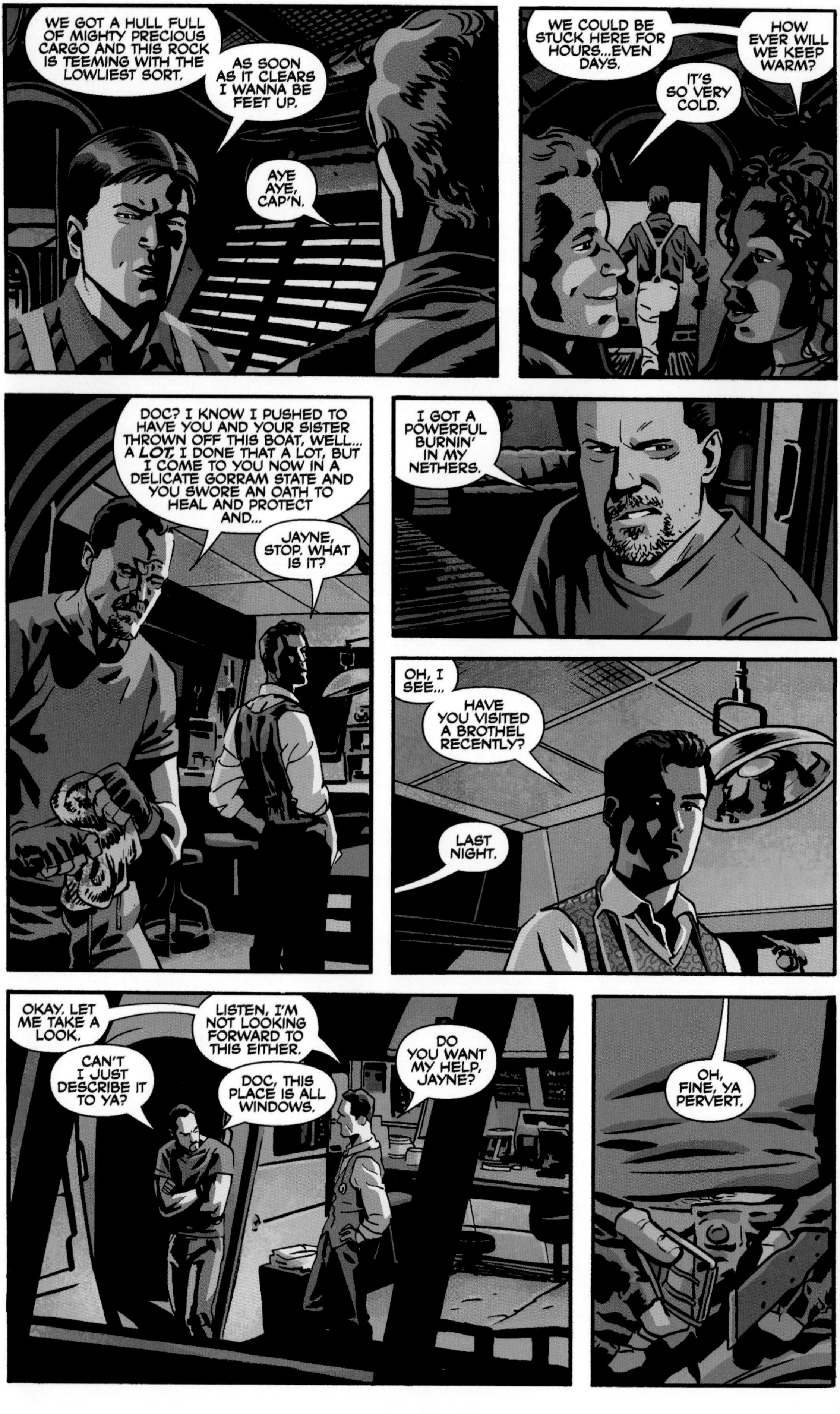
WE GOT A HULL FULL OF MIGHTY PRECIOUS CARGO AND THIS ROCK IS TEEMING WITH THE LOWLIEST SORT.
AS SOON AS IT CLEARS I WANNA BE FEET UP.
AYE AYE, CAP'N.
WE COULD BE STUCK HERE FOR HOURS...EVEN DAYS.
HOW EVER WILL WE KEEP WARM?
IT'S SO VERY COLD.
DOC? I KNOW I PUSHED TO HAVE YOU AND YOUR SISTER THROWN OFF THIS BOAT, WELL... A LOT, I DONE THAT A LOT, BUT I COME TO YOU NOW IN A DELICATE GORRAM STATE AND YOU SWORE AN OATH TO HEAL AND PROTECT AND...
JAYNE, STOP. WHAT IS IT?
I GOT A POWERFUL BURNIN' IN MY NETHERS.
OH, I SEE...
HAVE YOU VISITED A BROTHEL RECENTLY?
LAST NIGHT.
OKAY. LET ME TAKE A LOOK.
CAN'T I JUST DESCRIBE IT TO YA?
LISTEN, I'M NOT LOOKING FORWARD TO THIS EITHER.
DOC, THIS PLACE IS ALL WINDOWS.
DO YOU WANT MY HELP, JAYNE?
OH, FINE, YA PERVERT.

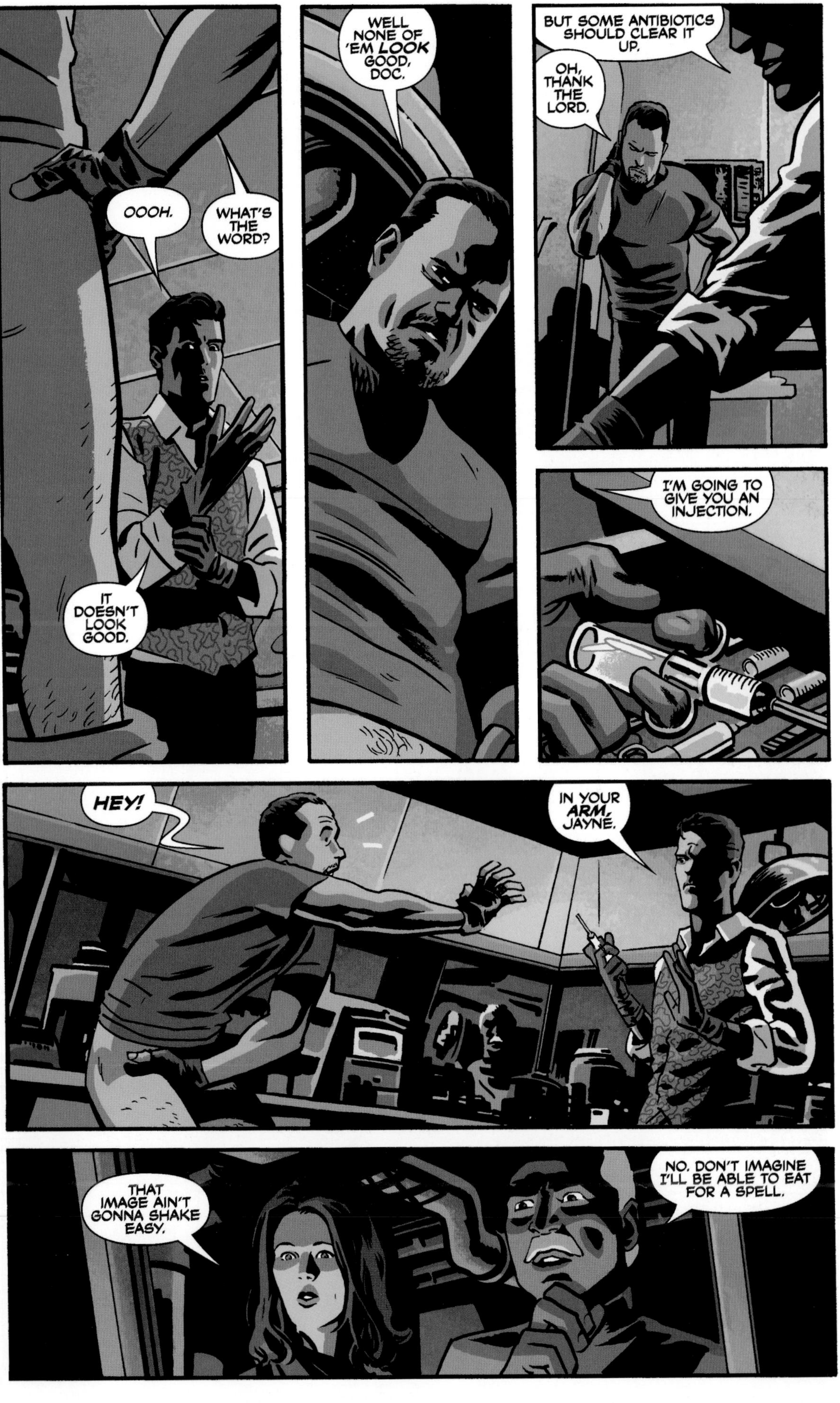
OOOH.
WHAT'S THE WORD?
IT DOESN'T LOOK GOOD.
WELL NONE OF 'EM LOOK GOOD, DOC.
BUT SOME ANTIBIOTICS SHOULD CLEAR IT UP.
OH, THANK THE LORD.
I'M GOING TO GIVE YOU AN INJECTION.
HEY!
IN YOUR ARM, JAYNE.
THAT IMAGE AIN'T GONNA SHAKE EASY.
NO. DON'T IMAGINE I'LL BE ABLE TO EAT FOR A SPELL.

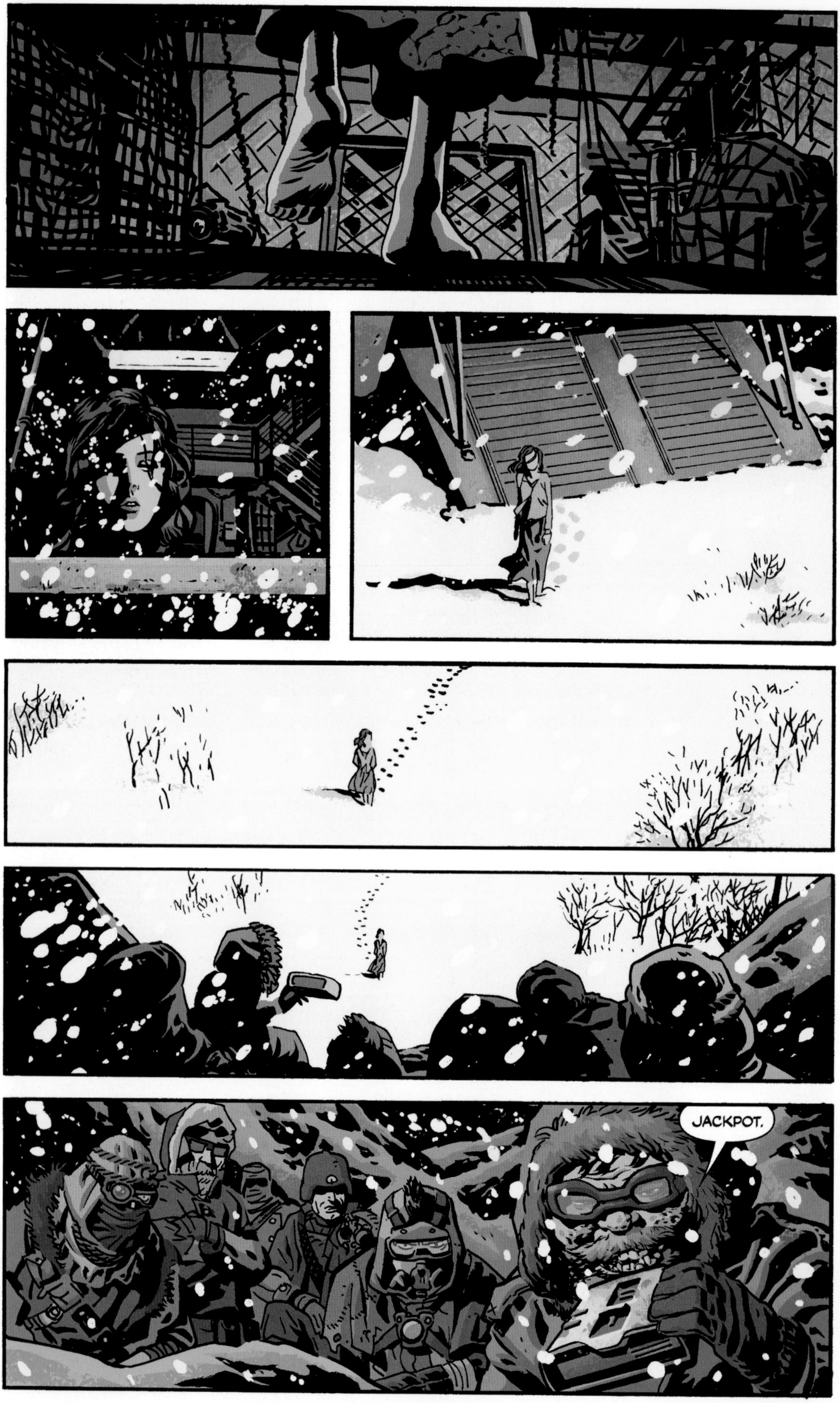
JACKPOT.

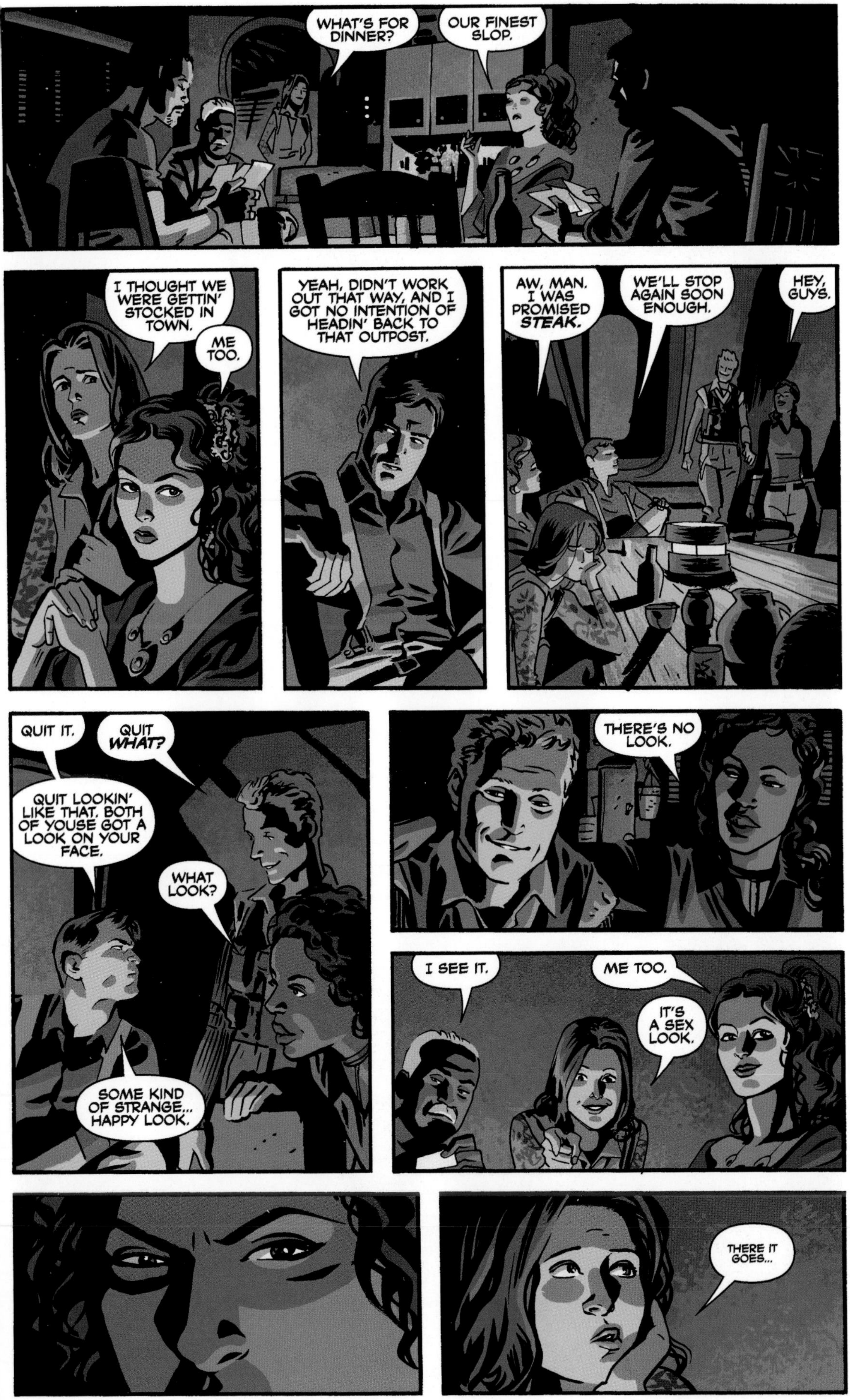
WHAT'S FOR DINNER?
OUR FINEST SLOP.
I THOUGHT WE WERE GETTIN' STOCKED IN TOWN.
ME TOO.
YEAH, DIDN'T WORK OUT THAT WAY, AND I GOT NO INTENTION OF HEADIN' BACK TO THAT OUTPOST.
AW, MAN. I WAS PROMISED STEAK.
WE'LL STOP AGAIN SOON ENOUGH.
HEY, GUYS.
QUIT IT.
QUIT WHAT?
QUIT LOOKIN' LIKE THAT. BOTH OF YOUSE GOT A LOOK ON YOUR FACE.
WHAT LOOK?
SOME KIND OF STRANGE... HAPPY LOOK.
THERE'S NO LOOK.
I SEE IT.
ME TOO.
IT'S A SEX LOOK.
THERE IT GOES...

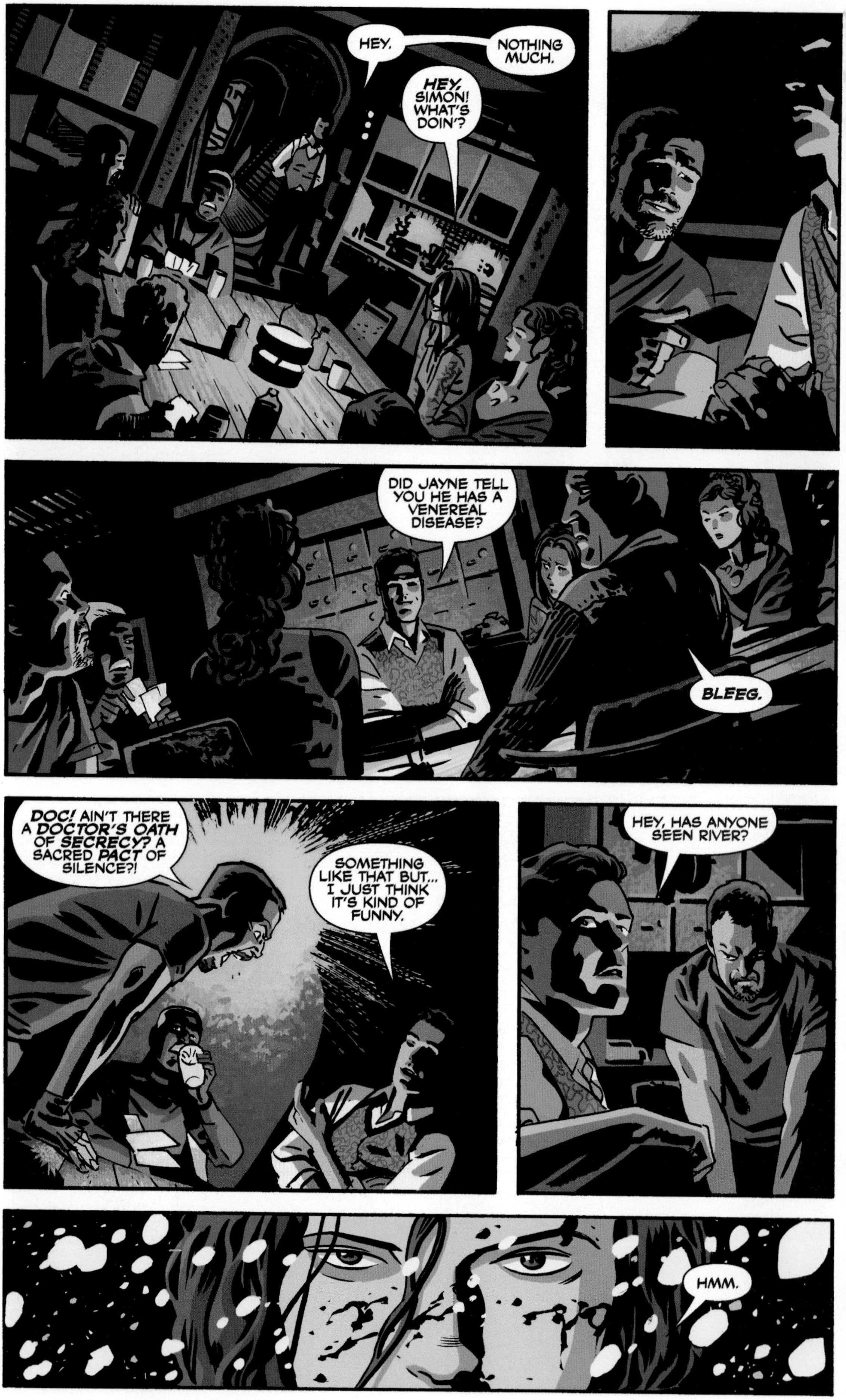
HEY.
HEY, SIMON! WHAT'S DOIN'?
NOTHING MUCH.
DID JAYNE TELL YOU HE HAS A VENEREAL DISEASE?
BLEEG.
DOC! AIN'T THERE A DOCTOR'S OATH OF SECRECY? A SACRED PACT OF SILENCE?!
SOMETHING LIKE THAT BUT... I JUST THINK IT'S KIND OF FUNNY.
HEY, HAS ANYONE SEEN RIVER?
HMM.

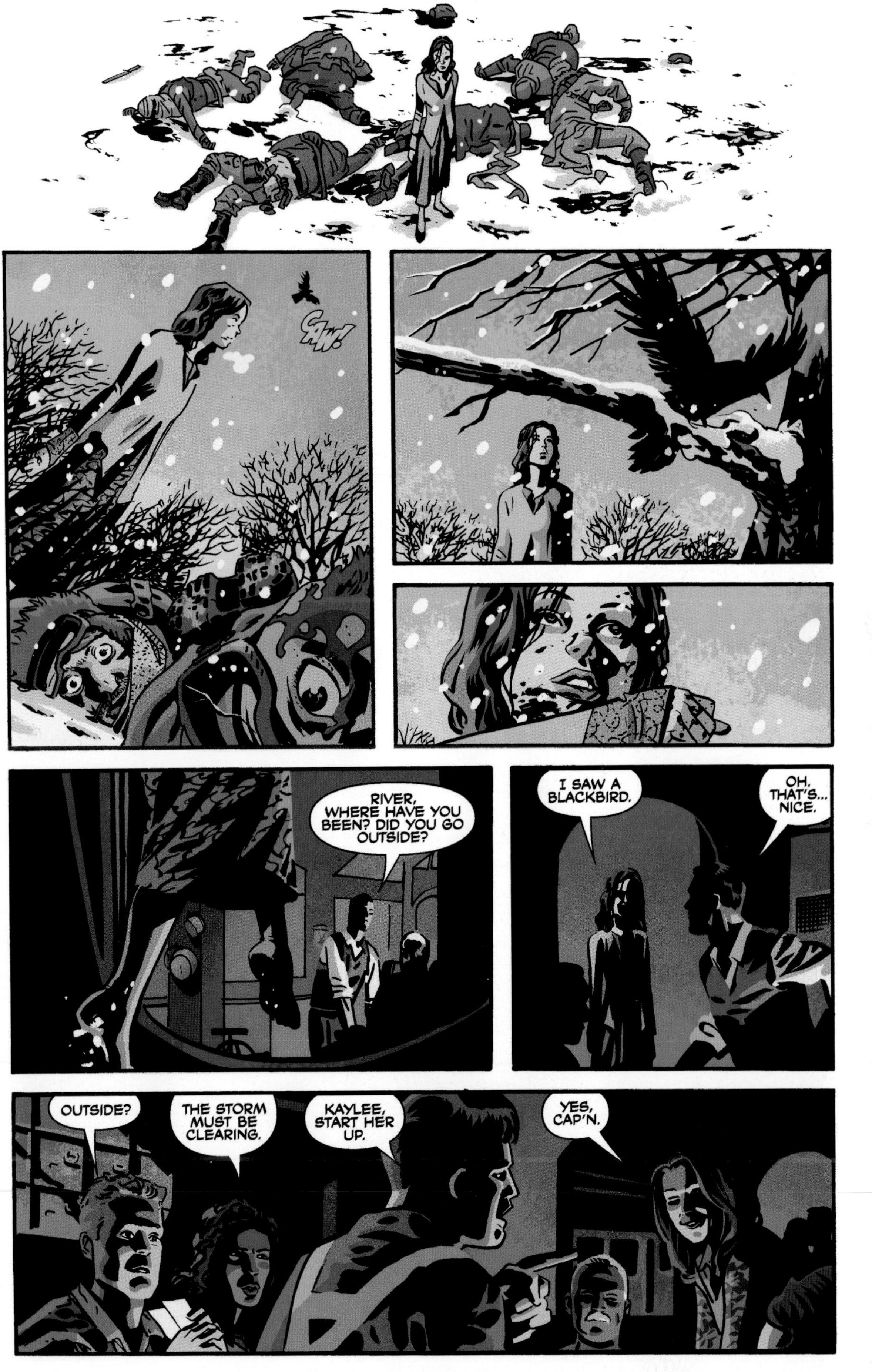
CAW!
RIVER, WHERE HAVE YOU BEEN? DID YOU GO OUTSIDE?
I SAW A BLACKBIRD.
OH, THAT'S... NICE.
OUTSIDE?
THE STORM MUST BE CLEARING.
KAYLEE, START HER UP.
YES, CAP'N.

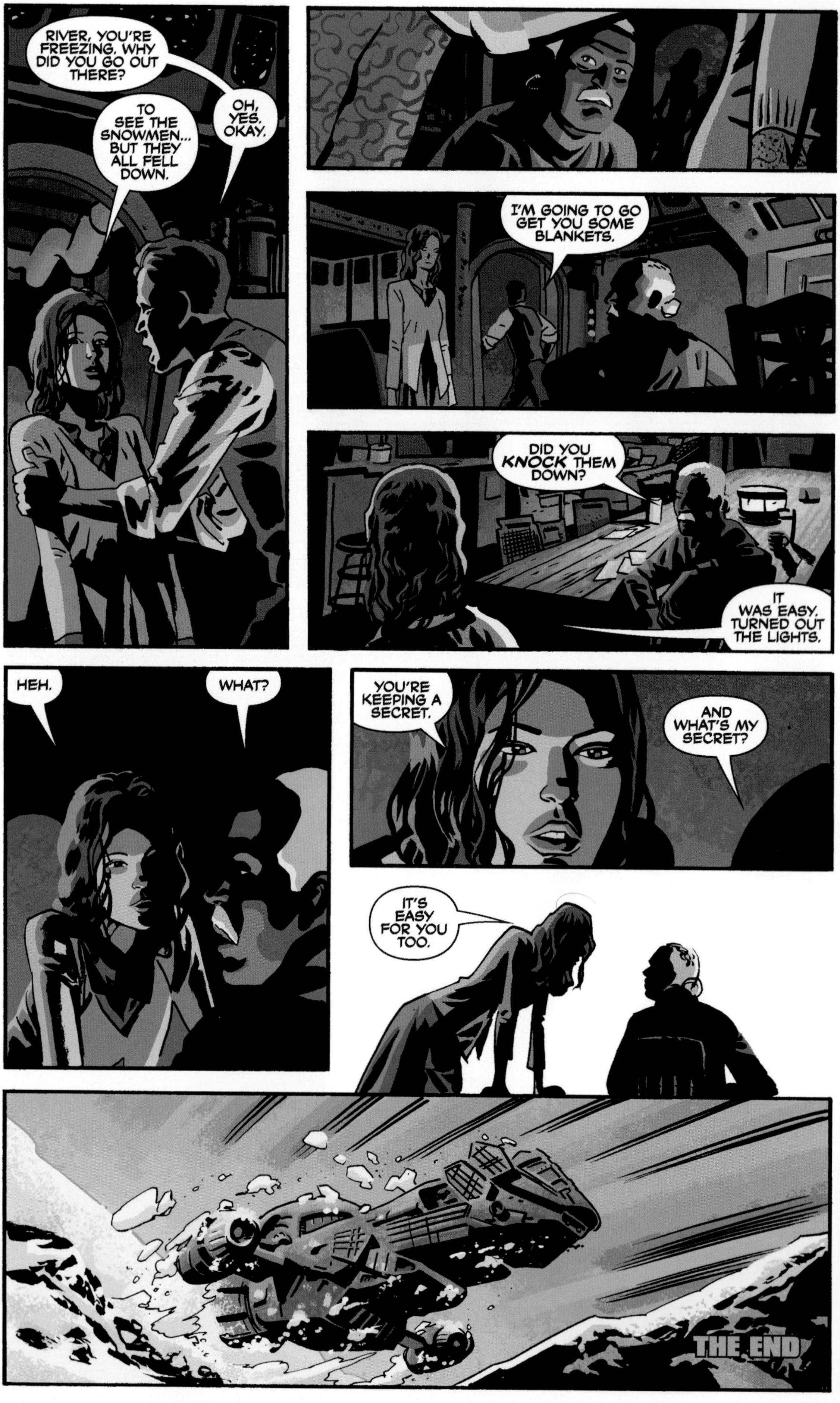
RIVER, YOU'RE FREEZING. WHY DID YOU GO OUT THERE?
TO SEE THE SNOWMEN... BUT THEY ALL FELL DOWN.
OH, YES. OKAY.
I'M GOING TO GO GET YOU SOME BLANKETS.
DID YOU KNOCK THEM DOWN?
IT WAS EASY. TURNED OUT THE LIGHTS.
HEH.
WHAT?
YOU'RE KEEPING A SECRET.
AND WHAT'S MY SECRET?
IT'S EASY FOR YOU TOO.
THE END

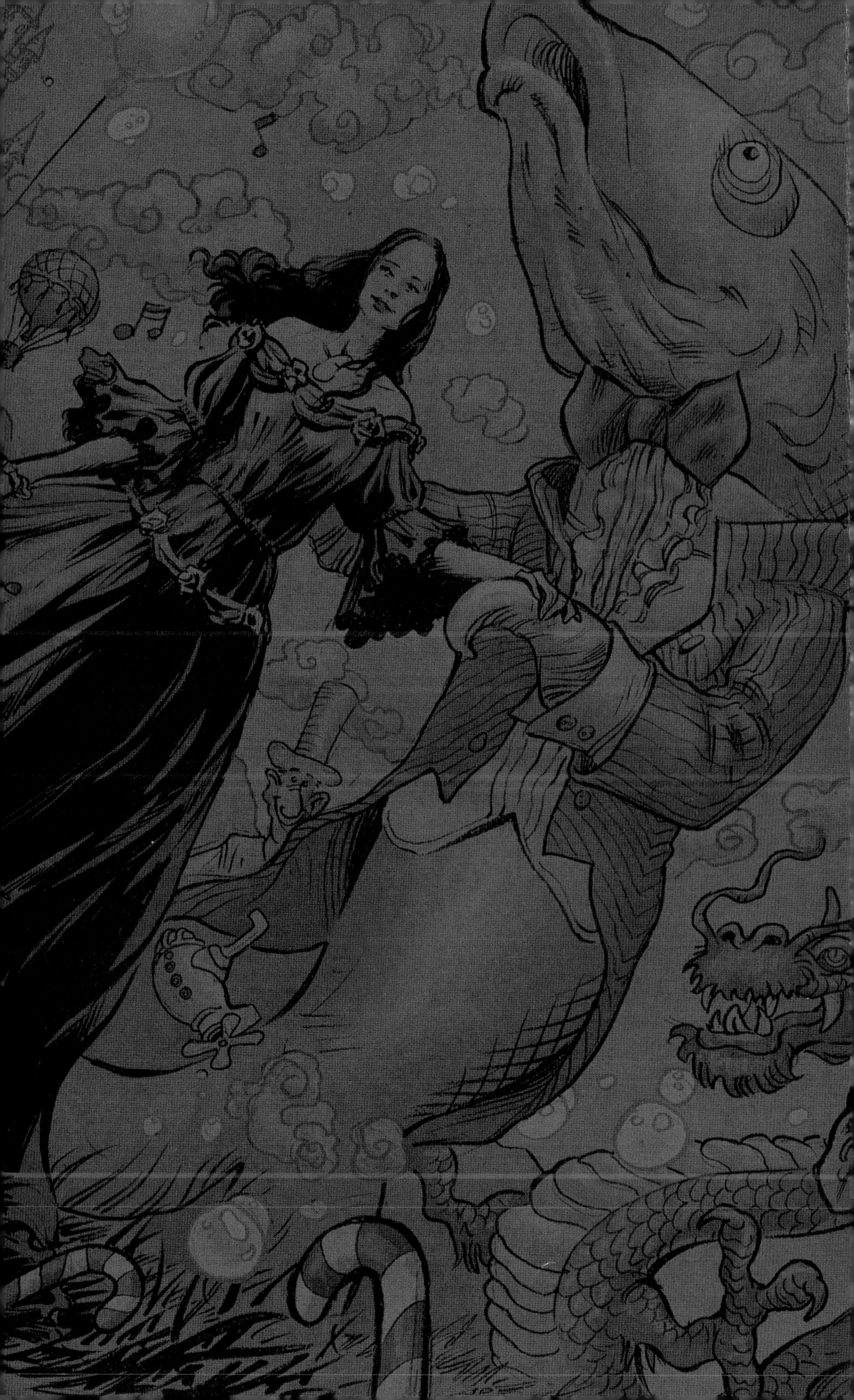

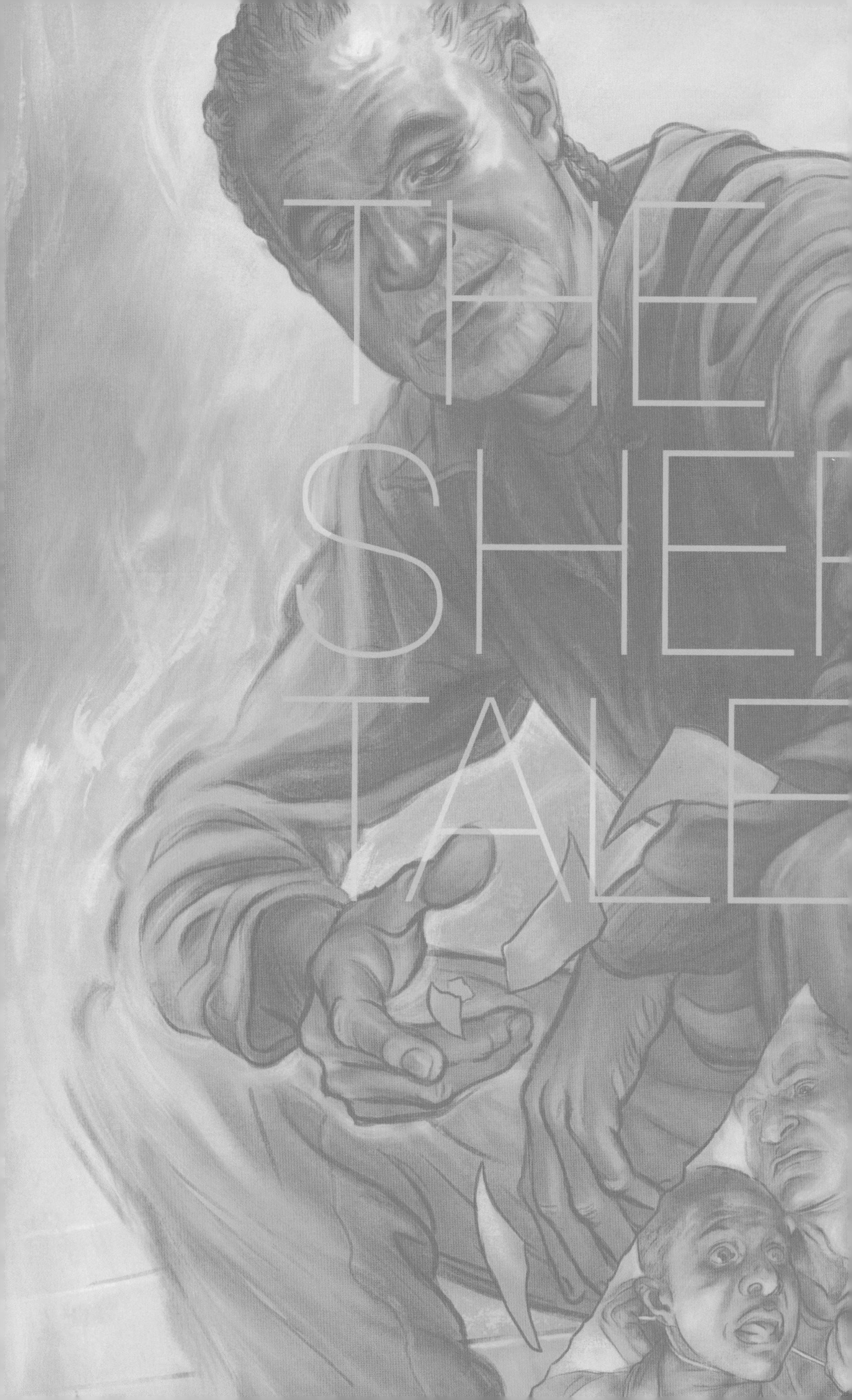
THE
SHE
TALE

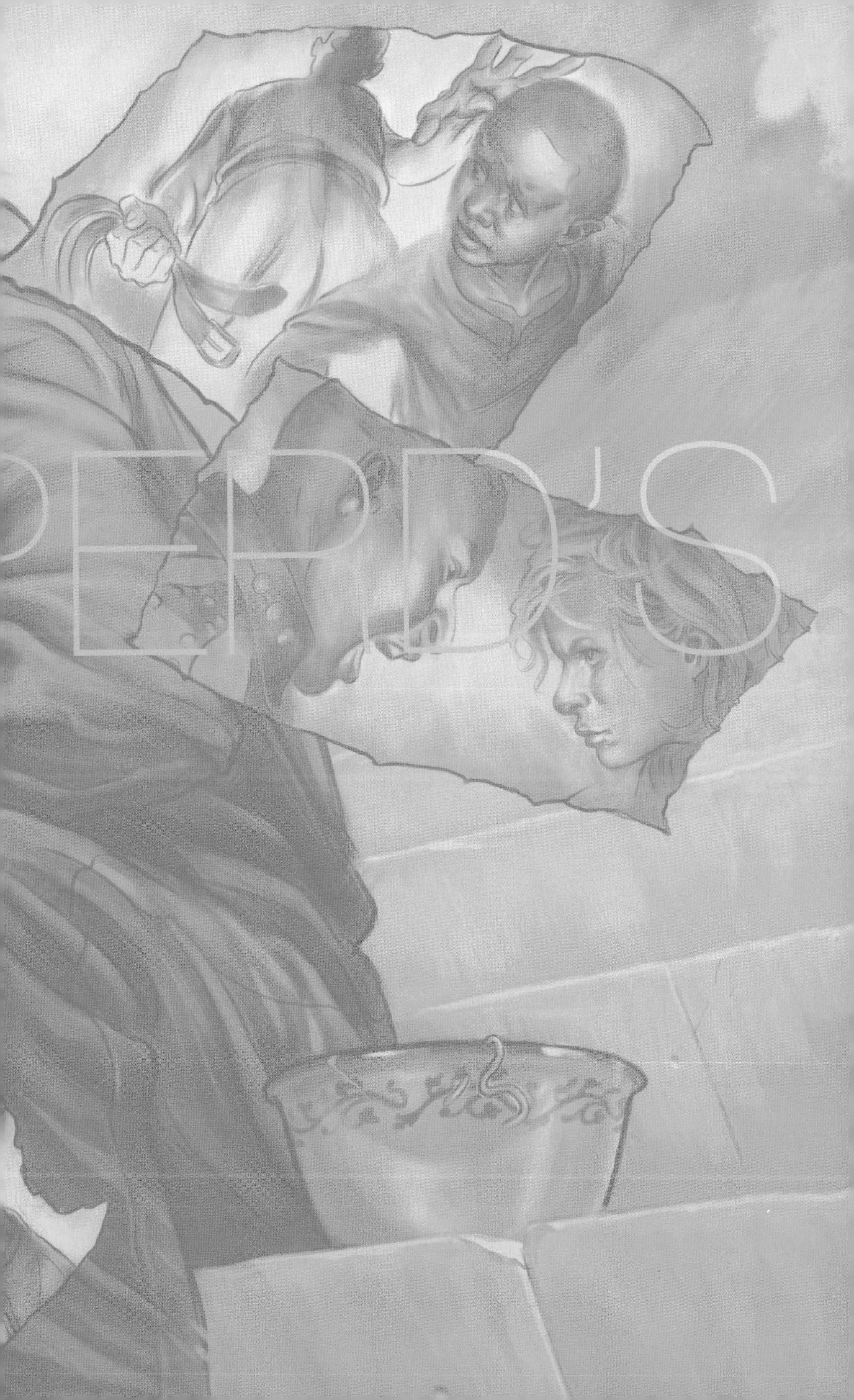

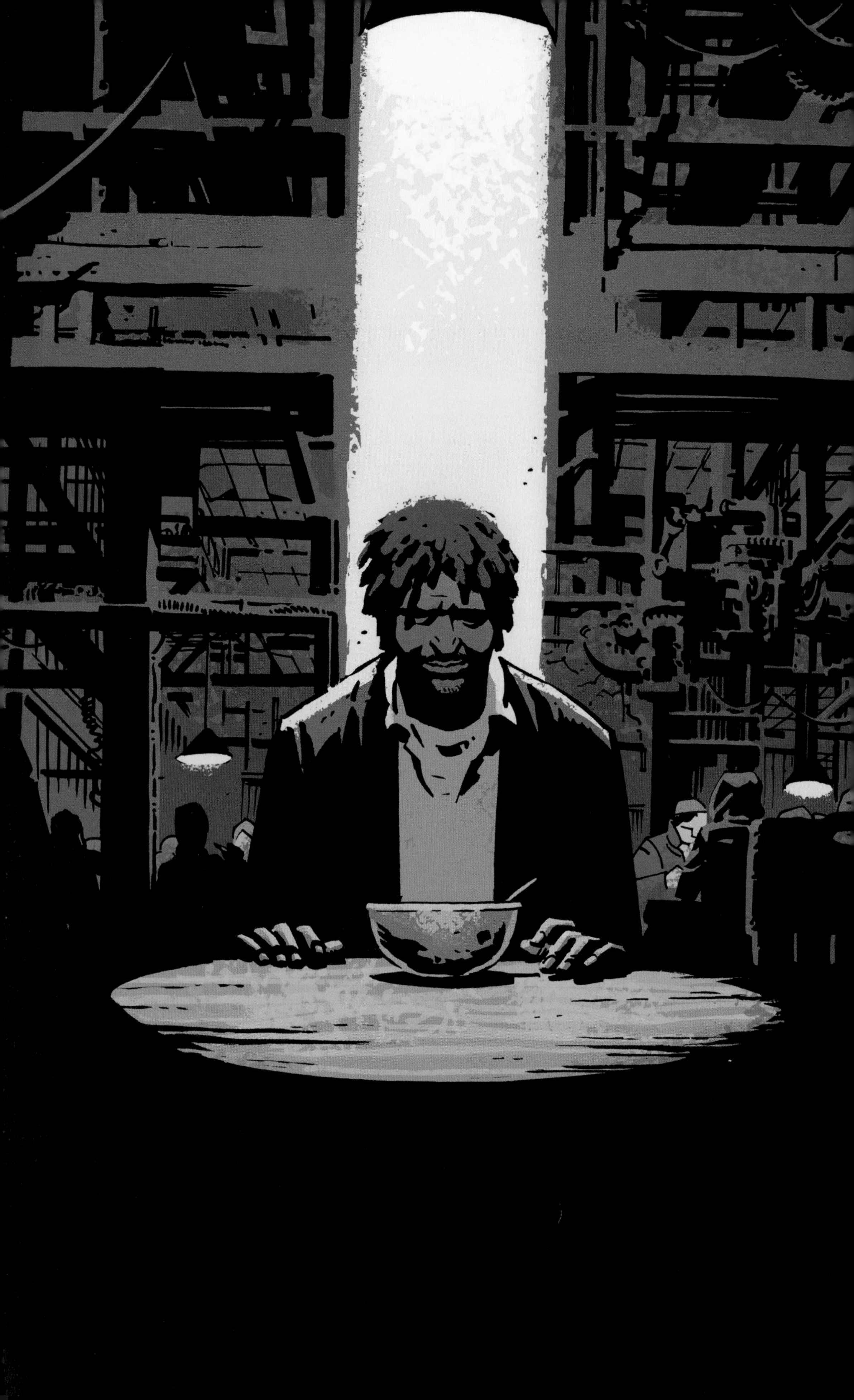

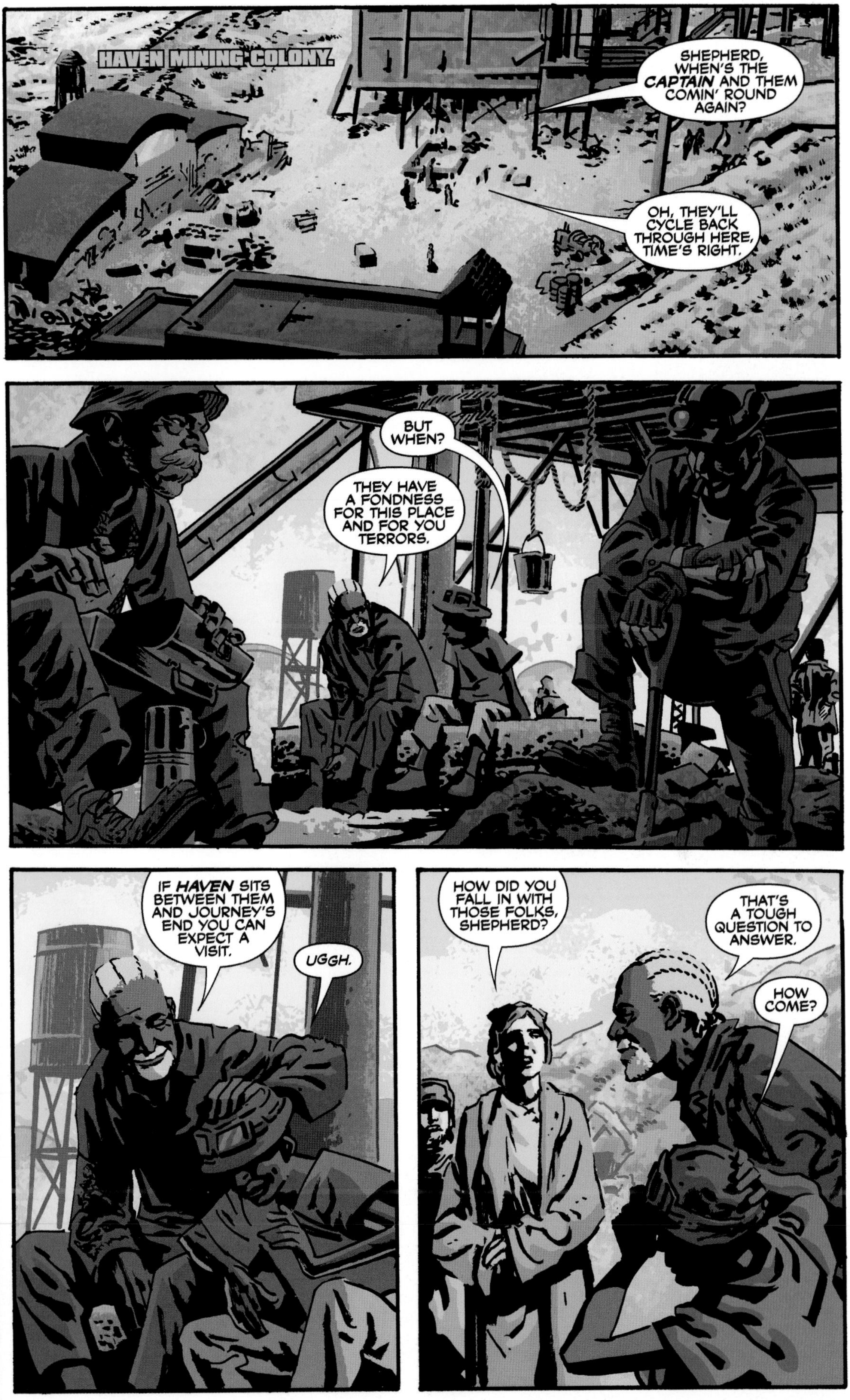
HAVEN MINING COLONY.
SHEPHERD, WHEN'S THE CAPTAIN AND THEM COMIN' ROUND AGAIN?
OH, THEY'LL CYCLE BACK THROUGH HERE, TIME'S RIGHT.
BUT WHEN?
THEY HAVE A FONDNESS FOR THIS PLACE AND FOR YOU TERRORS.
IF HAVEN SITS BETWEEN THEM AND JOURNEY'S END YOU CAN EXPECT A VISIT.
UGGH.
HOW DID YOU FALL IN WITH THOSE FOLKS, SHEPHERD?
THAT'S A TOUGH QUESTION TO ANSWER.
HOW COME?

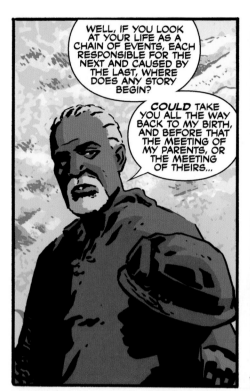

WELL, IF YOU LOOK AT YOUR LIFE AS A CHAIN OF EVENTS, EACH RESPONSIBLE FOR THE NEXT AND CAUSED BY THE LAST, WHERE DOES ANY STORY BEGIN?

COULD TAKE YOU ALL THE WAY BACK TO MY BIRTH, AND BEFORE THAT THE MEETING OF MY PARENTS, OR THE MEETING OF THEIRS...

I'M JUST ASKING HOW YOU MET THE GUY.

OF COURSE.

RUMM MMMBBBLLE

COMMERCIAL FREIGHTER. THEY COME BY HERE ALL THE TIME.

THAT'S NOT A FREIGHTER.

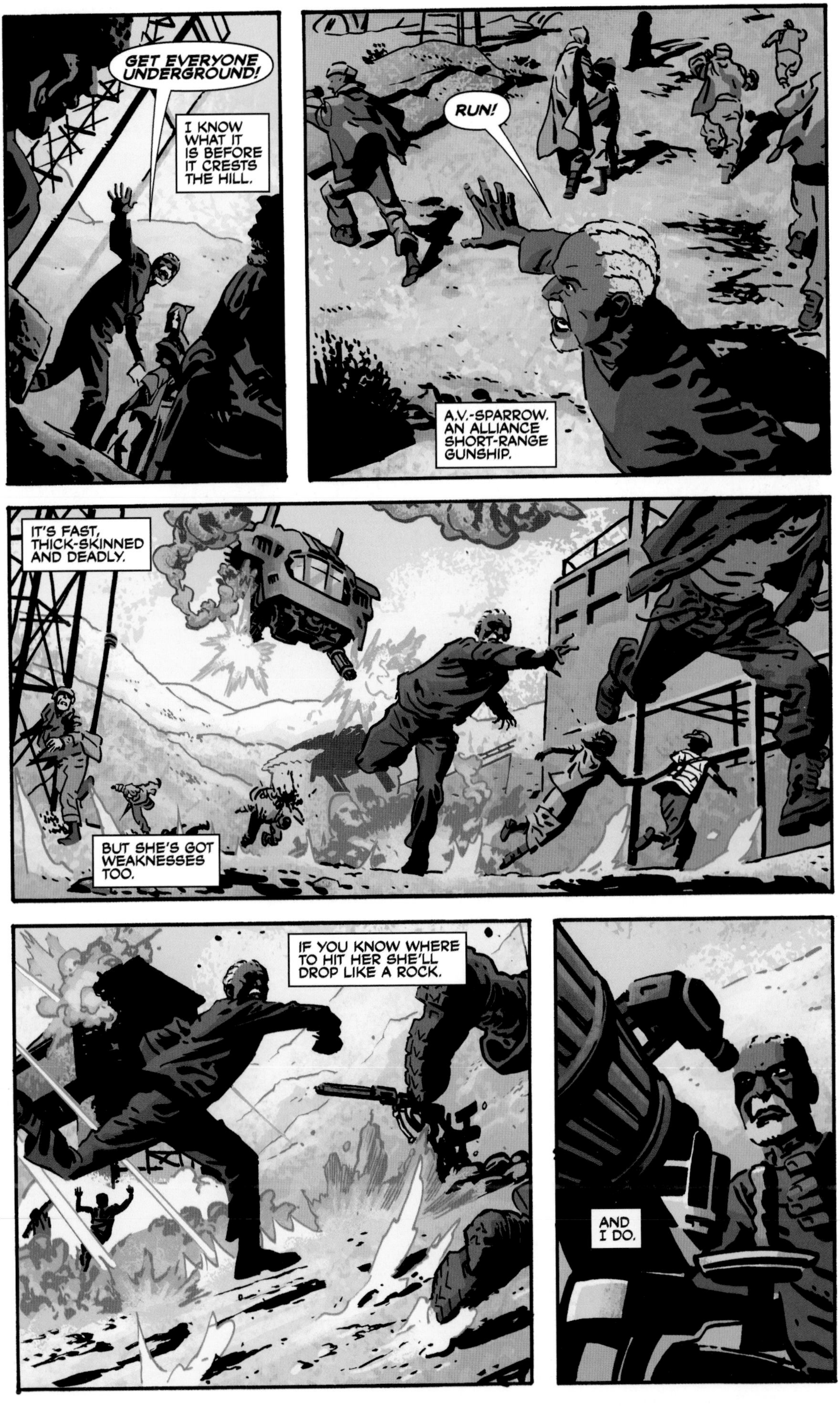
GET EVERYONE UNDERGROUND!
I KNOW WHAT IT IS BEFORE IT CRESTS THE HILL.
RUN!
A.V.-SPARROW. AN ALLIANCE SHORT-RANGE GUNSHIP.
IT'S FAST, THICK-SKINNED AND DEADLY.
BUT SHE'S GOT WEAKNESSES TOO.
IF YOU KNOW WHERE TO HIT HER SHE'LL DROP LIKE A ROCK.
AND I DO.

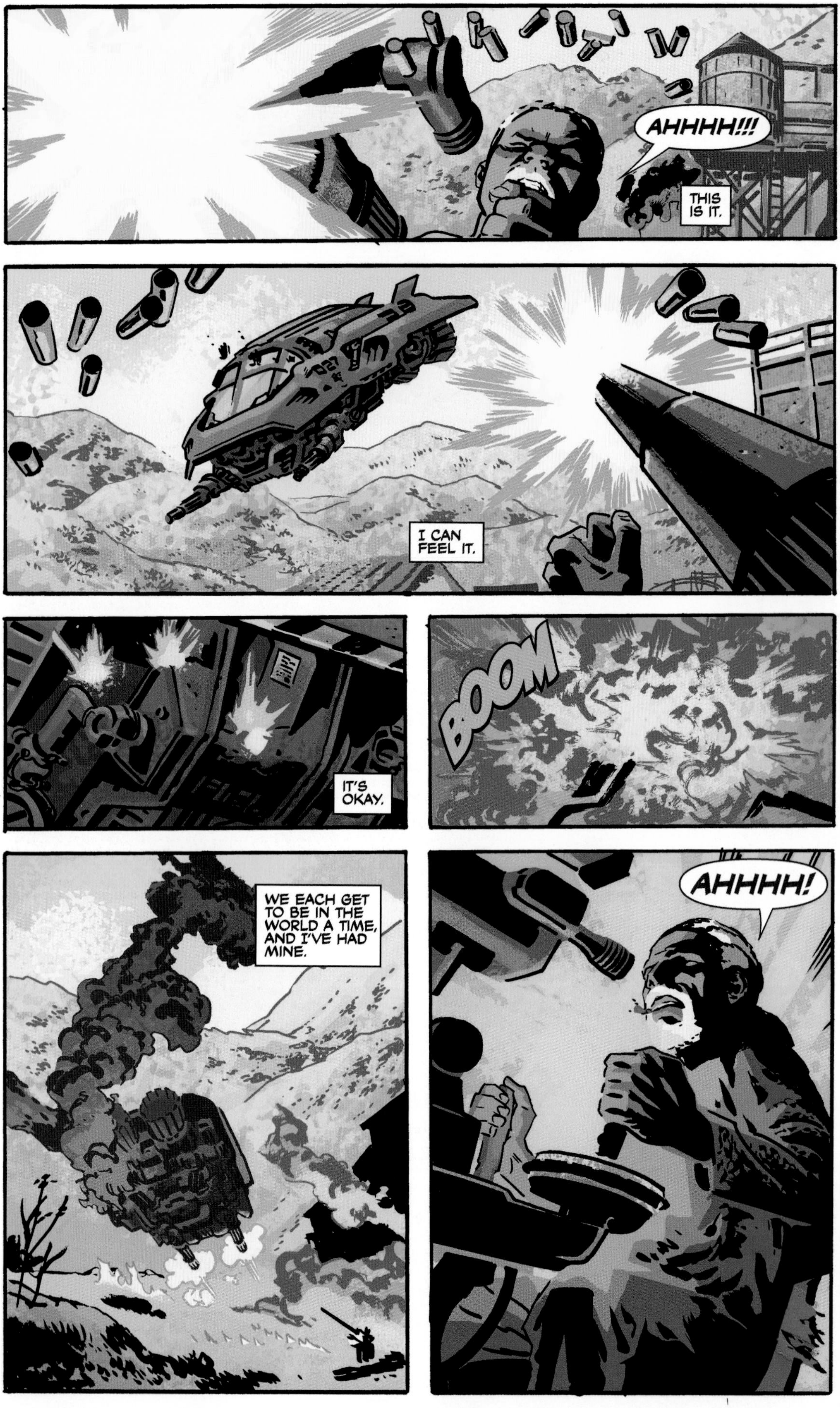
AHHHH!!!
THIS IS IT.
I CAN FEEL IT.
IT'S OKAY.
BOOM
WE EACH GET TO BE IN THE WORLD A TIME, AND I'VE HAD MINE.
AHHHH!

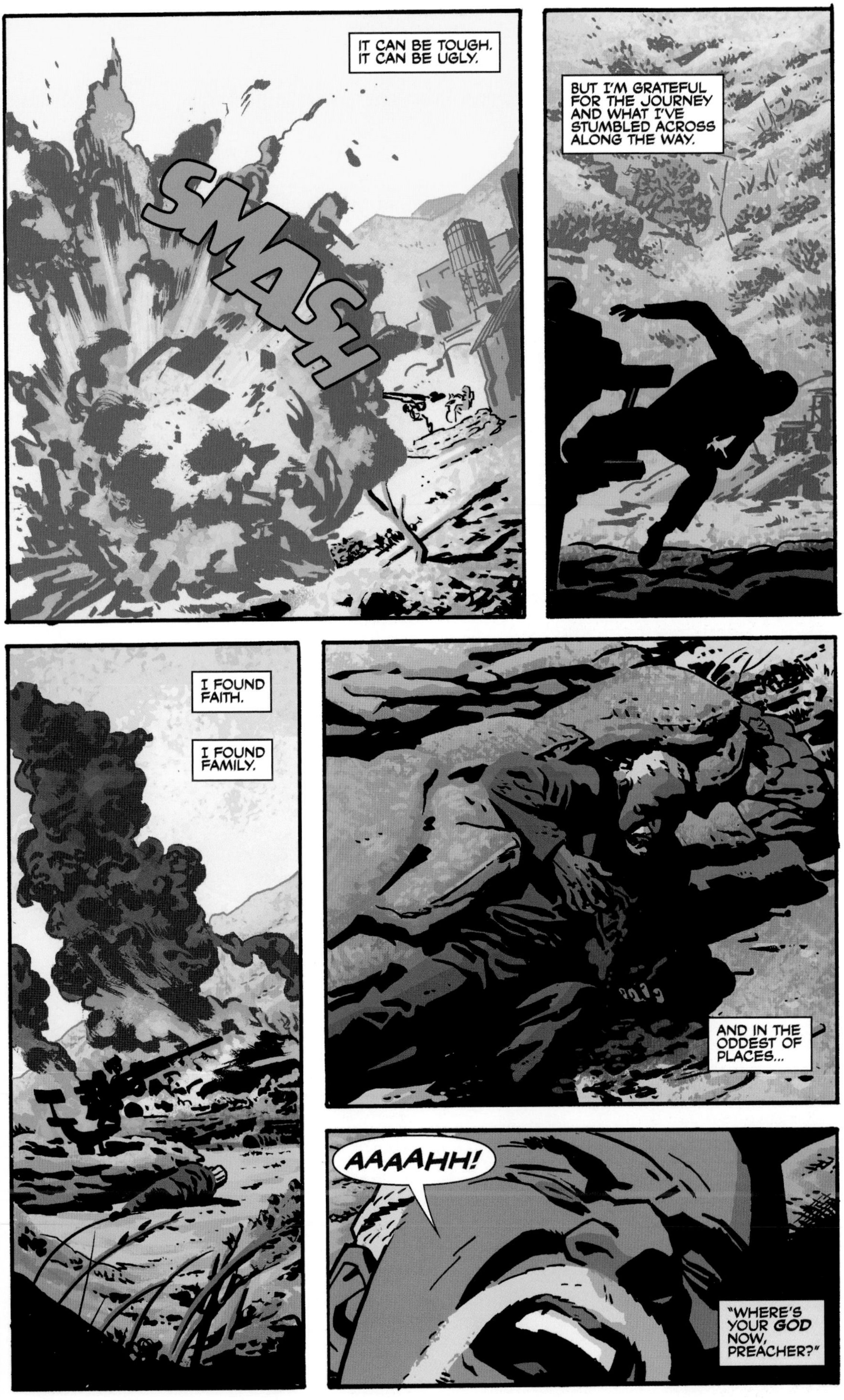
SMASH
IT CAN BE TOUGH. IT CAN BE UGLY.
BUT I'M GRATEFUL FOR THE JOURNEY AND WHAT I'VE STUMBLED ACROSS ALONG THE WAY.
I FOUND FAITH.
I FOUND FAMILY.
AND IN THE ODDEST OF PLACES...
AAAAHH!
"WHERE'S YOUR GOD NOW, PREACHER?"

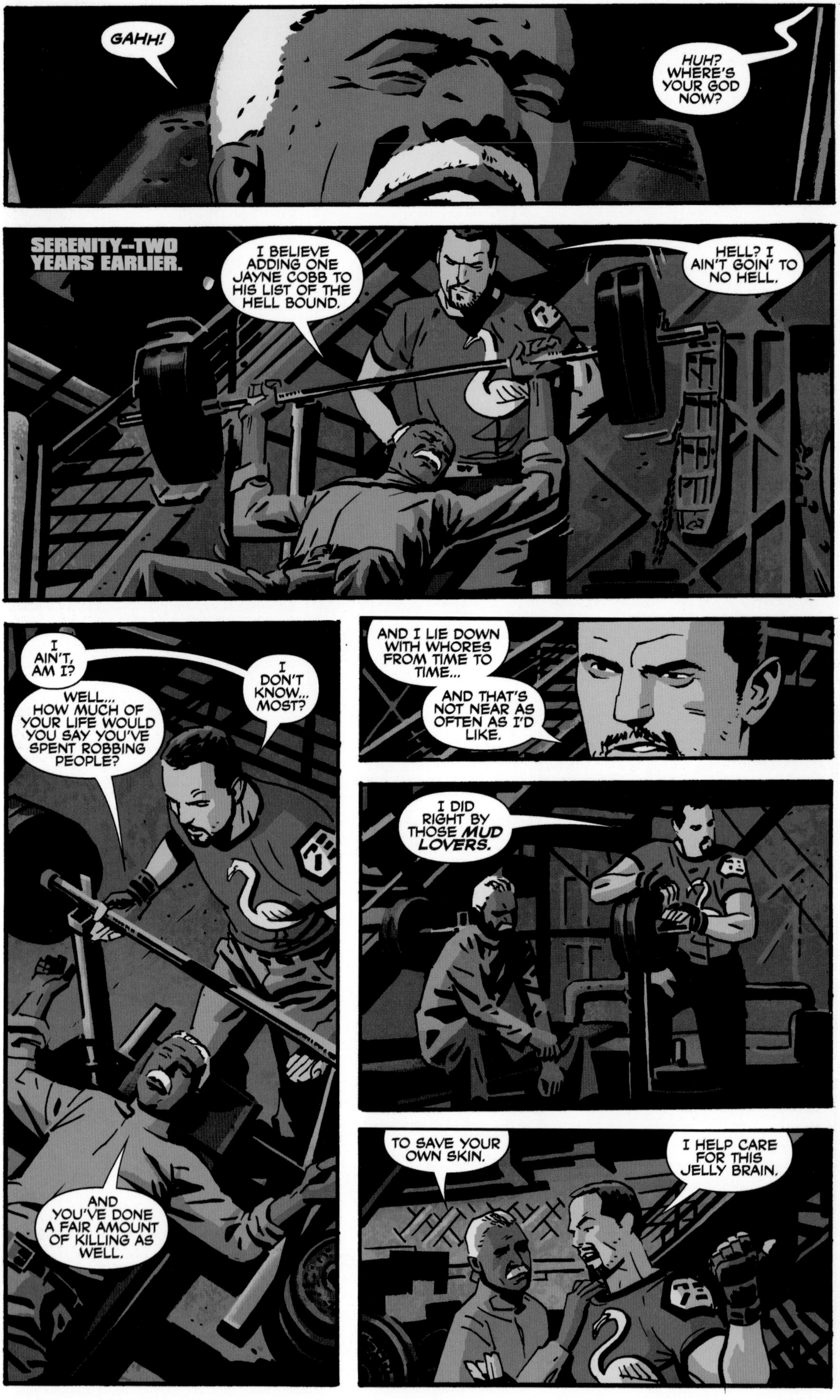
GAHH!
HUH? WHERE'S YOUR GOD NOW?
SERENITY--TWO YEARS EARLIER.
I BELIEVE ADDING ONE JAYNE COBB TO HIS LIST OF THE HELL BOUND.
HELL? I AIN'T GOIN' TO NO HELL.
I AIN'T, AM I?
WELL... HOW MUCH OF YOUR LIFE WOULD YOU SAY YOU'VE SPENT ROBBING PEOPLE?
I DON'T KNOW... MOST?
AND YOU'VE DONE A FAIR AMOUNT OF KILLING AS WELL.
AND I LIE DOWN WITH WHORES FROM TIME TO TIME...
AND THAT'S NOT NEAR AS OFTEN AS I'D LIKE.
I DID RIGHT BY THOSE MUD LOVERS.
TO SAVE YOUR OWN SKIN.
I HELP CARE FOR THIS JELLY BRAIN.

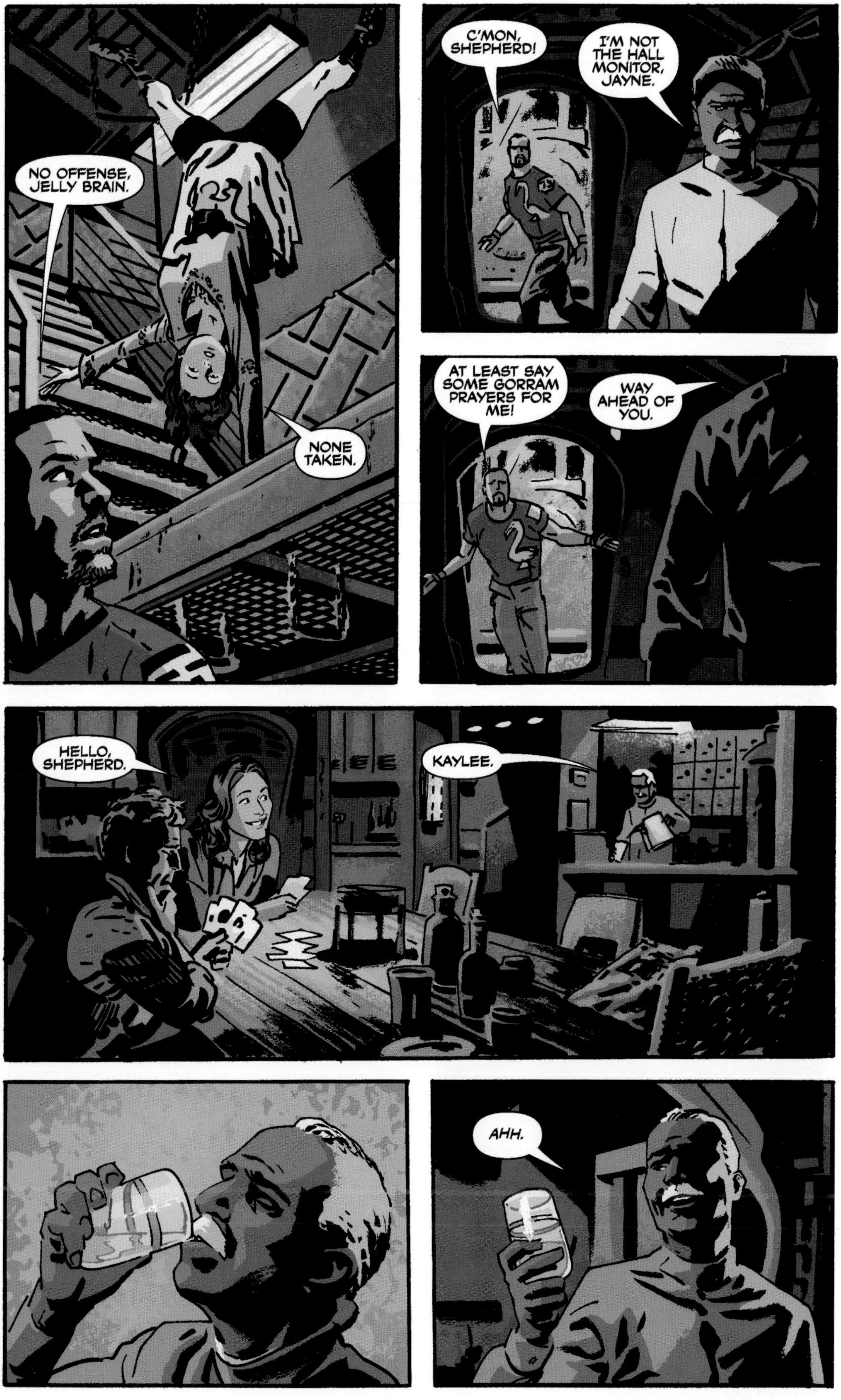
NO OFFENSE, JELLY BRAIN.
NONE TAKEN.
C'MON, SHEPHERD!
I'M NOT THE HALL MONITOR, JAYNE.
AT LEAST SAY SOME GORRAM PRAYERS FOR ME!
WAY AHEAD OF YOU.
HELLO, SHEPHERD.
KAYLEE.
AHH.

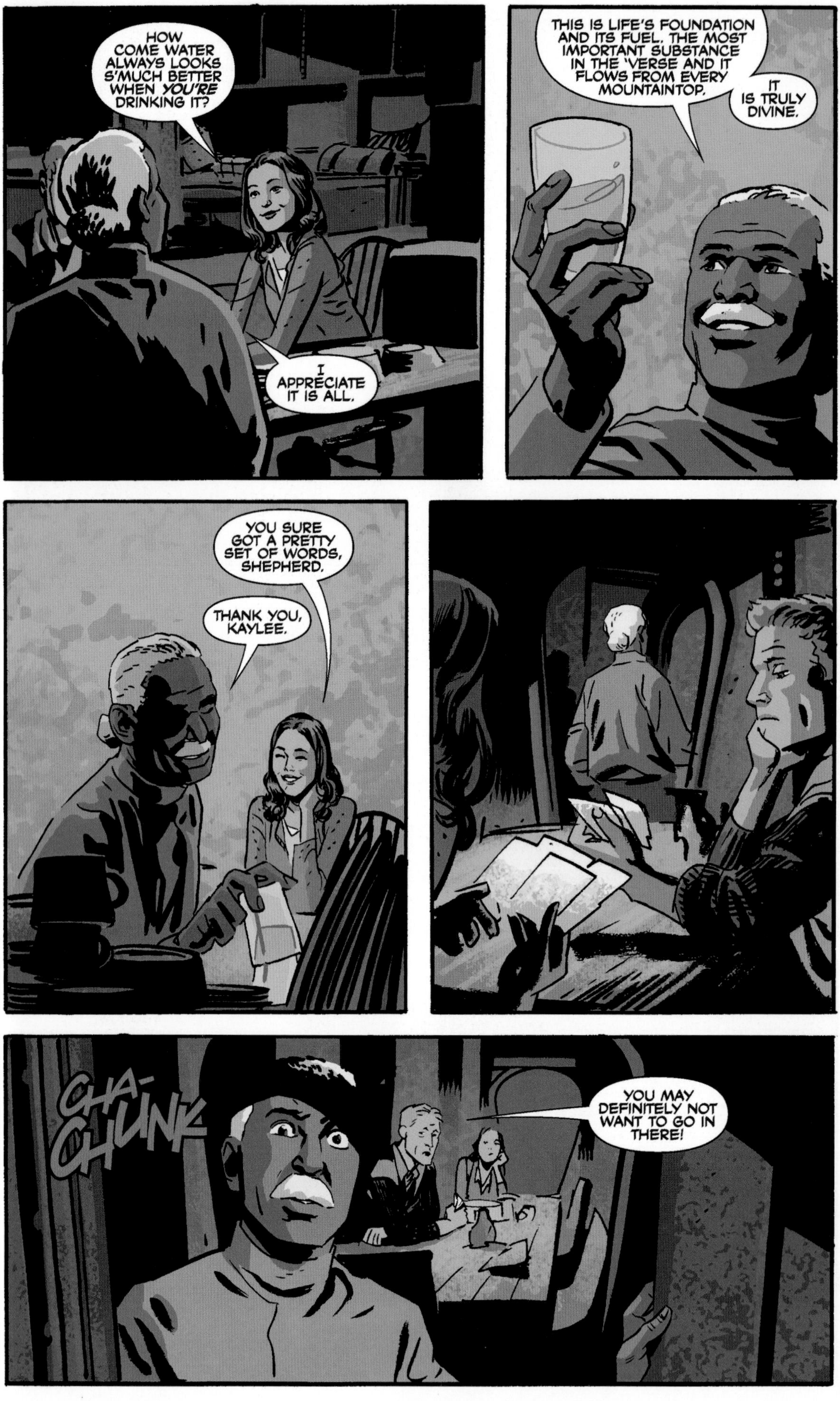
HOW COME WATER ALWAYS LOOKS S'MUCH BETTER WHEN *YOU'RE* DRINKING IT?
I APPRECIATE IT IS ALL.
THIS IS LIFE'S FOUNDATION AND ITS FUEL. THE MOST IMPORTANT SUBSTANCE IN THE 'VERSE AND IT FLOWS FROM EVERY MOUNTAINTOP.
IT IS TRULY DIVINE.
YOU SURE GOT A PRETTY SET OF WORDS, SHEPHERD.
THANK YOU, KAYLEE.
CHA-CHUNK
YOU MAY DEFINITELY NOT WANT TO GO IN THERE!

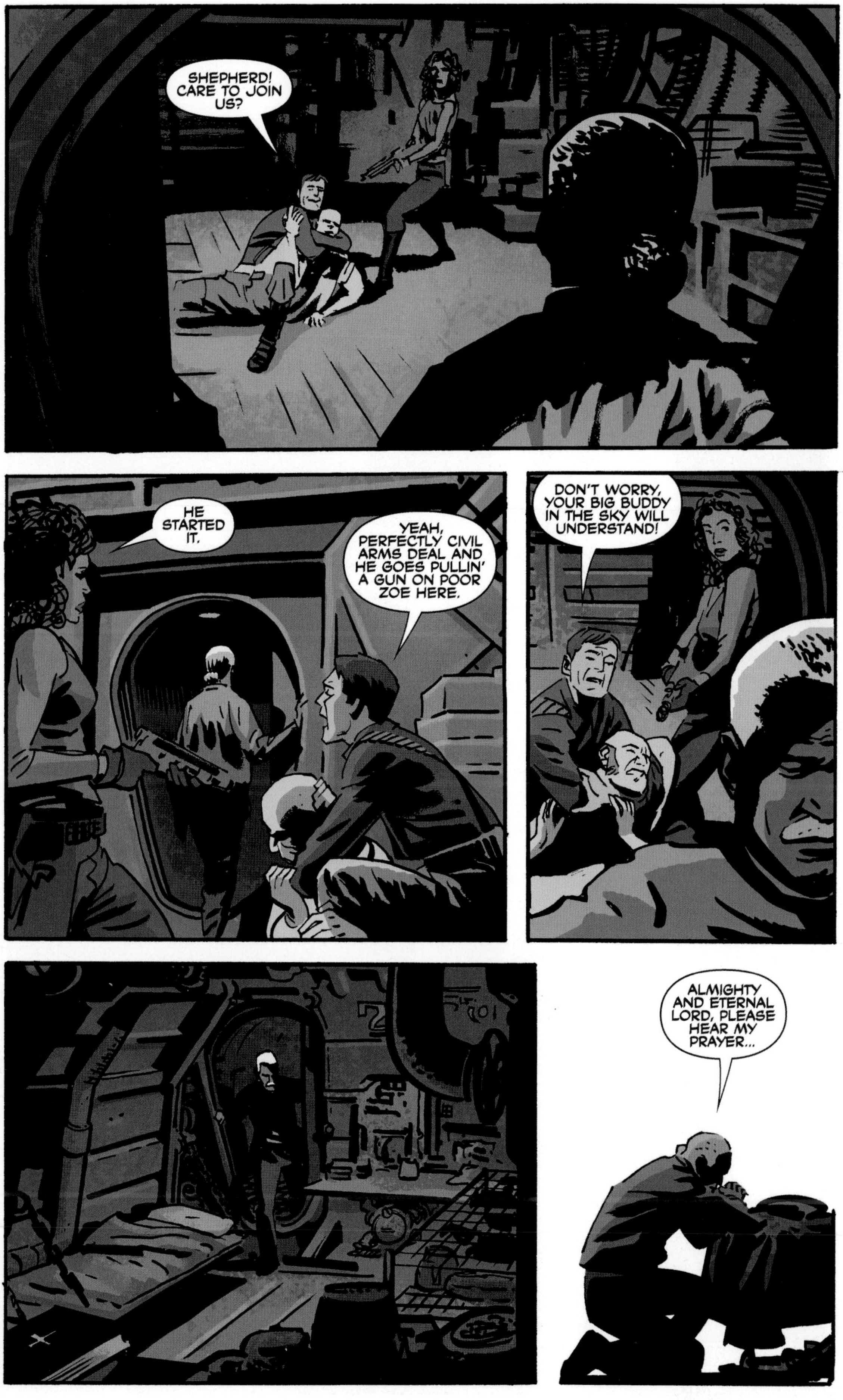
SHEPHERD! CARE TO JOIN US?
HE STARTED IT.
YEAH, PERFECTLY CIVIL ARMS DEAL AND HE GOES PULLIN' A GUN ON POOR ZOE HERE.
DON'T WORRY, YOUR BIG BUDDY IN THE SKY WILL UNDERSTAND!
ALMIGHTY AND ETERNAL LORD, PLEASE HEAR MY PRAYER...

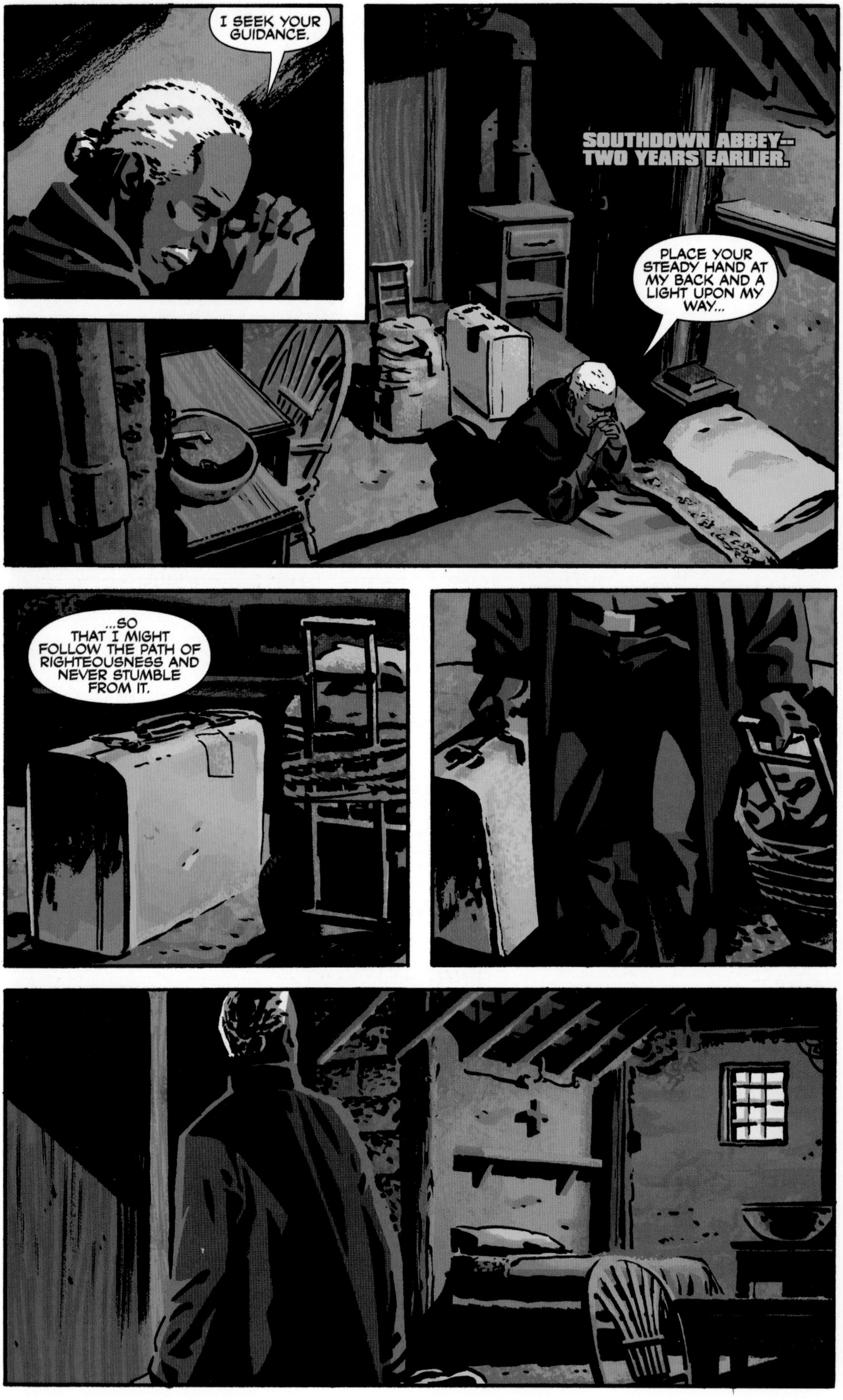
I SEEK YOUR GUIDANCE.
SOUTHDOWN ABBEY-- TWO YEARS EARLIER.
PLACE YOUR STEADY HAND AT MY BACK AND A LIGHT UPON MY WAY...
...SO THAT I MIGHT FOLLOW THE PATH OF RIGHTEOUSNESS AND NEVER STUMBLE FROM IT.

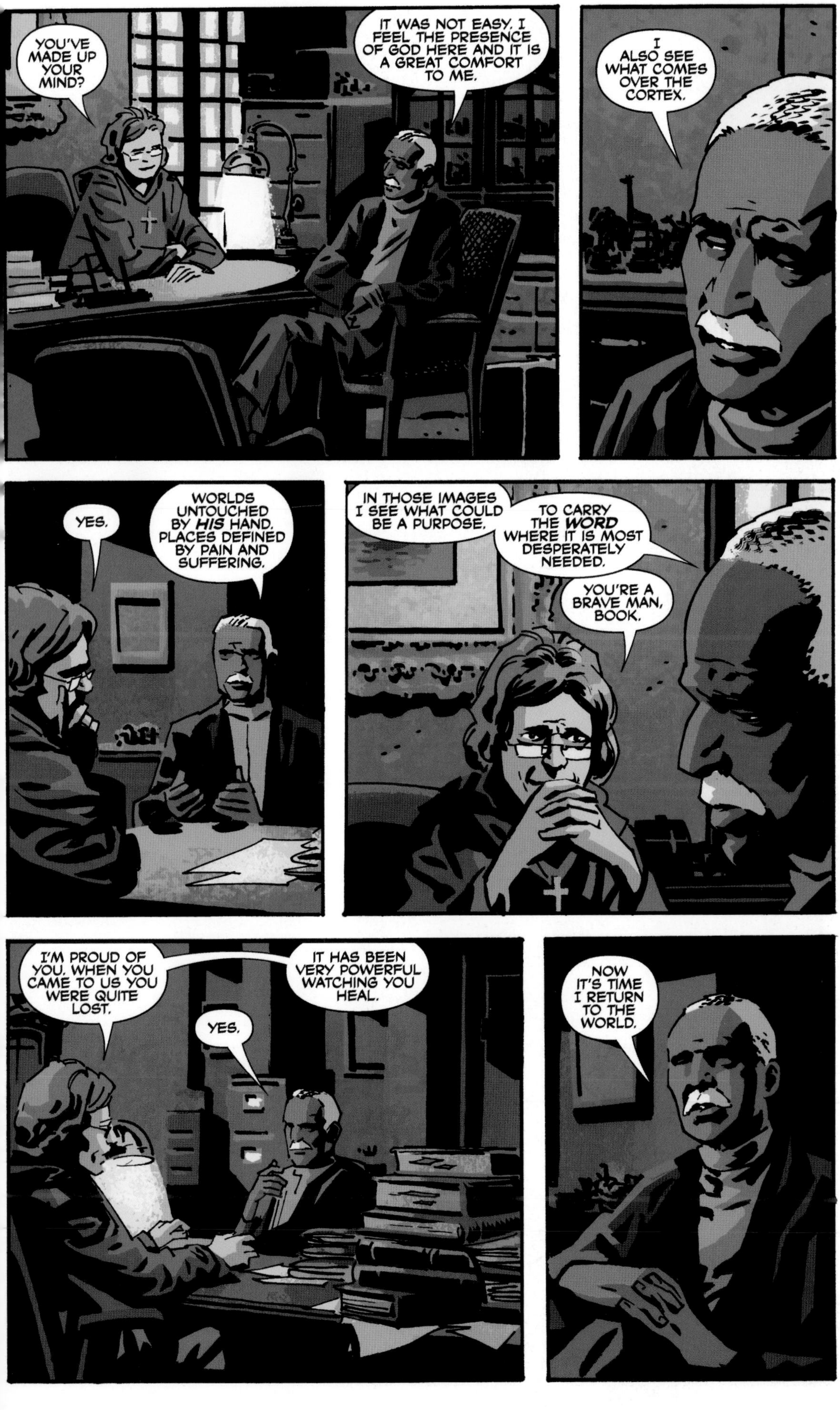
YOU'VE MADE UP YOUR MIND?
IT WAS NOT EASY. I FEEL THE PRESENCE OF GOD HERE AND IT IS A GREAT COMFORT TO ME.
I ALSO SEE WHAT COMES OVER THE CORTEX.
YES.
WORLDS UNTOUCHED BY *HIS* HAND. PLACES DEFINED BY PAIN AND SUFFERING.
IN THOSE IMAGES I SEE WHAT COULD BE A PURPOSE.
TO CARRY THE *WORD* WHERE IT IS MOST DESPERATELY NEEDED.
YOU'RE A BRAVE MAN, BOOK.
I'M PROUD OF YOU. WHEN YOU CAME TO US YOU WERE QUITE LOST.
IT HAS BEEN VERY POWERFUL WATCHING YOU HEAL.
YES.
NOW IT'S TIME I RETURN TO THE WORLD.

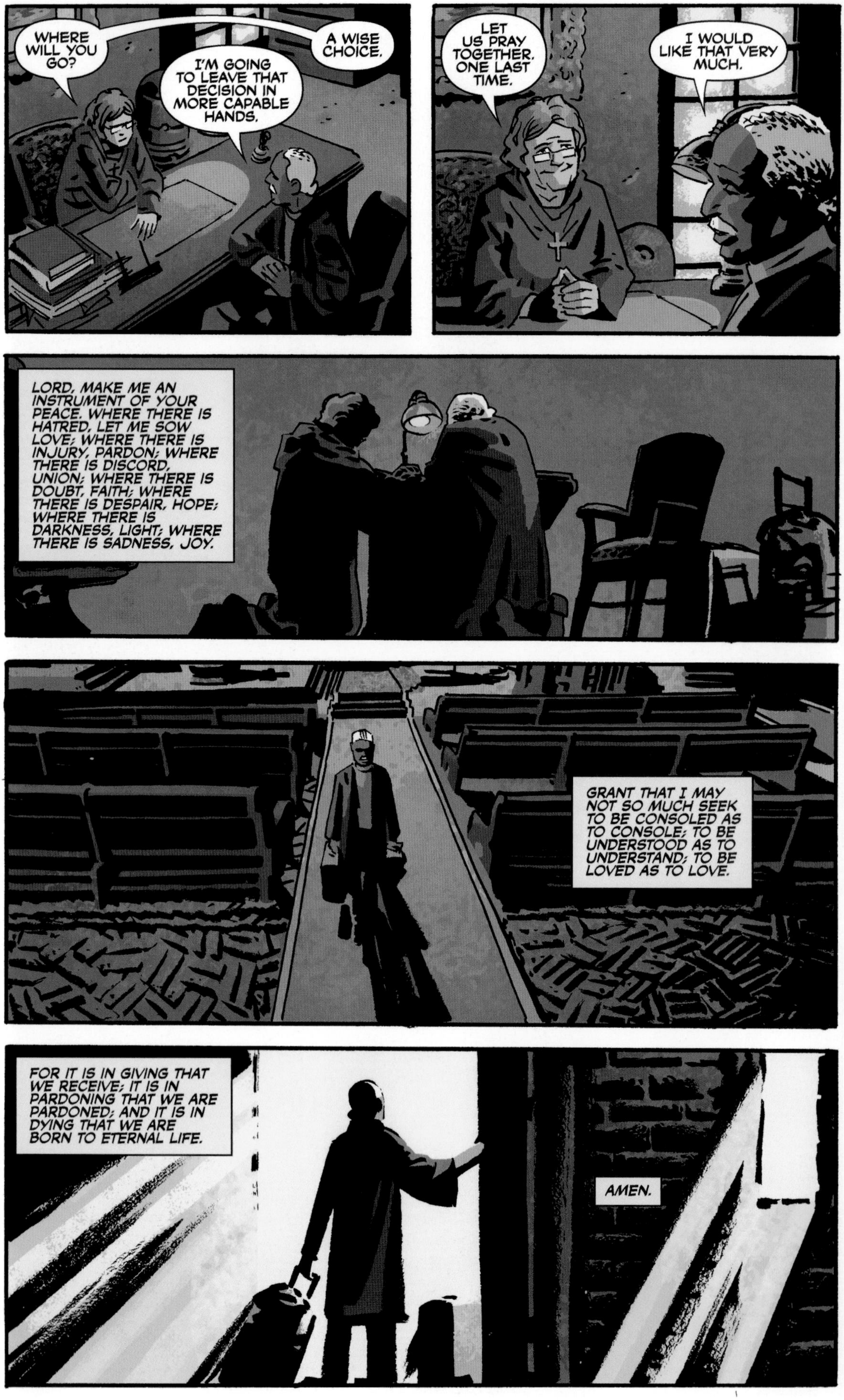
WHERE WILL YOU GO?
I'M GOING TO LEAVE THAT DECISION IN MORE CAPABLE HANDS.
A WISE CHOICE.
LET US PRAY TOGETHER. ONE LAST TIME.
I WOULD LIKE THAT VERY MUCH.
LORD, MAKE ME AN INSTRUMENT OF YOUR PEACE. WHERE THERE IS HATRED, LET ME SOW LOVE; WHERE THERE IS INJURY, PARDON; WHERE THERE IS DISCORD, UNION; WHERE THERE IS DOUBT, FAITH; WHERE THERE IS DESPAIR, HOPE; WHERE THERE IS DARKNESS, LIGHT; WHERE THERE IS SADNESS, JOY.
GRANT THAT I MAY NOT SO MUCH SEEK TO BE CONSOLED AS TO CONSOLE; TO BE UNDERSTOOD AS TO UNDERSTAND; TO BE LOVED AS TO LOVE.
FOR IT IS IN GIVING THAT WE RECEIVE; IT IS IN PARDONING THAT WE ARE PARDONED; AND IT IS IN DYING THAT WE ARE BORN TO ETERNAL LIFE.
AMEN.

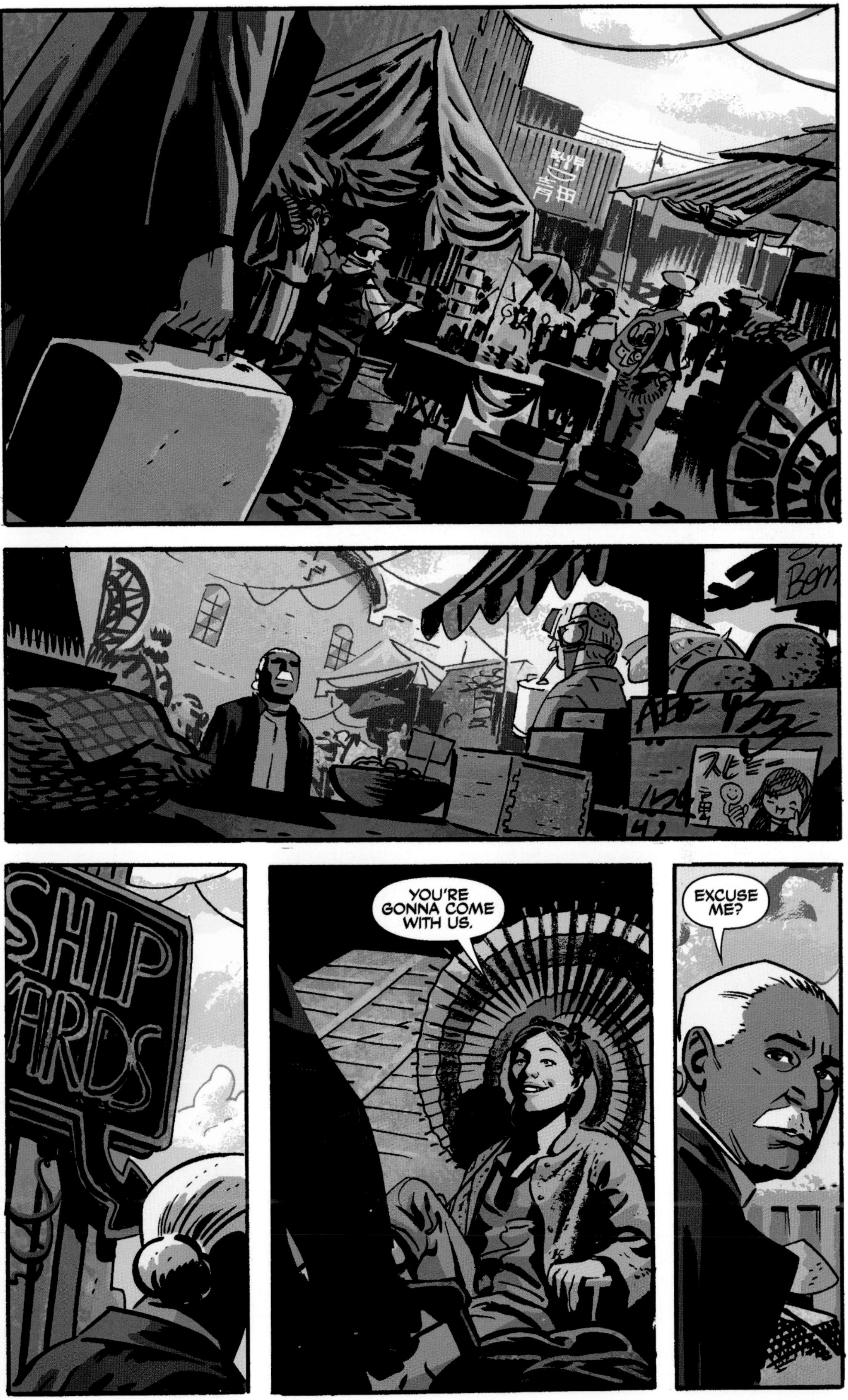
SHIP
YOU'RE GONNA COME WITH US.
EXCUSE ME?

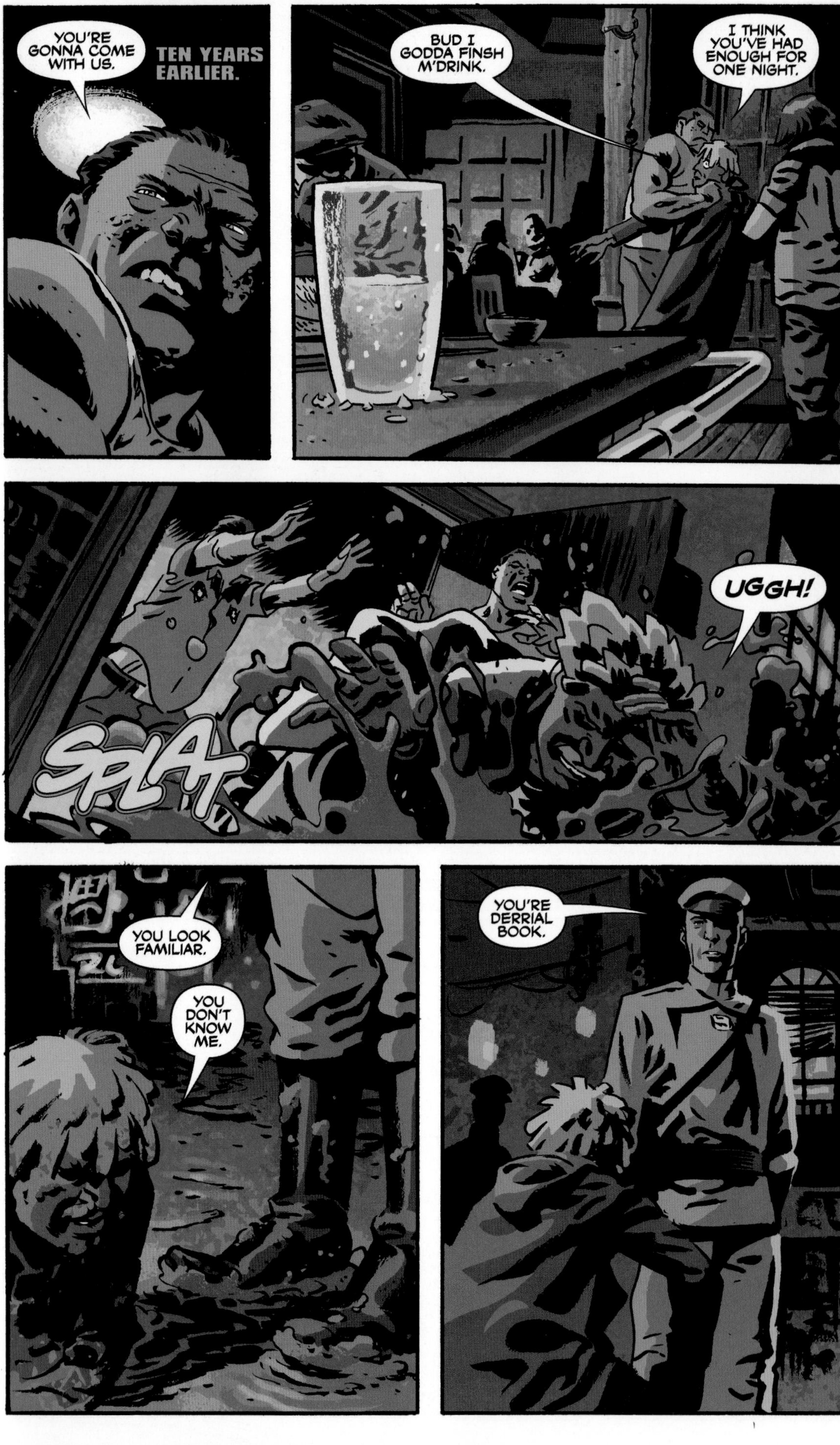
YOU'RE GONNA COME WITH US.
TEN YEARS EARLIER.
BUD I GODDA FINSH M'DRINK.
I THINK YOU'VE HAD ENOUGH FOR ONE NIGHT.
UGGH!
SPLAT
YOU LOOK FAMILIAR.
YOU DON'T KNOW ME.
YOU'RE DERRIAL BOOK.

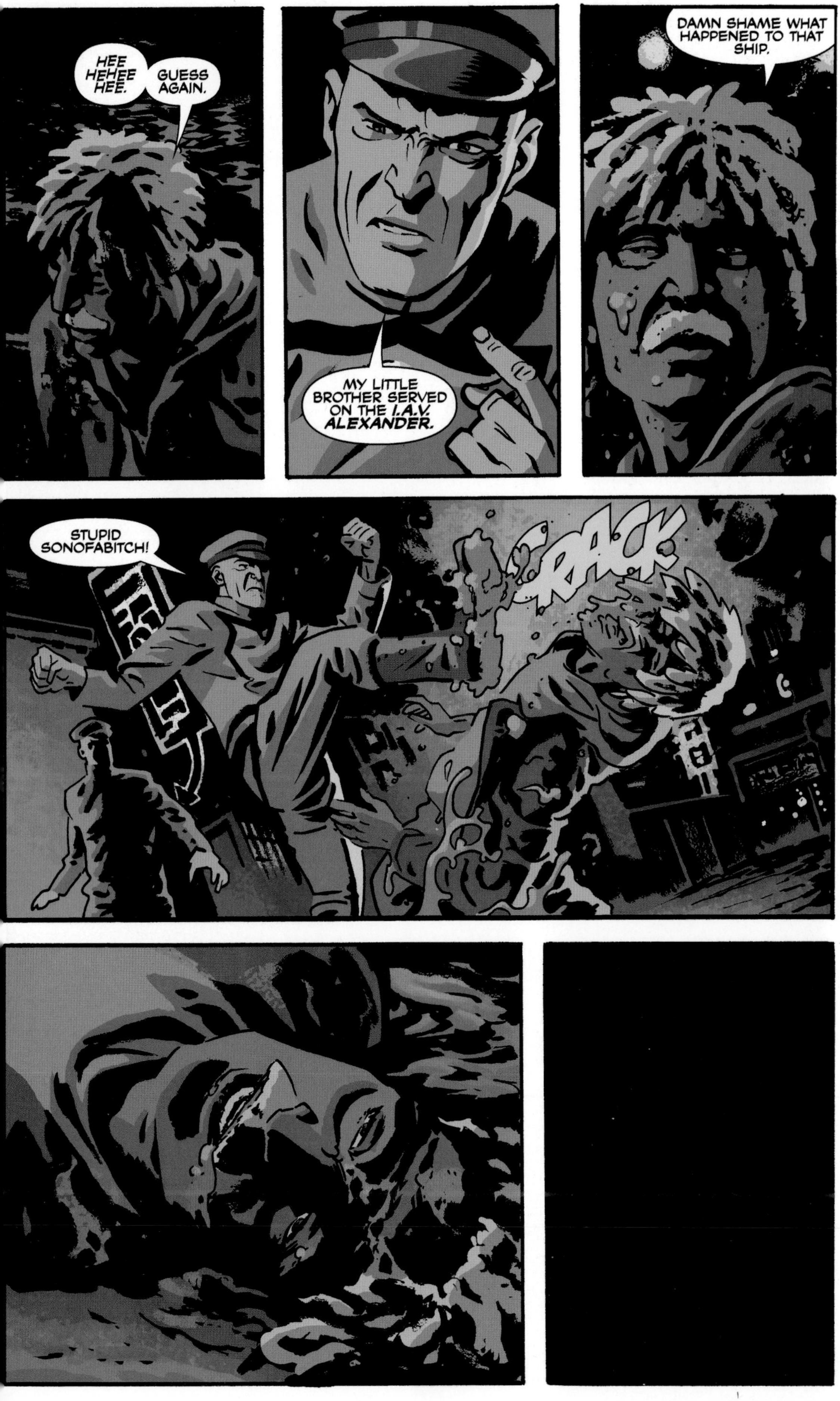
HEE HEHEE HEE.
GUESS AGAIN.
MY LITTLE BROTHER SERVED ON THE I.A.V. ALEXANDER.
DAMN SHAME WHAT HAPPENED TO THAT SHIP.
STUPID SONOFABITCH!
CRACK

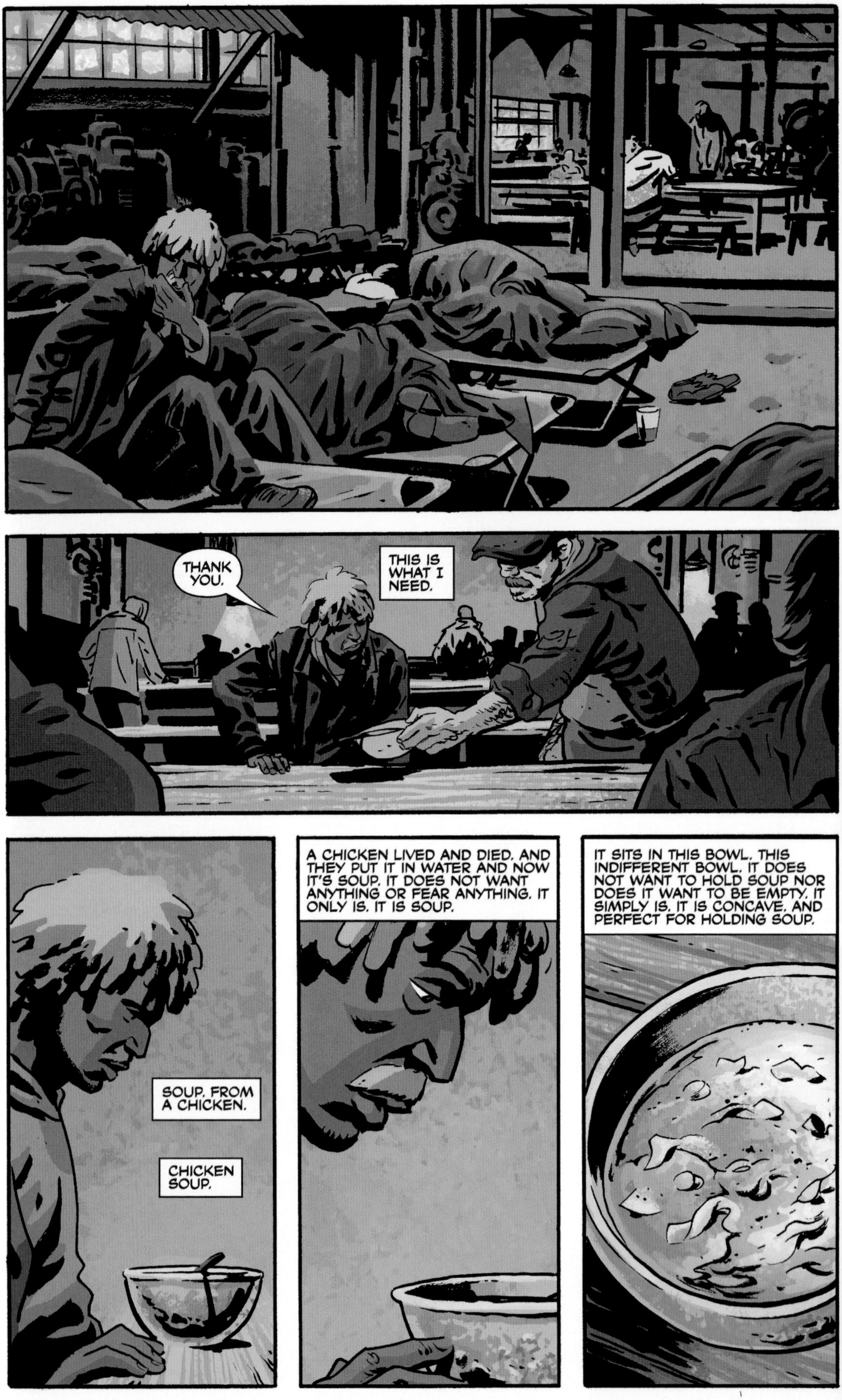
THANK YOU.
THIS IS WHAT I NEED.
SOUP. FROM A CHICKEN.
CHICKEN SOUP.
A CHICKEN LIVED AND DIED. AND THEY PUT IT IN WATER AND NOW IT'S SOUP. IT DOES NOT WANT ANYTHING OR FEAR ANYTHING. IT ONLY IS. IT IS SOUP.
IT SITS IN THIS BOWL. THIS INDIFFERENT BOWL. IT DOES NOT WANT TO HOLD SOUP NOR DOES IT WANT TO BE EMPTY. IT SIMPLY IS. IT IS CONCAVE. AND PERFECT FOR HOLDING SOUP.

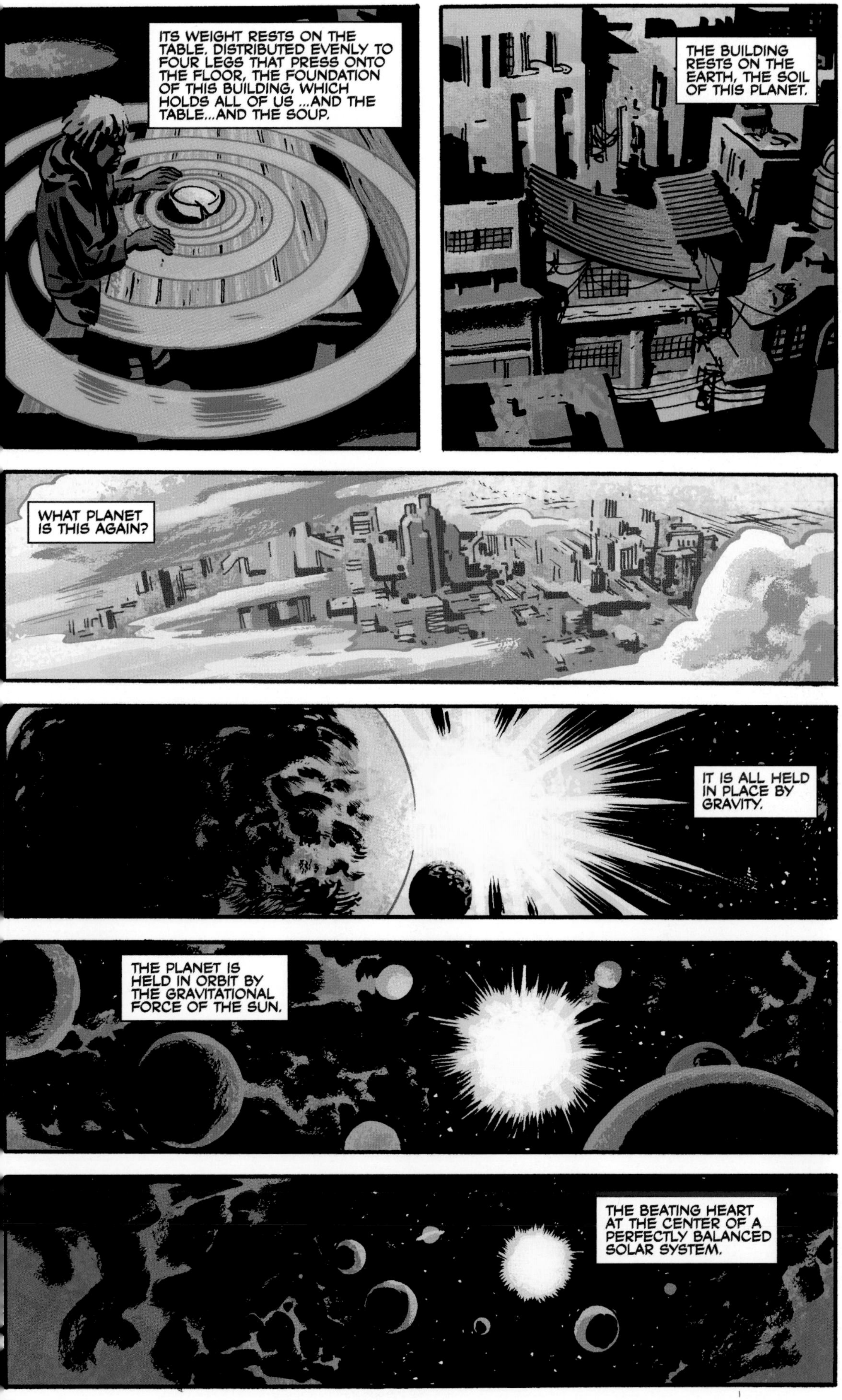
ITS WEIGHT RESTS ON THE TABLE, DISTRIBUTED EVENLY TO FOUR LEGS THAT PRESS ONTO THE FLOOR, THE FOUNDATION OF THIS BUILDING, WHICH HOLDS ALL OF US ...AND THE TABLE...AND THE SOUP.
THE BUILDING RESTS ON THE EARTH, THE SOIL OF THIS PLANET.
WHAT PLANET IS THIS AGAIN?
IT IS ALL HELD IN PLACE BY GRAVITY.
THE PLANET IS HELD IN ORBIT BY THE GRAVITATIONAL FORCE OF THE SUN.
THE BEATING HEART AT THE CENTER OF A PERFECTLY BALANCED SOLAR SYSTEM.

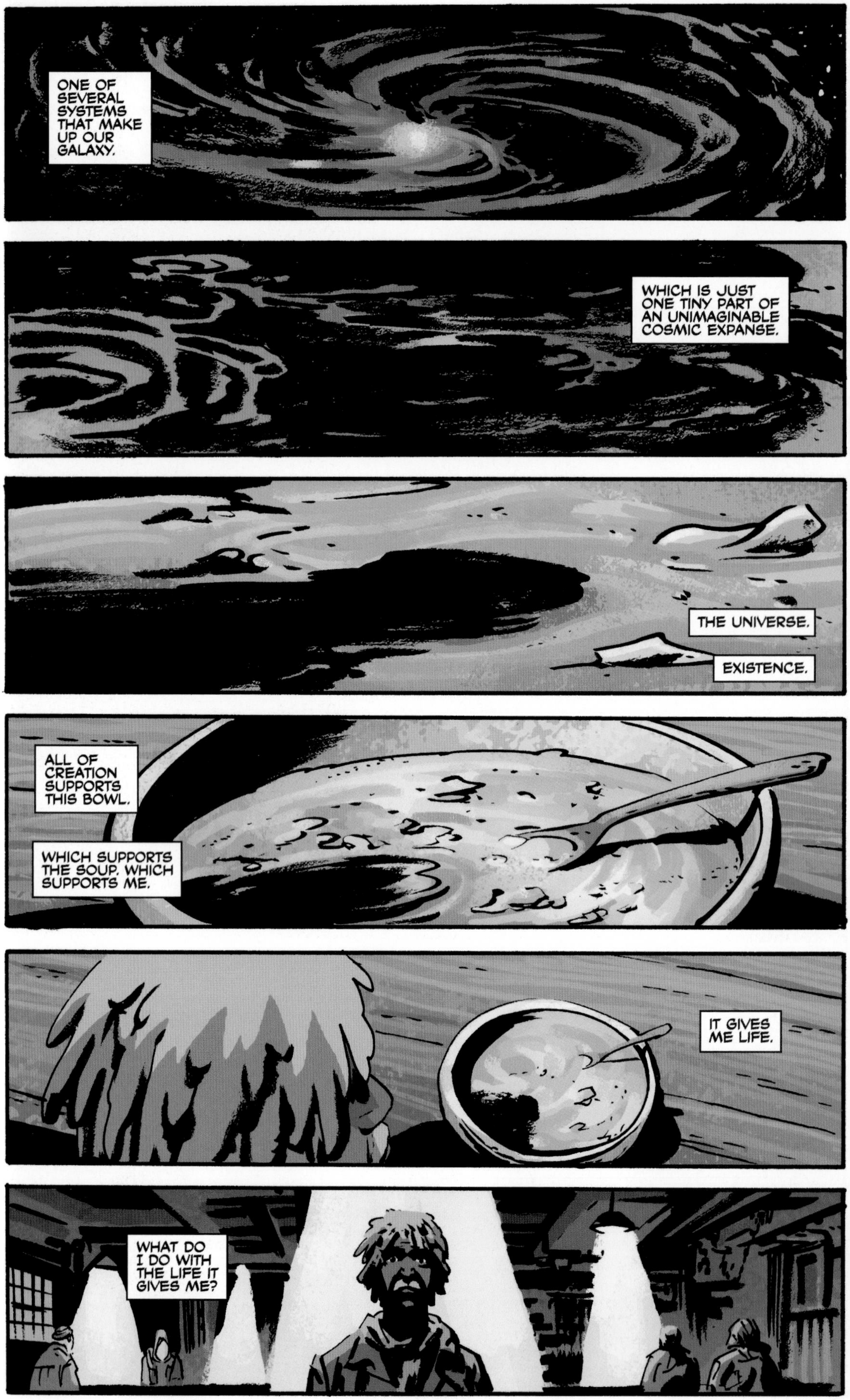
ONE OF SEVERAL SYSTEMS THAT MAKE UP OUR GALAXY.
WHICH IS JUST ONE TINY PART OF AN UNIMAGINABLE COSMIC EXPANSE.
THE UNIVERSE.
EXISTENCE.
ALL OF CREATION SUPPORTS THIS BOWL.
WHICH SUPPORTS THE SOUP. WHICH SUPPORTS ME.
IT GIVES ME LIFE.
WHAT DO I DO WITH THE LIFE IT GIVES ME?

GULP GULP GULP

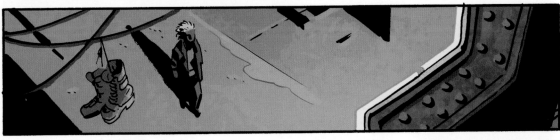

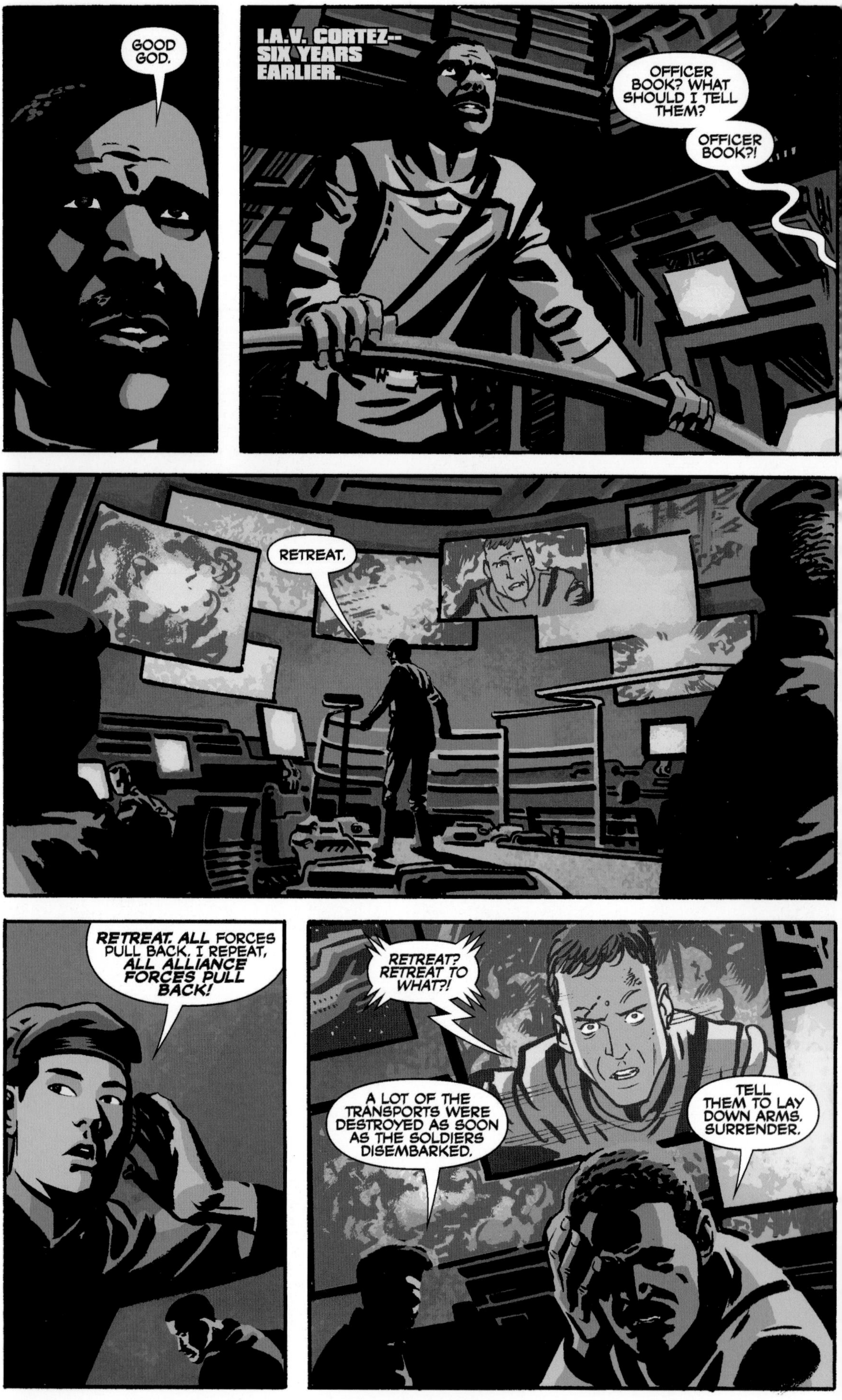
GOOD GOD.
I.A.V. CORTEZ-- SIX YEARS EARLIER.
OFFICER BOOK? WHAT SHOULD I TELL THEM?
OFFICER BOOK?!
RETREAT.
RETREAT. ALL FORCES PULL BACK. I REPEAT, ALL ALLIANCE FORCES PULL BACK!
RETREAT? RETREAT TO WHAT?!
A LOT OF THE TRANSPORTS WERE DESTROYED AS SOON AS THE SOLDIERS DISEMBARKED.
TELL THEM TO LAY DOWN ARMS. SURRENDER.

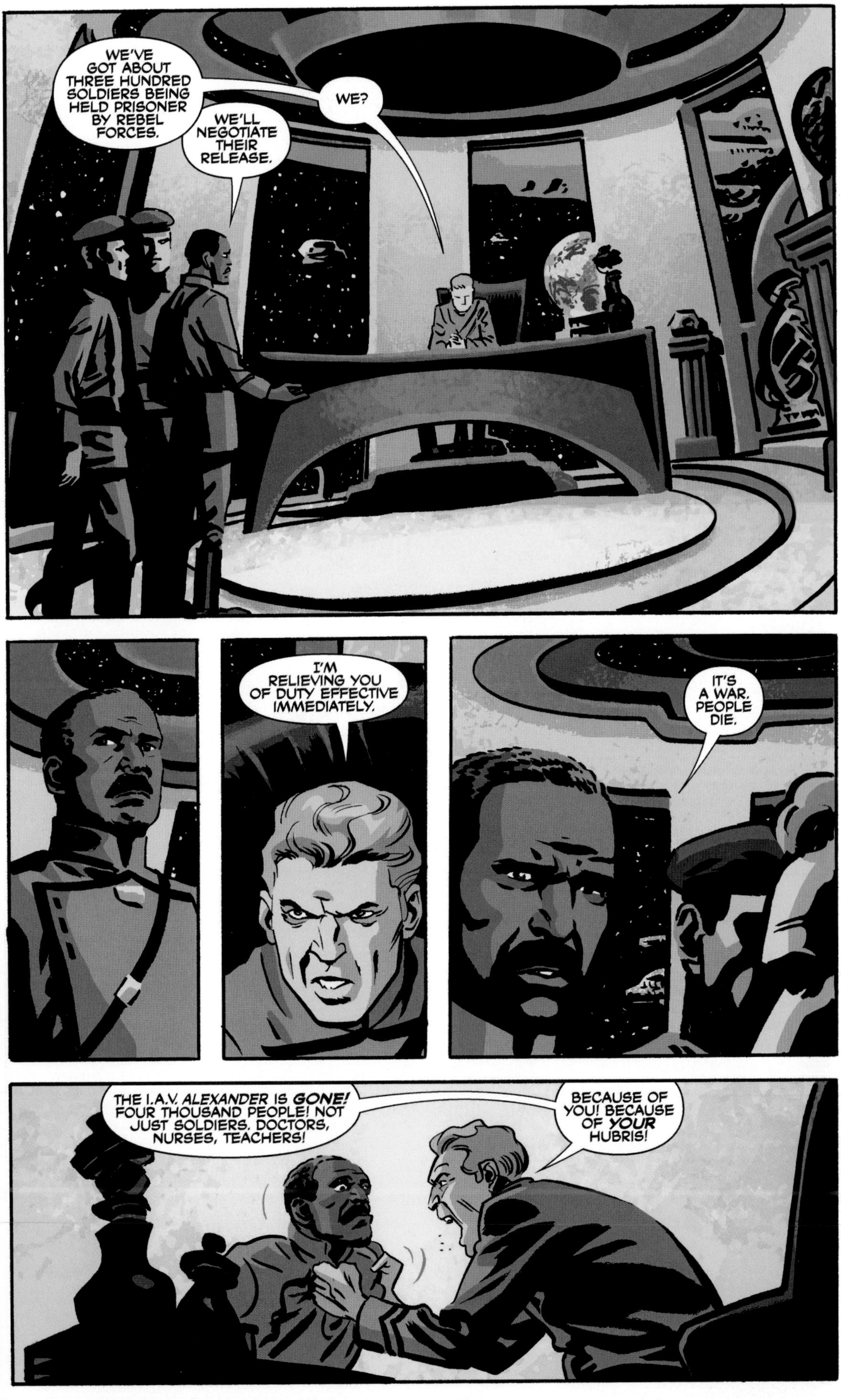
WE'VE GOT ABOUT THREE HUNDRED SOLDIERS BEING HELD PRISONER BY REBEL FORCES.
WE'LL NEGOTIATE THEIR RELEASE.
WE?
I'M RELIEVING YOU OF DUTY EFFECTIVE IMMEDIATELY.
IT'S A WAR. PEOPLE DIE.
THE I.A.V. *ALEXANDER* IS ***GONE!*** FOUR THOUSAND PEOPLE! NOT JUST SOLDIERS. DOCTORS, NURSES, TEACHERS!
BECAUSE OF YOU! BECAUSE OF ***YOUR*** HUBRIS!

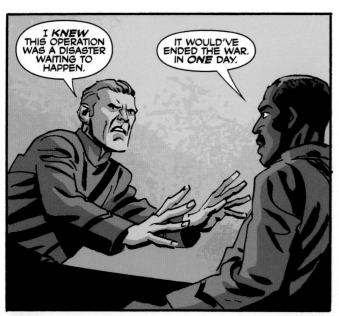

I **KNEW** THIS OPERATION WAS A DISASTER WAITING TO HAPPEN.

IT WOULD'VE ENDED THE WAR. IN **ONE** DAY.

IF YOU CONCERNED YOURSELF LESS WITH **PERSONAL GLORY** A LOT OF GOOD PEOPLE WOULD STILL BE ALIVE RIGHT NOW...

IT WASN'T EVEN A FIGHT. THEY WERE **WAITING** FOR US. MILES FROM ANYTHING, IN THE MIDDLE OF NOWHERE, OUR MEN OPENED UP THE DOORS OF THEIR TRANSPORTS AND WALKED INTO A WALL OF ENEMY FIRE.

EVERY SINGLE UNIT ON SIX DIFFERENT PLANETS, MILLIONS OF MILES AWAY FROM ONE ANOTHER, HAD THE SAME EXPERIENCE.

PUT ME IN CHARGE OF AN INVESTIGATIVE COMMITTEE. WE'LL FIND THE MOLES AND THEY'LL BE PUNISHED.

ARE YOU JOKING? ARE YOU OUT OF YOUR MIND?

SOLDIER, YOU JUST MASTERMINDED THE SINGLE GREATEST DISASTER IN ALLIANCE HISTORY. YOUR MILITARY CAREER IS OVER.

FOUR THOUSAND MEN, BOOK. DOES THAT MEAN ANYTHING TO YOU?

YOU KEEP TELLIN' YOURSELF THAT.

THIS ISN'T MY FAULT.

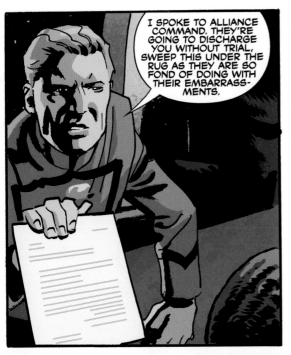

I SPOKE TO ALLIANCE COMMAND. THEY'RE GOING TO DISCHARGE YOU WITHOUT TRIAL, SWEEP THIS UNDER THE RUG AS THEY ARE SO FOND OF DOING WITH THEIR EMBARRASS-MENTS.

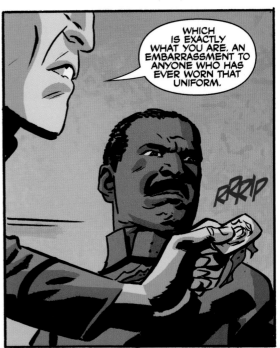

WHICH IS EXACTLY WHAT YOU ARE. AN EMBARRASSMENT TO ANYONE WHO HAS EVER WORN THAT UNIFORM.

RRRIP

I WANT YOU OFF MY SHIP IMMEDIATELY.

I'LL TAKE THE NEXT SHUTTLE.

NO, I SAID IMMEDIATELY. THESE MEN WILL ESCORT YOU TO AN ESCAPE VESSEL.

WHAT? YOU'RE NOT SERIOUS. THOSE THINGS ARE DEATH-TRAPS.

A HAPPY COINCIDENCE.

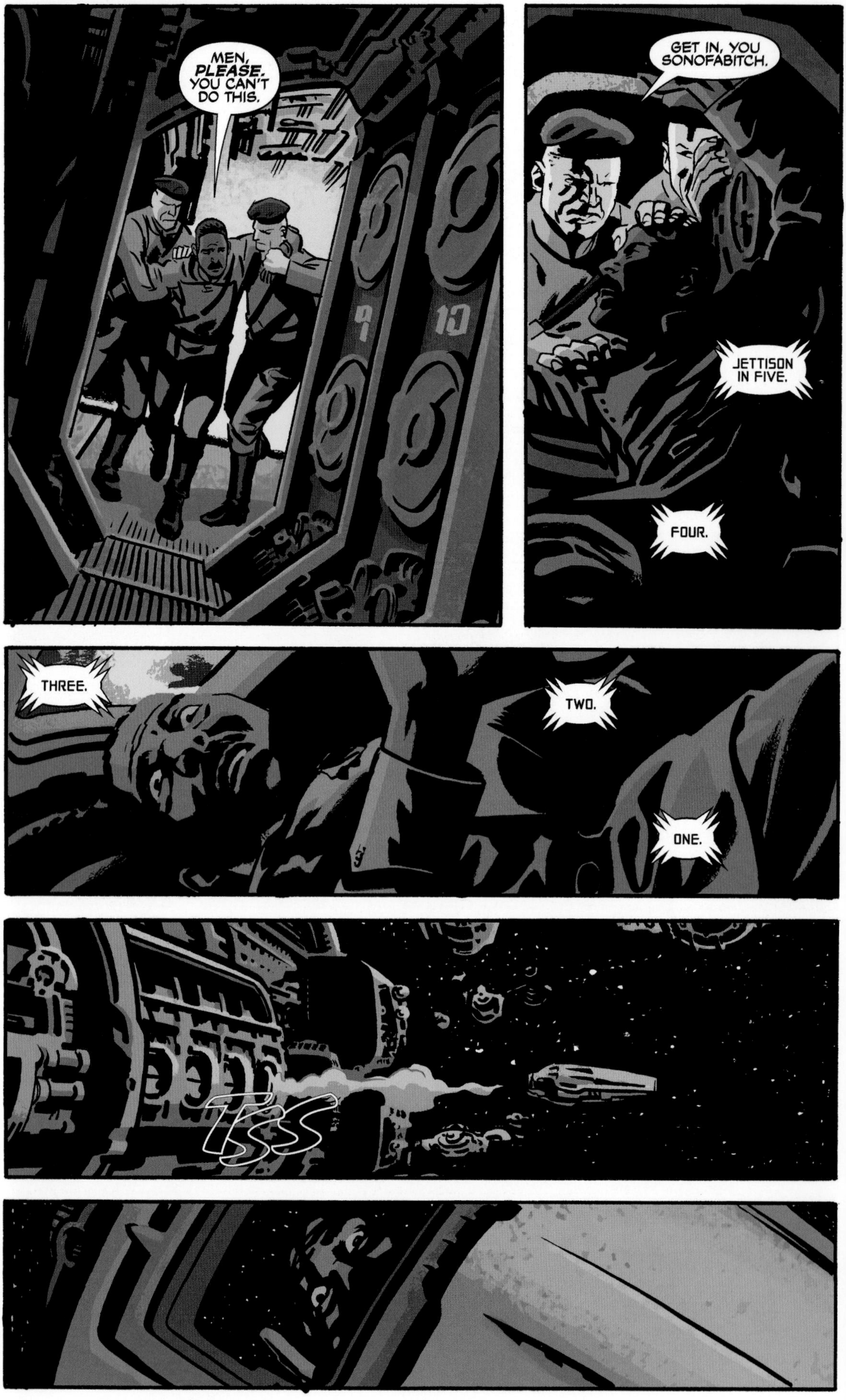
MEN, PLEASE. YOU CAN'T DO THIS.
9
10
GET IN, YOU SONOFABITCH.
JETTISON IN FIVE.
FOUR.
THREE.
TWO.
ONE.
TSS

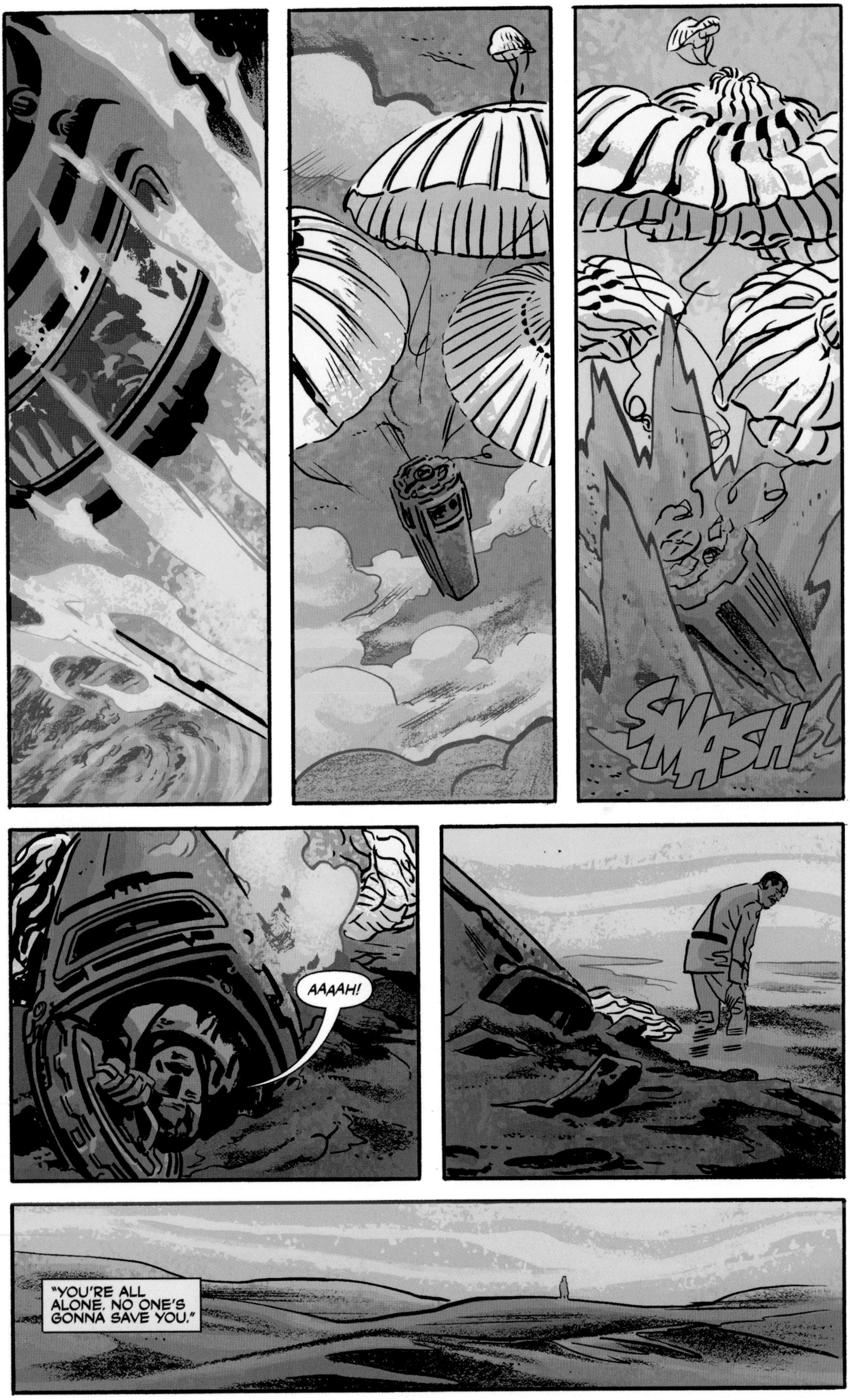
SMASH
AAAAH!
"YOU'RE ALL ALONE. NO ONE'S GONNA SAVE YOU."

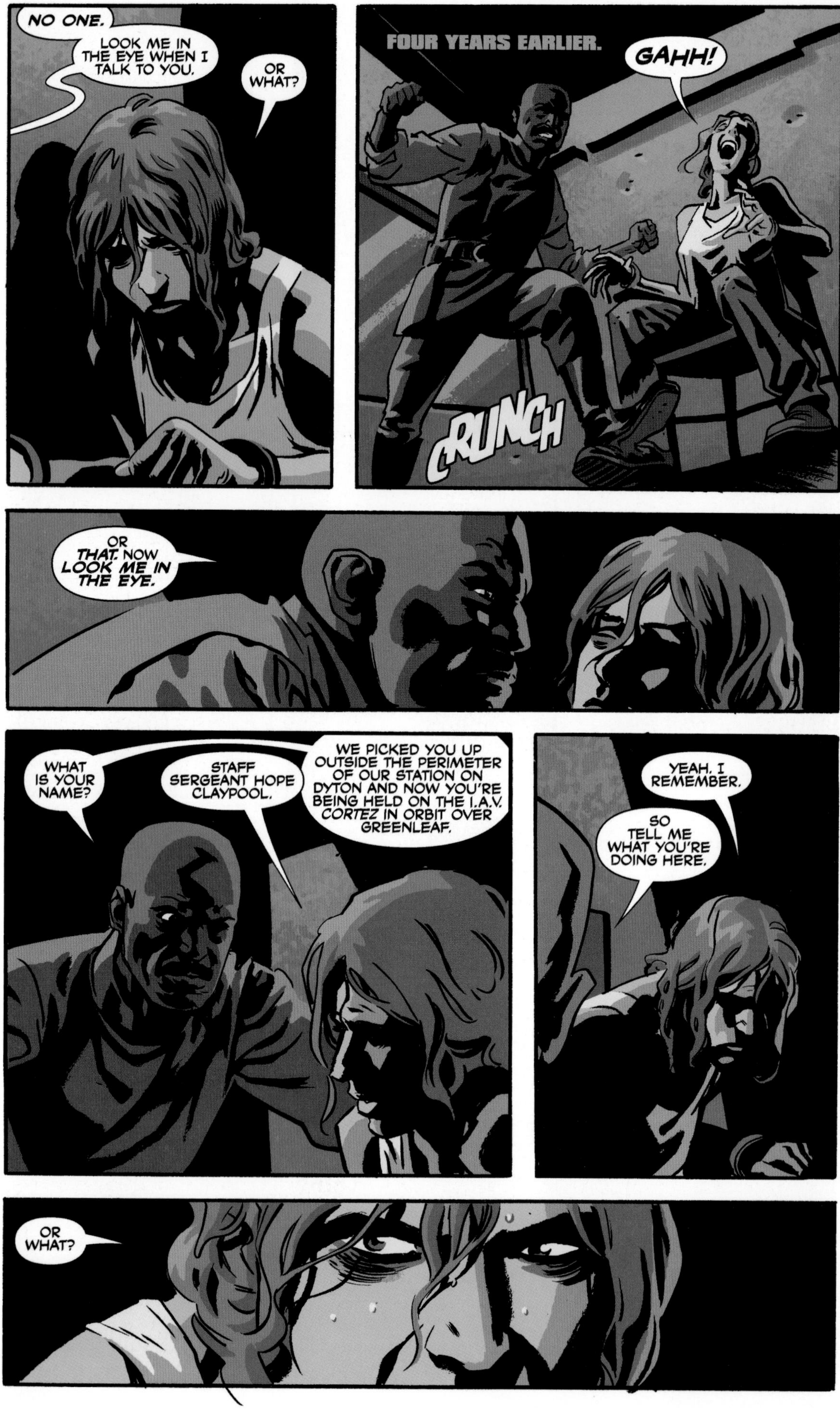
NO ONE.
LOOK ME IN THE EYE WHEN I TALK TO YOU.
OR WHAT?
FOUR YEARS EARLIER.
GAHH!
CRUNCH
OR THAT. NOW LOOK ME IN THE EYE.
WHAT IS YOUR NAME?
STAFF SERGEANT HOPE CLAYPOOL.
WE PICKED YOU UP OUTSIDE THE PERIMETER OF OUR STATION ON DYTON AND NOW YOU'RE BEING HELD ON THE I.A.V. CORTEZ IN ORBIT OVER GREENLEAF.
YEAH. I REMEMBER.
SO TELL ME WHAT YOU'RE DOING HERE.
OR WHAT?

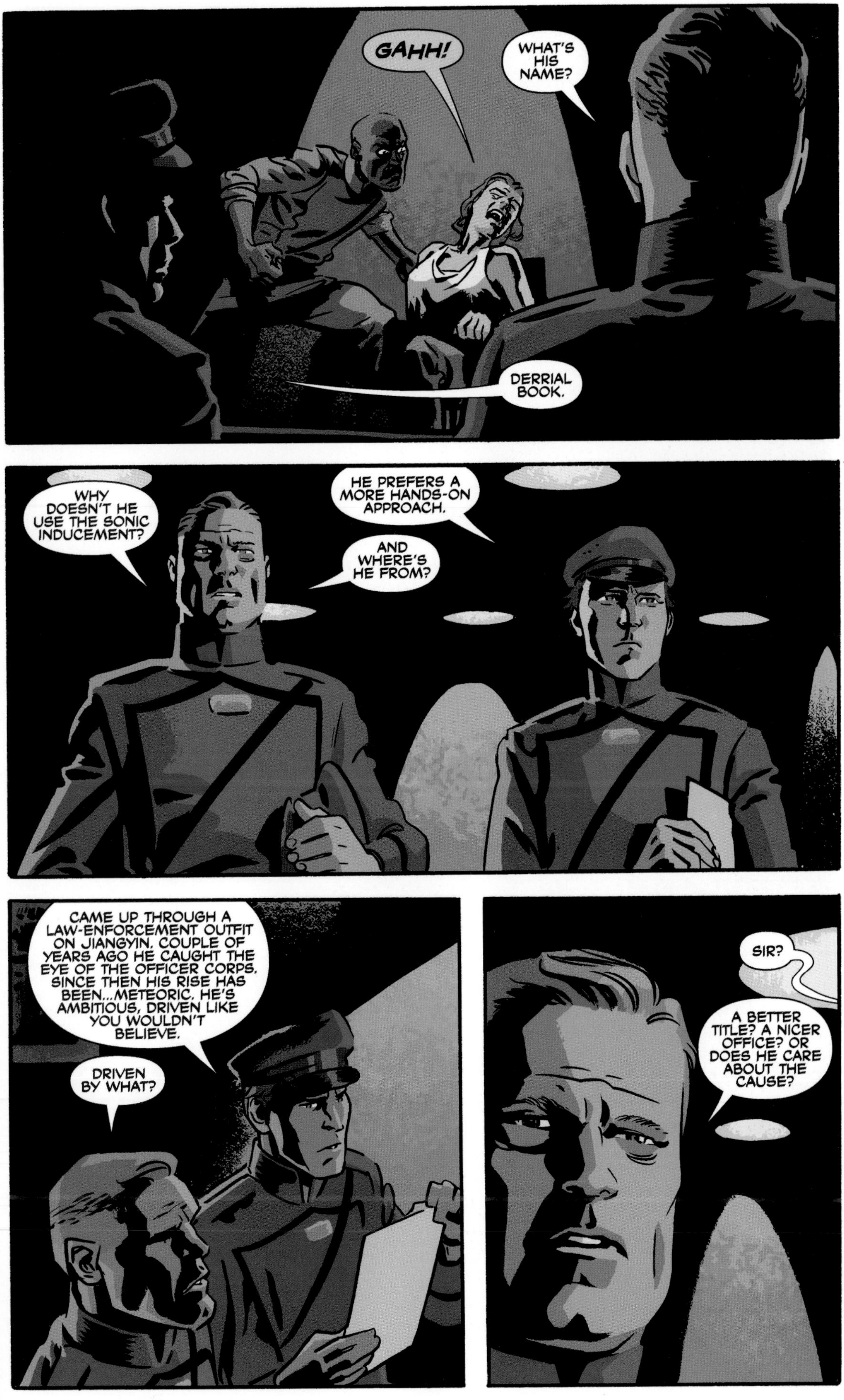
GAHH!
WHAT'S HIS NAME?
DERRIAL BOOK.
WHY DOESN'T HE USE THE SONIC INDUCEMENT?
HE PREFERS A MORE HANDS-ON APPROACH.
AND WHERE'S HE FROM?
CAME UP THROUGH A LAW-ENFORCEMENT OUTFIT ON JIANGYIN. COUPLE OF YEARS AGO HE CAUGHT THE EYE OF THE OFFICER CORPS. SINCE THEN HIS RISE HAS BEEN...METEORIC. HE'S AMBITIOUS, DRIVEN LIKE YOU WOULDN'T BELIEVE.
DRIVEN BY WHAT?
SIR?
A BETTER TITLE? A NICER OFFICE? OR DOES HE CARE ABOUT THE CAUSE?

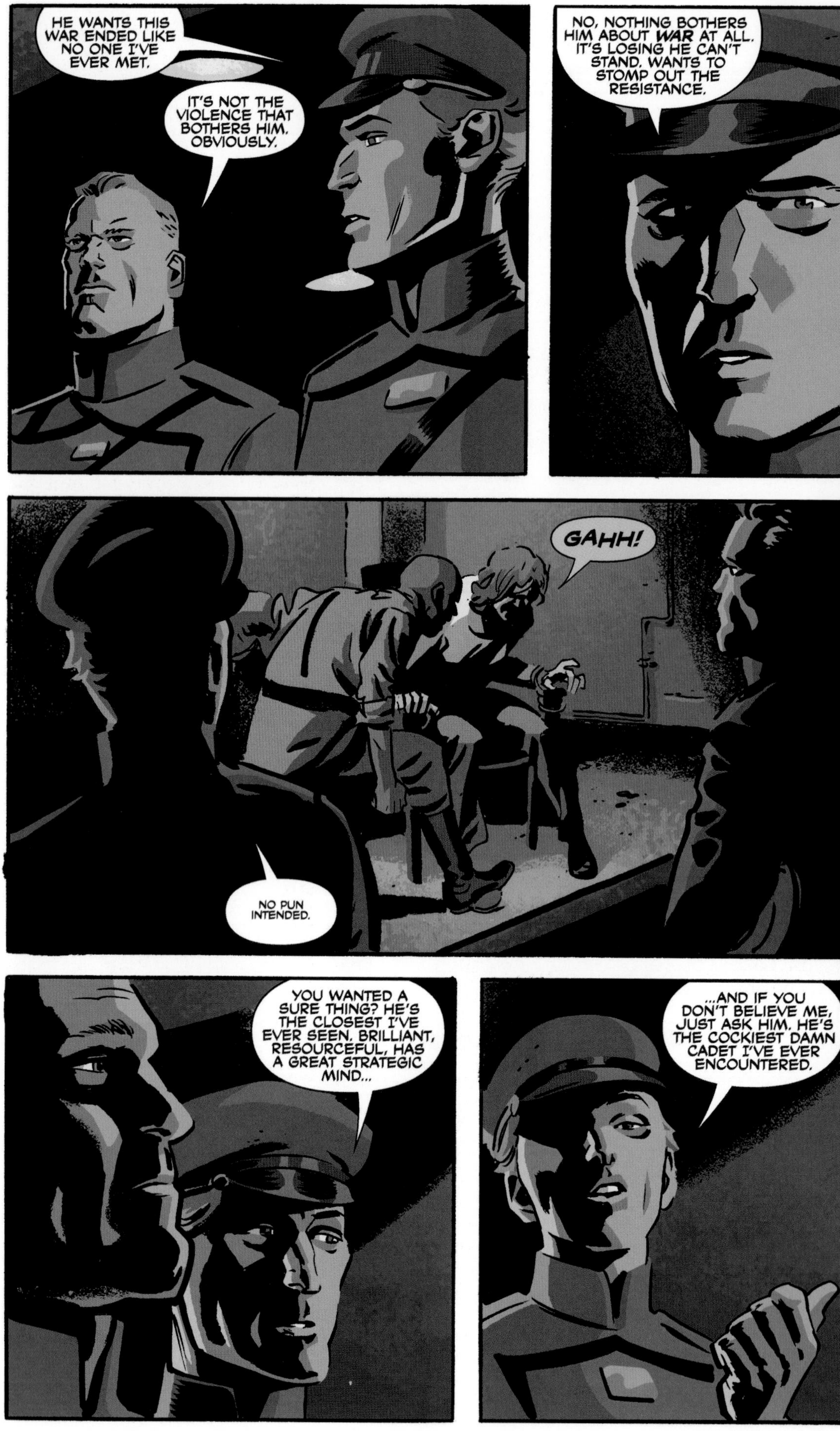
HE WANTS THIS WAR ENDED LIKE NO ONE I'VE EVER MET.
IT'S NOT THE VIOLENCE THAT BOTHERS HIM, OBVIOUSLY.
NO, NOTHING BOTHERS HIM ABOUT WAR AT ALL. IT'S LOSING HE CAN'T STAND. WANTS TO STOMP OUT THE RESISTANCE.
GAHH!
NO PUN INTENDED.
YOU WANTED A SURE THING? HE'S THE CLOSEST I'VE EVER SEEN. BRILLIANT, RESOURCEFUL, HAS A GREAT STRATEGIC MIND...
...AND IF YOU DON'T BELIEVE ME, JUST ASK HIM. HE'S THE COCKIEST DAMN CADET I'VE EVER ENCOUNTERED.

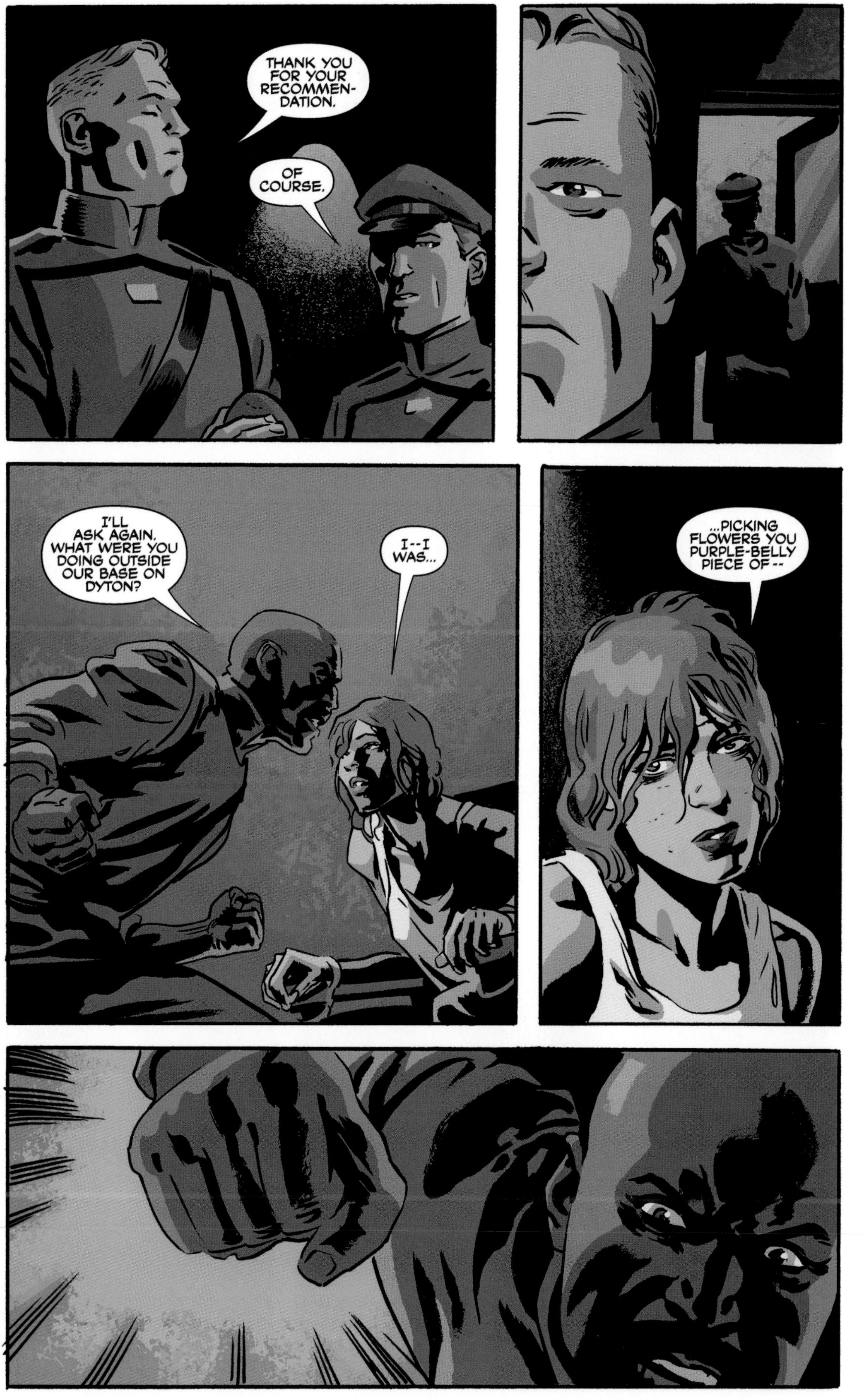
THANK YOU FOR YOUR RECOMMEN-DATION.
OF COURSE.
I'LL ASK AGAIN. WHAT WERE YOU DOING OUTSIDE OUR BASE ON DYTON?
I--I WAS...
...PICKING FLOWERS YOU PURPLE-BELLY PIECE OF --

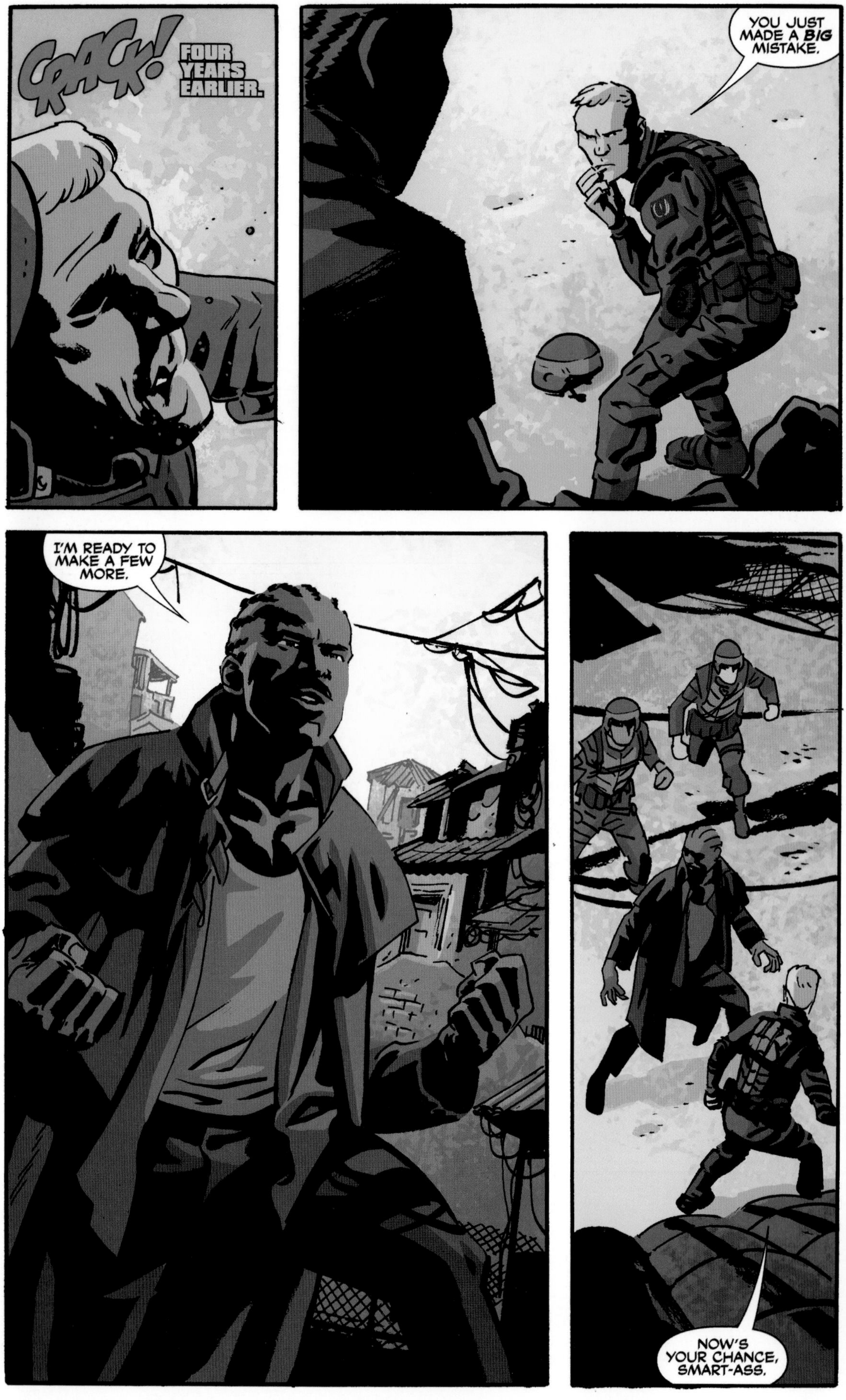
CRACK!
FOUR YEARS EARLIER.
YOU JUST MADE A *BIG* MISTAKE.
I'M READY TO MAKE A FEW MORE.
NOW'S YOUR CHANCE, SMART-ASS.

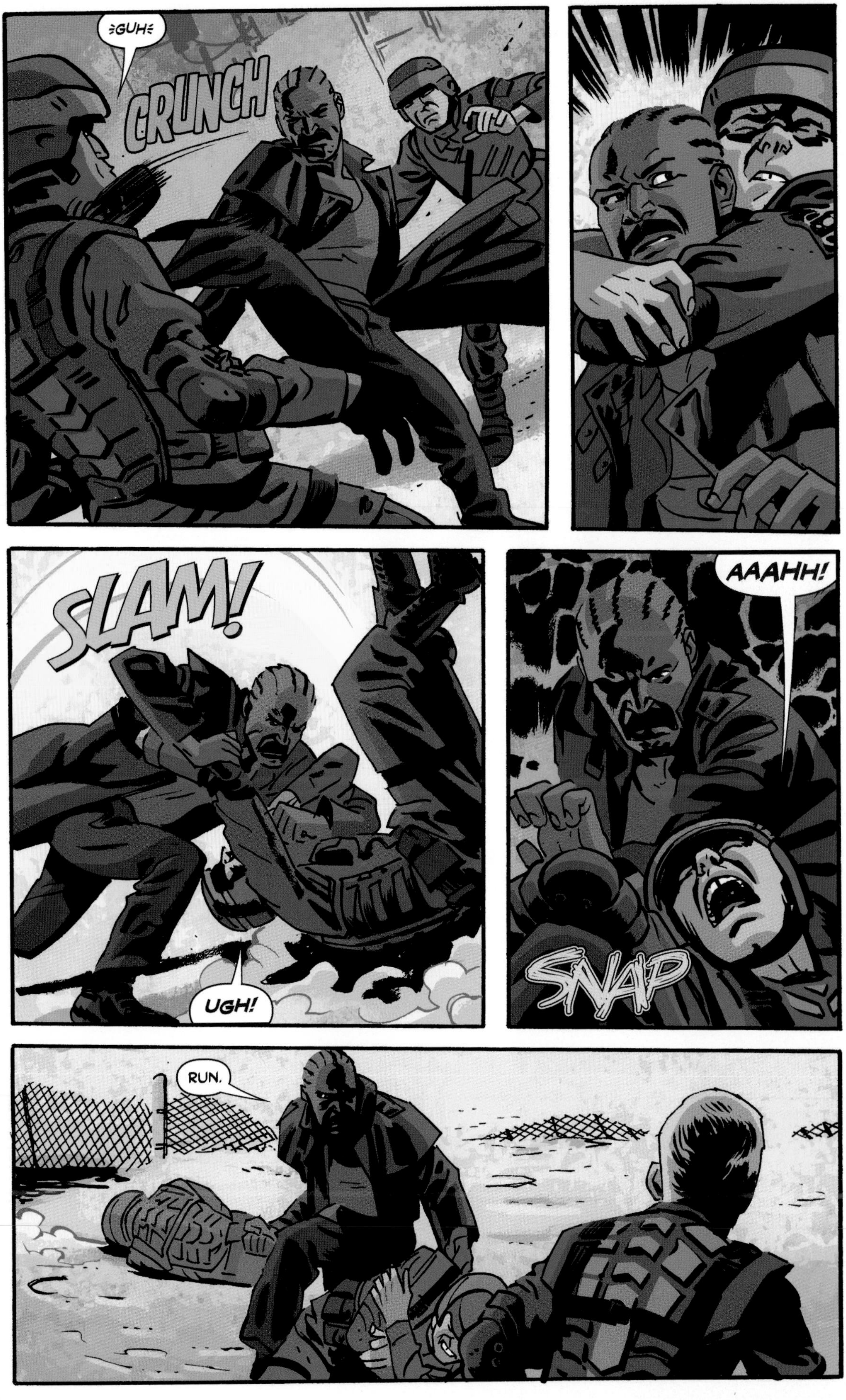
GUH
CRUNCH
SLAM!
UGH!
AAAHH!
SNAP
RUN.

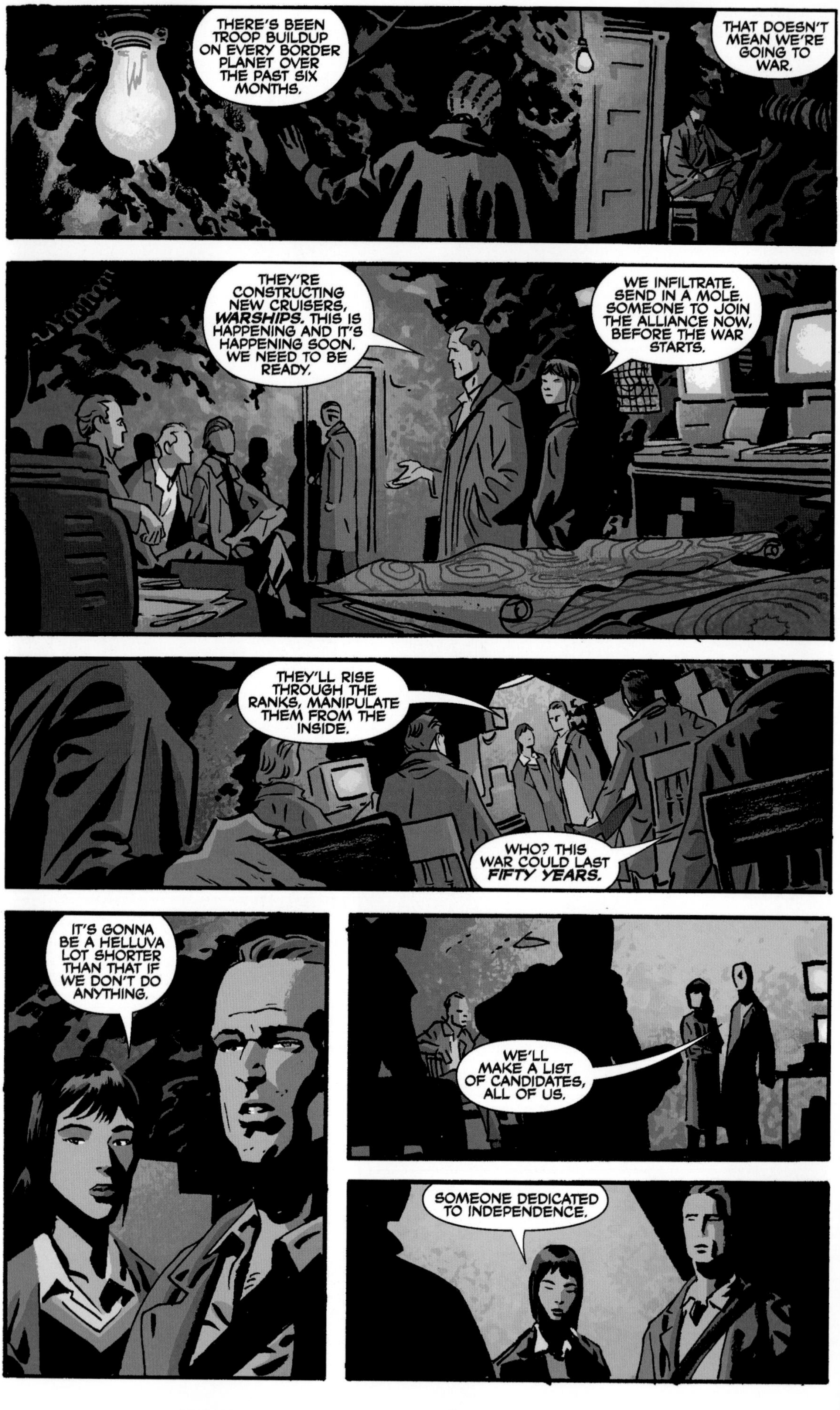
THERE'S BEEN TROOP BUILDUP ON EVERY BORDER PLANET OVER THE PAST SIX MONTHS.
THAT DOESN'T MEAN WE'RE GOING TO WAR.
THEY'RE CONSTRUCTING NEW CRUISERS, *WARSHIPS.* THIS IS HAPPENING AND IT'S HAPPENING SOON. WE NEED TO BE READY.
WE INFILTRATE. SEND IN A MOLE. SOMEONE TO JOIN THE ALLIANCE NOW, BEFORE THE WAR STARTS.
THEY'LL RISE THROUGH THE RANKS, MANIPULATE THEM FROM THE INSIDE.
WHO? THIS WAR COULD LAST *FIFTY YEARS.*
IT'S GONNA BE A HELLUVA LOT SHORTER THAN THAT IF WE DON'T DO ANYTHING.
WE'LL MAKE A LIST OF CANDIDATES, ALL OF US.
SOMEONE DEDICATED TO INDEPENDENCE.

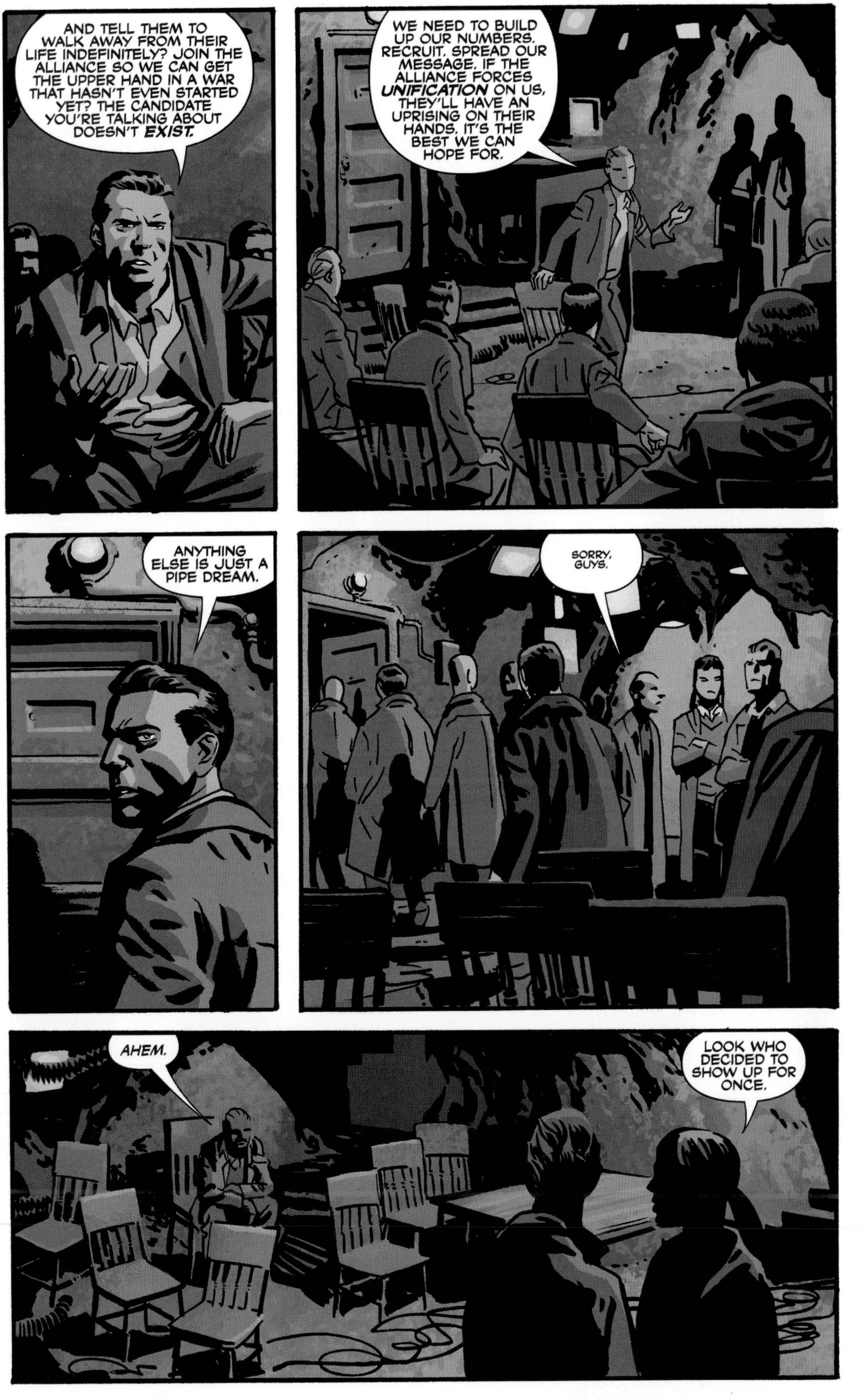
AND TELL THEM TO WALK AWAY FROM THEIR LIFE INDEFINITELY? JOIN THE ALLIANCE SO WE CAN GET THE UPPER HAND IN A WAR THAT HASN'T EVEN STARTED YET? THE CANDIDATE YOU'RE TALKING ABOUT DOESN'T EXIST.
WE NEED TO BUILD UP OUR NUMBERS. RECRUIT. SPREAD OUR MESSAGE. IF THE ALLIANCE FORCES UNIFICATION ON US, THEY'LL HAVE AN UPRISING ON THEIR HANDS. IT'S THE BEST WE CAN HOPE FOR.
ANYTHING ELSE IS JUST A PIPE DREAM.
SORRY, GUYS.
AHEM.
LOOK WHO DECIDED TO SHOW UP FOR ONCE.

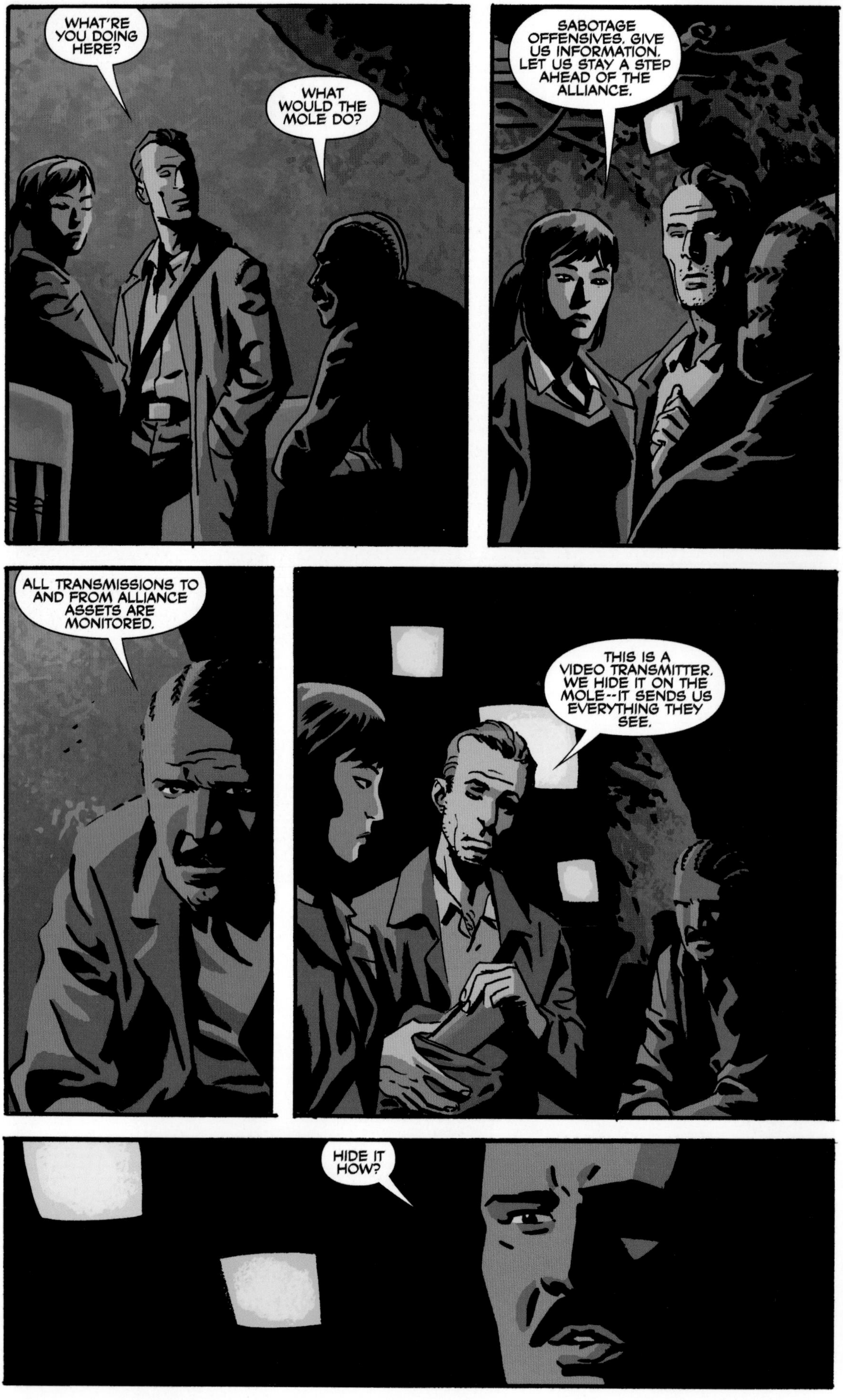
WHAT'RE YOU DOING HERE?
WHAT WOULD THE MOLE DO?
SABOTAGE OFFENSIVES. GIVE US INFORMATION. LET US STAY A STEP AHEAD OF THE ALLIANCE.
ALL TRANSMISSIONS TO AND FROM ALLIANCE ASSETS ARE MONITORED.
THIS IS A VIDEO TRANSMITTER. WE HIDE IT ON THE MOLE--IT SENDS US EVERYTHING THEY SEE.
HIDE IT HOW?

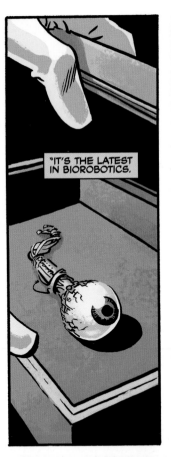

"IT'S THE LATEST IN BIOROBOTICS."

"A THERMAL-POWERED CAMERA AND MICRO-TRANSMITTER. IT INTEGRATES SEAMLESSLY WITH YOUR PHYSIOLOGY, CONNECTING TO YOUR OCULAR NERVE SO YOU CAN SEE."

"IT ALSO TRANSMITS ITS FEED BACK TO A RECEIVING UNIT HERE."

"WE'LL SURGICALLY REMOVE ONE OF YOUR EYES..."

"SOUNDS FUN."

"...AND REPLACE IT WITH THE IMPLANT."

"THEN WE'LL SEE WHAT YOU SEE."

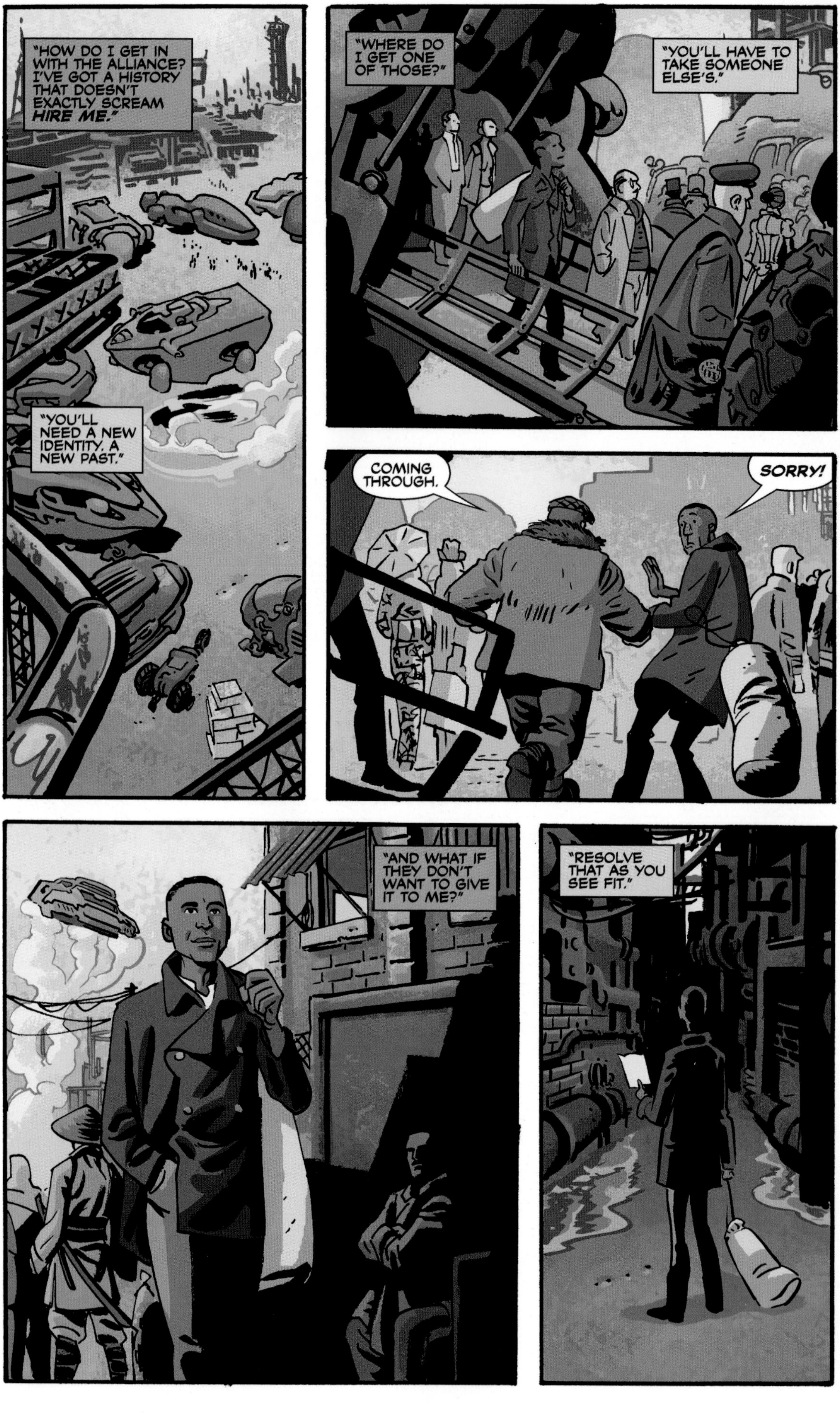
"HOW DO I GET IN WITH THE ALLIANCE? I'VE GOT A HISTORY THAT DOESN'T EXACTLY SCREAM *HIRE ME.*"
"YOU'LL NEED A NEW IDENTITY. A NEW PAST."
"WHERE DO I GET ONE OF THOSE?"
"YOU'LL HAVE TO TAKE SOMEONE ELSE'S."
COMING THROUGH.
SORRY!
"AND WHAT IF THEY DON'T WANT TO GIVE IT TO ME?"
"RESOLVE THAT AS YOU SEE FIT."

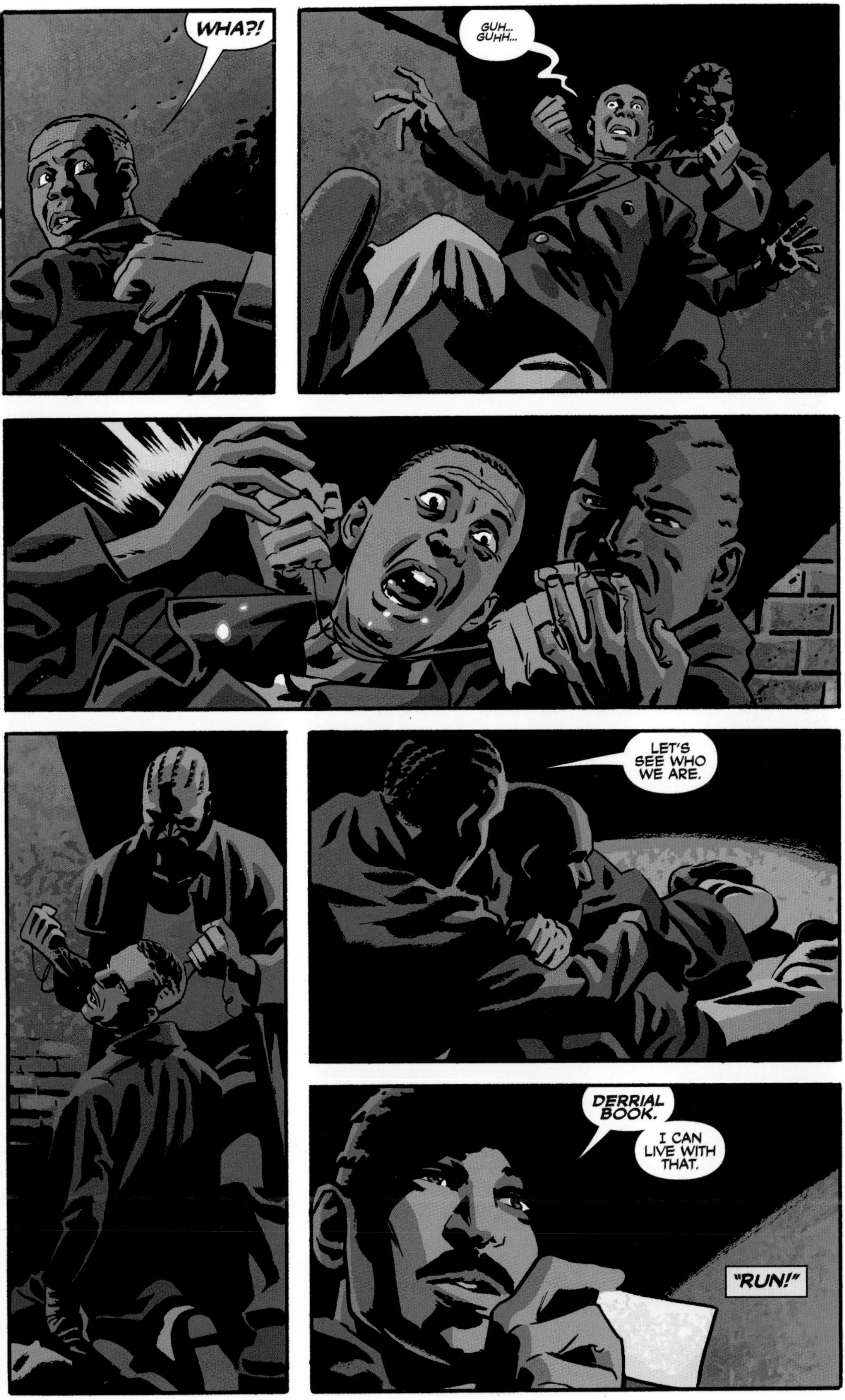
WHA?!
GUH... GUHH...
LET'S SEE WHO WE ARE.
DERRIAL BOOK.
I CAN LIVE WITH THAT.
"RUN!"

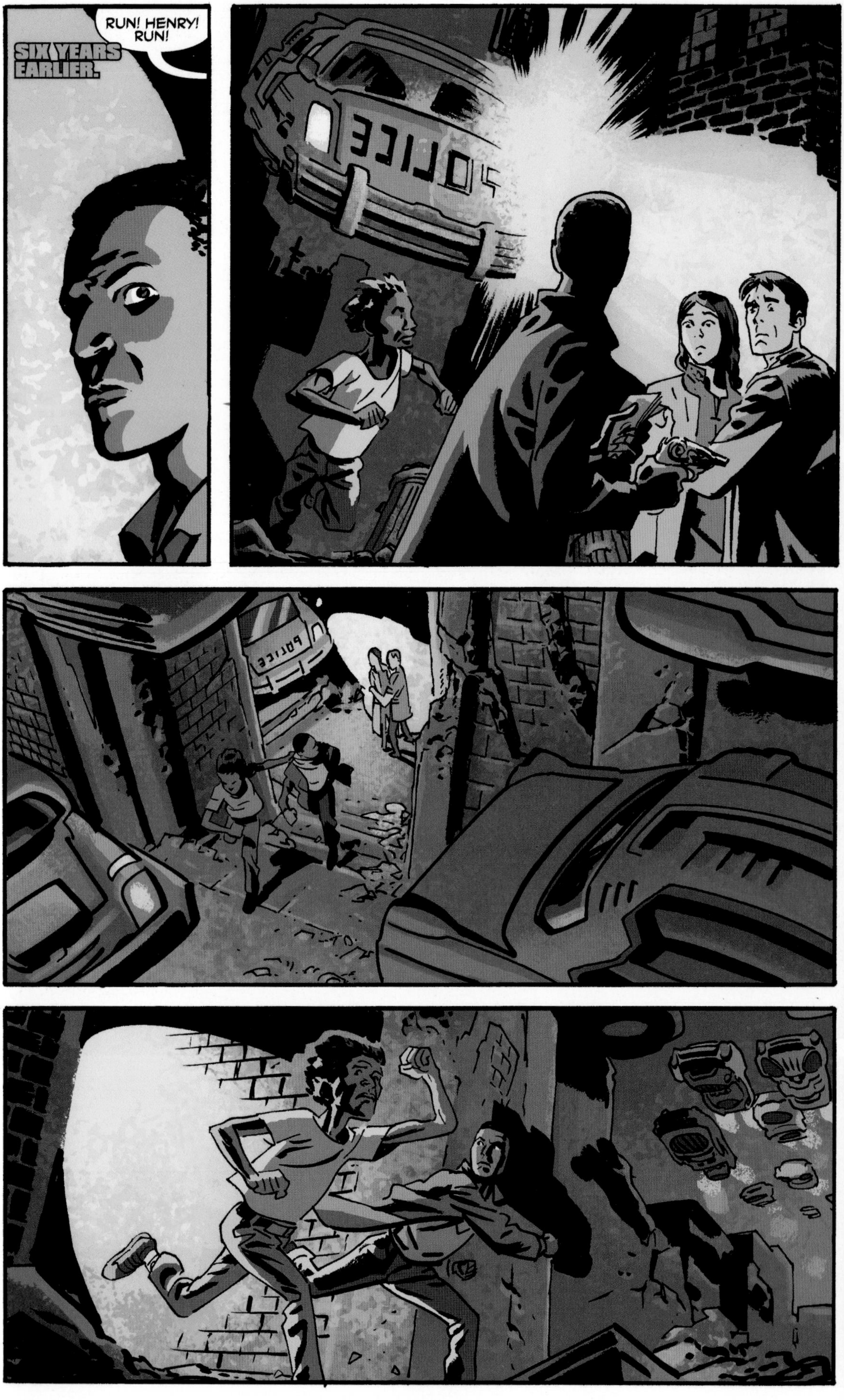
RUN! HENRY! RUN!
SIX YEARS EARLIER.

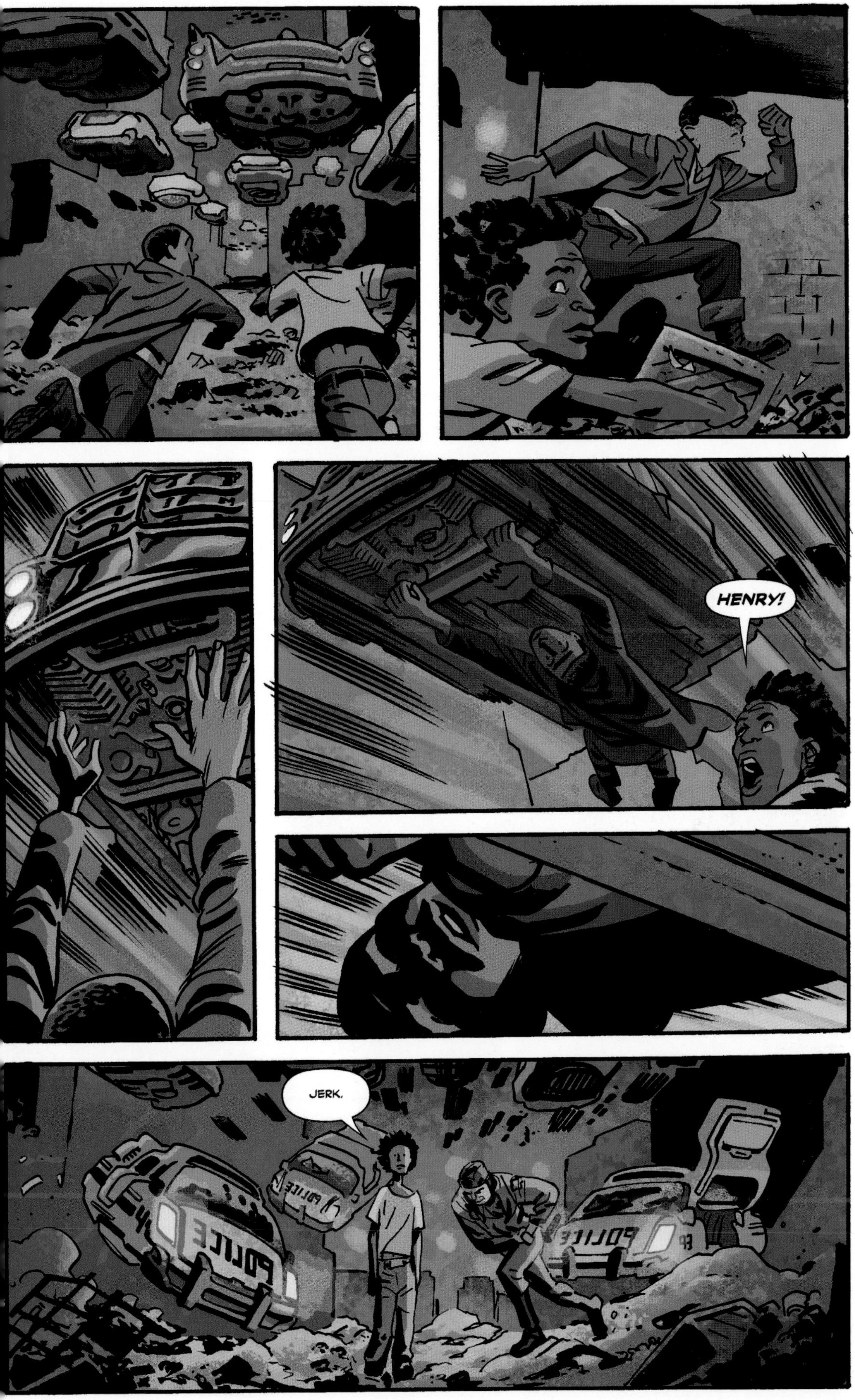
HENRY!
JERK.

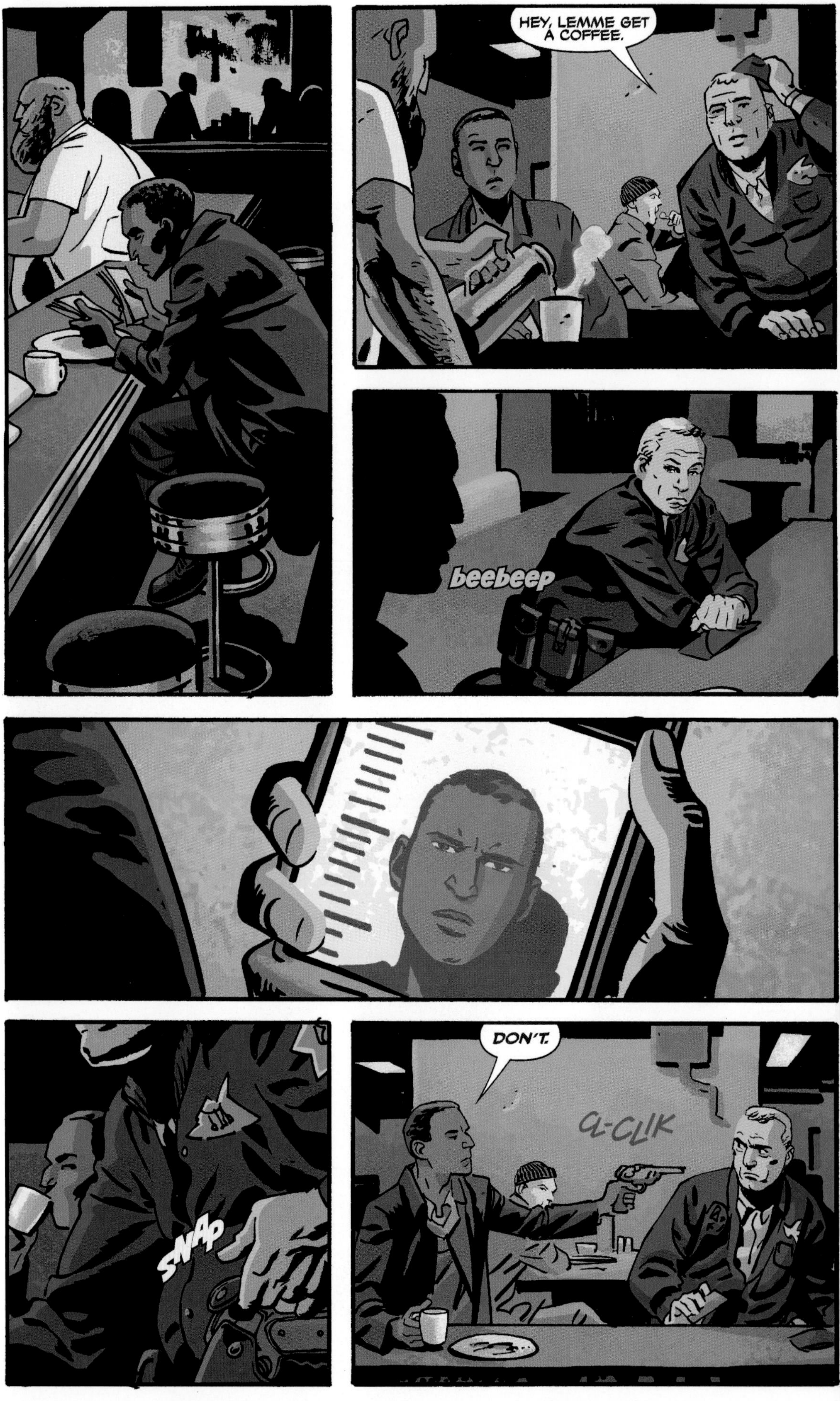
HEY, LEMME GET A COFFEE.
beebeep
SNAP
DON'T.
CL-CLIK

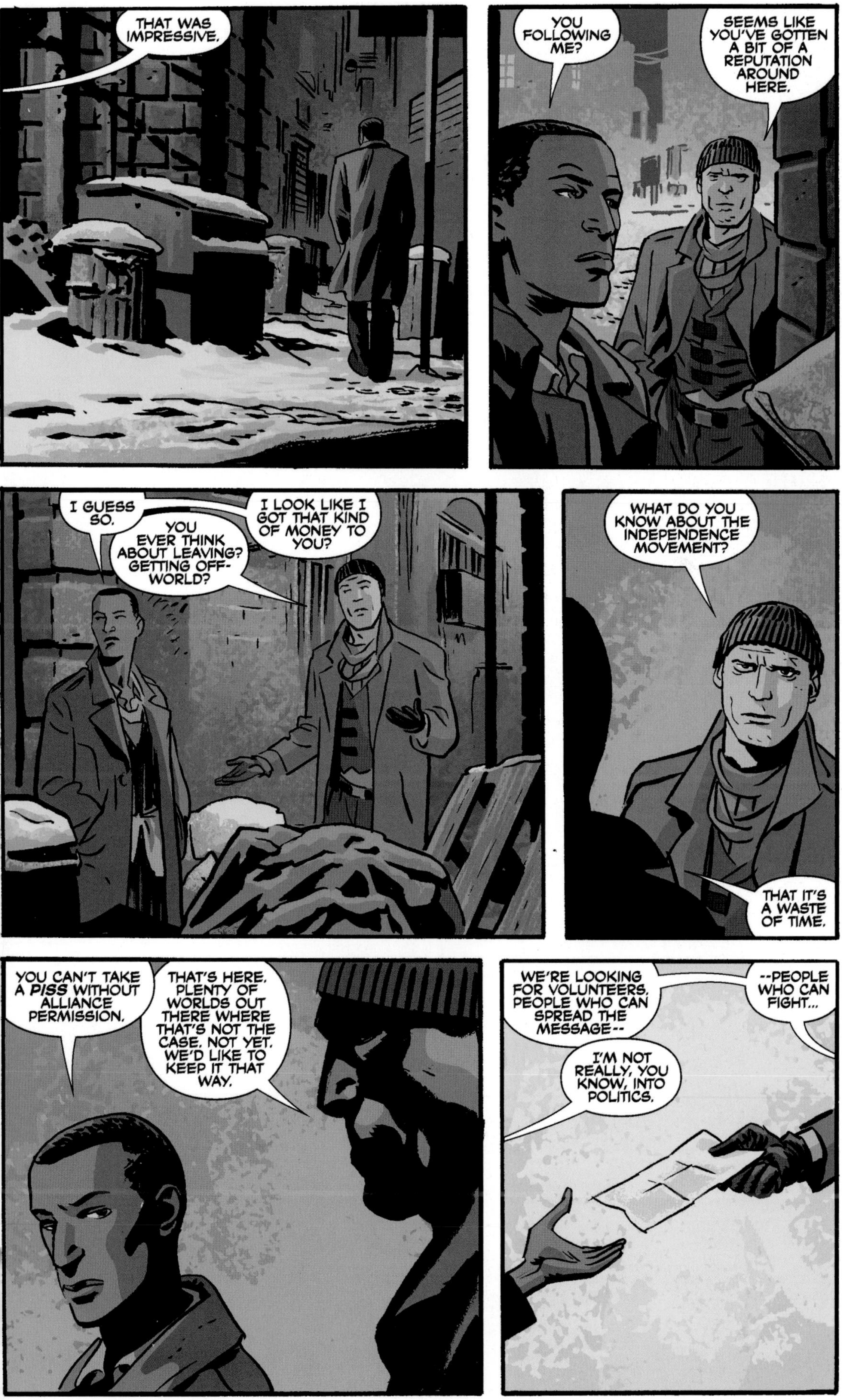
THAT WAS IMPRESSIVE.
YOU FOLLOWING ME?
SEEMS LIKE YOU'VE GOTTEN A BIT OF A REPUTATION AROUND HERE.
I GUESS SO.
YOU EVER THINK ABOUT LEAVING? GETTING OFF-WORLD?
I LOOK LIKE I GOT THAT KIND OF MONEY TO YOU?
WHAT DO YOU KNOW ABOUT THE INDEPENDENCE MOVEMENT?
THAT IT'S A WASTE OF TIME.
YOU CAN'T TAKE A *PISS* WITHOUT ALLIANCE PERMISSION.
THAT'S HERE. PLENTY OF WORLDS OUT THERE WHERE THAT'S NOT THE CASE. NOT YET. WE'D LIKE TO KEEP IT THAT WAY.
WE'RE LOOKING FOR VOLUNTEERS. PEOPLE WHO CAN SPREAD THE MESSAGE--
--PEOPLE WHO CAN FIGHT...
I'M NOT REALLY, YOU KNOW, INTO POLITICS.

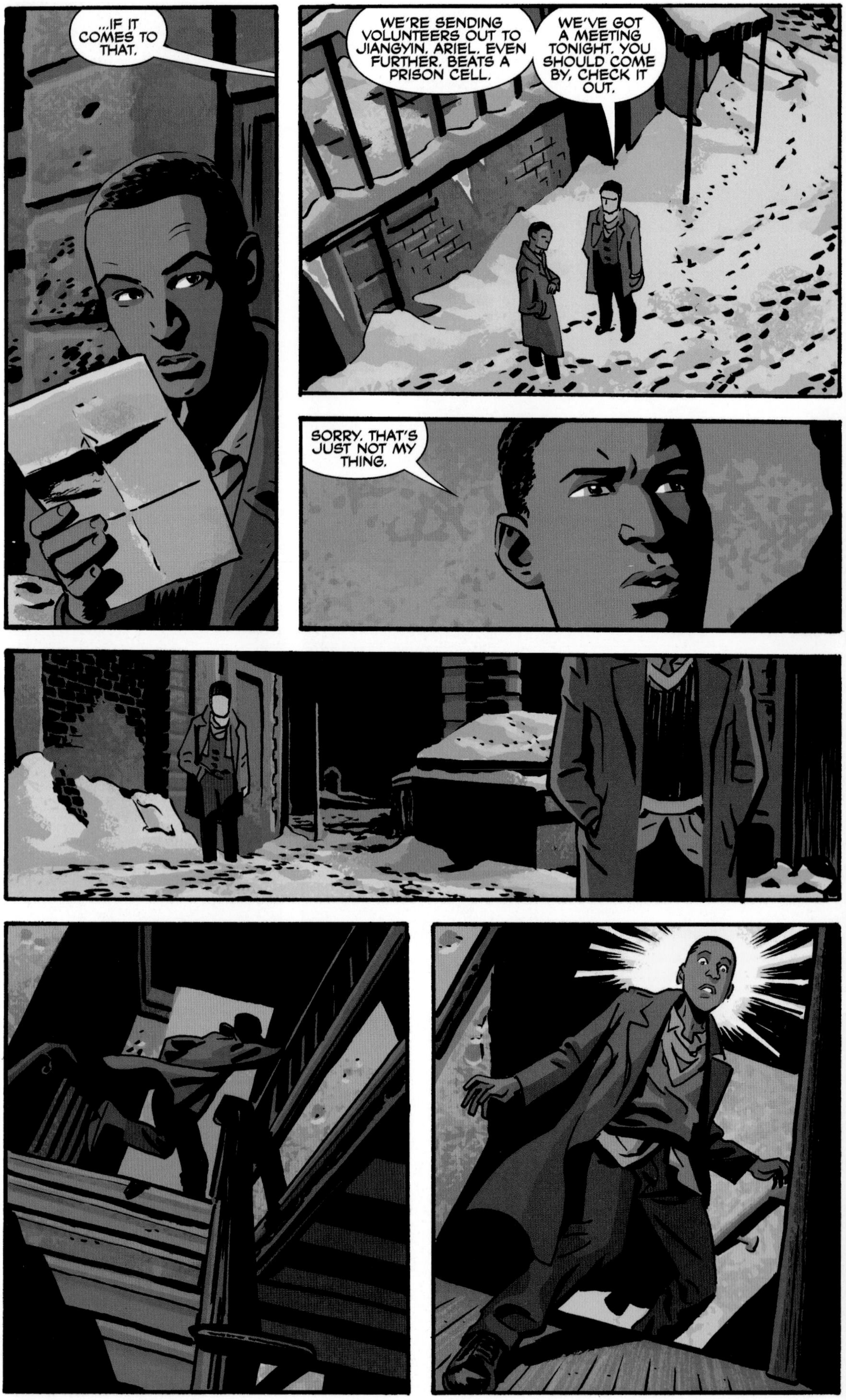
...IF IT COMES TO THAT.
WE'RE SENDING VOLUNTEERS OUT TO JIANGYIN, ARIEL. EVEN FURTHER. BEATS A PRISON CELL.
WE'VE GOT A MEETING TONIGHT. YOU SHOULD COME BY, CHECK IT OUT.
SORRY. THAT'S JUST NOT MY THING.

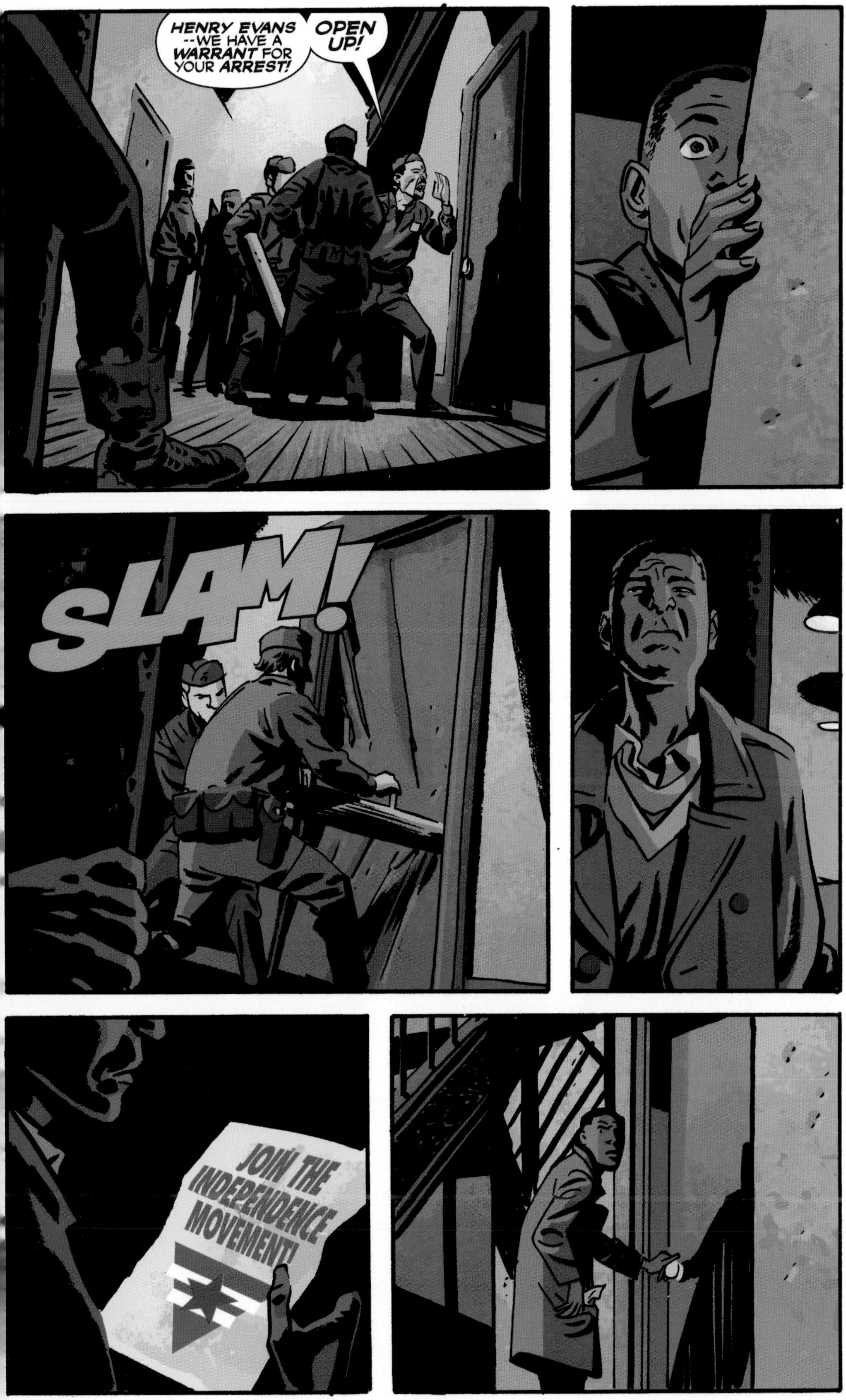
HENRY EVANS --WE HAVE A WARRANT FOR YOUR ARREST!
OPEN UP!
SLAM!
JOIN THE INDEPENDENCE MOVEMENT!

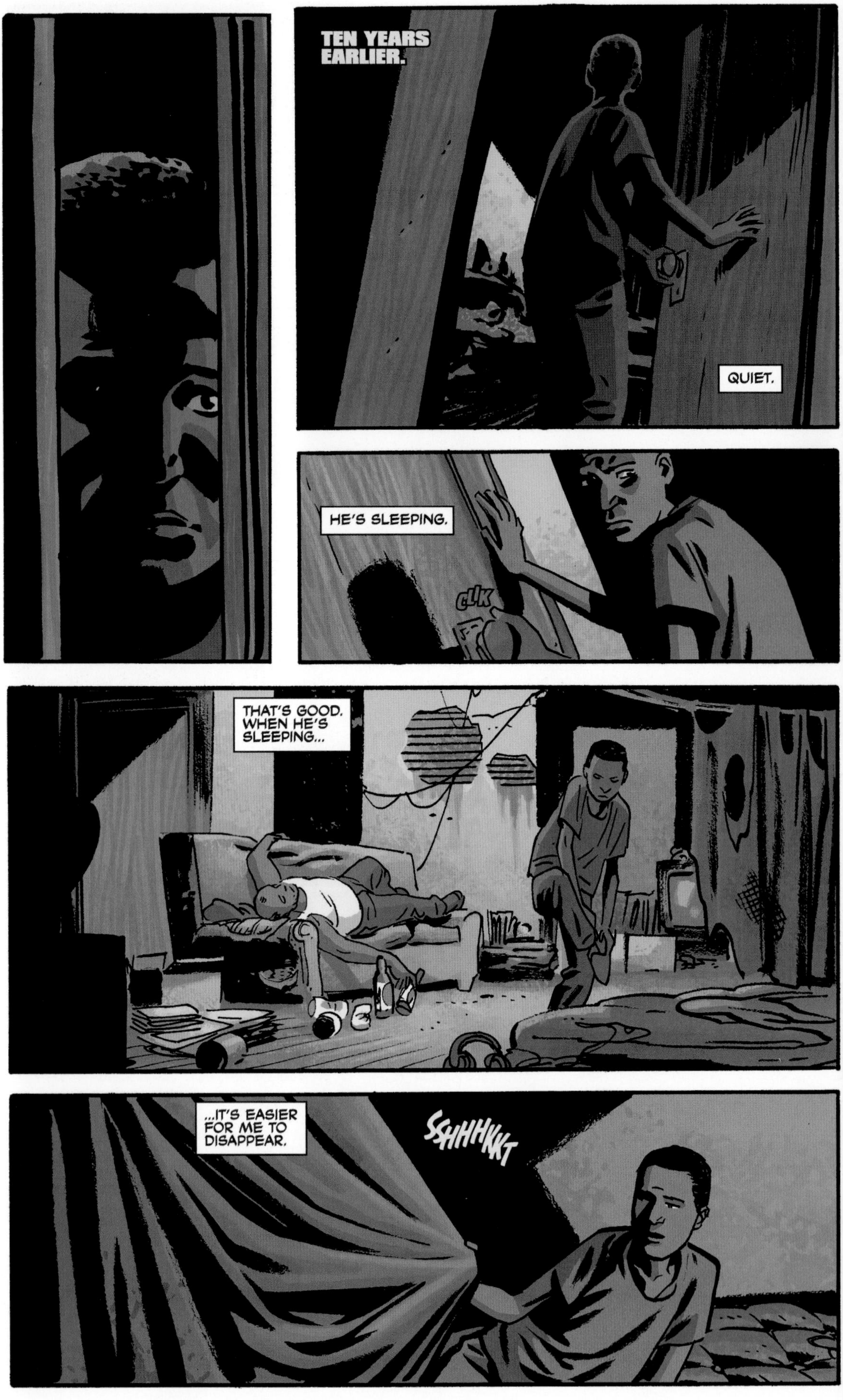
TEN YEARS EARLIER.
QUIET.
HE'S SLEEPING.
CLIK
THAT'S GOOD. WHEN HE'S SLEEPING...
...IT'S EASIER FOR ME TO DISAPPEAR.
SSHHHKKT

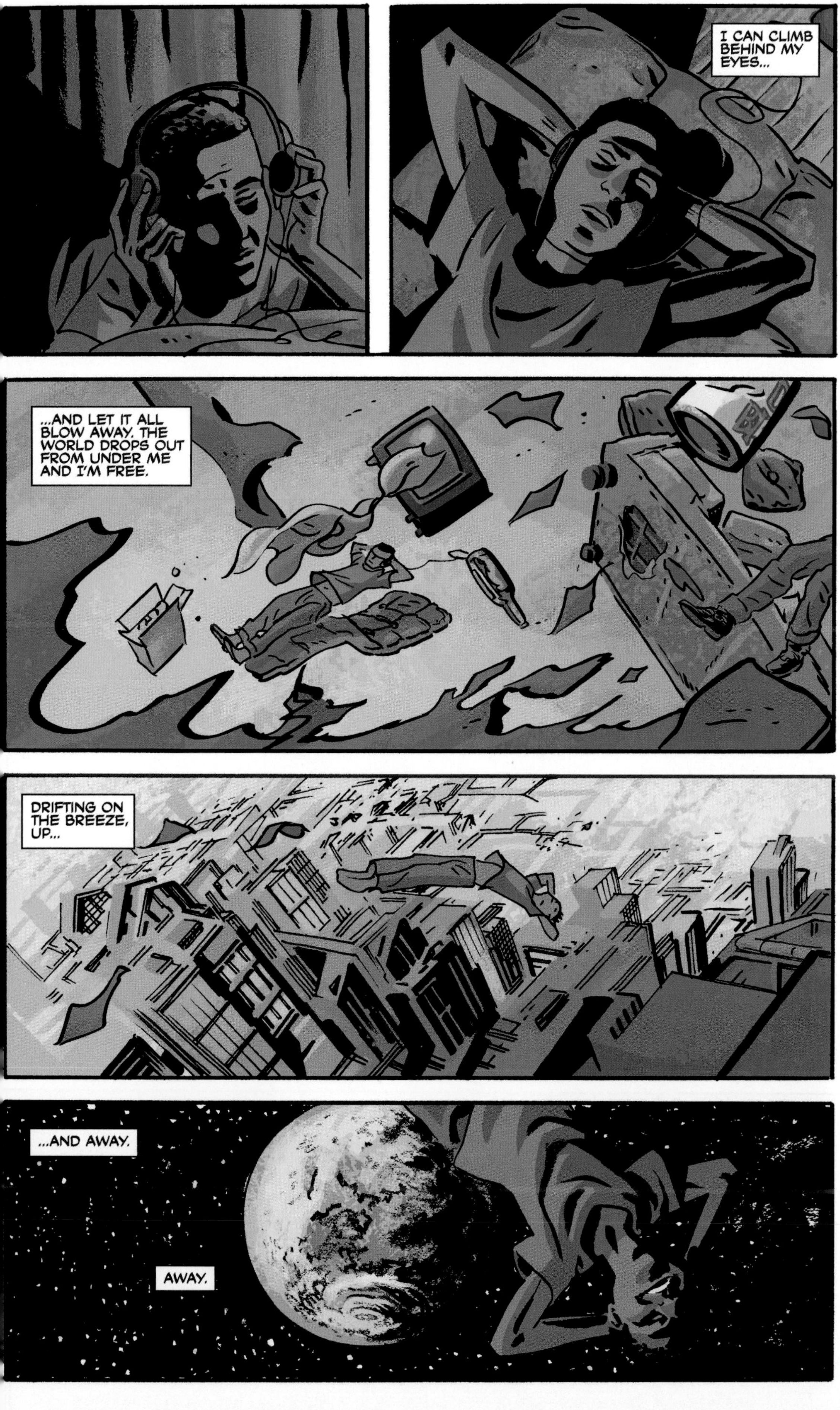
I CAN CLIMB BEHIND MY EYES...
...AND LET IT ALL BLOW AWAY. THE WORLD DROPS OUT FROM UNDER ME AND I'M FREE.
DRIFTING ON THE BREEZE, UP...
...AND AWAY.
AWAY.

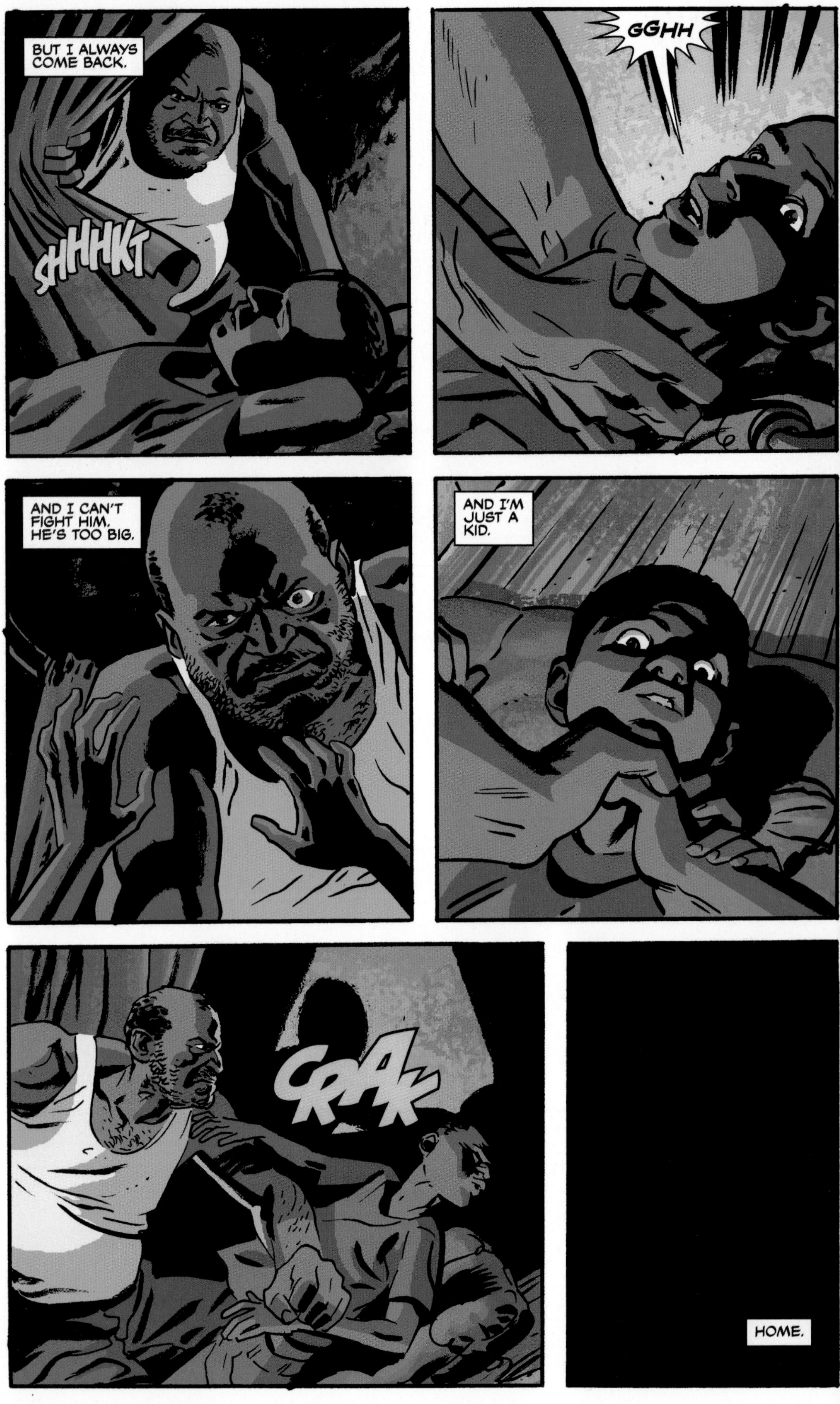
BUT I ALWAYS COME BACK.
SHHHKT
GGHH
AND I CAN'T FIGHT HIM. HE'S TOO BIG.
AND I'M JUST A KID.
CRAK
HOME.

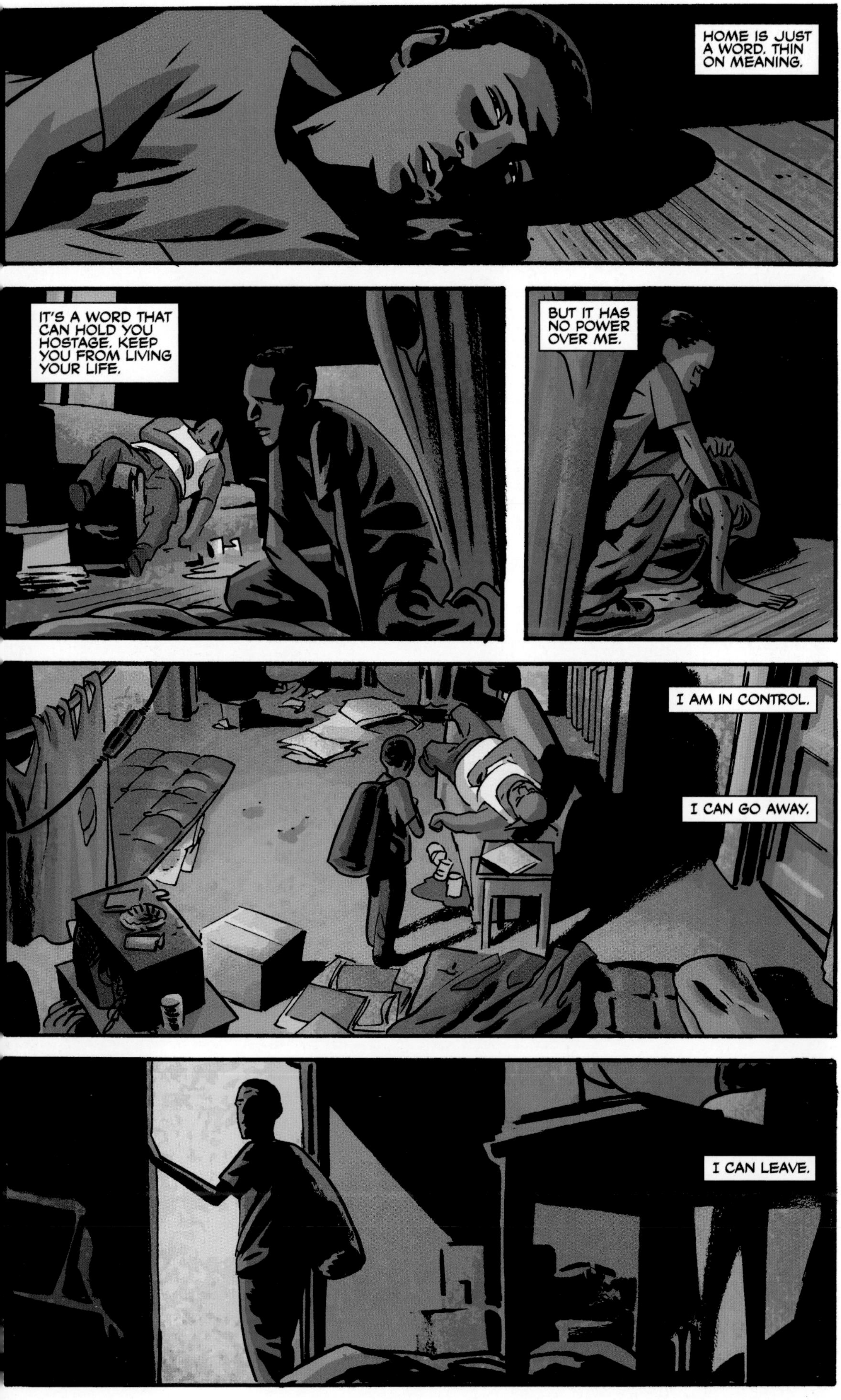
HOME IS JUST A WORD. THIN ON MEANING.
IT'S A WORD THAT CAN HOLD YOU HOSTAGE. KEEP YOU FROM LIVING YOUR LIFE.
BUT IT HAS NO POWER OVER ME.
I AM IN CONTROL.
I CAN GO AWAY.
I CAN LEAVE.

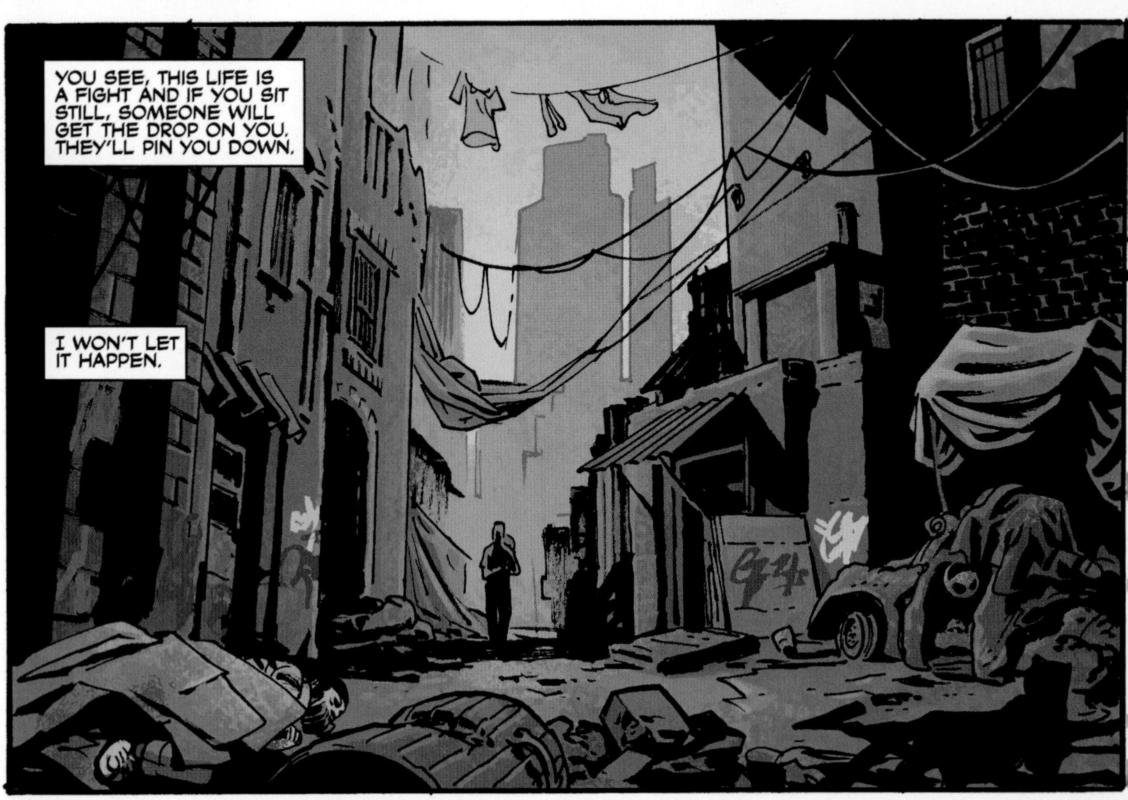
YOU SEE, THIS LIFE IS A FIGHT AND IF YOU SIT STILL, SOMEONE WILL GET THE DROP ON YOU. THEY'LL PIN YOU DOWN.
I WON'T LET IT HAPPEN.

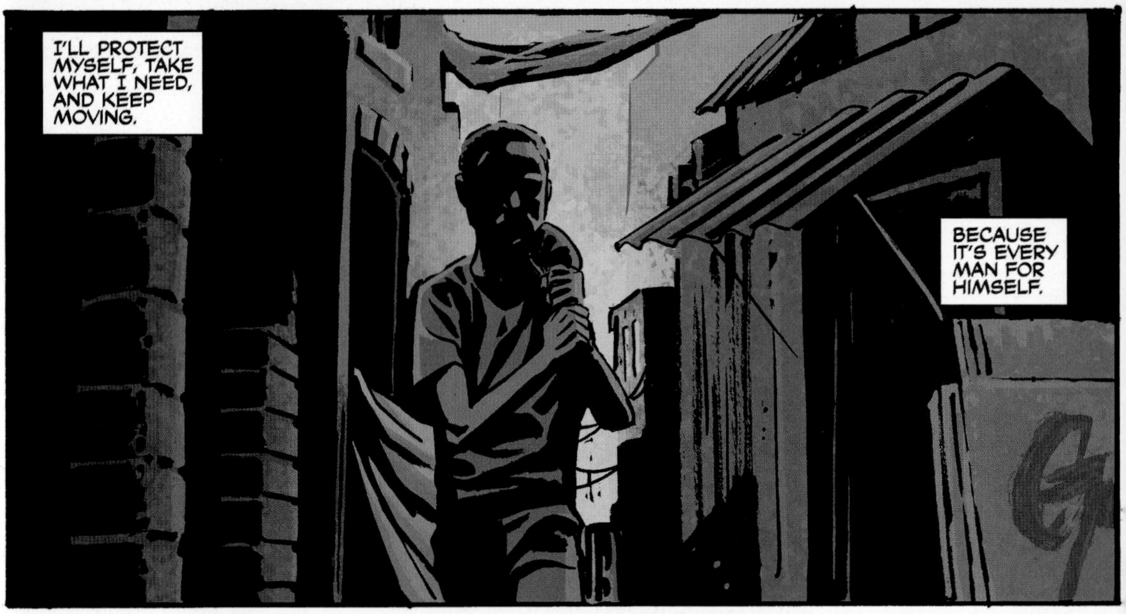
I'LL PROTECT MYSELF, TAKE WHAT I NEED, AND KEEP MOVING.
BECAUSE IT'S EVERY MAN FOR HIMSELF.

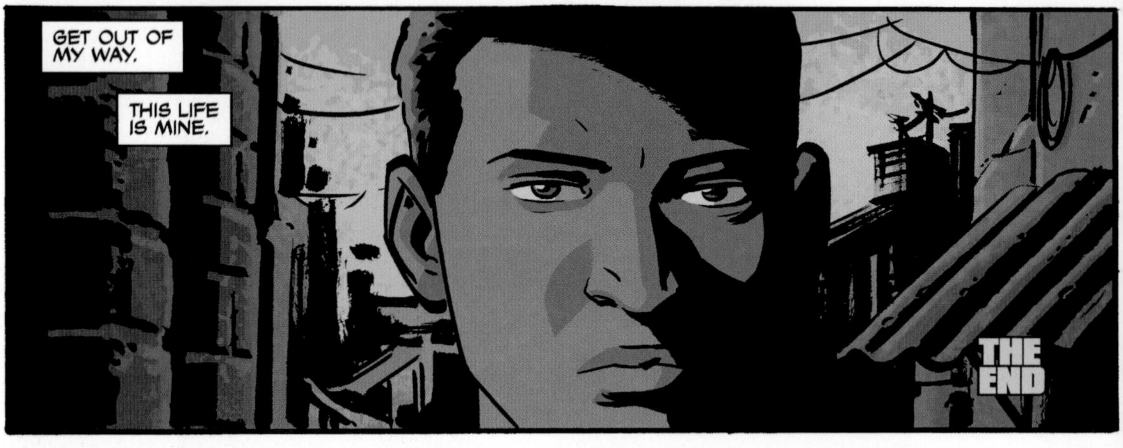
GET OUT OF MY WAY.
THIS LIFE IS MINE.
THE END

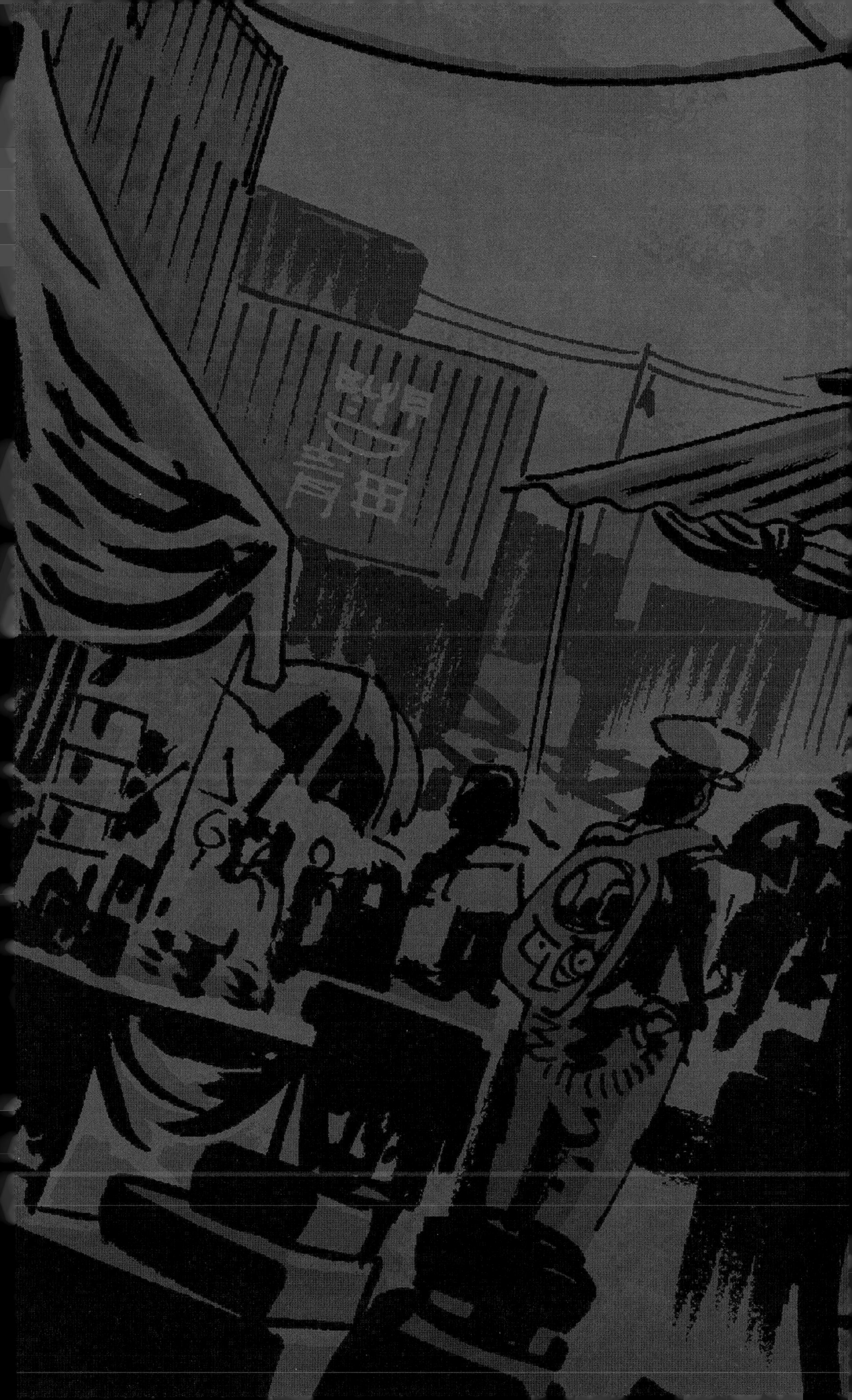

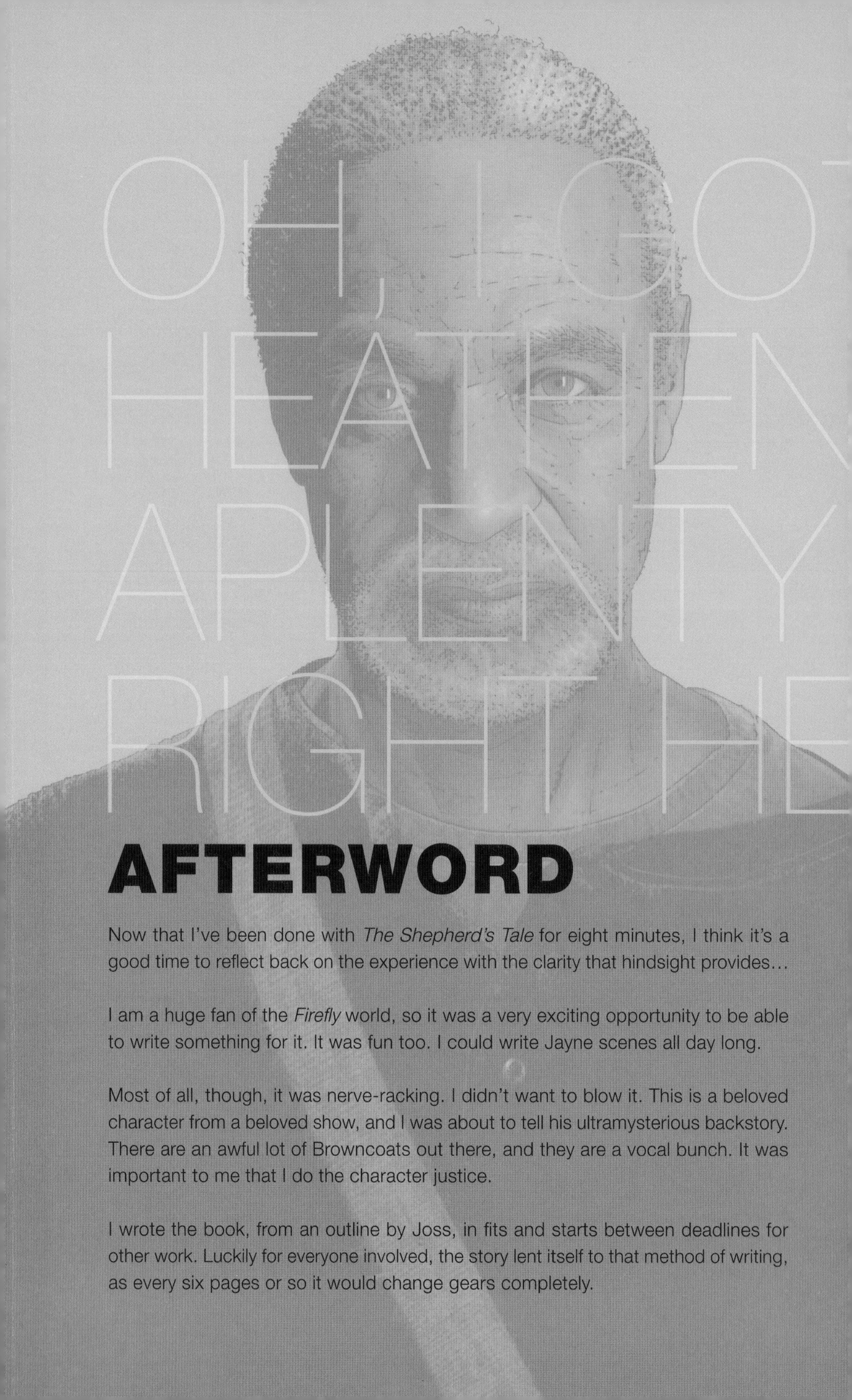
OH, I GOT
HEATHEN
APLENTY
RIGHT HE

AFTERWORD

Now that I've been done with *The Shepherd's Tale* for eight minutes, I think it's a good time to reflect back on the experience with the clarity that hindsight provides…

I am a huge fan of the *Firefly* world, so it was a very exciting opportunity to be able to write something for it. It was fun too. I could write Jayne scenes all day long.

Most of all, though, it was nerve-racking. I didn't want to blow it. This is a beloved character from a beloved show, and I was about to tell his ultramysterious backstory. There are an awful lot of Browncoats out there, and they are a vocal bunch. It was important to me that I do the character justice.

I wrote the book, from an outline by Joss, in fits and starts between deadlines for other work. Luckily for everyone involved, the story lent itself to that method of writing, as every six pages or so it would change gears completely.

As I got deeper into Book's past I found inspiration in odd places. ESPN's documentary *No Crossover: The Trial of Allen Iverson* was a particularly unlikely source. When you watch that movie, you can see Iverson changed by the trial. He begins as a gifted, trusting, wide-eyed kid, and by the end of the process you can see he no longer has much faith in anyone but himself. He's on his own. There is something very lonely about the state that he ends up in, and I thought that was exactly where Book lived much of his life, believing that in this world it's every man for himself.

If you are curious to know where I got the idea for Book's abusive home life, you should listen to *Hast Thou Considered the Tetrapod?* by The Mountain Goats. It's sort of a direct steal. Sorry, Mountain Goats.

The last thing I wrote was also the most difficult. It was Book's narration over his death and over his departure at the conclusion of the comic. Even though I'd spent a long time (I would tell you how long, but it's embarrassing) writing this story and thinking about this character, I was having a lot of trouble applying this finishing touch. I was tinkering with his death narration when I landed on a few lines that reminded me of one of Book's early encounters with Kaylee, when she asks him why he doesn't care what their destination is, and he replies, "Because the journey is the worthier part."

It struck me that Book is defined through and by movement. It's one of the reasons he fits in so well with the merry band of nomads aboard Serenity. It is a philosophy and a strategy. Keep moving.

As a young man Book mistakes movement for progress and runs away from things. He runs from abuse, imprisonment, and himself. He bounces around the 'Verse like a pinball. There isn't a tremendous amount of intent behind it beyond self-preservation. Hovering over a bowl of soup, there is a shift inside him, and his journey changes from one defined by what he is running from to one defined by what he is chasing: from self-preservation to self-discovery.

In remembering that moment from *Firefly*, I was able to uncover what the narration that ends the Book book should be. It's the journey that matters.

I have enjoyed my brief time in the 'Verse and hope that I've honored the amazing character Ron Glass created in the show. Chris Samnee obviously did an incredible job on his end. I was continually blown away by his work, as I'm sure you were.

Thank you for reading. It's been fun.

Zack Whedon

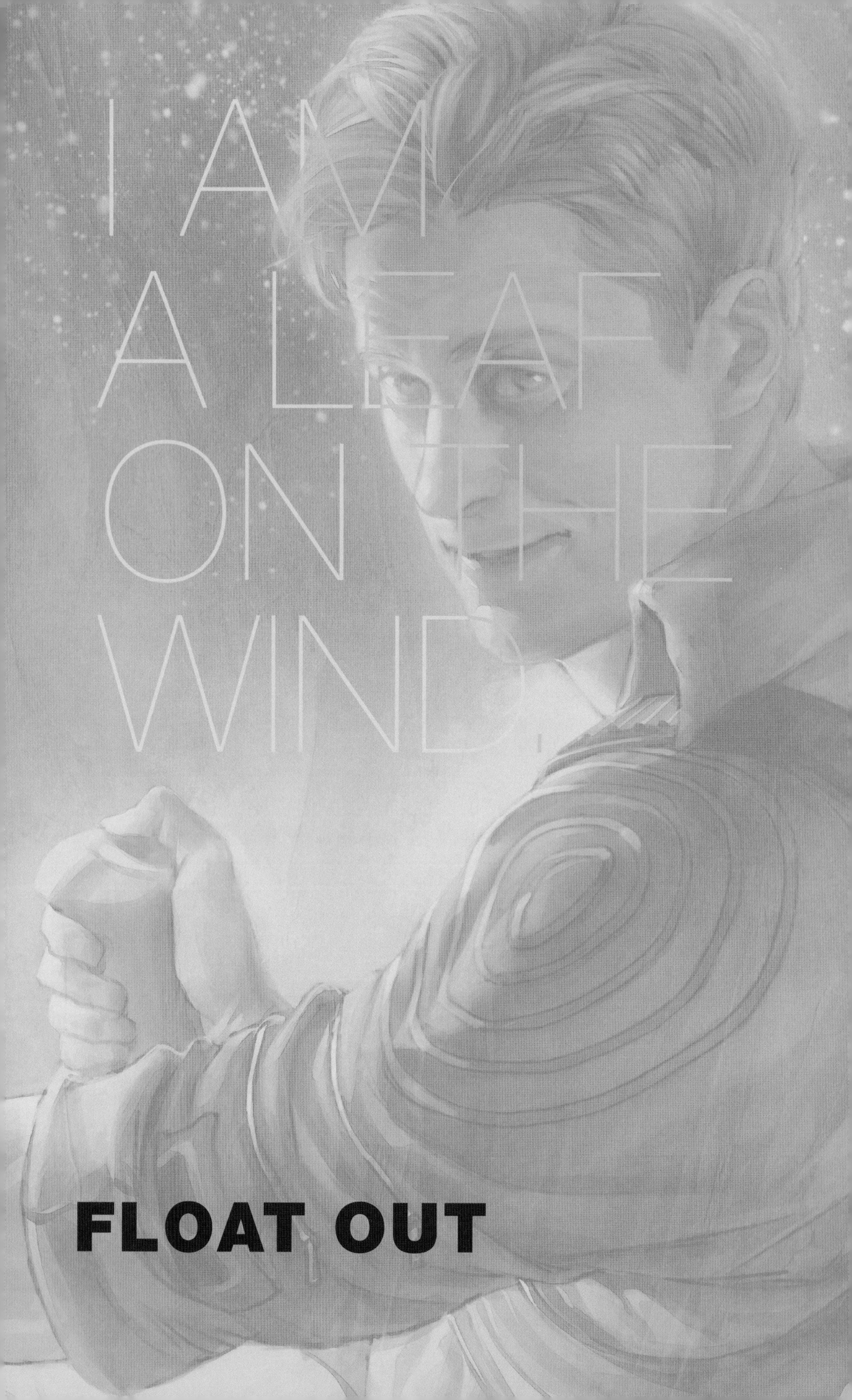
I AM
A LEAF
ON THE
WIND.
FLOAT OUT

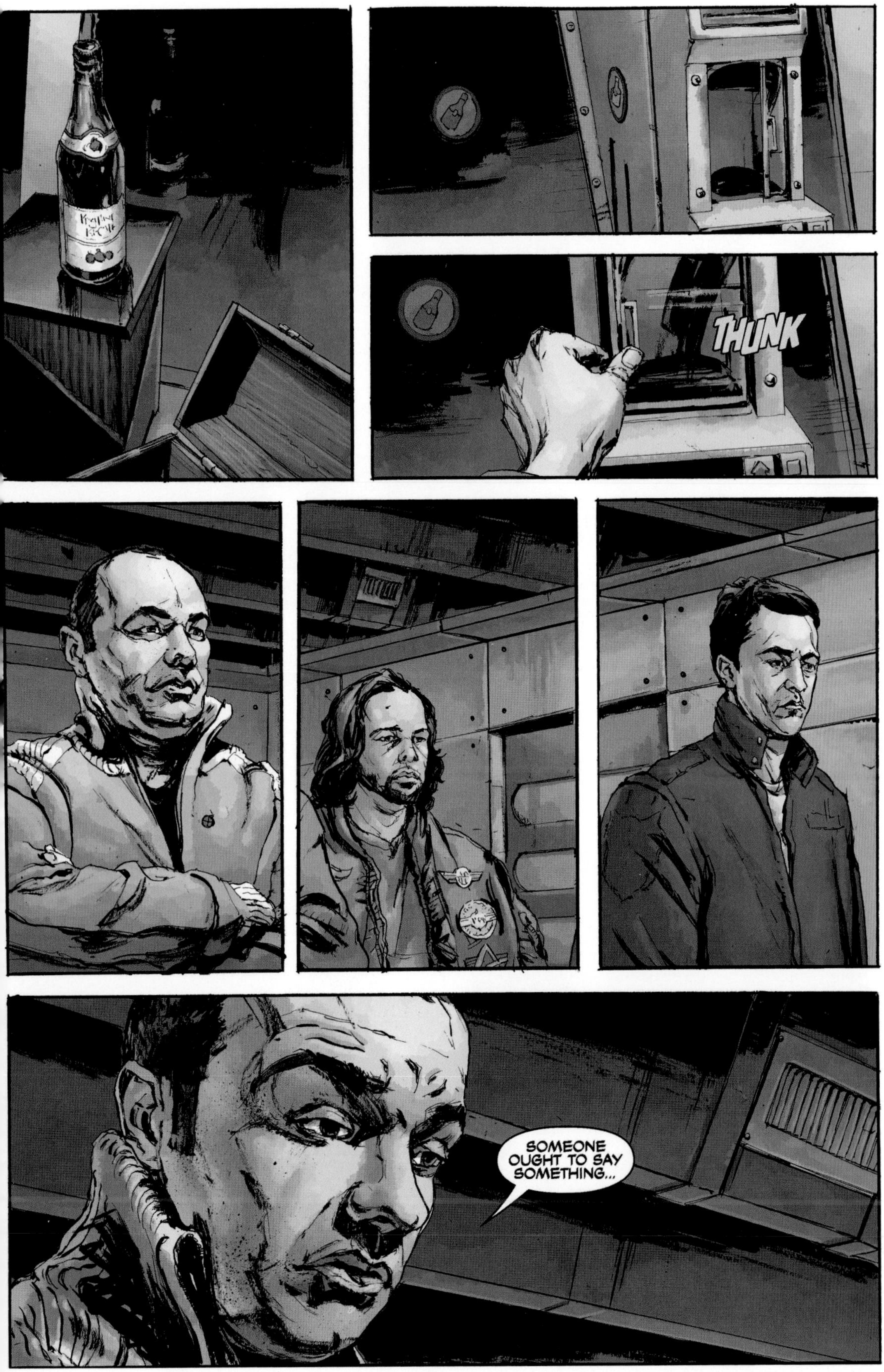
THUNK
SOMEONE OUGHT TO SAY SOMETHING...

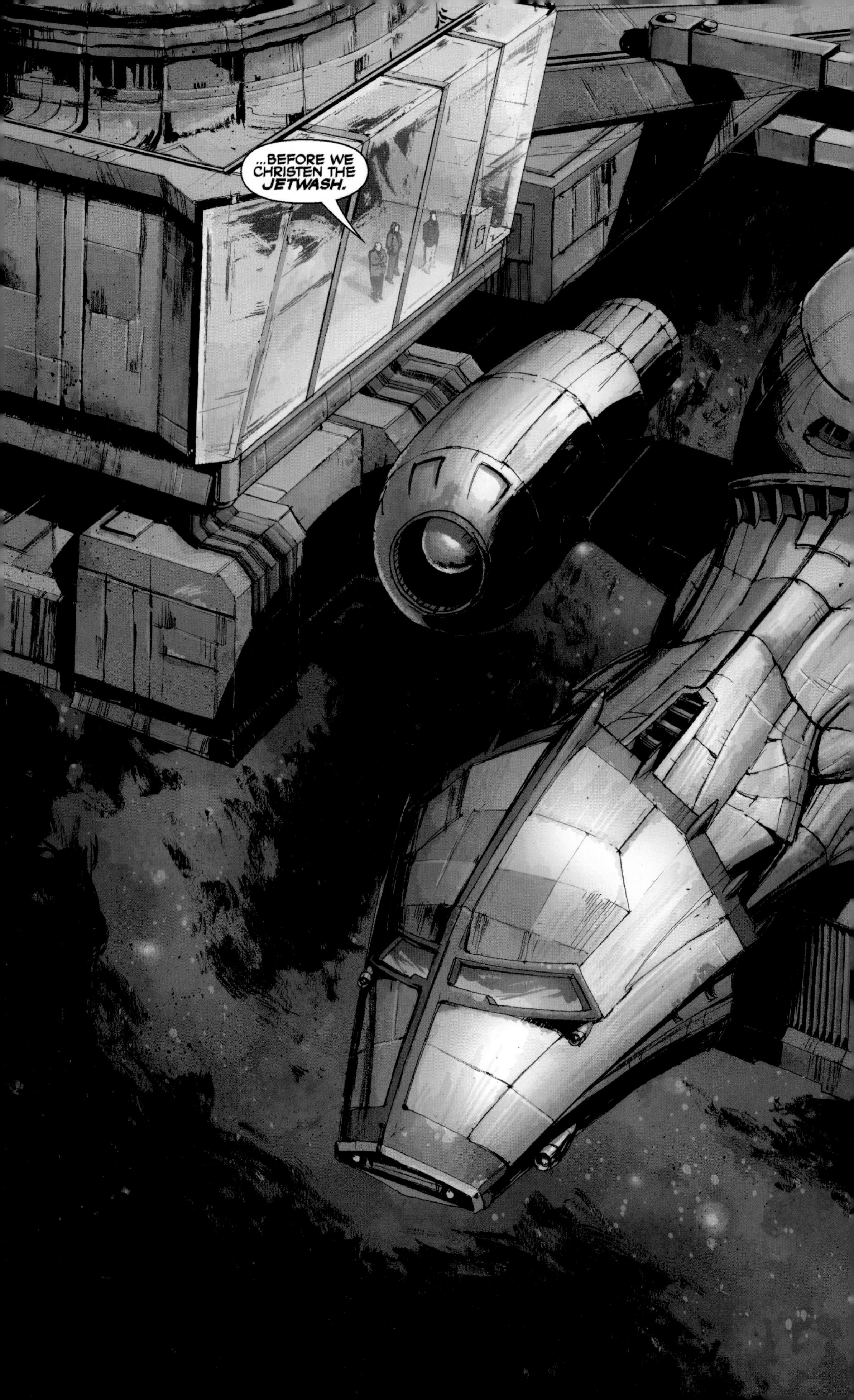
...BEFORE WE CHRISTEN THE JETWASH.

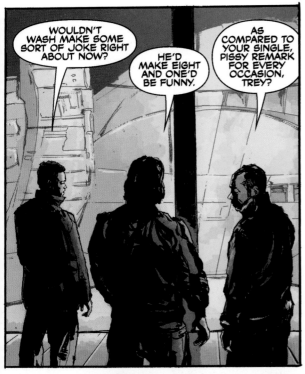

WOULDN'T WASH MAKE SOME SORT OF JOKE RIGHT ABOUT NOW?

HE'D MAKE EIGHT AND ONE'D BE FUNNY.

AS COMPARED TO YOUR SINGLE, PISSY REMARK FOR EVERY OCCASION, TREY?

BOTH OF YOU? I'M NOT SPLITTIN' DUTIES AS CAPTAIN AND PILOT OF THIS SHIP WITH YOU TWO WEASEL-BAGGING EVERY FIVE MINUTES.

DID *I* SAY I HAD AN ISSUE WITH LELAND?

WAIT, I THOUGHT WE WERE GETTING A PILOT. YOU'RE PUTTING *OUR* SHIP IN THE HANDS OF THE "ALMOST GHOST"?

THIRD OF IT'S MINE.

AND UNLESS WE SCARE UP A CHARTER, WE'VE GOT NO RATIONS, NO SICKBAY--

I KNEW WE SHOULD'VE GONE WITH AN OH-THREE-CLASS FIREFLY.

RELICS.

AFFORDABLE RELICS.

--AND ONE WEEK DOCKING ON THIS SLIP.

UNLESS YOU'VE GOT ANOTHER PALLET OF ALLIANCE GAUSS GUNS YOU CAN FENCE.

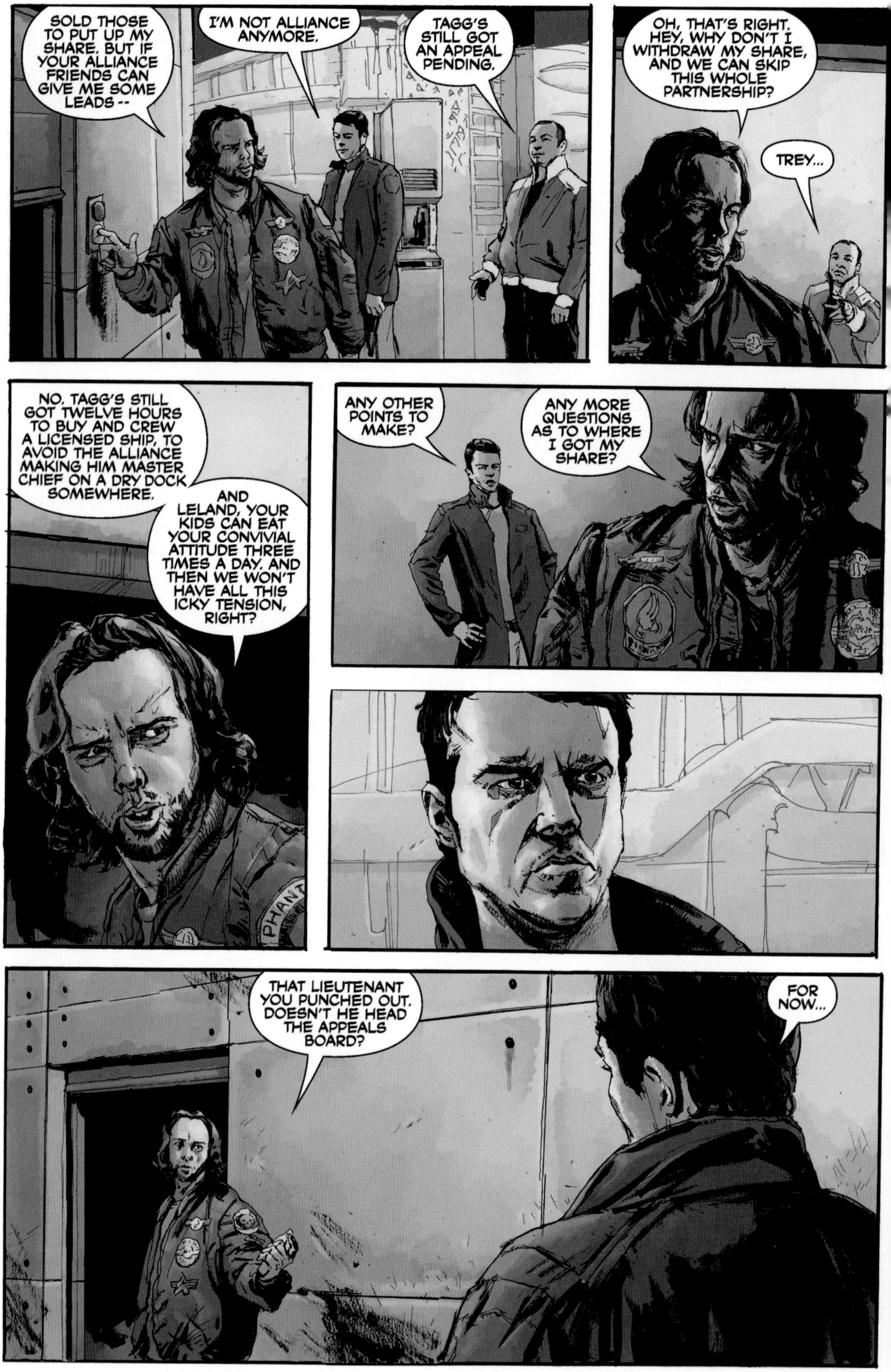
SOLD THOSE TO PUT UP MY SHARE. BUT IF YOUR ALLIANCE FRIENDS CAN GIVE ME SOME LEADS --
I'M NOT ALLIANCE ANYMORE.
TAGG'S STILL GOT AN APPEAL PENDING.
OH, THAT'S RIGHT. HEY, WHY DON'T I WITHDRAW MY SHARE, AND WE CAN SKIP THIS WHOLE PARTNERSHIP?
TREY...
NO. TAGG'S STILL GOT TWELVE HOURS TO BUY AND CREW A LICENSED SHIP, TO AVOID THE ALLIANCE MAKING HIM MASTER CHIEF ON A DRY DOCK SOMEWHERE.
AND LELAND, YOUR KIDS CAN EAT YOUR CONVIVIAL ATTITUDE THREE TIMES A DAY. AND THEN WE WON'T HAVE ALL THIS ICKY TENSION, RIGHT?
ANY OTHER POINTS TO MAKE?
ANY MORE QUESTIONS AS TO WHERE I GOT MY SHARE?
THAT LIEUTENANT YOU PUNCHED OUT. DOESN'T HE HEAD THE APPEALS BOARD?
FOR NOW...

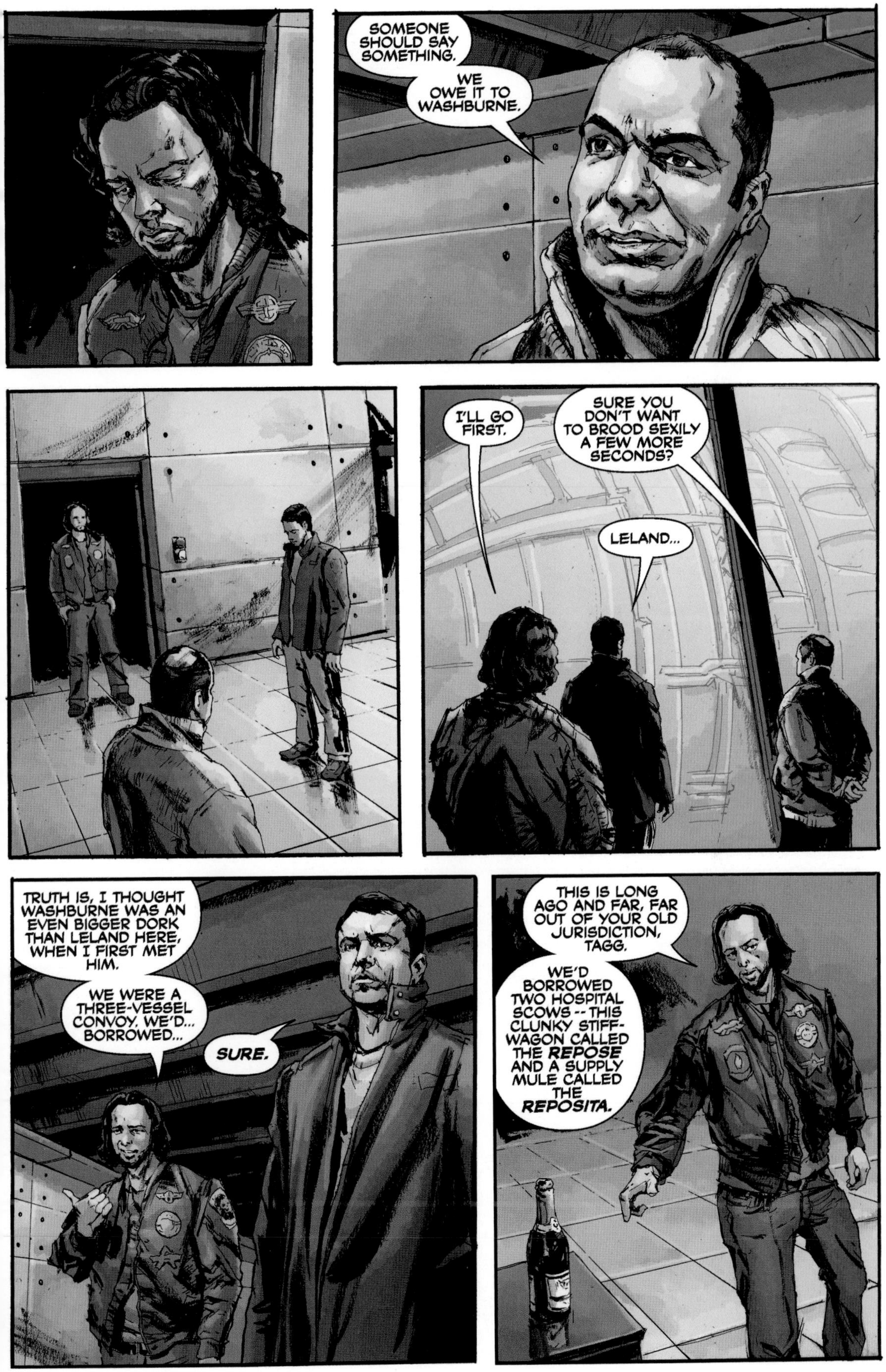
SOMEONE SHOULD SAY SOMETHING.
WE OWE IT TO WASHBURNE.
I'LL GO FIRST.
SURE YOU DON'T WANT TO BROOD SEXILY A FEW MORE SECONDS?
LELAND...
TRUTH IS, I THOUGHT WASHBURNE WAS AN EVEN BIGGER DORK THAN LELAND HERE, WHEN I FIRST MET HIM.
WE WERE A THREE-VESSEL CONVOY. WE'D... BORROWED...
SURE.
THIS IS LONG AGO AND FAR, FAR OUT OF YOUR OLD JURISDICTION, TAGG.
WE'D BORROWED TWO HOSPITAL SCOWS -- THIS CLUNKY STIFF-WAGON CALLED THE REPOSE AND A SUPPLY MULE CALLED THE REPOSITA.

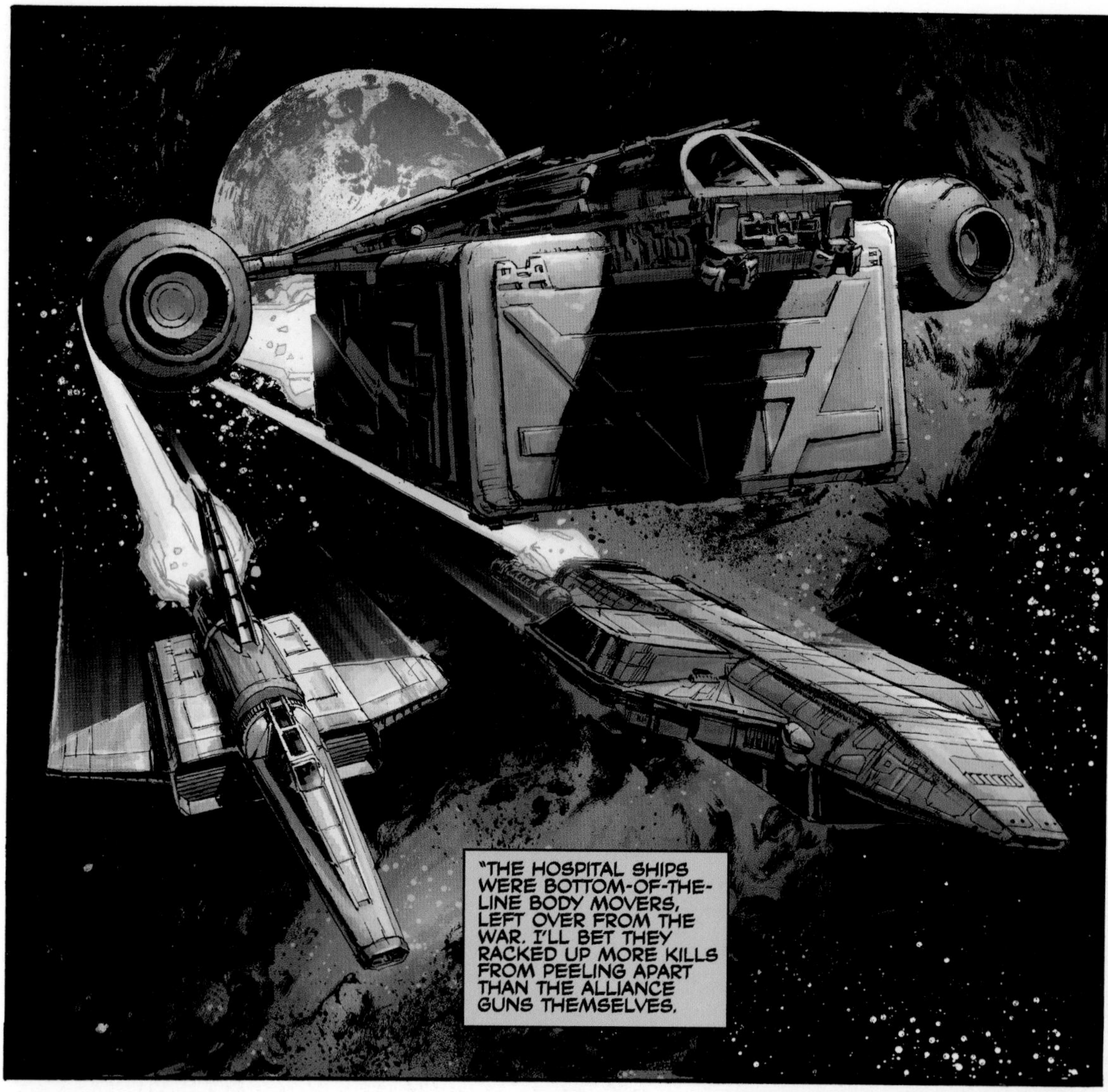
"THE HOSPITAL SHIPS WERE BOTTOM-OF-THE-LINE BODY MOVERS, LEFT OVER FROM THE WAR. I'LL BET THEY RACKED UP MORE KILLS FROM PEELING APART THAN THE ALLIANCE GUNS THEMSELVES.

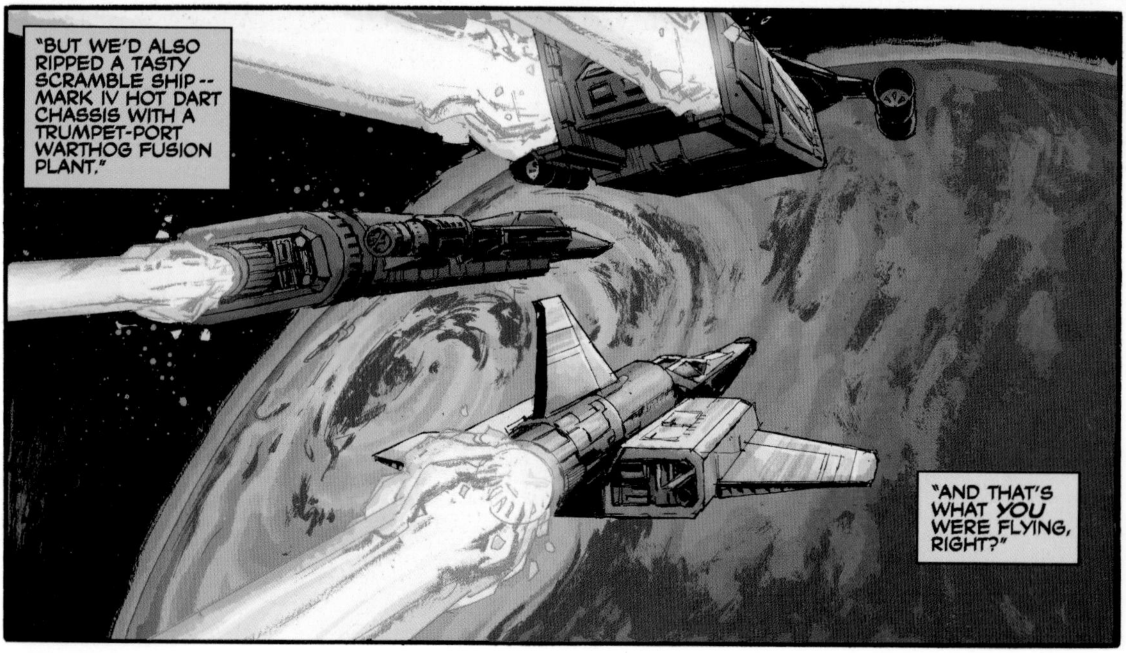
"BUT WE'D ALSO RIPPED A TASTY SCRAMBLE SHIP -- MARK IV HOT DART CHASSIS WITH A TRUMPET-PORT WARTHOG FUSION PLANT."
"AND THAT'S WHAT *YOU* WERE FLYING, RIGHT?"

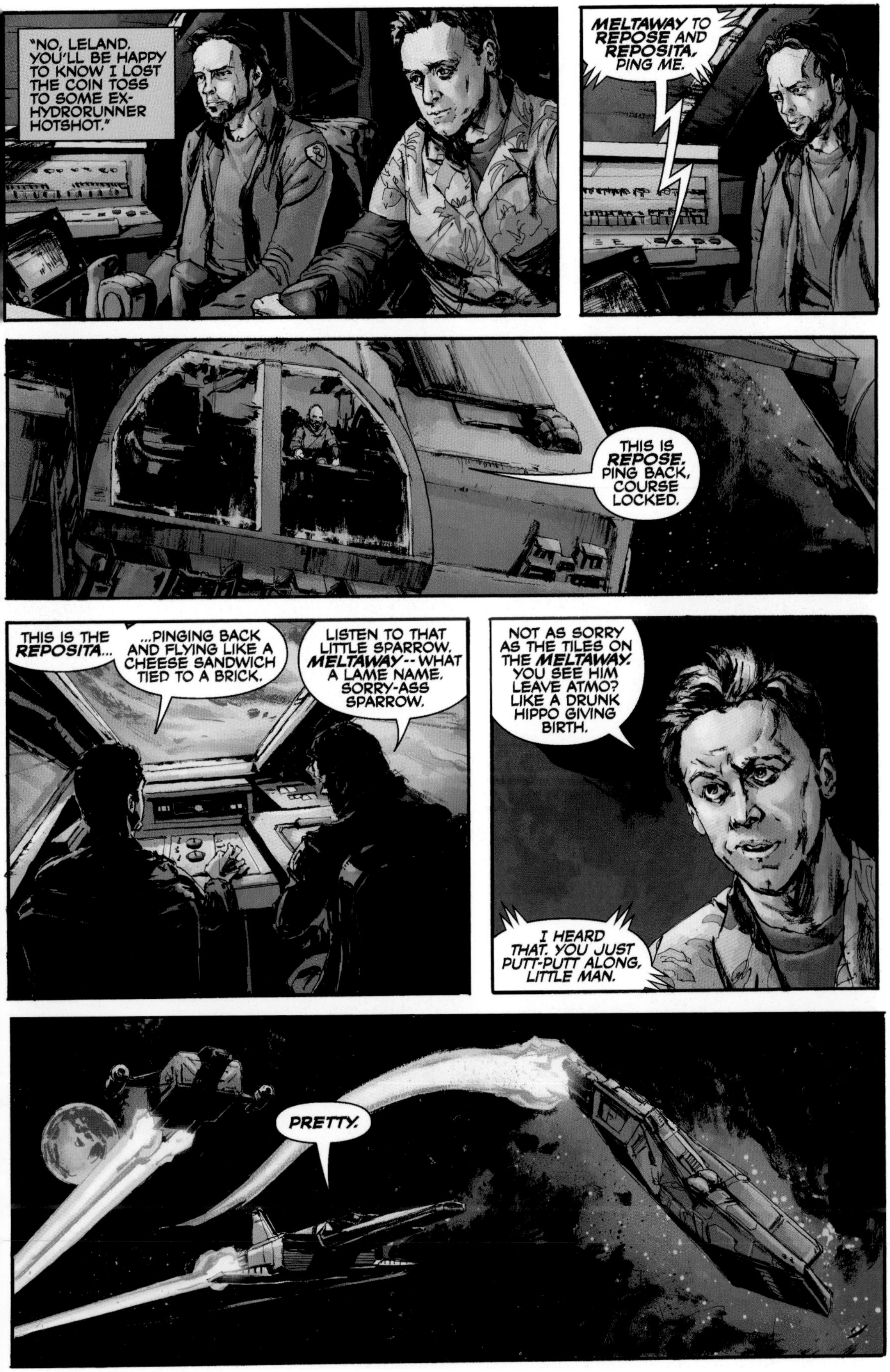
"NO, LELAND, YOU'LL BE HAPPY TO KNOW I LOST THE COIN TOSS TO SOME EX-HYDRORUNNER HOTSHOT."
MELTAWAY TO REPOSE AND REPOSITA, PING ME.
THIS IS REPOSE. PING BACK, COURSE LOCKED.
THIS IS THE REPOSITA...
...PINGING BACK AND FLYING LIKE A CHEESE SANDWICH TIED TO A BRICK.
LISTEN TO THAT LITTLE SPARROW. MELTAWAY--WHAT A LAME NAME. SORRY-ASS SPARROW.
NOT AS SORRY AS THE TILES ON THE MELTAWAY. YOU SEE HIM LEAVE ATMO? LIKE A DRUNK HIPPO GIVING BIRTH.
I HEARD THAT. YOU JUST PUTT-PUTT ALONG, LITTLE MAN.
PRETTY.

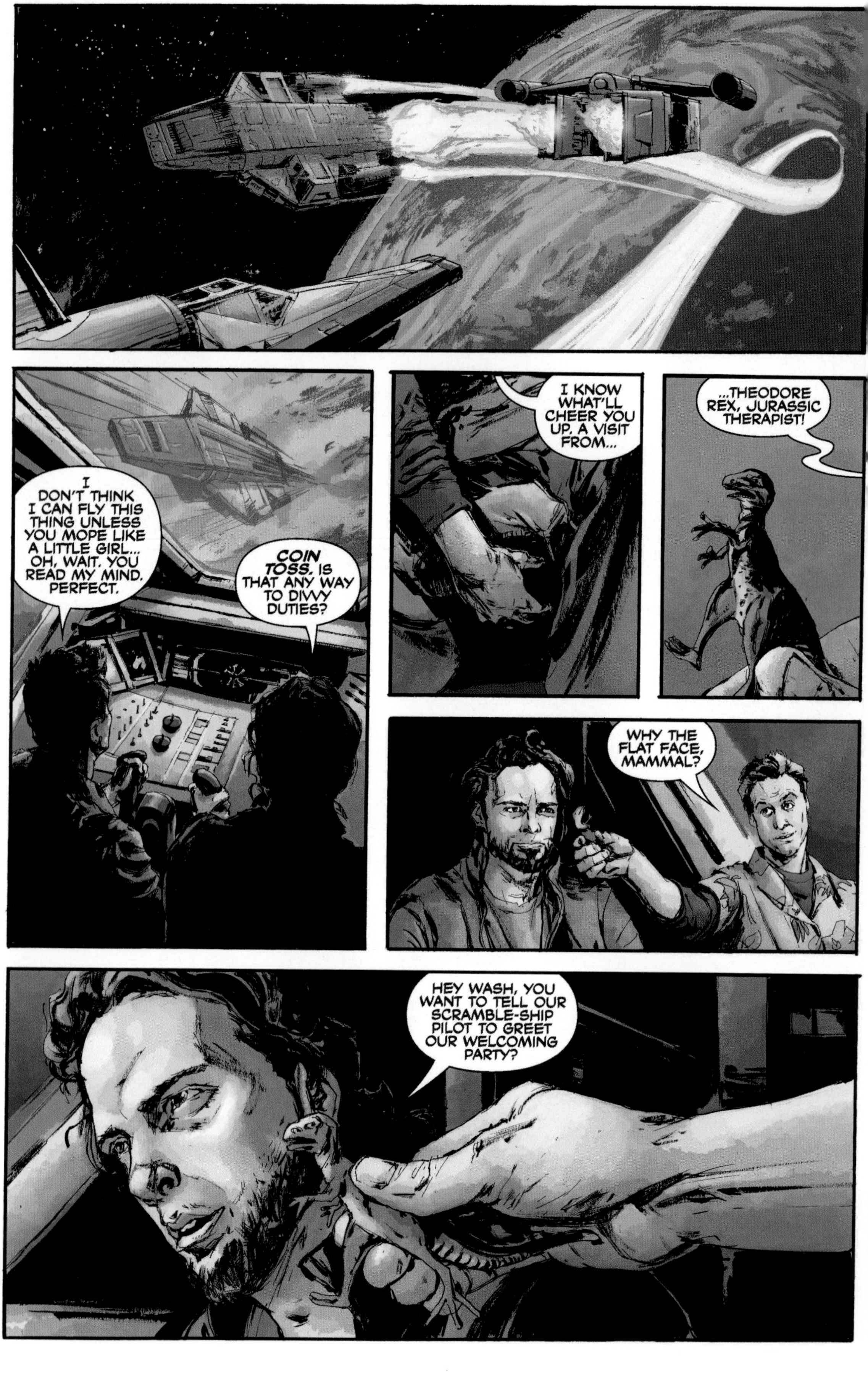
I DON'T THINK I CAN FLY THIS THING UNLESS YOU MOPE LIKE A LITTLE GIRL... OH, WAIT. YOU READ MY MIND. PERFECT.
COIN TOSS, IS THAT ANY WAY TO DIVVY DUTIES?
I KNOW WHAT'LL CHEER YOU UP. A VISIT FROM...
...THEODORE REX, JURASSIC THERAPIST!
WHY THE FLAT FACE, MAMMAL?
HEY WASH, YOU WANT TO TELL OUR SCRAMBLE-SHIP PILOT TO GREET OUR WELCOMING PARTY?

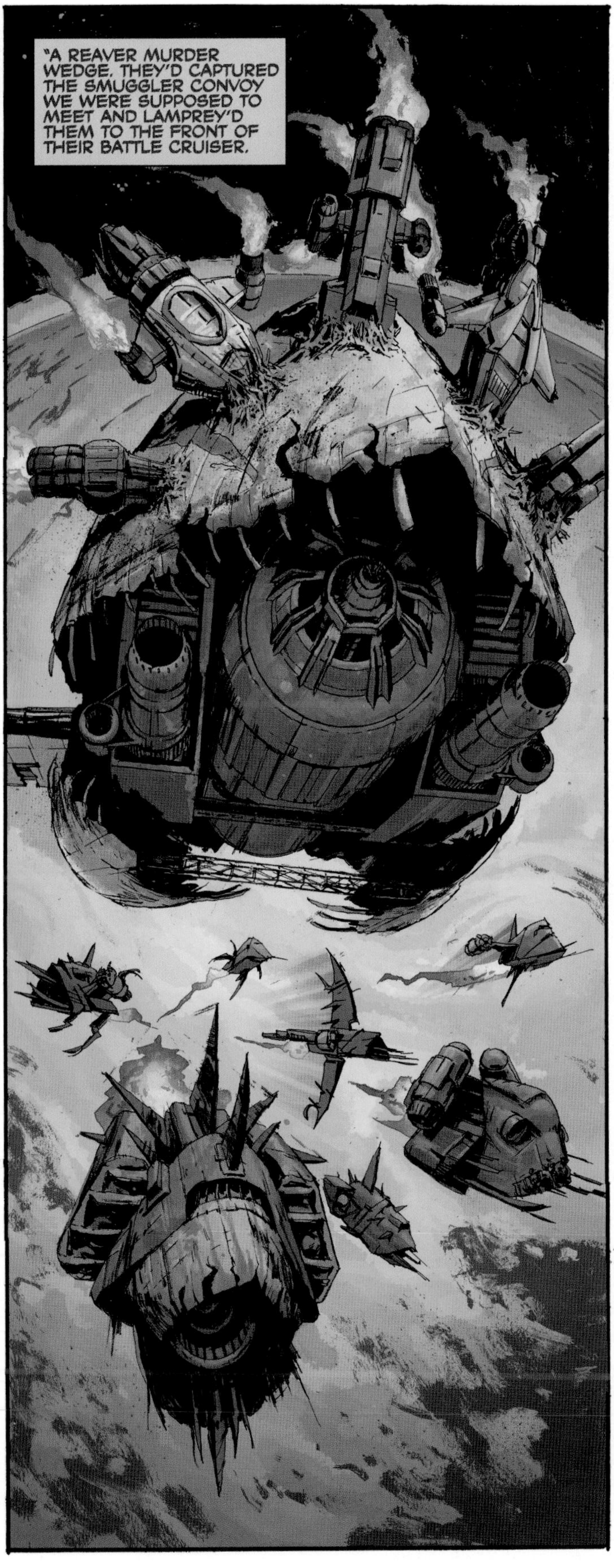
"A REAVER MURDER WEDGE. THEY'D CAPTURED THE SMUGGLER CONVOY WE WERE SUPPOSED TO MEET AND LAMPREY'D THEM TO THE FRONT OF THEIR BATTLE CRUISER.

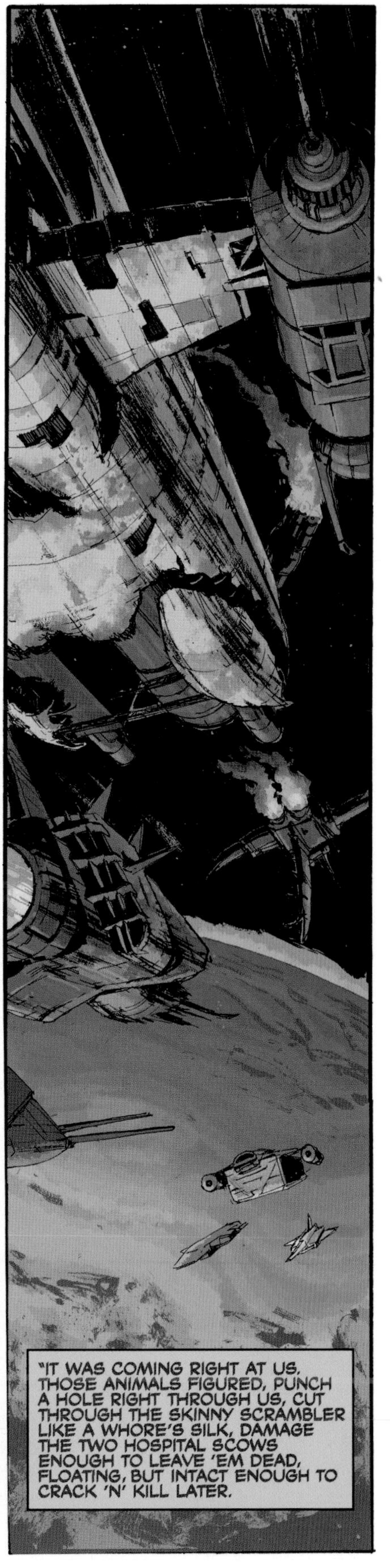
"IT WAS COMING RIGHT AT US. THOSE ANIMALS FIGURED, PUNCH A HOLE RIGHT THROUGH US, CUT THROUGH THE SKINNY SCRAMBLER LIKE A WHORE'S SILK, DAMAGE THE TWO HOSPITAL SCOWS ENOUGH TO LEAVE 'EM DEAD, FLOATING, BUT INTACT ENOUGH TO CRACK 'N' KILL LATER.

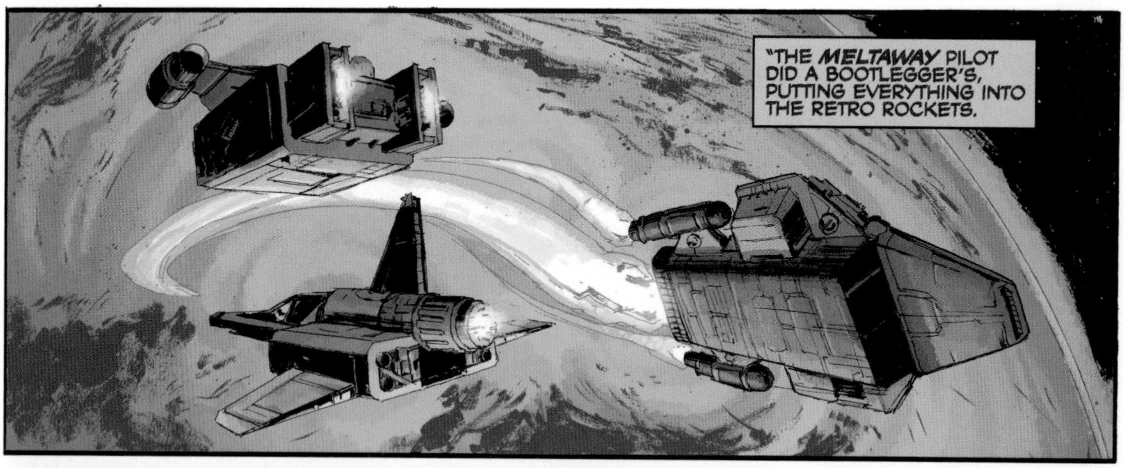
"THE MELTAWAY PILOT DID A BOOTLEGGER'S, PUTTING EVERYTHING INTO THE RETRO ROCKETS.

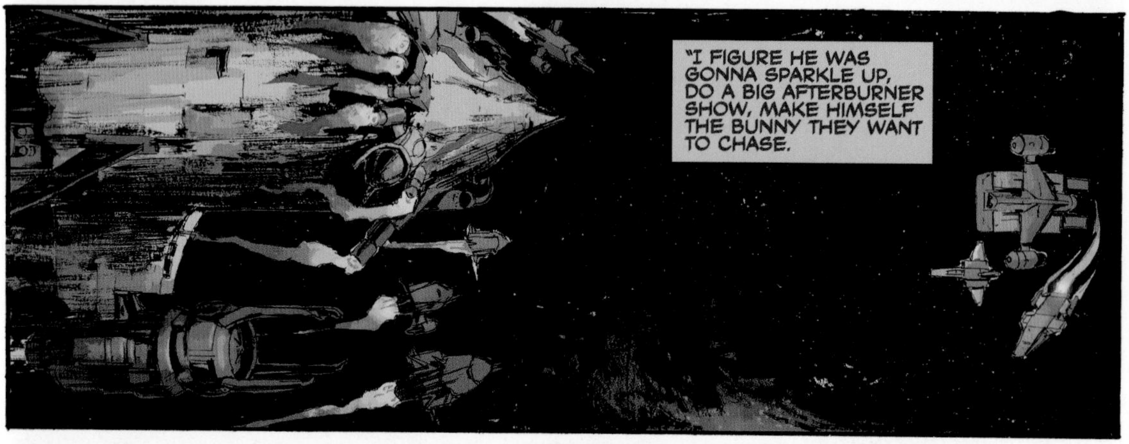
"I FIGURE HE WAS GONNA SPARKLE UP, DO A BIG AFTERBURNER SHOW, MAKE HIMSELF THE BUNNY THEY WANT TO CHASE.

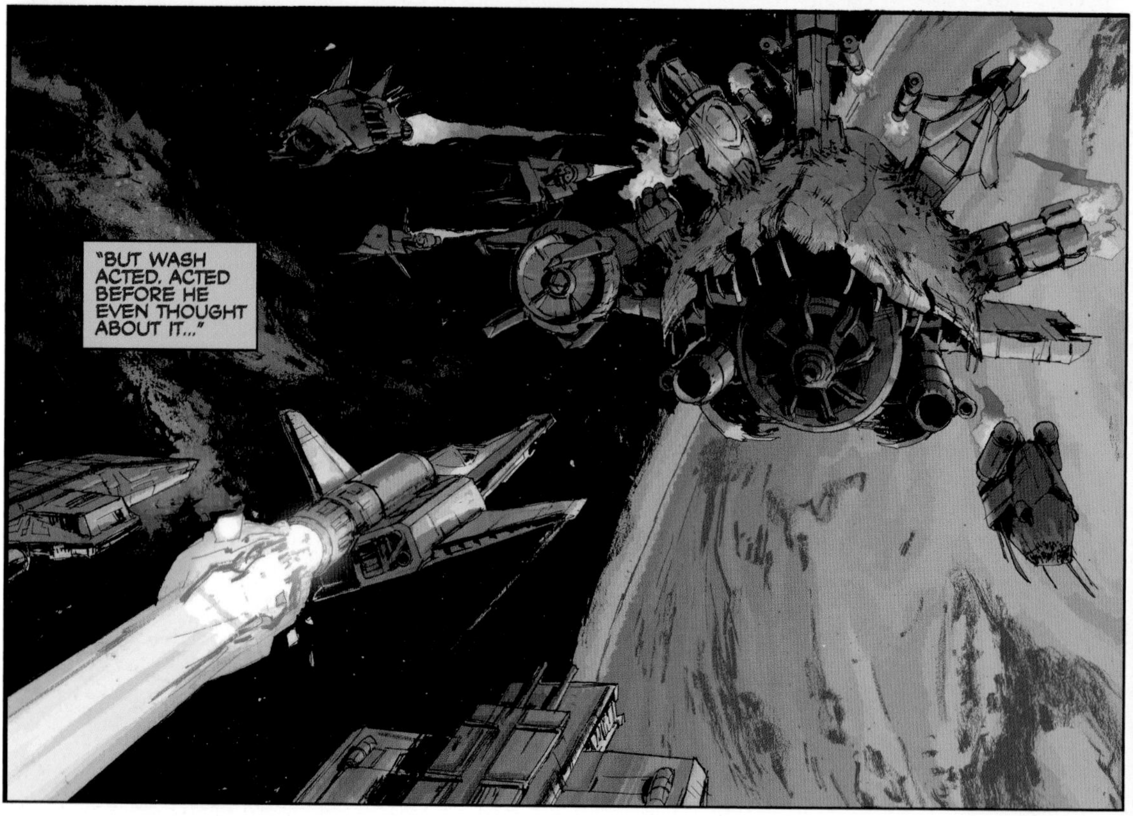
"BUT WASH ACTED. ACTED BEFORE HE EVEN THOUGHT ABOUT IT..."

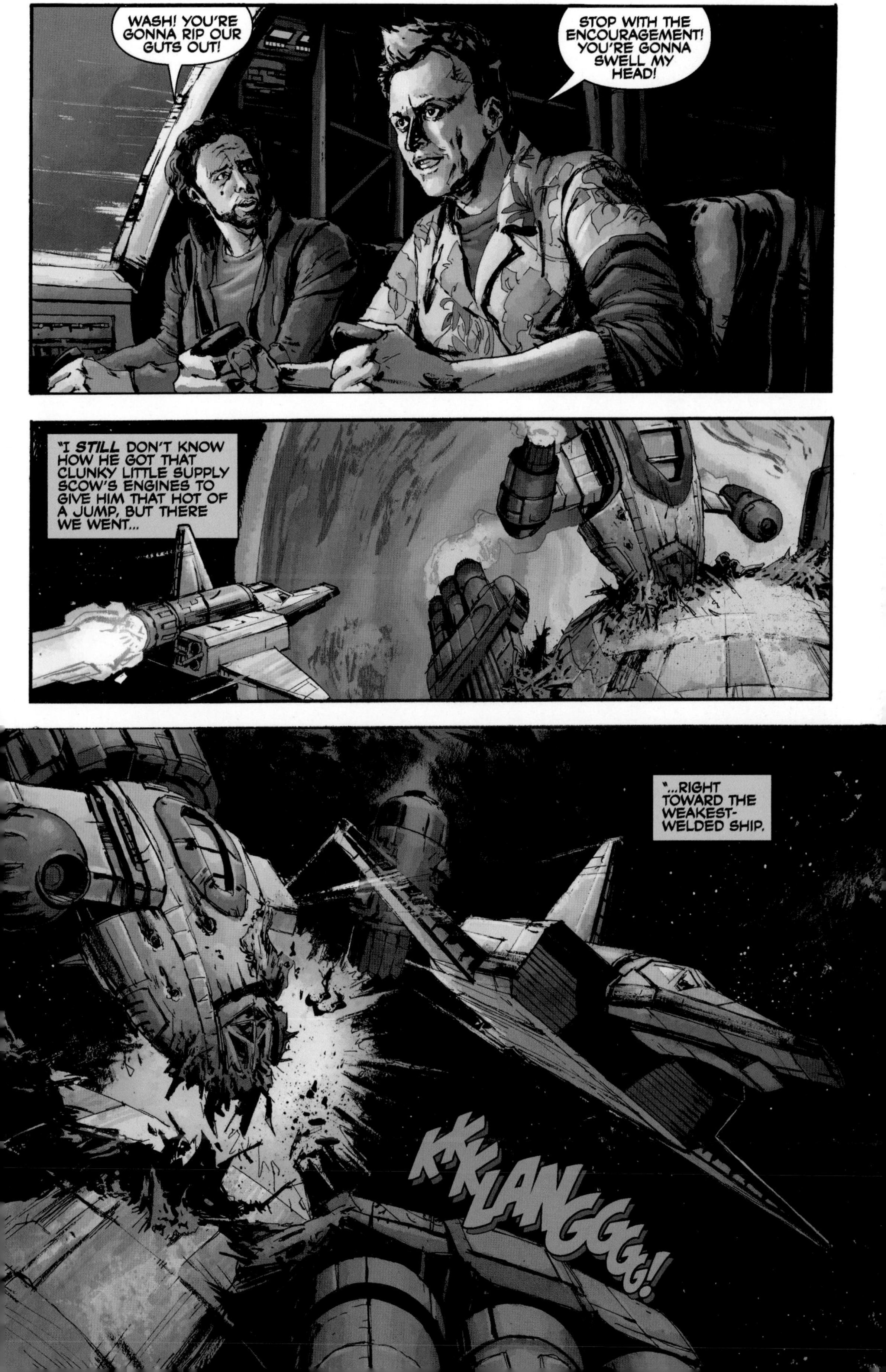
WASH! YOU'RE GONNA RIP OUR GUTS OUT!
STOP WITH THE ENCOURAGEMENT! YOU'RE GONNA SWELL MY HEAD!
"I STILL DON'T KNOW HOW HE GOT THAT CLUNKY LITTLE SUPPLY SCOW'S ENGINES TO GIVE HIM THAT HOT OF A JUMP, BUT THERE WE WENT...
"...RIGHT TOWARD THE WEAKEST-WELDED SHIP.
KKKLANGGGG!

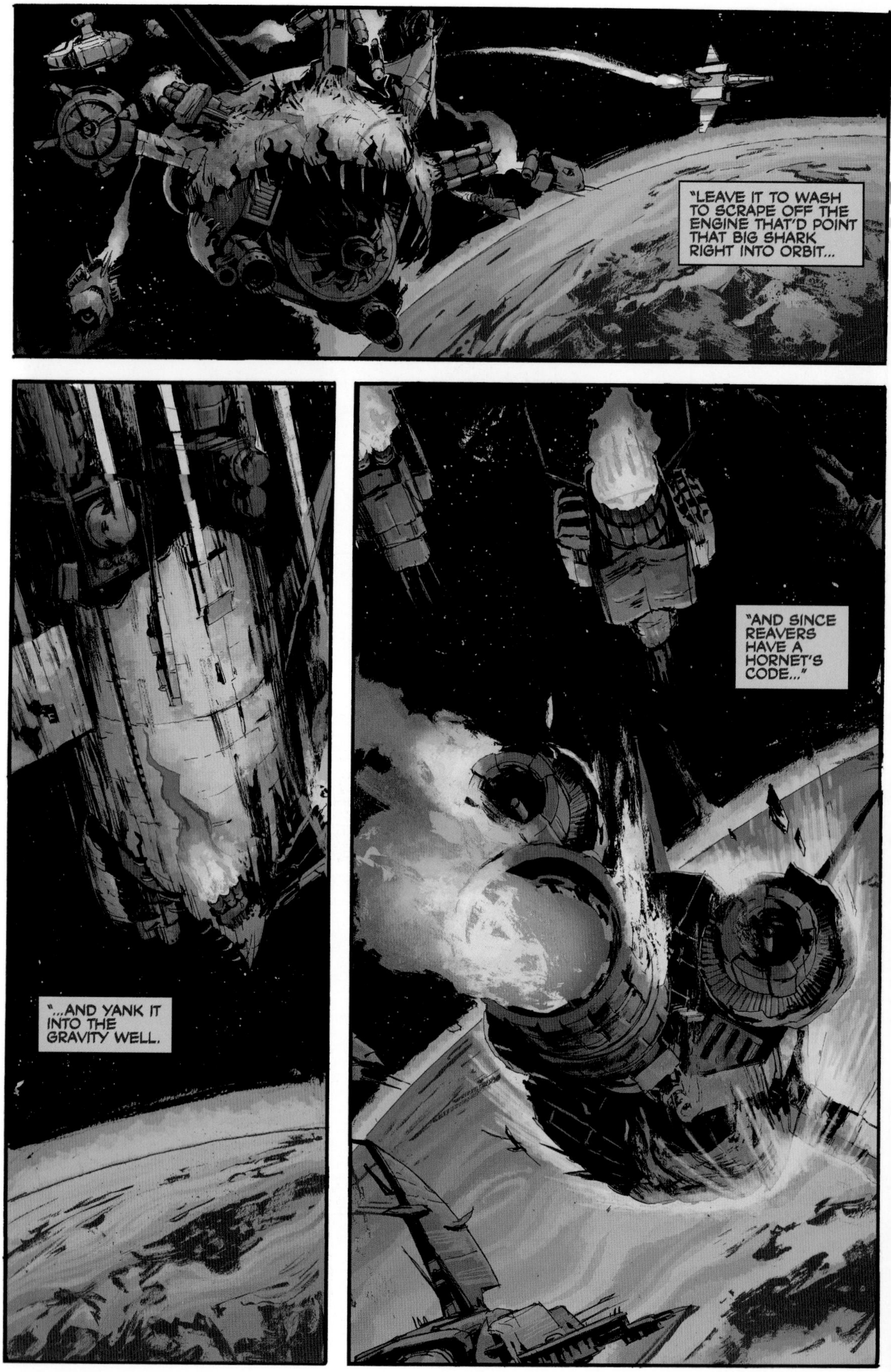
"LEAVE IT TO WASH TO SCRAPE OFF THE ENGINE THAT'D POINT THAT BIG SHARK RIGHT INTO ORBIT...
"...AND YANK IT INTO THE GRAVITY WELL.
"AND SINCE REAVERS HAVE A HORNET'S CODE..."

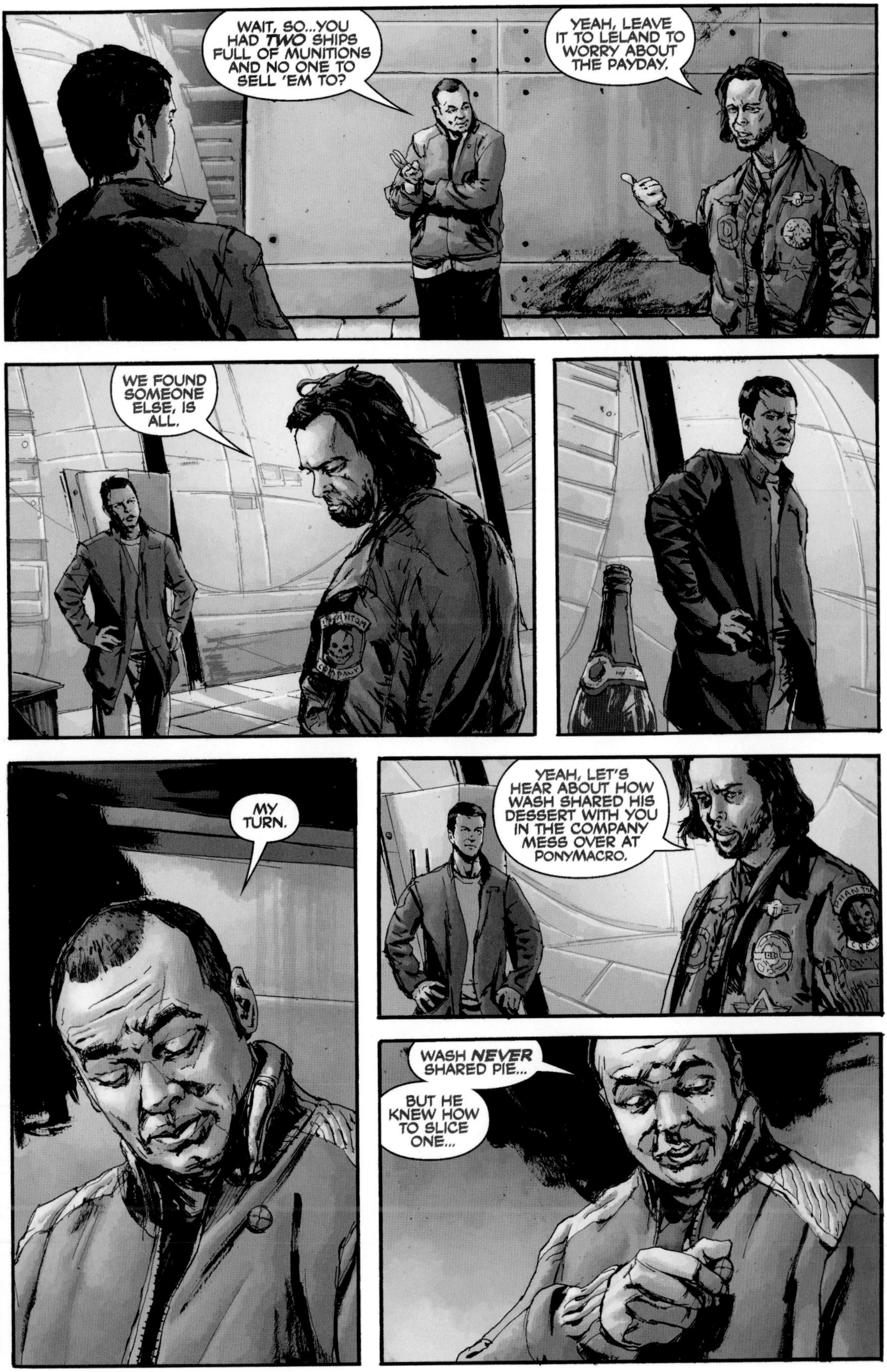
WAIT, SO...YOU HAD TWO SHIPS FULL OF MUNITIONS AND NO ONE TO SELL 'EM TO?
YEAH, LEAVE IT TO LELAND TO WORRY ABOUT THE PAYDAY.
WE FOUND SOMEONE ELSE, IS ALL.
PHANTOM COMPANY
MY TURN.
YEAH, LET'S HEAR ABOUT HOW WASH SHARED HIS DESSERT WITH YOU IN THE COMPANY MESS OVER AT PONYMACRO.
WASH NEVER SHARED PIE...
BUT HE KNEW HOW TO SLICE ONE...

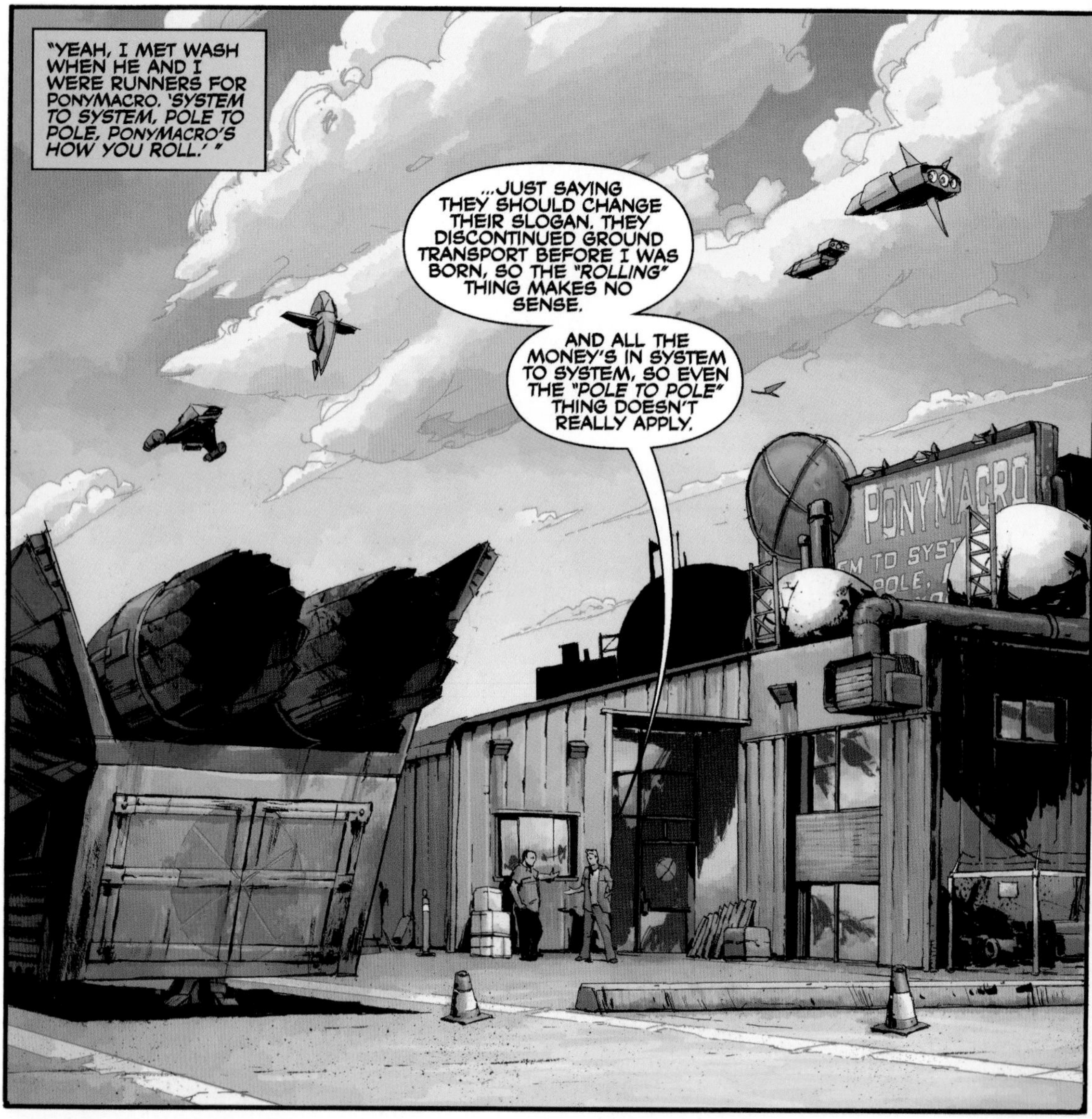
"YEAH, I MET WASH WHEN HE AND I WERE RUNNERS FOR PONYMACRO. 'SYSTEM TO SYSTEM, POLE TO POLE, PONYMACRO'S HOW YOU ROLL.' "
...JUST SAYING THEY SHOULD CHANGE THEIR SLOGAN. THEY DISCONTINUED GROUND TRANSPORT BEFORE I WAS BORN, SO THE "ROLLING" THING MAKES NO SENSE.
AND ALL THE MONEY'S IN SYSTEM TO SYSTEM, SO EVEN THE "POLE TO POLE" THING DOESN'T REALLY APPLY.
PONYMACRO

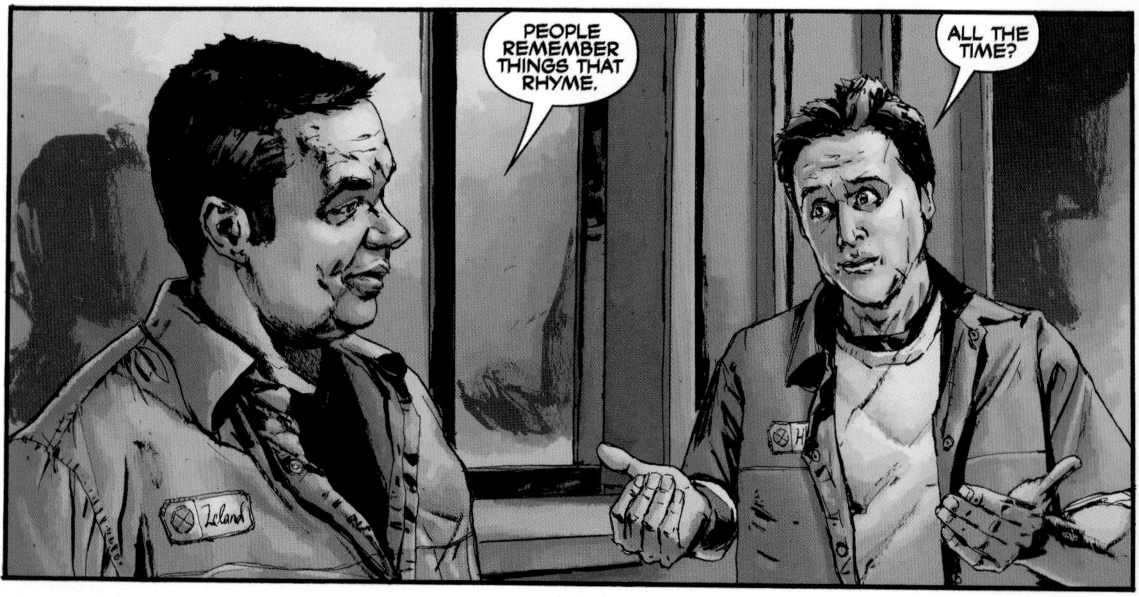
PEOPLE REMEMBER THINGS THAT RHYME.
ALL THE TIME?
Leland

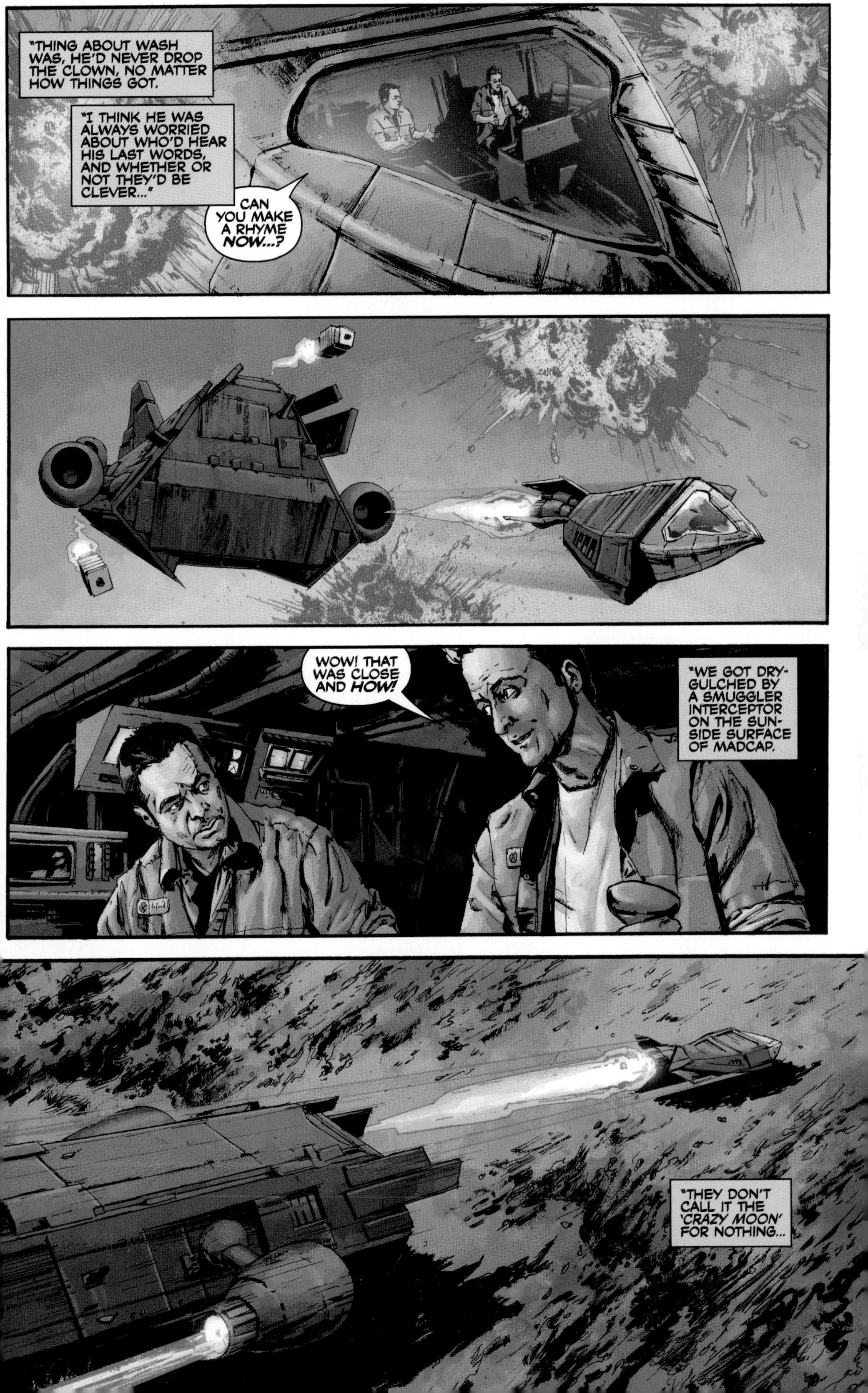
"THING ABOUT WASH WAS, HE'D NEVER DROP THE CLOWN, NO MATTER HOW THINGS GOT.
"I THINK HE WAS ALWAYS WORRIED ABOUT WHO'D HEAR HIS LAST WORDS, AND WHETHER OR NOT THEY'D BE CLEVER..."
CAN YOU MAKE A RHYME *NOW...?*
WOW! THAT WAS CLOSE AND *HOW!*
"WE GOT DRY-GULCHED BY A SMUGGLER INTERCEPTOR ON THE SUN-SIDE SURFACE OF MADCAP.
"THEY DON'T CALL IT THE '*CRAZY MOON*' FOR NOTHING...

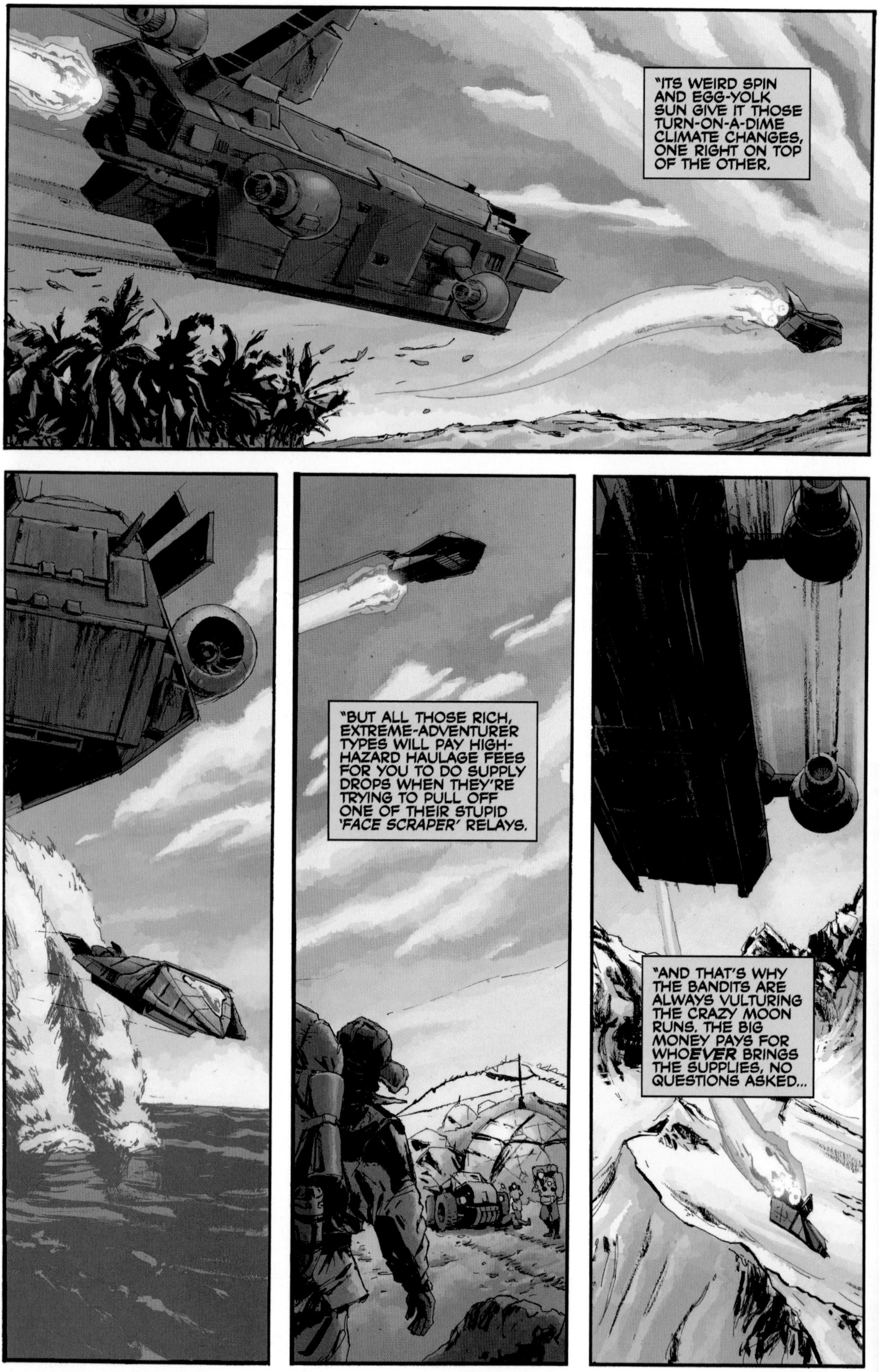
"ITS WEIRD SPIN AND EGG-YOLK SUN GIVE IT THOSE TURN-ON-A-DIME CLIMATE CHANGES, ONE RIGHT ON TOP OF THE OTHER.
"BUT ALL THOSE RICH, EXTREME-ADVENTURER TYPES WILL PAY HIGH-HAZARD HAULAGE FEES FOR YOU TO DO SUPPLY DROPS WHEN THEY'RE TRYING TO PULL OFF ONE OF THEIR STUPID '*FACE SCRAPER*' RELAYS.
"AND THAT'S WHY THE BANDITS ARE ALWAYS VULTURING THE CRAZY MOON RUNS. THE BIG MONEY PAYS FOR WHO*EVER* BRINGS THE SUPPLIES, NO QUESTIONS ASKED...

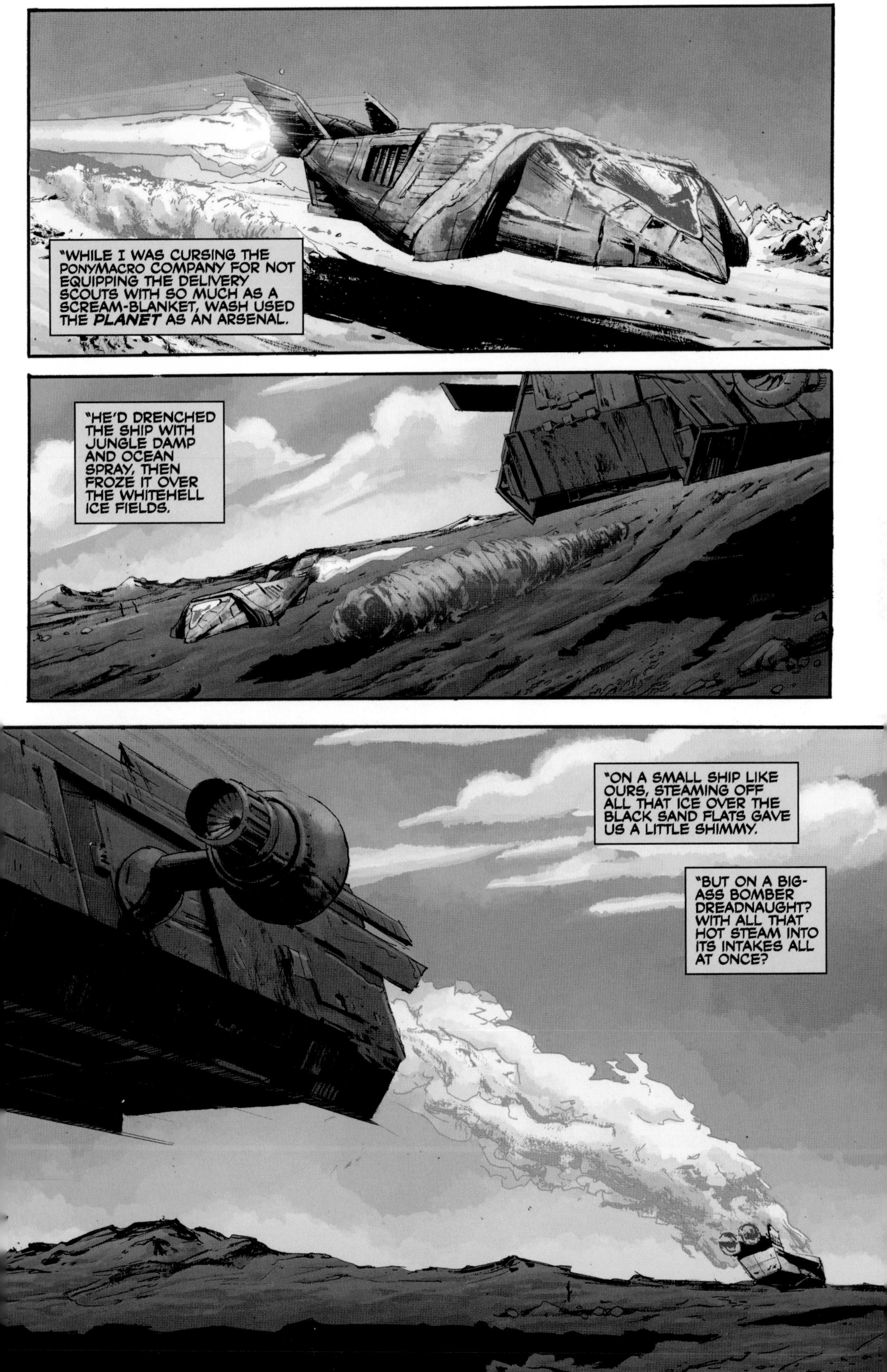
"WHILE I WAS CURSING THE PONYMACRO COMPANY FOR NOT EQUIPPING THE DELIVERY SCOUTS WITH SO MUCH AS A SCREAM-BLANKET, WASH USED THE *PLANET* AS AN ARSENAL.
"HE'D DRENCHED THE SHIP WITH JUNGLE DAMP AND OCEAN SPRAY, THEN FROZE IT OVER THE WHITEHELL ICE FIELDS.
"ON A SMALL SHIP LIKE OURS, STEAMING OFF ALL THAT ICE OVER THE BLACK SAND FLATS GAVE US A LITTLE SHIMMY.
"BUT ON A BIG-ASS BOMBER DREADNAUGHT? WITH ALL THAT HOT STEAM INTO ITS INTAKES ALL AT ONCE?

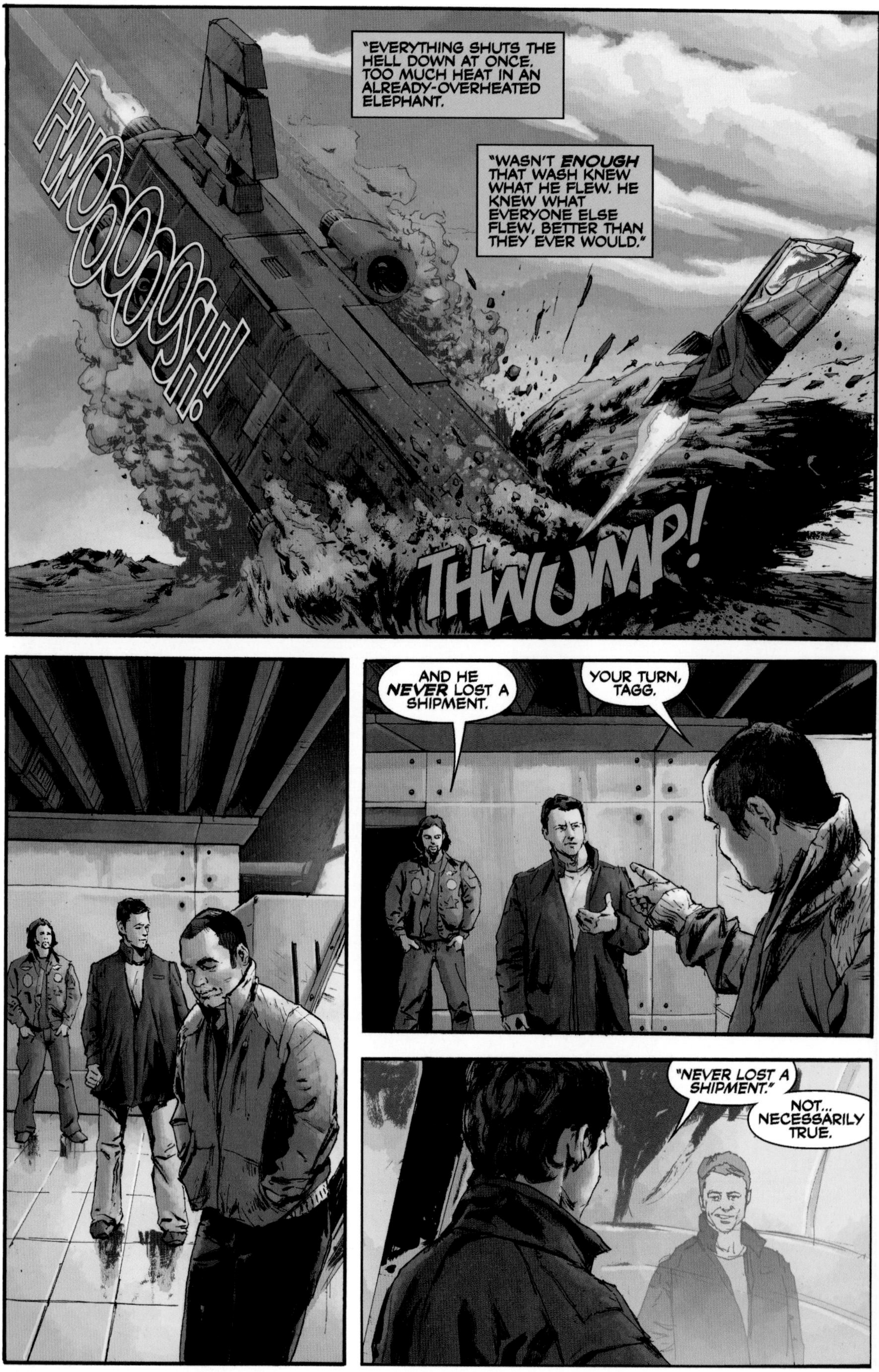
"EVERYTHING SHUTS THE HELL DOWN AT ONCE. TOO MUCH HEAT IN AN ALREADY-OVERHEATED ELEPHANT.
"WASN'T ENOUGH THAT WASH KNEW WHAT HE FLEW. HE KNEW WHAT EVERYONE ELSE FLEW, BETTER THAN THEY EVER WOULD."
FWOOOOSH!
THWUMP!
AND HE NEVER LOST A SHIPMENT.
YOUR TURN, TAGG.
"NEVER LOST A SHIPMENT."
NOT... NECESSARILY TRUE.

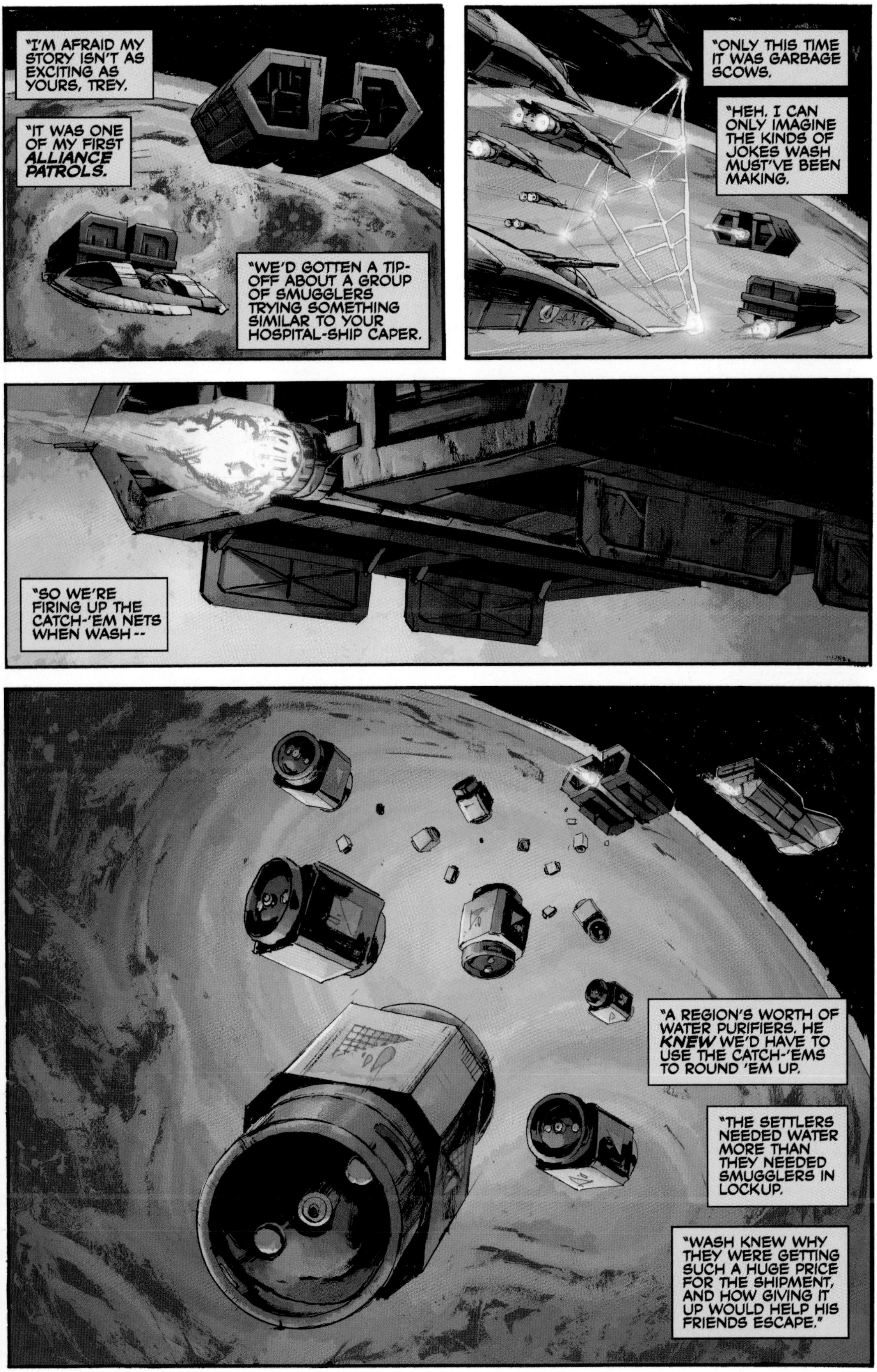
"I'M AFRAID MY STORY ISN'T AS EXCITING AS YOURS, TREY.
"IT WAS ONE OF MY FIRST *ALLIANCE PATROLS.*
"WE'D GOTTEN A TIP-OFF ABOUT A GROUP OF SMUGGLERS TRYING SOMETHING SIMILAR TO YOUR HOSPITAL-SHIP CAPER.
"ONLY THIS TIME IT WAS GARBAGE SCOWS.
"HEH, I CAN ONLY IMAGINE THE KINDS OF JOKES WASH MUST'VE BEEN MAKING.
"SO WE'RE FIRING UP THE CATCH-'EM NETS WHEN WASH --
"A REGION'S WORTH OF WATER PURIFIERS. HE *KNEW* WE'D HAVE TO USE THE CATCH-'EMS TO ROUND 'EM UP.
"THE SETTLERS NEEDED WATER MORE THAN THEY NEEDED SMUGGLERS IN LOCKUP.
"WASH KNEW WHY THEY WERE GETTING SUCH A HUGE PRICE FOR THE SHIPMENT, AND HOW GIVING IT UP WOULD HELP HIS FRIENDS ESCAPE."

I *REMEMBER* HEARING ABOUT THAT. A KING'S RANSOM IN CARGO, AND HE TOSSED IT?

SO HIS FRIENDS COULD GET AWAY.

HOW'D YOU KNOW IT WAS WASH?

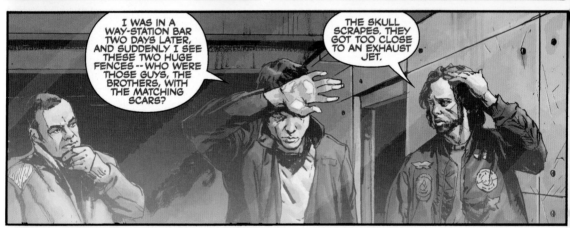

I WAS IN A WAY-STATION BAR TWO DAYS LATER, AND SUDDENLY I SEE THESE TWO HUGE FENCES -- WHO WERE THOSE GUYS, THE BROTHERS, WITH THE MATCHING SCARS?

THE SKULL SCRAPES. THEY GOT TOO CLOSE TO AN EXHAUST JET.

"THE SCRAPES ARE SCREAMING ABOUT THE WATER FILTERS, AND I KNOW, I *KNOW* THIS IS THE PILOT WHO DUMPED THEM.

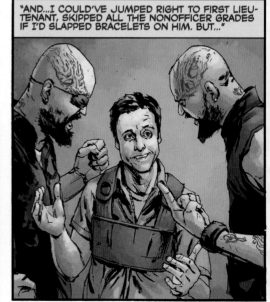

"AND...I COULD'VE JUMPED RIGHT TO FIRST LIEUTENANT, SKIPPED ALL THE NONOFFICER GRADES IF I'D SLAPPED BRACELETS ON HIM, BUT..."

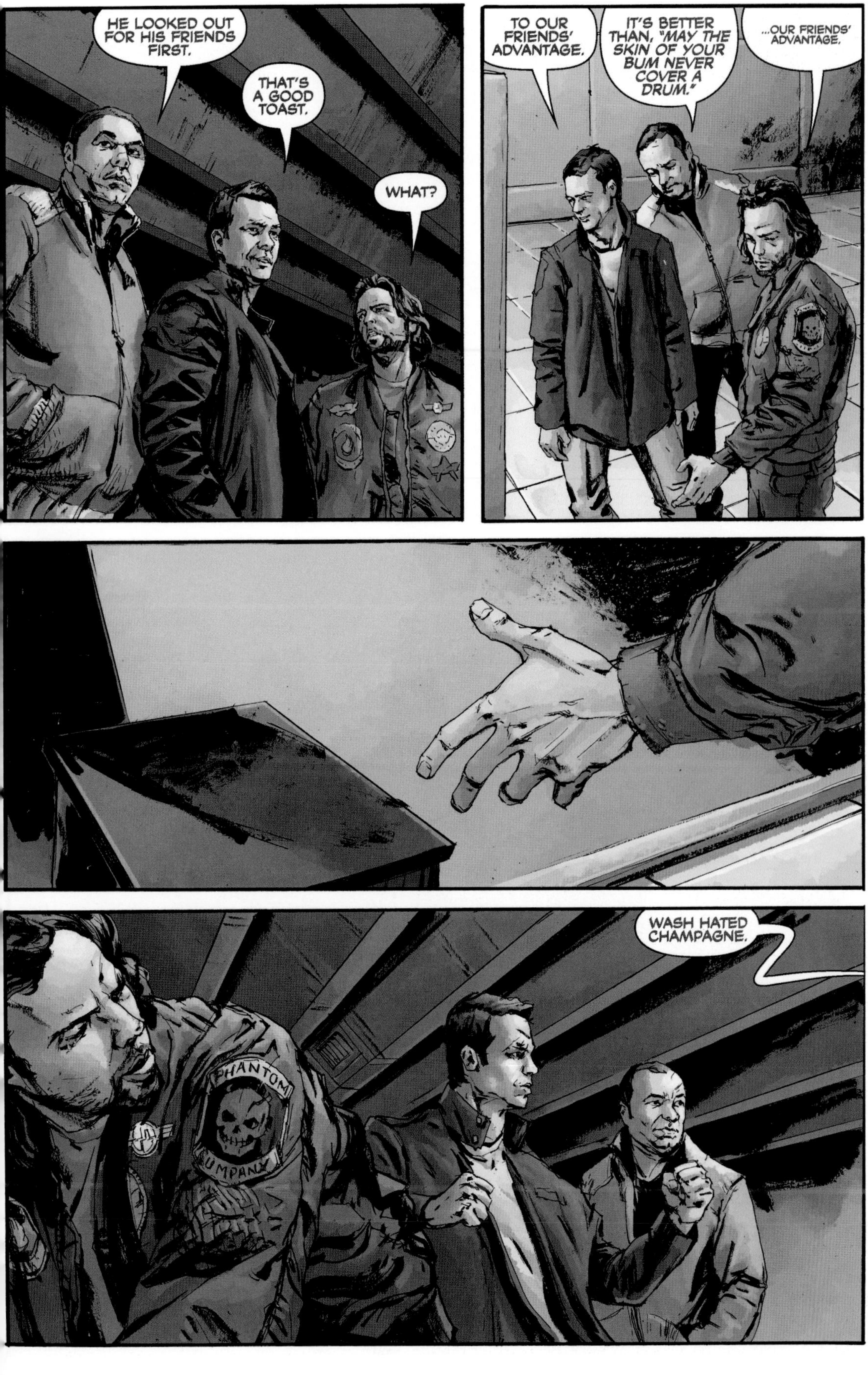
HE LOOKED OUT FOR HIS FRIENDS FIRST.
THAT'S A GOOD TOAST.
WHAT?
TO OUR FRIENDS' ADVANTAGE.
IT'S BETTER THAN, "MAY THE SKIN OF YOUR BUM NEVER COVER A DRUM."
...OUR FRIENDS' ADVANTAGE.
WASH HATED CHAMPAGNE.
PHANTOM
CUMPANY

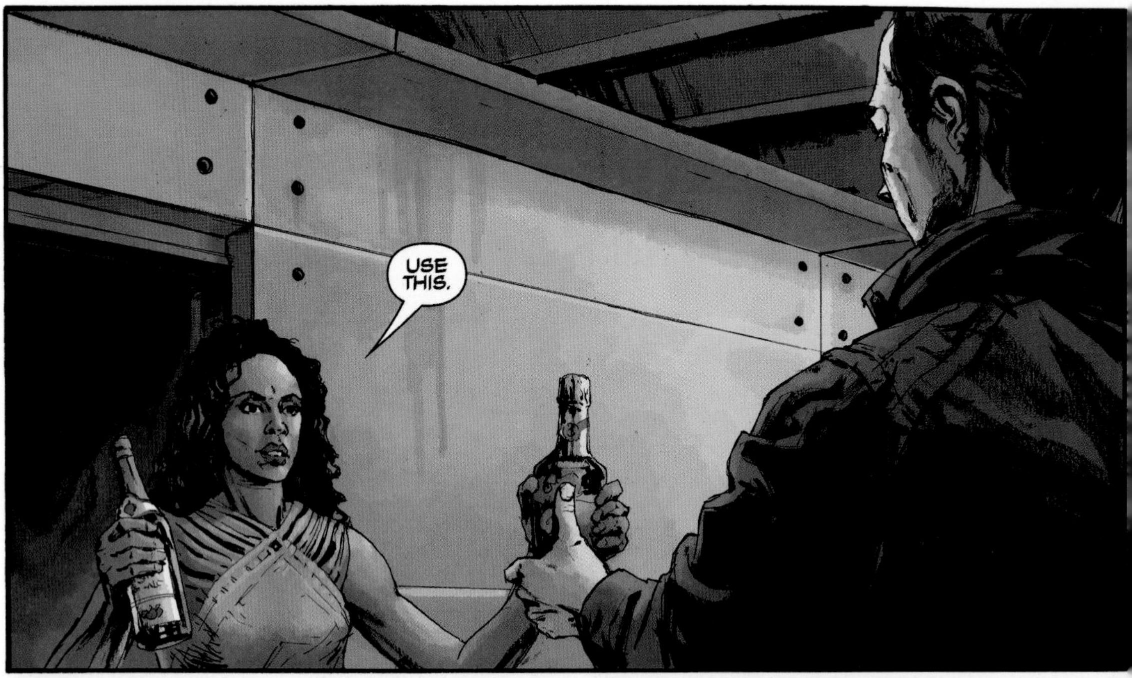
USE THIS.

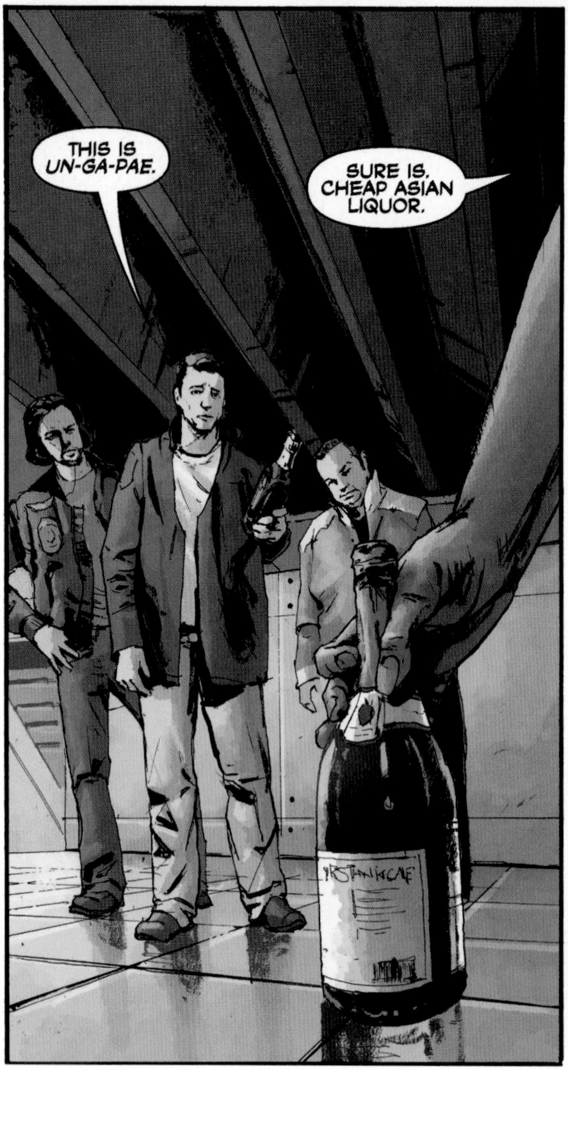
THIS IS UN-GA-PAE.
SURE IS. CHEAP ASIAN LIQUOR.

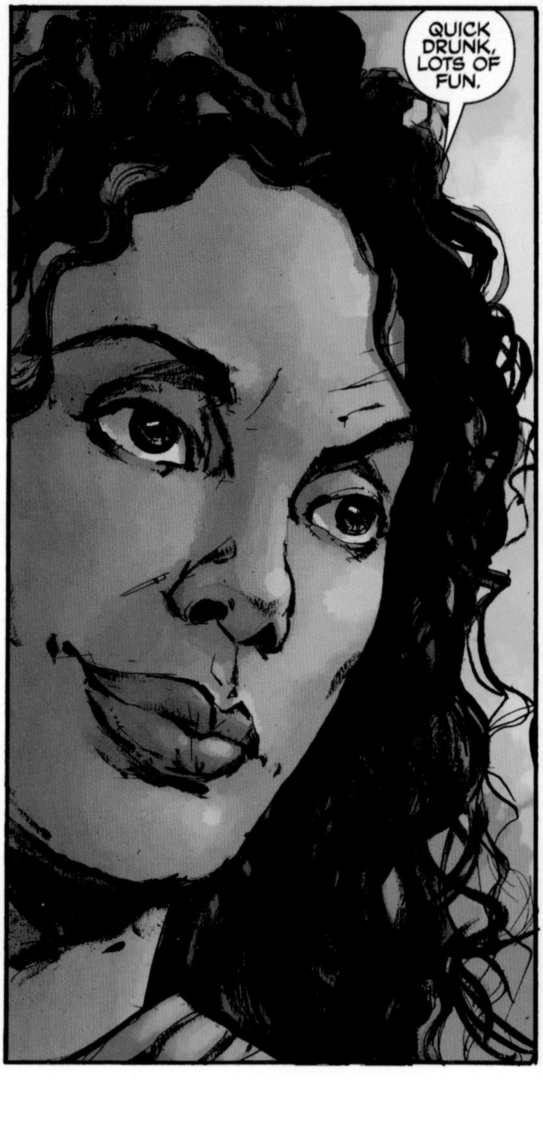
QUICK DRUNK, LOTS OF FUN.

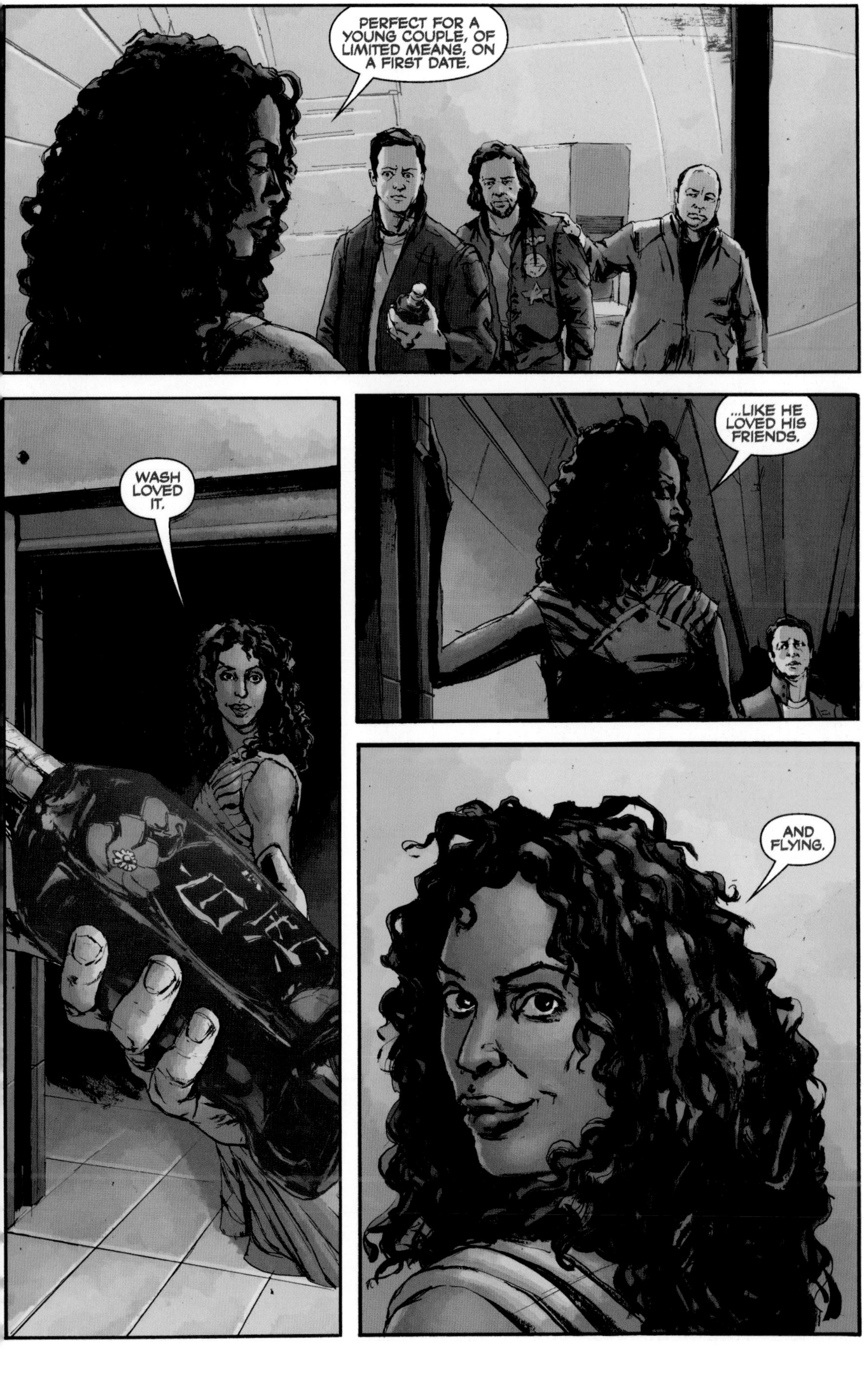
PERFECT FOR A YOUNG COUPLE, OF LIMITED MEANS, ON A FIRST DATE.
WASH LOVED IT.
...LIKE HE LOVED HIS FRIENDS.
AND FLYING.

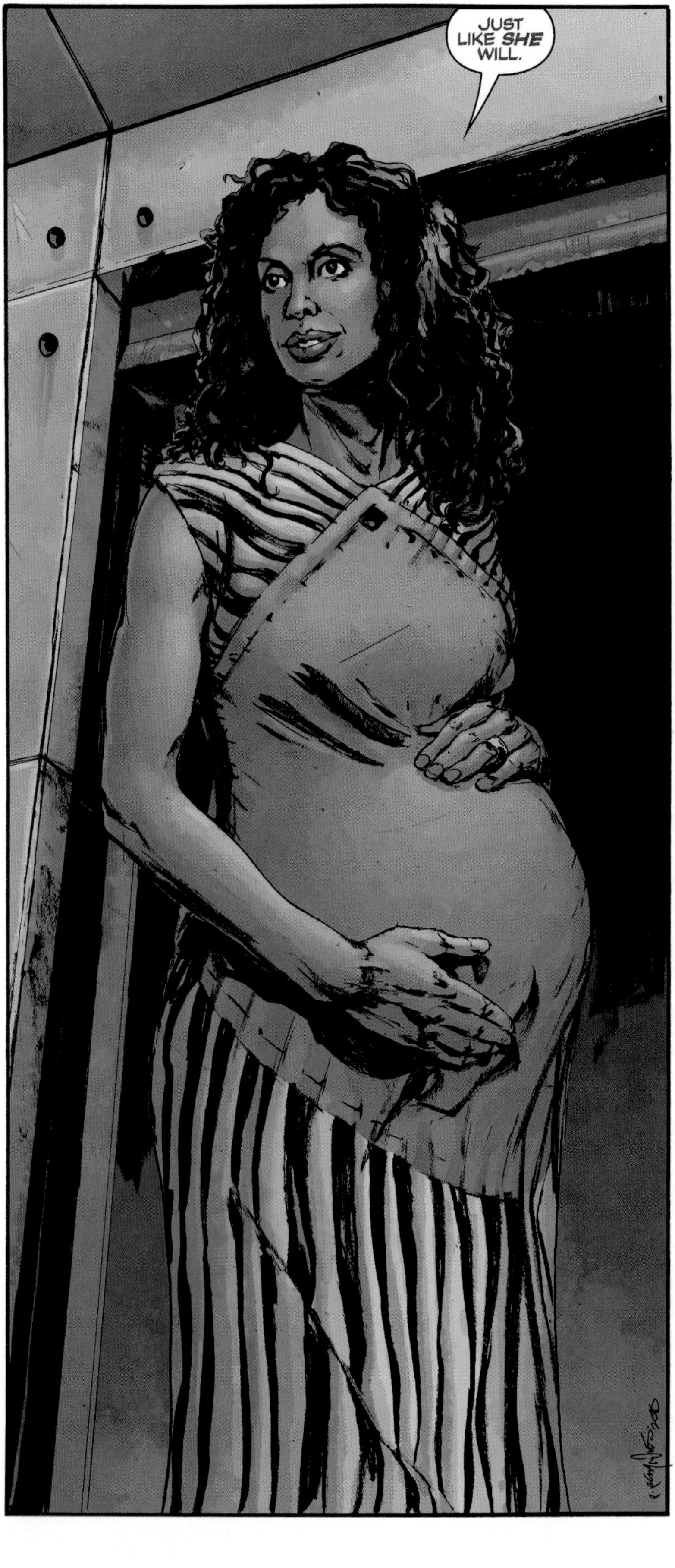
JUST LIKE SHE WILL.

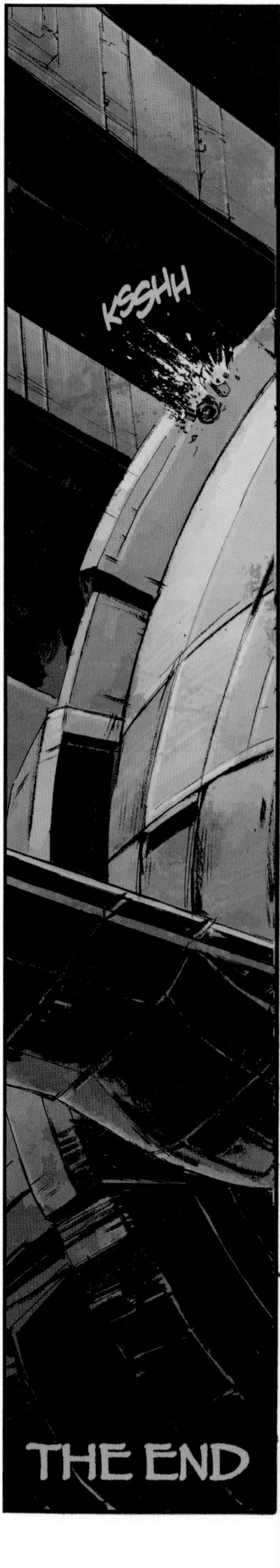
KSSHH
THE END

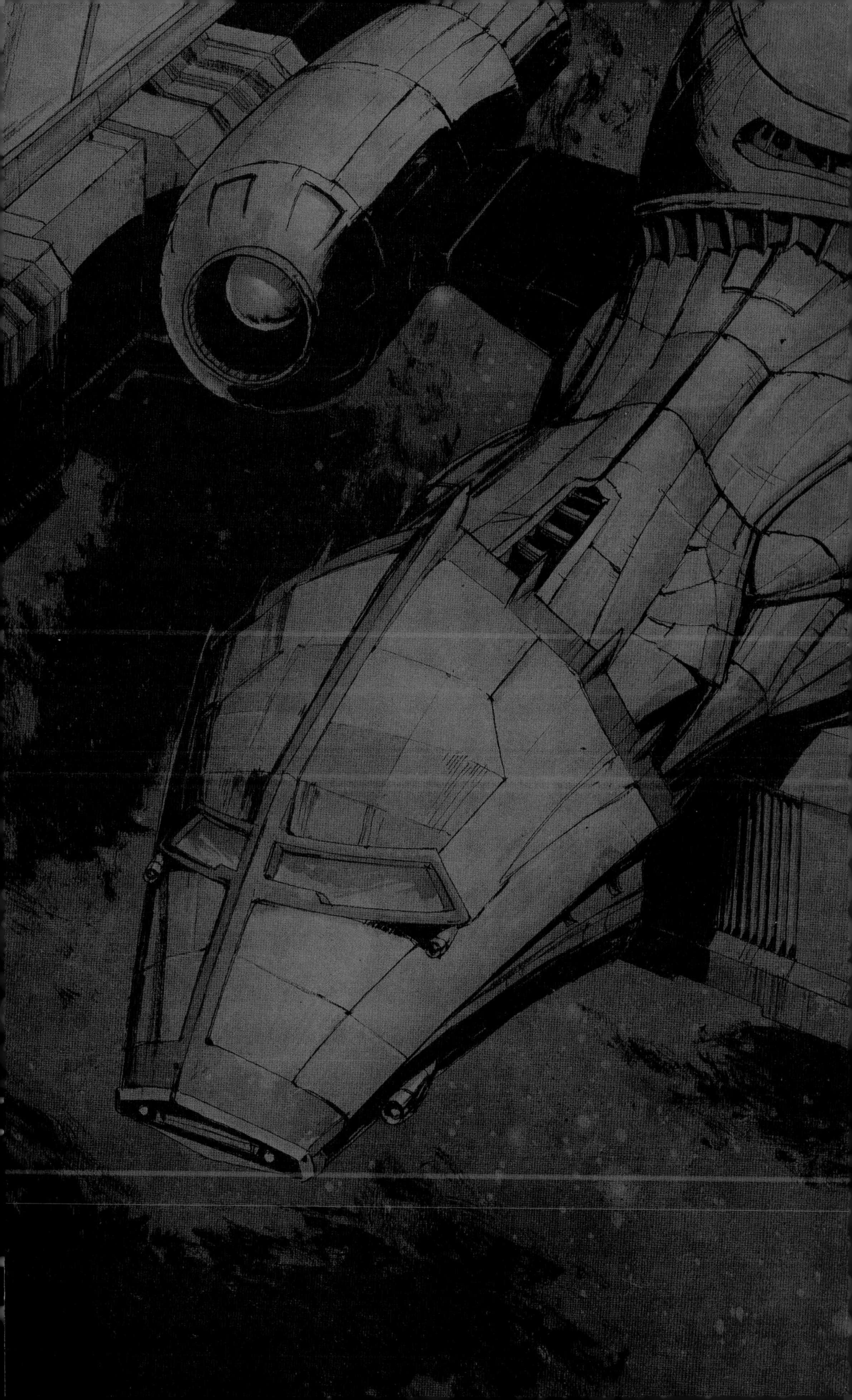

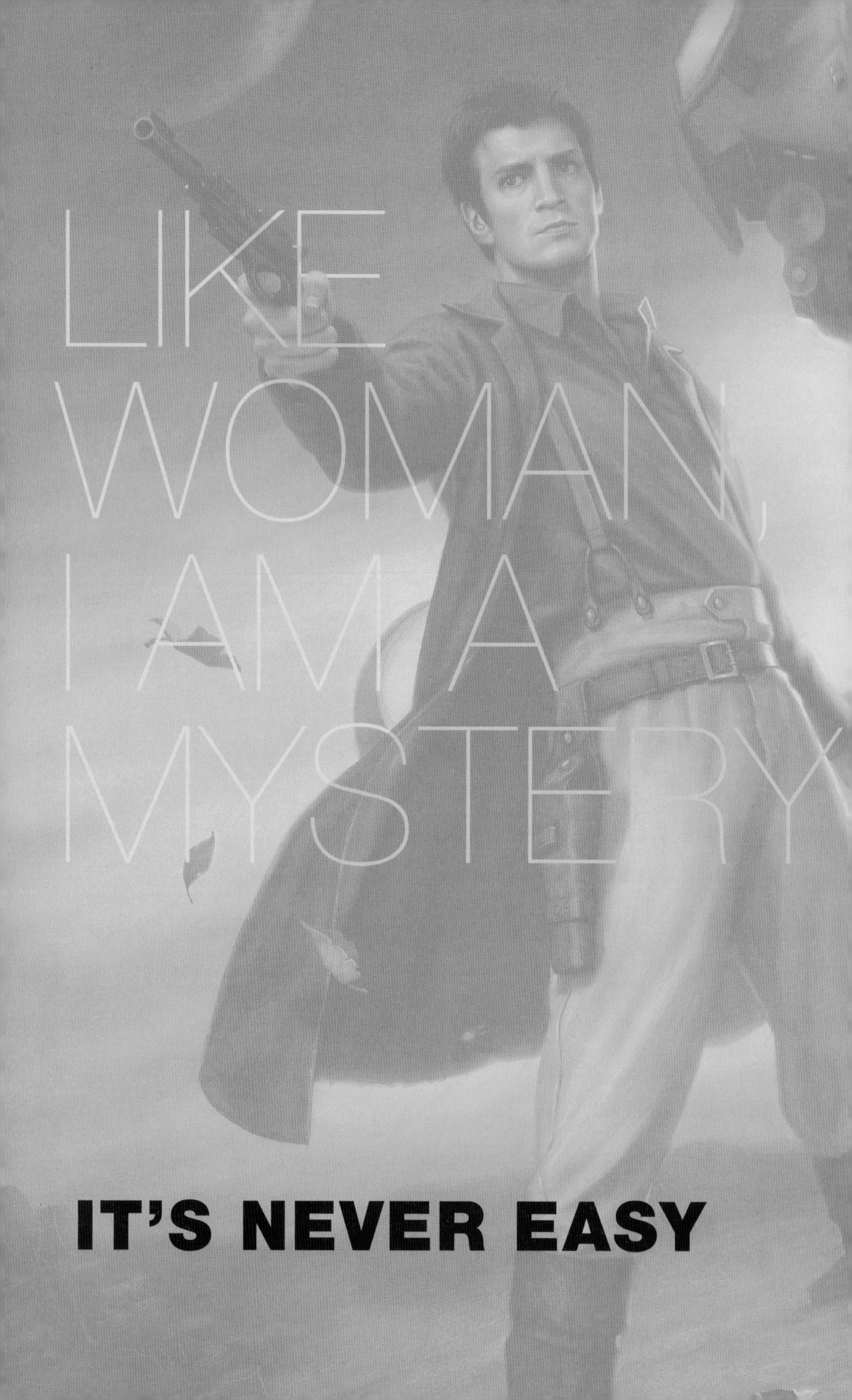
LIKE
WOMAN,
I AM A
MYSTERY
IT'S NEVER EASY

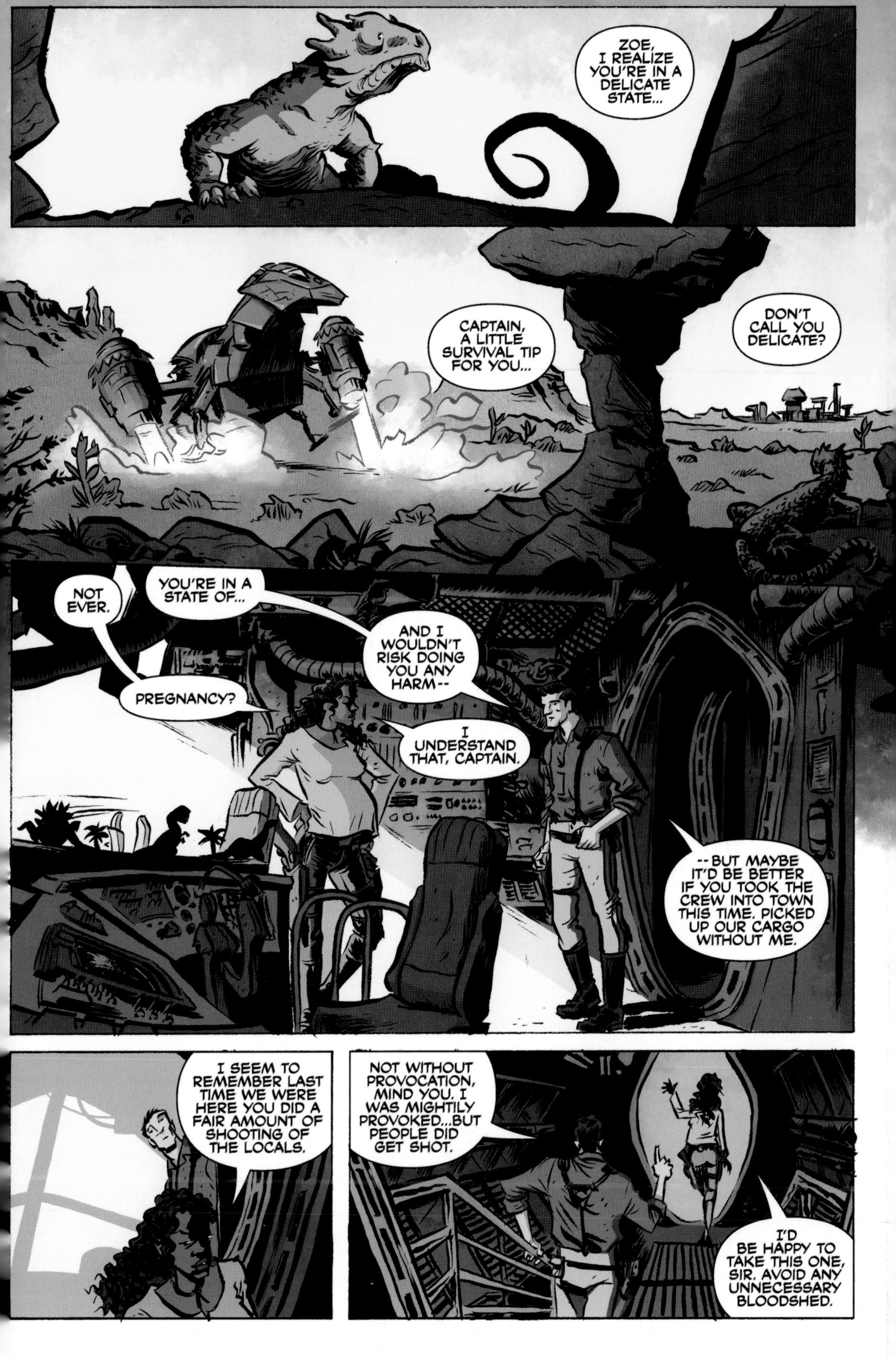
ZOE, I REALIZE YOU'RE IN A DELICATE STATE...
CAPTAIN, A LITTLE SURVIVAL TIP FOR YOU...
DON'T CALL YOU DELICATE?
NOT EVER.
YOU'RE IN A STATE OF...
PREGNANCY?
AND I WOULDN'T RISK DOING YOU ANY HARM--
I UNDERSTAND THAT, CAPTAIN.
--BUT MAYBE IT'D BE BETTER IF YOU TOOK THE CREW INTO TOWN THIS TIME. PICKED UP OUR CARGO WITHOUT ME.
I SEEM TO REMEMBER LAST TIME WE WERE HERE YOU DID A FAIR AMOUNT OF SHOOTING OF THE LOCALS.
NOT WITHOUT PROVOCATION, MIND YOU. I WAS MIGHTILY PROVOKED...BUT PEOPLE DID GET SHOT.
I'D BE HAPPY TO TAKE THIS ONE, SIR. AVOID ANY UNNECESSARY BLOODSHED.

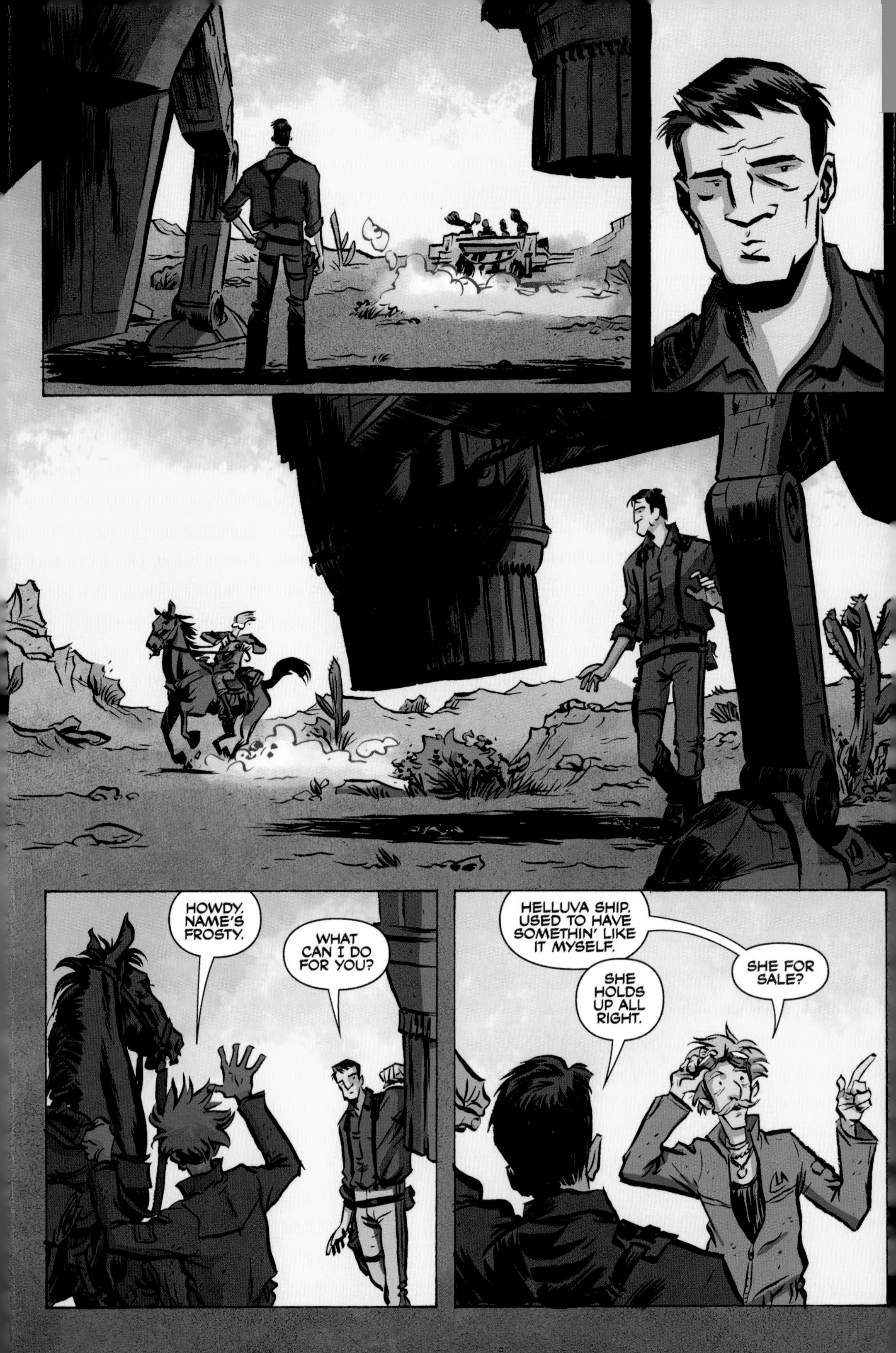
HOWDY. NAME'S FROSTY.
WHAT CAN I DO FOR YOU?
HELLUVA SHIP. USED TO HAVE SOMETHIN' LIKE IT MYSELF.
SHE FOR SALE?
SHE HOLDS UP ALL RIGHT.

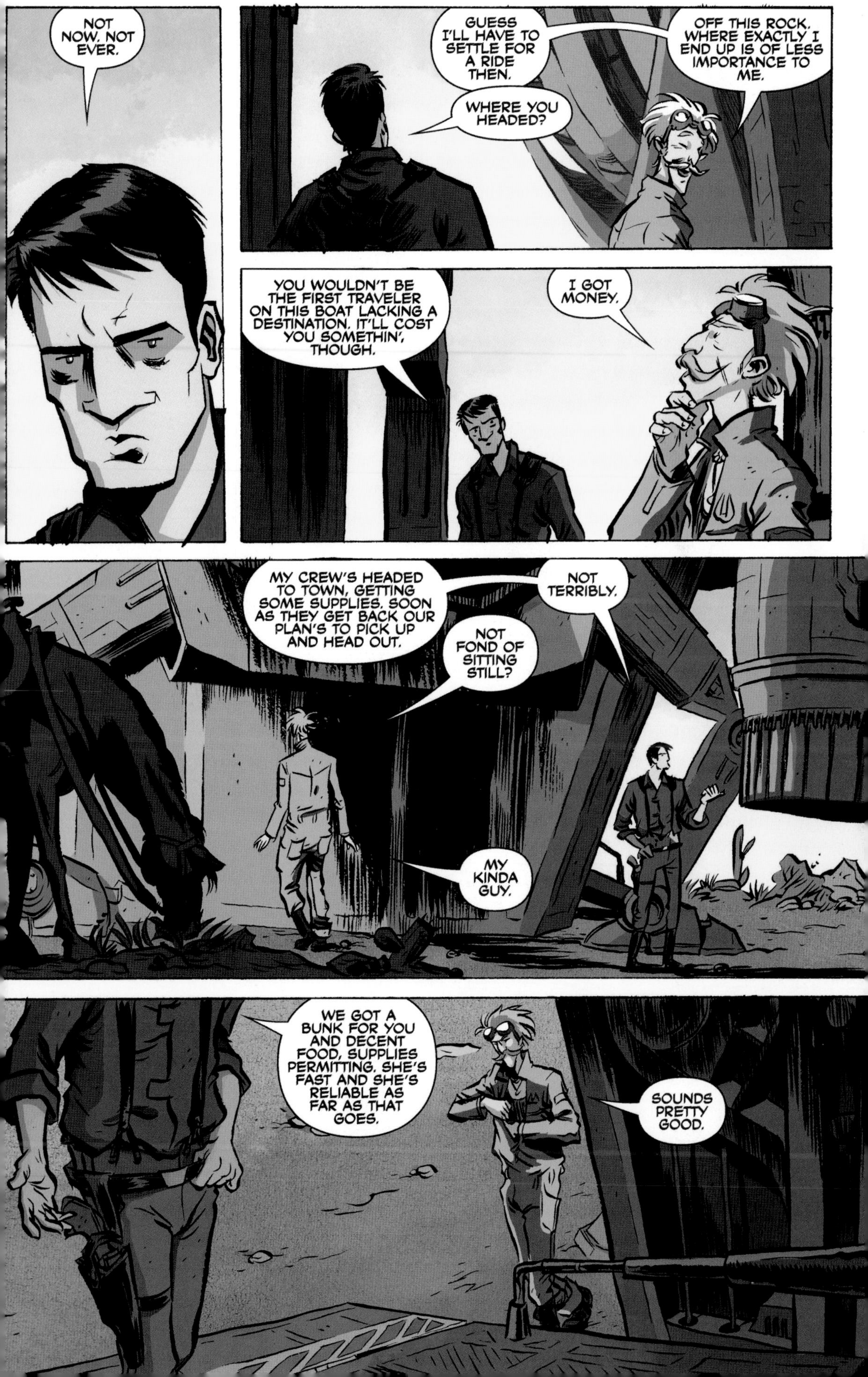
NOT NOW. NOT EVER.
GUESS I'LL HAVE TO SETTLE FOR A RIDE THEN.
OFF THIS ROCK. WHERE EXACTLY I END UP IS OF LESS IMPORTANCE TO ME.
WHERE YOU HEADED?
YOU WOULDN'T BE THE FIRST TRAVELER ON THIS BOAT LACKING A DESTINATION. IT'LL COST YOU SOMETHIN', THOUGH.
I GOT MONEY.
MY CREW'S HEADED TO TOWN, GETTING SOME SUPPLIES. SOON AS THEY GET BACK OUR PLAN'S TO PICK UP AND HEAD OUT.
NOT TERRIBLY.
NOT FOND OF SITTING STILL?
MY KINDA GUY.
WE GOT A BUNK FOR YOU AND DECENT FOOD, SUPPLIES PERMITTING. SHE'S FAST AND SHE'S RELIABLE AS FAR AS THAT GOES.
SOUNDS PRETTY GOOD.

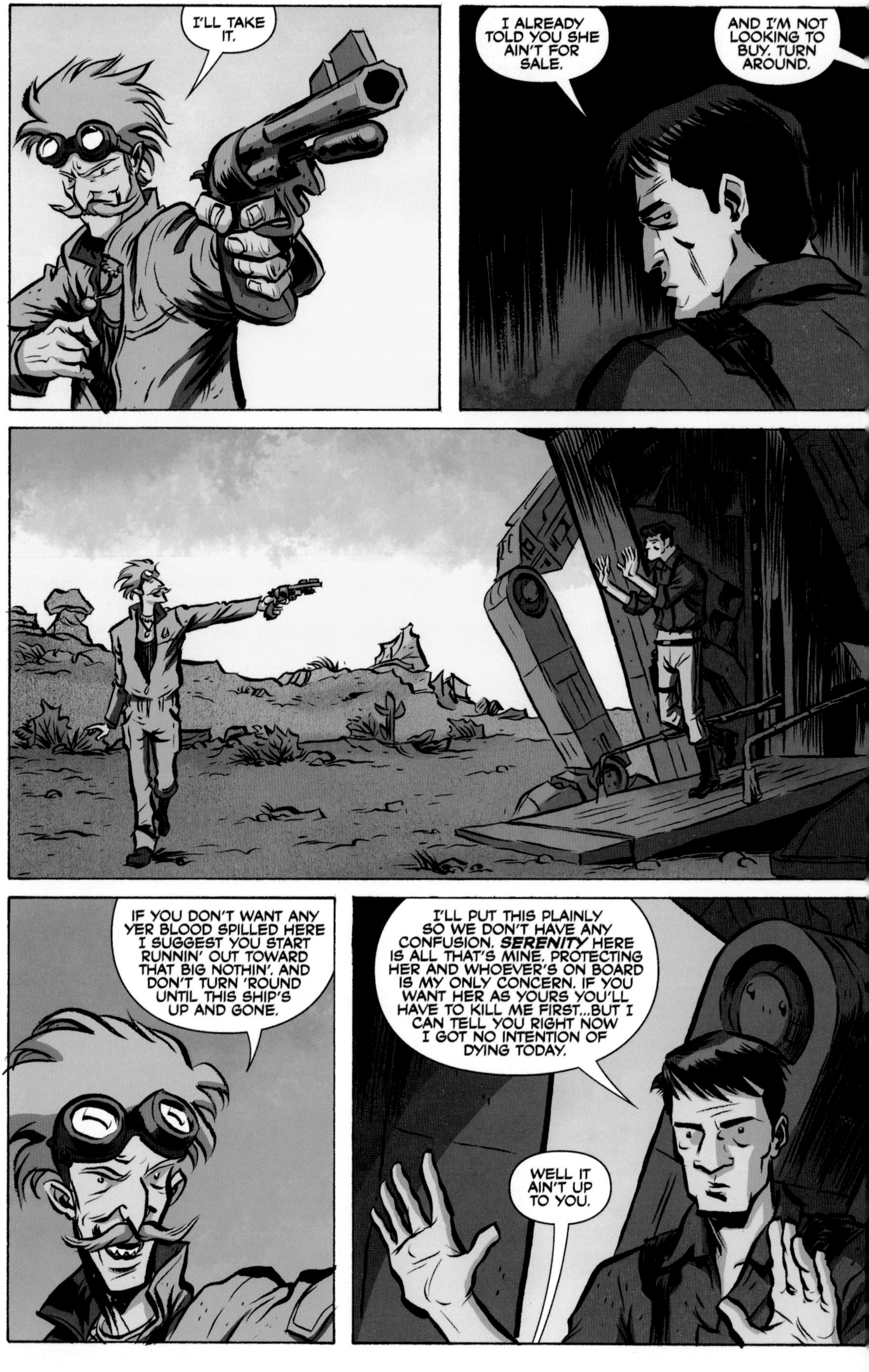
I'LL TAKE IT.
I ALREADY TOLD YOU SHE AIN'T FOR SALE.
AND I'M NOT LOOKING TO BUY. TURN AROUND.
IF YOU DON'T WANT ANY YER BLOOD SPILLED HERE I SUGGEST YOU START RUNNIN' OUT TOWARD THAT BIG NOTHIN', AND DON'T TURN 'ROUND UNTIL THIS SHIP'S UP AND GONE.
I'LL PUT THIS PLAINLY SO WE DON'T HAVE ANY CONFUSION. *SERENITY* HERE IS ALL THAT'S MINE. PROTECTING HER AND WHOEVER'S ON BOARD IS MY ONLY CONCERN. IF YOU WANT HER AS YOURS YOU'LL HAVE TO KILL ME FIRST...BUT I CAN TELL YOU RIGHT NOW I GOT NO INTENTION OF DYING TODAY.
WELL IT AIN'T UP TO YOU.

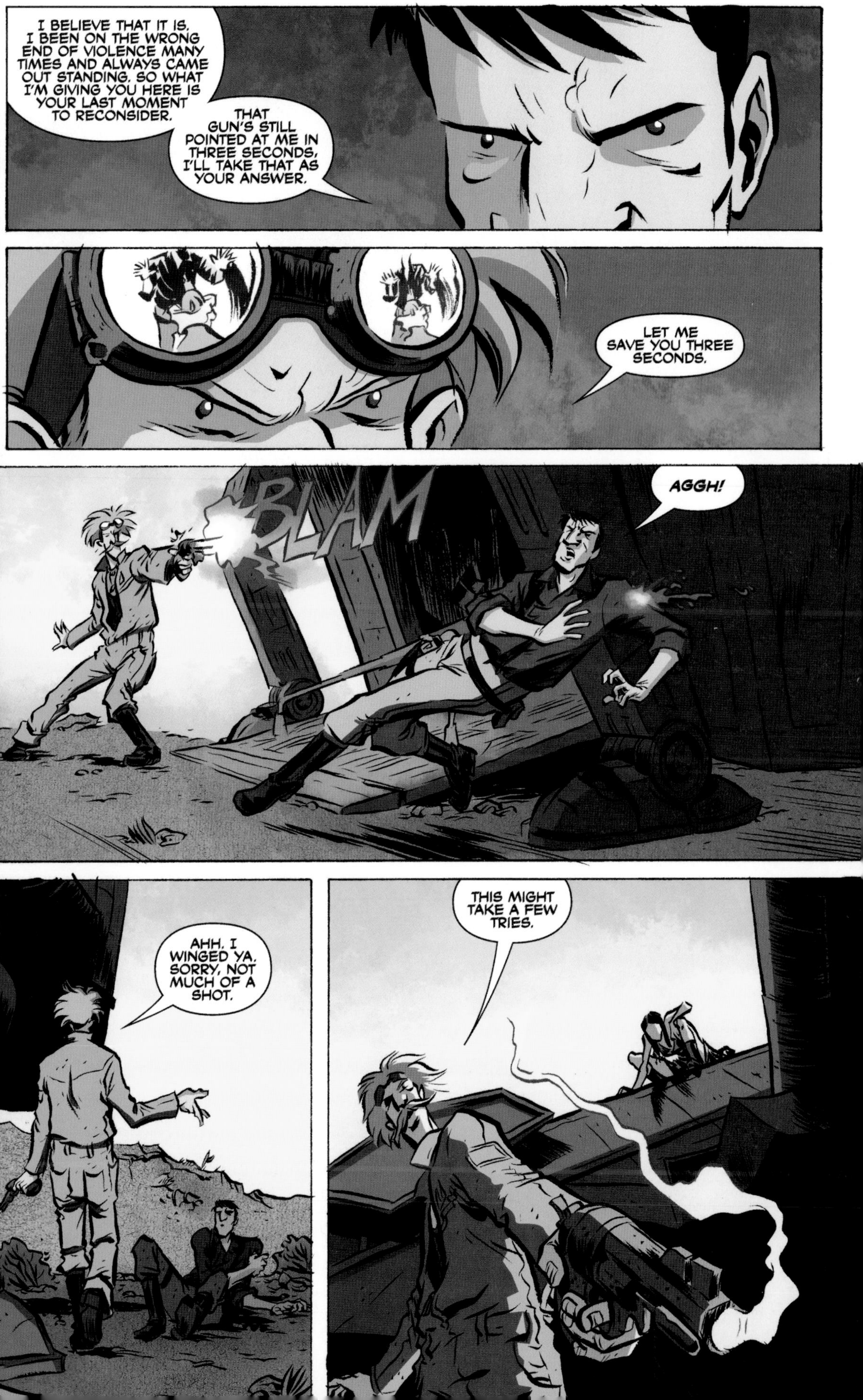
I BELIEVE THAT IT IS. I BEEN ON THE WRONG END OF VIOLENCE MANY TIMES AND ALWAYS CAME OUT STANDING. SO WHAT I'M GIVING YOU HERE IS YOUR LAST MOMENT TO RECONSIDER.
THAT GUN'S STILL POINTED AT ME IN THREE SECONDS, I'LL TAKE THAT AS YOUR ANSWER.
LET ME SAVE YOU THREE SECONDS.
BLAM
AGGH!
AHH. I WINGED YA. SORRY, NOT MUCH OF A SHOT.
THIS MIGHT TAKE A FEW TRIES.

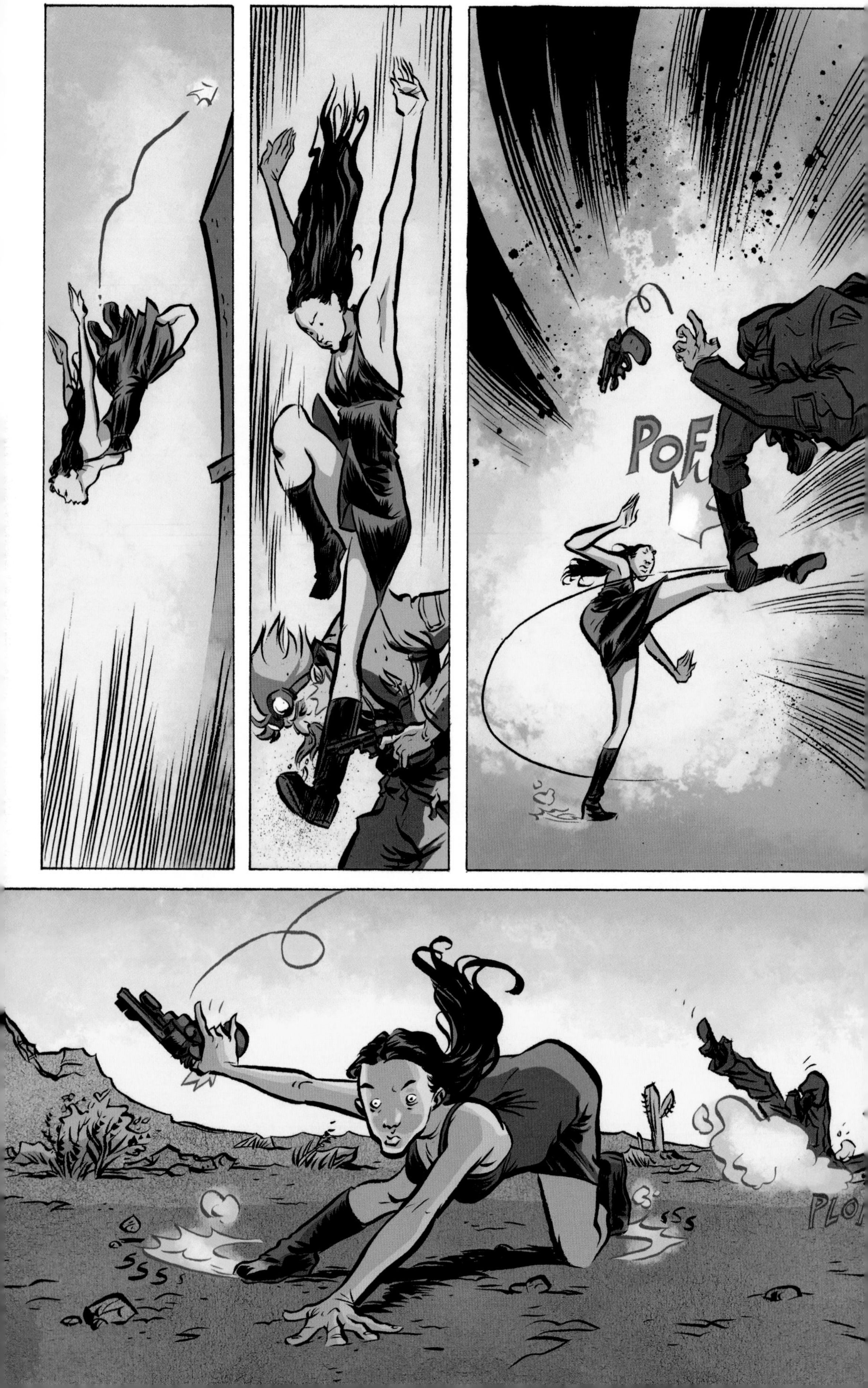

POF

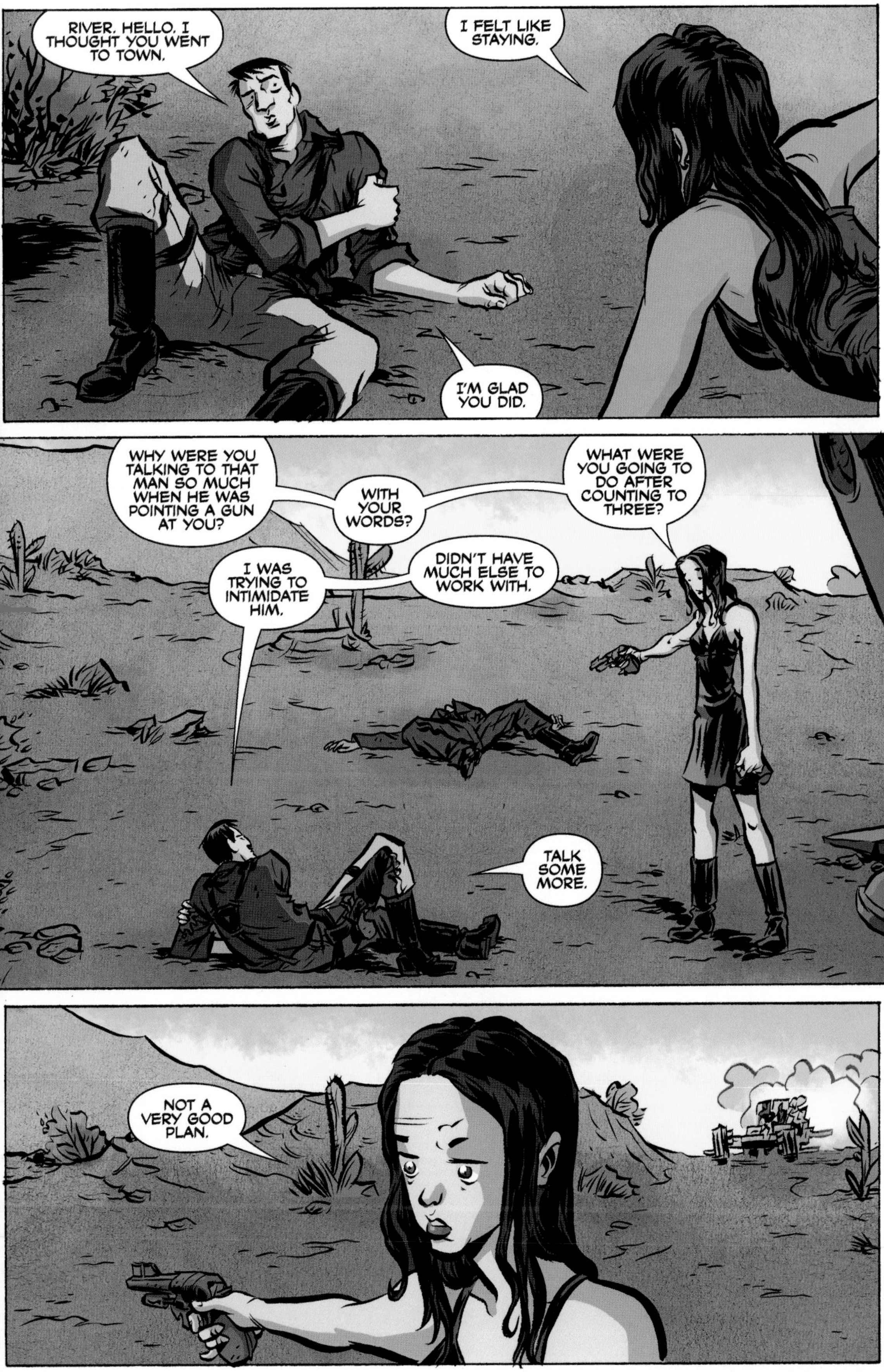
RIVER. HELLO. I THOUGHT YOU WENT TO TOWN.
I FELT LIKE STAYING.
I'M GLAD YOU DID.
WHY WERE YOU TALKING TO THAT MAN SO MUCH WHEN HE WAS POINTING A GUN AT YOU?
I WAS TRYING TO INTIMIDATE HIM.
WITH YOUR WORDS?
DIDN'T HAVE MUCH ELSE TO WORK WITH.
WHAT WERE YOU GOING TO DO AFTER COUNTING TO THREE?
TALK SOME MORE.
NOT A VERY GOOD PLAN.

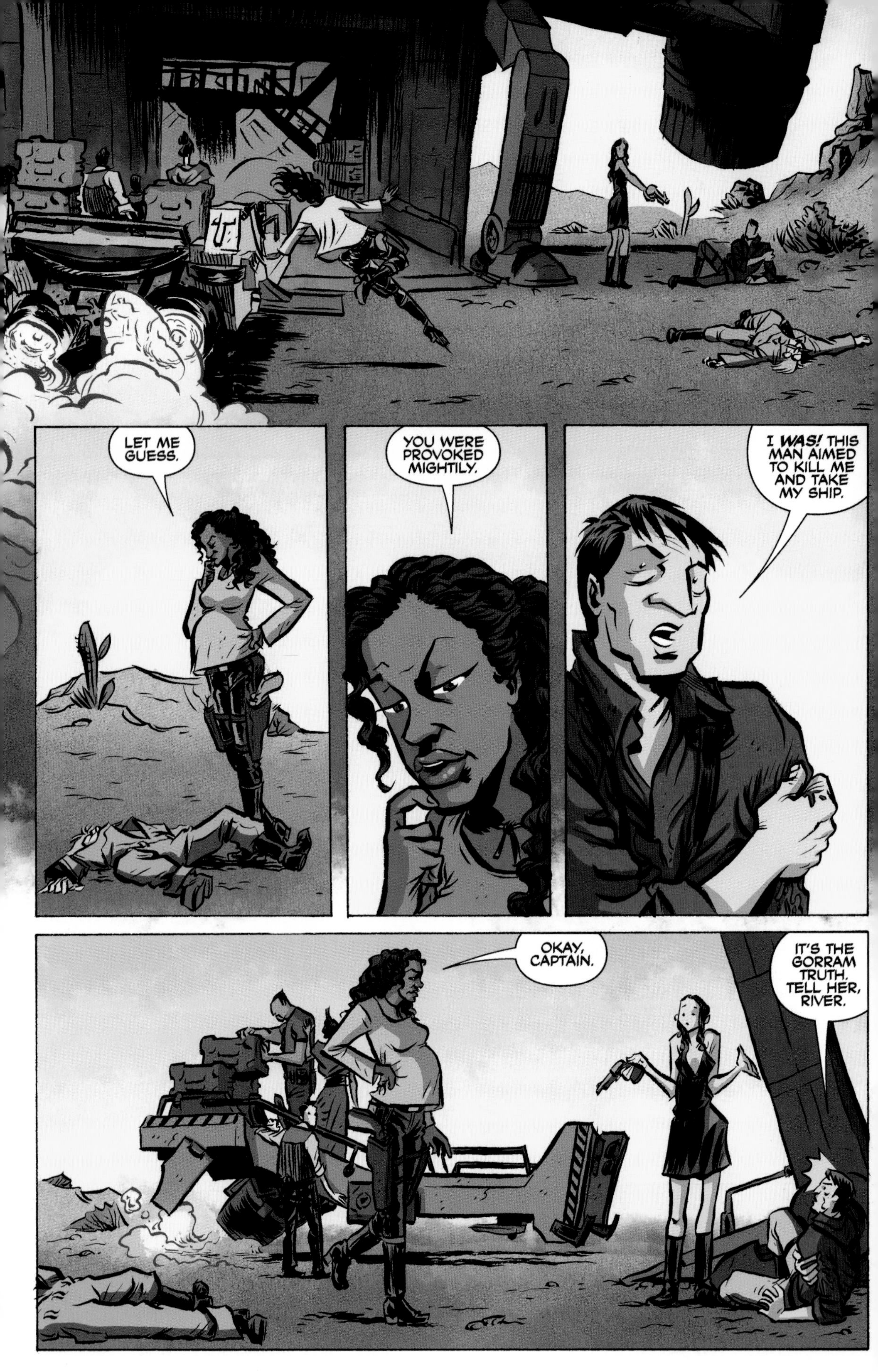
LET ME GUESS.
YOU WERE PROVOKED MIGHTILY.
I WAS! THIS MAN AIMED TO KILL ME AND TAKE MY SHIP.
OKAY, CAPTAIN.
IT'S THE GORRAM TRUTH. TELL HER, RIVER.

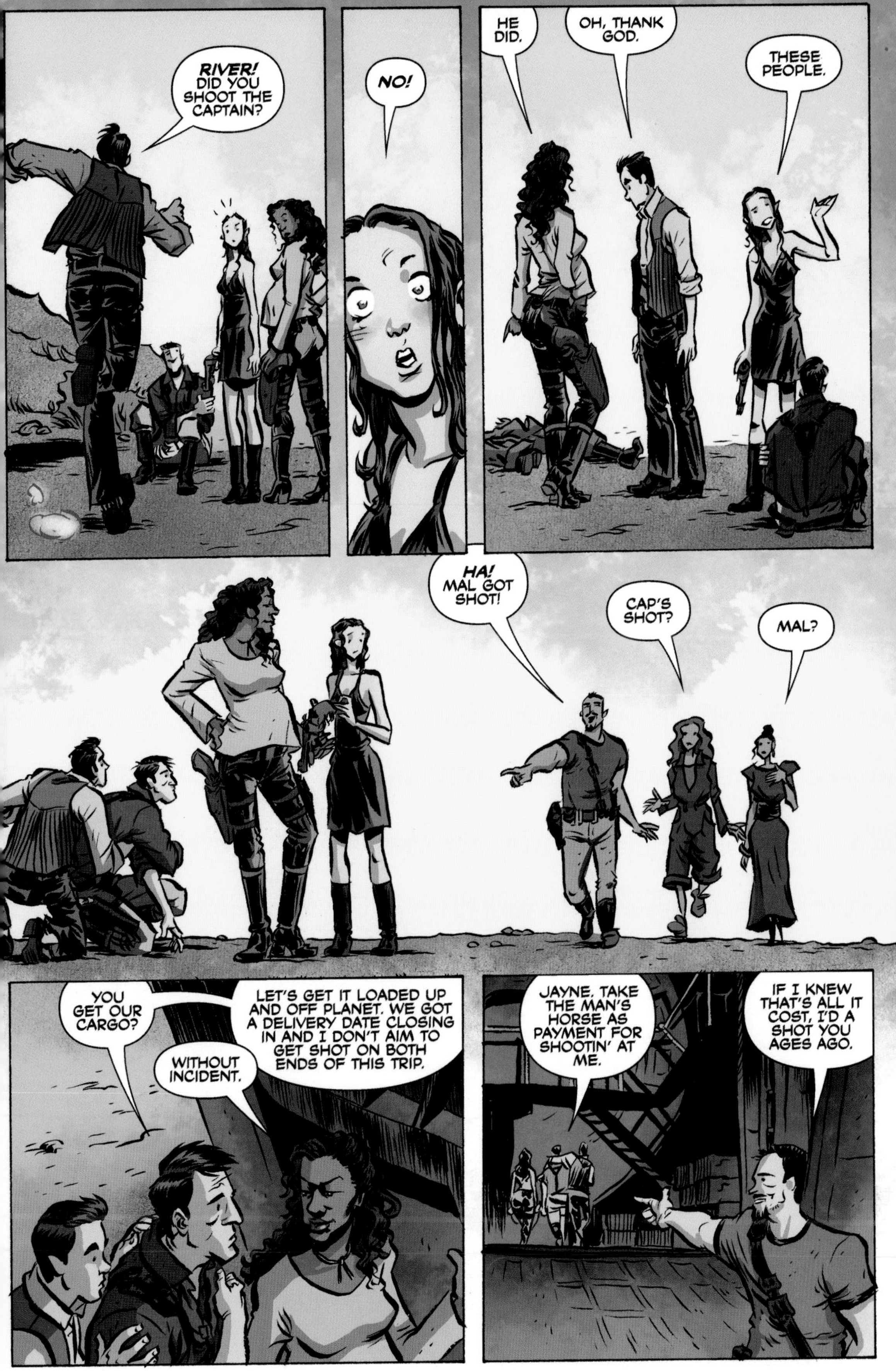
RIVER! DID YOU SHOOT THE CAPTAIN?
NO!
HE DID.
OH, THANK GOD.
THESE PEOPLE.
HA! MAL GOT SHOT!
CAP'S SHOT?
MAL?
YOU GET OUR CARGO?
WITHOUT INCIDENT.
LET'S GET IT LOADED UP AND OFF PLANET. WE GOT A DELIVERY DATE CLOSING IN AND I DON'T AIM TO GET SHOT ON BOTH ENDS OF THIS TRIP.
JAYNE, TAKE THE MAN'S HORSE AS PAYMENT FOR SHOOTIN' AT ME.
IF I KNEW THAT'S ALL IT COST, I'D A SHOT YOU AGES AGO.

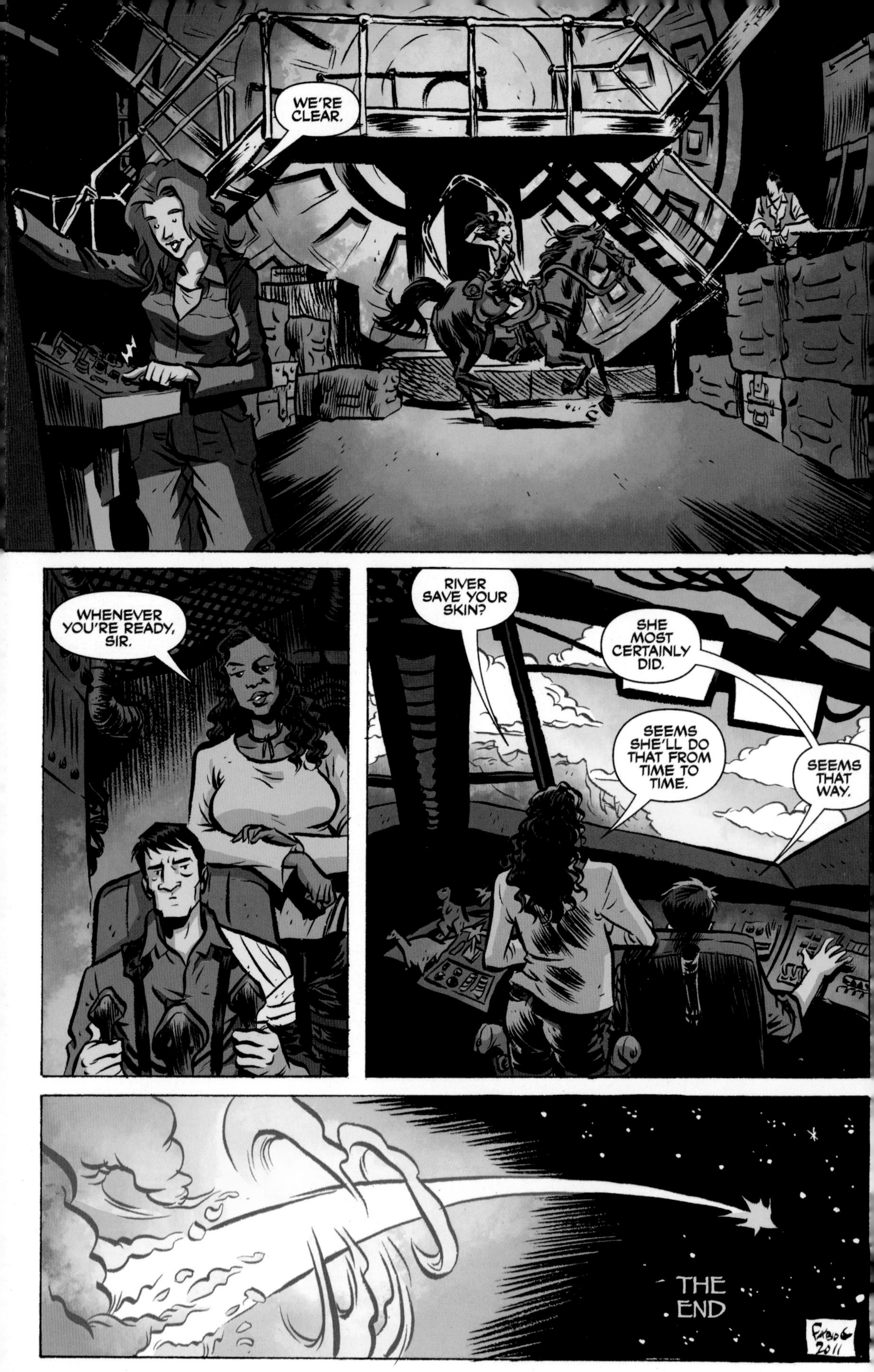
WE'RE CLEAR.
WHENEVER YOU'RE READY, SIR.
RIVER SAVE YOUR SKIN?
SHE MOST CERTAINLY DID.
SEEMS SHE'LL DO THAT FROM TIME TO TIME.
SEEMS THAT WAY.
THE END
2011

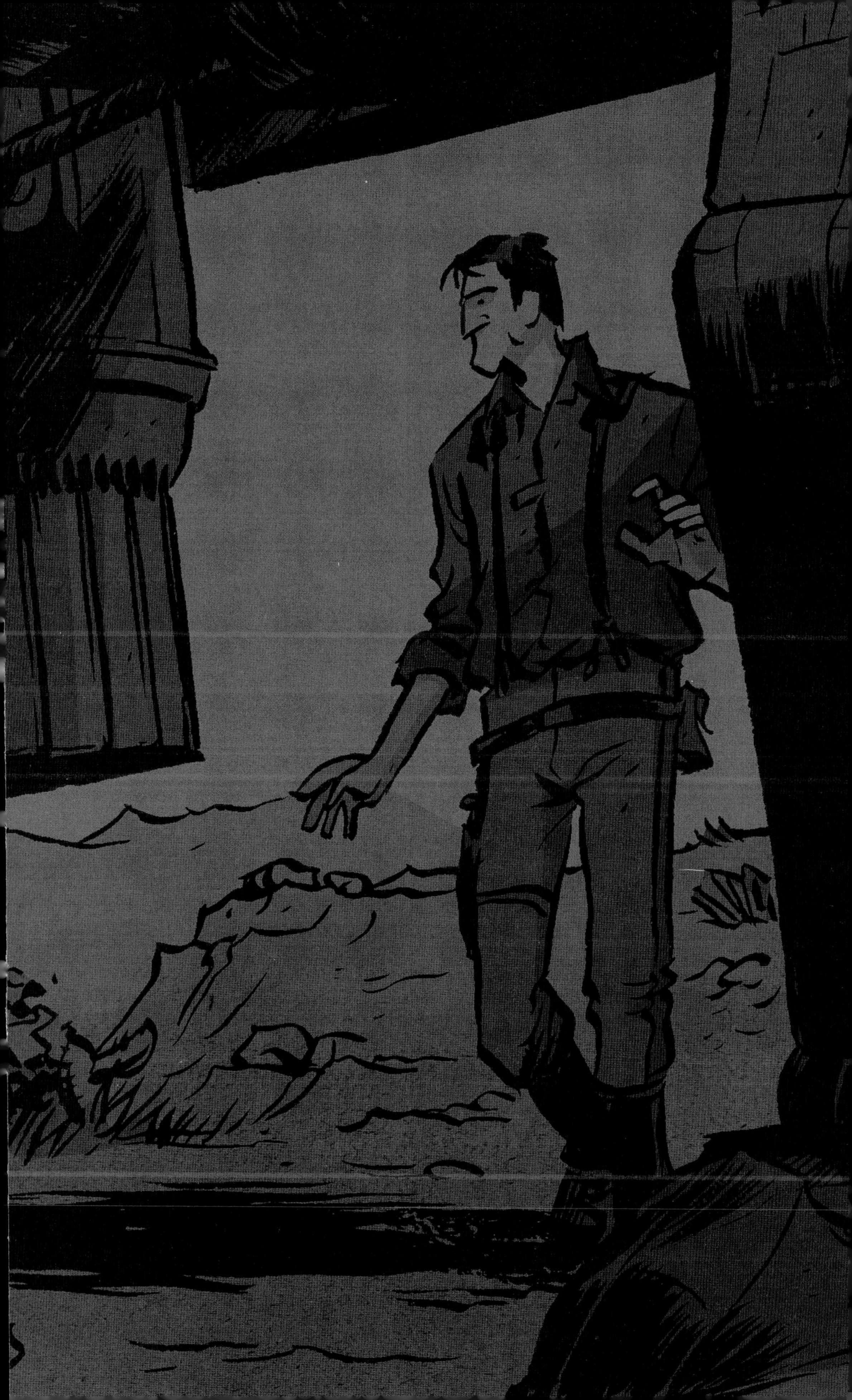

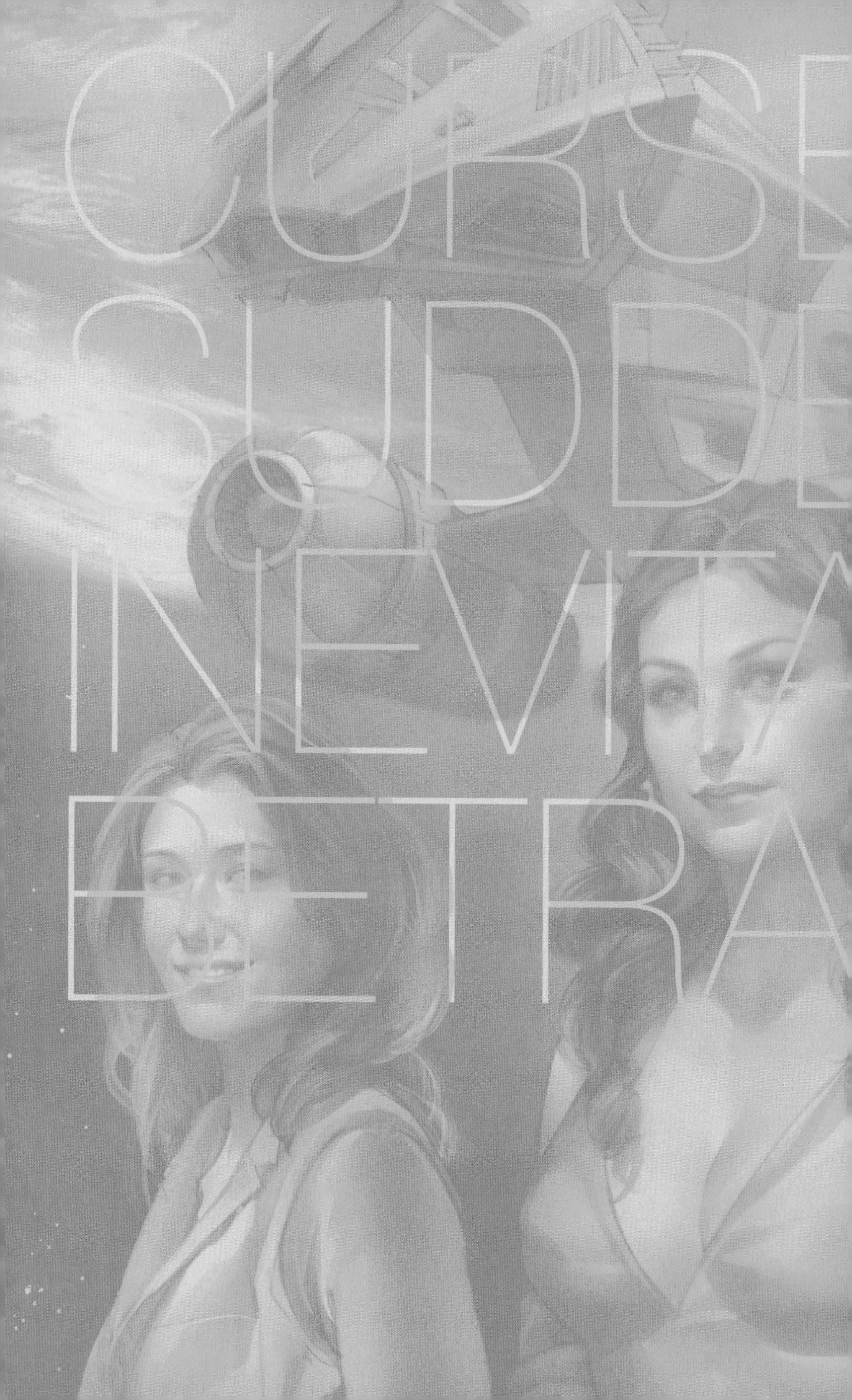
CURSE
SUDDE
INEVITA
DETRA

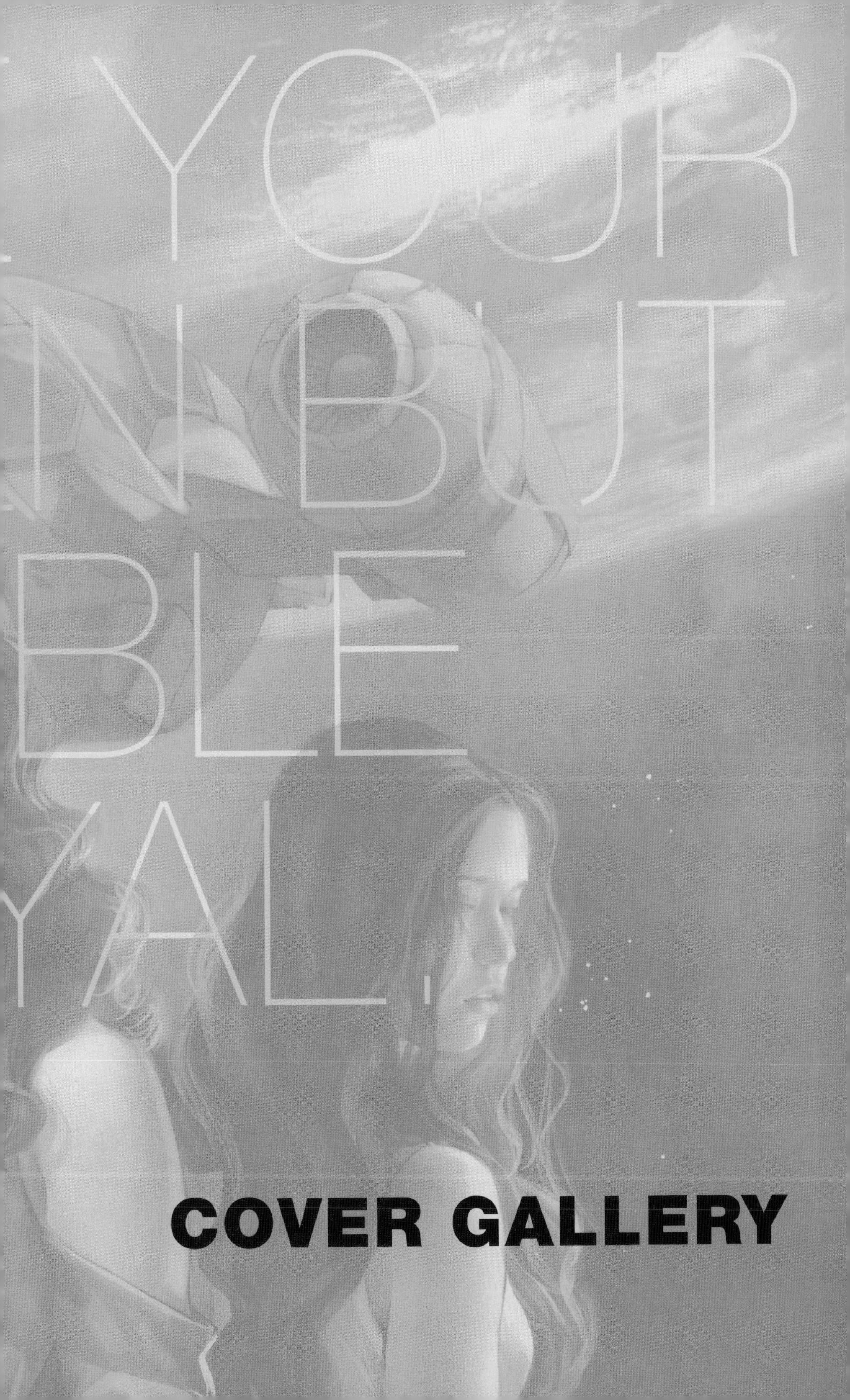

COVER GALLERY

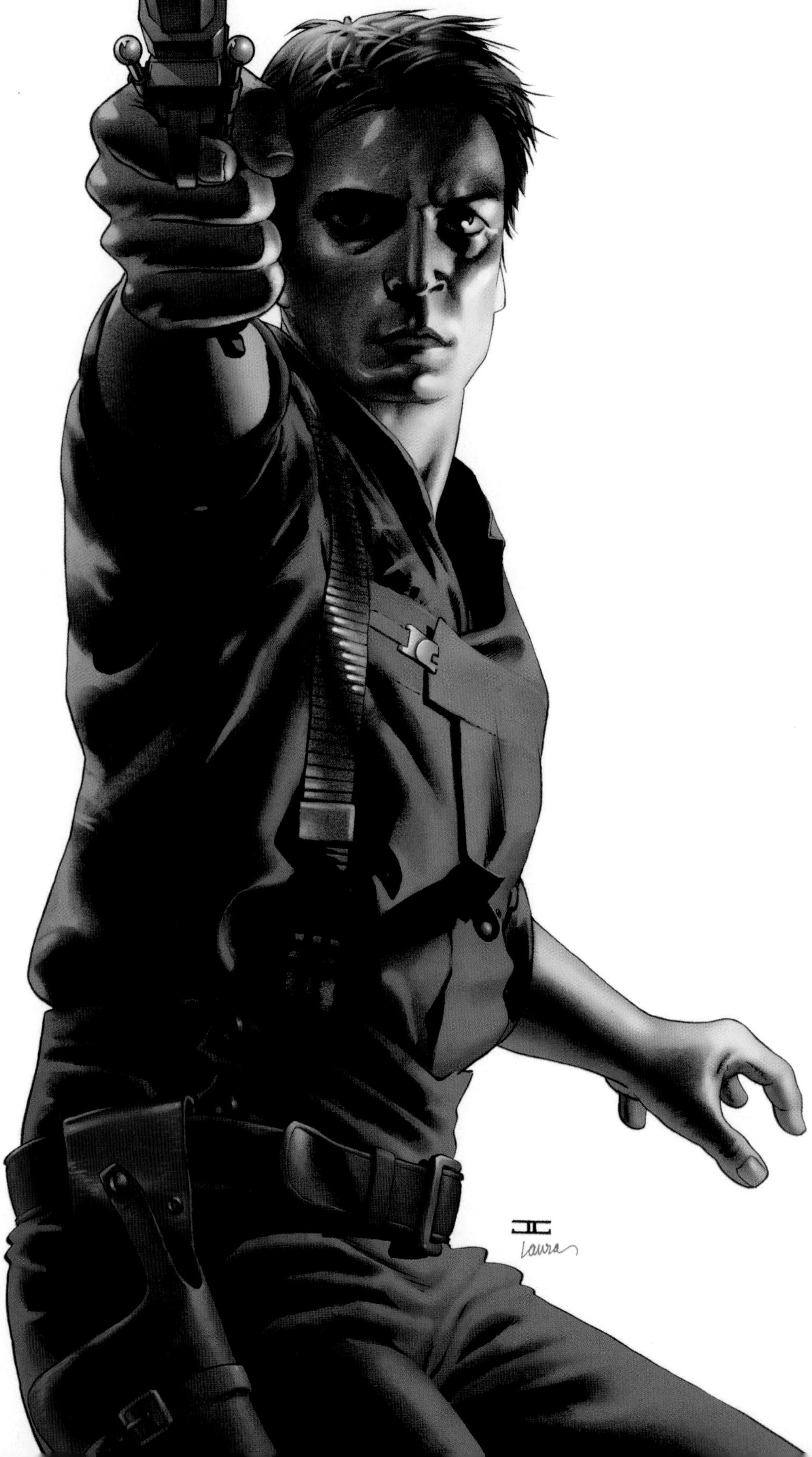

Serenity: Those Left Behind #1 Cover by
John Cassaday
with colors by **Laura Martin**

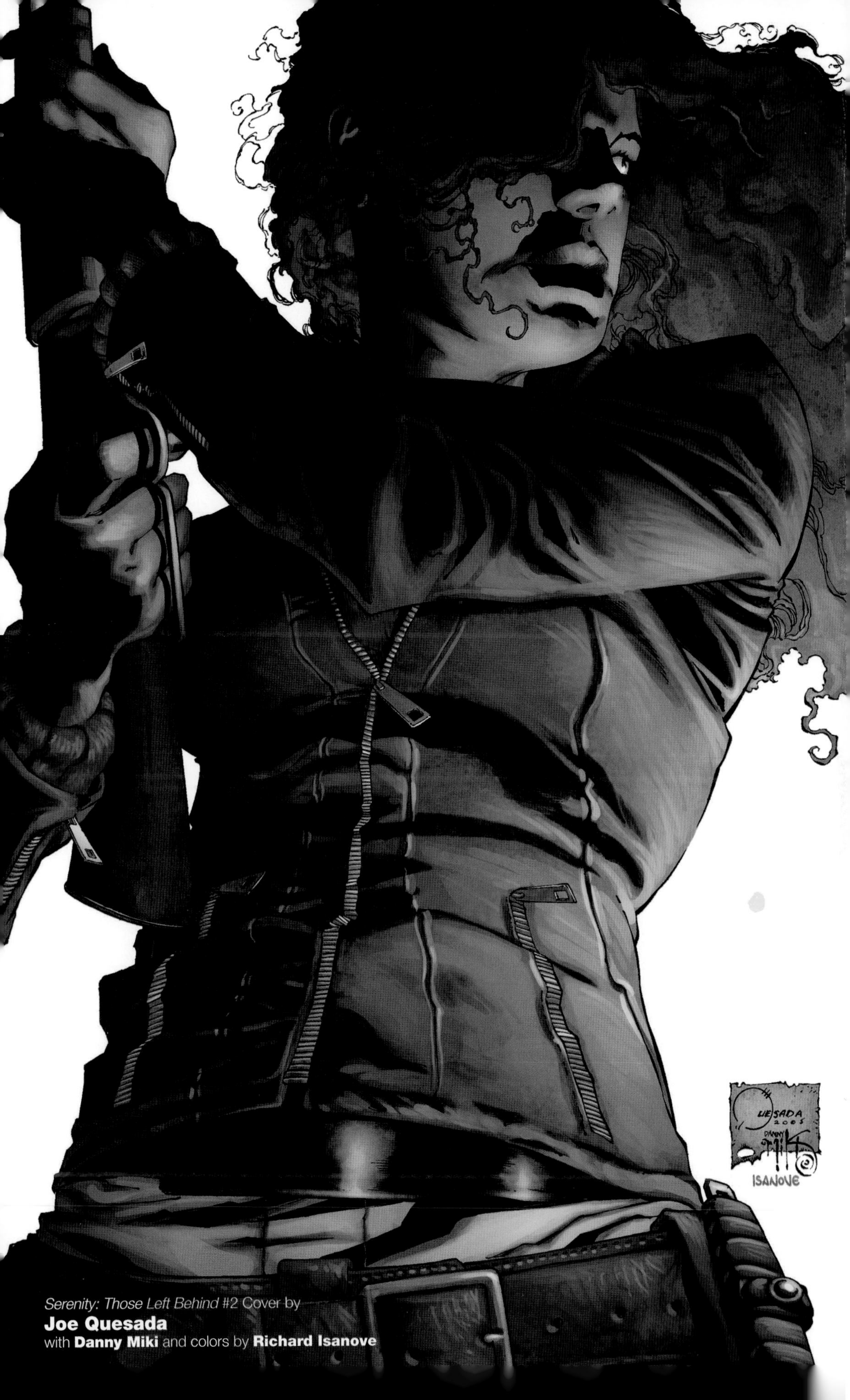
ISANOVE

Serenity: Those Left Behind #2 Cover by
Joe Quesada
with **Danny Miki** and colors by **Richard Isanove**

Serenity: Those Left Behind #3 Variant Cover by
Sean Phillips

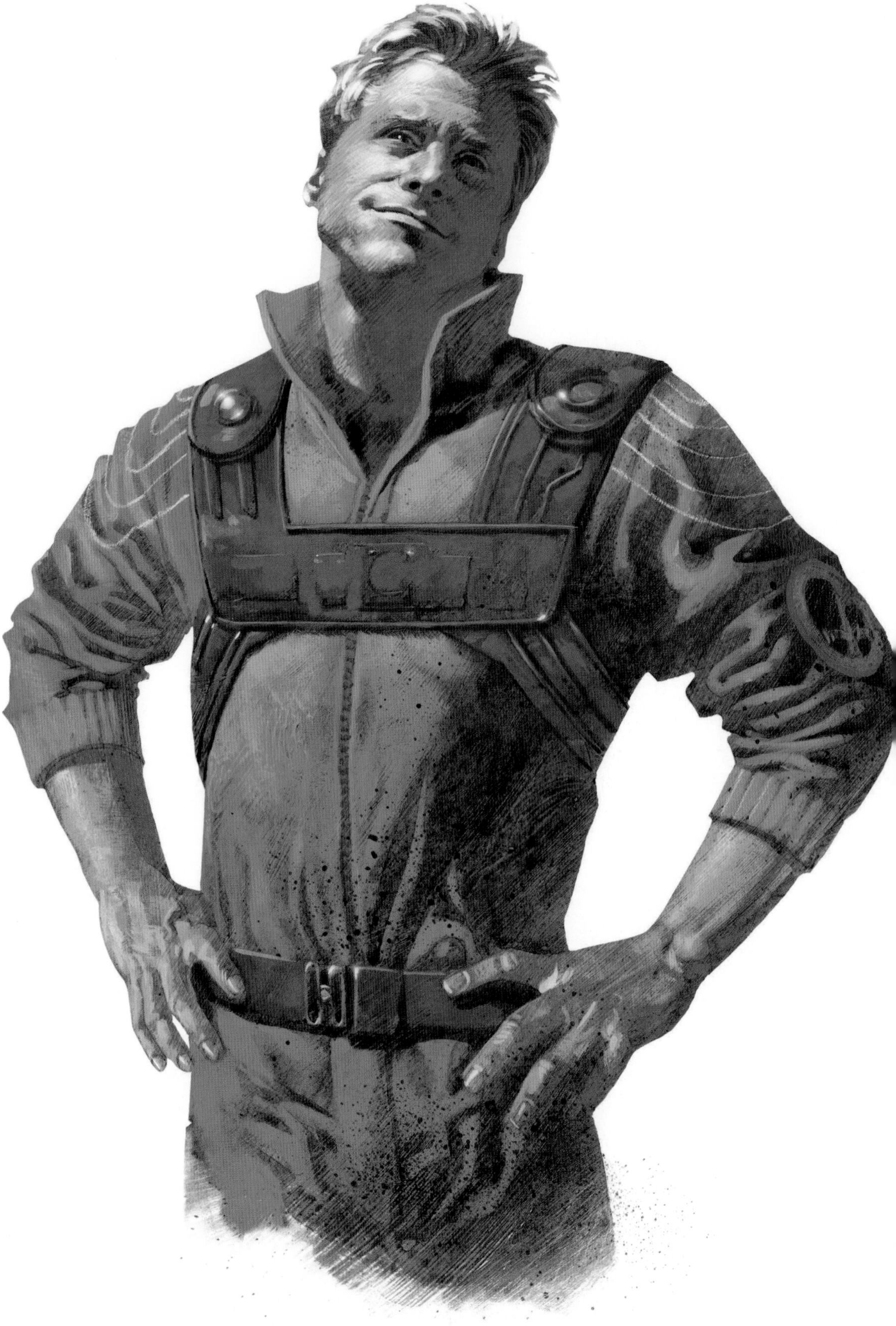

Serenity: Those Left Behind #1 Variant Cover by
JG Jones
with colors by **Laura Martin**

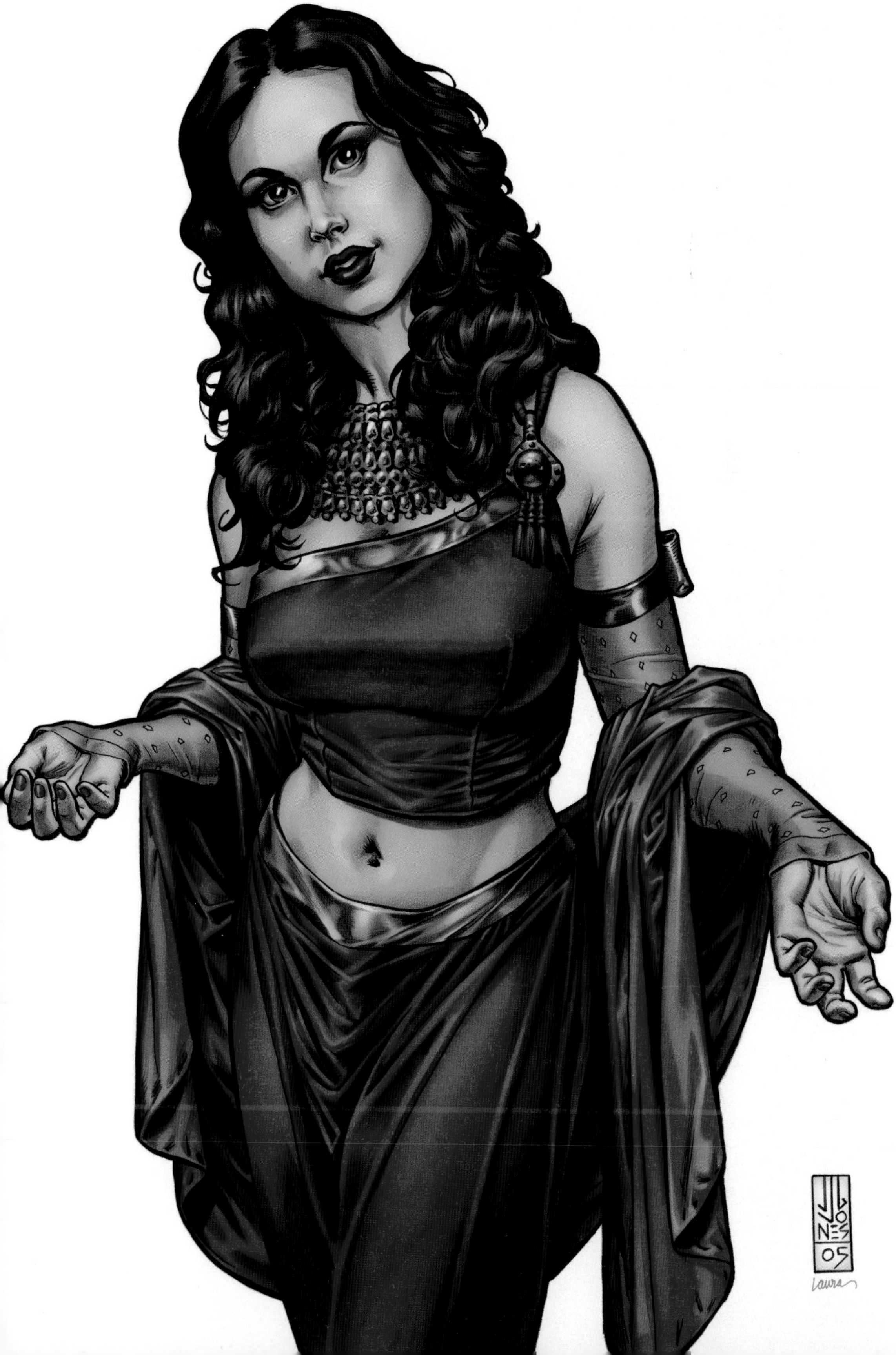

Serenity: Those Left Behind #2 Variant Cover by
Jo Chen

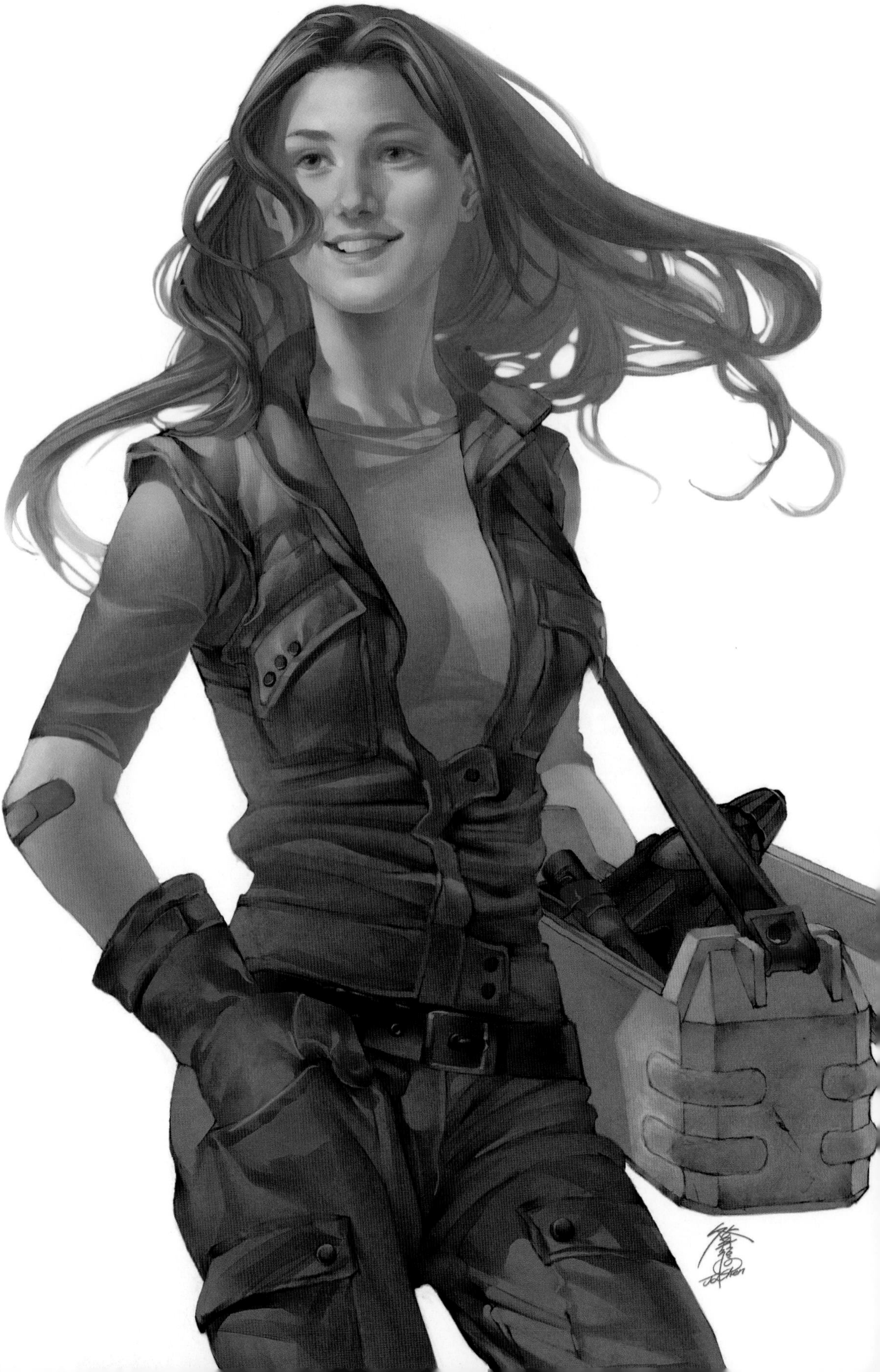

Serenity: Those Left Behind #1 Variant Cover by
Bryan Hitch
with colors by **Laura Martin**

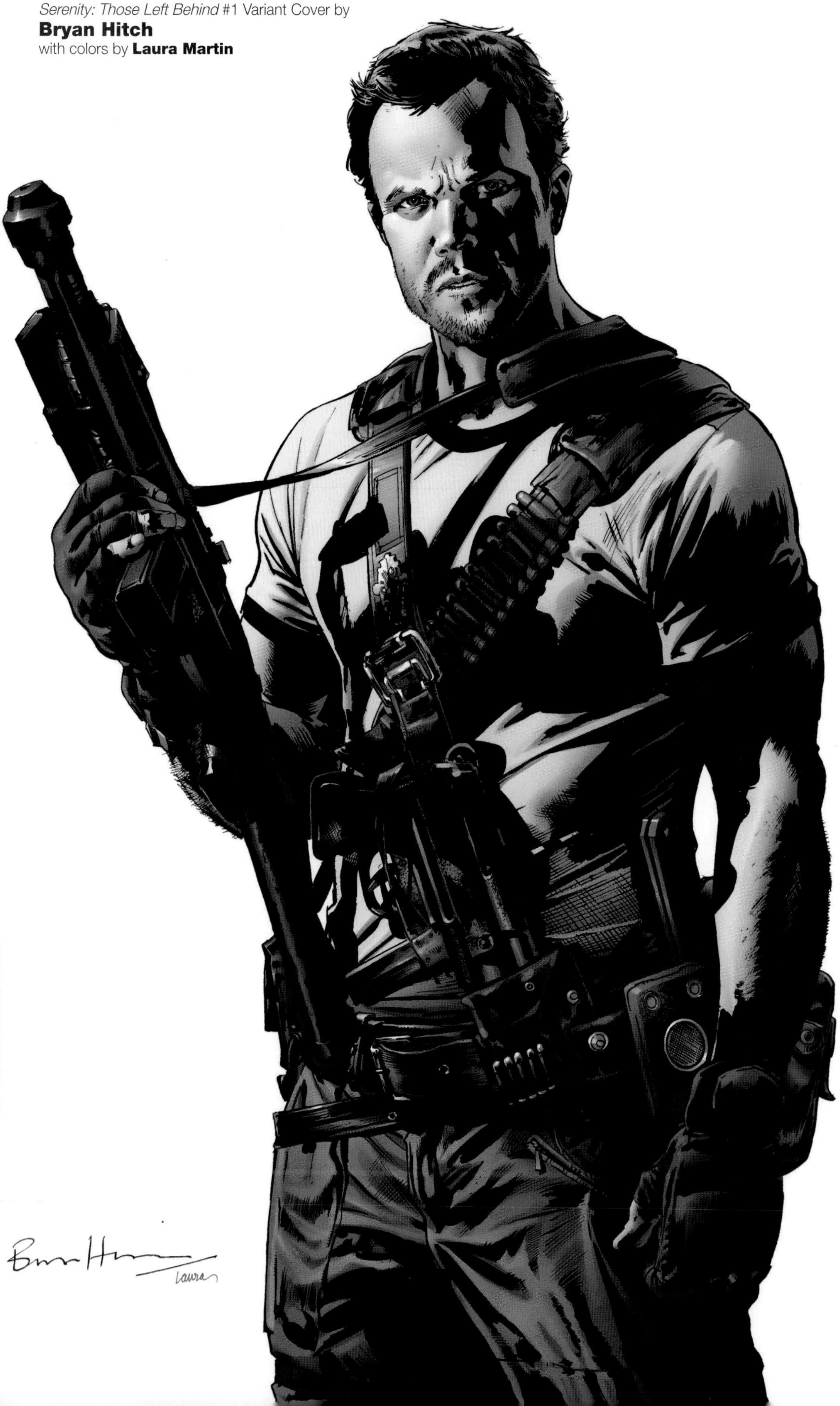

Serenity: Those Left Behind #3 Variant Cover by
Leinil Yu

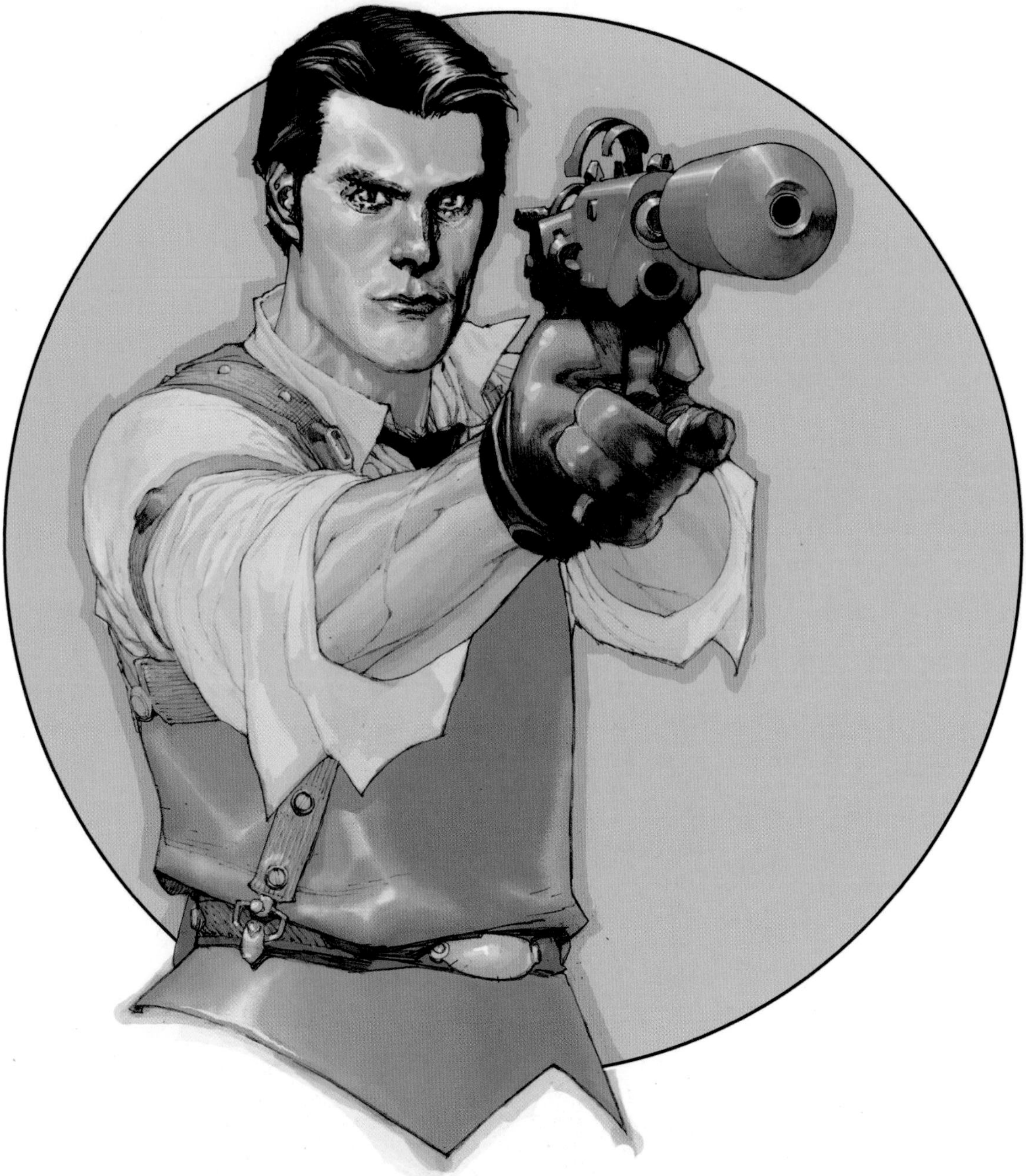

Serenity: Those Left Behind #3 Cover by
Joshua Middleton

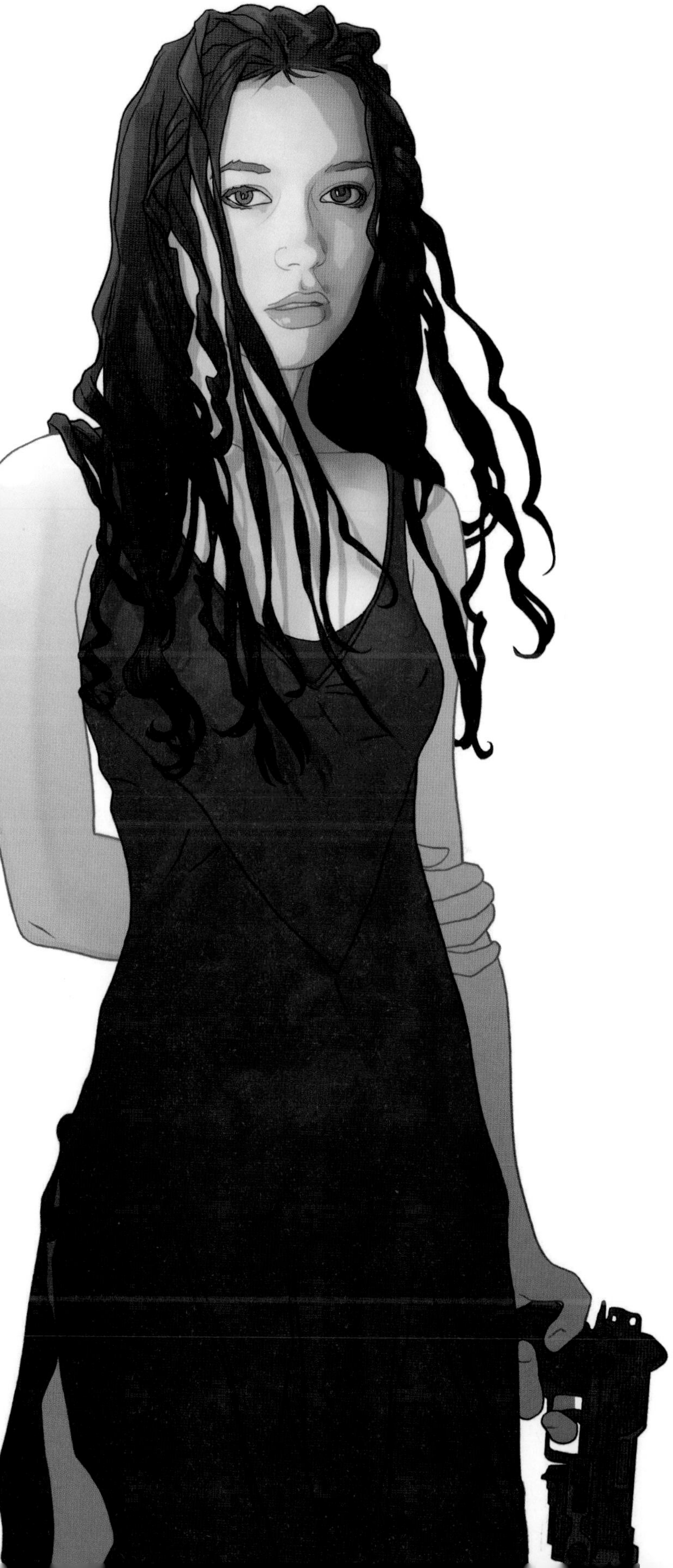

Serenity: Those Left Behind #2 Variant Cover by

Tim Bradstreet

with colors by **Grant Goleash**

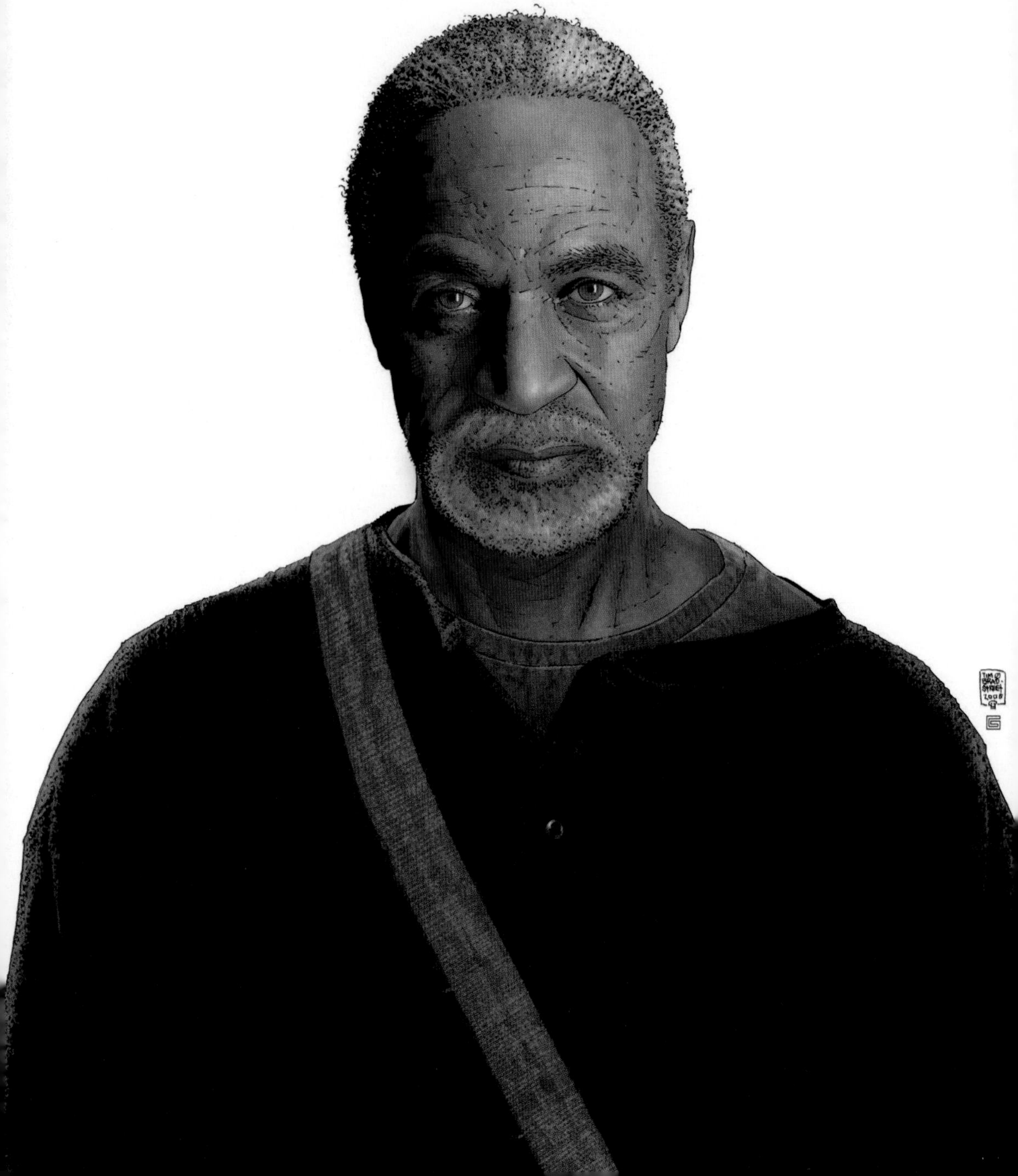

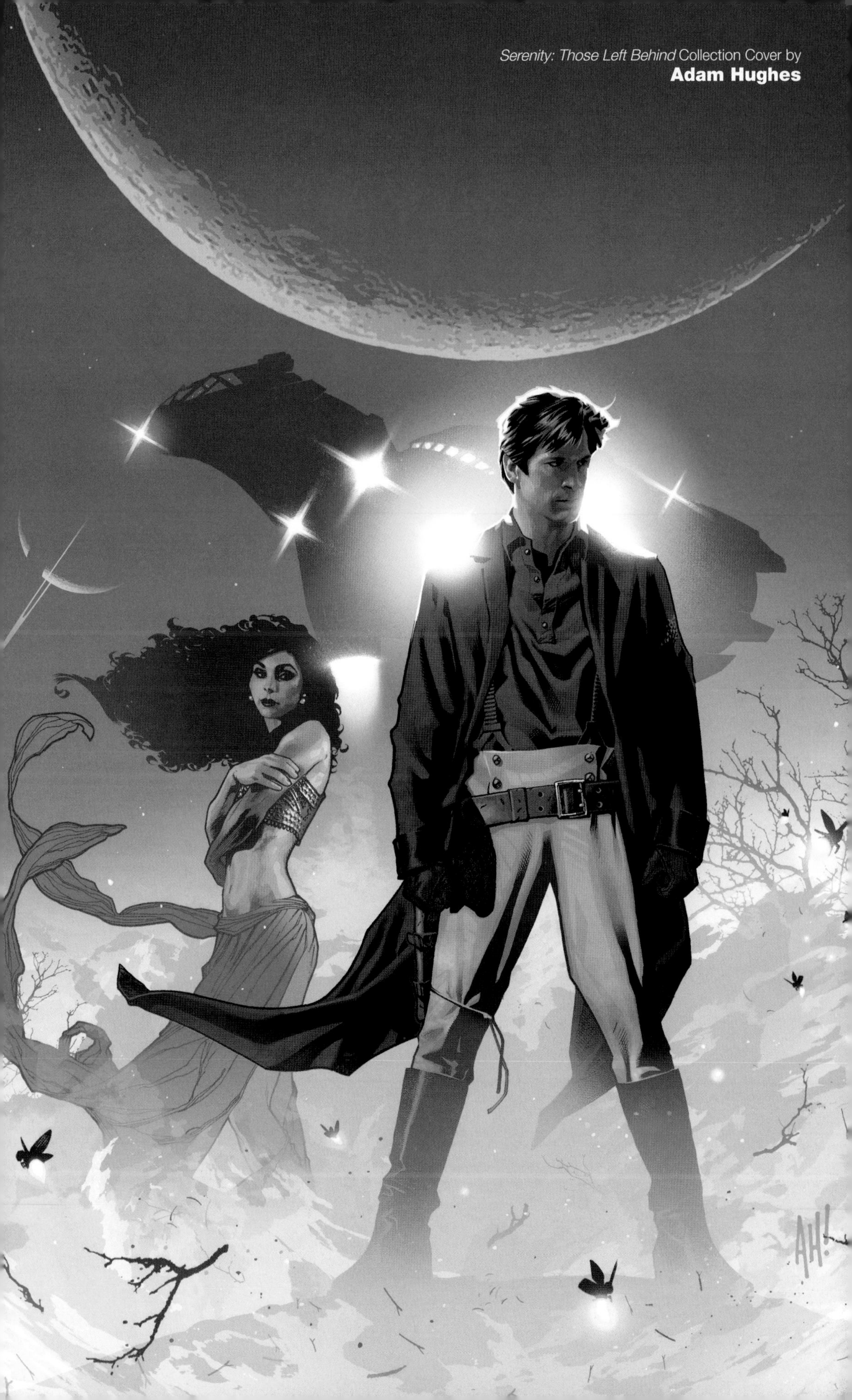

Serenity: Those Left Behind Collection Cover by
Adam Hughes

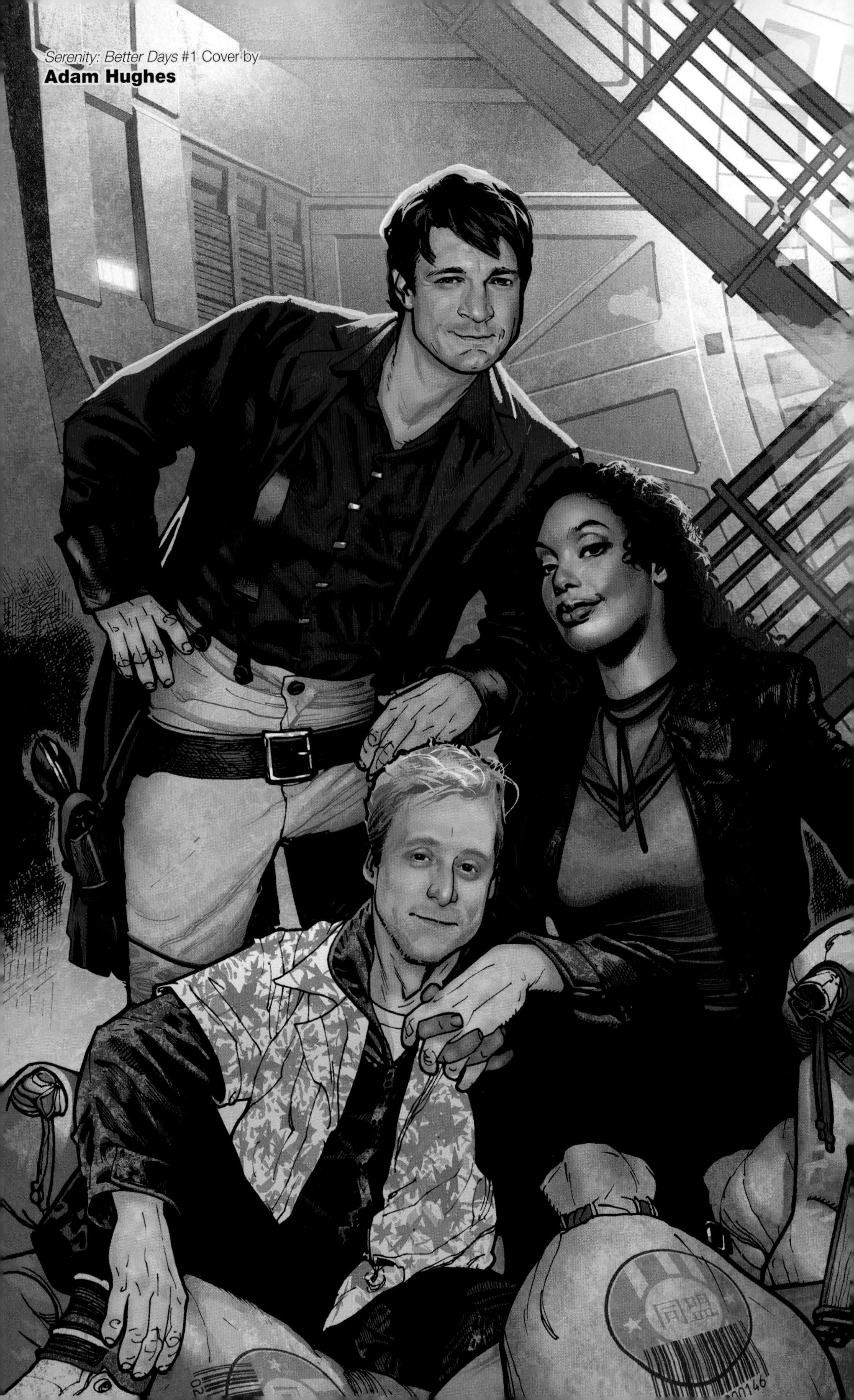
同盟

Serenity: Better Days #1 Cover by
Adam Hughes

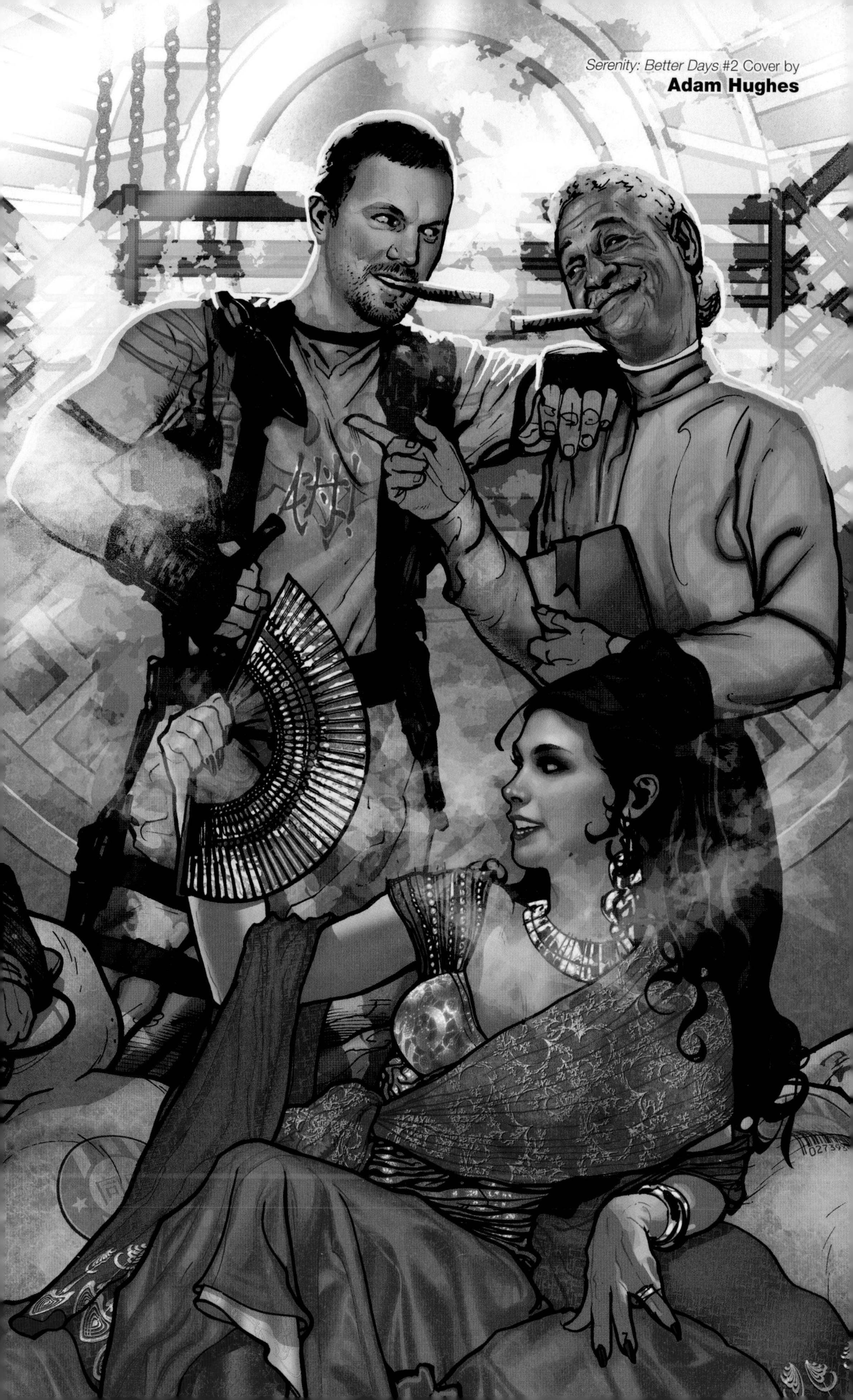

Serenity: Better Days #2 Cover by
Adam Hughes

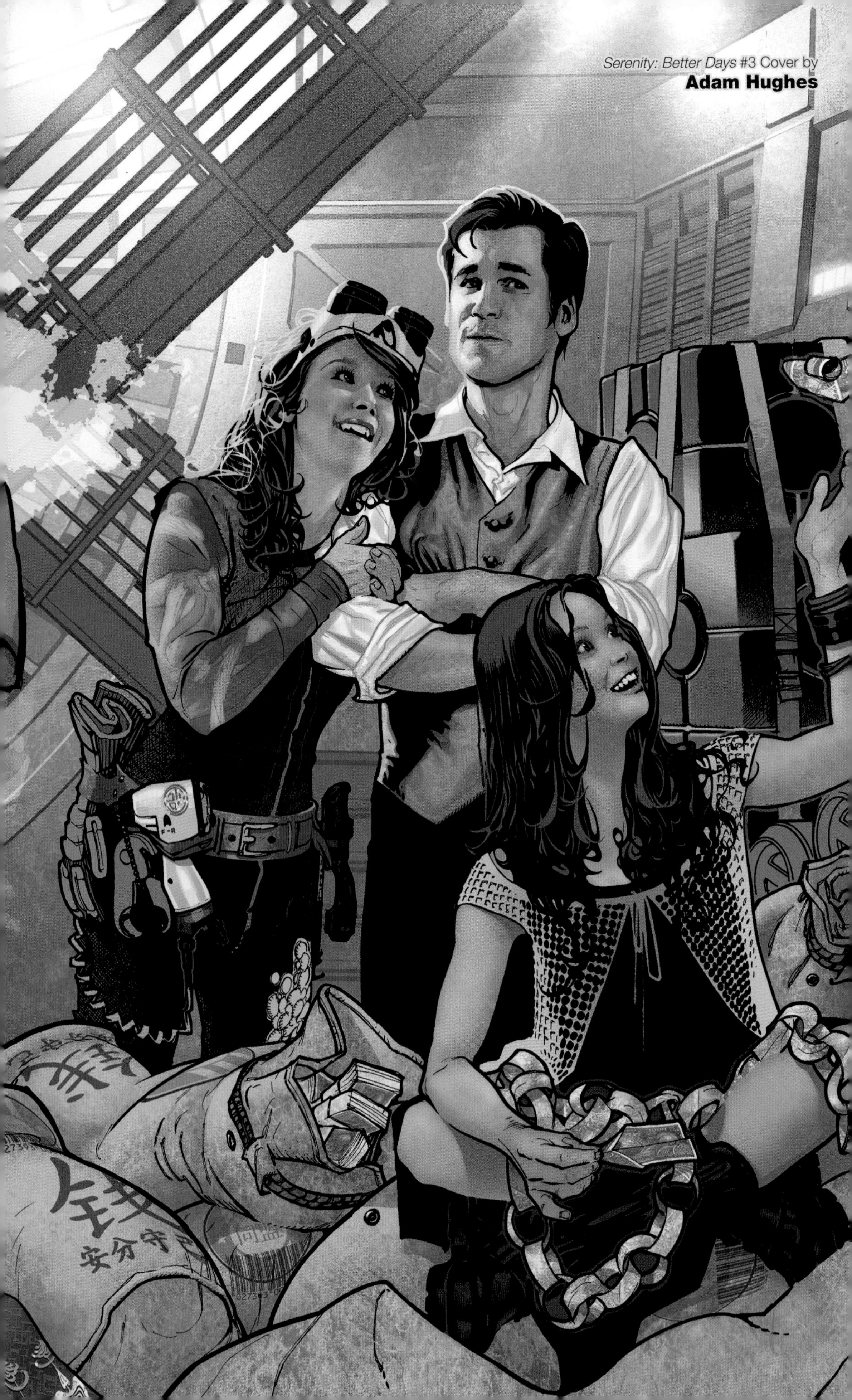
钱
安分守

Serenity: Better Days #3 Cover by
Adam Hughes

Serenity: Better Days Collection Cover by
Jo Chen

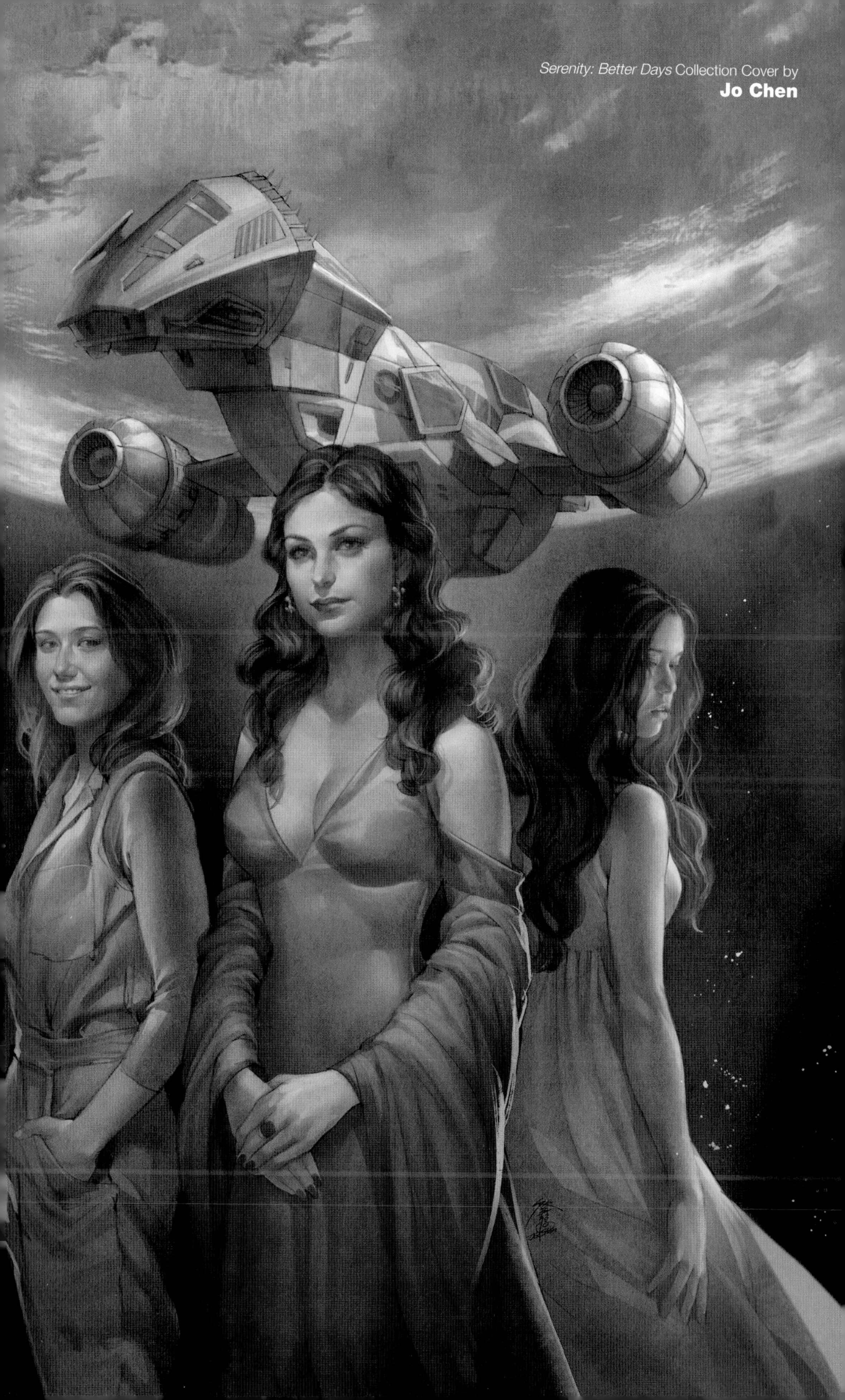

Serenity: The Shepherd's Tale Cover by
Steve Morris

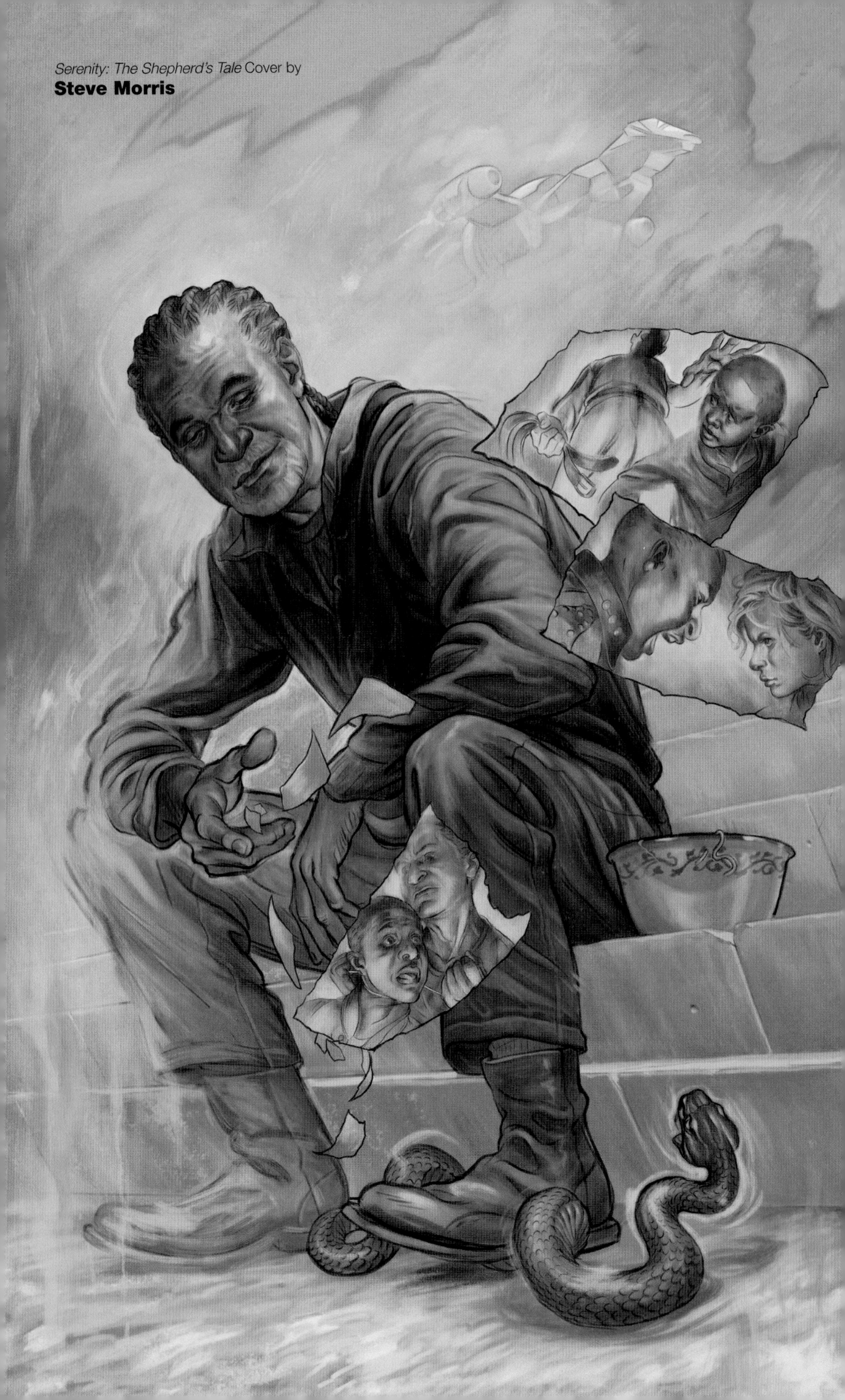

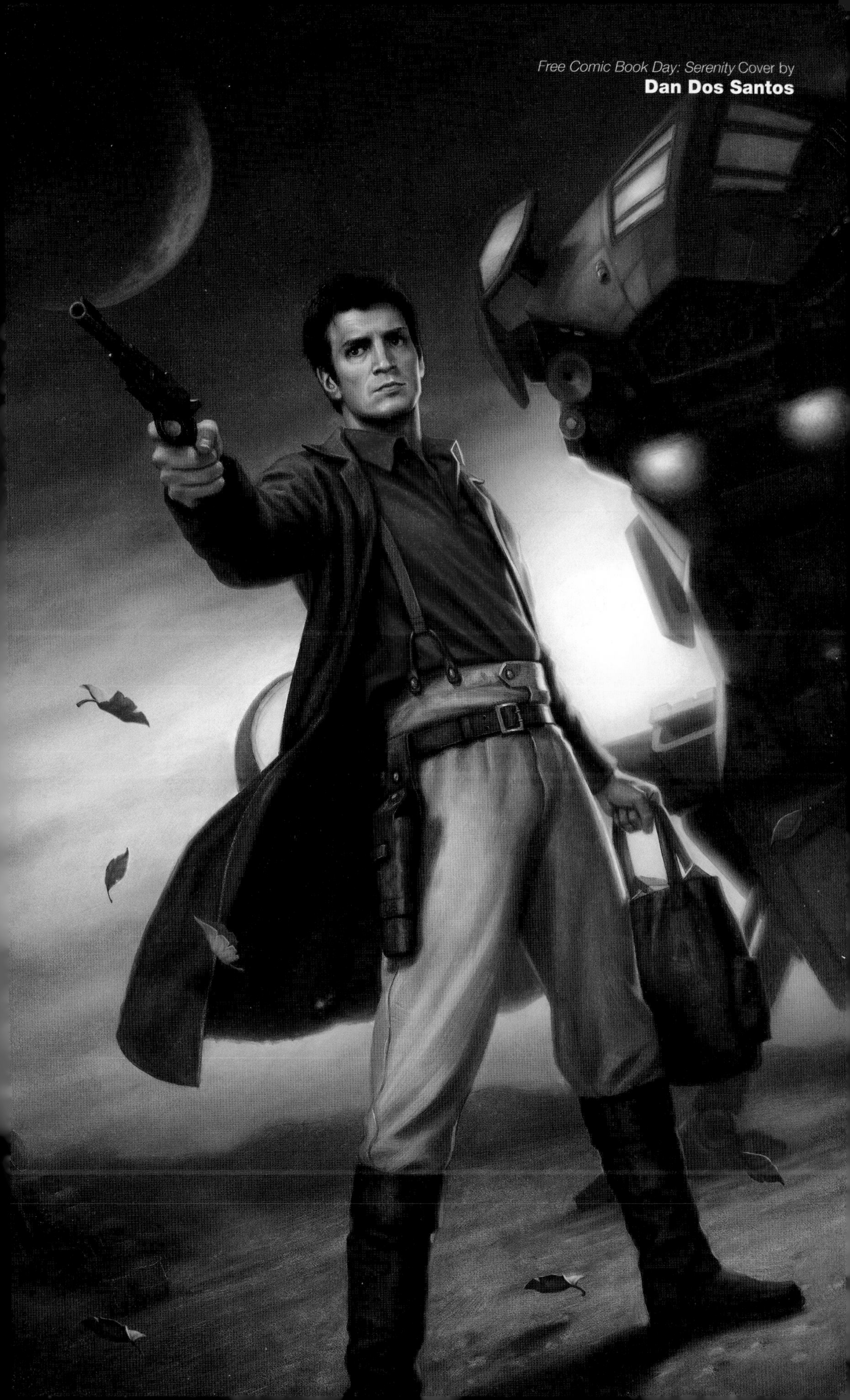

Free Comic Book Day: Serenity Cover by
Dan Dos Santos

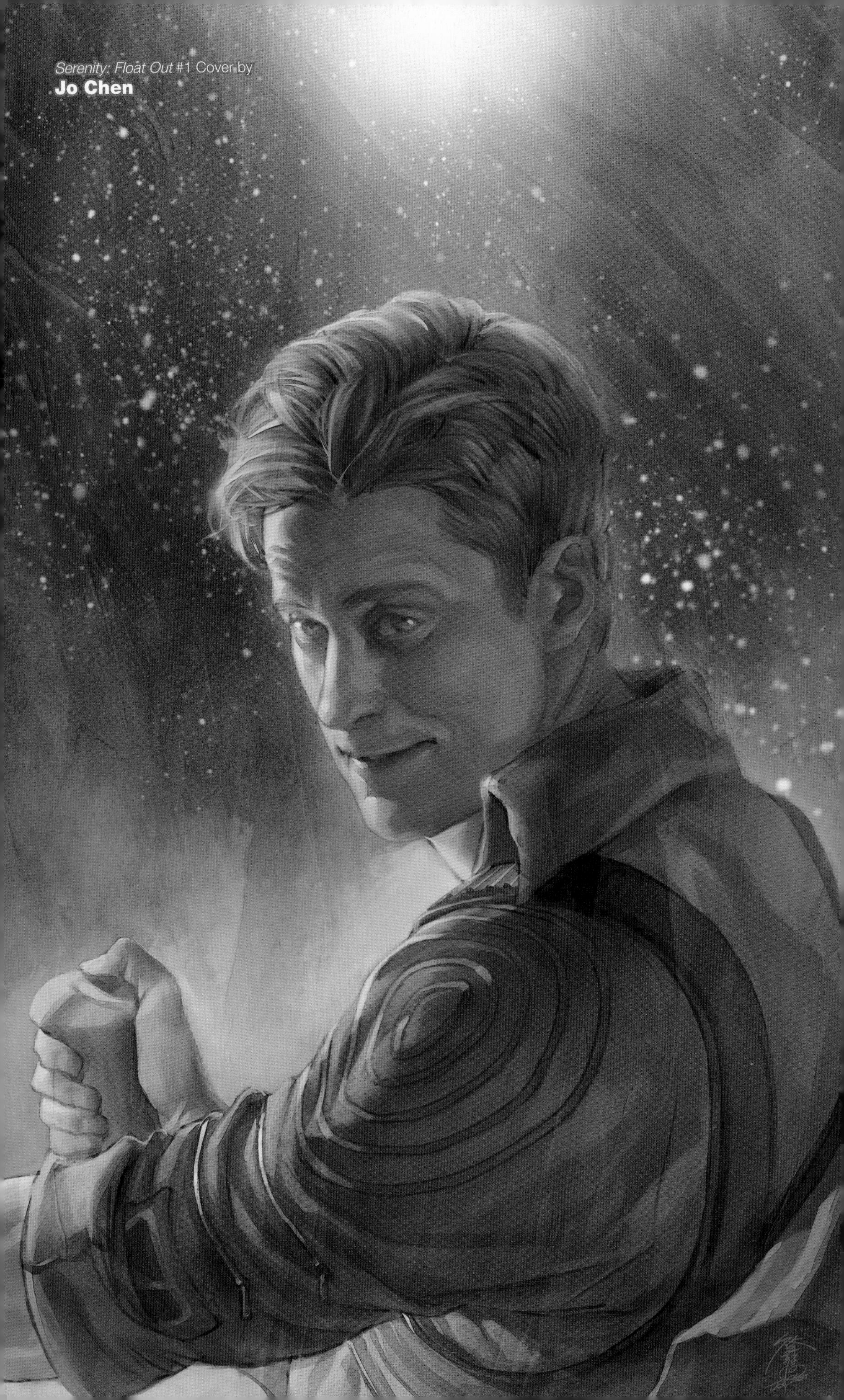

Serenity: Float Out #1 Cover by
Jo Chen

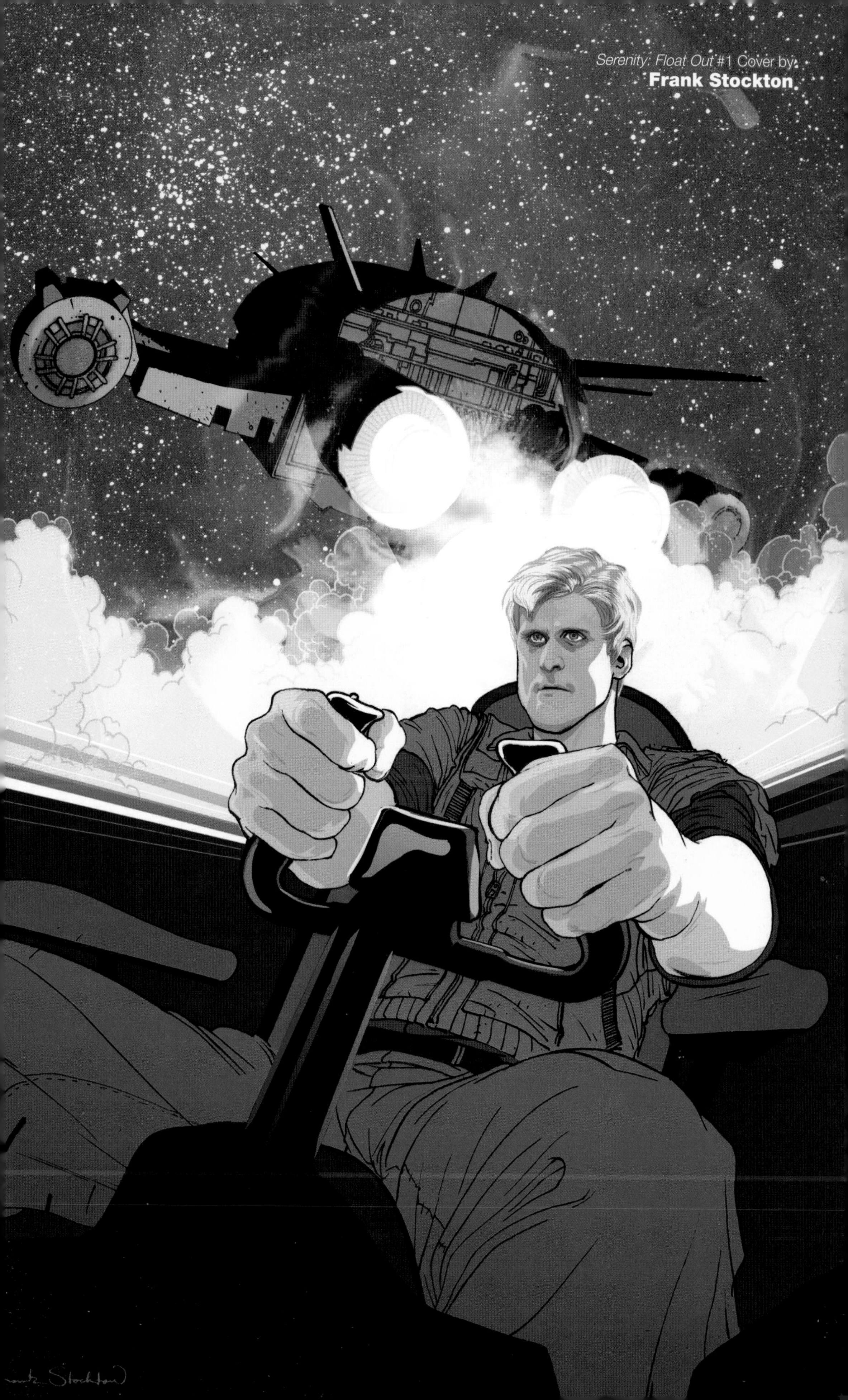

Serenity: Float Out #1 Cover by:
Frank Stockton

DISCOVER
VISIONARY CREATORS

THE WOODS
JAMES TYNION IV • MICHAEL DIALYNAS
VOL. 1
THE ARROW

"The Spire is fantastic! My kind of genre free-for-all."
—BRIAN K. VAUGHAN (Saga)
THE SPIRE
SIMON SPURRIER
JEFF STOKELY
ANDRÉ MAY

MARK WAID · PETER KRAUSE
IRREDEEMABLE
AFTERWORD BY GRANT MORRISON

J.G. JONES
MARK WAID
STRANGE FRUIT
Foreword by
ELVIS MITCHELL

MICHAEL ALAN NELSON
DAN MORA
GABRIEL CASSATA
HEXED
THE HARLOT & THE THIEF VOLUME ONE

ABNETT & CULBARD
WILD'S END
FIRST LIGHT
"IT'S REALLY GREAT!"
JEFF LEMIRE

BOOM! STUDIOS

AVAILABLE AT YOUR LOCAL COMICS SHOP AND BOOKSTORE
WWW.**BOOM-STUDIOS**.COM

James Tynion IV

The Woods
Volume 1
ISBN: 978-1-60886-454-6 | $9.99 US
Volume 2
ISBN: 978-1-60886-495-9 | $14.99 US
Volume 3
ISBN: 978-1-60886-773-8 | $14.99 US

The Backstagers
Volume 1
ISBN: 978-1-60886-993-0 | $14.99 US

Simon Spurrier

Six-Gun Gorilla
ISBN: 978-1-60886-390-7 | $19.99 US

The Spire
ISBN: 978-1-60886-913-8 | $29.99 US

Weavers
ISBN: 978-1-60886-963-3 | $19.99 US

Mark Waid

Irredeemable
Volume 1
ISBN: 978-1-93450-690-5 | $16.99 US
Volume 2
ISBN: 978-1-60886-000-5 | $16.99 US

Incorruptible
Volume 1
ISBN: 978-1-60886-015-9 | $16.99 US
Volume 2
ISBN: 978-1-60886-028-9 | $16.99 US

Strange Fruit
ISBN: 978-1-60886-872-8 | $24.99 US

Michael Alan Nelson

Hexed The Harlot & The Thief
Volume 1
ISBN: 978-1-60886-718-9 | $14.99 US
Volume 2
ISBN: 978-1-60886-816-2 | $14.99 US

Day Men
Volume 1
ISBN: 978-1-60886-393-8 | $9.99 US
Volume 2
ISBN: 978-1-60886-852-0 | $9.99 US

Dan Abnett

Wild's End
Volume 1: First Light
ISBN: 978-1-60886-735-6 | $19.99 US
Volume 2: The Enemy Within
ISBN: 978-1-60886-877-3 | $19.99 US

Hypernaturals
Volume 1
ISBN: 978-1-60886-298-6 | $16.99 US
Volume 2
ISBN: 978-1-60886-319-8 | $19.99 US

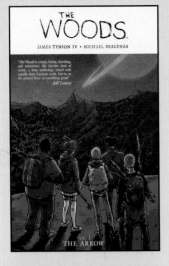

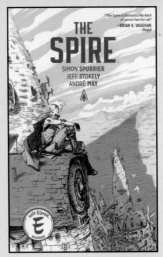

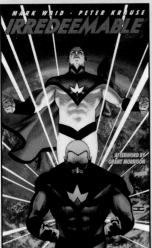

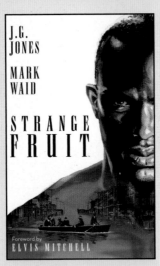

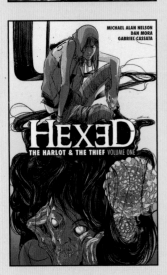

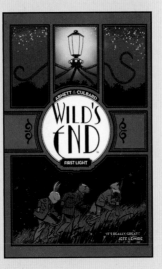

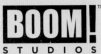